COMPLEX ORGANIZATIONS AND THEIR ENVIRONMENTS

Merlin B. Brinkerhoff
University of Calgary

Phillip R. Kunz
Brigham Young University

WM. C. BROWN COMPANY PUBLISHERS
Dubuque, Iowa

301.1832
B77c
88198
april 1974

Printed in the United States of America

1. *From Max Weber: Essays in Sociology,* edited and translated by H. H. Gerth and C. Wright Mills. Copyright 1946 by Oxford University Press, Inc. Reprinted with permission.

2. Talcott Parsons, "Suggestions for a Sociological Approach to the Theory of Organizations—I," *Administrative Science Quarterly,* June 1956, 1:63–69, 74–80. Reprinted with the permission of the author and publisher.

3. James G. March and Herbert A. Simon, *Organizations,* New York: John Wiley and Sons, Inc. 1958, pp. 84–93. Reprinted with permission.

4. Daniel Katz and Robert L. Kahn, "Organizations and the System Concept," *Social Psychology of Organizations,* New York: John Wiley and Sons, Inc. 1966, pp. 14–29. Reprinted with permission.

5. Charles Perrow, "A Framework for the Comparative Analysis of Organizations," *American Sociological Review,* 32 (April, 1967), pp. 194–208. Reprinted with the permission of the author and the publisher.

6. James S. Coleman, "Relational Analysis: The Study of Social Structure with Survey Methods," *Human Organization,* 17 (4) (1958–1959), pp. 28–33. Used with the permission of the author and the publisher.

7. W. Richard Scott, "Field Work in a Formal Organization," *Human Organization,* 22 (3) (1963), pp. 162–168. Used with the permission of the author and publisher.

8. James P. Spradley, "An Ethnographic Approach to the Study of Organizations: The City Jail." Used with the permission of the author.

9. Thomas E. Drabek and J. Eugene Hass, "Realism in Laboratory Simulation: Myth or Method?" *Social Forces,* 45 (March, 1967) pp. 337–346. Used with the permission of the authors and the publisher.

10. Arthur L. Stinchcombe, "Social Structure and Organizations," in James G. March (Ed.), *Handbook of Organizations,* Copyright 1965 by Rand McNally & Company, Chicago, pp. 146–160. Used with the permission of the publisher.

11. Philip Selznick, "Coöptation," *TVA and the Grass Roots,* Berkeley and Los Angeles: University of California Press, 1949 pp. 13–16, 219–226. Originally published by the University of California Press; reprinted by permission of The Regents of the University of California.

12. John Maniha and Charles Perrow, "The Reluctant Organization and the Aggressive Environment," *Administrative Science Quarterly,* September 1965, 10:238–257. Used with the permission of the authors and the publisher.

13. Peter M. Blau and W. Richard Scott, "Organizational Development," *Formal Organizations,* Scranton Pennsylvania: International Textbook Company, 1962, pp. 223–242.

14. Rita Braito, Steve Paulson, Gerald Klonglon, "Domain Consensus: A Key Variable in Interorganizational Analysis." Used with the permission of the authors.

15. Reprinted with permission from William G. Scott, The Management of Conflict, Homewood Illinois: Richard D. Irwin, Inc. pp. 114–126.

16. David J. Bordua and Albert J. Reiss, "Command, Control and Charisma: Reflections of Police Bureaucracy," *American Journal of Sociology,* 72 (July, 1966), pp. 68–76. Used with the permission of the authors and the publisher.

17. William R. Rosengren, "Structure, Policy, and Style: Strategies of Organizational Control," *Administrative Science Quarterly,* June, 1967, 12:140–164. Used with the permission of the author and the publisher.

18. Philip M. Marcus and Dora Marcus, "Control in Modern Organizations," *Public Administration Review,* 25 (2) (June, 1965), pp. 121–127. Used with the permission of the authors and the publisher.

19. Paul R. Lawrence and Jay W. Lorsch, "Organization and Environment," *Organization and Environment,* Boston: Graduate School of Business Administration, 1967, pp. 6–18. Used with the permission of the publisher.

20. James D. Thompson and William J. McEwen, "Organizational Goals and Environments," *American Sociological Review,* 23 (1958), pp. 23–31. Used with the permission of the author and the publisher.

21. F. E. Emery and E. L. Trist, "The Causal Texture of Organizational Environments," *Human Relations,* 18 (February, 1965), pp. 21–31. Used with the permission of the publisher.

22. Roy E. Rickson and Charles Simpkins, "Rational Organizations and Ecological Process: The Case of Pollution." Used with the permission of the authors.

23. Ruth C. Young and Olaf F. Larson, "The Contribution of Voluntary Organizations to Community Structure," *American Journal of Sociology,* Vol. LXXI, No. 2, (September, 1965) pp. 178–186. Used with the permission of the authors and the publisher.

24. Roland L. Warren, "The Interorganizational Field as a Focus for Investigation," *Administrative Science Quarterly,* December, 1967, 12:396–419. Used with the permission of the author and the publisher.

25. Reprinted from Approaches to Organizational Design, pp. 173–188, James D. Thompson, editor. Used with the permission of the University of Pittsburgh Press. Copyright 1966 by the University of Pittsburgh Press.

26. Sol Levine and Paul E. White, "Exchange as a Conceptual Framework for the Study of Interorganizational Relationships," *Administrative Science Quarterly,* March 1961, 5:583–601. Used with the permission of the authors and the publisher.

27. Burton R. Clark, "Interorganizational Patterns in Education," *Administrative Science Quarterly,* September 1965, 10:224–237. Used with the permission of the author and the publisher.

28. Michael Aiken and Jerald Hage, "Organizational Interdependence and Intraorganizational Structure," *American Sociological Review,* 33 (December, 1968) pp. 912–929. Used with the permission of the authors and the publisher.

29. Phillip R. Kunz, "Sponsorship and Organizational Stability: Boy Scout Troops," *American Journal of Sociology,* Vol. 74 No. 6, May 1969, pp. 666–675. Used with the permission of the publisher.

Contents

Introduction

As civilization has increased in complexity, we have become more involved in large-scale organizations. Many commentators on modern social life have observed wide-spread organizational involvement as a basic and pervasive characteristic of our current society. Modern man is man in organizations.[1]

Because of the extent to which we are involved in organizations, large-scale programs can be carried out for our mutual benefit. Furthermore, complex organizations, *per se,* as social realities, often relate to other organizations in a manner which permits them to utilize those organizations to attain some purpose or goal in which they have an interest.

Although sociologists have had a long-time interest in organizations, there has been a rapid expansion of effort to understand them during the last two decades. It is easy to document this recently increasing interest and to specify empirically the trends in organizational analysis by examining the bibliography at the end of this book or one found in such books as March and Simon's *Organizations,*[2] Blau and Scott's *Formal Organizations,*[3] or March's *Handbook of Organizations.*[4]

The vast number of organizations which are found in modern society is one of the characteristics which differentiates modern society from more traditional societies. Indeed, one might say that ours is an organizational society. Man is confronted with organizational demands from the time of his birth until his death. Many of these demands are couched within the setting of complex organizations. Man's adjustment to societal demands is facilitated by an increased understanding of

1. Peter M. Blau and W. Richard Scott, *Formal Organizations: A Comparative Approach* (San Francisco: Chandler Publishing Company, 1962), p. ix.
2. James G. March and Herbert A. Simon, *Organizations* (New York: John Wiley and Sons Inc.),1963.
3. Blau and Scott, *Formal Organizations.*
4. James G. March, *Handbook of Organizations* (Chicago: Rand McNally and Co.), 1965. This book includes extensive references following each of the chapters.

organizational life. This understanding may be part of the socialization process, hence not consciously perceived by many.

One of the earliest social observers, Saint-Simon, envisioned the significance of complex organizations for the emergence of modern society. He suggested that in the future the authority of the organizational administrators would be based upon scientific knowledge. Saint-Simon's conviction that the complex organization is a consciously planned entity differed from Comte, his student. Comte argued that future society would emerge spontaneously. That is, Comte, unlike Saint-Simon, failed to conceive of future societies as consciously derived social systems characterized by large-scale organizations.[5]

Max Weber must undoubtedly be considered among the greatest of the contributors to an understanding of the complex organization. Weber's work on bureaucracy has probably had greater influence on the conceptualizations and research which have been focused on complex organizations than the contributions of any other single person. Weber, just as Saint-Simon, envisioned the organization as characterized by rationality and expertise. Most of the selections in this book conceptualize organizations from perspectives based, at least in part, on the writings of Weber. That is, this perspective conceptualizes organizations as social units which have been deliberately established for the attainment of specific goals. Consequently, goal efficiency and effectiveness are dominant concerns for the theories of rational-legal organizations.

An approach within organizational theory known as Scientific Management[6] grew from an emphasis on goal attainment with the least expenditure of resources. Both economic incentives and job specialization were major characteristics of this approach. In addition, there was a specific interest in the physical setting as it relates to job specialization. For example, Scientific Management was concerned with the optimum amount of light for a specific task, or the relation of the width of a conveyor belt to the number of parts a worker could remove from it. Time and motion studies were extremely prevalent.

Mayo, Roethlisberger and Dickson's work suggested that factors other than economic affected the workers' productivity. In sum, their Human Relations[7] approach, as it came to be known, posited that interpersonal relations influence organizational goal attainment. As a consequence of their work, organizational analysis began to investigate

5. For an excellent, brief discussion of Saint-Simon and Comte's contributions to organizational analysis, see Alvin W. Gouldner, "Organizational Analysis," in Robert K. Merton, Leonard Broom and Leonard S. Cottrell, Jr., eds., *Sociology Today: Problems and Prospects* (New York: Basic Books, Inc., 1959), pp. 400–410.
6. Frederick W. Taylor, *Scientific Management* (New York: Harper and Brothers, 1947).
7. Elton Mayo, *The Social Problems of an Industrial Civilization* (Boston: Graduate School of Business Administration, Division of Research, 1945). Fritz J. Roethlisberger and William J. Dickson, *Management and the Worker* (Cambridge, Mass.: Harvard University Press, 1939).

the informal aspects of the organization. "Informal organization" then became a part of the considerations given to investigations of organizational matters.

Neither the rational model (sometimes referred to as the "formal organization") or the human relations model is complete. Both formal and informal elements must be taken into account if there is to be greater insight into organizations. The open systems model of the organization attempts to accomplish this.[8] This approach suggests that goal attainment is only one of many important organizational needs. An open systems approach, as presented by Katz and Kahn, for example, is characterized by the "recurrence of activities in relation to the energic input into the system, the transformation of energies within the system, and the resulting product or energic output."[9] Unlike previous theoretical approaches, this one emphasizes the relationship of the organization with the environment, which includes other organizations, natural resources, ideologies, etc. Open-systems theory suggests that the organization, which is the object of analysis, is only a part of a larger system, and is in continual interaction with other parts of the system because it is dependent upon them for resources as input and for recipients of the output.

The rational-legal model, which developed from the work of Weber, has been termed a closed-systems approach. However, the open-systems model, which we have discussed, is also concerned with rationality. It goes beyond the earlier model in its assumptions concerning the uncertainties which the organization encounters. This model suggests that complex organizations are "indeterminate and faced with uncertainty, but at the same time as subject to criteria of rationality and hence needing determinateness and certainty."[10] This model has been broadly referred to as the "contingency model."

While we have briefly summarized three basic models of organizations, we have not yet carefully delineated the definition of organization. Although all books which are addressed toward a particular subject may not at any point define the subject, it seems reasonable that they should do so. There are several terms which are sometimes employed interchangeably to refer to organizations but which should be differentiated.

Organization implies recurrent patterned relationships among various parts of some unit. This may be illustrated by the relationships which exist among the various parts of a watch, including the main-

8. See Etzioni's discussion in which he presents the structuralist model as a synthesis of the rational and human relations model. Amitai Etzioni, *Modern Organizations* (Englewood Cliffs, New Jersey: Prentice-Hall, Inc., 1964), pp. 20–49.
9. Daniel Katz and Robert L. Kahn, *The Social Psychology of Organizations* (New York: John Wiley and Sons, 1966), p. 17.
10. James D. Thompson, *Organizations in Action* (New York: McGraw-Hill, Inc., 1967), p.10.

spring, bearings, hairspring, balance wheel, etc. When these are properly fitted together (organized), there are patterned recurrent outcomes which are predictable with a high degree of probability. The watch may be an inadequate example of organization however, since it may unwarrantedly present a closed-system conception of organization.

Social organization occurs as the interaction of people becomes patterned and recurrent in a manner which creates social order.[11] This is possible only when the cultural orientations are shared, at least to some minimal degree. Social organization stems from the regularities which are social in origin, rather than those which are of a mechanical, psychological or physiological nature.

Neither organization nor social organization, as defined above, is the equivalent of complex organization. Rather, the concept of complex organization is a form or subtype of these. Etzioni, following the treatment of Parsons, defines organizations as "social units which are predominantly oriented to the attainment of specific goals."[12] Thus, General Motors, Ivy School, Tincan Company, or the Royal Canadian Mounted Police may all be examples of organizations. These examples can be treated as organizations because they have boundaries. An organization is differentiated from other elements in the environment by its boundaries. It should be recognized that organizational boundaries are not always easily identifiable or even agreed upon by different observers. Selections in the last two sections of this book illustrate some of the problems which are encountered when attempting to establish organizational boundaries. In addition, organizations are sometimes identified by names, charters, offices, etc.

While students of complex organizations frequently employ the terms *formal organization* and *complex organization* interchangeably, we would like to suggest the utility of treating the two terms as distinct in at least one way. Formal organization implies an organization which is deliberately established. This organization includes formal role prescriptions, a formal incorporation, bylaws, an organizational chart, etc. This definition, does not infer anything about the size and complexity of the organization, however. Thus, two or three persons could organize a company and pursue some goal, such as the manufacture of a toy. We would choose to treat this organization as an example of a formal organization, but *not* a complex organization.

The definition of a complex organization must include the same criteria as the definition of formal organization. But in addition, it must

11. For a discussion of the concept of social organization, see Marvin E. Olsen, *The Process of Social Organization* (New York: Holt, Rinehart and Winston, 1968).
12. Amitai Etzioni, *A Sociological Reader on Complex Organizations,* 2nd ed. (New York: Holt, Rinehart and Winston, Inc., 1969), p. vii.

include such notions as multiple hierarchical levels, multiple functions, or multiple role systems. By this formulation, an organization is not only formal, but also complex in its interrelationships. In contrast to the above toy company, which we call a formal organization, General Motors is complex. The complexity does not arise out of size alone, but out of the interrelationships among the parts of the organization. It is conceivable that a rather small organization which is characterized by functional differentiation, multiple levels of hierarchy, multiple communication levels, etc., is, in fact, a complex organization. In fact, Hall, Haas, and Johnson present a study which illustrates that size and complexity do not co-vary in a simplistic manner.[13] We present this conceptual distinction merely as a sensitizing notion. We do not suggest the exact number of levels of hierarchy, etc. which must be present for an organization to be considered complex rather than simply formal. In short, for the organizations which are considered in this text, the concept "formal organizations" is not sufficient. They are, in fact, complex.

Thus far, the historical development of complex organizations and some conceptual distinctions have been briefly summarized. Next, the major sections of this book and the common nexus which runs through them require some discussion.

The selections for this book were made on the basis of several criteria: (1) the articles pertain to organizational rather than to individual characteristics, (2) each selection stresses some theoretical or methodological position which gives continuity to the book, and (3) where possible, articles which are empirical in nature are utilized.

There have been various theoretical approaches to the field of complex organization. Consequently, because of the many articles which deal with organizational theory, there is a requirement for selectivity. Those theoretical approaches which are presented in chapter one tend to be of rather general interest. In addition, they are cumulative. Weber, for example, a pioneer in organizational theory, is initially presented, and is then followed by Parsons, a student of Weber. Finally, an extension of Parsons' work is found in Katz and Kahn's selection with an emphasis on organizations as open systems with varying technologies. It is immediately evident that this section fails to include some approaches which have been highly influential. For example, little has been included from the "human relations" school of thought.

The field of complex organization has long been dominated with an interest on the organization *per se,* as the object of analysis, rather than upon the organization as it relates to the outside environment, including other organizations. Both individuals who theorized about the orga-

---

13. Richard H. Hall, J. Eugene Haas, and Norman J. Johnson, "Organizational Size, Complexity and Formalization," *American Sociological Review* 32 (December, 1967):903–912.

nization and those who empirically examined the various formulations have usually been concerned with *intra*organizational considerations. For the most part, their orientations have been toward human relations. That is, they have been motivated toward investigation of psychological or social-psychological phenomena. The object of analysis has been the organization while the unit of analysis has usually been the individual within the organization or some department or division within the organization. For example, if the police department were the organization studied, the questions would most likely be related to morale, relationships between line and staff, the communications systems, turnover of department personnel, etc. Seldom would anyone be likely to examine the relation of the police department to the fire department, the court system, the schools, the city council, much less to historical considerations which may have had an impact upon the organization, or to the values of the society of which the department was a part.

We suggest, however, that the future trend in the field will be to examine the organization as the "unit of analysis," and to investigate the organization as it relates to its environment. Etzioni, for example, points out that substantial information is known about *individual* interaction, but little is known about organizational interrelationships; yet, modern society is a society of organizations.[14]

With this commitment to organizational interrelationships, concomitant with the pressure to be selective, certain theoretical approaches have not been emphasized, such as social psychological theories of organizations. In fact, it is our argument that such theorists can hardly explain interpersonal behavior within the organization without consideration of organizational interaction. In spite of this, there are a significant number of articles which are of importance to the organizational theorist who prefers to examine the interpersonal relations within the organization, such as Marcus and Marcus' article on organizational control in chapter four.

The reader should not be misled to believe that chapter one contains all important theoretical perspectives. The articles throughout the remaining sections were also selected because of their importance to organizational theory or because they contain empirical investigation of theoretical assumptions. For example, exchange theory is presented from March and Simon's perspective in chapter one, but it should be reconsidered when examining Levine and White's study of interorganizational relationships found in chapter six.

Articles have been included in the methodological section which explain the techniques and also provide an illustration of the organizational analyst in action. For example, Scott's selection in chapter two

14. Etzioni, *Modern Organizations,* pp. 110–113.

discusses the role of the observer while it describes his actual research behavior. Most of the articles in chapter two discuss methods applicable to the investigation of the internal organization. The same methods may also be utilized in interorganizational analysis. There are several articles which have been placed within the substantive areas which exemplify approaches which, in fact, have been employed for interorganizational analysis, such as Young and Larsen's discussion in chapter five. It may be argued that such approaches should be placed within the methodology section. However, this illustrates that all articles have been selected because they serve multiple purposes.

Complex Organizations and Their Environments is unusual in its treatment of the organization's life cycle. Although the authors risk being identified as members of an organismic cult, they are firmly committed to the proposition that the organization may be more fully understood when some life-cycle kinds of assumptions are posited. That is, there are factors which are relevant to the formation of an organization, to its development and change, and to its possible subsequent demise. Full understanding of a complex organization requires answers to such questions as: What are the factors which affect the formation of organizations? What are relevant historical conditions which affect the existence of current organizational structures? What happens when organizations attain their goals, or fail to attain their goals? How does change in one organization tend to influence or give rise to other organizations? This kind of approach has been previously exemplified in such works as Cottrell's "Death by Dieselization,"[15] and Haire's "Biological Models and Empirical Histories of the Growth of Organizations."[16]

The articles in chapter four discuss organizational control. This is an area which has been largely neglected. Some of the selections (e.g., Bordua and Reiss) utilize the organization as the unit of analysis, whereas others compare several organizations in order to explain more clearly the phenomena of intraorganizational control.

Just as man has memberships within various organizations, organizations are members of larger social systems. As man's role behavior must be controlled within the organization, the social system must and does control the behavior of its organizations. As an example, the National Basketball Association may be threatened with suits of anti-trust violation. The utilization of formal law within a society is, of course, not the only mechanism of organizational control. The Supreme Court, as

---

15. Leonard S. Cottrell, "Death by Dieselization: A Case Study in the Reaction to Technological Change," *American Sociological Review* 16 (June 1951): 358–365.
16. Mason Haire, "Biological Models and Empirical Histories of the Growth of Organizations," in Mason Haire, ed., *Modern Organizational Theory* (New York: John Wiley and Sons, Inc., 1959), pp. 272–306.

an organization, has a good deal to say about some kinds of organizational activity. The lower courts have a real impact upon the output or product of the police organization.

Within the external environment of the organization is an ideology which imposes restrictions on the organization. Since the organization derives its personnel from the environment, one would expect the personnel to "bear" the ideology of the environment, to a greater or lesser extent. Organizational decisions may be affected by this ideology. For example, Rickson and Simpkins argue in their original paper in this book that industrialized societies are characterized by an ideology which values economic advancement over aesthetic endeavors. Industrial organizations' efforts in pollution control are influenced by this ideology. Selznick, although addressing the intraorganizational level, stated it clearly:

> Organizations, like individuals, strive for a unified pattern of response. This integration will define in advance the general attitudes of personnel to specific problems as they arise. This means that there will be pressure within the organization, from below as well as from above, for unity, in outlook. As unity is approximated the character of the organization becomes defined.[17]

The society may be visualized as a composite structure of interrelated organizations. Thus, Congress, an organization, may vote to withhold funds for the development of new, larger aircraft. A large corporation which builds aircraft may be less able to function on their regular scale of operation. That, in turn, may affect literally hundreds of other organizations.

"Coordination," or "the orderly arrangement of group efforts,"[18] may also be a form of social control. When the U.S.S.R. surprised the United States with Sputnik, the U.S. government and various nongovernmental organizations began to coordinate their activities in terms of space exploration. The educational institutions were not unaffected by this coordination, inasmuch as they were called upon to train an increasing number of engineers. The creation of a market for the product of the school system (engineers) was partially controlled by this demand.

Up to this point we have suggested that society may control organizations through legislative and ajudication processes; they may also be controlled by ideologies (culture) and the coordination processes. These mechanisms of control are but a few of the alternatives which are

17. Philip Selznick, *TVA and the Grass Roots* (Berkeley: The University of California Press, 1953), p. 181.
18. For discussions on organizations discussed in terms of coordination, see: Chester I. Barnard, *The Functions of the Executive* (Cambridge, Massachusetts: Harvard University Press, 1938); Peter Blau, *Exchange and Power in Social Life* (New York: John Wiley and Sons, Inc., 1964); and James Mooney, "The Coordinative Principle," in Joseph A. Litterer (ed.) *Organizational Structure and Behavior* (New York: John Wiley and Sons, 1963), pp. 39–40.

employed for organizational control. In chapter five, for example, Thompson and McEwen, suggest that three types of cooperation (bargaining, cooptation, and coalition) as well as competition may serve as organizational control devices. To these, of course, should be added conflict, which may also be a controlling force. For example, conflict generated by minority groups has influenced recruiting policies of industrial organizations.

As has already been pointed out, the efforts of most organizational analysts have been directed toward internal analyses. However, recently social systems theory has stimulated an interest in the organization in interaction with its environment. However, this is still a relatively underdeveloped area in terms of empirical analyses. Chapters five and six are devoted to articles which specifically focus on the organization as it relates to its environment. The environment consists of other organizations, culture, natural resources, ecology, individuals, etc.

Organizations are mutually interdependent. The interrelationship which exists between Boy Scout troops and the organizations which sponsor them serves as an example of interdependence.[19] Essentially, the troop uses the organizational facilities, access, resources, etc. of the sponsoring organization to implement its own program. It is assumed that in most cases the organization which sponsors the troop will have some goals and purposes in mind for the troop beyond those of the national organization. These may in turn be reflected in the kinds of things which the troop does and the particular goals which they stress. Not only has the sponsor considered the Boy Scout organization in this way, but the Boy Scouts of America has taken the sponsors into account as well. The implementation of a special division consisting of representatives of sponsors has been effected to deal with relationships between the sponsors and the national organization. This should have some effects upon the sponsorship relationship.

It would seem evident that sponsorship is an important practical variable associated with Scouting. In the final analysis, the sponsor, with the activities it promotes and the manner in which it carries out programs which are devised to implement the goals of the national organization, will affect that organization. Knowledge of the types of sponsors that provide what the national organization needs in order to survive should be significant to them. In a similar manner other organizations have effects upon each other. What these effects are and how they may be changed are important questions which deserve consideration.

Along with the increasing complexity of society, there is a trend

19. Phillip R. Kunz, "The Relation of Sponsorship and Activity" (Unpublished paper read at the American Sociological Association, 1969).

toward larger organizations, which may further complicate an understanding of organizational concerns. Thus, three automobile firms
dominate an industry in which there were once many manufacturers.
It is assumed that about a third of all general merchandising in the
United States is accounted for by the three major catalog chain stores.
Mergers, acquisitions, and internal growth, along with bankruptcy, un-
adaptability, and the tremendous attrition rate among small organizations are the kinds of processes which encourage the growth of the
larger organizations.

The importance of organizations in our social life is evident, as may
be ascertained from the vast number of disciplines which currently
offer organizational courses in their curricula. Thus, the articles reported in this book examine such diverse organizations as hospitals,
business concerns, schools, jails, and welfare agencies, among others. In
other words, the selections in this collection include general concepts
which transverse many disciplines and present research which investigates the various types of organizations.

In modern society there exists an uneasiness with the status quo in
that a large percentage of the young people report that they are not
satisfied with the current institutions and organizations of which society
is comprised. It may be hypothesized that the recent decline in violent
protest may be a result of the recognition on the part of the young
people that they require more information about organizations. In order to initiate change, or to make an attempt to ameliorate society,
knowledge about organizations and their interrelationships is essential.
The article by Rickson and Simpkins, for example, suggests that in order
to control water pollution, we must concentrate our efforts on large-
scale industry. They argue that we must begin to articulate the need for
modifications of our basic values to the scientists and policy makers in
industry.

While we have made great strides in our knowledge of organizations, there appears to be much which we do not know. This knowledge
will accrue as we continue to utilize the methods of investigation which
have yielded information in other areas. We suggest that the field of
complex organizations will mature and be comprehended as rapidly as
we are willing to systematically unite the theoretical notions about
organizations and the proper methodological procedures to test and
revise those notions.

Acknowledgments

We want to express our appreciation to the many people who aided in the completion of this book. Chiefly, we want to acknowledge the authors of the selections which we have chosen to include in this book. In addition, we would like to thank Professors Donald Mills, Eugen Lupri, and Spencer Condie for their careful comments on various sections of the book. Mr. Robert Nash, editor for William C. Brown Company Publishers, proved especially helpful in the culmination of this project. Miss Vickie Hundley, Sandra Allen, and Michael Cooley were indispensable in the typing and the construction of the bibliography. And finally Gloria and Joyce, our wives, deserve a vote of appreciation for the understanding and support they extended during the time this book required.

Merlin B. Brinkerhoff
Phillip R. Kunz

CHAPTER ONE

ALTERNATIVE THEORETICAL APPROACHES TO COMPLEX ORGANIZATIONS

Since there are many different theoretical approaches to complex organizations, only selected ones can be presented. The theoretical approaches which are found in this section have been chosen because they provide a feeling for the development of current organizational theory, and because they, for the most part, examine the organization as it relates to the larger environment. Theory on organizations should provide an explanatory system by which the salient features of organizations might be better understood. The reader should not be misled into a belief that the theories presented here are the only possible theoretical approaches. In the remaining sections additional theoretical positions are explicated as they relate to more substantive problems. For example, in chapter six Levine and White suggest that interorganizational analysis can best be approached through an exchange framework.

Many of the current theorists in the area of complex organizations have been greatly influenced by Max Weber. "Legitimation" was a key concept upon which Weber based his conceptualization of organization. Simply stated, legitimation referred to the notion that the exercise of power is congruent with the values of the persons who are subjected to the power. Weber examined the sources and types of legitimation in the construction of his typology of authority. The three major types of authority which he posited were traditional, charismatic, and bureaucratic. Weber, as an organizational theorist, was primarily concerned

1

with the problem of rationality. For him, bureaucracy was the outcome of rational thought applied to organization.

For many people, bureaucracy implies red tape, delay, "the run-around," inefficiency, etc. They stress the disadvantages of bureaucracy, as they perceive it, or the dysfunctions which it may engender. Weber, however, visualized bureaucracy as a rational organization, and pointed to the advantages that derive from that type of organization.

Since Weber, many students of organization have attempted to reformulate his ideas, and some have attempted to empirically test his theoretical concepts. These attempts to refine Weber's concepts have been extremely useful to the growth of organizational theory. For example, Weber was not primarily interested in the internal relationships within the organization, such as job satisfaction and turnover, but in the organization as an outcome of rational thought. It is interesting to note, however, that many students of Weber have concerned themselves largely with relations internal to the organization. Such endeavors have, of course, also influenced organizational theory.

Parsons, a student of Weber, further developed the notion of the social system, and has translated this into his own conceptualization of complex organizations. He treats the organization primarily as a goal attainment mechanism whose boundaries may be understood by an investigation of input and output. Parsons' systems approach suggests that the output of one organization becomes the input for another.

Parsons' article, although written in 1956, precedes the more current organizational concern which relates the organization to its environment or one organization to another—problems which have long been neglected in this discipline. This neglect may have resulted, in part, from the misleading assumption that Weber focused only on the internal organization. In addition, Parsons' conceptualization of the organization includes the treatment of an organization as an adaptive system. He discusses the intricate relationship of its resources in this adaptive process.

The selection by March and Simon, not unlike the article by Parsons, also describes the organization from a social systems perspective. However, their selection examines the problem, internal to the organization, of motivating organizational participants to perform. They suggest that the participants receive inducements from the organization in exchange for the contributions they make to the organization. Because of this focus, their approach is often referred to as "exchange theory."

Although March and Simon concentrate on selected factors which are important in the motivation of employees within the organization, they also suggest that investors, external organizational units, and consumees are also participants with the organization. It should be immediately evident that the March and Simon model operates from the Weberian assumption of rationality within the social system.

Any collection of alternative theoretical approaches to complex organizations would be grossly incomplete without a more detailed discussion of the organization as an open system. The selection by Katz and Kahn delineates carefully the major characteristics of open systems. Furthermore, it suggests many questions which are critical to an understanding of complex organizations. For example, they raise the crucial problem of identifying organizational boundaries, i.e., how do you know that you are analyzing an organization? Katz and Kahn advise that there are several fallacies which are committed when an organization is identified by its goals. Goal-related concepts have been overemphasized. Instead, organizational concepts should concentrate upon the input, output, and functioning of the organization as an open social system and not upon the rational goals of the leaders.

Katz and Kahn are also extremely critical of most theoretical models of organizations because they fail to recognize that the organization is dependent upon inputs from the environment. That is, these models, which concentrate upon the internal functioning, fail to examine the interaction between the organization and the environment. Katz and Kahn outline several errors which result from the traditional closed-systems approach to organizations.

The article by Perrow provides a framework for comparing organizations. He treats technology, or the work done in organizations, as the major concept for comparison. He focuses upon two major aspects of technology: exceptions and search. Perrow envisions technology as a part of the overall structure of the organization. In fact, technology is that which influences the other aspects of structure. In this way, Perrow attempts to avoid the pitfalls of depending totally upon goals, functions, and organizational structure which have served as the bases of many other theories. That is, similarly to Katz and Kahn, Perrow sees the futility of utilizing only these concepts for organizational analysis. Instead, he treats these variables as dependent upon technology. Thus, although Perrow does not dismiss the notion of goals, he is concerned with the type of technology adapted to the goal, i.e., given the goal and the environment, a given technology is adapted to these variables, and the technology, in turn, influences yet other aspects of the internal structure. Perrow, in this scheme, provides one way of treating many different types of organizations, crosscutting several theoretical approaches, and avoiding many problems endemic to such approaches. Perrow's article, although not a theory in the most formal sense, does contain much of theoretical relevance, and serves well to bridge the gap between the theoretical and methodological sections.

---------------------------------- **1** ----------------------------------

FROM MAX WEBER
Essays in Sociology

H. H. Gerth and C. Wright Mills

CHARACTERISTICS OF BUREAUCRACY

Modern officialdom functions in the following specific manner:

I. There is the principle of fixed and official jurisdictional areas, which are generally ordered by rules, that is, by laws or administrative regulations.

1. The regular activities required for the purposes of the bureaucratically governed structure are distributed in a fixed way as official duties.
2. The authority to give the commands required for the discharge of these duties is distributed in a stable way and is strictly delimited by rules concerning the coercive means, physical, sacerdotal, or otherwise, which may be placed at the disposal of officials.
3. Methodical provision is made for the regular and continuous fulfilment of these duties and for the execution of the corresponding rights; only persons who have the generally regulated qualifications to serve are employed.

In public and lawful government these three elements constitute "bureaucratic authority." In private economic domination, they constitute bureaucratic "management." Bureaucracy, thus understood, is fully developed in political and ecclesiastical communities only in the modern state, and, in the private economy, only in the most advanced institutions of capitalism. Permanent and public office authority, with fixed jurisdiction, is not the historical rule but rather the exception. This is so even in large political structures such as those of the ancient Orient, the Germanic and Mongolian empires of conquest, or of many feudal structures of state. In all these cases, the ruler executes the most important measures through personal trustees, table-companions, or court-servants. Their commissions and authority are not precisely delimited and are temporarily called into being for each case.

II. The principles of office hierarchy and of levels of graded authority mean a firmly ordered system of super- and subordination in which there is a supervision of the lower offices by the higher ones. Such a system offers the governed the possibility of appealing the decision of a lower office to its higher authority, in a definitely regulated manner. With the full development of the bureaucratic type, the office hierarchy is monocratically organized. The principle of hierarchical office authority is found in all bureaucratic structures: in state and ecclesiastical structures as well as in large party organizations and private enterprises. It does not matter for the character of bureaucracy whether its authority is called "private" or "public."

When the principle of jurisdictional "competency" is fully carried through, hierarchical subordination—at least in public office—does not mean that the "higher" authority is simply authorized to take over the business of the "lower." Indeed, the opposite is the rule. Once established and having fulfilled its task, an office tends to continue in existence and be held by another incumbent.

III. The management of the modern office is based upon written documents ("the files"), which are preserved in their original or draught form. There is, therefore, a staff of subaltern officials and scribes of all sorts. The body of officials actively engaged in a "public" office, along with the respective apparatus of material implements and the files, make up a "bureau." In private enterprise, "the bureau" is often called "the office."

In principle, the modern organization of the civil service separates the bureau from the private domicile of the official, and, in general, bureaucracy segregates official activity as something distinct from the sphere of private life. Public monies and equipment are divorced from the private property of the official. This condition is everywhere the product of a long development. Nowadays, it is found in public as well as in private enterprises; in the latter, the principle extends even to the leading entrepreneur. In principle, the executive office is separated from the household, business from private correspondence, and business assets from private fortunes. The more consistently the modern type of business management has been carried through the more are these separations the case. The beginnings of this process are to be found as early as the Middle Ages.

It is the peculiarity of the modern entrepreneur that he conducts himself as the "first official" of his enterprise, in the very same way in which the ruler of a specifically modern bureaucratic state spoke of himself as "the first servant" of the state.[1] The idea that the bureau activities of the state are intrinsically different in character from the management of private economic offices is a continental European notion and, by way of contrast, is totally foreign to the American way.

IV. Office management, at least all specialized office management —and such management is distinctly modern—usually presupposes

1. Frederick II of Prussia.

thorough and expert training. This increasingly holds for the modern executive and employee of private enterprises, in the same manner as it holds for the state official.

V. When the office is fully developed, official activity demands the full working capacity of the official, irrespective of the fact that his obligatory time in the bureau may be firmly delimited. In the normal case, this is only the product of a long development, in the public as well as in the private office. Formerly, in all cases, the normal state of affairs was reversed: official business was discharged as a secondary activity.

VI. The management of the office follows general rules, which are more or less stable, more or less exhaustive, and which can be learned. Knowledge of these rules represents a special technical learning which the officials possess. It involves jurisprudence, or administrative or business management.

The reduction of modern office management to rules is deeply embedded in its very nature. The theory of modern public administration, for instance, assumes that the authority to order certain matters by decree—which has been legally granted to public authorities—does not entitle the bureau to regulate the matter by commands given for each case, but only to regulate the matter abstractly. This stands in extreme contrast to the regulation of all relationships through individual privileges and bestowals of favor, which is absolutely dominant in patrimonialism, at least in so far as such relationships are not fixed by sacred tradition.

THE POSITION OF THE OFFICIAL

All this results in the following for the internal and external position of the official:

I. Office holding is a "vocation." This is shown, first, in the requirement of a firmly prescribed course of training, which demands the entire capacity for work for a long period of time, and in the generally prescribed and special examinations which are prerequisites of employment. Furthermore, the position of the official is in the nature of a duty. This determines the internal structure of his relations, in the following manner: Legally and actually, office holding is not considered a source to be exploited for rents or emoluments, as was normally the case during the Middle Ages and frequently up to the threshold of recent times. Nor is office holding considered a usual exchange of services for equivalents, as is the case with free labor contracts. Entrance into an office, including one in the private economy, is considered an acceptance of a specific obligation of faithful management in return for a secure existence. It is decisive for the specific nature of modern loyalty to an office that, in the pure type, it does not establish a relationship to a *person,* like the vassal's or disciple's faith in feudal or in patrimonial relations of authority. Modern loyalty is devoted to impersonal and functional purposes. Behind the functional purposes, of course, "ideas of culture-values" usually stand. These are *ersatz* for the earthly or supra-mundane personal master: ideas such as "state," "church," "community," "party," or "enterprise" are thought of as being realized in a community; they provide an ideological halo for the master.

The political official—at least in the fully developed modern state —is not considered the personal servant of a ruler. Today, the bishop, the priest, and the preacher are in fact no longer, as in early Christian times, holders of purely personal charisma. The supra-mundane and sacred values which they offer are given to everybody who seems to be worthy of them and who asks for them. In former times, such leaders acted upon the personal command of their master; in principle, they were responsible only to him. Nowadays, in spite of the partial survival of the old theory, such religious leaders are officials in the service of a functional purpose, which in the present-day "church" has become routinized and, in turn, ideologically hallowed.

II. The personal position of the official is patterned in the following way:

1. Whether he is in a private office or a public bureau, the modern official always strives and usually enjoys a distinct *social esteem* as compared with the governed. His social position is guaranteed by the prescriptive rules of rank order and, for the political official, by special definitions of the criminal code against "insults of officials" and "contempt" of state and church authorities.

The actual social position of the official is normally highest where, as in old civilized countries, the following conditions prevail: a strong demand for administration by trained experts; a strong and stable social differentiation, where the official predominantly derives from socially and economically privileged strata because of the social distribution of power; or where the costliness of the required training and status conventions are binding upon him. The possession of educational certificates—to be discussed elsewhere[2]—are usually linked with qualification for office. Naturally, such certificates or patents enhance the "status element" in the social position of the official. For the rest this status factor in individual cases is explicitly and impassively acknowledged; for example, in the prescription that the acceptance or rejection of an aspirant to an official career depends upon the consent ("election") of the members of the official body. This is the case in the German army with the officer corps. Similar phenomena, which promote this guild-

2. Cf. *Wirtschaft und Gesellschaft,* pp. 73 ff. and part II. (German Editor.)

like closure of officialdom, are typically found in patrimonial and, particularly, in prebendal officialdoms of the past. The desire to resurrect such phenomena in changed forms is by no means infrequent among modern bureaucrats. For instance, they have played a role among the demands of the quite proletarian and expert officials (the *tretyj* element) during the Russian revolution.

Usually the social esteem of the officials as such is especially low where the demand for expert administration and the dominance of status conventions are weak. This is especially the case in the United States; it is often the case in new settlements by virtue of their wide fields for profit-making and the great instability of their social stratification.

2. The pure type of bureaucratic official is *appointed* by a superior authority. An official elected by the governed is not a purely bureaucratic figure. Of course, the formal existence of an election does not by itself mean that no appointment hides behind the election—in the state, especially, appointment by party chiefs. Whether or not this is the case does not depend upon legal statutes but upon the way in which the party mechanism functions. Once firmly organized, the parties can turn a formally free election into the mere acclamation of a candidate designated by the party chief. As a rule, however, a formally free election is turned into a fight, conducted according to definite rules, for votes in favor of one of two designated candidates.

In all circumstances, the designation of officials by means of an election among the governed modifies the strictness of hierarchical subordination. In principle, an official who is so elected has an autonomous position opposite the superordinate official. The elected official does not derive his position "from above" but "from below," or at least not from a superior authority of the official hierarchy but from powerful party men ("bosses"), who also determine his further career. The career of the elected official is not, or at least not primarily, dependent upon his chief in the administration. The official who is not elected but appointed by a chief normally functions more exactly, from a technical point of view, because, all other circumstances being equal, it is more likely that purely functional points of consideration and qualities will determine his selection and career. As laymen, the governed can become acquainted with the extent to which a candidate is expertly qualified for office only in terms of experience, and hence only after his service. Moreover, in every sort of selection of officials by election, parties quite naturally give decisive weight not to expert considerations but to the services a follower renders to the party boss. This holds for all kinds of procurement of officials by elections, for the designation of formally free, elected officials by party bosses when they determine the slate of candidates, or the free appointment by a chief who has himself been elected. The contrast, however, is relative: substantially similar conditions hold where legitimate monarchs and their subordinates appoint officials, except that the influence of the followings are then less controllable.

Where the demand for administration by trained experts is considerable, and the party followings have to recognize an intellectually developed, educated, and freely moving "public opinion," the use of unqualified officials falls back upon the party in power at the next election. Naturally, this is more likely to happen when the officials are appointed by the chief. The demand for a trained administration now exists in the United States, but in the large cities, where immigrant votes are "corraled," there is, of course, no educated public opinion. Therefore, popular elections of the administrative chief and also of his subordinate officials usually endanger the expert qualification of the official as well as the precise functioning of the bureaucratic mechanism. It also weakens the dependence of the officials upon the hierarchy. This holds at least for the large administrative bodies that are difficult to supervise. The superior qualification and integrity of federal judges, appointed by the President, as over against elected judges in the United States is well known, although both types of officials have been selected primarily in terms of party considerations. The great changes in American metropolitan administrations demanded by reformers have proceeded essentially from elected mayors working with an apparatus of officials who were appointed by them. These reforms have thus come about in a "Caesarist" fashion. Viewed technically, as an organized form of authority, the efficiency of "Caesarism," which often grows out of democracy, rests in general upon the position of the "Caesar" as a free trustee of the masses (of the army or of the citizenry), who is unfettered by tradition. The "Caesar" is thus the unrestrained master of a body of highly qualified military officers and officials whom he selects freely and personally without regard to tradition or to any other considerations. This "rule of the personal genius," however, stands in contradiction to the formally "democratic" principle of a universally elected officialdom.

3. Normally, the position of the official is held for life, at least in public bureaucracies; and this is increasingly the case for all similar structures. As a factual rule, *tenure for life* is presupposed, even where the giving of notice or periodic reappointment occurs. In contrast to the worker in a private enterprise, the official normally holds tenure. Legal or actual life-tenure, however, is not recognized as the official's right to the possession of office, as was the case with many structures of authority in the past. Where legal guarantees against arbitrary dismissal or transfer are developed, they merely serve to guarantee a strictly objective discharge of specific office duties free from all personal consid-

erations. In Germany, this is the case for all juridical and, increasingly, for all administrative officials.

Within the bureaucracy, therefore, the measure of "independence," legally guaranteed by tenure, is not always a source of increased status for the official whose position is thus secured. Indeed, often the reverse holds, especially in old cultures and communities that are highly differentiated. In such communities, the stricter the subordination under the arbitrary rule of the master, the more it guarantees the maintenance of the conventional seigneurial style of living for the official. Because of the very absence of these legal guarantees of tenure, the conventional esteem for the official may rise in the same way as, during the Middle Ages, the esteem of the nobility of office[3] rose at the expense of esteem for the freemen, and as the king's judge surpassed that of the people's judge. In Germany, the military officer or the administrative official can be removed from office at any time, or at least far more readily than the "independent judge," who never pays with loss of his office for even the grossest offense against the "code of honor" or against social conventions of the salon. For this very reason, if other things are equal, in the eyes of the master stratum the judge is considered less qualified for social intercourse than are officers and administrative officials, whose greater dependence on the master is a greater guarantee of their conformity with status conventions. Of course, the average official strives for a civil-service law, which would materially secure his old age and provide increased guarantees against his arbitrary removal from office. This striving, however, has its limits. A very strong development of the "right to the office" naturally makes it more difficult to staff them with regard to technical efficiency, for such a development decreases the career-opportunities of ambitious candidates for office. This makes for the fact that officials, on the whole, do not feel their dependency upon those at the top. This lack of a feeling of dependency, however, rests primarily upon the inclination to depend upon one's equals rather than upon the socially inferior and governed strata. The present conservative movement among the Badenia clergy, occasioned by the anxiety of a presumably threatening separation of church and state, has been expressly determined by the desire not to be turned "from a master into a servant of the parish."[4]

4. The official receives the regular *pecuniary* compensation of a normally fixed *salary* and the old age security provided by a pension. The salary is not measured like a wage in terms of work done, but according to "status," that is, according to the kind of function (the "rank") and, in addition, possibly, according to the length of service.

3. "Ministerialen."
4. Written before 1914. (German editor's note.)

The relatively great security of the official's income, as well as the rewards of social esteem, make the office a sought-after position, especially in countries which no longer provide opportunities for colonial profits. In such countries, this situation permits relatively low salaries for officials.

5. The official is set for a *"career"* within the hierarchical order of the public service. He moves from the lower, less important, and lower paid to the higher positions. The average official naturally desires a mechanical fixing of the conditions of promotion: if not of the offices, at least of the salary levels. He wants these conditions fixed in terms of "seniority," or possibly according to grades achieved in a developed system of expert examinations. Here and there, such examinations actually form a character *indelebilis* of the official and have lifelong effects on his career. To this is joined the desire to qualify the right to office and the increasing tendency toward status group closure and economic security. All of this makes for a tendency to consider the offices as "prebends" of those who are qualified by educational certificates. The necessity of taking general personal and intellectual qualifications into consideration, irrespective of the often subaltern character of the educational certificate, has led to a condition in which the highest political offices, especially the positions of "ministers," are principally filled without reference to such certificates.

* * *

TECHNICAL ADVANTAGES OF BUREAUCRATIC ORGANIZATION

The decisive reason for the advance of bureaucratic organization has always been its purely technical superiority over any other form of organization. The fully developed bureaucratic mechanism compares with other organizations exactly as does the machine with the non-mechanical modes of production.

Precision, speed, unambiguity, knowledge of the files, continuity, discretion, unity, strict subordination, reduction of friction and of material and personal costs—these are raised to the optimum point in the strictly bureaucratic administration, and especially in its monocratic form. As compared with all collegiate, honorific, and avocational forms of administration, trained bureaucracy is superior on all these points. And as far as complicated tasks are concerned, paid bureaucratic work is not only more precise but, in the last analysis, it is often cheaper than even formally unremunerated honorific service.

Honorific arrangements make administrative work an avocation and, for this reason alone, honorific service normally functions more slowly; being less bound to schemata and being more formless. Hence it is less precise and less unified than bureaucratic work because it is less dependent upon superiors and because the establishment and exploitation of the apparatus of subordinate officials and filing services are almost unavoidably less economical. Honorific service is less continuous than bureaucratic and frequently quite expensive. This is especially the case if one thinks not only of the money costs to the public treasury— costs which bureaucratic administration, in comparison with administration by notables, usually substantially increases—but also of the frequent economic losses of the governed caused by delays and lack of precision. The possibility of administration by notables normally and permanently exists only where official management can be satisfactorily discharged as an avocation. With the qualitative increase of tasks the administration has to face, administration by notables reaches its limits —today, even in England. Work organized by collegiate bodies causes friction and delay and requires compromises between colliding interests and views. The administration, therefore, runs less precisely and is more independent of superiors; hence, it is less unified and slower. All advances of the Prussian administrative organization have been and will in the future be advances of the bureaucratic, and especially of the monocratic, principle.

Today, it is primarily the capitalist market economy which demands that the official business of the administration be discharged precisely, unambiguously, continuously, and with as much speed as possible. Normally, the very large, modern capitalist enterprises are themselves unequalled models of strict bureaucratic organization. Business management throughout rests on increasing precision, steadiness, and, above all, the speed of operations. This, in turn, is determined by the peculiar nature of the modern means of communication, including, among other things, the news service of the press. The extraordinary increase in the speed by which public announcements, as well as economic and political facts, are transmitted exerts a steady and sharp pressure in the direction of speeding up the tempo of administrative reaction towards various situations. The optimum of such reaction time is normally attained only by a strictly bureaucratic organization.*

Bureaucratization offers above all the optimum possibility for carrying through the principle of specializing administrative functions according to purely objective considerations. Individual performances are allocated to functionaries who have specialized training and who by constant practice learn more and more. The "objective" discharge of

---

*Here we cannot discuss in detail how the bureaucratic apparatus may, and actually does, produce definite obstacles to the discharge of business in a manner suitable for the single case.

business primarily means a discharge of business according to *calculable rules* and "without regard for persons."

"Without regard for persons" is also the watchword of the "market" and, in general, of all pursuits of naked economic interests. A consistent execution of bureaucratic domination means the leveling of status "honor." Hence, if the principle of the free-market is not at the same time restricted, it means the universal domination of the "class situation." That this consequence of bureaucratic domination has not set in everywhere, parallel to the extent of bureaucratization, is due to the differences among possible principles by which polities may meet their demands.

The second element mentioned, "calculable rules," also is of paramount importance for modern bureaucracy. The peculiarity of modern culture, and specifically of its technical and economic basis, demands this very "calculability" of results. When fully developed, bureaucracy also stands, in a specific sense, under the principle of *sine ira ac studio.* Its specific nature, which is welcomed by capitalism, develops the more perfectly the more the bureaucracy is "dehumanized," the more completely it succeeds in eliminating from official business love, hatred, and all purely personal, irrational, and emotional elements which escape calculation. This is the specific nature of bureaucracy and it is appraised as its special virtue.

The more complicated and specialized modern culture becomes, the more its external supporting apparatus demands the personally detached and strictly "objective" *expert,* in lieu of the master of older social structures, who was moved by personal sympathy and favor, by grace and gratitude. Bureaucracy offers the attitudes demanded by the external apparatus of modern culture in the most favorable combination. As a rule, only bureaucracy has established the foundation for the administration of a rational law conceptually systematized on the basis of such enactments as the latter Roman imperial period first created with a high degree of technical perfection. During the Middle Ages, this law was received along with the bureaucratization of legal administration, that is to say, with the displacement of the old trial procedure which was bound to tradition or to irrational presuppositions, by the rationally trained and specialized expert.

─────────────────── **2** ───────────────────

SUGGESTIONS FOR A SOCIOLOGICAL APPROACH TO THE THEORY OF ORGANIZATIONS—I

Talcott Parsons

For the purposes of this article the term "organization" will be used to refer to a broad type of collectivity which has assumed a particularly important place in modern industrial societies—the type to which the term "bureaucracy" is most often applied. Familiar examples are the governmental bureau or department, the business firm (especially above a certain size), the university, and the hospital. It is by now almost a commonplace that there are features common to all these types of organization which cut across the ordinary distinctions between the social science disciplines. Something is lost if study of the firm is left only to economists, of governmental organizations to political scientists, and of schools and universities to "educationists."[1]

The study of organization in the present sense is thus only part of the study of social structure as that term is generally used by sociologists (or of "social organization" as ordinarily used by social anthropologists). A family is only partly an organization; most other kinship groups are even less so. The same is certainly true of local communities, regional subsocieties, and of a society as a whole conceived, for example, as a nation. On other levels, informal work groups, cliques of friends, and so on, are not in this technical sense organizations.

THE CONCEPT OF ORGANIZATION

As a formal analytical point of reference, *primacy of orientation to the attainment of a specific goal* is used as the defining characteristic of an organization which distinguishes it from other types of social systems. This criterion has implications for both the external relations and the internal structure of the system referred to here as an organization.

The attainment of a goal is defined as a *relation* between a system

1. There is already a considerable literature on organization which cuts across disciplinary lines. It is not the intention of this paper to attempt to review it. Three writers have been particularly important in stimulating the author's thinking in the field: Max Weber, Chester I. Barnard, and Herbert Simon. See particularly, Weber, *Theory of Social and Economic Organization* (New York, 1957), ch. iii; Barnard, *The Functions of the Executive* (Cambridge, Mass., 1938); Simon, *Administrative Behavior: A Study of Decision Making Processes in Administrative Organization* (New York, 1951).

(in this case a social system) and the relevant parts of the external situation in which it acts or operates. This relation can be conceived as the maximization, relative to the relevant conditions such as costs and obstacles, of some category of *output* of the system to objects or systems in the external situation. These considerations yield a further important criterion of an organization. An organization is a system which, as the attainment of its goal, "produces" an identifiable something which can be utilized in some way by another system; that is, the output of the organization is, for some other system, an input. In the case of an organization with economic primacy, this output may be a class of goods or services which are either consumable or serve as instruments for a further phase of the production process by other organizations. In the case of a government agency the output may be a class of regulatory decisions; in that of an educational organization it may be a certain type of "trained capacity" on the part of the students who have been subjected to its influence. In any of these cases there must be a set of consequences of the processes which go on within the organization, which make a difference to the functioning of some other subsystem of the society; that is, without the production of certain goods the consuming unit must behave differently, i.e., suffer a "deprivation."

The availability, to the unit succeeding the organization in the series, of the organization's output must be subject to some sort of terms, the settlement of which is analyzable in the general framework of the ideas of contract or exchange. Thus in the familiar case the economic producer "sells" his product for a money price which in turn serves as a medium for procuring the factors of production, most directly labor services, necessary for further stages of the productive process. It is thus assumed that in the case of all organizations there is something analogous to a "market" for the output which constitutes the attainment of its goal (what Chester I. Barnard calls "organization purpose"); and that directly, and perhaps also indirectly, there is some kind of exchange of this for entities which (as inputs into it) are important means for the organization to carry out its function in the larger system. The exchange of output for input at the boundary defined by the attainment of the goal of an organization need not be the only important boundary-exchange of the organization as a system. It is, however, the one most directly involved in defining the primary characteristics of the organization. Others will be discussed later.

The existence of organizations as the concept is here set forth is a consequence of the division of labor in society. Where both the "production" of specialized outputs and their consumption or ultimate utilization occur within the same structural unit, there is no need for the differentiation of specialized organizations. Primitive societies in so far as their units are "self-sufficient" in both economic and other senses generally do not have clear-cut differentiated organizations in the present sense.

In its internal reference, the primacy of goal-attainment among the functions of a social system gives priority to those processes most directly involved with the success or failure of goal-oriented endeavors. This means essentially the decision-making process, which controls the utilization of the resources of the system as a whole in the interest of the goal, and the processes by which those responsible for such decisions can count on the mobilization of these resources in the interest of a goal. These mechanisms of mobilization constitute what we ordinarily think of as the development of power in a political sense.

What from the point of view of the organization in question is its specified goal is, from the point of view of the larger system of which it is a differentiated part or subsystem, a specialized or differentiated function. This relationship is the primary link between an organization and the larger system of which it is a part, and provides a basis for the classification of types of organization. However, it cannot be the only important link.

This article will attempt to analyze both this link and the other principal ones, using as a point of departure the treatment of the organization as a social system. First, it will be treated as a system which is characterized by all the properties which are essential to any social system. Secondly, it will be treated as a functionally differentiated subsystem of a larger social system. Hence it will be the other subsystems of the larger one which constitute the situation or environment in which the organization operates. An organization, then, will have to be analyzed as the special type of social system organized about the primacy of interest in the attainment of a particular type of system goal. Certain of its special features will derive from goal-primacy in general and others from the primacy of the particular type of goal. Finally, the characteristics of the organization will be defined by the kind of situation in which it has to operate, which will consist of the relations obtaining between it and the other specialized subsystems of the larger system of which it is a part. The latter can for most purposes be assumed to be a society.

THE STRUCTURE OF ORGANIZATIONS

Like any social system, an organization is conceived as having a describable structure. This can be described and analyzed from two points of view, both of which are essential to completeness. The first is the "cultural-institutional" point of view which uses the values of the system and their institutionalization in different functional contexts as its point of departure; the second is the "group" or "role" point of view which takes suborganizations and the roles of individuals participating in the functioning of the organization as its point of departure. Both of these will be discussed, as will their broad relations to each other, but primary attention will be given to the former.

On what has just been called the cultural-institutional level, a minimal description of an organization will have to include an outline of the system of values which defines its functions and of the main institutional patterns which spell out these values in the more concrete functional contexts of goal-attainment itself, adaptation to the situation, and integration of the system. There are other aspects, such as technical lore, ideology, and ritual symbolization, which cannot, for reasons of space, be taken up here.

The main point of reference for analyzing the structure of any social system is its value pattern. This defines the basic orientation of the system (in the present case, the organization) to the situation in which it operates; hence it guides the activities of participant individuals.

In the case of an organization as defined above, this value system must by definition be a subvalue system of a higher-order one, since the organization is always defined as a subsystem of a more comprehensive social system. Two conclusions follow: First, the value system of the organization must imply basic acceptance of the more generalized values of the superordinate system—unless it is a deviant organization not integrated into the superordinate system. Secondly, on the requisite level of generality, the most essential feature of the value system of an organization is the evaluative *legitimation* of its place or "role" in the superordinate system.

Since it has been assumed that an organization is defined by the primacy of a type of goal, the focus of its value system must be the legitimation of this goal in terms of the functional significance of its attainment for the superordinate system, and secondly the legitimation of the primacy of this goal over other possible interests and values of the organization and its members. Thus the value system of a business firm in our society is a version of "economic rationality" which legitimizes the goal of economic production (specified to the requisite level of concreteness in terms of particular goods and services). Devotion of the organization (and hence the resources it controls) to production is legitimized as is the maintenance of the primacy of this goal over other functional interests which may arise within the organization. This is Barnard's "organization purpose."[2] For the business firm, money return is a primary measure and symbol of success and is thus *part* of the goal-structure of the organization. But it cannot be the primary organi-

2. Barnard, *op. cit.,* pt. II, ch. vii.

zation goal because profit-making is not by itself a function on behalf of the society as a system.

In the most general sense the values of the organization legitimize its existence as a system. But more specifically they legitimize the main functional patterns of operation which are necessary to implement the values, in this case the system goal, under typical conditions of the concrete situation. Hence, besides legitimation of the goal-type and its primacy over other interests, there will be legitimation of various categories of relatively specific subgoals and the operative procedures necessary for their attainment. There will further be normative rules governing the adaptive processes of the organization, the general principles on which facilities can be procured and handled, and there will be rules or principles governing the integration of the organization, particularly in defining the obligations of loyalty of participants to the organization as compared with the loyalties they bear in other roles.

A more familiar approach to the structure of an organization is through its constituent personnel and the roles they play in its functioning. Thus we ordinarily think of an organization as having some kind of "management" or "administration"—a group of people carrying some kind of special responsibility for the organization's affairs, usually formulated as "policy formation" or "decision-making." Then under the control of this top group we would conceive of various operative groups arranged in "line" formation down to the lowest in the line of authority. In a somewhat different relation we would also think of various groups performing "staff" functions, usually some kinds of experts who stand in an advisory capacity to the decision-makers at the various levels, but who do not themselves exercise "line" authority.

It seems advantageous for present purposes to carry through mainly with the analysis of the institutional structure of the organization. Using the value system as the main point of reference, the discussion of this structure can be divided into three main headings. The primary adaptive exigencies of an organization concern the procurement of the resources necessary for it to attain its goal or carry out its function; hence one major field of institutionalization concerns the modes of procurement of these resources. Secondly, the organization will itself have to have institutionalized procedures by which these resources are brought to bear in the concrete processes of goal-attainment; and, finally, there will have to be institutional patterns defining and regulating the limits of commitments to this organization as compared with others in which the same persons and other resource-controllers are involved, patterns which can be generalized on a basis tolerable to the society as a whole.

The resources which an organization must utilize are, given the social structure of the situation in which it functions, the factors of production as these concepts are used in economic theory. They are land, labor, capital, and "organization" in a somewhat different sense from that used mainly in this paper.[3]

THE MECHANISMS OF IMPLEMENTATION

The problem of mobilizing fluid resources concerns one major aspect of the external relations of the organization to the situation in which it operates. Once possessing control of the necessary resources, then, it must have a set of mechanisms by which these resources can be brought to bear on the actual process of goal-implementation in a changing situation. From one point of view, there are two aspects of this process. First is the set of relations to the external situation centering around the problem of "disposal" of the "product" of the organization's activities. This involves the basis on which the scale of operations is estimated and on which the settlement of terms with the recipients of this product is arrived at. In the economic context it is the problem of "marketing," but for present purposes it is necessary to generalize this concept to include all products of organization functioning whether they are "sold" or not; for example, the products of a military organization may be said to be disposed of immediately to the executive and legislative branches of the government and through them to the public, but of course in no direct sense are they sold. The second aspect of the process is concerned with the internal mechanisms of the mobilization of resources for the implementation of the goal. For purposes of the present analysis, however, it will not be necessary to treat these internal and external references separately. Both, as distinguished from the mobilization of resources, can be treated together as governed by the "operative code" of the organization.

This code will have to have an essential basis in the value system which governs the organization. In the case of mobilization of resources, this basis concerns the problem of the "claims" of the organization to the resources it needs and hence the settlement of the terms on which they would be available to it. In the operative case it concerns the manner of their utilization within the organization and the relation to its beneficiaries. We may speak of the relevant value-implementation as centering about the question of "authorization" of the measures involved in carrying through the processes of utilization of resources.

There is an important sense in which the focus of all these functions is the process ordinarily called "decision-making." We have assumed that goal-attainment has clear primacy in the functioning of the organization. The paramount set of decisions then will be, within the frame-

---

3. This possibly confusing terminological duplication is retained here because organization as a factor is commonly referred to in economic theory.

work of legitimation previously referred to, the set of decisions as to how, on the more generalized level, to take steps to attain the goal. This is what is generally thought of as the area of *policy* decisions. A second set of decisions concerns implementation in the sense of decisions about the utilization of resources available to the organization. These are the *allocative* decisions and concern two main subject matters: the allocation of responsibilities among personnel, i.e., suborganizations and individuals, and the allocation of fluid resources, i.e., manpower and monetary and physical facilities in accord with these responsibilities. Finally, a third set of decisions concerns maintaining the *integration* of the organization, through facilitating cooperation and dealing with the motivational problems which arise within the organization in relation to the maintenance of cooperation. The first two sets of decisions fall within the area which Barnard calls the problem of "effectiveness"; the third is the locus of the problem of "efficiency" in his sense.[4] Let us consider each of these decision areas in more detail.

POLICY DECISIONS

By policy decisions are meant decisions which relatively directly commit the organization as a whole and which stand in relatively direct connection to its primary functions. They are decisions touching such matters as determination of the nature and quality standards of "product," changes in the scale of operations, problems of the approach to the recipients of the product or service, and organization-wide problems of modes of internal operation.

Policy decisions as thus conceived may be taken at different levels of generality with respect to the functions of the organization. The very highest level concerns decisions to set up a given organization or, conversely, to liquidate it. Near that level is a decision to merge with one or more other organizations. Then the scale descends through such levels as major changes in type of product or in scale of operations, to the day-to-day decisions about current operation. Broadly, this level of generality scale coincides with a scale of time-span of the relevance of decisions; the ones touching the longer-run problems of the organization tend to be the ones on a higher level of generality, involving a wider range of considerations and leading to more serious commitments. An important task for the theory of organization is a systematic classification of these levels of generality of decisions.

As has been noted, the critical feature of policy decisions is the fact that they commit the organization as a whole to carrying out their implications. This area of decisions is the focus of the problem of responsibility. One but only one major aspect of responsibility in turn lies in

---

4. Barnard, *op. cit.,* pt. I, ch. v.

the fact that all operations of organization to some extent involve risks, and the decision-maker on the one hand is to some extent given "credit" for success, and on the other hand is legitimately held responsible for unfavorable consequences. One of the major features of roles of responsibility is the handling of these consequences; this becomes particularly complicated psychologically because it is often impossible to assess accurately the extent to which success or failure in fact stem from particular decisions or result from factors outside the control or predictive powers of the decision-maker. On high levels of responsibility conflicts of moral value may also operate.[5]

Because of the commitment of the organization as a whole, and through this of the interests of everyone participating in the organization to a greater or lesser degree, authorization becomes particularly important at the policy-decision level. This clearly connects with the value system and hence with the problem of legitimacy. It concerns not simply the content of particular decisions, but the right to make them.

Different organizations, according to scale and qualitative type, of course, have different concrete ways of organizing the policy-making process. Often the highest level of policy is placed mainly in the hands of some kind of a board; whereas "management" has responsibility for the next highest levels, with the still lower levels delegated to operative echelons.

ALLOCATIVE DECISIONS

Higher policy decisions will concern the general type and quantity of resources brought into the organization and the more general policies toward personnel recruitment and financing. But the operative utilization of these facilities cannot be completely controlled from the center. There must be some allocative organization by which resources are distributed within the organization, and responsibility for their utilization in the various necessary operative tasks is assigned. This means that specialization in the functions of administration or management precludes the incumbents of these functions from also carrying out the main technical procedures involved in the organization-goal, and hence making the main operating decisions at the "work" level. Thus, a commanding general cannot actually man a particular aircraft or command a particular battery of artillery; a university president cannot actively teach all the subjects of instruction for which the university is responsible.

From one point of view, these mechanisms of internal allocation may be treated as "delegations of authority," though this formula will have to be qualified in connection with various cross-cutting considera-

5. *Ibid.,* ch. xvii.

tions of types of competence and so forth. Thus a general, who by training and experience has been an artilleryman, when he is in command does not simply "delegate" authority to the air element under his command; he must in some way recognize the special technical competence of the air people in a field where he cannot have such competence. Similarly a university president who by academic training has been a professor of English does not merely delegate authority to the physicists on his faculty. Both must recognize an independent technical basis for "lower" echelons performing their functions in the ways in which their own technical judgment makes advisable. The technical man can reasonably be held responsible for the *results* of his operations; he cannot, however, be "dictated to" with respect to the technical procedures by which he achieves these results.

Seen in this light, there are two main aspects of the allocative decision process. One concerns mainly personnel (organized in suborganizations, for example, "departments"), the other financial and, at the requisite level, physical facilities. In the case of personnel the fundamental consideration is the allocation of responsibility. Using decisions as the reference point, the primary focus of the responsibility problem is allocation of the responsibility to decide, i.e., the "decision who should decide," as Barnard puts it. Technical operations as such may then be treated as controlled by the allocation of responsibility for decisions.

The second main aspect of the allocation process is the budget. Though generally formalized only in rather large and highly differentiated organizations, analytically the budget is a central conception. It means the allocation of fluid financial resources which in turn can be committed to particular "uses," namely, acquisition of physical facilities and employment of personnel. Allocation of responsibility is definition of the *functions* of humanly organized subsystems of personnel. Budget allocation is giving these suborganizations access to the necessary means of carrying out their assignment. There is a certain important crisscrossing of the two lines in that at the higher level the decision tends to be one of budget, leaving the employment of the relevant personnel to the subsystem to which funds are allocated. The people responsible at the level in question in turn divide the resource stream, devoting part of it to personnel the employment of whom is, subject to general policies, under their control, another part to subbudget allocation of funds to the uses of personnel they employ. This step-down series continues until the personnel in question are given only various types and levels of control or use of physical facilities, and not control of funds.

COORDINATION DECISIONS

Two types of operative decisions have so far been discussed, namely policy decisions and allocative decisions. There is a third category which may be called "decisions of coordination," involving what Barnard has called the problems of "efficiency." These decisions are the operative decisions concerned with the integration of the organization as a system. Our two types of fundamental resources have a sharply asymmetrical relation to these decisions as they do to the allocative decisions. Funds (considered apart from their lenders or other suppliers) and physical resources do not have to be motivated to cooperate in organizational tasks, but human agents do. Decisions of policy and decisions of the allocation of responsibility still leave open the question of motivation to adequate performance.

This becomes an integrative problem because the special types of performance required to achieve the many complex contributions to an organization goal cannot be presumed to be motivated by the mere "nature" of the participants independently of the sanctions operating in the organizational situation. What is coordination from the point of view of the operation of the organization is "cooperation" from the point of view of the personnel. The limiting case of noncooperation is declining to continue employment in the organization, a case of by no means negligible importance where a free labor market exists. But short of this, relative to the goals of the organization, it is reasonable to postulate an inherent centrifugal tendency of subunits of the organization, a tendency reflecting pulls deriving from the personalities of the participants, from the special adaptive exigencies of their particular job situations, and possibly from other sources.

In this situation the management of the organization must, to some degree, take or be ready to take measures to counteract the centrifugal pull, to keep employment turnover at least down to tolerable levels, and internally to bring the performances of subunits and individuals more closely into line with the requirements of the organization than would otherwise be the case. These measures can take any one or a combination of three fundamental forms: (1) coercion—in that penalties for noncooperation are set, (2) inducement—in that rewards for valued performance are instituted, and (3) "therapy"—in that by a complex and judicious combination of measures the motivational obstacles to satisfactory cooperation are dealt with on a level which "goes behind" the overt ostensible reasons given for the difficulty by the persons involved.[6]

6. The famous phenomenon of restriction of production in the informal group as reported by F. J. Roethlisberger and W. J. Dickson *(Management and the Worker* [Cambridge, Mass., 1939], pt. iv) is a case of relative failure of integration and hence, from one point of view, of failure of management in the function of coordination. It could be handled, from the present point of view, neither by policy decisions (e.g., not to hire "uncooperative workers") nor by allocative decisions (e.g., to hold the shop boss strictly responsible for meeting high production quotas), but only by decisions of coordination, presumably including "therapeutic" measures.

———————————— **3** ————————————

MOTIVATIONAL CONSTRAINTS
The Decision to Participate

James G. March and Herbert A. Simon

The Barnard-Simon theory of organizational equilibrium is essentially a theory of motivation—a statement of the conditions under which an organization can induce its members to continue their participation, and hence assure organizational survival. The central postulates of the theory are stated by Simon, Smithburg, and Thompson as follows:

1. An organization is a system of interrelated social behaviors of a number of persons whom we shall call the *participants* in the organization.
2. Each participant and each group of participants receives *from* the organization *inducements* in return for which he makes *to* the organization *contributions.*
3. Each participant will continue his participation in an organization only so long as the inducements offered him are as great or greater (measured in terms of *his* values and in terms of the alternatives open to him) than the contributions he is asked to make.
4. The contributions provided by the various groups of participants are the source from which the organization manufactures the inducements offered to participants.
5. Hence, an organization is "solvent"—and will continue in existence—only so long as the contributions are sufficient to provide inducements in large enough measure to draw forth these contributions.[1]

The theory, like many theoretical generalizations, verges on the tautological. Specifically, to test the theory, and especially the crucial postulate 3, we need independent empirical estimates of (*a*) the behavior of participants in joining, remaining in, or withdrawing from organizations; and (*b*) the balance of inducements and contributions for each participant, measured in terms of his "utilities."

The observation of participants joining and leaving organizations is comparatively easy. It is more difficult to find evidence of the value of variable (*b*) that does not depend on the observation of (*a*). Before we can deal with the observational problem, however, we must say a bit more about the concepts of inducements and contributions.

Inducements. Inducements are "payments" made by (or through)

1. H. A. Simon, D. W. Smithburg, V. A. Thompson, *Public Administration,* New York: Knopf, 1950, pp. 381–382.

the organization to its participants (e.g., wages to a worker, service to a client, income to an investor). These payments can be measured in units that are independent of their utility to the participants (e.g., wages and income can be measured in terms of dollars, service to clients in terms of hours devoted to him). Consequently, for an individual participant we can specify a set of inducements, each component of the set representing a different dimension of the inducements offered by the organization. Thus, each component of the inducements can be measured uniquely and independently of the utilities assigned to it by the participants.

Inducement utilities. For each component in the set of inducements there is a corresponding utility value. For the moment we will not be concerned with the shape of the utility function; but we do not exclude from consideration a step function. The utility function for a given individual reduces the several components of the inducements to a common dimension.

Contributions. We assume that a participant in an organization makes certain "payments" to the organization (e.g., work from the worker, fee from the client, capital from the investor). These payments, which we shall call contributions, can be measured in units that are independent of their utility to the participants. Consequently, for any individual participant we can specify a set of contributions.

Contribution utilities. A utility function transforming contributions into utilities of the individual contributor can be defined in more than one way. A reasonable definition of the utility of a contribution is the value of the alternatives that an individual foregoes in order to make the contribution. As we shall see below, this definition of contribution utilities allows us to introduce into the analysis the range of behavior alternatives open to the participant.

These definitions of inducements and contributions permit two general approaches to the observational problem. On the one hand, we can try to estimate the utility balance directly by observing the behavior (including responses to pertinent questions) of participants. On the other hand, if we are prepared to make some simple empirical assumptions about utility functions, we can make predictions from changes in the amounts of inducements and contributions, without reference to their utilities.

To estimate the inducement-contribution utility balance directly, the most logical type of measure is some variant of individual satisfaction (with the job, the service, the investment, etc.). It appears reasonable to assume that the greater the difference between inducements and contributions, the greater the individual satisfaction. However, the critical "zero points" of the satisfaction scale and the inducement-contribution utility balance are not necessarily identical. The zero point for the satisfaction scale is the point at which one begins to speak of degrees of "dissatisfaction" rather than degrees of "satisfaction." It is, therefore, closely related to the level of aspiration and is the point at which we would predict a substantial increase in search behavior on the part of the organism.

The zero point on the inducement-contribution utility scale, on the other hand, is the point at which the individual is indifferent to leaving an organization. We have ample evidence that these two zero points are not identical, but, in particular, that very few of the "satisfied" participants leave an organization, whereas some, but typically not all, of the "unsatisfied" participants leave.[2]

How do we explain these differences? The explanation lies primarily in the ways in which alternatives to current activity enter into the scheme (and this is one of the reasons for defining contribution utilities in terms of opportunities foregone). Dissatisfaction is a cue for search behavior. Being dissatisfied, the organism expands its program for exploring alternatives. If over the long run this search fails, the aspiration level is gradually revised downward. We assume, however, that the change in aspiration level occurs slowly, so that dissatisfaction in the short run is quite possible. On the other hand, the inducement-contribution utility balance adjusts quickly to changes in the perception of alternatives. When fewer and poorer alternatives are perceived to be available, the utility of activities foregone decreases; and this adjustment occurs rapidly.

Consequently, we can use satisfaction expressed by the individual as a measure of the inducement-contribution utility balance only if it is used in conjunction with an estimate of perceived alternatives available. Speaking roughly, only the desire to move enters into judgments of satisfaction; desire to move *plus* the perceived ease of movement enters into the inducement-contribution utility measure. Many students of mobility (particularly those concerned with the mobility of workers) have tended to ignore one or the other of these two facets of the decision to participate.[3]

Direct observation of the inducement-contribution utilities, however, is not the only possible way to estimate them. Provided we make certain assumptions about the utility functions, we can infer the utility balance directly from observations of changes in the inducements or contributions measured in nonutility terms. Three major assumptions are useful and perhaps warranted. First, we assume that the utility functions change only slowly. Second, we assume that each utility func-

2. L. G. Reynolds, *The Structure of Labor Markets,* New York: Harper, 1951.
3. A. K. Rice, J. M. M. Hill, and E. L. Trist, "The Representation of Labour Turnover as a Social Process," *Human Relations,* 1950, 3, pp. 349–372.

tion is monotonic with respect to its corresponding inducement or contribution. Although we may not know what the utility of an increase in wages will be, we are prepared to assume it will be positive. Third, we assume that the utility functions of fairly broad classes of people are very nearly the same; within a given subculture we do not expect radical differences in values. Also, we can expect that if an increase in a given inducement produces an increase in utility for one individual, it will produce an increase for other individuals.

There are other reasonable assumptions about individual utility functions; some will be indicated below when we relate individual participation to other factors. These three assumptions, however, in themselves lead to a variety of estimation procedures. Under the first assumption the short-run effect of a change in inducements or contributions will be uncontaminated by feedback effects. By the second assumption (particularly in conjunction with the third) a host of ordinal predictions can be made on the basis of knowledge of changes in the inducements and contributions. The third assumption permits us to estimate some of the cardinal properties of the inducements-contributions balance, avoiding the problem of interpersonal comparison of utilities.

Assumptions such as those listed have some a priori validity, but it is more important that much of the evidence currently available on the behavior of participants is consistent with them. Thus, predictions are frequently and often successfully made by businessmen as to the feasibility of proposed organizational plans.

Consider the analysis of a businessman exploring the feasibility of a business venture. His first step is to construct an operating plan showing what activities and facilities are required to carry on the proposed business, including estimates of the quantities of "inputs" and "outputs" of all categories. In the language of economics, he estimates the "production function." In the language of organization theory, the production function states the rates of possible conversion of contributions into inducements.[4]

His second step is to estimate the monetary inducements that will be needed to obtain the inputs in the amounts required, and the monetary contributions that can be exacted for the outputs—i.e., the prices of factors of production and of product. In estimating these monetary inducements, predictions are being made as to the inducements-contributions balances of various classes of participants. Let us give some hypothetical examples:

Salaries and wages. Information is obtained on "going rates of wages" for similar classes of work in other companies in the same area.

4. H. A. Simon, "A Comparison of Organization Theories," *The Review of Economic Studies,* 1952–53, 20, pp. 40–48.

An implicit *ceteris paribus* assumption is made with respect to other inducements, or (if the work, say, is particularly unpleasant, if proposed working conditions are particularly good or bad, etc.) the monetary inducement is adjusted upward or downward to compensate for the other factors. If the problem is to attract workers from other organizations, it is assumed that a wage differential or other inducement will be required to persuade them to change.

Capital. Information is obtained on "the money market"—i.e., the kinds of alternative investment opportunities that are available, the weight attached to various elements of risk, and the levels of interest rates. It is then assumed that to induce investment, the terms (interest rates, security, etc.) must be at least equal to the inducements available in alternative investments.

The same procedure is followed for the inducements to other participants. In each case, information is required as to the alternative inducements offered by other organizations, and these establish the "zero level" of the net inducement-contribution balance. If nonmonetary factors are not comparable among alternatives, an estimated adjustment is made of the monetary inducements by way of compensation. Of course, the adjustment may just as well be made in the nonmonetary factors (e.g., in product quality).

If the planned inducements, including the monetary inducements, give a positive balance for all groups of participants, the plan is feasible. If the plan is subsequently carried out, a comparison of the actual operations with the estimates provides an empirical test of the assumptions and the estimates. If the outcomes fail to confirm the assumptions, the businessman may still choose which of the two sets of assumptions he will alter. He may interpret the result as evidence that the basic inducements-contributions hypothesis is incorrect, or he may conclude that he has estimated incorrectly the zero points of one or more of the inducements-contributions balances. The fact is, however, that such predictions are frequently made with substantial success.

The testing of the theory is not confined to predicting the survival of new enterprises. At any time in the life of an organization when a change is made—that (a) explicitly alters the inducements offered to any group of participants; (b) explicitly alters the contributions demanded from them; or (c) alters the organizational activity in any way that will affect inducements or contributions—on any of these occasions, a prediction can be made as to the effect of the change on participation. The effects may be measurable in terms of turnover rates of employees, sales, etc., as appropriate.

The theory of organizational equilibrium, as we have formulated it here, implies a structure—an organization—underlying the equilibrium. Specifically, there must exist a social system involving the participants that exhibits both a high degree of interrelationship and substantial differentiation from other systems within the total social milieu.

Up to this point, we have not tried to be precise in defining participation. In fact, we must necessarily be somewhat arbitrary in identifying some particular individuals as participants in a given organization. A number of individuals other than those we will identify as principal participants in a business organization receive inducements from the organization and provide contributions to its existence, and under special circumstances such "participants" may assume a dominant role in determining the equilibrium of the organization. But when we describe the chief participants of most business organizations, we generally limit our attention to the following five major classes: employees, investors, suppliers, distributors, and consumers.

Most obvious in any catalogue of organizational participants are the employees, including the management. Ordinarily, when we talk of organizational participants what we mean are workers, and membership in a business organization is ordinarily treated as equivalent to employment. Employees receive wages and other gratuities and donate work (production) and other contributions to the organization. As will become obvious below, employment is the area of participation in organizations in which the most extensive research has been executed.

The role of investors as participants in the organization is explicit in the economic theory of the firm but has rarely been included in other analyses of organizational behavior. A close analogue is found in some treatises on public administration where external power groups are dealt with specifically.[5] Although the participation of investors in the activities of business firms is frequently less active than that of political power groups in the management of governmental units, the behavior of investing participants is not so insignificant in the general American business scene as to warrant excluding them from consideration.

The distinction between units in a production-distribution process that are "in" the organization and those that are "out" of the organization typically follows the legal definition of the boundaries of a particular firm. We find it fruitful to use a more functional criterion that includes both the suppliers and the distributors of the manufacturing core of the organization (or its analogue where the core of the organization is not manufacturing). Thus, in the automobile industry it is useful to consider the automobile dealers as component parts of an automobile manufacturing organization.

Finally, the role of consumers in an organization has, like the role

5. *Op. Cit.,* Simon, Smithburg and Thompson. D. B. Truman, *The Governmental Process,* New York: Knopf, 1951. J. L. Freeman, *The Political Process, Executive Bureau-Legislative Committee Relations,* New York: Doubleday, 1955.

of investors, been generally ignored except by economic theorists. Since consumers are clearly part of the equilibrating system, organization theory must include in its framework the major components of a theory of consumption.

Taken too literally, this conception of organizations incorporates almost any knowledge about human behavior as a part of organization theory. However, we will limit our primary attention here to the participation of employees. Labor mobility has been studied at some length by both economists and social psychologists. Consequently, we will be able to find at least some evidence for the propositions cited. In general, the areas of investment behavior, supplier behavior, and middleman behavior are less well developed; and their propositions less well documented. Consumer behavior presents a somewhat different case, being the subject of considerable research.[6]

EMPLOYEE PARTICIPATION: THE PARTICIPATION CRITERION

In one respect an employee's relation to the organization is quite different from that of other participants. In joining the organization he accepts an authority relation; i.e., he agrees that within some limits (defined both explicitly and implicitly by the terms of the employment contract) he will accept as the premises of his behavior orders and instructions supplied to him by the organization. Associated with this acceptance are commonly understood procedures for "legitimating" communications and clothing them with authority for employees. Acceptance of authority by the employee gives the organization a powerful means for influencing him—more powerful than persuasion, and comparable to the evoking processes that call forth a whole program of behavior in response to a stimulus.

On the assumption that employees act in a subjectively rational manner, we can make some predictions about the scope of the authority relation from our knowledge of the inducements and contributions of the employees and other organization members.[7] An employee will be willing to enter into an employment contract only if it does not matter to him "very much" what activities (within the area of acceptance agreed on in the contract) the organization will instruct him to perform, or if he is compensated in some way for the possibility that the organization will impose unpleasant activities on him. It will be advantageous for the organization to establish an authority relation when the employee activities that are optimal for the organization (i.e., maximize the inducement utility to other participants of the employee's activity) cannot be predicted accurately in advance.

6. L. H. Clark (ed.), *Consumer Behavior,* New York: Harper, 1958.
7. *Op. Cit.,* Simon.

These propositions can be restated in a form that permits them to be tested by looking at terms of the employment contract. A particular aspect of an employee's behavior can be (*a*) specified in the employment contract (e.g., as the wage rate usually is), (*b*) left to the employee's discretion (e.g., sometimes, but not always, whether he smokes on the job), or (*c*) brought within the authority of the employer (e.g., the specific tasks he performs within the range fixed by the job specification). The conditions that make it advantageous to stipulate an aspect of behavior in the contract are sharp conflict of interest (e.g., as to wage level) and some uncertainty as to what that interest is. It is advantageous to leave to the employee's discretion those aspects that are of little interest to the employer but great interest to the employee; and to subject the employee to the organization's authority in those aspects that are of relatively great interest to the employer, comparatively unimportant to the employee, and about which the employer cannot make accurate predictions much in advance of performance.

The authority relation is not a simple one. The problems of defining and enforcing the "employment contract" are a matter of concern and potential conflict for all organizational participants.

To construct a series of hypotheses relating employee participation to external variables, we must first establish a criterion for "participation." Three methods of measuring participation yield substantially different results. First, we can measure the quantity of production by the individual worker. Second, we can use an absence criterion. Permanent physical absence associated with leaving the company payroll represents the extreme value on the low side. Differences in on-the-job productivity are not captured by the absence criterion but employees are distinguished by their absence rates as well as their turnover rates. Third, we can use a turnover criterion: we can identify participation with the all-or-none phenomena of being on or off the organization payroll.

Although it may appear at first blush that these measures simply reflect different degrees of disassociation from the organization and, therefore, are simply different points on a common continuum, the available empirical evidence indicates no consistent relation among measures of production, absences, and voluntary turnover.[8] The correlations are sometimes high, sometimes low; and the antecedent conditions for each result are difficult to specify. Some reasons for these findings are suggested by the available research, although substantiation is difficult.

8. *The Action Society Trust, Size and Morale,* London: The Action Society Trust, 1953. N. C. Morse, *Satisfactions in the White-Collar Job,* University of Michigan: Survey Research Center, 1953. A. H. Brayfield and W. H. Crockett, "Employee Attitudes and Employee Performance," *Psychological Bulletin,* 1955, 52, pp. 396–424.

First, under what conditions should we expect to find low absence (and/or productivity) associated with high voluntary turnover? We might expect that if extreme penalties are imposed for absence (relative to those generally expected in the group employed), absence rates will tend to be low among those who choose to stay on the job. But we should also expect to find a high rate of exit from the job. Similarly, where the ability to leave the organization is restrained (e.g., by governmental fiat), we should expect to find low voluntary turnover rates but (particularly if labor is scarce) relatively high absence rates.[9]

Second, under what conditions should we expect to find a positive relation between absence and turnover? Assume (1) that motivation to avoid the demands (i.e., contributions) of the job situation stems primarily from dissatisfaction with the inducements-contributions balance, (2) that for most people motivation to seek relief through temporary absence occurs at a point related consistently to the point at which motivation to quit occurs, and (3) that the factors contributing to individual dissatisfaction are general to the population of workers rather than specific to individual workers. Under these assumptions absence and voluntary turnover will be positively related when the penalties associated with absence and withdrawal are "normal."

Although we have scarcely touched the complexity of the relation among absenteeism, sickness, and turnover, we can see that the choice of a criterion of participation will significantly affect the propositions about participation. We propose here to use a turnover criterion, both because there is some intuitive sense in which such a criterion is most meaningful and because we have already dealt with the production criterion (which is closely ralated, at least conceptually, to the absence criterion) in the previous chapter. At the same time, however, we will attempt to point out how an absence criterion would support similar or different propositions.

9. E. Mayo and G. F. Lombard, *Teamwork and Labor Turnover in the Aircraft Industry of Southern California*, Boston: 1944.

——————————————— **4** ———————————————

ORGANIZATIONS AND THE SYSTEM CONCEPT

Daniel Katz and Robert L. Kahn

     The aims of social science with respect to human organizations are like those of any other science with respect to the events and phenomena of its domain. The social scientist wishes to understand human organizations, to describe what is essential in their form, aspects, and functions. He wishes to explain their cycles of growth and decline, to predict their effects and effectiveness. Perhaps he wishes as well to test and apply such knowledge by introducing purposeful changes into organizations—by making them, for example, more benign, more responsive to human needs.

     Such efforts are not solely the prerogative of social sciences, however; common sense approaches to understanding and altering organizations are ancient and perpetual. They tend, on the whole, to rely heavily on two assumptions: that the location and nature of an organization are given by its name; and that an organization is possessed of built-in goals—because such goals were implanted by its founders, decreed by its present leaders, or because they emerged mysteriously as the purposes of the organizational system itself. These assumptions scarcely provide an adequate basis for the study of organizations and at times can be misleading and even fallacious. We propose, however, to make use of the information to which they point.

     The first problem in understanding an organization or a social system is its location and identification. How do we know that we are dealing with an organization? What are its boundaries? What behavior belongs to the organization and what behavior lies outside it? Who are the individuals whose actions are to be studied and what segments of their behavior are to be included?

     The fact that popular names exist to label social organizations is both a help and a hindrance. These popular labels represent the socially accepted stereotypes about organizations and do not specify their role structure, their psychological nature, or their boundaries. On the other hand, these names help in locating the area of behavior in which we are interested. Moreover, the fact that people both within and without an organization accept stereotypes about its nature and functioning is one determinant of its character.

The second key characteristic of the common sense approach to understanding an organization is to regard it simply as the epitome of the purposes of its designer, its leaders, or its key members. The teleology of this approach is again both a help and a hindrance. Since human purpose is deliberately built into organizations and is specifically recorded in the social compact, the by-laws, or other formal protocol of the undertaking, it would be inefficient not to utilize these sources of information. In the early development of a group, many processes are generated which have little to do with its rational purpose, but over time there is a cumulative recognition of the devices for ordering group life and a deliberate use of these devices.

Apart from formal protocol, the primary mission of an organization as perceived by its leaders furnishes a highly informative set of clues for the researcher seeking to study organizational functioning. Nevertheless, the stated purposes of an organization as given by its by-laws or in the reports of its leaders can be misleading. Such statements of objectives may idealize, rationalize, distort, omit, or even conceal some essential aspects of the functioning of the organization. Nor is there always agreement about the mission of the organization among its leaders and members. The university president may describe the purpose of his institution as one of turning out national leaders; the academic dean sees it as imparting the cultural heritage of the past, the academic vice-president as enabling students to move toward self-actualization and development, the graduate dean as creating new knowledge, the dean of men as training youngsters in technical and professional skills which will enable them to earn their living, and the editor of the student newspaper as inculcating the conservative values which will preserve the status quo of an outmoded capitalistic society.

The fallacy here is one of equating the purposes or goals of organizations with the purposes and goals of individual members. The organization as a system has an output, a product or an outcome, but this is not necessarily identical with the individual purposes of group members. Though the founders of the organization and its key members do think in teleological terms about organizational objectives, we should not accept such practical thinking, useful as it may be, in place of a theoretical set of constructs for purposes of scientific analysis. Social science, too frequently in the past, has been misled by such short-cuts and has equated popular phenomenology with scientific explanation.

In fact, the classic body of theory and thinking about organizations has assumed a teleology of this sort as the easiest way of identifying organizational structures and their functions. From this point of view an organization is a social device for efficiently accomplishing through group means some stated purpose; it is the equivalent of the blueprint for the design of the machine which is to be created for some practical objective. The essential difficulty with this purposive or design approach is that an organization characteristically includes more and less than is indicated by the design of its founder or the purpose of its leader. Some of the factors assumed in the design may be lacking or so distorted in operational practice as to be meaningless, while unforeseen embellishments dominate the organizational structure. Moreover, it is not always possible to ferret out the designer of the organization or to discover the intricacies of the design which he carried in his head. The attempt by Merton[1] to deal with the latent function is one way of dealing with this problem. The study of unanticipated consequences as well as anticipated consequences of organizational functioning is a similar way of handling the matter. Again, however, we are back to the purposes of the creator or leader, dealing with unanticipated consequences on the assumption that we can discover the consequences anticipated by him and can lump all other outcomes together as a kind of error variance.

It would be much better theoretically, however, to start with concepts which do not call for identifying the purposes of the designers and then correcting for them when they do not seem to be fulfilled. The theoretical concepts should begin with the input, output, and functioning of the organization as a system and not with the rational purposes of its leaders. We may want to utilize such purposive notions to lead us to sources of data or as subjects of special study, but not as our basic theoretical constructs for understanding organizations.

Our theoretical model for the understanding of organizations is that of an energic input-output system in which the energic return from the output reactivates the system. Social organizations are flagrantly open systems in that the input of energies and the conversion of output into further energic input consist of transactions between the organization and its environment.

All social systems, including organizations, consist of the patterned activities of a number of individuals. Moreover, these patterned activities are complementary or interdependent with respect to some common output or outcome; they are repeated, relatively enduring, and bounded in space and time. If the activity pattern occurs only once or at unpredictable intervals, we could not speak of an organization. The stability or recurrence of activities can be examined in relation to the *energic input* into the system, the *transformation of energies within the system,* and the *resulting product or energic output.* In a factory the raw materials and the human labor are the energic input, the patterned activities of production the transformation of energy, and the finished product the output. To maintain this patterned activity requires a con-

---

1. R. K. Merton, *Social Theory and Social Structure,* rev. ed., New York: Free Press, 1957.

tinued renewal of the inflow of energy. This is guaranteed in social systems by the energic return from the product or outcome. Thus the outcome of the cycle of activities furnishes new energy for the initiation of a renewed cycle. The company which produces automobiles sells them and by doing so obtains the means of securing new raw materials, compensating its labor force, and continuing the activity pattern.

In many organizations outcomes are converted into money and new energy is furnished through this mechanism. Money is a convenient way of handling energy units both on the output and input sides, and buying and selling represent one set of social rules for regulating the exchange of money. Indeed, these rules are so effective and so widespread that there is some danger of mistaking the business of buying and selling for the defining cycles of organization. It is a commonplace executive observation that businesses exist to make money, and the observation is usually allowed to go unchallenged. It is, however, a very limited statement about the purposes of business.

Some human organizations do not depend on the cycle of selling and buying to maintain themselves. Universities and public agencies depend rather on bequests and legislative appropriations, and in so-called voluntary organizations the output reenergizes the activity of organization members in a more direct fashion. Member activities and accomplishments are rewarding in themselves and tend therefore to be continued, without the mediation of the outside environment. A society of bird watchers can wander into the hills and engage in the rewarding activities of identifying birds for their mutual edification and enjoyment. Organizations thus differ on this important dimension of the source of energy renewal, with the great majority utilizing both intrinsic and extrinsic sources in varying degree. Most large-scale organizations are not as self-contained as small voluntary groups and are very dependent upon the social effects of their output for energy renewal.

Our two basic criteria for identifying social systems and determining their functions are (1) tracing the pattern of energy exchange or activity of people as it results in some output and (2) ascertaining how the output is translated into energy which reactivates the pattern. We shall refer to organizational functions or objectives not as the conscious purposes of group leaders or group members but as the outcomes which are the energic source for a maintenance of the same type of output.

This model of an energic input-output system is taken from the open system theory as promulgated by von Bertalanffy (1956). Theorists have pointed out the applicability of the system concepts of the natural sciences to the problems of social science. It is important, therefore, to examine in more detail the constructs of system theory and the characteristics of open systems.

System theory is basically concerned with problems of relation-ships, of structure, and of interdependence rather than with the con-stant attributes of objects. In general approach it resembles field theory except that its dynamics deal with temporal as well as spatial patterns. Older formulations of system constructs dealt with the closed systems of the physical sciences, in which relatively self-contained structures could be treated successfully as if they were independent of external forces. But living systems, whether biological organisms or social organizations, are acutely dependent upon their external environment and so must be conceived of as open systems.

Before the advent of open-system thinking, social scientists tended to take one of two approaches in dealing with social structures; they tended either (1) to regard them as closed systems to which the laws of physics applied or (2) to endow them with some vitalistic concept like entelechy. In the former case they ignored the environmental forces affecting the organization and in the latter case they fell back upon some magical purposiveness to account for organizational functioning. Biological theorists, however, have rescued us from this trap by point-ing out that the concept of the open system means that we neither have to follow the laws of traditional physics, nor in deserting them do we have to abandon science. The laws of Newtonian physics are correct generalizations but they are limited to closed systems. They do not apply in the same fashion to open systems which maintain themselves through constant commerce with their environment, i.e., a continuous inflow and outflow of energy through permeable boundaries.

One example of the operation of closed versus open systems can be seen in the concept of entropy and the second law of thermodynamics. According to the second law of thermodynamics, a system moves to-ward equilibrium; it tends to run down, that is, its differentiated struc-tures tend to move toward dissolution as the elements composing them become arranged in random disorder. For example, suppose that a bar of iron has been heated by the application of a blowtorch on one side. The arrangement of all the fast (heated) molecules on one side and all the slow molecules on the other is an unstable state, and over time the distribution of molecules becomes in effect random, with the resultant cooling of one side and heating of the other, so that all surfaces of the iron approach the same temperature. A similar process of heat ex-change will also be going on between the iron bar and its environment, so that the bar will gradually approach the temperature of the room in which it is located, and in so doing will elevate somewhat the previous temperature of the room. More technically, entropy increases toward a maximum and equilibrium occurs as the physical system attains the state of the most probable distribution of its elements. In social systems, however, structures tend to become more elaborated rather than less differentiated. The rich may grow richer and the poor may grow poorer. The open system does not run down, because it can import energy from the world around it. Thus the operation of entropy is counteracted by the importation of energy and the living system is characterized by negative rather than positive entropy.

COMMON CHARACTERISTICS OF OPEN SYSTEMS

Though the various types of open systems have common characteristics by virtue of being open systems, they differ in other characteristics. If this were not the case, we would be able to obtain all our basic knowledge about social organizations through studying the biological organisms or even through the study of a single cell.

The following nine characteristics seem to define all open systems.

1. *Importation of energy.* Open systems import some form of energy from the external environment. The cell receives oxygen from the blood stream; the body similarly takes in oxygen from the air and food from the external world. The personality is dependent upon the external world for stimulation. Studies of sensory deprivation show that when a person is placed in a darkened soundproof room, where he has a minimal amount of visual and auditory stimulation, he develops hallucinations and other signs of mental stress.[2] Deprivation of social stimulation also can lead to mental disorganization.[3] Köhler's[4] studies of the figural after-effects of continued stimulation show the dependence of perception upon its energic support from the external world. Animals deprived of visual experience from birth for a prolonged period never fully recover their visual capacities.[5] In other words, the functioning personality is heavily dependent upon the continuous inflow of stimulation from the external environment. Similarly, social organizations must also draw renewed supplies of energy from other institutions, or people, or the material environment. No social structure is self-sufficient or self-contained.

2. *The through-put.* Open systems transform the energy available to them. The body converts starch and sugar into heat and action. The personality converts chemical and electrical forms of stimulation into sensory qualities, and information into thought patterns. The organiza-

2. P. Solomon, et al. (eds.), *Sensory Deprivation,* Cambridge, Massachusetts: Harvard University Press, 1961.
3. R. A. Spitz, "Hospitalism: An Inquiry Into the Genesis of Psychiatric Conditions in Early Childhood," *Psychoanalytic Study of the Child,* 1945, 1, pp. 53–74.
4. W. Köhler, and D. Emery. "Figural After-Effects in the Third Dimension of Visual Space," *American Journal of Psychology,* 1947, 60, pp. 159–201.
5. R. Melzack and W. Thompson, "Effects of Early Experience on Social Behavior," *Canadian Journal of Psychology,* 1956, 10, pp. 82–90.

tion creates a new product, or processes materials, or trains people, or provides a service. These activities entail some reorganization of input. Some work gets done in the system.

3. *The output.* Open systems export some product into the environment, whether it be the invention of an inquiring mind or a bridge constructed by an engineering firm. Even the biological organism exports physiological products such as carbon dioxide from the lungs which helps to maintain plants in the immediate environment.

4. *Systems as cycles of events.* The pattern of activities of the energy exchange has a cyclic character. The product exported into the environment furnishes the sources of energy for the repetition of the cycle of activities. The energy reinforcing the cycle of activities can derive from some exchange of the product in the external world or from the activity itself. In the former instance, the industrial concern utilized raw materials and human labor to turn out a product which is marketed, and the monetary return is used to obtain more raw materials and labor to perpetuate the cycle of activities. In the latter instance, the voluntary organization can provide expressive satisfactions to its members so that the energy renewal comes directly from the organizational activity itself.

The problem of structure, or the relatedness of parts, can be observed directly in some physical arrangement of things where the larger unit is physically bounded and its subparts are also bounded within the larger structure. But how do we deal with social structures, where physical boundaries in this sense do not exist? It was the genius of F. H. Allport[6] which contributed the answer, namely that the structure is to be found in an interrelated set of events which return upon themselves to complete and renew a cycle of activities. It is events rather than things which are structured, so that social structure is a dynamic rather than a static concept. Activities are structured so that they comprise a unity in their completion or closure. A simple linear stimulus-response exchange between two people would not constitute social structure. To create structure, the responses of A would have to elicit B's reactions in such a manner that the responses of the latter would stimulate A to further responses. Of course the chain of events may involve many people, but their behavior can be characterized as showing structure only when there is some closure to the chain by a return to its point of origin with the probability that the chain of events will then be repeated. The repetition of the cycle does not have to involve the same set of phenotypical happenings. It may expand to

6. F. H. Allport, "A Structuronomic Conception of Behavior: Individual and Collective. I. Structural Theory and the Master Problem of Social Psychology," *Journal of Abnormal and Social Psychology,* 1962, 64, pp. 3–30.

include more sub-events of exactly the same kind or it may involve similar activities directed toward the same outcomes. In the individual organism the eye may move in such a way as to have the point of light fall upon the center of the retina. As the point of light moves, the movements of the eye may also change but to complete the same cycle of activity, i.e., to focus upon the point of light.

A single cycle of events of a self-closing character gives us a simple form of structure. But such single cycles can also combine to give a larger structure of events or an event system. An event system may consist of a circle of smaller cycles or hoops, each one of which makes contact with several others. Cycles may also be tangential to one another from other types of subsystems. The basic method for the identification of social structures is to follow the energic chain of events from the input of energy through its transformation to the point of closure of the cycle.

5. *Negative entropy.* To survive, open systems must move to arrest the entropic process; they must acquire negative entropy. The entropic process is a universal law of nature in which all forms of organization move toward disorganization or death. Complex physical systems move toward simple random distribution of their elements and biological organisms also run down and perish. The open system, however, by importing more energy from its environment than it expends, can store energy and can acquire negative entropy. There is then a general trend in an open system to maximize its ratio of imported to expended energy to survive and even during periods of crisis to live on borrowed time. Prisoners in concentration camps on a starvation diet will carefully conserve any form of energy expenditure to make the limited food intake go as far as possible.[7] Social organizations will seek to improve their survival position and to acquire in their reserves a comfortable margin of operation.

The entropic process asserts itself in all biological systems as well as in closed physical systems. The energy replenishment of the biological organism is not of a qualitative character which can maintain indefinitely the complex organizational structure of living tissue. Social systems, however, are not anchored in the same physical constancies as biological organisms and so are capable of almost indefinite arresting of the entropic process. Nevertheless the number of organizations which go out of existence every year is large.

6. *Information input, negative feedback, and the coding process.* The inputs into living systems consist not only of energic materials which become transformed or altered in the work that gets done. Inputs are also informative in character and furnish signals to the struc-

7. E. Cohen, *Human Behavior in the Concentration Camp,* London: Jonathan Cape, 1954.

ture about the environment and about its own functioning in relation to the environment. Just as we recognize the distinction between cues and drives in individual psychology, so must we take account of information and energic inputs for all living systems.

The simplest type of information input found in all systems is negative feedback. Information feedback of a negative kind enables the system to correct its deviations from course. The working parts of the machine feed back information about the effects of their operation to some central mechanism or subsystem which acts on such information to keep the system on target. The thermostat which controls the temperature of the room is a simple example of a regulatory device which operates on the basis of negative feedback. The automated power plant would furnish more complex examples. Miller[8] emphasizes the critical nature of negative feedback in his proposition: *"When a system's negative feedback discontinues, its steady state vanishes, and at the same time its boundary disappears and the system terminates"* (p. 529). If there is no corrective device to get the system back on its course, it will expend too much energy or it will ingest too much energic input and no longer continue as a system.

The reception of inputs into a system is selective. Not all energic inputs are capable of being absorbed into every system. The digestive system of living creatures assimilates only those inputs to which it is adapted. Similarly, systems can react only to those information signals to which they are attuned. The general term for the selective mechanisms of a system by which incoming materials are rejected or accepted and translated for the structure is coding. Through the coding process the "blooming, buzzing confusion" of the world is simplified into a few meaningful and simplified categories for a given system. The nature of the functions performed by the system determines its coding mechanisms, which in turn perpetuate this type of functioning.

7. *The steady state and dynamic homeostasis.* The importation of energy to arrest entropy operates to maintain some constancy in energy exchange, so that open systems which survive are characterized by a steady state. A steady state is not motionless or a true equilibrium. There is a continuous inflow of energy from the external environment and a continuous export of the products of the system, but the character of the system, the ratio of the energy exchanges and the relations between parts, remains the same. The catabolic and anabolic processes of tissue breakdown and restoration within the body preserve a steady state so that the organism from time to time is not the identical organism it was but a highly similar organism. The steady state is seen in clear

---

8. J. G. Miller, "Toward a General Theory for the Behavioral Sciences," *American Psychologist,* 1955, 10, pp. 513–531.

form in the homeostatic processes for the regulation of body temperature; external conditions of humidity and temperature may vary, but the temperature of the body remains the same. The endocrine glands are a regulatory mechanism for preserving an evenness of physiological functioning. The general principle here is that of Le Châtelier (see Bradley and Calvin[9]) who maintains that any internal or external factor making for disruption of the system is countered by forces which restore the system as closely as possible to its previous state. Krech and Crutchfield[10] similarly hold, with respect to psychological organization, that cognitive structures will react to influences in such a way as to absorb them with minimal change to existing cognitive integration.

The homeostatic principle does not apply literally to the functioning of all complex living systems, in that in counteracting entropy they move toward growth and expansion. This apparent contradiction can be resolved, however, if we recognize the complexity of the subsystems and their interaction in anticipating changes necessary for the maintenance of an overall steady state. Stagner has pointed out that the initial disturbance of a given tissue constancy within the biological organism will result in mobilization of energy to restore the balance, but that recurrent upsets will lead to actions to anticipate the disturbance:

> We eat before we experience intense hunger pangs. . . . energy mobilization for forestalling tactics must be explained in terms of a *cortical tension* which reflects the visceral-proprioceptive pattern of the original biological disequilibration. . . . *Dynamic homeostasis* involves the maintenance of tissue constancies by establishing a constant physical environment—by reducing the variability and disturbing effects of external stimulation. Thus the organism does not simply restore the prior equilibrium. A new, more complex and more comprehensive equilibrium is established.[11]

Though the tendency toward a steady state in its simplest form is homeostatic, as in the preservation of a constant body temperature, the basic principle is *the preservation of the character of the system.* The equilibrium which complex systems approach is often that of a quasi-stationary equilibrium, to use Lewin's concept.[12] An adjustment in one direction is countered by a movement in the opposite direction and both movements are approximate rather than precise in their compensatory nature. Thus a temporal chart of activity will show a series of ups and downs rather than a smooth curve.

In preserving the character of the system, moreover, the structure

9. D. F. Bradley and M. Calvin, "Behavior: Imbalance in a Network of Chemical Transformations," *General Systems,* Yearbook of the Society for the Advancement of General Systems Theory, 1956, 1, pp. 56–65.
10. D. Krech and R. Crutchfield, *Theory and Problems of Social Psychology,* New York: McGraw-Hill, 1948.
11. R. Stagner, *The Psychology of Industrial Conflict,* New York: Wiley, 1956, p. 5.
12. K. Lewin, "Frontiers in Group Dynamics," *Human Relations,* 1947, 1, pp. 5–41.

will tend to import more energy than is required for its output, as we have already noted in discussing negative entropy. To insure survival, systems will operate to acquire some margin of safety beyond the immediate level of existence. The body will store fat, the social organization will build up reserves, the society will increase its technological and cultural base. Miller[13] has formulated the proposition that the rate of growth of a system—within certain ranges—is exponential if it exists in a medium which makes available unrestricted amounts of energy for input.

In adapting to their environment, systems will attempt to cope with external forces by ingesting them or acquiring control over them. The physical boundedness of the single organism means that such attempts at control over the environment affect the behavioral system rather than the biological system of the individual. Social systems will move, however, towards incorporating within their boundaries the external resources essential to survival. Again the result is an expansion of the original system.

Thus, the steady state which at the simple level is one of homeostasis over time, at more complex levels becomes one of preserving the character of the system through growth and expansion. The basic type of system does not change directly as a consequence of expansion. The most common type of growth is a multiplication of the same type of cycles or subsystems—a change in quantity rather than in quality. Animal and plant species grow by multiplication. A social system adds more units of the same essential type as it already has. Haire[14] has studied the ratio between the sizes of different subsystems in growing business organizations. He found that though the number of people increased in both the production subsystem and the subsystem concerned with the external world, the ratio of the two groups remained constant. Qualitative change does occur, however, in two ways. In the first place, quantitative growth calls for supportive subsystems of a specialized character not necessary when the system was smaller. In the second place, there is a point where quantitative changes produce a qualitative difference in the functioning of a system. A small college which triples its size is no longer the same institution in terms of the relation between its administration and faculty, relations among the various academic departments, or the nature of its instruction.

In fine, living systems exhibit a growth or expansion dynamic in which they maximize their basic character. They react to change or they anticipate change growth which assimilates the new energic inputs to the nature of their structure. In terms of Lewin's quasi-station-

13. *Op. Cit.,* J. G. Miller.
14. M. Haire, "Biological Models and Empirical Histories of the Growth of Organizations," in M. Haire (ed.), *Modern Organization Theory,* New York: Wiley, 1959, pp. 272–306.

ary equilibrium the ups and downs of the adjustive process do not always result in a return to the old level. Under certain circumstances a solidification or freezing occurs during one of the adjustive cycles. A new base line level is thus established and successive movements fluctuate around this plateau which may be either above or below the previous plateau of operation.

8. *Differentiation*. Open systems move in the direction of differentiation and elaboration. Diffuse global patterns are replaced by more specialized functions. The sense organs and the nervous system evolved as highly differentiated structures from the primitive nervous tissues. The growth of the personality proceeds from primitive, crude organizations of mental functions to hierarchically structured and well-differentiated systems of beliefs and feelings. Social organizations move toward the multiplication and elaboration of roles with greater specialization of function. In the United States today medical specialists now outnumber the general practitioners.

One type of differentiated growth in systems is what von Bertalanffy terms progressive mechanization. It finds expression in the way in which a system achieves a steady state. The early method is a process which involves an interaction of various dynamic forces, whereas the later development entails the use of a regulatory feedback mechanism. He writes:

> It can be shown that the *primary* regulations in organic systems, that is, those which are most fundamental and primitive in embryonic development as well as in evolution, are of such nature of dynamic interaction. . . . superimposed are those regulations which we may call *secondary,* and which are controlled by fixed arrangements, especially of the feedback type. This state of affairs is a consequence of a general principle of organization which may be called progressive mechanization. At first, systems—biological, neurological, psychological or social —are governed by dynamic interaction of their components; later on, fixed arrangements and conditions of constraint are established which render the system and its parts more efficient, but also gradually diminish and eventually abolish its equipotentiality.[15]

9. *Equifinality*. Open systems are further characterized by the principle of equifinality, a principle suggested by von Bertalanffy in 1940. According to this principle, a system can reach the same final state from differing initial conditions and by a variety of paths. The well-known biological experiments on the sea urchin show that a normal creature of that species can develop from a complete ovum, from each half of a divided ovum, or from the fusion product of two whole ova. As open systems move toward regulatory mechanisms to control their operations, the amount of equifinity may be reduced.

15. L. von Bertalanffy, "General Systems Theory," *General Systems,* Yearbook of the Society for the Advancement of General Systems Theory, 1956, 1, p. 6.

SOME CONSEQUENCES OF VIEWING ORGANIZATIONS AS OPEN SYSTEMS

In subsequent writings, we shall inquire into the specific implications of considering organizations as open systems and into the ways in which social organizations differ from other types of living systems. At this point, however, we should call attention to some of the misconceptions which arise both in theory and practice when social organizations are regarded as closed rather than open systems.

The major misconception is the failure to recognize fully that the organization is continually dependent upon inputs from the environment and that the flow of materials and human energy is not a constant. The fact that organizations have built-in protective devices to maintain stability and that they are notoriously difficult to change in the direction of some reformer's desires should not obscure the realities of the dynamic interrelationships of any social structure with its social and natural environment. The very efforts of the organization to maintain a constant external environment produce changes in organizational structure. The reaction to changed inputs to mute their possible revolutionary implications also results in changes.

The typical models in organizational theorizing concentrate upon principles of internal functioning as if these problems were independent of changes in the environment and as if they did not affect the maintenance inputs of motivation and morale. Moves toward tighter integration and coordination are made to insure stability, when flexibility may be the more important requirement. Moreover, coordination and control become ends in themselves rather than means to an end. They are not seen in full perspective as adjusting the system to its environment but as desirable goals within a closed system. In fact, however, every attempt at coordination which is not functionally required may produce a host of new organizational problems.

One error which stems from this kind of misconception is the failure to recognize the equifinality of the open system, namely that there are more ways than one of producing a given outcome. In a closed physical system the same initial conditions must lead to the same final result. In open systems this is not true even at the biological level. It is much less true at the social level. Yet in practice we insist that there is one best way of assembling a gun for all recruits, one best way for the baseball player to hurl the ball in from the outfield, and that we standardize and teach these best methods. Now it is true under certain conditions that there is one best way, but these conditions must first be established. The general principle, which characterizes all open systems, is that there does not have to be a single method for achieving an objective.

A second error lies in the notion that irregularities in the functioning of a system due to environmental influences are error variances and should be treated accordingly. According to this conception, they should be controlled out of studies of organizations. From the organization's own operations they should be excluded as irrelevant and should be guarded against. The decisions of officers to omit a consideration of external factors or to guard against such influences in a defensive fashion, as if they would go away if ignored, is an instance of this type of thinking. So is the now outmoded "public be damned" attitude of businessmen toward the clientele upon whose support they depend. Open system theory, on the other hand, would maintain that environmental influences are not sources of error variance but are integrally related to the functioning of a social system, and that we cannot understand a system without a constant study of the forces that impinge upon it.

Thinking of the organization as a closed system, moreover, results in a failure to develop the intelligence or feedback function of obtaining adequate information about the changes in environmental forces. It is remarkable how weak many industrial companies are in their market research departments when they are so dependent upon the market. The prediction can be hazarded that organizations in our society will increasingly move toward the improvement of the facilities for research in assessing environmental forces. The reason is that we are in the process of correcting our misconception of the organization as a closed system.

Emery and Trist have pointed out how current theorizing on organizations still reflects the older closed system conceptions. They write:

> In the realm of social theory, however, there has been something of a tendency to continue thinking in terms of a "closed" system, that is, to regard the enterprise as sufficiently independent to allow most of its problems to be analyzed with reference to its internal structure and without reference to its external environment. . . . In practice the system theorists in social science . . . did "tend to focus on the statics of social structure and to neglect the study of structural change." In an attempt to overcome this bias, Merton suggested that "the concept of dysfunction, which implied the concept of strain, stress and tension on the structural level, provides an analytical approach to the study of dynamics and change." This concept has been widely accepted by system theorists but while it draws attention to sources of imbalance within an organization it does not conceptually reflect the mutual permeation of an organization and its environment that is the cause of such imbalance. It still retains the limiting perspectives of "closed system" theorizing. In the administrative field the same limitations may be seen in the otherwise invaluable contributions of Barnard and related writers.[16]

16. F. E. Emery and E. L. Trist, "Socio-technical Systems." in *Management Sciences Models and Techniques,* Vol. 2, London: Pergamon Press, 1960, p. 84.

SUMMARY

The open-system approach to organizations is contrasted with common-sense approaches, which tend to accept popular names and stereotypes as basic organizational properties and to identify the purpose of an organization in terms of the goals of its founders and leaders.

The open-system approach, on the other hand, begins by identifying and mapping the repeated cycles of input, transformation, output, and renewed input which comprise the organizational pattern. This approach to organizations represents the adaptation of work in biology and in the physical sciences by von Bertalanffy and the others.

Organizations as a special class of open systems have properties of their own, but they share other properties in common with all open systems. These include the importation of energy from the environment, the through-put or transformation of the imported energy into some product form which is characteristic of the system, the exporting of that product into the environment, and the reenergizing of the system from sources in the environment.

Open systems also share the characteristics of negative entropy, feedback, homeostasis, differentiation, and equifinality. The law of negative entropy states that systems survive and maintain their characteristic internal order only so long as they import from the environment more energy than they expend in the process of transformation and exportation. The feedback principle has to do with information input, which is a special kind of energic importation, a kind of signal to the system about environmental conditions and about the functioning of the system in relation to its environment. The feedback of such information enables the system to correct for its own malfunctioning or for changes in the environment, and thus to maintain a steady state or homeostasis. This is a dynamic rather than a static balance, however. Open systems are not at rest but tend toward differentiation and elaboration, both because of subsystem dynamics and because of the relationship between growth and survival. Finally, open systems are characterized by the principle of equifinality, which asserts that systems can reach the same final state from different initial conditions and by different paths of development.

Traditional organizational theories have tended to view the human organization as a closed system. This tendency has led to a disregard of differing organizational environments and the nature of organizational dependency on environment. It has led also to an overconcentration on principles of internal organizational functioning, with consequent failure to develop and understand the processes of feedback which are essential to survival.

---------------------------------- **5** ----------------------------------

A FRAMEWORK FOR THE
COMPARATIVE ANALYSIS OF
ORGANIZATIONS

Charles Perrow

This paper presents a perspective on organizations that hopefully will provide a basis for comparative organizational analysis, and also allow one to utilize selectively the existing theories of organizational behavior. There are four characteristics of this perspective.

First, technology, or the work done in organizations, is considered the defining characteristic of organizations. That is, organizations are seen primarily as systems for getting work done, for applying techniques to the problem of altering raw materials—whether the materials be people, symbols or things. This is in contrast to other perspectives which see organizations as, for example, cooperative systems, institutions, or decision-making systems.

Second, this perspective treats technology as an independent variable, and structure—the arrangements among people for getting work done—as a dependent variable. Goals are conceived of as being in part a dependent variable. What is held to be an independent and dependent variable when one abstracts general variables from a highly interdependent and complex social system is less of an assertion about reality than a strategy of analysis. Thus, no claim is made that for all purposes technology need be an independent variable.

Third, this perspective attempts to conceptualize the organization as a whole, rather than to deal only with specific processes or subparts. Thus, while the importance of technology has often been demonstrated within work groups or for particular organizational processes, here it will be used as a basis for dealing with the organization as an organization.

Finally, and in the long run perhaps most importantly, the perspective holds that technology is a better basis for comparing organizations than the several schemes which now exist.[1]

Revision of a paper read at the 1966 Annual Meeting of the American Sociological Association. This paper was prepared during the course of research on industrial corporations supported by Grant No. GS-742, National Science Foundation. Numerous colleagues criticized an earlier version unstintingly, but I would like to single out Ernest Vargas, Geoffrey Guest and Anthony Kovner, who transcended their graduate student roles at the University of Pittsburgh during the formulation of these ideas in sticky field situations.
1. E.g., social function (schools, business firms, hospitals, etc.), as used by Talcott Parsons in *Structure and Process in Modern Society*, Glencoe, Ill.: The Free Press, 1960, pp. 44–47; who benefits, proposed

None of these points in itself is new, and the last section of this article discusses the uses to which the concept of technology has been put by others. However, the attempt to deal with all four points simultaneously, or, to put it differently, to pay systematic attention to the role of technology in analyzing and comparing organizations as a whole, is believed to be distinctive.

TECHNOLOGY AND RAW MATERIALS

By technology is meant the actions that an individual performs upon an object, with or without the aid of tools or mechanical devices, in order to make some change in that object. The object, or "raw material," may be a living being, human or otherwise, a symbol or an inanimate object. People are raw materials in people-changing or people-processing organizations; symbols are materials in banks, advertising agencies and some research organizations; the interactions of people are raw materials to be manipulated by administrators in organizations; boards of directors, committees and councils are usually involved with the changing or processing of symbols and human interactions, and so on.

In the course of changing this material in an organizational setting, the individual must interact with others. The form that this interaction takes we will call the structure of the organization. It involves the arrangements or relationships that permit the coordination and control of work. Some work is actually concerned with changing or maintaining the structure of an organization. Most administrators have this as a key role, and there is a variety of technologies for it. The distinction between technology and structure has its gray areas, but basically it is the difference between an individual acting directly upon a material that is to be changed and an individual interacting with other individuals in the course of trying to change that material. In some cases the material to be changed and the "other individuals" he interacts with are the same objects, but the relationships are different in each case.

There are a number of aspects of technology which are no doubt important to consider in some contexts, such as the environment of the work (noise, dirt, etc.) or the possibilities of seductive or exploitative relationships with clients, patients or customers. For our purposes, however, we are concerned with two aspects of technology that seem to be directly relevant to organizational structure. The first is the number of exceptional cases encountered in the work,[2] that is, the degree to

by Peter M. Blau and William R. Scott in *Formal Organizations,* San Francisco: Chandler, 1962, pp. 42–45; or compliance structure, as used by Amitai Etzioni, *A Comparative Analysis of Complex Organizations,* New York: The Free Press, 1961.

2. Cf. James March and Herbert Simon, *Organizations,* New York: Wiley, 1958, pp. 141–142, where a related distinction is made on the basis of search behavior. In our view the occurrence of an exceptional case is prior to search behavior, and various types of search behavior can be distinguished.

which stimuli are perceived as familiar or unfamiliar. This varies on a scale from low to high.

The second is the nature of the search process that is undertaken by the individual when exceptions occur. We distinguish two types of search process. The first type involves a search which can be conducted on a logical, analytical basis. Search processes are always exceptional actions undertaken by the individual. They are nonroutine. No programs exist for them. If a program exists, only a very trivial search is involved in switching from one program to another program when the stimuli change.[3] But though nonroutine, one type of search may be logical, systematic and analytical. This is exemplified by the mechanical engineering unit of a firm building large machinery, or by programmers writing individual programs for slow readers in a special school. The second type of search process occurs when the problem is so vague and poorly conceptualized as to make it virtually unanalyzable. In this case, no "formal" search is undertaken, but instead one draws upon the residue of unanalyzed experience or intuition, or relies upon chance and guesswork. Examples would be work with exotic metals or nuclear fuels, psychiatric casework, and some kinds of advertising. We can conceive of a scale from analyzable to unanalyzable problems.

If we dichotomize these two continua into the presence or absence of exceptional cases and into the presence or absence of analyzable problems, we have a four-fold table as in Figure 1. The upper right-hand quadrant, cell 2, where there are many exceptional cases and a few analytic techniques for analyzing them, is one extreme to which we will refer as nonroutine. In the lower left-hand quadrant, cell 4, we have the routine extreme, where there are few exceptions and there are analytic techniques for handling those that occur. A one-dimensional scheme would follow the dotted line from routine to nonroutine. But note that the other two quadrants may represent viable cases in themselves and they have been labeled with some industrial examples. Few cases would probably fall in the upper left-hand corner of cell 1, or lower right-hand corner of cell 3, but otherwise many organizations are expected to appear in these two cells.

Techniques are performed upon raw materials. The state of the art of analyzing the characteristics of the raw materials is likely to determine what kind of technology will be used. (Tools are also necessary, of course, but by and large, the construction of tools is a simpler problem than the analysis of the nature of the material and generally follows the analysis.) To understand the nature of the material means to be able to control it better and achieve more predictability and efficiency in transformation. We are not referring here to the "essence" of the material, only to the way the organization itself perceives it.

3. *Ibid.*, p. 142.

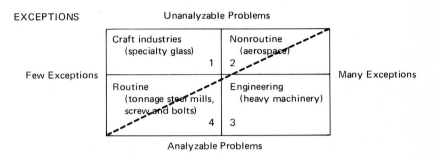

Figure 1.

The other relevant characteristic of the raw material, besides the understandability of its nature, is its stability and variability; that is, whether the material can be treated in a standardized fashion or whether continual adjustment to it is necessary. Organizations uniformly seek to standardize their raw material in order to minimize exceptional situations. This is the point of de-individualizing processes found in military academies, monasteries and prisons, or the superiority of the synthetic shoe material Corfam over leather.

These two characteristics interact, of course. On the one hand, increased knowledge of the nature of the material may lead to the perception of more varieties of possible outcomes or products, which in turn increases the need for more intimate knowledge of the nature of the material. Or the organization, with increased knowledge of one type of material, may begin to work with a variety of related materials about which more needs to be known, as when a social service agency or employment agency relaxes its admission criteria as it gains confidence, but in the process sets off more search behavior, or when a manufacturing organization starts producing new but related products. On the other hand, if increased knowledge of the material is gained but no expansion of the variety of output occurs, this permits easier analysis of the sources of problems that may arise in the transformation process. It may also allow one to prevent the rise of such problems by the design of the production process.

A recent analysis of a public defender system by Sudnow highlights the twin characteristics of the material variable.[4] On the one hand, offenders are distributed into uniform categories by means of the con-

4. David Sudnow, "Normal Crimes: Sociological Features of the Penal Code in a Public Defender Office," *Social Problems,* 12 (Winter, 1965), pp. 255–276.

ception of the "normal crime," and on the other hand, control over the individual offender is insured because the public defender well understands the offender's "nature"—that is, his low status, limited understanding and intellectual resources, and his impecunious condition. The technology, then, can be routine because there are few exceptions (and these are handled by a different set of personnel) and no search behavior on the public defender's part is required. The lawyer in private practice, of course, is a contrasting case.[5]

It will readily be seen that these two characteristics of the raw material are paralleled in the four-fold table of technology (Figure 2). If the technology of an organization is going to move from cell 2 to any of the other cells, it can only do so either by reducing the variability of the material and thus the number of exceptional cases that occur, or by increasing the knowledge of the material and thus allowing more analytic techniques to be used, or both. One may move from cell 2 to cell 1 with increasing production runs, clients served, accounts handled, research projects underway, agency programs administered and so forth, since this allows more experience to be gained and thus reduces the number of stimuli seen as exceptions. If technical knowledge increases, increasing the reliability of search procedures, one may move from cell 2 to cell 3. If both things happen—and this is the aim of most organizations—one may move from cell 2 to cell 4.[6]

TASK AND SOCIAL STRUCTURE

For our purpose, the task structure of an organization is conceived of as consisting of two dimensions, control and coordination. Control itself can be broken up into two components. They are the degree of discretion an individual or group possesses in carrying out its tasks, and the power of an individual or group to mobilize scarce resources and to control definitions of various situations, such as the definition of the nature of the raw material. Discretion here does not mean freedom from supervision or freedom simply to vary task sequences or pace of work. Both of these are compatible with routine activities, and some nonroutine tasks must be closely supervised or have precise sequences of tasks, once a program is selected, because of their critical nature. Nor does the length of time between performance reviews[7] necessarily indicate discretion. Rather, discretion involves judgments about whether close supervision is required on one task or another, about

---

5. For a more extensive treatment of raw material somewhat along these lines, see David Street, Robert Vinter and Charles Perrow, *Organization for Treatment, A Comparative Study of Institutions for Delinquents,* New York: The Free Press, 1966, Chap. 1.
6. Some organizations, such as mental hospitals, perceive that their technology is inadequate to their goals, and try to move from cell 4 to cell 2 in the search for a new technology.
7. Eliot Jaques, *The Measurement of Responsibility,* Cambridge: Harvard University Press, 1959.

Raw Material Variables
(People-Changing Examples)
PERCEIVED NATURE OF RAW MATERIAL

VARIABILITY   Not Well Understood
OF MATERIAL

Socializing instit. (e.g. some schools) 1	Elite psychiatric agency 2
Custodial institutions, vocational traning 4	Programmed learning school 3

Perceived as Uni-form and Stable

Perceived as Non-uniform and Stable

Well Understood

Figure 2.

changing programs, and about the interdependence of one's task with other tasks.[8] Discretion and power may often be correlated,[9] but there is an important distinction. Power affects outcomes directly because it involves choices regarding basic goals and strategies. Discretion relates to choices among means and judgments of the critical and interdependent nature of tasks. The consequences of decisions in the case of discretion have no direct influence on goals and strategies; these decisions are formed within the framework of accepted goals and strategies.

Coordination, on the other hand, can be achieved through planning or feedback, to use the terms proposed by March and Simon.[10] Coordination by planning refers to the programmed interaction of tasks, which interaction is clearly defined by rules or by the very tools and machinery or the logic of the transformation process. Coordination by feedback, on the other hand, refers to negotiated alterations in the nature or sequence of tasks performed by two different units.

It is now necessary to distinguish three functional or task areas

8. This raises serious operationalization problems. In my own work, first-line supervisors were said to have considerable independence in some routine production situations, and to have little in some nonroutine situations, according to a questionnaire, though it was observed that the former had little discretion and the latter a good deal. Kovner found the same kind of responses with a similar question regarding control of job and pace of work among nurses in routine and nonroutine nursing units. See Anthony Kovner, "The Nursing Unit: A Technological Perspective," unpublished Ph.D. dissertation, University of Pittsburgh, 1966. See also the discrepancy between scores on a similar matter resulting from different interpretations of discretion in two studies: Rose L. Coser, "Authority and Decision-Making in a Hospital," *American Sociological Review*, 23 (February, 1958), pp. 56–64, and James L. Hawkins, and Eugene Selmanoff, "Authority Structure, Ambiguity of the Medical Task, Absence of Doctor from the Ward, and the Behavior of Nurses," Indiana University, mimeo.
9. See, for example, a developmental scheme which holds that critical tasks requiring considerable discretion are the basis for group domination in hospitals and other organizations, in Charles Perrow, "Analysis of Goals in Complex Organizations," *American Sociological Review,* 26 (April, 1961), pp. 335–341. See also the compelling illustration presented in the discussion of maintenance personnel in a thoroughly routinized cigarette factory by Michel Crozier, *The Bureaucratic Phenomenon,* Chicago: University of Chicago Press, 1964, Chap. 4.
10. March and Simon, *op. cit.,* p. 160.

within management in organizations. Area One, the design and planning function, entails such major decisions as what goods or services are to be produced, who the customers will be, the technology employed, and the source of legitimacy and capital. Area Two, the technical control and support of production and marketing, includes such functions (to use industrial terms) as accounting, product and process research, quality control, scheduling, engineering, plant management, purchasing, customer service, advertising, market research, and general sales management. (Not all are important, or even existent, of course, in all industrial organizations.) This is distinguished as a function, though not necessarily in terms of actual persons or positions, from Area Three, the supervision of production and marketing. This area involves the direct supervision of those dealing with the basic raw materials and those doing direct selling.[11] In the subsequent discussion we shall ignore marketing, and, for a time, Area One.

Figure 3 shows crudely the kinds of values that might be expected to appear in the task structure, considering only Areas Two and Three —technical control and support of production, and the supervision of production. Some global organizational characterizations of structure are given at the bottom of each cell. Those familiar with Burns and Stalker's work will recognize cell 2 as closest to the organic structure and cell 4 as closest to the mechanistic structure.[12]

Task Structure
Task-Related Interactions

	Discretion	Power	Coord. w/in gp.	Interdependence of groups	Discretion	Power	Coord. w/in gp.	Interdependence of groups
Technical Superv.	Low	Low	Plan	Low	High	High	Feed	High
	High	High	Feed		High	High	Feed	
	Decentralized				Flexible, Polycentralized			
				1	2			
				4	3			
Technical Superv.	Low	High	Plan	Low	High	High	Feed	Low
	Low	Low	Plan		Low	Low	Plan	
	Formal, Centralized				Flexible, Centralized			

Figure 3.

11. The distinction between Areas Two and Three is based upon a more limited distinction used by Joan Woodward in her brilliant study, *Industrial Organization,* London: Oxford University Press, 1965.
12. Tom Burns and G. M. Stalker, *The Management of Innovation,* London: Tavistock Publications, 1961.

In cell 2, we have nonuniform raw materials in both areas which are not well understood, and thus present many occasions for exceptional handling. However, the search required cannot be logically conducted, but must involve a high degree of experimentation and "feel." In such a technological situation, the discretion of both those who supervise the transformation of the basic raw material, and those who provide technical help for this process, must be high. The supervisors will request help from technical personnel rather than receive orders from them, or there may not even be a clear line of distinction between the two in terms of persons. That is, the clinical psychologist or the quality control engineer will find himself "on the line" so to speak, dealing directly with patients or exotic metals and working side by side with the supervisors who are nominally of lower status. The power of both groups will be high, and not at the expense of each other. The coordination will be through feedback—that is, considerable mutual adjustment must be made. The interdependence of the two groups will be high. The development of product groups and product managers in industry provides an example, as does the somewhat premature attempt of one correctional institution to utilize a cottage system bringing both clinical and line personnel together with joint responsibility for running autonomous cottages.[13]

In the case of cell 4, uniform stable materials whose relevant nature is perceived as well understood can be handled with few exceptions occurring, and those that do occur can be taken care of with analytical search processes. In such a situation the discretion of both groups is likely to be low. This is a well-programmed production process and there is no need to allow much discretion. Indeed, there is danger in doing so. However, the power of the technical group over the supervisory group is high, for they direct the activities of the supervisors of production on the basis of routine reports generated by the supervisors. Those in Area Three are likely to see those in Area Two as hindrances to their work rather than aides. Coordination can be through planning in both groups, and the interdependence of the two groups is low; it is a directive rather than an interdependent relationship.

Cell 3 represents a variation from either of these extremes, for here, in contrast to cell 2, the existence of many exceptions which require search procedures increases both the power and the discretion of the technical group, which handles these exceptions, at the expense of the supervisory group. The supervisors of production respond to the results of these search processes rather than undertake search themselves. In the case of cell 1, the situation is reversed. Because search cannot be logical and analytical, when the infrequent exceptions occur

13. Street, *et al., op. cit.,* Chaps. 5, 6. The organization is called Milton.

they are handled by those in closest contact with the production process such as teachers and skilled craftsmen, and there is minimal development of administrative services. Of course, in schools that attempt to do little socialization but simply offer instruction and provide custody, technical (administrative) services grow and we move to cell 2.

Having thus related technology to task structure, let us turn to another aspect of structure—the non-task-related but organizationally relevant interactions of people. We call this the social structure.

(Social Structure)
The Bases of Non-Task-Related Interaction

Social identity (communal)	Goal identification (mission, "character" of organization, distinctive competence, etc.)
1	2
4	3
Instrumental identity (job security, pay, protection from arbitrary power)	Work or task identification (technical satisfactions)

Figure 4.

Figure 4 follows our previous four-fold classification and indicates the variety of bases for non-task-related interactions. All are present in all organizations, but the saliency varies. In cell 2, these interactions are likely to revolve more around the mission, long-range goals, and direction of development of the organizations than around the other three bases. This is because of the task structure characteristic of a flexible, polycentric organization, or at least is related to it. The category "social identity" in cell 1 is meant to convey that the non-task-related interactions of personnel that are organizationally relevant revolve around communal or personal satisfactions born of long tenure and close working relationships. This is true especially at the supervisory level, which is a large management group in this type of structure. However, it is very possible, as Blauner and others have shown, for communal relations to develop in cell 4 types of organizations if the organization is located in a rural area where kinship and rural ties are strong.[14] The basis of interaction in cell 3 is instrumental identity and in cell 4, work or task identification. These would also be predicted upon the basis of the technology.

14. Robert Blauner, *Alienation and Freedom: The Factory Worker and His Industry,* Chicago: University of Chicago Press, 1964, Chap. 4. Blauner's theory, incidentally, is entirely consistent with the perspective proposed here, even though we do not concern ourselves explicitly in this article with the morale of hourly employees.

So far we have ignored Area One—design and planning. This area receives more inputs from the environment than the other areas, and thus its tasks and technologies are derived from both internal and external stimuli. If the product environment of the organization—a term meant to cover competitors, customers, suppliers, unions and regulatory agencies—were the same in all four cells of Figure 3, we would expect the design and planning areas in cell 4 to have routine tasks and techniques, and nonroutine ones in cell 2. This is because the occasions for design and long-range planning would be few in the one and many in the other. For example, at least until very recently, the decisions that executives in the primary metals industries, railroads and surface mining had to make were probably rather routine, while those of executives in new industries such as electronics and aerospace were probably nonroutine.[15] One would expect that cell 1 would also be routine, and cell 3 somewhat nonroutine. But the product environment can alter all this. Organizations in cell 4 can be in a rapidly changing market situation even though the technical control and the supervision of production are fairly routine. Consumer goods industries probably deal with many decisions where the search behavior confronts unanalyzable problems such as the hemline of women's clothes, fads in the toy industry, or the length of time that tail fins or the boxy look in autos will last. Generally speaking, however, though the intrinsic characteristics of the product remain the same, rapid changes in the extrinsic characteristics will introduce nonroutine tasks in the design and planning area, even though it hardly alters the routine character of the technical control and the supervision of production.[16]

These are industrial examples, but it also seems likely that the tasks of Area One in custodial mental hospitals are quite different from those in treatment-oriented hospitals. Relations with the regulatory agencies, supplying agencies, the consumers such as courts and families, and the other agencies that compete for funds or clients, will be rather routine in the first, while they will be quite nonroutine and sensitive in the second. This would not be true, of course, if the latter have the means of isolating themselves from their environment.[17] Similarly, the market situation of vocational training institutions may change rather quickly as industrial technologies change, requiring changes in the design and

15. On the former see Alfred D. Chandler, Jr., *Strategy and Structure,* Cambridge, Mass.: MIT Press, 1962, pp. 329–330, and Chap. 7 in general. The discussion of social structure and time periods by Stinchcombe can be interpreted in this manner also. Those exceptions that occur in his data appear to be examples of nonroutine technologies established in periods of predominantly routine technologies, or *vice versa.* See Arthur Stinchcombe, "Social Structure and Organizations" in James March (ed.) *Handbook of Organizations,* Chicago: Rand McNally, 1965, pp. 142–169, esp. p. 158.

16. On the distinction between intrinsic and extrinsic prestige, see Charles Perrow, "Organizational Prestige, Some Functions and Dysfunctions," *American Journal of Sociology,* 66 (January, 1961), pp. 335–341.

17. Cf. Street, *et al., op. cit.,* Chap. 4.

planning of the institution, while the market of a public school that attempts to socialize youths will not change as often.

GOALS

Finally, let us turn to the last major variable, goals. Three categories of goals can be distinguished for present purposes.[18] These are system goals, which relate to the characteristics of the system as a whole, independent of its products; product characteristic goals, which relate to the characteristics of the products the organization decides to emphasize; and derived goals, which refer to the uses to which power generated by organizational activities can be put, independent of system or product goals.

Goals

System	Product	Derived	System	Product	Derived
Stability Few risks Moderate to low profit emphasis	Quality No innovations	Conserv. 1	High growth High risks Low emphasis on profit	High quality Innovative	Liberal 2

Stability
Few risks
High profit
  emphasis
	Quantity
	No innovations
		4
		Conserv.
			3
			Moderate growth
			Some risks
			Moderate profit
			  emphasis
				Reliability
				Moderate
				innovations
					Liberal

Figure 5.

We would expect completely routinized organizations to stress those "system" goals of organizational stability, low risk, and perhaps high profits or economical operations rather than growth. (See Figure 5.) In terms of "product characteristic" goals, they would be more likely to emphasize quantity than quality, stable lines over unstable or diversified lines, superficial transformations (e.g., instilling discipline in deviant clients) over basic transformation (such as character restructuring), and so forth. Their "derived" goals are likely to emphasize conservative attitudes towards the government, conservative political philosophies, conservative forms of corporate giving. Also, they are perhaps more likely to have individuals who exploit, for their own benefit, relations with suppliers, and who have collusive arrangements with competitors and devious and excessive forms of management compensation. Obvi-

18. For a full discussion of these and three others see Charles Perrow, "Organizational Goals," *International Encyclopedia of the Social Sciences,* (rev. ed.), forthcoming. (Draft copies, mimeo. 18 pp., can be obtained from the author.)

ously, these comments upon possible goals are open to serious question. For one thing, we lack such data on goals for a large number of organizations. Furthermore, personalities and the environment may shape goals more than the other variables of technology and structure. Finally, the link between structure and goals is an intuitive one, based upon unproven assumptions regarding attitudes generated by task relations. But the comments are meant to suggest how goals may be shaped or constrained, though hardly specified, through the influence of technology and structure.

SOME CAUTIONS

This truncated perspective ignores the role of the cultural and social environment in making available definitions of raw material, providing technologies, and restricting the range of feasible structures and goals.[19] It also ignores, for the most part, the role of the product environment—customers, competitors, suppliers, unions and regulatory agencies—and the material and human resources. These will have their independent effect upon the major variables.

In addition, it is not proposed here that there are four types of organizations. The two-dimensional scheme is conceived of as consisting of two continua. Nor are the dimensions and the specifications of the variables necessarily the best. It is argued, however, that the main variables—raw materials, technology, task and social structure, goals, and some differentiation of task areas within organizations, are critical ones. As to the assignment of independent and dependent variables, occasions can be readily cited where changes in goals, for example those brought about by changes in the market place or the personalities of top executives, have brought about changes in the technology utilized. The argument is somewhat more subtle than one of temporal priorities. Rather, it says that structure and goals must adjust to technology or the organization will be subject to strong strains. For a radical change in goals to be a successful one, it may require a change in technology, and thus in structure, or else there will be a large price paid for the lack of fit between these variables.[20] Furthermore, as one proceeds, analytically, from technology through the two kinds of structure to goals, increasingly the prior variable only sets limits upon the range of possible variations in the next variable. Thus, technology may predict task

19. The role of the cultural and social environment is developed in somewhat more detail in a review of studies of general and mental hospitals in Charles Perrow, "Hospitals. Technology, Structure and Goals," in James March, *op. cit.,* Chap. 22.
20. This is argued in detail in Perrow, *ibid.,* pp. 926–946. Kovner finds those nursing units with the greatest divergence between technology and structure to have the lowest scores on a dimension of goal realization. *Op. cit.,* pp. 96–97.

structure quite well in a large number of organizations,[21] but these two predict social structure less well, and these three only set broad limits upon the range of possible goals.

COMPARATIVE ANALYSES

If all this is at all persuasive, it means that we have a powerful tool for comparing organizations. The first implication of this for comparative studies is that we cannot expect a particular relationship found in one organization to be found in another unless we know these organizations are in fact similar with respect to their technology. Thus, the fact that the cosmopolitan-local relationship that worked so well in Antioch College was not found in the outpatient department of a hospital should not surprise us; the work performed by the professionals in each case was markedly different.[22] That morale was associated with bureaucracy in fairly routine public schools, but not in research organizations, is understandable.[23] Less obvious, however, is the point that types of organization—in terms of their function in society—will vary as much within each type as between types. Thus, some schools, hospitals, banks and steel companies may have more in common, because of their routine character, than routine and nonroutine schools, routine and nonroutine hospitals, and so forth. To assume that you are holding constant the major variable by comparing several schools or several steel mills is unwarranted until one looks at the technologies employed by various schools or steel mills. In fact, the variations within one type of organization may be such that some schools are like prisons, some prisons like churches, some churches like factories, some factories like universities, and so on.[24] Once this is recognized, of course, analysis of the differ-

21. Unfortunately, verification of the predicted relationships would require a large sample of organizations since there are bound to be many examples of incompatibility between the variables. However, even in a small sample, those whose structure was appropriate to their technology should have fewer "strains" than those whose structure was inappropriate. Joan Woodward, using a similar approach with 100 industrial firms found strong relationships between production systems and certain aspects of structure, though the rudimentary information and analysis on the 100 firms leaves one in doubt as to how strong. See Joan Woodward, *op. cit.*
22. Cf. Alvin Gouldner, "Cosmopolitans and Locals: Toward an Analysis of Latent Social Roles," *Administrative Science Quarterly,* 2 (December, 1957, March, 1958), pp. 281–306, 444–480, and Warren G. Bennis, N. Berkowitz, M. Affinito, and M. Malone, "Reference Groups and Loyalties in the Out-Patient Department," *Administrative Science Quarterly,* 2 (March, 1958), pp. 481–500.
23. Gerald H. Moeller and W. W. Charters, "Relation of Bureaucratization to Sense of Power Among Teachers," *Administrative Science Quarterly,* 10 (December, 1966), pp. 444–465. In addition, for this reason one becomes wary of propositional inventories that fail to make sufficient distinctions among organizations, but attempt to support the propositions by illustrations that are likely to restrict the scope of the proposition to the particular type of organization used in the illustration. For the most recent example, see William A. Rushing, "Organizational Rules and Surveillance: Propositions in Comparative Organizational Analysis," *Administrative Science Quarterly,* 10 (December, 1966), pp. 423–443.
24. Many of the frameworks for comparative analysis, such as those cited in footnote 1, break down because of their broad categories. The failure of some of these schemes to meaningfully order the data from a large sample of a great variety of organizations is discussed in J. Eugene Haas, Richard H. Hall and Norman J. Johnson, "Toward an Empirically Derived Taxonomy of Organizations," in Raymond V. Bowers (ed.), *Studies on Behavior in Organizations,* Atlanta: University of Georgia Press, 1966, pp. 157–180.

ences between churches or whatever can be a powerful tool, as witness the familiar contrast of custodial and treatment-oriented people-changing institutions.

Another implication is that there is little point in testing the effect of a parameter variable, such as size, age, auspices, geographical dispersion, or even national culture, unless we control for technology. For example, in the case of size, to compare the structure of a small R and D lab where the tasks of all three areas are likely to be quite nonroutine with the structure of a large bank where they are likely to be quite routine is fruitless. The nature of their tasks is so different that the structures must vary independently of their different sizes.[25] A meaningful study of the effect of size on structure can be made only if we control for technology, and compare, say, large and small banks all of which have similar services, or large and small R and D labs. Similarly, though the brilliant work of Crozier on French culture is very suggestive, many of his conclusions may stem from the fact that only very routine organizations were studied, and even those lacked many critical elements of the bureaucratic model.[26] Equally routine organizations in a protected product environment in the U.S. might have displayed the same characteristics.

Finally, to call for decentralization, representative bureaucracy, collegial authority, or employee-centered, innovative or organic organizations—to mention only a few of the highly normative prescriptions that are being offered by social scientists today—is to call for a type of structure that can be realized only with a certain type of technology, unless we are willing to pay a high cost in terms of output. Given a routine technology, the much maligned Weberian bureaucracy probably constitutes the socially optimum form of organizational structure.

If all this is plausible, then existing varieties of organizational theory must be selectively applied. It is increasingly recognized that there is no "one best" theory (any more than there is "one best" organizational structure, form of leadership, or whatever) unless it be so general as to be of little utility in understanding the variety of organizations. The perspective proposed here may allow us to utilize existing theories selectively.

For example, a characteristic of thoroughly routinized organizations is the programmatic character of decisions, and perhaps the infrequency with which important decisions have to be made. A decision-making framework that attempts to simulate executive behavior would be fruitful in such cases, for decisions are programmed and routinized. There are fairly clear guidelines for decisions, and clear routing maps, flow charts, and so forth. (See the examples in the second

25. This may be a basic error in the ambitious survey conducted by Haas and his associates, *ibid.*
26. Crozier, *op. cit.*

half of the Cyert and March volume, *The Behavioral Theory of the Firm*.[27]) However, a decision-making perspective which emphasizes uncertainty, such as Herbert Simon's, or that illustrated in the first part of the Cyert and March volume, would not be fruitful here.[28] It would be fruitful where nonroutine tasks are involved.

The study of organizations with a moderate or high component of nonroutine activities, especially at the design and planning level, would benefit from the institutional analysis proposed by Selznick, whereas more routine organizations would not. Selznick, himself, would see them as technical tools. The Communist Party is engaged in nonroutine activities and Selznick chose to analyze the nonroutine rather than the routine aspects of the multi-organization, the Tennessee Valley Authority.[29] Except for its Bell Laboratories, the American Telephone and Telegraph Corporation is probably a rather routine organization in a stable product environment and Barnard's equilibrium analysis works well.[30] Equilibrium analysis also works well for the routine operatives at the production level in economic organizations that constitute most of the subjects for the discussion by March and Simon of the contribution-inducement model.[31] Where nonroutine activities are involved, however, the measurement of both inducements and contributions tends to be difficult, and little is gained by this model except the unenlightening assertion that if the person stays in the organization and produces, there must be some kind of an inducement at least to match his contribution.[32]

There are, of course, many aspects of the general perspectives or theories of organizations that apply to all organizations, and many more will be forthcoming. What is asserted here is that we know enough about organizations in general, at this point, to suggest that more of our effort should be directed toward "middle range" theories which attempt to increase their predictive power by specifying the types of organizations to which they apply. To do this we need far better classification systems than we now have. A better classification system will be based upon a basic aspect of all organizations. In this paper we have suggested that a better system would be one which conceptualizes

27. Richard M. Cyert and James G. March, *The Behavioral Theory of the Firm*, Englewood Cliffs, New Jersey: Prentice-Hall, 1963, Chaps. 7–11.
28. *Ibid.*, Chaps. 1–4, 6.
29. Philip Selznick, *The Organizational Weapon*, New York: McGraw-Hill, 1952, and *TVA and The Grass Roots*, Berkeley: University of California Press, 1949. See also *Leadership in Administration*, Evanston, Ill.: Row, Peterson, 1957, Chap. 1.
30. Chester Barnard, *The Functions of the Executive*, Cambridge: Harvard University Press, 1938.
31. March and Simon, *op. cit.*, Chap. 4.
32. Woodward's remarkable book offers several implicit examples of selective utility. It seems clear, for example, that firms in her middle category (large batch, assembly and mass production) exhibit the characteristics of political science models such as Melville Dalton (*Men Who Manage*, New York: Wiley, 1959) and the first part of Cyert and March *(op. cit.)*. But this view would not illuminate the other two categories in her scheme; application must be selective.

organizations in terms of the work that they do rather than their structure or their goals.

OTHER STUDIES UTILIZING TECHNOLOGY

If there is anything novel in the present essay it is the setting forth of an integrated and somewhat comprehensive viewpoint on technology and complex organizations. Numerous studies have dealt with specific aspects of this viewpoint and some are discussed here.

There have been a few general theoretical statements regarding technology and structure. The one closest to the perspective presented here is a seminal essay by Litwak[33] which distinguishes uniform and nonuniform tasks. His framework received some empirical support in an interesting essay by Hall.[34] One of the first attempts to specify some structural and goal concomitants of technology in general terms was by Thompson and Bates.[35] March and Simon,[36] and Simon alone,[37] proposed and discussed a distinction between programmed and nonprogrammed decisions in general terms. Bennis[38] verges upon a technological conceptualization in parts of his excellent review of leadership theory and administrative behavior.

There have been numerous studies of the role of technology in work groups and small groups. One of the most widely cited is that of the long-wall coaling method by Trist and Bamforth.[39] In our terms this represents a premature attempt at rationalizing nonroutine activities. An assembly-line work layout was imposed on a craft and job-shop operation which was essentially nonroutine, and the results were predictably unfortunate, as were similar attempts to impose a bureaucratic

33. Eugene Litwak, "Models of Organization Which Permit Conflict," *American Journal of Sociology,* 67 (September, 1961), pp. 177–184.
34. Richard H. Hall, "Intraorganizational Structural Variation: Application of The Bureaucratic Model," *Administrative Science Quarterly,* 7 (December, 1962), pp. 295–308. However, the normative anti-bureaucratic tone of many of Hall's questionnaire items precludes an adequate test. An affirmative response to an item such as "I have to ask my boss before I do almost anything" probably indicates a very poor boss, rather than a situation where a bureaucratic structure is viable. A factor analysis of Hall's items was utilized to construct several discrete dimensions of some aspects of bureaucracy in connection with research reported by Aiken and Hage. It appears that the groupings are not on the basis of content, but on the evaluative wording of the items. Those stated negatively, as in the above example, group together, and those implying "good" leadership techniques (rather than bureaucratic or nonbureaucratic techniques) group together. It is doubtful that anything but good or bad leadership in a gross sense is being tested here. A valid item for degree of bureaucratization would permit respondents to approve of the necessity for close supervision, for example, as well as to indicate it is not appropriate. See Michael Aiken and Jerald Hage, "Organizational Alienation: A Comparative Analysis," *American Sociological Review,* 31 (August, 1966), pp. 497–507.
35. James D. Thompson and Frederick L. Bates, "Technology, Organization, and Administration," *Administrative Science Quarterly,* 2 (March, 1957), pp. 325–343.
36. James March and Herbert Simon, *Organizations,* New York: Wiley, 1958.
37. Herbert Simon, *The New Science of Management Decisions,* New York: Harper, 1960.
38. Warren G. Bennis, "Leadership Theory and Administrative Behavior: The Problem of Authority," *Administrative Science Quarterly,* 4 (1959), pp. 259–301.
39. Eric L. Trist and E. K. Bamforth, "Some Social and Psychological Consequences of the Long-Wall Method of Coal-Getting," *Human Relations,* 4 (1951), pp. 3–38.

structure on the nonroutine underground mining operations described by Gouldner.[40] Those interested in human relations in organizations have increasingly toyed with technology as an independent variable, but with mixed feelings and reluctance, since it appears to jeopardize some implicit values of this school of thought. See, for example, the curious chapter in Likert[41] where many of the central hypotheses of previous and subsequent chapters are undermined by observing that the consequences of leadership style varied with the routine and non-routine nature of the work. More sophisticated statements of the impact of technology upon work groups can be found in Dubin[42] and in the comparative study of Turner and Lawrence.[43] The most sophisticated statement of the impact upon workers is presented by Blauner,[44] who uses a comparative framework to great effect; he also summarizes the vast literature on this topic which need not be cited here. Studies of experimental groups have provided evidence of the effect of technology upon small group structure. See the work of Bavelas,[45] Guetzkow and Simon,[46] and Leavitt.[47]

The impact of routine technologies upon both managerial and non-managerial personnel is apparent, though not explicit, in Argyris' study of a bank,[48] in Sudnow's study of a court system,[49] and in two studies of French organizations by Crozier.[50]

Technology plays an explicit and important role in a number of studies of single types of organizations, such as Janowitz's outstanding study of the military,[51] and Rose Coser's contrast of two units in a long-term hospital.[52] It is implicit in her contrast of a medical and a surgical ward.[53] It is also implicit in Rosengren's analysis of milieu

40. Alvin W. Gouldner, *Patterns of Industrial Bureaucracy,* Glencoe, Ill.: The Free Press, 1954.
41. Rensis Likert, *New Patterns of Management,* New York: McGraw-Hill, 1961, Chap. 7.
42. Robert Dubin, "Supervision and Productivity: Empirical Findings and Theoretical Considerations," in Robert Dubin, George C. Homans, Floyd C. Mann and Delbert C. Miller, *Leadership and Productivity,* San Francisco: Chandler, 1965, pp. 1–50.
43. Arthur N. Turner and Paul R. Lawrence, *Industrial Jobs and the Worker,* Cambridge: Harvard University Press, 1965.
44. Robert Blauner, *Alienation and Freedom: The Factory Worker and His Industry,* Chicago: University of Chicago Press, 1964.
45. Alex Bavelas, "Communication Patterns in Task-Oriented Groups," *Journal of the Statistical Society of America,* 22 (1950), pp. 725–730.
46. Harold Guetzkow and Herbert Simon, "The Impact of Certain Communication Nets Upon Organization and Performance in Task-Oriented Groups," in Albert H. Rubenstein and Chadwick J. Haverstroh, eds. *Some Theories of Organization,* Homewood, Ill.: The Dorsey Press, 1960, pp. 259–277.
47. Harold J. Leavitt, "Some Effects of Certain Communication Patterns on Group Performance," *Readings in Social Psychology,* Eleanor Maccoby, *et al.,* eds., New York: Holt, Rinehart & Winston Inc., 1958, pp. 546–563.
48. Chris Argyris, *Organization of a Bank,* New Haven, Conn.: Yale University Press, 1954.
49. David Sudnow, "Normal Crimes: Sociological Features of the Penal Code in a Public Defender Office," *Social Problems,* 12 (Winter, 1965), pp. 255–276.
50. Michel Crozier, *The Bureaucratic Phenomenon,* Chicago: University of Chicago Press, 1964.
51. Morris Janowitz, *The Professional Soldier,* Glencoe, Ill.: The Free Press, 1960.
52. Rose L. Coser, "Alienation and the Social Structure: A Case Analysis of a Hospital," in Eliot Freidson (ed.), *The Hospital in Modern Society,* New York: The Free Press, 1963, pp. 231–265.
53. Rose L. Coser, "Authority and Decision-Making in a Hospital," *American Sociological Review,* 23, (February, 1958), pp. 56–64.

therapy.[54] It plays the key role in the author's analysis of the literature on general and mental hospitals,[55] and in his longitudinal study of a maximum security institution for juveniles.[56] It plays an ambiguous role in the Street, et al., study of six correctional institutions where its impact is obscured by a competing emphasis upon executive goals and behavior, and an inappropriate reliance upon a simple custodial-treatment continuum which leads to many ambiguities about the middle organizations where components of treatment vary independently.[57]

Explicit contrasts of organizations have utilized technological variables. The most ambitious, of course, is Udy's analysis of simple organizations in nonindustrial societies where the emphasis upon technology is explicit.[58] Unfortunately, it is difficult to import his techniques of operationalization and his theory into the world of complex organizations in industrialized societies. As is noted in the preceding essay, technology is a relevant variable, and is sometimes made explicit, in Stinchcombe's discussion of structure and time periods.[59] It also plays a role, though not the key one, in his discussion of craft and bureaucratic organization.[60] The key role is reserved for market factors, and this is true of two other comparative studies—the study of two business concerns by Dill[61] and an ambitious study of two industrial firms by Lorsch.[62] In both these cases it would appear that technology is an important variable but is absorbed in the broader variable, environment. A study of several British firms by Burns and Stalker[63] uses technology as an important variable, though in a quite nonrigorous fashion; their one explicit comparison of a routine and a nonroutine firm is excellent.[64]

The most ambitious and stimulating comparative study using technology as an independent variable is Joan Woodward's survey of 100 industrial organizations.[65] Her independent variable is not, strictly speaking, technology, but is a mixture of type of production, size of

54. William R. Rosengren, "Communication, Organization and Conduct," *Administrative Science Quarterly,* 9 (June, 1964), pp. 70–90.
55. Charles Perrow, "Hospitals: Technology Structure and Goals," in James March, ed., *Handbook of Organizations,* Chicago: Rand McNally, 1965, Chap. 22.
56. Charles Perrow, "Reality Adjustment: A Young Organization Settles for Humane Care," *Social Problems,* 14 (Summer, 1966), pp. 69–79.
57. David Street, Robert Vinter and Charles Perrow, *Organization for Treatment: A Comparative Study of Institutions for Delinquents,* New York: The Free Press, 1966.
58. Stanley Udy, *Organization of Work,* New Haven: Human Relations Area Files Press, 1959.
59. Arthur L. Stinchcombe, "Social Structure and Organization," in James March (ed.), *Handbook of Organizations,* Chicago: Rand McNally, 1965, Chap. 4.
60. Arthur L. Stinchcombe, "Bureaucratic and Craft Administration of Production: A Comparative Study," *Administrative Science Quarterly,* 4 (September, 1959) pp. 168–187.
61. William Dill, "Environment as an Influence on Managerial Autonomy," *Administrative Science Quarterly,* 2 (March, 1958), pp. 409–443.
62. Jay W. Lorsch, *Product Innovation and Organization,* New York: Macmillan, 1965.
63. Tom Burns and G. M. Stalker, *The Management of Innovation,* London: Tavistock Publications, 1961.
64. *Ibid.,* Chap. 5.
65. Joan Woodward, *Industrial Organization: Theory and Practice,* London: Oxford University Press, 1965.

production run, layout of work and type of customer order. These distinctions overlap and it is difficult to decide how a particular kind of organization might be classified in her scheme, or how she made her final classification. An examination of the actual types of organizations (bakery, electronic firm, etc.) utilized in her study, kindly provided by Miss Woodward, suggests that most of those in the general category "small batch and unit" are probably involved in nonroutine production; those in the "large batch and unit" are probably involved in routine production; those in the "large batch and mass production" category have a mixture of routine and nonroutine technologies, but are predominantly routine. If so, her findings would be consistent with our perspective. However, her analysis of continuous process firms unfortunately cannot easily be incorporated in the scheme advanced here. Efforts to do so after her book appeared floundered because of lack of crucial data.

Considering the strong empirical tradition of sociology, it is surprising that so few studies actually give details regarding the kind of work performed in organizations that permit technological generalizations. Two of the best are Gouldner's contrast of mining and manufacturing within a gypsum plant,[66] and Blau's implicit contrast of a routine employment agency and a nonroutine regulatory agency.[67] The works of Argyris,[68] Crozier,[69] Sudnow,[70] and Trist and Bamford[71] also are exceptions.

Finally, we should mention the problem of operationalizing the various concepts of technology—programmed and nonprogrammed decisions, uniform and nonuniform events, routine and nonroutine techniques, simple and complex technologies, and so forth. This has rarely been systematically handled. Udy's procedures do not seem to be applicable to complex organizations.[72] Neither Lorsch[73] nor Hall[74] indicate in detail how they make their distinctions. March and Simon provide some general guidelines,[75] but Litwak[76] provides none. It is impossible to determine how Woodward[77] or Burns and Stalker[78] arrived at their classifications of companies. Street, *et al.,*[79] provide

66. Gouldner, *op. cit.*
67. Peter Blau, *Dynamics of Bureaucracy,* Chicago: University of Chicago Press, 1955.
68. Argyris, *op. cit.*
69. Crozier, *op. cit.*
70. Sudnow, *op. cit.*
71. Trist and Bamford, *op. cit.*
72. Udy, *op. cit.*
73. Lorsch, *op. cit.*
74. Hall, *op. cit.*
75. March and Simon, *op. cit.,* pp. 142–143.
76. Litwak, *op. cit.*
77. Woodward, *op. cit.*
78. Burns, *op. cit.*
79. Street, *et al., op. cit.*

indications of operationalization, but these are not particularly applicable to other types of organizations nor are the authors particularly sensitive to the problem. Only Turner and Lawrence[80] have approached the problem systematically and fully described in an appendix the measurement of their variables. The level of conceptualization is not general enough to apply to other types of organizations than industrial firms, and the material is limited to blue-collar workers, but it is at least encouraging that in our own study of industrial firms we arrived independently at some roughly similar measures.

Udy, in a discussion of this paper, aptly noted the difficulty of reconciling the respondent's perception of the nature of his work with the observer's perception, which is based upon a comparative view. Few organizations will characterize themselves as routine, and most employees emphasize the variability of their jobs and the discretion required. Nevertheless, contrasts between extreme examples of a single type of organization appear to present no problem. It seems clear that the technology of custodial and therapeutic mental hospitals, or of firms producing ingot molds and those producing titanium-based metals, differ greatly. On the other hand, to say precisely wherein these differences occur, and how one might compare the two routine examples, is far more difficult. Such operationalization, however, depends first upon adequate conceptualization. That proposed in this essay—the two continua of exceptions and search procedures—hopefully can be operationalized for a variety of settings. (An attempt is made, with fair success, by Kovner in his study of nursing units.[81]) But much more research and theory will be required to determine if these concepts are relevant and adequate. Meanwhile, we are aware of a number of other studies of technology and organization currently under way or even in press; other concepts will no doubt be formulated and perhaps will be given systematic operational definition.

80. Turner, *op. cit.*
81. Anthony Kovner, "The Nursing Unit: A Technological Perspective," unpublished Ph.D. dissertation, University of Pittsburgh, 1966.

CHAPTER TWO

METHODOLOGICAL APPROACHES TO THE STUDY OF COMPLEX ORGANIZATIONS

Knowledge about complex organizations will accumulate as they are increasingly subjected to empirical investigation. The various methodological approaches to the investigation of social science phenomena are relevant to the study of complex organizations. The articles selected for this section represent important research techniques and, in addition, give examples of organizational research conducted in a creative manner. Whereas in the last article of the previous chapter Perrow presented a conceptual framework for comparative analysis, in the first article of this chapter James Coleman illustrates specific research methods for the analysis of complex organizations.

The article by Coleman is extremely important in any book which deals with organizational analysis in that he focuses on relational analysis and contrasts it with the individual-oriented approach which much of organizational research stresses. Coleman presents a discussion on research design and methods of sampling which are useful in the implementation of survey research among large organizations. He then presents four different analytical methods in which survey analysis can treat problems which tend to involve social structure. The specific analytical methods which he presents are contextual analysis, boundaries of homogeneity, pair analysis, and analysis by partitioning into cliques. Coleman also provides two very good examples of contextual and comparative analysis in this article. The interested reader is urged to consult the original source which includes two appendices which exemplify relational analysis with its mathematical bases.

W. Richard Scott's paper provides an excellent example of field research conducted in complex organizations. His paper describes the study of a social welfare agency. He carefully delineates the role of the sociological observer in a field study within organizations. Scott clearly discusses selected problems which are encountered in field research. For example, he describes reactions of personnel within the organization to the observations of the field researcher. In addition, he presents some of the factors which tend to facilitate participant observation.

Whereas Scott discusses some of the general problems confronted in field research, the original paper by Spradley presents a specific method for gathering data in the field. Spradley, a social anthropologist, utilizes a method known as ethnoscience to examine the social organization of a city jail. Spradley's major theme is that complex organizations are, in fact, culturally constituted and that the investigator must examine the organization not in terms of his own culture but in terms of the organization's cultural setting. For example, in order to understand the city jail, it should be realized that the respondents do not communicate in terms of the investigator's vocabulary but in terms of the vocabulary of their own normative system. This tends to diminish cultural bias and, as a consequence, furnishes a more exacting description of the complex organization.

The problem of realism versus artificiality is a concern of many people who have attempted to study organizations (or small groups, for that matter) in the laboratory setting. The problem which always arises is whether the artificially contrived experiment is realistic. Drabek and Haas recast the problem and ask what it is that makes an experiment realistic. For example, the specific variables studied, contextual situations, etc., must be taken into account before one can determine the extent of the realism of the experiment. Can the findings from laboratory experiments be generalized to real life settings? Drabek and Haas spell out the properties of a method of research which they have labeled *realistic simulation,* that is, a technique whereby a simulant which behaves exactly as its real counterpart is constructed and manipulated.

The type of method used will, of course, vary with level of abstraction and theory development. Thus, a laboratory study may be very appropriate for highly abstract variables, where an enthnographic method, such as Spradley's, may be used when theory is relatively absent.

6

RELATIONAL ANALYSIS
The Study of Social Organizations with Survey Methods

James S. Coleman

Survey research methods have often led to the neglect of social structure and of the relations among individuals. On the other hand, survey methods are highly efficient in bringing in a large volume of data —amenable to statistical treatment—at a relatively low cost in time and effort. Can the student of social structure enjoy the advantages of the survey without neglecting the relationships which make up that structure? In other words, can he use a method which ordinarily treats each individual as an isolated unit in order to study social structure?

The purpose of this paper is to describe some important developments in survey research which are giving us a new way of studying social organization.

It is useful to trace briefly the history of survey research, to indicate how it has grown from "polling" to the point where it can now study problems involving complex human organization. A look at this history indicates two definite stages. The first was a polling stage which was concerned with the *distribution* of responses on any one item: What proportion favored Roosevelt in 1936? What proportion was in favor of labor unions? This type of concern continues even today among pollsters, and to the lay public it is still the function of surveys to "find out what people think" or to see just how many feel thus and so.

Among sociologists, however, this purely descriptive use of survey research was soon supplanted by an *analytical* one. First there began to be a concern with how different subgroups in the population felt or behaved. From this, the analysts moved on to further cross-tabulation. Finally, some survey analysts began, through cross-tabulations and correlations, to study complicated questions of why people behaved as they did. By relating one opinion item to another, attitude configurations and clusters of attitudes emerged; by relating background information to these attitudes, some insight was gained into the *determinants* of attitudes. It was in this analytical stage, then, beyond the simple description of a population, that survey research began to be of real use to social science.

But throughout all this one fact remained, a very disturbing one to the student of social organization. The *individual* remained the unit of analysis. No matter how complex the analysis, how numerous the correlations, the studies focused on individuals as separate and independent units. The very techniques mirrored this well: samples were random, never including (except by accident) two persons who were friends; interviews were with one individual, as an atomistic entity, and responses were coded onto separate IBM cards, one for each person. As a result, the kinds of substantive problems on which such research focused tended to be problems of "aggregate psychology," that is, *within*-individual problems, and never problems concerned with relations between people.

Now, very recently, this focus on the individual has shown signs of changing, with a shift to groups as the units of analysis, or to networks of relations among individuals. The shift is quite a difficult one to make, both conceptually and technically, and the specific methods used to date are only halting steps toward a full-fledged methodology. Nevertheless, some of these methods are outlined below, to indicate just how, taken together, they can even now provide us with an extremely fruitful research tool. This tool has sometimes been used for the study of formal organization but more often for the study of the informal organization which springs up within a formal structure. In both cases, it shows promise of opening to research, problems which have been heretofore the province of speculation.

PROBLEMS OF DESIGN AND SAMPLING

The break from the atomistic concerns of ordinary survey analysis requires taking a different perspective toward the individual interview. In usual survey research and statistical analysis, this interview is regarded as *independent* of others, as an entity in itself. All cross-tabulations and analyses relate one item in that questionnaire to another item in the same questionnaire. But, in this different approach, an individual interview is seen as a *part* of some larger structure in which the respondent finds himself: his network of friends, the shop or office where he works, the bowling team he belongs to, and so on. Thus, as a part of a larger structure, the individual is *not* treated independently. The analysis must somehow tie together and interrelate the attributes of these different parts of the structure.

So much for the basic change in perspective—away from the atomistic treatment of the individual interview, and toward the treatment of each interview as a part of some larger whole. This basic perspective has several implications for the kind of data collected and for the sample design. Perhaps the most important innovation in the kind of data collected is sociometric-type data in the interview, that is, explicit questions about the respondent's relation to other specific individuals. Each person may be asked the names of his best friends, or the names of his subordinates in the shop upon whom he depends most, or any one of a multitude of *relational* questions. For example, in a study of two housing projects by Merton, Jahoda, and West,[1] one way to map out the informal social structure in the community was to ask people who their best friends were. Having obtained such data from all the families in the project, so that each family could be located in the network of social relations in the community, it was then possible to examine the relation between this social structure, on the one hand, and various values and statuses on the other. Specifically, this information allowed these authors to show that in one housing project social ties were based very largely on similarities in background and religion; in the other, social relations were more often built around common leisure interests and participation in community organizations.

More generally, the incorporation of sociometric-type data into survey research allows the investigator to *locate* each interviewed individual within the networks of voluntary relations which surround him. In some cases, these networks of voluntary relations will be superimposed on a highly articulated formal structure. In a department of a business, for example, there are numerous hierarchical levels and there are numerous work relations which are imposed by the job itself. In such cases, sociometric-type questions can be asked relative to these formal relations, e.g.: "Which supervisor do you turn to most often?" or, "Which of the men in your own workgroup do you see most often outside of work?" or, "When you want X type of job done in a hurry to whom do you go to get it done?" or, "When you need advice on such-and-such a problem, whom do you usually turn to?".

Another kind of data is that which refers to some larger social unit. For example, in some research on high schools currently being carried out at the University of Chicago, it is necessary to find the paths to prestige within a school, so that the boys are asked: "What does it take to be important and looked up to by the other fellows here at school?". Then the responses to this question—aggregated over each school separately—can be used to characterize the *school* as well as the individual. Because of this, the question itself makes explicit reference to the school.

But apart from the kinds of data collected, there are also important *sampling* considerations. In this kind of research, it is no longer possible to pull each individual out of his social context and interview him as an independent entity. It is necessary to sample parts of that context as well or, to say it differently, to sample explicitly with reference to the social structure. There are numerous ways of doing this; only a few, which have been successfully tried, are mentioned below.

1. Robert K. Merton, Patricia S. West, and Marie Jahoda, *Patterns of Social Life: Explorations in the Sociology of Housing,* forthcoming.

SNOWBALL SAMPLING

One method of interviewing a man's immediate social environment is to use the sociometric questions in the interview for sampling purposes. For example, in a study of political attitudes in a New England community, Martin Trow has used this approach: first interviewing a small sample of persons, then asking these persons who their best friends are, interviewing these friends, then asking *them* their friends, interviewing these, and so on.[2] In this way, the sampling plan follows out the chains of sociometric relations in the community. In many respects, this sampling technique is like that of a good reporter who tracks down "leads" from one person to another. The difference, of course, is that snowball sampling in survey research is amenable to the same scientific sampling procedures as ordinary samples. Where the population in ordinary samples is a population of individuals, here it is two populations: one of individuals and one of *relations* among individuals.

SATURATION SAMPLING

Perhaps a more obvious approach is to interview *everyone* within the relevant social structure. In a study of doctors in four communities, *all* the doctors in these communities were interviewed.[3] Sociometric-type questions were then used to lay out the professional and social relations existing among these doctors. This "saturation" method or complete census was feasible there, because the total number of doctors in these communities was small—less than three hundred. But in the study mentioned earlier which used snowball sampling, such an approach would have been practically impossible, for the community was about 15,000 in size. Thus this "saturation sampling" is only feasible under rather special circumstances. A borderline case is the study of high schools mentioned earlier. There are 9,000 students in the ten schools being studied. Only because these students are given self-administered questionnaires, rather than interviews, is it possible to use a saturation sample, and thereby characterize the complete social structure.

DENSE SAMPLING

Another approach is to sample "densely." This is a compromise between the usual thinly-dispersed random sample and the saturation sample. An illustration will indicate how this may be useful. In a study of pressures upon the academic freedom of college social science teachers, carried out by Paul Lazarsfeld, at least *half* of the social science

2. Martin A. Trow, "Right Wing Radicalism and Political Intolerance: A Study of Support for McCarthy in a New England Town." Unpublished Ph.D. dissertation, Columbia University, 1957.
3. J. S. Coleman, E. Katz, and H. M. Menzel, "Diffusion of an Innovation Among Physicians," *Sociometry,* XX (Dec. 1957).

faculty in every college in the sample was interviewed.[4] Thus, by sampling densely, enough men were interviewed in each college so that the climate of the college could be characterized, as well as the attitudes of the individual respondent.

MULTI-STAGE SAMPLING

Any of the above approaches to sampling can be combined with an element found in many sample designs: the multi-stage sample. For example, in the academic freedom study referred to above, it would have been impossible to have a dense sample of social science teachers in *all* the colleges in the United States, so a two-stage sample was used: first sampling colleges, and then teachers within colleges. In doing this, of course, the crucial question is what balance to maintain between the sampling of colleges and the sampling of teachers within colleges. Enough colleges are needed to have representativity, yet few enough so that the sampling within each one can be dense. In a study of union politics, reported in *Union Democracy,*[5] we perhaps made a wrong decision: we interviewed in 90 printing shops, spreading the interviews so thinly that only one man out of three—at most—was interviewed within the shop. This meant that we had only a very few interviews in each shop, and could not use the interview material to characterize the climate or atmosphere of the shops, except in the very largest ones.

These sampling procedures are, of course, not the only possible ones. An infinite degree of variation is possible, depending upon the problem and upon the kind of social structure involved. The most important point is that the individual interview can no longer be treated as an independent entity, but must be considered as a part of some larger whole: in the sampling, in the questions asked, and in the subsequent analysis.

ANALYTICAL METHODS

The real innovations in this new kind of research are in the techniques of analysis. I will mention several of these with which I am most familiar, to give an indication of the kinds of problems this research examines and the way it examines them.

CONTEXTUAL ANALYSIS

The first, and the one closest to usual survey research, might be termed contextual analysis. In essence, it consists of relating a characteristic of the respondent's social context—and the independent vari-

4. P. F. Lazarsfeld and Wagner Thielens, *The Academic Man: Social Scientists in a Time of Crisis,* The Free Press, Glencoe, Ill., 1956.
5. S. M. Lipset, M. A. Trow, and J. S. Coleman, *Union Democracy,* The Free Press, Glencoe, Ill., 1956.

able—to a characteristic of the individual himself.[6] A good example of this occurred in *The American Soldier,* where the attitudes of inexperienced men, in companies where most others were inexperienced, were compared to attitudes of similarly inexperienced men in companies where most others were veterans. It was found that inexperienced men in green companies felt very differently about themselves, and about combat, than their counterparts in veteran companies. That is, when men were characterized by both individual characteristics and by their social surroundings, the latter were found to have an important effect on their attitudes.

In the union politics study mentioned above, one of the major elements in the analysis was an examination of the effect of the shop context on the men within the shop. We had access to voting records in union political elections for these shops, and these made it possible to characterize the shop as politically radical or politically conservative and as high or low in political consensus. Then we could examine the different behavior or attitudes of men in different kinds of shops and compute a "shop effect." An example is given in Table I. Each man is in a shop of high or low political consensus, depending on whether the men in the shop vote alike or are evenly split between the radical and conservative parties. And each man has a certain degree of political activity. In this table, the shop's political consensus and the man's political activity are related. The table indicates that in shops of high consen-

Table 1

		Shops of High Political Consensus	Shops of Low Political Consensus
Percent of men active in union politics		29%	7%
	N	(125)	(28)

sus, men are politically more active than in shops of low consensus. The inference might be that high consensus provides a kind of resonance of political beliefs which generates a greater interest in politics. In any case, the table exemplifies the use of an attribute of a *shop* related to an attribute of a *man* in the shop. This general kind of analysis, which bridges the gap between two levels of sociological units—the individual

6. Peter Blau has emphasized the importance of such analysis in formal organizations for locating the "structural effects" of a situation upon the individuals in it. See his "Formal Organization: Dimensions of Analysis," *American Journal of Sociology,* LXIII (1957), 58–69.

and his social context—seems to be a very basic one for this "structural" approach to survey research.

BOUNDARIES OF HOMOGENEITY

A second kind of analysis attempts to answer the question: How homogeneous are various groups in some belief or attitude? In a medical school, for example, are a student's attitudes toward medicine more like those of his fraternity brothers or more like those of his laboratory partners? This question, incidentally, has been posed in a study of medical students presently being carried out at Columbia University.[7] The answer is, in the particular medical school being studied, that his attitudes are far more like those of his fraternity brothers. In other words, in this medical school, the "boundaries of homogeneity" of certain attitudes about medicine coincide very largely with fraternity boundaries.

The major problems in answering questions of group homogeneity are problems of index construction. Consider the above example: each student has twenty or thirty fraternity brothers, but only three laboratory partners in anatomy lab. How can the effects of variability between groups, due to small numbers in a group, be separated out from the actual tendency toward homogeneity of attitude? It can be done, and indices have been developed to do so. The indices, incidentally, are much like the formulas by which statisticians measure the effects of clustering in a random sample.

An example of group homogeneity may indicate more concretely how this approach can be useful in research. In the study of doctors in four communities mentioned earlier, we were interested in the social processes affecting the physicians' introduction of a new drug into their practices. Through interviewing all doctors and asking sociometric questions in the interview, we were able to delineate seven "cliques" of doctors who were sociometrically linked together. (How to reconstruct such cliques is another problem, which will be considered shortly.) The question, then, became this: At each point in time after the drug was marketed, were cliques homogeneous or not in their members' use or non-use of the drug? If they were homogeneous, then this was evidence that some kind of social influence or diffusion was going on in relation to the measured sociometric ties. If not, this indicated that the cliques delineated on the basis of questions in the interview had little relevance to drug adoption. Table 2 shows, for several time periods, just how much homogeneity there was in the cliques, beyond that

7. Some of the work in this study (though not the work mentioned here) is reported in P. F. Kendall, R. K. Merton, and G. S. Reader (eds.), *The Student Physician*, Commonwealth Fund, New York, 1957.

which would arise by chance. An index value of 1.0 means each clique is completely homogeneous in its use or non-use of the drug. An index value of 0 means there is no more homogeneity than would arise through chance variation between groups.

Table 2 shows that there was no homogeneity until around seven months after the drug was introduced, that is, until over 50 percent of the doctors had used the drug. The maximum homogeneity was reached at about eleven months, when three-fourths of the doctors had begun to use the drug. Then after that, the homogeneity receded to zero again.

Table 2

Months After Drug was Marketed	Amount of Clique Homogeneity	Percent of Doctors Who Had Used the Drug
1	No	14
3	No	32
5	No	49
7	.07	66
9	.12	71
11	.18	76
13	.03	83
15	No	86

This result helped to reinforce a conclusion derived from other findings in the study: that the social networks measured in the study were effective as paths of diffusion at certain times but not at others. However, apart from the substantive results of the study, this example indicates how such analysis of the boundaries of homogeneity may be useful for the study of the functioning of various social organizations.

PAIR ANALYSIS

Neither of the above kinds of analysis has required the use of sociometric-type data. An important kind of analysis which does use such direct data on relationships is the analysis of *pairs*. Here, the pair formed by A's choosing B becomes the unit of analysis. Speaking technically, "pair cards" may be constructed for each sociometric choice, and then these cards used for cross-tabulations. In other words, instead of cross-tabulating a man's attitude toward Russia with his attitude toward the United Nations, we can cross-tabulate the man's attitude toward Russia with the attitude toward Russia of the man he eats lunch with at the cafeteria.

One of the most important problems which has been studied in this way is the similarity or difference in attitudes or backgrounds between the two members of a pair. That is, do people have friendship relations with those who are like them politically, with people of the same age, with persons in the same occupation?

This kind of problem can be illustrated by Table 3, which contains hypothetical data. This table, which looks very much like an ordinary contingency table, must be treated in a slightly different fashion. It allows us to raise the question: do boys tend to choose boys more than would be expected by chance? and, do girls tend to choose girls more than would be expected by chance? The answer, of course, depends upon what we take as chance. However, chance models have been worked out, so that one can assign measures of the tendency to choose others of one's own kind. For the above example, this measure (varying between 0 and 1) says that the tendency to in-choice for boys is .38 and that for girls is .17. By comparing such indices for numerous attributes, one could get a good glimpse into the informal social organization of the group. For example, in the medical study mentioned earlier which is being carried out at Columbia University, the values of in-choice tendency for friends shown in Table 4 were found:

Table 3

Chosen

		Boy	Girl	
Chooser	Boy	45	15	60
	Girl	20	20	40
				100

Table 4

Subgroups	Tendencies Toward in-Choice
Class in school	.92
Fraternity	.52
Sex	.33
Marital status	.20
Attitudes toward national health insurance	.37

By looking at the relative sizes of these index values, we get an idea of just how the informal social relations—that is, the friendship choices—

at this medical school mesh with the formal structure, and with the distribution of attitudes.

In the study mentioned above of drug introduction by doctors, these pair relations were used as the major aspect of the analysis: by examining how close in time a doctor's first use of a new drug was to the first use of the doctor he mentioned as a friend, it was possible to infer the functioning of friendship networks in the introduction of this drug.

These examples of pair analysis give only a crude picture of the kinds of problems which can be studied in this fashion. The important matter is to break away from the analysis of *individuals* as units to the study of *pairs* of individuals. To be sure, this involves technical IBM problems and problems of index construction along with conceptual problems, but the difficulties are not great.

PARTITIONING INTO CLIQUES

Another important kind of problem is the partitioning of a larger group into cliques by use of sociometric choices. This problem is a thorny one, for it involves not only the delineation of cliques, but, even prior to this, the *definition* of what is to constitute a clique. Are cliques to be mutually exclusive in membership, or can they have overlapping memberships? Are they to consist of people who all name one another, or of people who are tied together by more tenuous connections? Such questions must be answered before the group can be partitioned into cliques.

A good review of some of the methods by which cliques and sub-groups can be treated is presented in Lindzey and Borgotta.[8] The two most feasible of these are the method of matrix multiplication[9] and the method of shifting rows and columns in the sociometric choice matrix until the choices are clustered around the diagonal.[10] This last tech-nique is by far the more feasible of the two if the groups are more than about twenty in size. When the groups are on the order of a hundred, even this method becomes clumsy. An IBM technique was successfully used in the study of doctors and the study of medical students, both mentioned above, in which the groups were 200–400 in size. At the University of Chicago, a program has been developed for Univac, using a method of shifting rows and columns in a matrix, which can handle groups up to a thousand in size.[11] The necessity for some such method

8. G. Lindzey (ed.), *Handbook of Social Psychology,* Addison-Wesley, Cambridge, 1956, Chap. II.
9. See L. Festinger, "The Analysis of Sociograms Using Matrix Algebra," *Human Relations,* II, No. 2 (1949), 153–158 and R. D. Luce, "Connectivity and Generalized Cliques in Sociometric Group Struc-ture," *Psychometrika,* XV (1950), 169–190.
10. C. O. Beum and E. G. Brundage, "A Method for Analyzing the Sociomatrix," *Sociometry,* XIII (1950), 141–145.
11. A description of this program, written by the author and Duncan McRae, is available upon request from the author and the program itself is available for copying, for those who have access to a Univac I or II.

becomes great when, for example, one wants to map out systematically the informal organization of a high school of a thousand students.

CONCLUSION

These four kinds of analysis, contextual analysis, boundaries of homogeneity, pair analysis, and partitioning into cliques, are only four of many possibilities. Several other approaches have been used, but these four give some idea of the way in which survey analysis can come to treat problems which involve social structure. In the long run, these modes of analysis will probably represent only the initial halting steps in the development of a kind of structural research which will represent a truly sociological methodology. In any case, these developments spell an important milestone in social research, for they help open up for systematic research those problems which have heretofore been the province of the theorist or of purely qualitative methods.

There is one new development which should be mentioned, although the frontier is just opened, and not at all explored. This development is the construction of electronic computers with immediate-access storage capacities a hundred times the size of an 80-column IBM card. Such computers make it possible, for the first time, to lay out a complex social structure for direct and systematic examination. Instead of examining the similarity of attitudes between socially-connected pairs, after laborious construction of "pair cards," it becomes possible to trace through a whole structural network, examining the points in the network where attitudes or actions begin to diverge. Methods for doing this have not yet been developed but, for the first time, the technical facilities exist, and it is just a matter of time until analytical methods are developed. IBM cards and counter-sorters were methodologically appropriate for the individualistic orientation which survey research has had in the past; electronic computers with large storage capacities are precisely appropriate for the statistical analysis of complex social organization.

Unfortunately, it has not been possible here to present any of the tools discussed above fully enough to show precisely how it is used. In giving a broad overview of a number of developments, my aim has been to point to an important new direction in social research, one which may aid significantly in the systematic study of social organization.

7

FIELD WORK IN A FORMAL ORGANIZATION
Some Dilemmas in the Role of Observer

W. Richard Scott

With an increasing number of field studies of formal organizations being carried out, it is important that more attention be given the role of sociological observer as it functions in this context since this role in part determines the kind and quality of data collected. Such accounts of research roles and relationships, apart from their use to qualify and interpret the particular data collected, are useful in and of themselves for the clarification, development, and teaching of this aspect of the role of sociologist.[1]

My experience with the role of sociological observer came in connection with a study carried out in a medium-sized county welfare agency located in a large city in a Midwestern state. I was completely independent of the organization studied, being at this time a graduate student doing research for a dissertation and enjoying the financial support of an outside agency. In return for his staff's cooperation, the director of the welfare organization asked only that I forward to them a copy of the completed dissertation. The study was focused on the professional employees (i.e., the casework field staff) and began with an extended period of observation and informal interviewing in the agency.[2] My comments on the role of the observer stem from the three- or four-month period spent gaining familiarity with this agency and its staff.

The research experience reported in this paper was made possible by a Social Science Research Council predoctoral training fellowship. An earlier version of this paper was read at the Pacific Sociological Association's annual meetings in Tucson, Arizona on April 14, 1961. The author is indebted to Peter M. Blau for his critical reading of an earlier draft of this report and to Morris J. Daniels for the constructive comments made in his role of discussant at the Tucson meetings.

1. For only a few of the better examples of this kind of report on the relation of the sociologist to the organization analyzed, see the following accounts: Robert K. Bain, "The Researcher's Role: A Case Study," *Human Organization,* IX (Spring, 1950), 23–28; Alvin W. Gouldner, *Patterns of Industrial Bureaucracy,* The Free Press, Glencoe, Illinois, 1954, pp. 247–69; Elliott Jaques, *The Changing Culture of a Factory,* The Dryden Press, New York, 1952, pp. 3–23; Alfred H. Stanton and Morris S. Schwartz, *The Mental Hospital,* Basic Books, New York, 1954, pp. 426–37; and papers in the first section of Richard N. Adams and Jack J. Preiss (eds.), *Human Organization Research; Field Relations and Techniques,* Dorsey Press, Homewood, Illinois, 1960.

2. A complete report of this study will be found in W. Richard Scott, "A Case Study of Professional Workers in a Bureaucratic Setting," unpublished Ph.D. dissertation, Department of Sociology, University of Chicago, 1961.

PURPOSES OF THE OBSERVATION PERIOD

Although the study was guided from the outset by a general theoretical orientation and by certain specific hypotheses, it was necessary to formulate these ideas and operationalize the concepts in such a way that they would meaningfully apply to the particular organization under study. It was also necessary to adapt research techniques to the peculiarities of the organization.[3] It would seem that no amount of preliminary planning or previous experience would obviate the need for intimate familiarity with the organization studied in the final formulation of concepts and techniques. The observation period furnished this familiarity.

Since my primary source of information was the staff of the agency itself, it was essential that rapport be established with the members of the organization. This could best be accomplished through frequent and informal contacts with individual staff members. A period of observation made these contacts possible.

Many sociological studies—of organizations as well as of other areas —depend exclusively for their data on questionnaires, interviews, or other similar devices. Such techniques are limited in that they do not necessarily provide valid, reliable materials on the activities and interactions of respondents. While both the questionnaire and the interview were employed to gather data on such areas as worker sentiments and background characteristics, the observation period allowed me to gather both anecdotal and systematic data on the actual behavior of staff members as they performed in their work setting.

Finally, a period of observation seemed particularly desirable in a study which was partly exploratory in character since it would furnish opportunities for closer contact with the operating levels of the organization. Keeping in mind these varied purposes, let us briefly examine some aspects of the role of the observer as it was performed in connection with this study.

THE ROLE OF OBSERVER

EXPLANATIONS

The overall purposes of the study were explained to the entire staff of the agency in a general meeting held prior to the commencement of the field work in the organization. In my statement I attempted to establish my identity as a sociologist (explaining the differences and similarities of this role to that of the social worker) and as a graduate

3. See Frank B. Miller, " 'Resistentialism' in Applied Social Research," *Human Organization*, XII (Winter, 1954), 5, on the notion that data imbedded in a given research context are often stubbornly resistant to prefabricated means of attack.

student. My independence from the organization itself was emphasized. The study was described as one of work and of work groups
concentrating on activities, interpersonal relations, and attitudes. It was
explained that over the next several months I would be observing the
work of the agency and visiting informally with members of the staff
and that later in the study some of the staff would be asked to fill out
a questionnaire or participate in an interview. Finally, the confidential-
ity of the data was discussed, and it was pointed out that the final report
would contain data summaries so that no individual respondent could
be identified.

STAFF REACTIONS

This initial appearance before the entire staff gave me a kind of
"legitimacy" and enough prestige so that many doors were opened to
me which might otherwise have remained closed. In general, I seemed
to be successful in conveying the message that I was (1) an outsider and
(2) conducting some sort of study. My introductory statement, however,
was probably unsatisfactory to many organization members since I attempted to keep my discussion both general and somewhat vague. This
was essential if my major hypotheses were not to be revealed—a circumstance which could bias the very behavior to be utilized as evidence for their confirmation or rejection. My vagueness seemed to
generate some suspicion and several misconceptions of my role—the
latter taking three more or less distinct forms.

First, several workers seemed to identify me as some sort of "efficiency engineer." These people came to me in the early weeks of the
study to report certain physical defects or deficiencies in their work
settings that they presumably felt I could remedy, such as lack of space
between desks or the need for additional phones. A second group of
workers perceived that I was some sort of "junior administrator"
present to check on their behavior. Thus, one worker came in a few
minutes late after lunch and told me,

We had a credit board meeting so don't mark me late!

Another worker whose duties required him to constantly be in and out
of the room where I was observing came over to explain what he was
doing because, as he put it,

I don't want you to think I'm just running around.

On more than one occasion my approach to an informal collection of
workers elicited the joking but significant warning from one worker to
the others:

Oh, oh! Cheese it, the cops!

A third misconception took the form of my being perceived as an "expert" in social work by some of the workers. Thus, one worker asked me to read a case record and tell him how he could improve his casework and recording; several workers discussed their case problems with me, many apparently hoping and some explicitly asking for advice. All of these contacts provided opportunities for me to clarify my role by tactfully rejecting the role that was being ascribed to me.

In addition to these rather specific misconceptions of my role which occurred during the early phases of the study, other more generalized negative reactions were observed. Two of these will be described.

ANXIETY

Probably a certain amount of anxiety will always accompany the entrance of an observer into a social organization no matter what his purposes may be. Staff anxiety focused on the observer can have many roots. In my case, I was an outsider and a stranger; I also had access to powerful people in the organization. Of course, my presence may have been gratifying to some who considered the organization's selection as a research site to be a matter of pride; however, others no doubt harbored feelings of hostility at being reduced to the status of "mere subjects or objects" by the study. Perhaps the most important source of staff anxiety in connection with my study was the fact that I stationed myself at an empty desk in various departments and observed the activities of work groups over considerable periods of time; in fact, to some I must have appeared to be virtually omnipresent. Having no conflicting duties—as did supervisors, for example—I could *constantly* observe the behavior of the particular group under study for shorter or longer periods. Merton has rightly pointed out that few if any groups will readily accept full and unrestricted observability of their behavior. This would seem to be largely because

> ... *some* measure of leeway in conforming to role-expectations is presupposed in all groups. To have to meet the strict requirements of a role at all times, without some degree of deviation, is to experience insufficient allowances for individual differences in capacity and training and for situational exigencies which make strict conformity extremely difficult.[4]

Of course, the workers being observed could not know that I was not primarily concerned with checking on their conformity to role-expectations. But even were this realized, the workers could hardly help feeling some anxiety. The fact that they could not be certain as to just what my interests were (and I could not be overly explicit about them for fear of introducing bias into the behavior of my subjects) was *in itself* no

4. Robert K. Merton, *Social Theory and Social Structure*, The Free Press, Glencoe, Illinois, 1957, p. 343.

doubt a major cause for anxiety. How does one behave "properly" under observation when the observer's standards for proper behavior are not known?

The major evidence for the presence of anxiety among the groups observed in the study was the rather frequent attempt of many of the staff to explain or justify to me some action of theirs. The staff member mentioned earlier who felt compelled to explain his actions because he did not want me to think that he was "just running around" is a good example of this behavior. The most extreme example of mistrust occurred when one staff member accused me of having written a disparaging newspaper article concerning the agency and its program.[5] Fortunately, the organization studied was not in the throes of major changes, staff satisfaction was high,[6] and in general there were good relations between workers and the administration. Had any of these factors been otherwise it could have made for serious problems. Anxieties created by the organization itself could easily find a convenient scapegoat in the "meddling outsider" and thus make his task difficult if not impossible.[7]

ENVY

A second type of negative reaction to the presence of the observer may be characterized as envy. Like anxiety, this reaction appears to have several sources—many of which are endemic to the observation situation. In connection with the present study, my role must have appeared to be an exceedingly pleasant one to the organization member. There seemed to be no specific work I had to accomplish; no supervisors were in sight making demands on me and controlling my work. I was not required to keep definite hours but came and went at will. I was not confined to one desk or place of work but could range freely throughout the organization. I had access to the top-level organization personnel and meetings and was privy to many secrets of the organization which were withheld from rank-and-file members. My work consisted of "just talking and visiting" with people and recording notes. In short, I appeared to have a "soft" and interesting job.

While this is in many respects a distorted picture of the role of observer there was evidence that some agency members felt that it was an accurate one and on the basis of this view exhibited rather distinct

---

5. It developed that this article, which had *not* appeared in a local paper but had been sent to the worker by his mother, concerned a welfare department in another state but in a county of the same name.
6. In the questionnaire returned by virtually all of the workers, 89 percent stated that they were either "satisfied" or "highly satisfied" with their work situation.
7. For an elaboration of this point and some suggestions as to how the researcher may avoid this situation, see Jaques, *op. cit.,* pp. 11-12.

signs of envy. For example one worker approached a second in my presence and said:

I'm going to give up this business and get my doctor's degree.

I asked,

Would you like a job like mine?

and he responded,

I sure would.

Of course, respondent envy directed toward the observer is only a problem to the extent that it inhibits the development of confidence in and openness with him.

If there were some staff members who misinterpreted my role in the early days of the study and some who reacted to my presence somewhat negatively, many others did not, and after a few weeks most if not all appeared to have developed a reasonably accurate picture of my identity and the nature of my study. In fact, I encountered no active resistance during the entire period of study in the agency. No staff member refused to answer my questions and none seemed overly disturbed by my presence. Indeed, there were a few workers who became active collaborators in the study, telling and reminding me of meetings, providing reports and personal documents pertaining to their work or to the agency, and helping in other ways.

ROLE ATTRIBUTES OF THE OBSERVER

Having dealt with some specific misconceptions of and some general staff reactions to the role of observer—I have concentrated on the negative ones since these seemed to be the more instructive—we are ready to consider several specific role attributes of the observer. These attributes are designed to aid in reducing the disturbances created by his presence in the organization, but, as will be suggested, while each of these characteristics solves some problems, it appears to raise others.[8] This discussion of the observer may be considered to be a brief essay on his problems in what Goffman has aptly labeled the "art of impression-management."[9] The observer must manage his impression both in what he does and says—in the expressions given and the expressions given off—if he is to be judged "sincere" in his performance. For the observer is also the observed and while he has only one pair of eyes and ears, his "subjects" numbered in the dozens are ever alert for the

---

8. Our discussion will be couched in general terms since it is felt that these attributes are often associated with the role of observer; however, it should be kept in mind that the observer's role-attributes will vary from situation to situation.

9. Erving Goffman, *The Presentation of Self in Everyday Life,* Doubleday Anchor Books, Garden City, New York, 1959.

tell-tale smile of condescension, the frown of displeasure, or the casual comment voiced in an unguarded moment which will furnish them with some key as to his "real" reactions to them and to events occurring in the organization.

IMPARTIALITY

The first canon governing the role of observer is that all members of the organization should have approximately equal access to his attention. The avoidance of bias in the selection of cases is a problem in all situations where data are collected; it is particularly a problem in the research situation under discussion where the "cases" exercise considerable discretion in deciding whether or not they will be "available" to the observer. Impartiality is particularly vital when different and possibly conflicting groups are being studied. Thus, in my study, it was important that I not spend too much time with either the workers or the supervisors. The fact that the supervisors and the higher administrative staff were included in the scope of the study seemed to be a source of satisfaction to the workers; however, had too much time been spent with supervisors I might have become identified with them in the minds of the workers and hence have been cut off from certain worker attitudes and sentiments. And, of course, the reverse is equally true.

One of the means I employed to assure some impartiality and a maximum spread of contacts among workers was to change each day my location in the room under observation. Another was to consciously seek out and visit with the more passive members of the staff. In a few cases, auxiliary workers were interviewed more because it was perceived that they were anxious about my presence or felt slighted by the lack of attention given to them than because I needed the data they could provide.

Of course, impartiality remained only an ideal. On the one hand, some workers were much more active in seeking me out and so received a relatively greater amount of attention. Although it is difficult to generalize here, it appears that these workers were predominantly (1) students doing their field-work in the agency, who perhaps tended to identify with me because they were more nearly my age or because they had a better idea of the nature of my interests and work; (2) the more competent workers, who were glad to discuss their work and who because of their competence had more time at their disposal for social interaction; and (3) deviants, who were partial isolates and so hungry for social contacts or who were anxious to give some voice to their grievances.

On the other hand, in spite of my best intentions I was not completely successful in distributing my attentions evenly. Contacts with certain respondents proved to be more rewarding—both socially and in terms of information received—than did contacts with others and so the former were the more frequently contacted.[10] It should be remembered that particularly during the first few weeks of observation the observer is to a degree an isolate[11] and thus somewhat subject to feelings of anxiety and loneliness. Outgoing respondents who are friendly and accepting help relieve these feelings and so quite naturally receive more than their share of the observer's attention.

NEUTRALITY

By word and action the sociological observer should attempt to be neutral and non-judgmental in his reactions to all members of the staff.[12] This attitude is essential if he is to avoid involvement in the organization with a consequent loss of objectivity and if he is not to inhibit the responses of the informants. However, this is a difficult attitude to maintain consistently. First, as Bain has pointed out,[13] staff members will attempt to obtain the observer's opinion on various controversial matters partly because this is one way by which they can identify him. They must know *who* he is in terms of his attitudes and values if they are to relate themselves to him. Another problem is that a completely neutral, non-judgmental person may be perceived as rather dull, and staff members may very quickly become annoyed with noncommittal or evasive responses to their assertions and questions. Such considerations are important because social interaction with the observer must be rewarding to the staff members or he will soon find himself an isolate ignored by all. A partial solution I employed to avoid this irksome neutrality was to attempt to assume a non-judgmental attitude only in relation to matters connected with the agency and social work in general. In other matters—particularly in non-workplace encounters—I did not constantly strive for neutrality but now and then allowed myself the luxury of expressing attitudes and judgments of various kinds.

10. Note that Homans' notions on the relations between sentiment and interaction appear to apply to the observer and his subjects as well as to members of a common group. See George C. Homans, *The Human Group,* Harcourt, Brace, New York, 1950, p. 133.
11. Not only is he an isolate but he is confronted by an ongoing network of interpersonal relations in the organization observed which can only serve to emphasize by contrast his own relative isolation. Compare the comments of Blau on the discomfort of "being alone and feeling disoriented while witnessing the cohesiveness of others." Peter M. Blau, *The Dynamics of Bureaucracy,* The University of Chicago Press, Chicago, 1955, p. 157.
12. Impartiality is always only striven for, never attained. The subtle manner in which the observer's interests can lead to bias in his contacts with respondents may be hinted at. One of the major concerns of our study was to differentiate between workers with "professional" and those with "bureaucratic" orientations. Everett C. Hughes, in a private conversation with the author, has indicated his belief that studies dealing with this topic may be subject to considerable bias in that the observer will more often than not be identified as a "professional" himself and so have differential contacts with the two types of respondents.
13. Bain, *op. cit.,* pp. 24–25, n.3.

NON-EXPERTNESS

Another characteristic of the sociological observer is that he does not pose as an expert, at least with regard to the tasks being performed in the organization studied. Such a role would be too threatening to the staff since his observation would be interpreted as a search for areas of ignorance or for inappropriate actions. The sociologist is or should be an "expert" in his own discipline, but the role of observer does not afford many opportunities for displaying his special skills and knowledge to his respondents.[14]   Indeed, one could argue that the most effective observer is the one whose words and actions are so unremarkable that they go virtually unnoticed among his respondents, for the observer enters a situation to learn, not to impress or teach. The attribute of non-expertness is important, then, if the observer is to avoid threatening the staff under observation. However, to pose as an amateur seeking information may damage the status of the observer impairing his attractiveness to the staff and his own self-confidence. The observer will find himself being taught things which he knows to be incorrect; and some respondents may decide that since the observer does not argue with and contradict them, he is gullible and ignorant and hence not worthy of further attention.

No general solution to this dilemma can be proposed. In connection with the present study, my age allowed me to adopt at least in part the role of "student"—by definition not an expert, but not necessarily an amateur—and this stance met some of the problems posed by this aspect of the role of the observer.

PASSIVITY

The sociological observer must behave in a fairly passive manner if he is not to disrupt or overly influence the behavior of those under observation. Of course, the mere presence of such an observer will not be without its effects on those observed, but the observer can do much to minimize his influence on respondents by a quiet and unobtrusive manner. In general, in my periods of observation in the agency I attempted to remain alert and interested in my reactions but to keep my own participation to a minimum.

The problems associated with this role characteristic are not unlike those connected with non-expertness and neutrality. As in the case of neutrality, passivity may be interpreted as dullness. Bales' findings[15]

14. This seems to be a special case of the more general problem that Goffman has discussed under the label of the "dramatic realization" of work performances. Some types of work are of the sort which do not lend themselves to dramatic expression: the sociological observer cannot display his skills to his subjects in the same way as can, for example, the surgeon or the violinist. See Goffman, *op. cit.*, pp. 30–34.
15. See Robert F. Bales, "Some Uniformities of Behavior in Small Social Systems," in Swanson, Newcomb, and Hartley (eds.), *Readings in Social Psychology*, Henry Holt, New York, 1952, p. 154.

that persons most active in participation in groups are likely to be considered the most "productive" and the most "popular" by other members is not a source of comfort to the observer playing a passive role. Thus, this characteristic of the role of observer appears to aggravate certain of the status problems already made sensitive by other aspects of the role.

GENERAL PROBLEMS CONFRONTING THE OBSERVER

Many of the problems referred to in this discussion of the role attributes of the observer have been associated with the development and maintenance of the observer's status in the eyes of his respondents. The observer's status is of concern, as we have noted, since it is one of the means by which he maintains his attractiveness and thus facilitates his interactions with organization members. But why should problems arise in this area? Underlying the specific problems associated with the several role attributes we have considered appears to be a more general structural condition. It is suggested that status problems arise for the sociological observer because his role has little or no legitimacy within the system in which his research is carried out. He is in the organization but not of it. The significant members of his role set[16] are not the staff of the organization studied but his sociological colleagues to whom he will report, and his activities within the organization gain legitimacy and meaning only from their relation to the norms and standards of the scientific community of which he is a part. Since his respondents do not (necessarily) share these norms, the observer's activities may hold little meaning or significance from their point of view: his activities are irrelevant from the standpoint of their social system or, indeed, may violate some of its norms and values. It is because of these circumstances that the researcher is faced with the problem of achieving sufficient status among the organization's personnel to allow him to carry out his study, and it is to achieve this end that he must employ some of the informal, interpersonal techniques suggested in the above discussion.

A second set of problems which confronts the observer is that of maintaining a favorable balance of obligations between himself and his respondents. The observer finds himself constantly in the position of asking—for information, materials, time, opinions. Unless he finds ways of repaying his social obligation to staff members he may become weighted down by the burden of unpaid social debts. Fortunately, the observer is in a position to offer some rewards to his respondents. In addition to being helpful and friendly as specific occasions demand, the observer provides respondents with opportunities to express opinions

16. Robert K. Merton, "The Role Set," *British Journal of Sociology*, VIII (June, 1957), 106–20.

and attitudes without fear of contradiction,[17] opportunities to interact with a social scientist and a person of considerable education; and a chance to contribute to a scientific study of their organization and occupational group. These are experiences which most persons find satisfying. The observer must understand the nature of the rewards he dispenses if he is to maintain the balance of social obligations between himself and his respondents.

FACTORS FACILITATING OBSERVATION IN AN ORGANIZATION

Our survey of some of the difficulties and dilemmas attending the role of the observer in the organization may have left the impression that this research approach is beset with severe problems and consequently has little to recommend it over alternative strategies. To counterbalance this negative appraisal, we would like to suggest two advantages offered by this method of data collection lacking in other approaches.

THE BINDING NETWORK OF RELATIONS

There is always some question as to the degree to which the presence of the observer affects the behavior of the persons observed and thus introduces bias into his observations. Although this is an important concern and one which the observer must take into consideration, there are certain forces within the situation itself which serve to reduce this danger. The most important of these factors is the network of relations and activities extant within the organization. Although the presence of the observer may (particularly at first) be an overriding concern to some of the workers, the fact is that little is changed. There is familiar work to do, and the worker is surrounded by his fellow workers all of whom have come to develop particular kinds of relations with or expectations of him. In most cases the worker will feel it is more important to continue to meet these expectations and maintain these relations than to deviate from them because of the presence of the observer. Note that these same safeguards do not operate in, for example, the interview situation. Here the worker is temporarily separated from his social context and may distort his comments in any way he sees fit without fear of retaliation from his peer group. It is our impression that in general more reliable data may be gathered in the observation situation because of the sustaining influence of the work being per-

17. On this point see Theodore Caplow, "The Dynamics of Information Interviewing," *American Journal of Sociology*, LXII (September, 1956), 165–71.

formed and of the network of interpersonal relations in which the worker is embedded.[18]

THE BIAS-CORRECTING ACTIONS OF WORKERS

Closely related to the first point is the fact that staff members are generally anxious that the observer obtain what they consider to be a "true" picture of their activities and feelings. Thus in my study, time and again the comments of some worker to the observer would be overheard by other workers and challenged on the spot. A good example of this bias-correcting function of the presence of other workers is contained in the following incident:

> I had just completed the observation of a conference between a worker, Jones, and her supervisor. The worker came over to me and said: "I enjoyed having you sit in on my conference, Mr. Scott." Brown [another worker] overhearing this comment says: "You get along with her [the supervisor] because you never argue." Jones: "Yes I do. There were some differences of opinion, weren't there, Mr. Scott?" I say yes. Jones continues: "I enjoy my conference periods; it's a good chance to learn something." At this point a third worker, Smith, comments to Jones: "Who learns, you or her?" Jones: "I do." Brown: "Oh, come off it Jones; you're not in there [with the supervisor] now!"

It seems clear from this incident that Brown and Smith felt that Jones was not being sincere with the observer in her comments concerning her conference and they refused to "let her get away with it." Obviously, I as the observer could not have challenged the sincerity of Jones' comments; but other workers could and did, partly in the interests of providing a more accurate picture of the situation for the observer although a variety of motives were no doubt involved.

Another method utilized by workers to aid in evaluating the statements of other workers was to point out privately to me which workers they considered to be "deviant" or marginal to the group. On several occasions I was warned against taking too seriously the remarks of one worker and was provided with several anecdotes of her unacceptable behavior in the past. Note that the social situation—the presence of other workers—is the crucial factor permitting this bias-correcting behavior. Had the investigator been closeted with individual workers during the whole of the study, he would have had no basis for evaluating

---

18. Of course, it is possible for the respondents under observation to agree privately to behave in an atypical manner during periods of observation. Examples of this kind are reported in the literature. (See, for example, William F. Whyte *et al.*, *Money and Motivation: An Analysis of Incentives in Industry*, Harper, New York, 1955, pp. 15–16.) But they usually occur where the observer is perceived as a real threat by all members of the group under observation, for example, when the observer is responsible for setting the rates at which workers will be paid. It is felt that few sociological observers will be considered dangerous enough to merit such concerted action on the part of the respondents.

the remarks of any single respondent; but in the social situation of the work group other members readily provided such evaluations.

CONCLUSION

This paper has considered some problems relating to the role of the sociological observer as that role was played in connection with a case study of a public welfare organization. In addition to considering some of the reactions of respondents to this role—specifically, their misinterpretations of it—we have examined some of the dilemmas raised by certain of its attributes: impartiality, neutrality, non-expertness, and passivity. Finally, we turned to consider some of the factors which impede and others which facilitate the collection of reliable and valid data in this research context.

8

AN ETHNOGRAPHIC APPROACH TO THE STUDY OF ORGANIZATIONS
The City Jail

James P. Spradley

INTRODUCTION

Complex organizations are culturally constituted. Social interaction is based on certain definitions of the situation shared by some or all members. Whether in a tribal clan or an urban corporation, individuals acquire a body of folk knowledge which enables them to function in an acceptable manner within that organization. They learn to locate it in space and time. They are taught to identify its physical features, time schedules, categories of personnel, and variety of routines. They learn to recognize and interpret symbols which represent the significant aspects of organizational life. While these may include flags, signs, colors, songs, uniforms, and other paraphernalia, specialized languages are inevitably a major feature of every organization. As an individual acquires these meaning systems, he learns to anticipate events and behave in a manner which other members consider appropriate. In short, the culture of an organization refers to the knowledge which members learn and employ to organize their behavior. It is the characteristic ways in which they categorize, code, and define their experience.

Ethnography, the description of a culture, is carried out through many different methods. Whatever approach is used the researcher must select a set of *descriptive units* for ordering his data. Instead of selecting categories for this purpose from his own culture or using those invented by social scientists, the ethnographer's goal is to *discover* the categories used by informants. He will, in a sense, undergo a form of socialization which will enable him to define, interpret and anticipate life in the organization in the same way members do.[1] He will avoid the temptation to pour the content of one culture into the structure of another—even if that structure is made up of the categories of social science. In order to map the content and structure of the symbolic world of organizational members, it is necessary to study their language. Although this will not exhaust their system of cultural symbols, it will certainly tap a major portion of it. Ethnographic description in one's own society will probably not involve a study of the phonology and grammar of language, but it will require a semantic analysis. To the investigator interested in an organization's culture,

> the semantics of the language of the people in whom he is interested is a subject of considerable interest since it presents him with a practically exhaustive classification of the objects in the cultural universe of speakers.[2]

If descriptive units are to be derived from the classification system of those studied, the meaning and use of such units must conform to their culture. This requires more than simply getting the names people use to identify the objects and events in their experience. Suppose one wishes to study interaction among factory workers. He will certainly ask workers to identify the types of employees, the products they are assembling, their activities, and where these are performed. He will record many linguistic labels—the folk terminologies for the things he observes. Such terms as "assembly line," "foreman," "punch clock," "lunch room," "coffee break," and "company picnic," will begin to fill his field notes. But it is not sufficient to use these labels in the description unless one discovers their meaning to the workers. It is often the case that investigators *assume* they know the referents of such terms but the arbitrary nature of symbols means this cannot be taken for granted.[3] Frake has summarized this point very well.

1. Paul Kay, "Some Theoretical Implications of Ethnographic Semantics," In *Current Directions in Anthropology*, Bulletin of the American Anthropological Association, 1970, Vol. 3, No. 3, Part 2, pp. 19–35.
2. Joseph H. Greenberg, "Linguistics and Ethnology," *Southwestern Journal of Anthropology*, 1948, 4, pp. 140–147.
3. Howard S. Becker and Blanche Greer, "Participant Observation and Interviewing: A Comparison," *Human Organization*, 1957, 16, No. 3, pp. 28–32.

If, however, instead of 'getting words for things,' we redefine the task as one of finding the 'things' that go with the words, the eliciting of terminologies acquires a more general interest. In actuality not even the most concrete, objectively apparent physical object can be identified apart from some culturally defined system of concepts (Boas 1911:24–25; Bruner *et al.*, 1956; Goodenough 1957). An ethnographer should strive to define objects according to the conceptual system of the people he is studying.[4]

During the last few years anthropologists have been developing more systematic methods for mapping the cognitive systems which make up a culture.[5] Let us consider these methods in the context of an ethnographic study of a city jail.

ETHNOGRAPHY OF A JAIL

The research[6] reported here was carried out from July, 1967 to August, 1968, in Seattle, Washington. Data were gathered by means of participant observation in an alcoholism treatment center, on Skid Road, in a municipal court, and to a lesser extent within the city jail. The first few months were spent in observation and informal interviews with individuals who had been in this jail. This was followed by more formal ethnographic interviews to elicit and define the categories used by members of this organization. In addition to interviews with a small number of experienced informants, an extensive questionnaire was administered to a sample of one hundred men who had been in this jail on at least one occasion.

During the early phase of the project I was faced with the problem of how to select and organize the data related to social interaction within the jail. One of the main functions of an *explicit* theoretical orientation and related hypotheses is to avoid being influenced by *implicit* notions of relevance. Without such a guiding theory, how does the researcher select and organize his data with a minimum of bias? I began by listening to individuals talk about life in jail and recording what was said. Such conversations occurred in jail, in the court docket, and at the alcoholism treatment center. This corpus of linguistic data was then examined for relevant categories. Some terms used by informants ap-

4. Charles O. Frake, "The Ethnographic Study of Cognitive Systems," In *Anthropology and Human Behavior*, T. Gladwin and W. C. Slurtevant (eds.), Washington: Anthropological Society of Washington, 1962, pp. 72–85.
5. Harold C. Conklin, "Ethnography," *International Encyclopedia of Social Sciences*, Crowell Colliers, and Macmillan, Inc., 1967. Charles O. Frake, "Notes on Queries in Ethnography," In *Transcultural Studies in Cognition*, A. Kimball Romney and Rog G. D'Andrade (eds.), *American Anthropologist*, 1964, 66, pp. 132–145, (Part 2). *Op. Cit.*, James P. Spradley.
6. Some of the data reported here appeared in *You Owe Yourself a Drunk: An Ethnography of Urban Nomads*, (James P. Spradley, Boston: Little, Brown and Co., 1970). Those who are interested in additional data on the jail studied using the ethnographic methods discussed here should consult this source.

peared to refer to individuals within the jail. Consider the following statements:

> (1) Those *guys* in for worse than shoplifting, fighting, *drunks,* and car prowling are not made *trusty.* (2) Some *guys* might brown nose by passing things to *bulls* that aren't his business. (3) A *garage man* gets nickel candy bars and sells them for a dime.

A long list of terms for people in this organization was thus compiled from recorded material and also by asking informants directly, "What are all the different kinds of people in the jail?"

Classification systems are more than lists of linguistic labels. Categories are *organized* into systematic relationships which must be discovered rather than imposed from the outside. One relationship among classes which appears to be a universal feature of human communication is an *hierarchical* one. This occurs when a general concept includes more specific ones. Walker has summarized this kind of relationship:

> The members of a speech community necessarily share a common core of highly codable reference categories, since this is a prerequisite to any sort of communication. But hierarchically structured taxonomies are not essential since, even without them, the speakers of a language might communicate anything which they were capable of imagining. The apparent universality of hierarchical taxonomies in language is clearly due to the enormous increase in efficiency of communication which they provide. With the invention of the generic term, man was for the first time permitted to suspend temporarily irrelevant discriminations; and, also for the first time, he could indicate a large reference category without listing its many subdivisions. He could, in other words, refer to *pines* as *trees,* if their pineness was irrelevant. He could also indicate trees without an exhaustive list of pines, oaks, etc., etc. The hierarchical taxonomy, in a word, permits the speaker to refocus his hearer's attention to any degree of abstraction provided by the various levels of the hierarchy. This refinement is quite possibly unique for human communications systems.[7]

The ethnographer who has discovered *lists* of reference categories (in this case, categories of people in the jail) must also discover how they are *organized.* Without such a discovery one is still in danger of imposing his boundaries upon the data collected—in effect, he may classify oranges and apples together with cars and call them all vegetables. When I began to investigate how informants classified parts of the jail it included places I thought were outside the jail. For example, the places labeled drunk tank, standup cell, court docket, courtroom, and judge's bench were all identified by informants as integral parts of the

7. Willard Walker, "Taxonomic Structure and the Pursuit of Meaning," *Southwestern Journal of Anthropology,* 1965, 21, pp. 265–275.

jail. Such inclusion relationships are often covert and must be inferred from the way informants use various terms.

There are several ways to discover whether one reference category is included in another or whether a general category includes more specific ones.[8] When informants apply different names to the same object it may be that one is included in the other. Consider the following cases: it is a carrot—it is a vegetable; she is a student—she is a freshman; that is a car—that is a Ford; and, he is a garage man—he is a trusty. Care must be taken to eliminate cases where distinct names are synonyms as in the statement: he is an inmate—he is a prisoner. Also, reference terms applied to an object may actually refer to an *aspect* rather than the object itself. Terms for individuals usually refer not to the person but to one of his identities. When an informant says, "He is a trusty, a father, and a Negro," numerous identities have been referred to. On the other hand, when one says, "He is a garage man, a trusty, and an inmate," a single identity has been labeled at three levels of generality. When different names are used for the same object, they can be further tested for inclusion by asking, "Are *all* trusties inmates?" and "Are *all* inmates trusties?" Another way to discover and test when the relationship of inclusion occurs is to ask, for each member of a list, whether there are other "kinds." For example, "Are there different kinds of trusties?" resulted in a long list of identities, one of which was a garage man. The question, "Are there different kinds of garage men?" resulted in only two included identities, neither of which was labeled "trusty." Thus, through observation of usage in natural settings and carefully controlled elicitation during interviews, hierarchical relationships among categories were discovered. A partial taxonomy of the various identities people have when they are members of this organization is shown in Figure 1. The most extensive category was the one labeled *trusty* which included more than fifty different classes of trusties. Only the sixteen core terms which are immediately included in the cover term for this class are shown in Figure 1. One category (floor man) included sixteen more specific classes while another (kitchen man) included fourteen. The actual number of men who assumed these identities at one time ranged from one hundred and twenty-five to one hundred and fifty.

DIMENSIONS OF MEANING

During ethnographic field work one is constantly faced with the temptation to use invented categories rather than ones *discovered*

8. Charles O. Frake, "The Diagnosis of Disease Among the Surbanun of Mindanas," *American Anthropologist*, 1961, 63, pp. 113–132. Harold C. Conklin, "Lexicographical Treatment of Folk Taxonomies," In *Problems in Lexicography*, F. W. Householder and S. Saperta, (eds.), *Indiana University Research Center in Anthropology, Folklore, and Linguistics Publication* 21, pp. 119–141.

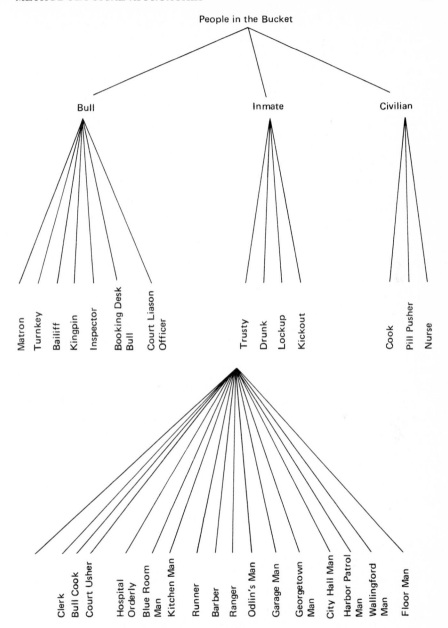

Figure 1. Taxonomy of Jail Identities.

from informants. The investigator is confronted with a great many stimuli and must selectively attend to some while ignoring others. This creates pressure to classify and order the data by using concepts and criteria derived from social science. It would have been possible to explain the behavior of inmates or trusties in terms of characteristics and traits which I considered important. But inmates also selectively perceived their environment. They attended to some characteristics of those they defined as inmates and ignored others. Whether they used attributes similar to those employed by social scientists—age, sex, race, educational achievement, income, etc.—was an empirical problem. It could not be answered by simply asking informants to answer questions about these criteria. Such an approach would have fallen into the trap of describing the inmates' culture in terms of the investigator's culture. Those who become inmates learn to define all the different kinds of inmate identities, and I was interested in this body of coded information. In short, it was necessary to examine another way in which semantic systems are organized.

As noted above, reference categories are related hierarchically in terms of different degrees of generalization and specification. When an informant states that George is a *runner* and Bill is a *bull cook,* he is implicitly indicating that they are both trusties. If he says that they are both trusties, he has called attention to the fact that their identities are similar. But how does a runner differ from a bull cook? What information is required to enable us to distinguish these identities in the same manner as our informants? Contrasts among categories are made in terms of certain attributes which we shall call "dimensions of meaning." One's mother and father are contrasted, in part, on the dimension of sex. The values of male and female on that dimension distinguish these kinsmen. A radio and television set are distinguished by noting whether or not they receive signals which are represented visually. A watch and a clock are usually contrasted on the dimension of size. When a large number of categories which informants group together are contrasted, a great many dimensions of meaning emerge. While these do not tell us everything that one can know about that class of categories, they tell us some of the most important information employed by informants in their actions toward these categories. We may examine some of the methods for discovering this type of semantic organization by considering the sixteen categories of trusties which are immediately included in the cover term for that taxonomy (Figure 1).

The dimensions of meaning for this set were discovered by examining statements from informants, asking them to indicate the difference among pairs of categories, and by means of a triadic sorting task. In the latter method, which proved most useful, an inmate was presented with three category terms. He was then asked, "Which two of these are most alike and which one is different?" For example, he would be asked to sort kitchen man, bull cook, and georgetown man into two groups. This sorting task was designed to produce a decision about both similarities and differences among categories.[9] A typical response for these three kinds of trusties was: "Oh, kitchen men and bull cooks—they're more alike and the georgetown man is different." A query as to the reason for such a decision led to the response: "Well, they are both trusties who stay inside the jail while the other is an outside trusty." It was then possible to ask the informant to map this dimension of meaning onto each of the other categories. Often an informant would ask, "How do you mean, different and alike?" At this point, it would have been possible to provide him with criteria which I considered important. Instead, I asked, "Can you tell me any important way *you think* they are alike or different?" In nearly every case informants were able to report their perception of similarity and difference. There are a large number of combinations possible with sixteen terms. It was not necessary to use all of them but only enough to generate an adequate number of dimensions to define each category in this set.

Five major dimensions of meaning emerged from this investigation. The first refers to the degree to which a trusty experiences *restricted mobility* (A). Incarceration may appear to be a similar experience for all inmates but informants perceived radical differences depending on one's identity. The men in the drunk tank have little freedom to move around and their resources are extremely limited. If a man becomes a lockup, he continues to feel restricted, he must "lay it out on the steel." Each day he will be allowed to leave the cell to pick up his meals, and he may have a brief "walk time" in the late afternoon. Otherwise he remains confined to a cell with other men. The mobility of all trusties is much less restricted than other inmates. A man might work many hours each day as a trusty, but he will be free to move about and that is worth a great deal. At the same time, restrictions on mobility vary among the various kinds of trusties. The most important distinction is between those outside and those inside the jail. In fact, many men refer to other trusties, not by the name for a specific type, but rather as "outside men" or "inside men." If an inmate has a sentence which is longer than thirty days he may not be allowed to become an outside man because of the temptation to "rabbit" or escape. The two values then, on this dimension of meaning indicate whether a particular trusty is inside (1) or outside (2) of the jail.

Although it took little time to discover these two classes of restriction, it was not readily apparent that informants made finer distinctions. It turned out that those who worked outside still did not have equal *freedom* (B), nor did those who worked inside experience the same degree of *confinement* (C). As individuals sorted the various terms for outside trusties they made distinctions such as the following:

9. George A. Kelly, *The Psychology of Personal Constructs*, Vols. I and II, New York: Norton, 1955.

> A harbor patrol man has more freedom than other outside trusties. He
> doesn't have to be in at a certain time. He gets money each day for
> lunch while the ranger has to take his lunch. Harbor patrol man stays
> somewhere else, he stays on the job while others go out and come in.
> A ranger for instance goes out once in the morning and comes back
> at night but a city hall man and a garage man come in two times a day.
> A ranger and a Georgetown man stay out all day.

Four values appeared to be important in distinguishing among different
kinds of trusties on this dimension of meaning. (1) Some lived outside
the jail in another part of town, ate at restaurants, and had the right to
go to stores, attend movies, and receive visitors. (2) A second group left
the jail each morning and returned in the late afternoon at the end of
their work day. They ate a lunch prepared in the jail kitchen and had
only limited opportunity to go to stores. If they purchased items to be
brought back into the jail, they had to smuggle them past the "shake-
down." (3) Other trusties left each morning to work at the police garage
or the city hall. They returned to the jail at noon for lunch and then
went back to their work stations until late in the afternoon. (4) Finally,
one group of trusties went out of the jail but never left the building
where it was located. They also returned each day at noon for lunch.

While these distinctions may appear trivial to those outside this
culture, they have crucial significance to inmates. Different degrees of
freedom determine, in part, whether a prisoner does *hard time* or *easy
time.* Trusties who live outside the jail during their entire sentence are
the envy of all inmates. Those who have access to stores can hustle other
prisoners and thus earn money while in jail. Candy bars can be purchased and sold to lockups for at least 100 per cent profit. The outside
trusty who doesn't leave the building may be glad he isn't confined to
one floor in the jail, but he is cut off from many opportunities available
to others. One man recalled: "A trusty who works on the range has his
friends bring him some instant coffee and he peddles it to the men in
lockup or other trusties." Increased freedom also carries with it a
greater sense of psychological distance from the jail—an institution
which most inmates intensely dislike. When one man tells another, "Joe
is a ranger," or "I hope to be a bull cook," he has more in mind than
simply jobs performed by prisoners. The terms signify important values
on this dimension of freedom.

Inside trusties are defined by three values on the dimension of
confinement (C). (1) Kitchen men leave the sixth and seventh floor
where the jail is located, but they do not leave the jail. They take a
restricted elevator and travel to the first floor of the public safety building where the jail kitchen is located. This kind of ambiguity is a feature
of many systems of folk knowledge. (2) Runners remain in the jail but
have access to almost every part of it as they carry messages and run

errands for the officers. As one man stated, "A runner sees the most, he knows what is going on in the jail." Another recalled, "I was on as a runner and so could hustle the drunk tank. I peddled cups of coffee to some of the drunks for fifty cents." (3) Finally, a group of trusties are confined to a limited or restricted area on a single floor. This may be the barber shop, hospital area, the officer's coffee room, or an entire floor. Although restricted, one still has more freedom than the men in lockup do and he can use his freedom for a variety of purposes.

When an inmate becomes a trusty, it involves work and its meaning is partially shared by the officers in the jail. Trusties provide janitorial services to the jail and other agencies of government. They cut hair for officers and inmates, prepare and serve food, maintain vehicles, and work in many other ways. While trusties engage in many tasks, each identity has a particular *work focus* (D). These include (1) guns, (2) buildings, (3) wheeled vehicles, (4) boats, (5) food, and (6) people. When a man is assigned to a trustee position, he knows what he must work with; a fact of great significance for his stay in jail. Informants specified these contrasts in statements such as, "He does janitor work but the others wait on the cops," or "Those trusties wash cars but the others work only with food." The most desirable work focus is food because it provides an opportunity to reduce one of the most persistent frustrations in this jail—hunger. In a sample of ninety-eight men, seventy-nine felt that in a lockup there was never enough to eat or the menu was a "starvation diet." In a sample of sixty-two men, only twenty-four reported that they had enough to eat as trusties. One man's complaint shows how access to food is a feature of the meaning of work for trusties.

> Procedure for meals for trusties should be changed. The guys that usually work hard are the ones who don't get a chance for seconds, as instance, garage (men). Cause there's so little time between being left and picked up by head mechanic. Guys who hand out meals usually wind up kniving extra sandwiches for themselves or selling them.

Another man described the special opportunities of kitchen men:

> A kitchen trusty makes a sandwich in the kitchen and sticks it inside his sock to get by the shakedown when he returns from work. He then peddles this for pills, cigarettes, or something else to men in lockup.

Another dimension of meaning used to define this domain was the persons to whom a trusty must provide *direct service* (E). Social interaction varies from one identity to another. Trusties do not simply work, they work for others. Sometimes it is for those who have immense power over their lives, while at other times, it is for lockups who are beneath them in the jail hierarchy. Some trusties must serve one class of persons, others are required to serve several different groups. In distinguishing among trusty identities, informants reported, "He has to get people for the bull," "He takes people to court," or "He is under the jurisdiction of the nurse." The knowledge of who must be served not only tells a man the strains to be faced but also the opportunities to be enjoyed. Consider the man who becomes a barber:

> The barber who cuts the officers hair does more brown-nosing. Brown-nosing is passing things on to the bulls that aren't his business such as saying, "Old so and so had three extra trays today and I only got one, I'm still hungry." Now some guys brown nose or kiss ass in order to be able to do other things like running a game. He might engratiate himself to them so he can run the game. He may need to kiss ass to protect himself if suspected or caught.

Service to officers may give one new opportunities to hustle other prisoners or to help his friends, as in the following examples:

> An inmate in lockup wants his comb from his property. He tells the trusty, "Can you see the bulls about getting my comb? I'll give you a candy bar." A clerk might be able to get another clerk out of lockup. The inmate may say, "Harry, can you get me out of lockup?" and the clerk will get a bull to get him sprung as a favor to the clerk.

The values for these five dimensions are mapped onto the sixteen terms for trusties in Figure 2. The meanings are sufficient to distinguish each reference category from all the others in the set. At the same time they do not exhaust informants' sense of what it means to be any one

Dimensions of Meaning

Trusty	A Restricted Mobility	B Freedom	C Confinement	D Work Focus	E Direct Service
Ranger	a_2	b_2	c_0	d_1	e_1
Odlin's man	a_2	b_4	c_0	d_2	e_1
Garage man	a_2	b_3	c_0	d_3	e_1
Georgetown man	a_2	b_2	c_0	d_2	e_1
City Hall man	a_2	b_3	c_0	d_2	e_2
Harbor Patrol man	a_2	b_1	c_0	d_4	e_1
Wallingford man	a_2	b_1	c_0	d_2	e_1
Floor man	a_1	b_0	c_3	d_2	e_4
Clerk	a_1	b_0	c_3	d_6	e_1
Bull cook	a_1	b_0	c_3	d_2	e_3
Court usher	a_1	b_0	c_3	d_6	e_5
Hospital orderly	a_1	b_0	c_3	d_6	e_6
Blue Room man	a_1	b_0	c_3	d_5	e_1
Kitchen man	a_1	b_0	c_1	d_5	e_6
Runner	a_1	b_0	c_2	d_6	e_4
Barber	a_1	b_0	c_3	d_6	e_4

Figure 2. Paradigm of Trusty Identities.

of these kinds of trusties. For one thing, some of the work groups wear special uniforms that are a distinguishing feature of the identity. A bull can immediately tell what kind of trusty an inmate is by noting whether he is wearing "stripes," "whites," or some other special clothing. There are differences in the amount of work a man must do from one position to another. One inmate stated: "The court usher is different from a bull cook or a clerk—he works only two hours a day and then can go relax in the tank." Undoubtedly there are other dimensions of referential and connotative meaning learned by trusties and employed to organize their behavior while in jail.

CONCLUSION

A complete ethnographic description would include all the other category systems of those who are members of this organization. In this paper I have presented an analysis of one domain in order to illustrate some of the discovery procedures which are useful in the ethnographic study of complex organizations. The aim of this kind of investigation is the adequate description of specific cultures. As Goodenough has said,

> . . . a society's culture consists of whatever it is one has to know or believe in order to operate in a manner acceptable to its members, and do so in any role that they accept for any one of themselves. . . . By this definition, we should note that culture is not a material phenomenon; it does not consist of things, people, behavior, or emotions. It is rather an organization of these things. It is the forms of things that people have in mind, their models for perceiving, relating, and otherwise interpreting them.[10]

The study of an organization's culture involves an investigation of the cognitive maps employed by members to organize their behavior. It is maintained here that an important starting point is the language of informants. This symbolic system is used in every society to organize the phenomenal world. Discrete objects and events are classified together, linguistically labeled, and treated as if they were equivalent. Several strategies were presented for mapping the hierarchical relationships among categories and the dimensions of meaning which distinguish one category from another. The description which results from this approach is intended to provide a cultural grammar, a set of rules for defining objects, anticipating events, and judging whether behavior is appropriate.

---

10. Ward H. Goodenough, "Cultural Anthropology and Linguistics," in Report of the Seventh Annual Round Table Meeting on Linguistics and Language Study, (P. L. Garvin, ed.), Washington: Georgetown University Monograph Series on Language and Linguistics, No. 9, 1957, p. 167.

9

REALISM IN LABORATORY SIMULATION
Myth or Method?

Thomas E. Drabek and J. Eugene Haas

There is increasing interest in laboratory simulation by sociologists.[1] A wide range of research efforts have been categorized as "simulations" which on the surface appear to have little similarity. Some researchers have restricted their efforts to computer programming, e.g., simulation of voting behavior and other social processes.[2] Efforts also have been made to combine the use of computers and human subjects in a variety of experiments.[3] Other researchers have restricted their efforts to the use of human subjects, but these experiments which are labeled "simulations" are a marked contrast to traditional "small group" research.[4] Yet despite differences in appearance, these varied studies, all labeled simulations, have a basic underlying principle in

Revision of a paper presented at the annual meeting of the American Sociological Association, Chicago, Illinois, September 1965. Financial support for this research was provided by United States Air Force Grant #AF-AFOSR-572-65, monitored by the Air Force Office of Scientific Research of the Office of Aero Space Research.

1. It is of special interest that a recent introductory methods text includes a chapter on simulation; see Bernard S. Phillips, *Social Research: Strategy and Tactics* (New York: The Macmillan Co., 1966), pp. 145–152.

2. Ithiel de Sola Pool and Robert Anderson, "The Simulmatics Project," *Simulation in Social Science,* (ed.) Harold Guetzkow (Englewood Cliffs, New Jersey: Prentice-Hall, 1962), pp. 70–81. Three such papers were presented at the annual meeting of the American Sociological Association, September 1965, Chicago, Illinois, in a section entitled "Three Models Simulating Work and its Discontents": Raymond Breton, "Output Norms and Productive Behavior In Non-Cooperative Work Groups" (Johns Hopkins University); R. R. RiHi and C. P. Fair, "Simulating the Behavioral Consequences of Changes in Organizational Systems" (IBM, Armonk); and John T. Gullahorn and Jeanne E. Gullahorn, "Computer Simulation of Role Conflict Resolution" (Michigan State University).

3. The work of Sydney and Beatrice Rome is most notable; see Sydney C. Rome and Beatrice K. Rome, "The Leviathan Technique for Large Group Analysis," *Behavioral Science,* 6 (April 1961), pp. 148–152; and "Computer Simulation Toward a Theory of Large Organizations," *Computer Applications in the Behavioral Sciences,* (ed.) Harold Borko (Englewood Cliffs, New Jersey: Prentice-Hall, 1962), pp. 523–555.

4. Three sets of experiments are most well-known: (1) Robert L. Chapman and John L. Kennedy, "The Background and Implications of the RAND Corporation Systems Research Laboratory Studies," *Some Theories of Organization,* (eds.) Albert H. Rubenstein and Chadwick J. Haberstroh (Homewood, Illinois: The Dorsey Press, 1960), pp. 139–146; John L. Kennedy, "The System Approach: Organizational Development," *Human Factors,* 4 (February 1962), pp. 25–52; and Robert L. Chapman *et al.,* "The Systems Research Laboratory's Air-Defense Experiments," Guetzkow, *op. cit.;* (2) W. M. Evan and Morris Zelditch, Jr., "A Laboratory Experiment on Bureaucratic Authority," *American Sociological Review,* 26 (December 1961), pp. 883–893; Morris Zelditch, Jr. and William M. Evan, "Simulated Bureaucracies: A Methodological Analysis," Guetzkow, *op. cit.;* (3) L. Wesley Wager and Ernest G. Palola, "The Miniature Replica Model and Its Use in Laboratory Experiments of Complex Organizations," *Social Forces,* 42 (May 1964), pp. 418–429.

common—emphasis is placed on the construction and manipulation of a "simulate" which behaves in a way identical to a natural system.[5]

A large body of research, often labeled "small group" research, may provide significant insights for future simulation efforts. However, analysis of this literature reveals certain assumptions which are not often explicated. Our objective here is to briefly analyze certain of these assumptions and to offer a framework whereby a clearer statement of the relationship between traditional laboratory research, simulation experiments, and field studies of groups might be derived.

A variety of criticisms have been made of traditional small group research. Perhaps none have been so frequent as the general argument that while what occurs in a laboratory is interesting, it has dubious generalizability to the "real world." In fact, it has been suggested that some research efforts have been labeled "simulation studies" to avoid association (and resulting "guilt") with traditional small group research. As Weick recently stated, "By labeling their experiments as a simulation, experimenters seem to be making an effort to forestall criticism that the experiment has nothing to do with actual organizations."[6] It is our thesis that the entire issue of "realism versus artificiality" has been oversimplified. Future development following the reasoning presented here should serve to clarify both the interpretation of previous research and the design of future investigations whereby the existing gap between field and laboratory research might be narrowed.

Discussions of artificiality versus realism in laboratory research have assumed many forms. In the literature, for example, frequent use is made of such labels as "natural" groups, "field-experimental" groups, ad hoc groups, etc. Obviously even the most cursory glance at small group research reveals these kinds of distinctions. Researchers focusing on natural groups such as Whyte[7] and the Sherifs[8] have emphasized

5. Richard E. Dawson, "Simulation in the Social Sciences," Guetzkow, op. cit., p. 3. This definition includes computer simulation which requires (1) A source of input data, often obtained from surveys and (2) a set of propositions or operations by which the data will be manipulated. Thus, an operating model is created through the use of the computer. See Ithiel de Sola Pool, "Simulating Social Systems," International Science and Technology (March 1964), pp. 62–70 and John T. Gullahorn and Jeanne E. Gullahorn, "Some Computer Applications In Social Science," American Sociological Review, 30 (June 1965), pp. 353–365. The "natural system" may, of course, be one abstractly conceived rather than one empirically existing in a concrete form.

6. Karl E. Weick, "Laboratory Experimentation with Organizations" in Handbook of Organizations, (ed.) J. G. March (Chicago: Rand McNally & Co., 1965), p. 200.

7. W. F. Whyte, Street Corner Society: The Social Structure of an Italian Slum (Chicago: University of Chicago Press, 1943).

8. Muzafer Sherif and Carolyn W. Sherif, Reference Groups: Exploration Into Conformity and Deviation of Adolescents (New York: Harper & Row, 1964). The "wholistic" view presented in the present research and in previous research such as that cited here by the Sherifs, is a direct contrast to the "isolationistic" view that variables can meaningfully be related while others are held constant by their absence from the research design. By virtue of their absence from the design, these variables are not controlled, but become part of the "experimental conditions." Researchers thus have no way of

factors which other researchers using "artificial" settings have selected to ignore. Thus, synthesis of research findings has been most difficult.[9]

While the distinctions between such labels as *ad hoc* or natural groups often become blurred, it is apparent that most previous small group research has focused on *ad hoc* groups in laboratory settings.[10] This fact is often explained by suggestions that greater control over the variables under investigation is a major advantage of such research methods. Also, ingenious manipulation and elaborate designs are available in more artificial settings. However, as Olmstead has noted, "It is nonetheless important to ask whether behavior observed in the laboratory and that observed in the 'real' world are the same in fact or in name only."[11] Similarly McGrath and Altman have pointed out that "By highly disproportionate use of laboratory settings alone, we may gain much information about behavior in the laboratory but we may neglect the bridge from laboratory to real-life settings."[12]

Relevance to real world phenomena is often questioned when sociologists discuss a somewhat extreme case such as Mintz's study in which he purported to analyze panic behavior by having subjects quickly remove small paper cones from a bottle to which strings had been attached.[13] Some would agree with Mintz's argument that the chief characteristic of panic flight is an unstable reward structure, i.e., individual escape is threatened when others push toward limited exit points, thus individuals will seek their own escape at the possible expense of the group. We would suggest, however, that a qualitative difference exists between the two situations; research results based on individuals removing cones from a bottle are *not* directly applicable to panic behavior in the real world.

Rather than engage in verbal battles as to which method is superior, recent statements have offered a new perspective. Weick, for example, has suggested that there are clearly advantages and disadvantages to laboratory research which is either artificial or realistic.[14] He argued that such decisions should be determined by the research objec-

knowing the experimental conditions which exist only in the laboratory. Extreme caution is therefore due in efforts to generalize results to the "outside world" where behavior is determined by a complex network of variables which exist as an "interacting whole." See Weick, *op. cit.* pp. 199–207, for a clear statement of this position. Leik presents an intriguing analysis of the unknown factors introjected into experiments through the use of stooges. Robert K. Leik, "Irrelevant Aspects of Stooge Behavior: Implications for Leadership Studies and Experimental Methodology," *Sociometry,* 27 (September 1965), pp. 259–271.

9. Joseph E. McGrath and Irwin Altman, *Small Group Research: A Synthesis and Critique of the Field* (New York: Holt, Rinehart & Winston, 1966), pp. 67–77.

10. *Ibid.,* p. 51.

11. Michael S. Olmstead, *The Small Group* (New York: Random House, 1956), p. 76.

12. McGrath and Altman, *op. cit.,* p. 68.

13. A. Mintz, "Non-Adaptive Group Behavior," *Journal of Abnormal and Social Psychology,* 46 (May 1951), pp. 150–159.

14. Weick, *op. cit.,* pp. 199–254.

tives. While in agreement with this position, we would suggest that the argument of realism versus artificiality requires further analysis.

Our view is similar to Goffman's who suggests that *ad hoc* groups are not groups, but actually "gatherings." Researchers using *ad hoc* groups are " . . . studying processes characteristic of focused interaction, (3) rather than groups as such."[15] Thus, beneath all of the arguments about the merits of artificial experiments, there remains the crucial issue as to whether qualitative differences may exist between *ad hoc* groups or gatherings and "real" groups.

WHAT IS A "REAL" GROUP?

In a classic article, Warriner outlined an attack on nominalistic tendencies in sociology.[16] Taking the position of Durkheim[17] and others,[18] he described what he labeled "modern realism."

> This doctrine holds that (1) the group is just as real as the person, but that (2) both are abstract, analytical units, not concrete entities, and that (3) the group is understandable and explicable solely in terms of distinctly social processes and factors, not by reference to individual psychology.[19]

From this perspective, groups are viewed as meaningful units of analysis, which possess properties independent of individuals. Of course, much small group research has been completed by psychologists who presumably are interested in individual variation. It is thus understandable why many of these experimenters have utilized *ad hoc* groups. However, sociologists, interested in studying social systems in a laboratory setting, must first have a social system, i.e., a real group. It should be emphasized that we think of a group, not as a collection of individuals, but as a relatively permanent and uncomplicated interaction system.[20]

Bales and his colleagues have demonstrated that when a collection

15. Erving Goffman, *Encounters* (Indianapolis: The Bobbs-Merrill Co. 1961), pp. 10–11. Goffman's footnote indicated by the (3) in this quote is especially good and reads as follows: "A similar argument is presented by Hans Zetterberg in 'Compliant Actions,' *Acta Sociologica*, quote: 'What is important to us here is to note that most laboratory experiments on small groups are experiments with action systems. They are usually *not* experiments with "social groups" in the complex sense in which sociologists use this term.' "

16. Charles K. Warriner, "Groups Are Real: A Reaffirmation," *American Sociological Review*, 21 (October 1956), pp. 549–554.

17. Emile Durkheim, *The Rules of Sociological Method*, (trans.) Sarah A. Solovay and John H. Mueller (London: The Free Press—Collier-Macmillan, 1964), (original French publication, 1895).

18. For example, Smelser and Smelser state: "A description of a social system cannot be reduced to the psychological states of the persons in that system; a social system must be described in terms of roles, organizations, norms, etc." Neil J. Smelser and William T. Smelser, *Personality and Social Systems* (New York: John Wiley & Sons, 1963), p. 3.

19. Warriner, *op. cit.*, p. 550.

20. J. Eugene Haas, *Role Conception and Group Consensus* (Columbus, Ohio: Ohio State University, Bureau of Business Research, 1964), pp. 25–26.

of individuals are assembled together and given a task, patterns of interaction will slowly emerge.[21] More recent studies have emphasized that such groups appear to evolve through certain "phases."[22] Over time, "role" differentiation will occur and eventually a relatively stable pattern of interaction will become crystallized.[23] Thus, it is in these developments, which Bales labels phases and Newcomb refers to as the acquaintance process,[24] that result in the establishment of expectations or sets of norms about how each group member ought to behave.

It is in the sense that there exists a pattern of interaction, which has developed through time, and not just a collection of individuals, that sociologists use the term "real group." Group interaction patterns result from shared norms and interlocking role relationships. In *ad hoc* groups, which typically have a history of less than an hour, such shared expectations are not present.[25] As a result we would argue that a qualitative difference exists between *ad hoc* groups and real groups.

Previous research tends to support this position. For example, Taylor, Berry, and Block compared brainstorming effectiveness of different types of groups.[26] Their results indicated that "nominal groups," i.e., *ad hoc* groups in which members had not previously met, were significantly superior in brainstorming activity when contrasted to real groups. These findings were interpreted as indicative of the presence of various group pressures, e.g., fear of criticism by well-known group members, tendency of real groups to limit their attention to "one path" of analysis, and so on.

Leik has also reported specific empirical findings which suggest that qualitative differences exist between *ad hoc* and real groups.[27] In

21. Robert F. Bales, "The Equilibrium Problem in Small Groups," *Small Groups: Studies in Social Interaction,* (eds.) A. Paul Hare, Edgar F. Borgatta, and Robert F. Bales (New York: Alfred A. Knopf, 1955), pp. 424–456; Robert F. Bales and Fred L. Strodtbeck, "Phases in Group Problem Solving," *Group Dynamics, Research and Theory,* (eds.) Dorwin Cartwright and Alvin Zander (2d ed.; Evanston, Illinois: Row, Peterson & Co., 1960), pp. 624–638.
22. More recent studies include Theodore M. Mills, *Group Transformation: An Analysis of a Learning Group* (Englewood Cliffs, New Jersey: Prentice-Hall, 1964); and Dexter C. Dunphy, "Social Change in Self-Analytic Groups," paper presented at the annual meeting of the American Sociological Association, Chicago, Illinois, September 1965.
23. Some research has focused on prediction of "role differentiation," e.g., Philip E. Slater, "Role Differentiation in Small Groups," in Hare, Borgatta and Bales, *op. cit.,* pp. 498–515; and David Moment and Abraham Zaleznik, *Role Development and Interpersonal Competence: An Experimental Study of Role Performances in Problem Solving Groups* (Cambridge: Harvard University Press, 1963). However, our interest here is not to analyze the process, but only to indicate its presence and importance.
24. Theodore M. Newcomb, *The Acquaintance Process* (New York: Holt, Rinehart & Winston, 1961).
25. We refer to norms and interpersonal relationships specific to the group members. Obviously, interaction in *ad hoc* groups is patterned to a degree as a result of general societal norms which members bring into such groups.
26. Donald W. Taylor, Paul C. Berry, and Clifford H. Block, "Does Group Participation When Using Brain-Storming Facilitate or Inhibit Creative Thinking?" *Administrative Science Quarterly,* 3 (June 1958), pp. 23–47.
27. Robert K. Leik, "Instrumentality and Emotionality in Family Interaction," *Sociometry,* 26 (June 1963), pp. 131–145. More recently Leik has indicated that assessment of leadership patterns using *ad hoc* groups as a basis of investigation may not be applicable to other types of groups, i.e., real groups such as family units. See Leik, "Irrelevant Aspects of Stooge Behavior, . . . ," *op. cit.*

a rather ingenious study he compared interaction in three different structural settings: (1) family; all three group members constituted a real family, (2) structured; a three-member group was formed with positions of mother, father, and daughter, but no position incumbents were actually related and, (3) *ad hoc;* a three-member group with identical positions, e.g., all fathers, all mothers, all daughters. The same persons participated in all three situations. When the interaction patterns in the different structures were compared, they were found to be different. For example, it appeared that, " . . . family consensus involves more than those facets which would be found in the laboratory study of *ad hoc* groups."[28]

Upon reviewing data from the entire study, Leik concluded:

> In general, the relevance of instrumentality and emotionality is quite different for family interaction than for interaction among strangers. This major finding poses new problems for the theoretical integration of family research with that based on *ad hoc* experimental groups. Such integration is possible only through a recognition of the fact that the context of interaction with strangers places a meaning on particular acts which is different from the meaning of acts within the family group.[29]

Other studies, of course, have also suggested that qualitative differences may exist between real groups and *ad hoc* groups. For example, Strodtbeck, attempted to test Mills' conclusions about power in three-person groups.[30] Strodtbeck concluded that many of Mills' propositions were not valid for real groups such as three-person families. Results obtained by Torrence also suggest differences between permanent and temporary groups.[31] Similarly, Talland indicated that while Bales' model of successive cycles of equilibrium described a laboratory group engaged in problem-solving discussion, the model did not fit a therapy group.[32]

Groups, viewed as interaction systems have certain properties. What little evidence is available suggests that qualitative distinctions may exist between *ad hoc* groups and real groups. By the term real groups, sociologists refer to relatively permanent interaction systems which result from shared norms and interlocking roles. These groups have histories or "cultures," and knowledge of this is essential in understanding their behavior.

28. Leik, "Instrumentality and Emotionality in Family Interaction," *op. cit.,* p. 144.

29. *Ibid.,* p. 145.

30. Fred L. Strodtbeck, "The Family as a Three-Person Group," *American Sociological Review,* 19 (February 1954), pp. 23–29.

31. E. Paul Torrence, "Some Consequences of Power Differences on Decision Making in Permanent and Temporary Three-Man Groups," in Hare, Borgatta, and Bales, *op. cit.,* pp. 482–492.

32. George A. Talland, "Task and Interaction Process: Some Characteristics of Therapeutic Group Discussion," in Hare, Borgatta, and Bales, *op. cit.,* pp. 457–463.

DIMENSIONS OF REALISM

In the literature the term "realism" is used in a variety of ways. Occasionally, it has referred to experiments in which real groups were used. Other properties have also been suggested. Just as different experimental results may be obtained between *ad hoc* and real groups, so also may variation exist between experimentally created systems which differ in other properties. Instead of dichotomizing experiments into "realistic" and "artificial" and arguing that either method is superior, is it not more meaningful to ask, what is it that makes an experiment "realistic"?

These characteristics might then be used to construct a typology of "class defining properties." These properties could serve to specify the experimental conditions under which relationships between variables were tested. Comparisons within classes of units, i.e., those with identical experimental characteristics, could be made. Testing hypotheses within each "class" would serve to clarify relationships between the variables under study. Further elaboration and specification of these experimental conditions will allow more precise control and greater assurity that relationships discovered are truly products of the variables investigated and not of the experimental conditions.

The intriguing analysis of Zelditch and Hopkins as well as Wager and Palola is somewhat similar to this view. For example, Zelditch and Hopkins suggested that laboratory experiments might be classified according to their relevance for organizations.[33] They formulated four social units each of which was differentiated from the other by specific properties.[34] Wager and Palola[35] added two additional properties to the miniature replica model of Zelditch and Hopkins, and emphasized support for the view that efforts to simulate organizations might be guided by the selection of "class defining properties."

From this perspective, then, the issue of artificiality versus realism is seen as an oversimplification of a more fundamental problem. Realism in laboratory research represents a *method of research* in which an experimental system is created which behaves exactly as its real counterpart. Hence, the connection with simulation should be more clear.

33. Morris Zelditch and Terence K. Hopkins, "Laboratory Experiments with Organizations," *Complex Organizations: A Sociological Reader,* (ed.) Amitai Etzioni (New York: Holt, Rinehart & Winston, 1961).
34. *Ibid.,* see pp. 472–478; four types were constructed, (a) the miniature replica—highly formalized and highly differentiated social system which is integrated through strictly defined subordination and is structurally complex, i.e., has at least three subunits; (b) the part replica—has all elements of "a" except structural complexity, i.e., lack of subunits; (c) the "near" organization—has all or some of the minimum number of units and ranks, and at least one but not all three of the other criteria; and (d) the simple structural unit—a single unit with none of the defining properties of an organization.
35. Wager and Palola, *op. cit.,* pp. 420–423. Two properties added were: "(1) primacy of orientation to the formulation, attainment, and appraisal of goals, and (2) formalized patterns of recruitment, socialization, and termination of participants" (p. 421).

If, such experimentally created systems are to be compared to their "real counterparts," then fundamental points of comparison must be specified. We are again forced to ask, what is it that makes a system realistic?

It must be emphasized that we are not suggesting that other types of laboratory research are without merit. Instead our thesis is that it is essential to recognize that *different relationships may exist between variables if tested under different experimental conditions.* Indeed, such differences may not only be "differences in degree" but also "differences in kind." Therefore, what is required is analysis of those variables which are crucial in defining different experimental properties so that a typology of such might be constructed.

We have initially identified five such properties which appear to be significant. They were derived by asking the question, what is it that makes an experiment realistic? Presumably, a research technique, which we have labeled realistic simulation, would be one in which all five of these properties were present, i.e., they are the class defining properties, the characteristics of the experimental system.

The first requisite for a realistic simulation is that a real group be utilized. Some experimenters have used real groups by manipulating natural groups in natural settings,[36] others have attempted to bring real groups into the laboratory,[37] and some have allowed the units to develop over a long period of time in the laboratory.[38]

It was indicated that individuals who meet together over a prolonged period of time will behave differently than an *ad hoc* group. It is not the fact of time spent together that is crucial, however, but rather the development of a set of norms and an interlocking system of roles. Also, members of such groups often expect the group to persist for an indefinite period of time. Alternative behavioral actions are thus evaluated in terms of possible future consequences.[39] It is the presence of this group culture, reflected by a relatively stable pattern of interaction, that is the defining property of a real group.

Second, the type of task, activity, or demand placed on groups must be appraised. The point is not that "parlor games" are less realistic than other types of tasks, but that group interaction observed under such

36. Best known perhaps is the early study by K. Lewin, R. Lippitt, and R. K. White, "Patterns of Aggressive Behavior in Experimentally Created 'Social Climates,'" *Journal of Social Psychology,* 10 (May 1939), pp. 271–299.

37. Thomas E. Drabek, *Laboratory Simulation of A Police Communication System Under Stress* (Columbus, Ohio: Ohio State University, Disaster Research Center, in press).

38. Chapman *et al., op. cit.;* Wager and Palola, *op. cit.*

39. For example, status differentials are much more likely to be maintained in real groups whose members know they will return to work tomorrow with their same superior, than in *ad hoc* groups where status differentials are assigned for the duration of an experiment which subjects know will terminate in an hour or two.

circumstances may not be generalized as the typical interaction pattern unless the major activity of the group is such. Different sets of norms may apply to such game situations. Thus, investigators seeking to use the method of realistic simulation, would provide group tasks identical to those with which their experimental groups were normally confronted.

Tasks resulting in group discussion have been widely used by previous researchers. While such tasks are appropriate for certain groups, our thesis is that the social meaning of the task for the group is often overlooked. For example, in one of our recent experiments,[40] groups of college students were given the task of discussing a series of topics. Social meaning was provided by linking the group activity to a wider frame of reference. These students were actually enrolled in a credit course; topics were assigned by their professor; and discussion results were written up in the form of brief critiques which served as partial bases for evaluation in the course. While tasks requiring group discussion have frequently been used in previous research, wider social meaning for the subjects is often absent.

Again our point is not that there should be a termination of experiments in which groups are given tasks outside their typical sphere of activity. Instead, we emphasize that experimenters must be aware of the fact that different sets of norms may apply to such situations. Thus, task assignment is another major variable which contributes to the specification of experimental conditions. Variation, of course, may range from assignment of tasks which are exact duplicates of those normally incurred by the groups, to tasks totally outside the groups' experience.

Third, the ecological setting in which a unit is located may significantly affect resulting interaction patterns. Several researchers have emphasized the impact of ecological variables on interaction. Sommer, for example, reports a series of studies which illustrate the importance of seating arrangements and selections.[41] Similarly, Strodtbeck and Hook[42] have studied these same phenomena, and the more recent work of Argyle and Dean[43] has focused on what was often suggested to be the crucial variable, eye contact. Thus, while the theoretical frameworks have ranged from elaborations of "field theory" (Sommer)

40. Results of these experiments conducted at the Disaster Research Center at The Ohio State University are, as yet, unpublished.
41. Robert Sommer, "Studies in Personal Space," *Sociometry,* 22 (September 1959), pp. 244–260.
42. Fred L. Strodtbeck and L. Harmon Hook, "The Social Dimensions of a Twelve-Man Jury Table," *Sociometry,* 24 (December 1961), pp. 397–415.
43. Michael Argyle and Janet Dean, "Eye-Contact, Distance and Affiliation," *Sociometry,* 27 (September 1965), pp. 289–304.

to focus on a specific variable such as eye contact,[44] the importance of ecological variables is clear.

Our point is more general. The method of realistic simulation: would require that all ecological arrangements be maintained, i.e., between the simulate and its real counterpart. Similarly, since ecological factors may be crucial to any system, especially those involving different status levels, this variable is another facet of the experimental conditions. Other than saying they are "important," we have little knowledge of the degree to which ecological factors may affect interaction. Until such knowledge is obtained, generalizations between studies should be restricted to those where ecological factors have been controlled in a similar fashion.

Fourth, social systems exist in, and interact with an environment. Whether the focus of study is a small work group, or an entire organization, relationships with other units nearly always exist. Such activity is often crucial to group functioning. Interunit interaction, be it basic "input" information, "feedback" data, etc., must be socially meaningful to experimental subjects. As Kennedy has commented:

> Our first attempt to study organizations used a highly abstract and very constrained laboratory model. But the people in this model behaved either like automatons or, as a reaction to the short constraints, like 'gamesmen' who took advantage of every artificiality of the situation to stay in a position of 'one-upness' in relation to the experimenters. We learned the hard way something that is probably common knowledge to anthropologists—that people start behaving like people only when the environment they are behaving in has 'reality' for them; in particular, that they start to exhibit the full range of adaptation and learning which is the 'essence of humanness' only when the environment is complex, rich, and challenging.[45]

Empirical support for the argument that variation in environmental conditions may produce variation in results is suggested by O'Rourke[46] in his study of family interaction. "The results of the experiment indicate that both the quantity and the quality of the groups' interactive behavior changed as they moved from home to laboratory."[47] The point was further stressed at the conclusion of the article.

> ... the laboratory situation works a definite distortion on the experimental outcomes. At present we do not know whether the directions

44. Argyle and Dean report what is perhaps the ultimate of specialization in research on eye contact. " ... it was found that subjects would stand closer to a second person when his eyes were shut ... " *Ibid.*, p. 289.
45. John L. Kennedy, "A 'Transition-Model' Laboratory for Research on Culture Change," *Human Organization*, 14 (Fall 1955), pp. 16–17.
46. J. F. O'Rourke, "Field and Laboratory: The Decision-Making Behavior of Family Groups in Two Experimental Conditions," *Sociometry*, 26 (December 1963), pp. 422–435.
47. *Ibid.*, p. 434.

or degrees of distortion will be the same for all types of groups. This and questions about other variables in the interaction situation can be answered only by further research. It must be emphasized that, if the object of small groups research is generalization out of laboratory situations, the conduct of these researches is of a crucial nature.[48]

The fifth, and final variable we encountered in our analysis of realism is that of the subjects' knowledge that they were participating in an experiment. Much has recently been written about variation in behavior depending on whether one is "on" or "off" stage.[49] It is clear that much interaction in the real world is guided in large part by perceived longer term consequences. Such analyses have an obvious relevance for laboratory research.

The method of realistic simulation would require that subjects be unaware that they are participating in an experiment.[50] Observed behavior will not be altered by this experimental condition. A different set of norms will not be imposed. Subjects will behave according to the norms of "real life," and not according to the norms of "laboratory life." Since such norms specify the appropriate degree of "involvement," mode of discussion, restrictions on behavior, etc., it is clear that this variable is highly significant.

The five dimensions, while not inclusive, cover most of the varied meanings which have been implied by the term "realism." In short, they are the properties which make an experiment realistic. Thus, the method of realistic simulation refers to a research technique in which these five dimensions are considered. It is a technique of research and as such, realism is not to be considered as a goal in and of itself.

This perspective also permits a more fruitful approach to future synthesis of small group research. Viewed as properties or characteristics which define the experimental conditions in which hypotheses are tested, a typology can be constructed. Comparison of results within classes could then be made. Also, future elaboration and more precise specification of these dimensions will not only result in more systematic statements of experimental conditions in which hypotheses are tested, but will also permit analysis of the effects of such conditions on the relationships between variables.

Familiarity with the method we have labeled realistic simulation[51] immediately reveals that often large amounts of equipment and technical skill are required.[52] While the sheer mechanical difficulties of using

48. *Ibid.,* p. 435.
49. Erving Goffman, *Presentation of Self in Everyday Society* (New York: Doubleday Anchor, 1959).
50. The obvious ethical problems raised by this point are briefly discussed later in this article.
51. Examples are the studies previously cited in footnote 4.
52. For example, in our own work involving simulation of a police communication system, which was activated by four police officers, a staff of 26 was required during the operation of the simulate. Drabek, *op. cit.*

this method are enormous, there are two basic problems inherent in the method. These are discussed below.

BASIC PROBLEMS: CONTROL AND ETHICS

It should be obvious that the degree of realism varies inversely with the range of manipulation and control open to experimenters. As Wager and Palola note, " ... the closer the experimental 'groups' or organization match the miniature replica type, the greater the difficulty in achieving the desired control over the empirical system and the measurement process."[53] Their experience further confirmed observations first made by those associated with the RAND experiments,[54] that when a high level of realism is achieved, laboratory groups or organizations behave like real ones, i.e., they change, "grow," or "develop." At times, such behavior is not desired by the experimenter since it may be contrary to his design.

Use of ongoing groups, selected from the real world on the basis of criteria which meet the experimenter's objectives, may partially solve both problems of system and measurement control. Such systems have already evolved. Within the limits of these systems, controls are already present. Long periods of laboratory time are not required for system development. Certain measurement can be taken in different settings without revealing connections with laboratory work. For example, if an ongoing work group is used in the laboratory part of one day over a several week period, certain measurements can be obtained, e.g., via paper and pencil, or interview, under a different guise while the subjects are at work. Similarly subjects may, under certain conditions, be brought into the laboratory with incomplete knowledge about the experiment, or that they are even participating in an experiment. No method is without limitations and anticipated manipulation must always be evaluated considering both distraction from realism and the research objectives. This technique is no panacea, but its uses are many, and as yet, it remains relatively unexplored.

In simulations where emphasis is on realism, experimenters must be mindful of ethical considerations. As scientists, experimenters may see the need for persons to participate in experiments without prior knowledge that they are in an experiment or with "faulty" knowledge about the true nature of the experiment. However, researchers cannot escape their ethical responsibilities in such instances. The issue cannot be hidden within a "cloak of scientific objectivity." Also, "higher" and

53. Wager and Palola, *op. cit.,* p. 424.
54. Chapman and Kennedy, "The Background and Implications of the RAND Corporation Systems Research Laboratory Studies," *op. cit.*

"more noble" justifications such as "it's in the best interest of science" or "others will benefit" are inadequate, given the values of our society.[55] We argue that intentional manipulation of human behavior is accompanied by a series of highly significant ethical responsibilities. Human subjects must never be "sacrificed" for the "best" interests of an organization, society, or science.

While members of *ad hoc* groups may never see each other again, use of ongoing groups or creation of "real" laboratory groups requires that experimenters be especially cognizant of ethical considerations. Groups may be markedly changed due to experimental manipulation, and group members may strongly resent such changes especially when they find out that the events were part of a carefully executed experiment. Just as juries do not forget words spoken by witnesses over lawyers' objections, even though the statement may be stricken from the record, so also group members may not be able to return to their original relationships when informed that "it was all an experiment, just forget everything that happened."

Experimenters should note Strodtbeck's statement which he made after his research on three-person families.

> There was every reason to believe that after the experimental session was over they would pick up their daily relations very much as they had been in the past. Their actions in the experimental session proceeded on a broad basis of common knowledge and their behavior in the experimental situation could very well have consequences in their interpersonal relations at a later time.[56]

There are times, of course, when it is hoped that certain changes, both in groups and individuals, will occur. In these instances manipulation is done explicitly with this objective, e.g., classrooms, group therapy sessions, and industrial settings where training is a major or minor objective.[57] However, experimenters not primarily interested in such "applied" objectives should be aware that their experimental groups will change. Such change must not violate the professional ethics of the experimenter.

55. The "justifications" offered by Nazi physicians when questioned about their "experiments" is the logical extreme of the argument which we refute. Ethical issues relevant to certain methodological techniques will probably receive increased attention by social scientists; see for example, Herbert C. Kelman, "The Human Use of Human Subjects: The Problem of Deception In Social-Psychological Experiments," paper presented at the annual meeting of the American Psychological Association, Chicago, Illinois, September 1965. In June 1966 the National Institutes of Health sponsored a three-day conference held at the University of Denver at which 30 nationally-known behavioral scientists discussed various ethical issues related to current research. These discussions indicate that dissension exists within the scientific community as to what, if any, ethical responsibilities social scientists have regarding their subjects.
56. Strodtbeck, *op. cit.,* p. 28.
57. Olmstead has suggested use of therapy settings, Olmstead, *op. cit.,* pp. 77–79; and researchers at Harvard and elsewhere have used "self-analytic" student groups, e.g., Philip E. Slater, *Microcosm* (New York: John Wiley & Sons, 1966).

In this brief analysis we have endeavored to clarify the debate over realism versus artificiality. It appeared to us that asking "which method is superior?" was the wrong question. As an alternative we asked, "what is it that makes an experiment realistic?" By asking this question we were able to draw four major conclusions: (1) Relationships between variables may vary significantly under different sets of experimental conditions and such conditions need, therefore, to be specified; (2) This prospective presents definite implications for a more meaningful synthesis of small groups research, in that comparisons of results could be made between experiments which possess similar experimental conditions, i.e., which occupy the same positions in a typology of experimental conditions; (3) The perspective more clearly identifies the properties of a method of research which we labeled realistic simulation; i.e., a technique whereby a simulate which behaves exactly as its real counterpart is constructed and manipulated; and (4) Inherent in the method of realistic simulation are two fundamental problems—control and ethics. While not a panacea, the technique appears to have much potential and is yet relatively unexplored.

CHAPTER THREE

LIFE CYCLE OF ORGANIZATIONS: EMERGENCE, ADAPTATION, AND DISSOLUTION

An area of organizational concern which has largely been neglected by social scientists is the life cycle of organizations. Upon emergence, organizations encounter many contingencies, both internal and external to the organization. Unless they can adapt to these contingencies they will cease to exist. What are the factors which give rise to these events? Most people know of many organizations which did not survive very long. What factors are associated with short-lived organizations and with long-lived ones? For example, what factors account for the persistence of the Roman Catholic Church which has existed for many centuries?

Organizations never exist in isolation, but are continuously interacting with other organizations. This interaction often results in some modification of each organization. The organization is always found within an environmental context which also may serve as an impetus for change in the organization. Organizations, differentiated by function, are often changed as a result of the necessary interaction among their parts.

The article by Stinchcombe examines the relationship of social structure to organizations. His major interests are in the explanation of the organization's formation, the liability of newness, and the organization's demise. The article treats some of the variables which affect the organizing capacity of a society, and also develops a discussion of the founding of organizations. The selection examines the manner in which historical events and existing social structures have influenced contemporary organizations. Stinchcombe's article is abundant with exciting ideas which merit empirical examination.

Selznick's definition of cooptation, which stemmed from his study of the T.V.A., identifies it as a process "of absorbing new elements into the leadership or policy determining structure of an organization as a means of averting threats as to its stability or existence." The selection from this classical work illustrates one of the processes by which an organization is able to remain viable through time. Thus the T.V.A. strengthened its own position by co-opting the Farm Bureau and other organizations.

When an organization is created, it is generally assumed that there are reasons for its birth and development. The article by Maniha and Perrow discusses an organization which apparently had little reason to be formed and no explicit goals to direct it. Later, however, through interaction with other organizations, it became a viable organization with an explicit *raison d' etre*.

The process through which the organization moves from a position of "meager hope" for stability and power to one of purpose is demonstrated to be significant as an area for study. Interestingly, this article suggests that even an organization without purpose still is a power, in embryo, because it has organizational characteristics—an office, an address, a potential voice in the community.

Dilemmas, or "choices between alternatives in which any choice must sacrifice some valued object in the interest of another," are germane to Blau and Scott's treatment of adaptation. They assume that problems are endemic, and therefore serve as a continual source of change. Thus, change is internally generated. The rate of growth of an organization varies according to the internal adjustments and changes which are required of the organization.

Blau and Scott's presentation of the concepts "bureaucratization" and "debureaucratization" posits them as forms of adaptations. As an organization increases in size and complexity, it tends to increase in bureaucratization. However, bureaucratization is a process which also may require additional adaptations. For example, a danger of bureaucratization is that the original organizational goals may be neglected as a result of preoccupation with administrative problems.

The selection by Katz and Kahn in chapter one demonstrated some of the difficulties which the organizational analyst encounters when he attempts to ascertain the boundaries of the organization. The original selection by Braito, Paulson and Klonglan contains an empirical investigation of this problem by examining "domain" and "domain consensus." As the authors point out, domain consensus is of particular significance for organizations concerned with problem areas, such as organizations or agencies which deal with alcohol, crime, health problems, etc. They suggest that "an organization may be highly committed (self-definition of domain) to the reduction of a specific problem, but unless they receive the support from other organizations in their environment (domain consensus), they will have little success working with other organizations within the problem area." Because of the nature of the organizations, and the specific problems around which domain and domain consensus are established, we have placed this selection in this chapter; however, it might also be examined in light of other sections such as chapter six, Interorganizational Analysis.

The paper by Braito, Paulson and Klonglan investigates the problem of organizational participation in a new program on smoking and health. They present data with which they suggest that domain consensus, their dependent variable, is a function of the organization's domain or claims to a problem area which it sets out for itself, and not a function of general organizational characteristics such as complexity or formalization. This, of course, suggests that it may be necessary to examine these concepts in light of organizations which are not so highly problem oriented, such as industrial organizations.

--------------------------------- **10** ---------------------------------

SOCIAL STRUCTURE AND ORGANIZATIONS

Arthur L. Stinchcombe

The postulates which can be extracted from the literature on the conditions under which people will be motivated to form organizations to achieve various special purposes are the following: People found organizations when (a) they find or learn about alternative better ways of doing things that are not easily done within existing social arrangements; (b) they believe that the future will be such that the organization will continue to be effective enough to pay for the trouble of building it and for the resources invested; (c) they or some social group with which they are strongly identified will receive some of the benefits of the better way of doing things; (d) they can lay hold of the resources of wealth, power, and legitimacy needed to build the organization; and (e) they can defeat, or at least avoid being defeated by, their opponents, especially those whose interests are vested in the old regime. These characteristics of individual motivation are affected by the social struc-

The source references for the Stinchcombe article may be found in the bibliography at the end of the book.

ture. Better ways are communicated socially; the future is partly guaranteed by social arrangements and disrupted by social convulsions; the pattern of identifications of individuals with groups which will benefit, and the legal protection of the appropriated benefits, are social phenomena; the patterns of trust and of mobility of resources which determine whether resources can be moved to innovators are socially patterned; and the distribution of power in society is an aspect of social structure. In short, the probability that a man or group of men will be motivated to start an organization is dependent on the social structure and on the position of men within it.

The effect of condition (a), the degree of knowledge of alternatives,[1] is illustrated by the predominant role in innovation played today in new nations by Western or Japanese-educated elites, or by the role of German-educated scholars in the restructuring of American colleges into universities during the last century. Organizational forms from abroad are very generally found most frequently in metropolises, where there is extensive communication with other nations. Presumably the same factor would operate to cause more rapid change of organizational charts in companies with research and development staffs than in companies without them.

The effect of condition (b), predictable future benefits, is suggested by Weber's strong emphasis on the effect of calculable law, calculable taxation, and military security on the rate of formation of rational bourgeois enterprise (1927, pp. 94–114, 122–135, 276–277). The effect of condition (c), that some of the benefits accruing from the organizational innovation be appropriated by some group with whom the innovator is identified (very generally his family), is, of course, at the center of the debate on income inequalities, taxation of profits, and the like, in the United States, and plays a role in speculations on the significance of the bureaucratization of management, divorcing executives from appropriation of profits (Gordon, 1952; Linter, 1959). The problem of how much or what kind of benefits (in prestige, money, or power) must go to the innovators, or the question of how precarious the status of innovators must be for them to put forth their best efforts need not be discussed. All that is necessary here is to point out the obvious fact that most people are little motivated to start organizations if they anticipate the benefits will all be appropriated by others whom they do not love.[2]

1. "Knowledge" is a very rough word for what we are really interested in, namely, the conviction that the alternative will work. Such conviction derives from personal contact with operative alternative patterns over long periods, or contact with others who believe in the alternative, or personal pain from the defects of the old regime. As Pascal suggested, a pain in the bowels may be enough to start a man reforming the world as well as pain really attributable to the old regime; for instance, Key (1952), pp. 302, 410, suggested that farmers around the rim of the great Western desert (where they are much subject to drought, although Key's explanation runs in terms of the length of political tradition) have sponsored a disproportionate share of political innovations.
2. The "altruistic" component, serving those with whom one identifies, is often quite strong for military, religious, scientific, and political innovators. And, particularly in these fields, but more

The effect of condition (d), the mobility of resources, is most easily seen by imagining societies in which resources are fully committed to particular purposes and persons. In societies where most of the land passes through inheritance and is not freely alienable outside the family, where labor's obedience is to its traditional lord rather than to the highest bidder, where wealth stays in bags in the lord's warehouse to be used to support retainers rather than for investment, the rate of organization formation is low. The importance of savings banks which mobilize capital for innovation, the role of free alienability of land in medieval cities in encouraging commercial innovation, or Weber's analysis of formally free labor as a condition for capitalism, all illustrate the extent to which mobility of resources is essential for innovators. A money economy and universalistic law distribute money and power more equally between the elites of the old regime and the new elites, and free resources to move to innovators.[3]

The effect of condition (e), ability to avoid defeat by interests vested in the old regime, is illustrated by the fact that the chief industrial development in England took place in the newer northern cities rather than in London (S. M. Lipset called my attention to this fact), or that modern civil-service principles were applied in India before they were applied in metropolitan England, or by the capacity to form new types of organizations that often shows up in postrevolutionary times. There is, of course, no necessary relation between the existence of possible opponents in the same city or country and the likelihood of being defeated by them, so that many organizations grow best in precisely the environment which grows their opponents.

THE "LIABILITY OF NEWNESS"

Aside from these conditions encouraging men to start new organizations, there are poorly understood conditions that affect the comparative death rates of new and old organizations. As a general rule, a higher proportion of new organizations fail than old. This is particularly true of new organizational *forms,* so that *if an alternative requires new organization,* it has to be much more beneficial than the old before the

generally also, if a very small part of the total benefit of an innovation goes to the innovator or to people with whom he is identified, it may be sufficient motivation. Perhaps under other institutional conditions this would be more true of economic innovators than it seems to have been in the Occident. Dudintsev's novel *Not by Bread Alone* (which is really about the sacredness of the mission of material advance), when compared with, for example, the Marquand novels, suggests that the altruistic component in economic innovation may be greater in the Soviet Union. See also the account of self-denying service to agricultural innovation after the Meiji Restoration in Japan (Dore, 1960, pp. 73, 75, 86).
3. A new treatment of the conditions encouraging extraordinarily rapid mobility of resources into new fields is Smelser's discussion of the "craze" (1963, 170–221). This came to my attention too late to be adequately incorporated into the present treatment. Some of the conditions specified by Smelser are similar to those developed here, and some (such as the importance of prior structural differentiation in the society) are additions which need to be made to the treatment. Some are, I believe, contradictory, at least involving different weights to different causes. The degree of formality of the theoretical structure developed by Smelser is substantially greater than that used in this chapter.

flow of benefits compensates for the relative weakness of the newer social structure. If there are, therefore, populations in which the "liability of newness" is exceptionally great, organizational innovation will tend to be carried out only when the alternatives are stark (generally in wartime). What sorts of things, then, make up the liability of newness, and how do social conditions affect the degree of liability?

(a) New organizations, especially new types of organizations, generally involve new roles, which have to be learned. In old organizations former occupants of roles can teach their successors, communicating not only skills but also decision criteria, responsibilities to various people who have relations to the role occupant, devices for smoothing over persistent sources of tension and conflict, generalized loyalty to the organization, what sort of things can go wrong with routine procedures, and so on. New organizations have to get by with generalized skills produced outside the organization, or have to invest in education (including especially the cost of inefficiency until people learn their roles). Clearly, the distribution and generality of skills outside the organization, the socially induced capacity to learn new roles (especially without visible role models), and the ease of recruitment of skills to new organizations will affect the degree of disadvantage of organizational innovations.

(b) The process of inventing new roles, the determination of their mutual relations and of structuring the field of rewards and sanctions so as to get maximum performance, have high costs in time, worry, conflict, and temporary inefficiency. For some time until roles are defined, people who need to know things are left to one side of communication channels. John thinks George is doing what George thinks John is doing. Bottlenecks which experience will smooth out create situations that can only be solved with a perpetual psychology of crisis. No one has yet realized that under existing rules, the keeper of the tool bin is implicitly rewarded for keeping tools out of the hands of the workers.

Standard social routines in the organizational culture of the population which solve many such problems (e.g., cost accounting, inventory control systems, standard report forms put out by people who specialize in printing them) clearly reduce the liability of newness. Probably more important still is the degree of initiative—the sense of responsibility for getting the job done rather than doing as they are told—in the labor force as a whole. Such a disciplined and responsible work force, combined with social routines for letting them exercise initiative, greatly reduces the liability of newness. The strength of the norm of initiative in the American labor force shows up clearly in their indignant reaction to the norm that basic trainees in the army are not supposed to show initiative in telling sergeants how the job might be done more effi-ciently.[4]

(c) New organizations must rely heavily on social relations among strangers. This means that relations of trust are much more precarious in new than old organizations—trust that a stranger will do the job he says he will, that his promises to pay actually bind the resources he says they do, that the new goods he describes are something like what he says they are, that he will not divert organizational funds into his own pocket beyond tolerable levels, that he will make personnel decisions largely on the basis of competence rather than (or at least along with) kinship, and so forth. (An explanation of backwardness in terms of extensive incapacity to trust strangers, who are expected to be loyal only to kin, is in Banfield, 1958.) A cultural tradition in which obligations to kin and friends invariably override obligations to strangers, or in which loyalty to the implicit promises of the employment contract to work at the job is very low, limits organizational structure to that which can be built out of combinations of kinship loyalty and force. Many types of organizations cannot be efficiently built on this basis.

Universalistic religions making oaths to strangers sacred, universal-istic law making contracts between strangers binding, reliable negotia-ble instruments so that one can trust the paper and not the man, ethics of achievement according to impersonal standards in occupational life, rather than interpenetration of occupational and kinship life, all clearly make it easier to construct social systems out of groups of strangers (Weber (1958), or more clearly in Bendix's summary, 1960, pp. 285–297, 385–457. See also Udy, 1959, pp. 55–71, 88–94, 136–138). That is, al-though strangers almost always are less trusted than people with whom we have had long experience, some kinds of social structure reduce drastically the amount of difference in trustworthiness between stran-gers and kin or friends. Such a reduction greatly reduces the liability of newness.

(d) One of the main resources of old organizations is a set of stable ties to those who use organizational services. Old customers know how to use the services of the organization, have built their own social systems to use the old products or to influence the old type of govern-ment, are familiar with the channels of ordering, with performance qualities of the product, with how the price compares, and know the people they have to deal with—whom to call up to get action, for instance. There are generally two necessary adoption units for a new

4. As armies have come to rely more and more on rapid reorganization to adapt to technical change, they have developed routines for encouraging initiative, among other things by changing the shape of their stratification system (see Janowitz, 1959, pp. 36–42). For the reasons specified, revolutionary armies depend much more on initiative than older armies, a fact reflected in their administrative ideology.

practice or product—the producer and the consumer, the politician and the voter, the teacher and the student. The stronger the ties between old organizations and the people they serve, or the larger the component of personal loyalty in the consumer-producer relations, the tougher the job of establishing a new organization.

Obviously, many social conditions will affect the strength of the tie between consumer and producer. To take an extreme case, if an illiterate peasantry depends on the same man to mediate between themselves and a literate world market, to grant credit to buy seed, to rent them their land, and to advise on agricultural practices, they are unlikely to be willing to risk alienating him for a small advantage in only one of these areas. At the other extreme, when literate housewives read their own advertisements, borrow from the bank, rent from a real estate company, and get advice from newspapers, they can easily substitute a supermarket for the local grocer.

BASIC VARIABLES AFFECTING ORGANIZING CAPACITY

Clearly, with so many variables immediately affecting the likelihood of starting new organizations and the likelihood of their living, any complete treatment of the social sources of organizing capacity could be as complex as we have time for. Rather than trace each one of these variables back along all possible causal chains, we can specify and discuss a number of basic variables which affect many of these intermediate variables: (a) general literacy and specialized advanced schooling; (b) urbanization; (c) a money economy; (d) political revolution; (e) the density of social life, including especially an already rich organizational life.

(a) Perhaps the most fundamental difference between men for the social scientists' purposes is the difference between functionally literate men and illiterates: certainly, societies made up primarily of literate men are fundamentally different from those made up primarily of illiterates. Even the existence of a small literate elite is the generally accepted line of demarcation between "primitive" cultures and civilizations. Schools differentiated from real life depend on learning from books. Checks and money orders, as well as orders for goods, have to be written for extensive trade. Alternative ways of doing things come to the attention of prospective innovators more rapidly and cheaply through print than any other way. Writing down the law makes it easily available to many people as a basis for their calculations, and tends to increase the degree of formality and stability of legal arrangements. One central way of giving agricultural laborers guaranteed rights is to demand that the labor contract be written, for example. Nicely concerted action of physically dispersed people, such as a railroad system entails, is greatly facilitated by written communication. Solidarity and empathy between people who do not know each other depends on written communication between them—written histories and holy books that define their common loyalties and written literature to communicate their common emotions, desires, hopes, and problems (Lerner, 1958, especially pp. 43–75). Bureaucracies can hardly function without written tax rolls, accounts receivable and payable, manuals of procedure, payrolls, notices of pending disciplinary action, and printed application forms. Men cannot easily start their own Christian sect unless someone can read the Scriptures. Every study of political apathy in every country shows that interest in the distant public realm and the decisions of nations, as opposed to involvement in private concerns, is directly and strongly related to the number of years of education and to the amount of current reading. And, of course, the existence of political interest-group organization depends on interest in public issues among the population.

In short, literacy and schooling raise practically every variable which encourages the formation of organizations and increases the staying power of new organizations. It enables more alternatives to be posed to more people. It facilitates learning new roles with no nearby role model. It encourages impersonal contact with customers. It allows money and resources to be distributed more easily to strangers and over distances. It provides records of transactions so that they can be enforced later, making the future more predictable. It increases the predictability of the future environment of an organization by increasing the available information and by making possible a uniform body of law over a large area.

The speed of industrial advance is an indicator of the organization-forming capacity of a population. And in every case of exceptionally rapid industrial advance that I know of, a rapid advance in literacy is an outstanding characteristic of the population. Protestants, especially sectarians who had to read the Book themselves, were much more literate during early industrialization than Catholics. (In my opinion, literacy is the fundamental spurious variable in Max Weber's argument [1930]. If the connection between Protestantism and industrial capitalism indeed exists, and there is some dispute about the facts, it may well be because of Protestants' superior literacy.) The introduction of free elementary education (especially in the Jacksonian period in the North and West, later and less universally in the South) preceded the great boom of the middle of the nineteenth century in the United States. Japan has fewer illiterates by far than other countries with a comparable degree of economic development and has a growth rate only just behind those of the most rapidly growing Communist states. The Soviet Union wrote grammars in the minority languages, herded everyone into schools, and increased literacy almost as fast as steel production.

One of the major postrevolutionary reforms in Mexico was massive school building, and Mexican national income has been quite steadily increasing at about 7 per cent a year—even faster than the population, a substantial accomplishment indeed.

The same sort of observation could be made about the connection between literacy and the rate of formation of voluntary associations, political party branches, income tax departments,[5] vocational schools, effective police departments, and so on.

(b) Urbanization, particularly when it is slow enough to allow routines of urban living to develop without being swamped by new waves of rustics, has the same effect of facilitating organization formation that literacy does. Socially differentiated urban populations present alternatives to each other, and most innovations can find a home in some social segment. Urban agglomerations are always made up of people who are mutually strangers, and social devices for regularizing these relations tend to be invented in cities—guilds, written laws, checks, ethics of commercial social relations, and so forth. These facilitate the formation of new organizations and ease the transfer of customers from old to new suppliers and products. Devices for mobilizing resources and moving them to innovators (e.g., legal alienability of land, stock exchanges) are developed in cities. The generally greater universalism and probably higher rates of social mobility[6] in cities encourage free choice of roles by the young and stimulate the formation of schools as placement agencies. Both because writing is more useful and because a larger proportion of the young go to school, literacy rates are nearly always higher in cities (Belgium is the only exception I know of). Writers and other originators of ideas and proposals head for New York, London, Paris, Rome, Berlin, Moscow, Peking, Tokyo, and Calcutta, where there are publishers and theaters, a massed public, and other writers. Any organization depending on political activity needs at least representatives in the capital, which in recent times is always a city. In general, then, urbanization increases the organizational competence of populations in much the same way, although perhaps not in the same degree, as literacy. The classic statement of one form of this generalization is Durkheim's (1949).

---

5. One reason for the popularity of tariffs and expropriation in the fiscal system of underdeveloped countries is the difficulty of finding literate young women to process income tax forms.

6. We are unfortunately finding that impressions about the social mobility rates of different populations are worthless as evidence. For instance, there is no conclusive evidence that such rates differ among the urban populations of industrial countries, all impressions of higher American mobility to the contrary (see Lipset & Bendix 1959, pp. 11–75). For some qualifications, see Janowitz (1958), and on rural-urban differences Stinchcombe (1961, p. 165). Likewise, the truism that medieval cities had lower social mobility rates is disproved by the extraordinarily high rates found in the only good study I know of, Thrupp (1948), although the influence of the plague makes the generality of this observation problematic. Thus, I would not be surprised to see the judgement that social mobility is generally higher in cities go the way of the rest of folk knowledge on this topic.

(c) A money economy liberates resources so that they can be more easily recruited by new organizations, facilitates the formation of free markets so that customers can transfer loyalties, depersonalizes economic social relations, simplifies calculation of the advantages of alternative ways of doing things, and allows more precise anticipation of the consequences of future conditions on the organization. Weber's thorough treatment of this question (and its almost axiomatic nature) obviates the necessity of elaboration here (1957, pp. 173–212).

(d) Political revolutions can drastically shift the relative advantage of vested interests and new organizations by changing the normative basis on which interests are vested and by redirecting the armies and police that are the means of vesting. Besides this crucial factor, revolutions very often "create" resources, particularly of loyalty, terror, political power and in modern times education, which were not at anyone's disposal under the old regime. Generally when we contrast "totalitarianism" with "traditional autocracy," we are referring to the greater capacity of postrevolutionary regimes to reorganize the social structure. The eulogistic equivalents of the dyslogistic "totalitarianism" are such phrases as "the creativity of the masses," the ability to use "revolutionary justice on the enemies of the people," or "bringing educational progress." The Meiji Restoration in Japan, the great Mexican Revolution of the first part of this century, and the Russian Revolution come to mind as outstanding cases where creation of new resources for founding economic organizations followed upon political revolution, and probably the Nazi revolution should be included in the list.

(e) The main way to learn to form organizations is to form them. Beginning businessmen are more likely to succeed if they have failed before (Mayer & Goldstein, 1961, pp. 138–139). The 1905 revolution in Russia taught many of the organizational forms that were used in 1917 and tempered the leadership that led successfully another time. The fact that one learns to lead liberal organizations by leading them is shown by the interlocking directorates of such organizations.[7] In short, the level of organizational experience of a population is a main determinant of their capacity to form new organizations.

Not only the level of organizational experience determines organizational capacity. More generally, the richer the social life of a group, the more likely it is to have the resources to build new organizations. This is particularly true of organizations depending primarily on ties of loyalty and trust, such as voluntary associations. But on the other hand, richer social life generally means that many important vestable inter-

7. Somehow, this does not shake liberals' conviction that interlocking directorates of corporations are the product of conspiracy. Corporation directors see liberal conspiracies, too. The point is that organizations requiring similar talents and training tend to have interlocking directorates.

ests become vested, so new organizations very often fail, or at least are forced to reduce their utopias to concrete negotiable goals. Ordinarily, new organizations with narrow purposes grow rapidly in an already rich environment. The wider the claims of a new organization, the more likely is it to run into vested interests.

In summary, because literacy, urbanization, money economy, political revolution, and previously existing organizational density affect the variables leading to high motivation to found organizations and the variables increasing the chances for success of new organizational forms, they tend to increase the rate at which new organizational forms are developed. Such, at least, is the current theory, which remains at a relatively low level of verification. Better verification awaits solution of the problem of counting new organizations in widely different social structures, and particularly the problem of counting new organizational *forms.*

Before we leave the topic, one other important fact should be noted. Certain kinds of organizations are themselves crucial aspects of the social structure determining the rate of formation of new organizations. In some ways the great industrial empires are fundamentally "organization-creating mechanisms" rather than organizations properly speaking, giving birth at frequent intervals to new corporate units with new purposes, new social structures, and new markets (I owe this observation to Fred Gouldner). Similarly, in many of the new nations or nations recently having had a revolution, the majority political party is itself the main agent in creating interest groups to influence policy. In Mexico, for instance, the *Partido Revolutionario Institutional* (engagingly called "the official party") organized most of the agrarian, trade-union, and petty bourgeois organizations, which remain tied to the party much as Buick remains tied to General Motors. The rapid, deliberate creation of nationality organizations, trade unions, and so forth by the Communist parties where they have come to power is well known. Not much is known about the conditions under which such "organization-forming organizations" originate, nor about the types of continuing organization-forming mechanisms, nor about the conditions under which an umbrella organization can recruit generalized resources for later use in creating specific organizations.

SOCIAL STRUCTURE AND THE FOUNDING OF ORGANIZATIONS[8]

This section will be concerned with the implications of the fact that organizational forms and types have a history, and that this history

8. The relation of the age of organizations to their social structure is one of several topics on which Robert Blauner and I have had extensive correspondence and discussion over several years. I can no

determines some aspects of the present structure of organizations of that type. The organizational inventions that can be made at a particular time in history depend on the social technology available at the time. Organizations which have purposes that can be efficiently reached with the socially possible organizational forms tend to be founded during the period in which they have become possible. Then, both because they can function effectively with those organizational forms, and because the forms tend to become institutionalized, the basic structure of the organization tends to remain relatively stable.

For example, the present urban construction industry, with specialized craft workers, craft-specialized subcontractors, craft trade unions, and a relation of contract between the construction enterprise and the consumer, was developed in European cities before the industrial revolution. Such an organization requires relatively dense settlement, some detachment of socialization for occupational roles from families to be vested in guild-like organizations of craftsmen, contracts enforceable in the law, free wage labor which can move to some extent from job to job and employer to employer, and so on. Such conditions do not normally exist in agrarian societies. This craft form of organization has persisted partly because it is well adapted to the problems of the building industry and partly because of the force of tradition and vested interest, except in certain circumstances. In the Soviet Union, which had a quite normal-looking construction industry in the cities before the Revolution, a combination of forces (government being virtually the only consumer, industrial building being emphasized in contrast to residential and commercial building, the destruction of autonomous power of trade unions) has resulted in the thoroughgoing destruction of the craft system. During the 1930's there were actually fewer apprentices (a characteristic feature of craft systems) in construction than in the steel industry, even though the construction industry grew much faster during the period. Except in these circumstances (up to now, fortunately, exceptional cases), the basic craft organization has persisted and has distinguished construction from more "modern" industries.

Looked at another way, an examination of the history of almost any type of organization shows that there are great spurts of foundation of organizations of the type, followed by periods of relatively slower growth, perhaps to be followed by new spurts, generally of a fundamentally different kind of organization in the same field. For instance, most men's national social fraternities were founded in one of three periods, 1840–1850, 1865–1870, and 1900–1920. The first wave were founded mainly at northern colleges that later became liberal arts colleges and

longer sort out which ideas are his, which are mine, and which are my projections of what he would say if he considered some particular aspect of the problem. The responsibility of publishing these ideas before the difficulties are cleared up is, however, entirely mine.

seem to have had something to do with the secularization of student culture in reaction to previous evangelical currents, and perhaps also functioned as a defense against the high tide of Jacksonian democracy. Fraternities in the second wave were founded in the South, later spreading to the North, and clearly had something to do with the difficulties of Northerners and Southerners being "brothers" right after the Civil War. Several were founded in Lexington, Virginia, where Robert E. Lee headed Washington College, which is suggestive of the symbolic conditions surrounding their founding. The third wave was of "anti-fraternity fraternities," especially of Jews, Negroes, Catholics, and students at teachers' colleges, with a heavy outpouring of anti-discrimination statements and praise of poor college students in the chartering documents. (These observations are based on my own tabulations from fraternity handbooks.)

Our interest in these spurts derives from the fact that organizations formed at one time typically have a different social structure from those formed at another time. Further the slow rate of growth after the spurts generally indicates that few organizational restructurings are taking place, hence the *date of the spurts* is highly correlated with the *present social structure* of the organization whose type originates in one of these spurts. These spurts are best documented in the field of economic organizations, largely because of the influence of Schumpeter (1934; 1939; 1951; Conrad, 1961), who thought they were fundamental to the explanation of business cycles. But the history of virtually any type of organization suggests the same pattern.

Thus, there was a rash of savings bank formations in the 1830's. The first factory industry, textiles, developed in its factory form in England mainly between 1800 and 1830, and was imported pretty much in that form to the United States toward the end of that period. Railroads, and consequently new communities and counties, and, of course, great steel companies, had their great period of organization in the 1850's and again in the 1870's. Organized socialist parties spread throughout western Europe after the organization of the Second International. New universities were founded in the United States mainly from 1870 to 1900, and the universities "founded" before or after that time are mainly other types of schools (especially liberal arts colleges or land grant colleges) on their way up. Practically no private liberal arts colleges, and very few liberal arts colleges of any kind, have been founded since 1900. At present, junior colleges are being organized at a high rate.

Most of the national (or "International") craft trade unions were founded between the Civil War and the beginning of the twentieth century. They had great growth in local organizations and membership in the World War I decade. The next great spurt of union foundation was, of course, the organization of CIO unions in the 1930's, especially 1937. Streetcar companies and electricity-producing companies were all the rage from 1887 to 1910. The combination of the streetcar and the railroad was at the back of the great reorganization of retail trade by department stores (Macy's, 1858; Marshall Field's, 1852), chain stores (A & P, 1901; Woolworth's, 1879), and mail-order houses (Sears, Roebuck, 1886; Montgomery Ward, 1872). (All dates are from *Moody's Industrial Manual.*) The automobile revolution, and consequently the foundation of the great automobile companies and the rapid growth of the oil and rubber industries, came in the 1920's. Roughly concomitant was the rise of the industrial chemicals industry and (shortly following the reorganization of medical education in the first decade of the twentieth century) the reorganization and centralization of the pharmaceutical trade. Mass production of airplanes and regular air transportation became important during and after World War II. The data processing industries are still going through the throes of organization. The mass communications industries were mostly organized in the 1920's, although the fundamental mass communications industry, printing and publishing, derives from before the factory production period. Retail trade and many of the service industries derive mainly from the preindustrial city and farming is obviously a prefactory industry.

STABILITY OF TYPES OVER TIME

All this would be merely an interesting facet of social history, if it could not be shown that certain structural characteristics of a type of organization are remarkably stable over time. But Hoselitz, for example, has provided data on the proportion of workers in enterprises with more than 200 persons in different industries in Germany in 1882 and 1956 (1961, p. 545). Even though the average size of enterprise in all industries (except printing, which seems to be due to changes in census coverage with the partition of Germany) increased steadily throughout the period, the Spearman rank correlation of proportions of firms with more than 200 employees in 1882 and 1956 is 0.74. That is, if an industry was a small firm industry in 1882, it was very probably still a small firm industry in 1956, though the absolute size of a "small" firm was likely to be somewhat higher.

An even more direct indication of the power of persistence of organizational forms comes from a study of Japanese manufacturing (Rosovsky & Ohkawa, 1961). The authors classified branches of industry into those making products in general use before the Meiji Restoration in 1868, when Japan's rapid modernization of the economy started (but apparently there had been relatively rapid economic growth in the previous period, particularly a great increase in the productivity of land). Manufacturing enterprises in the traditional sector are much smaller, much less capital-extensive, less oriented to a luxury market. For instance, among all manufacturing industries, only 35.0 per cent of the labor force was employed by firms of size 4–29; among indigenous industries, the proportion was 74.4 per cent. The unweighted mean of urban expenditure elasticities (cross-section) for indigenous commodities was only .401; for modern commodities it was 1.022.[9]

In general, in Japan, as in other industrialized countries, unpaid family labor is most prevalent in agriculture, somewhat less prevalent in retail and personal service industries, less yet in urban construction (apparently the heavily male character of the industry somewhat overcomes the normal expectation that this industry should be highly involved in families), and much less in the thoroughly modern economic sectors. *Within* manufacturing, 8.7 per cent of the workers in 55 indigenous industries were unpaid family workers, while the national average for all industry included in the Census of Manufactures is 3.2 per cent.

For the United States, Table 1 presents statistics on various aspects of the social structure of industries by a rough age-of-industry classification.[10] I have had to leave many industries out because of my ignorance of their history, and at best the age classification represents my impressions from a casual reading of economic history. Some better criterion of the "age" of a product (such as that used by Rosovsky & Ohkawa) is needed, but this would necessitate a much finer industrial classification than is available, and a separate research project in the history of American technology.

The first two columns are proportions of the labor force involved in the kinship sector of the labor market, of self-employed and unpaid family workers. The third column is the proportion of clerical workers in the "middle-class administrative personnel" group made up of clerical workers, professionals, proprietors, managers, and officals. Two industries, telecommunications and the Post Office, are not reported in this column because their operative personnel are classified by the census as clerical workers, so the proportion reported is not a good index of "bureaucratization." The fourth column reports the porportion of all "top status people," i.e., professionals and proprietors, managers,

9. Expenditure elasticities are low when a smaller proportion of higher incomes is spent on a commodity, high when higher incomes lead to increased proportional expenditures on the commodity (i.e., high for "luxuries," low for "necessities"). An elasticity of 1.00 would mean that the proportion spent on the commodity was the same for all ranges of income. Later industries were, of course, started when income was higher, so their current higher elasticities are probably an indication of preservation of organizational characteristics, in the sense that they are oriented to the same markets which had newly appeared when they were founded, while older industries are still oriented to markets that existed long ago.
10. It is unnecessary to say that the age of an industry is not the average age of firms in the industry. Very few construction firms are as old as almost any railroad firm, although rails are clearly a newer industry. Most retail firms showing a highly "traditional" organization are much younger than Sears, Roebuck, with a "modern" organization.

and officials who are professionals, thus providing an index of the development of staff structures.

The first column shows that the prefactory industries still involve unpaid family workers to a greater extent than any of the industries developed after that time. There are three cells in the column that deviate from this pattern (deviant cells are starred for ease in locating them). Two of these come from industries which are deviant in *all* cells, namely Ship and Boat Building and Automobile Repair. Ship and Boat Building is much more modern on all criteria than would be anticipated on the basis of its age, and Automobile Repair is a twentieth-century traditional industry. The other exception in the first column is Water Transportation. (Clearly the introduction of the steamship, diesel propulsion, and the steel hull reorganized the shipbuilding and water-transportation industries much more than I had anticipated.) With these exceptions, all the prefactory industries are above 0.15 per cent in the porportion of unpaid family workers, and all those whose organizational forms were determined after the beginning of the nineteenth century are below 0.15 per cent. On this basis, we can hazard the historical guess that the first stage of "bureaucratization of industry" was the differentiation of the work role from family life. Note also that the level of unpaid family labor in all United States industries except agriculture is below that of manufacturing as a whole in Japan, as reported above. This suggests that unpaid family labor declines with time and modernization in both the traditional and modern sectors, but the difference between these two sectors remains even in advanced industrial countries.

In the second column there are indications of a slightly different relation of kinship institutions to the organization. "Self-employment" is an indication of the "employment" of "unpaid family labor" in the work of *managing* the enterprise. Thus, the two breaks in the column indicate the present results of the historical process of differentiating managerial roles from kinship roles. Prefactory industries are at 5.9 per cent or above in the proportion in the kinship sector (two exceptions), early nineteenth century industries between 3.0 and 6.0 per cent (one exception), railroad age and later industries are below 3.0 per cent (two exceptions). Before commenting on this, we will treat the closely related third column.

In the third column, the decisive break is again between prefactory industries and all later ones, the former running below 45 per cent clerical workers among administrators, the later above (five exceptions). Since the proportion of clerical workers among administrators is a good indication of the development of files, regularized communications channels using written communication between designated officials,

Table 1[a]

Characteristics of the Labor Force of Industries Classified by Age

Industry	% Unpaid Family Workers	% Self-Employed & Family Workers	Clerical as % Administrative Workers	Professionals as % Authority
Prefactory				
Agriculture	13.3	76.3	0.4	0.7
Forestry, fisheries	0.5	33.2	14	79*
Retail trade	1.4	23.7	26	7
Construction	0.2	19.2	20	31
Hotels, lodging	1.0	17.8	37	9
Logging	0.5	15.4	18	21
Wholesale trade	0.2	13.3	47*	11
Printing, publishing	0.2	5.9	51*	54*
Ship, boat building	0.1*	2.9*	55*	64*
Water transportation	0.0*	1.7*	36	12
Early nineteenth century				
Woodworking industries	0.1	6.0	45	14
Stone, clay, glass	0.1	5.4	48	45*
Leather, except footwear	0.1	3.0	52	22
Apparel	0.0	3.4	53	18
Textile industries	0.0	1.2*	62	36
Banking, finance	0.0	4.2	69	15
Railroad age				
Post office	––	––	not relevant (mail carriers)	3
Railroads, railway express	0.0	0.1	70	17
Street railroads, buses	0.1	2.0	68	28
Coal mining	0.1	2.7	45	31
Metal extraction and fabrication	0.0	1.6	54	54*
Railroad and miscellaneous transportation equipment	0.1	0.9	58	66*
Modern				
Automobile repair	0.5*	23.7*	23*	4*
Telecommunications	0.1	0.4	not relevant (operators)	51
Crude petroleum, natural gas	0.0	5.7*	35*	55
Rubber products	0.0	0.6	59	60
Motor vehicles and equipment	0.0	0.5	63	63
Electrical and gas utilities	0.0	0.3	62	65
Chemicals and allied	0.1	2.5	49	69
Air transport	0.1	2.5	49	69
Petroleum, coal production	0.0	0.9	48	71
Electrical machinery and equipment	0.0	1.0	53	73
Aircraft and parts	0.0	0.4	46	89

* Cells deviant from hypotheses.

the origin of "bureaucratic" administration of production (in this sense) can be roughly located in the early nineteenth century.

Combining these results, we see two crucial stages of the "bureaucratization of industry." The first took place at the beginning of the factory age and involved the introduction of written and filed communication into factory administration and the differentiation of both work roles and lower management from family institutions. But the top administration was still in the hands of owners, and the factory was still an element in the family estate of the top management. Authority can become more hierarchical, can have more levels, with impersonal written communications and filed records. The superior efficiency of a bureaucratic communications apparatus for large-scale administration allows the size of the enterprise to expand somewhat, resulting in fewer top administrators (reflected in fewer "self-employed" than in the prefactory period). But top management is still not a normal career stage in the life plan of a subordinate official, for the top managers are still "self-employed," and their positions depend on their success (or the success of their ancestors) in building up a family estate.

Later, in the railroad age, top managerial positions were differentiated from kinship institutions and made into "occupations" of employed career officials. Capital was now frequently recruited by the sale of corporate securities on the open market, and the size of the business

Table 1

a. Based on my computations from U.S. Bureau of the Census, 1952, pp. 290-291. Comparison with figures for 1960, for those industries in which comparable data are available, shows a virtually identical ranking of industries by criteria of professionalization of authority and the proportion of clerical workers among all administrative workers. All industries but one (out of 14 where comparable data are available) have become more professionalized in authority. All prefactory industries but one (out of the five where data are available) have become more "bureaucratic," in the sense that a higher proportion of administrators are clerks in 1960 than in 1950. All but one of the early nineteenth-century, railroad age, and modern industries have become less "bureaucratic" by this criterion. The drifts over a decade within industries are small compared with the differences among industries at the starting point, which accounts for the preservation of relative positions.

(Note: I have combined "Sawmills and Planning Mills," "Furniture," and "Miscellaneous Wood Products" into a general category of "Woodworking Industries." Also I have combined "Primary Iron and Steel Extraction," "Non-ferrous Metal Extraction," and "Metal Fabrication" into a general category of "Metal Extraction and Fabrication." The individual subindustries in these cases are similar on all the indices computed here and generally originated at about the same periods, so no confusion in the general picture should result from these combinations.

did not depend on the size of the family estate inherited by top management. Top managerial positions became a career stage in the life of
employed officials, rather than a prerogative of sons and husbands. The
same process apparently took place in the old industries of Ship and
Boat Building and Water Transportation, while in Automobile Repair
and Crude Petroleum and Natural Gas Extraction traditional forms
have been introduced into new industries.

The fourth column represents roughly the development of staff
departments. In organizations originating before the modern age, less
than 35 per cent of the top status people (those who occupy positions
of authority either by virtue of their office or proprietorship or by virtue
of professional training) are made up of professional people (six exceptions). After the beginning of the twentieth century, at least half of the
authority positions are occupied in new industries by professionals (one
exception). Two of the exceptions are accidental features of the data.
The government departments concerned with forestry and conservation (which are relatively new) are disproportionately made up of
professionals, and account for a large share of the professionals found
in these industries. So here the index does not represent the development of staff departments, but the dominance of new departments of
the government. Second, writers and editors are counted as professionals, but are not generally in staff departments, so the misplacement of
printing and publishing is not really meaningful.

Discounting "accidental" exceptions which reflect inadequacies in
the data we have used, the main exceptions to the generalizations are
in the "machine-building" industries. These industries, whether building ships, locomotives and railroad cars, machine tools, automobiles,
aircraft, electrical machinery, or other machinery, all have modern
forms of organization, whatever their age.

For economic organizations where the data are fairly readily available, structural characteristics of a type of organization tend to persist,
and consequently there is a strong correlation between the age at which
industries were developed and their structure at the present time.

Probably other organizations as well still have traces of their time
of origin. It seems very unlikely that national social fraternities being
organized now would have racial and religious exclusion clauses. The
representatives of national fraternities or sororities who visit campuses
during rushing seasons are sometimes provided with printed instructions and arguments to help them deal with chapters that want to
pledge a minority-group member. If the unprejudiced forces are so
strong as to require special efforts of national officers to overcome them,
newly founded groups without a tradition to defend would probably

save themselves the trouble.[11] If working-class parties in Europe were organized without reference to tradition now, the overhanging revolutionary mood of Marxist ideology would probably be dispensed with. If universities were just being organized now, the federal government and its research arms would undoubtedly play more of a role in university government. If the YMCA were organized now, it would very likely be a secular agency more similar to the mental health movement. And so on.

11. The fact that almost all fraternities founded between 1900 and 1920 were "anti-fraternity" fraternities of ethnic or nonsectarian groups, without exclusion clauses, is only slight support for this guess, if any, for these fraternities were reacting to previously established fraternity systems, not starting anew.

—————————————— 11 ——————————————

COÖPTATION

Philip Selznick

Coöptation[1] *is the process of absorbing new elements into the leadership or policy-determining structure of an organization as a means of averting threats to its stability or existence.* With the help of this concept, we are enabled more closely and more rigorously to specify the relation between TVA and some important local institutions and thus uncover an important aspect of the real meaning and significance of the Authority's grass-roots policy. At the same time, it is clear that the idea of coöptation plunges us into the field of bureaucratic behavior as that is related to such democratic ideals as "local participation."

Coöptation tells us something about the process by which an institutional environment impinges itself upon an organization and effects changes in its leadership, structure, or policy. Coöptation may be formal or informal, depending upon the specific problem to be solved.

Formal coöptation.—When there is a need for the organization to publicly absorb new elements, we shall speak of formal coöptation. This involves the establishment of openly avowed and formally ordered relationships. Appointments to official posts are made, contracts are

1. With some modifications, the following statement of the concept of coöptation is a repetition of that presented in the author's "Foundations of the Theory of Organization," *American Sociological Review,* XIII, 1 (February, 1948), pp. 33–35. For further discussion of coöptation see below, pp. 259–261.

signed, new organizations are established—all signifying participation in the process of decision and administration. There are two general conditions which lead an organization to resort to formal coöptation, though they are closely related:

1. When the legitimacy of the authority of a governing group or agency is called into question. Every group or organization which attempts to exercise control must also attempt to win the consent of the governed. Coercion may be utilized at strategic points, but it is not effective as an enduring instrument. One means of winning consent is to coöpt into the leadership or organization elements which in some way reflect the sentiment or possess the confidence of the relevant public or mass and which will lend respectability or legitimacy to the organs of control and thus reëstablish the stability of formal authority. This device is widely used, and in many different contexts. It is met in colonial countries, where the organs of alien control reaffirm their legitimacy by coöpting native leaders into the colonial administration. We find it in the phenomenon of "crisis-patriotism" wherein normally disfranchised groups are temporarily given representation in the councils of government in order to win their solidarity in a time of national stress. Coöptation has been considered by the United States Army in its study of proposals to give enlisted personnel representation in the courts-martial machinery—a clearly adaptive response to stresses made explicit during World War II. The "unity" parties of totalitarian states are another form of coöptation; company unions or some employee representation plans in industry are still another. In each of these examples, the response of formal authority (private or public, in a large organization or a small one) is an attempt to correct a state of imbalance by formal measures. It will be noted, moreover, that what is shared is the responsibility for power rather than power itself.

2. When the need to invite participation is essentially administrative, that is, when the requirements of ordering the activities of a large organization or state make it advisable to establish the forms of self-government. The problem here is not one of decentralizing decision but rather of establishing orderly and reliable mechanisms for reaching a client public or citizenry. This is the "constructive" function of trade unions in great industries where the unions become effective instruments for the elimination of absenteeism or the attainment of other efficiency objectives. This is the function of self-government committees in housing projects or concentration camps, as they become reliable channels for the transmission of managerial directives. Usually, such devices also function to share responsibility and thus to bolster the legitimacy of established authority. Thus any given act of formal coöptation will tend to fulfill both the political function of defending

legitimacy and the administrative function of establishing reliable channels for communication and direction.

In general, the use of formal coöptation by a leadership does not envision the transfer of actual power. The forms of participation are emphasized but action is channeled so as to fulfill the administrative functions while preserving the locus of significant decision in the hands of the initiating group. The concept of formal coöptation will be utilized primarily in the analysis of TVA's relation to the voluntary associations established to gain local participation in the administration of the Authority's programs.

Informal coöptation.—Coöptation may be, however, a response to the pressure of specific centers of power within the community. This is not primarily a matter of the sense of legitimacy or of a general and diffuse lack of confidence. Legitimacy and confidence may be well established with relation to the general public, yet organized forces which are able to threaten the formal authority may effectively shape its structure and policy. The organization faced with its institutional environment, or the leadership faced with its ranks, must take into account these outside elements. They may be brought into the leadership or policy-determining structure, may be given a place as a recognition of and concession to the resources they can independently command. The representation of interests through administrative constituencies is a typical example of this process. Or, within an organization, individuals upon whom the group is dependent for funds or other resources may insist upon and receive a share in the determination of policy. This type of coöptation is typically expressed in informal terms, for the problem is not one of responding to a state of imbalance with respect to the "people as a whole" but rather one of meeting the pressure of specific individuals or interest groups which are in a position to enforce demands. The latter are interested in the substance of power and not necessarily in its forms. Moreover, an open acknowledgment of capitulation to specific interests may itself undermine the sense of legitimacy of the formal authority within the community. Consequently, there is a positive pressure to refrain from explicit recognition of the relationship established. This concept will be utilized in analyzing the underlying meaning of certain formal methods of coöperation initiated in line with the TVA's grass-roots policy.

Coöptation reflects a state of tension between formal authority and social power. This authority is always embodied in a particular structure and leadership, but social power itself has to do with subjective and objective factors which control the loyalties and potential manipulability of the community. Where the formal authority or leadership reflects real social power, its stability is assured. On the other hand, when it

becomes divorced from the sources of social power its continued existence is threatened. This threat may arise from the sheer alienation of
sentiment or because other leaderships control the sources of social
power. Where a leadership has been accustomed to the assumption that
its constituents respond to it as individuals, there may be a rude awak-
ening when organization of those constituents creates nucleuses of
strength which are able to effectively demand a sharing of power.

The significance of coöptation for organizational analysis is not
simply that there is a change in or a broadening of leadership, and that
this is an adaptive response, but also *that this change is consequential
for the character and role of the organization or governing body.* Coöptation results in some constriction of the field of choice available to the
organization or leadership in question. The character of the coöpted
elements will necessarily shape the modes of action available to the
group which has won adaptation at the price of commitment to outside
elements. In other words, if it is true that the TVA has, whether as a
defensive or as an idealistic measure, absorbed local elements into its
policy-determining structure, we should expect to find that this process
has had an effect upon the evolving character of the Authority itself.
From the viewpoint of the initiators of the project, and of its public
supporters, the force and direction of this effect may be completely
unanticipated.

The important consideration is that the TVA's choice of methods
could not be expected to be free of the normal dilemmas of action. If
the sentiment of the people (or its organized expression) is conservative,
democratic forms may require a blunting of social purpose. A perception of the details of this tendency is all important for the attempt to
bind together planning and democracy. Planning is always positive—
for the fulfillment of some program,—but democracy may negate its
execution. This dilemma requires an understanding of the possible
unanticipated consequences which may ensue when positive social
policy is coupled with a commitment to democratic procedure.

FORMAL COÖPTATION AND AGRICULTURAL DEMOCRACY

The use of voluntary associations is not new, and is far from unique
or peculiar to the program or administration of the Tennessee Valley
Authority.[2] Indeed, it is useful to think of the coöptation of citizens into

2. Perhaps as testimony to the effectiveness with which the grass-roots doctrine is circulated within
the TVA, there appears to have developed a feeling that the Authority has somehow originated a
unique administrative device, binding the agency to its client public in some special way. This is partly
referrable to enthusiasm, partly to the prevalent idea that other federal agencies, lacking the halo of
regional decentralization, are unlikely to be really interested in democratic administration. It is hardly
necessary to enter that controversy here, or to lay undue emphasis upon it. Yet although the grass-roots

an administrative apparatus as a general response made by governments to what has been called "the fundamental democratization" of
society.[3] The rise of the mass man,[4] or at least the increasing need for
governments to take into account and attempt to manipulate the sentiments of the common man, has resulted in the development of new
methods of control. These new methods center about attempts to organize the mass, to change an undifferentiated and unreliable citizenry
into a structured, readily accessible public. Accessibility for administrative purposes seems to lead rather easily to control for the same or
broader purposes. Consequently, there seems to be a continuum between the voluntary associations set up by the democratic (mass) state
—such as committees of farmers to boost or control agricultural production—and the citizens' associations of the totalitarian (mass) state. Indeed, the devices of corporatism emerge as relatively effective
responses to the need to deal with the mass, and in time of war the
administrative techniques of avowedly democratic countries and
avowedly totalitarian countries tend to converge.

Democracy in administration rests upon the idea of broadening
participation. Let the citizen take a hand in the working of his government, give him a chance to help administer the programs of the positive
state. At its extreme, this concept of democracy comes to be applied to
such structures as conscript armies, which are thought to be democratic
if they include all classes of the population on an equal basis. If analysis
and appraisal is to be significant, however, it is necessary to inquire into
the concrete meaning of such an unanalyzed abstraction as "participation." In doing so, we shall have to distinguish between substantive
participation, involving an actual role in the determination of policy,
and mere administrative involvement. In the conscript army, we have
a broadening involvement of citizens, with a concomitant abdication of
power. The same may be said of the Japanese *tonari gumi,* neighborhood associations which helped to administer rationing and other wartime programs. Such organizations, which have had their counterparts
in many parts of the world, involve the local citizens, but primarily for
the convenience of the administration. It is easy enough for administrative imperatives which call for decentralization to be given a halo; that
becomes especially useful in countries which prize the symbols of
democracy. But a critical analysis cannot overlook that pattern which

method is considered one of the major collateral objectives of the Authority, relatively little attention
has been paid to the mechanics of its implementation and certainly the experience of other organizations facing the same problems and using voluntary associations has not been seriously studied inside
the Authority.
3. Karl Mannheim, *Man and Society in an Age of Reconstruction* (New York: Harcourt, Brace, 1941),
pp. 44 ff.
4. See Jose Ortega y Gasset, *The Revolt of the Masses* (New York: Norton, 1932).

simply transforms an unorganized citizenry into a reliable instrument for the achievement of administrative goals, and calls it "democracy."[5]

The tendency for participation to become equivalent to involvement has a strong rationale. In many cases, perhaps in most, the initiation of local citizens' associations comes from the top, and is tied to the pressing problem of administering a program. The need for uniformity in structure; for a channel through which directives, information, and reports will be readily disseminated; for the stimulation of a normally apathetic clientele; and for the swift dispatch of accumulated tasks—these and other imperatives are met with reasonable adequacy when involvement alone has been achieved. Some additional impetus, not provided for in the usual responsibilities of the administrative agency, is normally required if the process is to be pushed beyond the level of involvement. Indeed, it is doubtful that much can be achieved beyond that level. Such associations, voluntary or compulsory,[6] are commonly established *ad hoc,* sponsored by some particular agency.[7] That agency is charged with a set of program responsibilities. These cannot be readily changed, nor can they be effectively delegated. As an administrative organization, the agency cannot abandon the necessity for unity of command and continuity of policy—not only over time but down the hierarchy as well. What, therefore, can be the role of the coöpted local association or committee? It cannot become an effective part of the major policy-determining structure of the agency.[8] In practice only a limited sphere of decision is permitted, involving some adaptation of general directives to local conditions, and within that circumscribed sphere the responsible (usually paid) officials of the agency will play an effective part.

With these general considerations in mind, it may be well to mention at least one phase of the historical context within which the TVA's use of voluntary associations has developed. Especially in the field of agricultural administration, the TVA's methods have paralleled an emerging trend in the administration of the federal government. This

5. This is no necessary reflection on the integrity or the intentions of the responsible leadership. It is normal for programs infused with a moral content to be reduced to those elements in the program which are relevant to action. Thus the moral ideal of socialism has been reduced rather easily to concrete objectives, such as nationalization of industry. Administrative objectives, such as the establishment of a ramified system of citizens' committees, are similar.

6. This distinction tends to melt away as the program administered comes closer to becoming an exclusive means of distributing the necessities of life, or if inducements are such as to eliminate any practical alternatives to participation.

7. This may be the effective situation, even where there is not legal sponsorship. Thus, the local soil conservation districts are creatures of the state legislatures, but serviced by the Department of Agriculture's Soil Conservation Service. It is probably not inappropriately that they have been known in some areas as "SCS" districts.

8. This might happen if the local groups formed an independent central organization, but that is not envisioned by the administrative agency, unless it already has control of a preëxisting central organization, as when a national government utilizes a preëxisting party structure to aid in the administration of its program.

is not often recognized within the Authority, but there can be little doubt that the United States Department of Agriculture has gone much farther in developing both the theory and the practice of citizen participation than has the TVA. The emergence of this trend accompanied the construction of a vast apparatus to administer an action program reaching virtually every farmer in the nation.

One formulation of the idea of "agricultural democracy" was undertaken in 1940 by M. L. Wilson, Director of Extension Work of the Department of Agriculture.[9] Wilson noted the movement toward a greater group interest on the part of farmers, and the pressure for equality through government intervention, culminating in the enactment of the Agricultural Adjustment Act of 1933 and subsequent New Deal agricultural legislation. The administration of the new government programs was based on the ideal of coöperation and voluntary participation, leading to a set of procedures which, in Wilson's view, can be thought of as the general principles of agricultural democracy:

1. Decentralized administration in varying degrees through community, county, and state farmer committees, elected by coöperating farmers or appointed by the Secretary of Agriculture.
2. The use of referendums in determining certain administrative policies, especially those having to do with quotas, penalties, and marketing agreements.
3. The use of group discussion and other adult education techniques as a means of promoting understanding of the problems and procedures involved in administration of the various programs and referendums.
4. Coöperative planning in program formulation and localization of programs.[10]

This program emphasizes the importance of participation within the democratic pattern of culture. Moreover, in theory, participation includes both policy-forming and administrative functions.

The technique of coöpting local citizens through voluntary associations and as individuals into the administration of various agricultural programs was widely developed during the nineteen-thirties. In 1940, it was reported that over 890,000 citizens were helping to plan and operate nine rural action programs:[11] community, county, and state committees of the Agricultural Adjustment Administration, operating

9. "A Theory of Agricultural Democracy," an address before the American Political Science Association, Chicago, December 28, 1940. Published as Extension Service Circular 355, March, 1941 (mim.). See also M. L. Wilson, *Democracy Has Roots* (New York: Carrick & Evans, 1939), chap. vii. Also, Howard R. Tolley, *The Farmer Citizen at War* (New York: The Macmillan Co., 1943), Pt. V.

10. Wilson, "A Theory of Agricultural Democracy," p. 5. It is interesting to note that Mr. Wilson, Director of Extension Work, considered the AAA program to have represented the practical beginning of agricultural democracy. The TVA agriculturists, loyal essentially to the local extension service organizations, would not have made such a statement.

11. Carleton R. Ball, "Citizens Help Plan and Operate Action Programs," *Land Policy Review* (March-April, 1940), p. 19.

through over 3,000 county agricultural associations; land-use planning committees organized through the Bureau of Agricultural Economics; farmer associations aiding in the administration of Farm Credit Administration loans; rehabilitation and tenant-purchase committees organized by the Farm Security Administration; local district advisory boards for the Grazing Service; coöperatives dealing with the Rural Electrification Administration; government boards of soil conservation districts serviced by Soil Conservation Service; these together form an administrative pattern of which the TVA ventures along this line were only a part. Mr. Ball's summary of participating citizens is reprinted as table 1.

Table 1

Summary of Assisting Citizens in U.S. Agricultural Programs 1939

Name of citizen group	Members
AAA: local committees	135,591
County land-use committees	72,000
Extension Service: volunteer program leaders	586,600
FCA: association directors and committees	36,574
FSA: local committees	26,753
Grazing Service: district advisory boards	547
REA: association directors	4,900
Soil conservation district supervisors	855
Tennessee Valley committees and test-demonstrators	29,035
	892,855

Source: Carleton R. Ball. "Citizens Help Plan and Operate Action Programs." *Land Policy Review* (March–April, 1940), p. 26. In 1942, just prior to the withdrawal of federal support from the program, membership in state, county, and community land-use planning committees reached 125,000, according to the Report of the Chief of the BAR, 1942.

The trend toward coöptation of farmers in the administration of a national agricultural program reached a high point with the organization of the county land-use planning program in 1938. The idea of democratic planning with farmer participation was given considerable attention, and an attempt was made to construct a hierarchy of representative committees which would embody the democratic ideal.[12] At the same time, the achievement of a primary administrative objective was envisioned. The land-use planning organization program received its impetus from a conference of representatives of the Department of

12. See "The Land Use Planning Organization," County Planning Series No. 3, Bureau of Agricultural Economics, May, 1940; also, *Land Use Planning Under Way,* prepared by the BAE in coöperation with the Extension Service, BSA, SCA, AAA, and Forest Service, USDA, Washington, July, 1940; and John M. Gaus and Leon O. Wolcott, *Public Administration and the U.S. Department of Agriculture* (Chicago: Public Administration Service, 1940), pp. 151 ff.

Agriculture and the Association of Land-Grant Colleges and Universities held at Mt. Weather, Virginia, in July, 1938. The Mt. Weather Agreement[13] recommended a system of coördinated land-use planning to overcome the confusion created by the existence of a large number of points of contact between governmental agencies and local farmers. By providing that local officials of the national agricultural agencies would be represented on the farmer committees, it was felt that a single point of contact would be established. It is possible that the land-use planning system would have been established without this impetus from a pressing administrative imperative, but it is clear that the latter was the occasion for the new organization. The problems of the officialdom were primary, and logically so, for their responsibilities had to do with the efficient execution of statutory programs—not the creation of new culture patterns. The latter might, time and resources permitting, have become an effective collateral objective, but it would be idle to suppose that the requirements of administration would not assume priority within the system.

The coöptative construction of systems of voluntary associations fulfills important administrative needs. These are general, and include:

1. The achievement of ready accessibility, which requires the establishment of routine and reliable channels through which information, aid, and requests may be brought to segments of the population. The committee device permits the assembling of leading elements on a regular basis, so that top levels of administration may have reason to anticipate that quota assignments will be fulfilled; and the local organization provides an administrative focus in terms of which the various line divisions may be coördinated in the field.

2. As the program increases in intensity it becomes necessary for the lower end of administration to be some sort of group rather than the individual citizen. A group-oriented local official may reach a far larger number of people by working through community and county organizations than by attempting to approach his constituency as individuals. Thus the voluntary association permits the official to make use of untapped administrative resources.

3. Administration may be decentralized so that the execution of a broad policy is adapted to local conditions by utilizing the special knowledge of local citizens; it is not normally anticipated, however, that the policy itself will be placed in jeopardy.

4. The sharing of responsibility, so that local citizens, through the voluntary associations or committees, may become identified with and

13. Reprinted as an appendix to Gaus and Wolcott, *op. cit.* Russell Lord (*The Agrarian Revival,* p. 193) notes extension service references to this agreement as "The Truce of Mt. Weather." Truce indeed, for by the middle of 1942 the Congress had scuttled the program, with the support of the American Farm Bureau Federation. See Charles M. Hardin, "The Bureau of Agricultural Economics Under Fire: A Study in Valuation Conflicts," *Journal of Farm Economics,* Vol. 28 (August, 1946).

committed to the program—and, ideally, to the apparatus—of the operating agency.

These needs define the relevance of the voluntary-association device to the organizational problems of those who make use of it. It is only as fulfilling such needs as these that the continuity—in both structure and function—of this type of coöptation under democratic and totalitarian sponsorship can be understood.

From the above it is not surprising that criticisms of the county planning program have stressed deviations from the democratic ideal, particularly in lack of representativeness and the tendency for established organizations such as the Farm Bureau to take control of the local committees.[14] Insofar, however, as this represents criticism of a program developing toward complete fulfillment of the ideal, it is not basic. More significant for this analysis are such criticisms as the following:

> ... it is the central thesis of this paper that county planning did not succeed because no desire to solve community and county problems was created in the population of the area in which the county planning program was to function. ... Most administrators of county planning conceive of rural planning as another administrative problem, as a procedure.[15]

The normal pattern—perhaps inevitable because of the rapid creation of a nationally ramified system of committees—established an organization set down from above, oriented toward the administration of the national program. As a consequence, the problems of the local official *qua* official assumed priority. "One needed only to talk with representatives of the several agencies engaged in trying to "enforce" the county planning system to recognize how ubiquitous this condition [of apathy] was."[16] To the extent that the problems of the officialdom are sufficiently pressing to stamp the character of the organization, it may be expected that involvement rather than meaningful participation will prevail. This same point is made in another way by John D. Lewis, in tracing one of the bases for the lack of complete representativeness.

> The pressure to "get things done" has tended to encourage appointment rather than election. The Division in Washington naturally expects its field agents to report results that will justify the high hope with which the program was launched, and the state office in turn pushes the county agents for progress reports with which to appease

14. See John D. Lewis, "Democratic Planning in Agriculture," *American Political Science Review,* XXXV (April and June, 1941); also Neal C. Gross, "A Post Mortem on County Planning," *Journal of Farm Economics,* XXV (August, 1943); and Bryce Ryan, "Democratic Telesis and County Agricultural Planning," *Journal of Farm Economics,* XXII (November, 1940).

15. Gross, p. 647.

16. *Ibid.,* p. 653. Mr. Gross also points out that the units of planning tended to follow the convenience of the administrators, rather than local interest patterns.

Washington administrators. Democratic procedure is notoriously slow procedure. Consequently the first thought of an overworked county agent, unless he is genuinely impressed by the importance of finding a truly democratic committee, will be to find a group of industrious and coöperative farmers who can be depended upon to work together harmoniously. With the best of intentions and with no thought of deliberately stacking the committee, he may set up a committee of "outstanding leaders" who have a sincere desire to act in the interest of the whole county, but who have only a second-hand knowledge and indirect concern about the problems of less successful farmers in the county.[17]

In effect, those responsible for organizing the system of committees or associations are under pressure to shape their actions according to exigencies of the moment, and those exigencies have to do primarily with the needs of administration. As the needs of administration become dominant, the tendency for democratic participation to be reduced to mere involvement may be expected to increase. At the extreme, the democratic element drops out and the coöptative character of the organizational devices employed becomes identified with their entire meaning.[18]

17. Lewis, *op. cit.,* p. 247.
18. Unless "democracy" is reinterpreted, so that it reaches a higher level with the subordination of the mass to the organization. The above account, one sided in its emphasis, in no way deprecates the democratic aims of the initiators of the planning program. We are concerned here only with the explication of underlying trends to which the concept of coöptation lends significance.

─────────────────── **12** ───────────────────

THE RELUCTANT ORGANIZATION AND THE AGGRESSIVE ENVIRONMENT

John Maniha and Charles Perrow

Organizations are usually defined as rational systems for co-ordinating the efforts of individuals towards a goal or goals. Increasingly, attention has been focused upon such topics as informal goals, the succession of goals, adaptation to the environment, intended rationality, and so on.[1] The nonrational, informal, and adaptive aspects generally appear with growing institutionalization, as Selznick persuasively argues.[2] But implicit in this view is the assumption that organizations start out as rationally designed instruments with a charter directed toward a clear set of goals designed to fulfill some social need. The distinctively sociological analysis is relevant when the compromises and affective networks of history have accumulated and fleshed out the structure and processes of the organization. We would like to present one case history where an organization had every reason not to be born, and had no goals to guide it. It was used by other organizations for their own ends, but in this very process it became an organization with a mission of its own, in spite of itself, and even while its members denied it was becoming an action group.

The organization under study is the Youth Commission made up of nine private citizens appointed by the mayor of a city of some 70,000 persons. The origins and first year of the Commission were reconstructed from structured interviews with most of the principals concerned, within and without the organization, the minutes of the Commission, documents and letters in their file, and newspaper accounts. In the second year the meetings of the Commission were observed, and interviews were held with the heads of other agencies, public officials, and private citizens involved in or concerned with the affairs of the Commission. All Commission members, except one who had moved away, were interviewed at length at least once.[3] The account is basically historical, starting with the community environment, the specific origins of the Commission, its search for a role, its utilization by other groups and, finally, its emergence as an organization with an action role.

SETTING

Collegetown considers itself a progressive community with few major problems. As the mayor once put it, when speaking of youth problems, "We've always known about the 'five per cent' of the kids who go bad, but we've always felt that Collegetown had only two per

1. For a representative sampling see Philip Selznick, "Foundations of the Theory of Organization," *American Sociological Review*, 13 (1948), pp. 25–35; David Sills, *The Volunteers* (Glencoe, Ill.: Free Press, 1957); Herbert Simon, *Administrative Behavior* (2nd ed.; New York: Macmillan, 1957), especially the introduction; and James D. Thompson *et al.*, *Comparative Studies in Administration* (Pittsburgh: University of Pittsburgh, 1959).

2. Philip Selznick, *Leadership and Administration* (New York: Row, Peterson, 1957).

3. The Commission agreed to serve as a research site for a seminar paper in organizational analysis, with the chairman hoping thereby that the role of the Commission in the community might be clarified. J. Maniha conducted the field work, while C. Perrow had primary, though not exclusive, responsibility for the framework of the analysis and much of the writing.

cent." Much of this image comes from the view that not only does the city have a large percentage of well-educated professional citizens—university professors, scientists and engineers—but that it draws these citizens into government through the use of semiofficial commissions. The commissions are made up of a cross section of the community elite —wealthy landowners, the business elite, representatives of the leading Protestant churches, university people, and sometimes representatives of the new electronics and aerospace industries. Commissions informally share responsibility for legislation passed by the City Council and serve as sounding boards of elite public opinion on some of the issues upon which the Council should act.

Some commissions are noncontroversial as, for example, the group of seven citizens formed to advise the Council on how Collegetown could, according to the mayor, retain its "character ... by trying to strike a balance between progress, as defined by growth, and the traditional character of our community." The Citizens Recreation Commission at the time of the study was somewhat more powerful, since it influenced the allocation of recreation resources. The Human Relations Commission, dealing with more explosive issues, such as civil rights, minority housing, and zoning, had been forced into a controversial role by the pressure of liberal organizations. The Youth Commission started out innocuously enough, but by the end of its second year was making headlines, and was even accused by members of the Human Relations Commission of invading their strife-ridden domain. In view of its origins, the change was significant.

ORIGINS

The formation of the Youth Commission was not prompted by any dramatic evidence of need in the area, nor by demands of agencies dealing with youth, citizen groups, or political groups. Several cities in the region were reported to be forming youth commissions, but generally in response to dramatic evidence of problems. During the preceding administration a small group had looked into the problems of youth and made at least one report to the City Council, but it received no publicity and little could be learned of its activities.

The idea of forming the Youth Commission came from a councilman who was a candidate for re-election. He initially explored the idea with his friends, some of whom were prominent in youth affairs; and while they agreed there might be some value in it, reportedly they expressed concern that the service might be a duplication of existing facilities. The Director of the YMCA had a more explicit caution. He recalled that he told the councilman that he "thought it was a good idea but expressed the hope that the Commission would not be an action group." The councilman used the proposal as a campaign plank during the election. Surprise was expressed by workers in both parties when, following his re-election, he continued to pursue the idea. He presented it to the Council as an ordinance, which then required two readings and a vote. One member of the Council characterized the atmosphere at the first reading as apathetic. The ordinance passed and came up again one month later for final action. At this point another councilman, a retired businessman and past chairman of the United Fund and Community Chest, proposed that the word "commission" be changed to "committee"—a term connoting less stature and influence. His proposal was defeated, and with the second councilman registering the only nay, the ordinance was officially passed, again apathetically.

The official goals of the charter were sufficiently straightforward to confer upon it the broad responsibility of appraising conditions and influences affecting youth, evaluating existing services, and recommending to the Council measures which it could take "to promote the best interests of children and youth in the city." It was to report to the Council every four months, advising the Council of current developments relating to youth. Just how the Commission was to go about its tasks was not spelled out. It was noted in the charter that it "shall not undertake or carry out youth projects," but this was followed by the ambiguous qualification "though after specific request therefrom may render such assistance as it deems appropriate to other agencies supporting youth projects or actions." What "appropriate assistance" might be, or the scope of support, was apparently left to the Commission to decide. They decided quite early; indeed, by the time the members were selected other agencies had, in effect, decided for them.

FORMING A RELUCTANT ORGANIZATION

As soon as the ordinance was passed, the town newspaper informed the public of the "appraising, evaluating, and recommending" goals of the Commission. The mayor immediately received queries from the heads of agencies concerned with youth. They wished to know what was to be appraised, who was to be evaluated, and whether this was not a duplication of existing services. It appeared that the autonomy and integrity of some 29 existing agencies were threatened. The Commission was not the mayor's idea, and he attempted to assuage their fears. His nine appointments to the Commission can be interpreted in this light:

1. *High School Principal*—The group's first chairman. He was head of the city's only public high school, which served about 2,000 students

and held a very visible position in the community. He was highly respected by all the Commission members for his knowledge of youth problems and his candid and forthright approach. The high school had been a focal point for some disturbances in the past, and thus had a more than usual interest in youth problems.

2. *YMCA Director*—Representative of one of the organizations most conscious of public relations. He was a friend or acquaintance of the mayor and several councilmen, as well as most of the other heads of agencies serving youth in Collegetown. The YMCA had also had problems with juvenile disturbances on its premises and had been criticized for this in the past.

3. *Catholic*—Athletic coach at a Catholic high school. He rarely came to meetings and took almost no part in them. He was interested in pursuing his sports activities with youth and working with them on a face-to-face basis, and felt the Commission should be talking with the youth of the community. In an interview, he said, "I was asked to be on the Commission because they needed a Catholic. There aren't a lot of us here, but enough to be represented."

4. *Negro Woman*—She also recognized why she was appointed and was frank about it. She belonged to a great many other organizations, including the Human Relations Commission, and was a friend of the mayor and several powerful families in Collegetown. White leaders depended upon her to be prudent about the race issue, and she was in great demand for organizations requiring a Negro representative. Vocal elements in the Negro civil rights movement did not feel she spoke for her race, and she in turn did not strongly identify with the Negro community in Collegetown.

5. *Junior High School Teacher*—A son of the mayor. His access to City Hall was utilized by the Commission in technical matters, and he may also have informed his father about developments in the group. He did not appear to find the connection between his relationship to the mayor and his Commission membership awkward.

6. *Protestant Minister*—Four of the eight other members of the Commission belonged to his church. The minister clearly represented organized religion and Christian morality, reminding members, for example, that even so-called unenforceable laws must be observed. He can be seen as the link between the Commission and the powerful Collegetown Ministerial Association.

7. *Physician*—Professor of public health at the University. He was elected chairman at the close of the Commission's first year. He was interested in the welfare of youth and was also acting chairman of a state-wide health organization dealing with children. The pres-

ence of a physician would ordinarily be a requisite of such an organization.

8.   *University Faculty Member*—In physical education. He belonged to a great many service groups and was active in many phases of community work. He was very interested in the affairs of the Commission and probably the most vocal member of the group. But his role was mainly that of a public-spirited citizen and a concerned father of an adolescent. He was also at the same time the Chairman of the Citizens Recreation Commission.

9.   *Nurse*—She replaced another woman who moved away and who had been president of the Women's Auxiliary of the Junior Chamber of Commerce and, as secretary of the group, was said to have played almost no role in deliberations. Her replacement, the nurse, was also promptly made the group's secretary. She said she was appointed to the Commission because "they needed a housewife." Her role was subordinate; she rarely spoke at meetings; and she admitted to being awed by the other "strong members who are authorities on youth."

The appointments, then, covered two of the powerful agencies most involved with youth—the high school and the YMCA—and added representatives from four other obvious fields: religion, recreation, medicine, and housewifery. Two minority groups were included: a Negro and a Catholic. The ruling political party was represented at least by the mayor's son, and initially also by the representative from the Junior Chamber of Commerce. It can be assumed that most of the members were in sympathy with the political party in office. None of the many authorities in delinquency from the university, such as social workers, sociologists, or psychologists, were included, nor was a representative of the major Negro youth organization, which had programs similar to the YMCA. Any of these might have urged a more active role for the Commission.

At the organization meeting of the group, the mayor discussed the implications of the creation of a group to study youth problems in a city which prided itself on the lack of such problems. He said he was "not sure" Collegetown had any youth problems, but if it did he "certainly wanted to know about them." He would also co-operate in any way he could with the group, and if the Commission needed anything to let him know. One member recalls that he mentioned stamps and envelopes. He then explicitly advised them to move very slowly and cautiously in order to allay the suspicions of several agencies. He concluded by expressing his admiration for the fine group of public-spirited citizens he had chosen, and appointed the high school principal as chairman.

THE FIRST YEAR: PROTECTING THE MINIMAL ROLE

"Goals appear to grow out of interaction both within the organization and between the organization and its environment."[4] In the case of the Commission, much of the salient environment was built into the organization—representation of the two largest youth organizations in the city, and of the city administration. The high school principal and the director of the YMCA immediately became the key personnel in the Commission. They were instrumental in defining a no-action study-group role for the Commission at its first meeting. The goals of the Commission had been clearly set forth in the charter—appraise, evaluate and recommend—but appraisal, or more accurately, "listening," became the only operative goal.[5]

During its first year, and for some months after, the agency invited the heads of the major youth agencies in the city to describe the program and problems of their agencies. Each presentation was followed by a polite question-and-answer period. The presentations of the agencies appear to have been optimistic and self-satisfied, and the questions of the members were innocuous. Even so, some of the members felt that the agencies mimimized their problems. For example, the head of the county health agency announced that there were almost no health problems among the youth in the city, and that this could be attributed to the fine cooperation between private physicians and his department. Several Commission members, not particularly prone to gloomy views, privately debunked the statement. They had enough contact with juveniles to know that many poor children suffered from inadequate health facilities, and even the mayor was reportedly surprised when informed of the presentation. But the head of the agency was not questioned about this in the discussion session.

It was a Commission member, the minister, who tested the reluctance of the Commission to become active. Assigned to report on what the churches were doing with youth, with a panel discussion of his report by a group of ministers to follow at a later session, the minister stated that, in fact, the churches were doing virtually nothing and deplored the fact. The report was quickly tabled and the panel discussion cancelled. One Commission member, a member of the minister's congregation, said, "We decided the panel should be postponed until further study could be made of the report. Of course, it never was. The

4. James D. Thompson and William J. McEwen, "Organizational Goals and Environment: Goal Setting as an Interaction Process," *American Sociological Review* 23 (1958), 28–29.
5. On the concept of "operative goals," see Charles Perrow, "The Analysis of Goals in Complex Organization," *American Sociological Review,* 26 (1961), 854–866.

report would have set up barriers." The minister subsequently played a minor role at the meetings.

More informal means were used to allay the suspicion of groups. The YMCA director, a self-proclaimed listening post in the town, informed the chairman that the head of the Juvenile Division of the Police Department was suspicious of the role of the Commission. This led to an informal meeting, and in the Commission's first annual report, the Commission supported the Police Department's request for more personnel.

Sensitivity to public criticism characterized the two dominant men in the Commission in its first year, the principal and the YMCA director, and concern with the image of the town became a preoccupation of the group. The high school principal set the tone of cautious procedure for the Commission. The high school was occasionally the scene of vandalism and delinquency, and he was sensitive to potential criticisms. In the second year he was involved in a direct controversy with the local newspaper, which, he claimed, was placing the school in an unfavorable light by publishing accounts of delinquency by high school students— he argued that they could just as well have been identified as College-town youths, or the children of certain families. He felt the school was being made to look like "a training school for punks." The YMCA director also had similar experiences in which his organization was criticized for lack of supervision during its functions. He took on the role of seeing that no one was misquoted, misinterpreted or otherwise compromised in dealing with the press. Another member was quite concerned that Collegetown had a reputation among other cities as being a "hoody town." All agreed with the statement of one member that "throwing these accusations and sensational terms around indiscreetly can give our town a bad reputation that will stick for years."

During the first year several formal and informal attempts by relatively weak groups were made to enlist the help of the Commission in meeting problems related to youth. The Commission resisted these attempts on the grounds of the no-action policy made explicit by the two dominant members and shared by others. For example, a local Protestant minister tried to get the Commission interested in doing something about all-night parties after the senior prom at the high school. The minister was referred to the PTA, since his proposal was "beyond the role of the Commission, because we are not an action group." A more constructive role for the Commission was sought by the head of the City Recreation Board, who attempted to enlist the Commission's aid in keeping city recreation facilities open on school nights. Although the Commission did not refuse to consider the proposal, it ignored it, and no formal action was taken on it, even though a member of the Citizens Recreation Commission was on the Youth Commission.

At the end of the year the Youth Commission was required to submit an annual report to the City Council. Perhaps in keeping with the Commission's minimal role, it had only had a few carbon copies made. To the surprise of the members, there were a number of requests for copies from agencies and citizens following the announcement of the report in the newspaper. The report was then mimeographed and distributed to those who requested it. The interest probably reflected both a concern with problems of youth by the citizens and a concern with the role and recommendations of the Commission. The report, however, did much to allay the suspicions of the agencies. It was non-controversial and minimized youth problems. It contained a few minor recommendations, and was full of praise for the work the community youth agencies were doing, given the limitations that were beyond agency control. The report reaffirmed that the Commission was "fully cognizant of its legal limitation to require action on its recommendations by any agency, civil or legal body. The Commission's prime responsibility is to bring to the attention of the community and the several responsible agencies, through its report to the city council, the results of its findings and its recommendations for the alleviation or resolution of problems and issues of the youth of Collegetown." The report ended with a section on proposed plans for the coming year, one of which reads, "Make a more detailed analysis of the role of the Youth Commission."

The distribution of mimeographed copies of the annual report marked the end of the first phase of the Commission's development—the study-group role—and the beginning of its second phase, involving an action role. The annual report was more than a symbolic calendaring of a new year; it stirred interest in the group by others in the community, allayed suspicions, and prompted criticism. At the same time, the term of the high school principal as chairman expired, and he did not wish to serve as chairman for another year. A new chairman was elected, the public health physician. This, it turned out, was a fateful decision. The physician differed from the other members in not having a local constituency—he did not represent the schools, the YMCA, the recreation department, Catholics, Negroes, or housewives. He might be seen as representing physicians or the university, but neither of these was involved, as an organization, in community youth affairs. Without a constituency, the physician could act as a free agent. He alone seems to have played the role of member of a Commission rather than a representative of some interest group. In fact, at the end of the second year, he remarked that he was not so sure that the YMCA director and the high school principal really ought to be on the Commission: "They have difficulty separating their roles as director and principal from their roles as Commission members. They often speak and act in terms of their own organizations and not the Commission." As a corollary of the physician's role, he did not have great public visibility and was able to move inconspicuously in informal negotiations with groups.

THE EMERGING ACTION ROLE

There was nothing to indicate that the Youth Commission would do more than continue its role as a study group in its second year. Because it existed, however, it was there for others to utilize. As the head of the Juvenile Division of the Police Department put it, "The Commission can do a lot to help all agencies. We all need support. People listen to them because their opinions carry weight and prestige."

There were some who urged the Commission to take a more active, constructive role. In the early part of the second year, they asked an expert in juvenile delinquency and related community problems from the university to address them. He exhorted them to make an aggressive and sincere effort to attack the city's many youth problems. Members replied that this was "not the Commission's role," but the faculty member then read them the official goals as stated in their charter and reminded them that their role was to appraise, evaluate, and recommend programs. Furthermore, he reminded them that other organizations in the city, like the Human Relations Commission, had not let their official charter goals stand in the way of the development of an aggressive approach to community problems. The Commission appeared unmoved.

Shortly after this, the Commission invited an official of the State Youth Commission, which had no affiliation with the local one, to address them on youth problems. He praised their annual report, but then told them that they should seize the opportunity created by good feeling and the interest in the Commission to forge ahead with some kind of constructive program. Again, the members listened but did not discuss these exhortations nor apparently take them seriously at the time.

The Commission continued its study role but was pressed into a more active role by the City Council itself. A well-publicized brawl broke out between a group of high school youths and students from the university. Publicity in the newspaper, letters to the editor, letters to the mayor and City Council, and direct pressure upon the Council from some of the citizens, who protested the lack of control by the police, demanded some kind of response. The response was an ordinance drafted by the city attorney, which would give the police power to arrest those whom they suspected of being about to cause a disturbance. The mayor and the Council were reluctant to handle the ordinance from the start. Casting about for a device to suggest action while delaying any, the Council seized upon the Commission. As one councilman said, when he was asked why the Commission had been brought into the matter, "We didn't know what to do with the ordinance and needed more time to think about it and test out more opinions." A joint meeting between the Council and the Commission was called.

The meeting illustrated both the ambiguous role of the Commission and the apprehensions which some Council members had about its goals. The high school principal began the discussion by stating frankly that he did not know what the Council expected of the group and was waiting for positive leadership from the Council. All evening the Council and mayor solicited opinions from Commission members about various aspects of the youth problem: Could we use a dragstrip? What sort of problems do the schools have? Are youth at the YMCA hard to control? Do you think the police juvenile division needs more men? The Commission members gave their opinions and attempted, in some cases, to speak for the community at large; but several times they sought from the Council a definite statement of purpose for their organization. None was forthcoming. Indeed, the councilman who had voted against the Commission, felt that he should warn the Commission to proceed slowly and be very careful about recommendations. He feared that "half-baked schemes" might be proposed by the Commission. "Just because something worked in another city, doesn't mean it will work in Collegetown," he added. Finally, the mayor asked the Commission to make a recommendation on the proposed ordinance and submit it to the Council.

The Commission met, but there was little consensus at first. The YMCA director was immediately concerned about public opinion and, in effect, admitted that a no-action role was no longer feasible. "We have to recommend the ordinance. If we don't and it's not passed, the first time something happens we'll be blamed for it. Anyway, the ordinance won't do any good, but if they think they need it then give it to them." But some other members felt the ordinance was potentially threatening to civil rights. The principal was not present but sent a letter stating that he was against the ordinance because it was unconstitutional. Finally, the new chairman reluctantly formulated a compromise agreeable to the YMCA director. It met its obligation to the city administration by recommending passage, but qualified its support by adding that it should be passed only if some means could be found to protect civil rights, and that other so-called "unenforceable" laws were attended to.

Opposition to the ordinance from groups concerned with civil liberties eventually caused the mayor to postpone action indefinitely. Although the newspapers gave prominence to the recommendations of the Commission, its members did not feel that they had been compromised by the administration's decision to postpone action. Most of them, when interviewed, said that their actions as an organization were not especially noticed by the community.

The next group to seize upon the potentialities of the Youth Commission was the United Fund. This organization had originally been suspicious of the Youth Commission. Following the issuance of the Commission's annual report, the planning committee of the United Fund asked the principal of the high school to discuss the Commission and its role with them. This meeting apparently allayed many suspicions since, shortly afterwards, the head of the United Fund wrote to the Commission regarding the meeting saying, "You have focused for this committee what the committee already knew and was concerned about; and you have done it with a realistic appreciation of the limitations we have in the face of so exacting and imperative a task and, finally, you have pointed the way to our working together." The planning committee of the United Fund decided that it would be beneficial to have a discussion comparable to that held with the high school principal on a community-wide basis. A seminar was proposed which would be cosponsored by the United Fund and the Youth Commission. This proposal was made to the YMCA director, suggesting that the new chairman of the Commission was still not visible or believed to be a powerful member. The YMCA director and the principal decided that the Commission should not cosponsor the seminar because they were "not an action group," and so informed the United Fund. They rather casually informed the other members of the request and the group agreed with their action. All agreed, however, that the Commission should at least go on record as actively supporting the project, though it could not cosponsor it.

Less than three months later, at least partly through the leadership of the new chairman of the Youth Commission, the Commission found itself cosponsoring the seminar. The proposal received favorable publicity in the press, which commended the Commission and the United Fund for this constructive and positive step.

The City Council and the United Fund were both influential agencies in the community. So was the Probate Court, and the third and even more significant line of action that engaged the Commission stemmed from this source. A judge from the court, who was an officer in a state-wide group promoting a project concerned with protective services for juveniles, met with the chairman of the Youth Commission and urged him to look into the project, which involved setting up protective services for children, which fell outside the jurisdiction or responsibility of existing youth agencies. For example, a community agency could be established to assume responsibility for the prosecution of parents of abused children. The initial step would be a survey of the

community resources to see if a protective-service agency was needed.
At the urging of the judge, the Commission met with a representative
of the state-wide project. During the meeting, the judge stated frankly
that he saw a real need for the program and would like to see the
Commission sponsor it. Whatever their individual feelings, the Commission members must have found it difficult to turn down a request
from this influential source.

The Commission was now pressed to explore the role of recommending to other agencies a study by an outside group, which would
assess the effectiveness of agencies in the community and might propose yet another agency to fill in the gaps. The implications of perhaps
finding such a need were not lost upon agency heads. There would be
implied criticism of existing facilities. A new organization might be
created which would upset the balance of power and the accommodative division of labor existing among some 29 community agencies, and
affect the distribution of United Fund resources. At a joint meeting of
the agency heads, some sought to avoid the responsibilities and the
burdens that such an organization might exact from them, and others
attempted to place themselves in a position where they could have a
share in its control. At the conclusion of our field work, agency heads
had only agreed to confer with their respective organizations to see if
approval would be given for a study in which they would have to
cooperate, and even this agreement was reluctant in many cases.

By this time—the end of the Commission's second year—meetings
were lively and participation was more enthusiastic. This change had
begun when the antibrawling ordinance had been discussed, and quick-
ened further during the planning of the seminar. A good deal of excite-
ment was now generated in connection with the protective-service
project. As one member put it with enthusiasm, "We are about to
commit ourselves." The YMCA director characteristically saw the
project as "a major test for the Commission since it involves an expenditure of a lot of money and other responsibilities." While it certainly
seemed as if they had compromised their hard-earned nonintervention
reputation, the action implications of the project appeared to have been
lost upon most of the Commission members. In final interviews, all
members (except the chairman, who recognized the action role implicit
in current developments) affirmed that the Commission should not be
an action group, nor should it be granted any more formal powers than
it had. They affirmed that the group had no authority to go to any
agency with plans, and that they had merely to keep themselves informed and await requests from others for their advice and information. The mayor's son summed it up well:

> "Working with a lot of different groups as we are, groups like the
> churches, the city agencies, and private agencies, all of which are

separate and autonomous, the city really can't give us any more power than we already have. All must work co-operatively and without force with these separate groups. We can only study the situation and wait for others to ask our opinion."

The study-group role was even pressed anew by some members in the final interviews. One said, somewhat wistfully, "We haven't talked to all the agencies yet." Another complained, "We haven't talked to the kids yet."

A postscript to our study was provided just one year after the end of the field work. A newspaper story reported that a survey initiated by the Youth Commission and the Probate Court had found that "at least 1,350 children in the county are known to suffer from neglect by their parents or guardians." The mayor, in summoning the Commission, councilmen, judges, and police department to a meeting, stated again his belief that only about two per cent of the youthful population were in trouble with authorities, but he stressed that, "The Community must take constructive action; it must stop dividing itself."

The chairman of the Youth Commission, who had been unanimously encouraged by members to continue in office another year, was reported to be contacting those in charge of welfare matters in the state "to seek possibilities for state support for a protective service here." Even more significantly, the Commission was also "considering the addition of a staff person to co-ordinate the work of all involved groups." The role of action and controversy, which had been so predictably rejected by the carefully selected members of the Commission, had been embraced.

DISCUSSION

There are many conclusions on organizational analysis to be drawn from this modest analysis of a modest organization. For one thing, not all organizations start out as rationally designed instruments directed toward a predetermined goal specified in their charter. As obvious as this may seem, there has been little attempt to explore the origins of organizations in these terms. Such an exploration immediately confronts one with the influence of the environment upon organizational behavior—a point analyzed systematically by Selznick from the beginning of his work[6] but still receiving only scattered attention in its own right.[7]

Other organizations constituted the most significant part of the

6. Philip Selznick, *op. cit.;* also *TVA and the Grass Roots* (Berkeley: University of California, 1949).
7. See, for example, Sol Levine and Paul E. White, "Exchange as a Conceptual Framework for the Study of Interorganizational Relationships," *Administrative Science Quarterly,* 5 (1961), 583–601; Eugene Litwak and Lydia Hylton, "Inter-organizational Analysis," *Administrative Science Quarterly,* 6 (1962), 395–421; and Thompson and McEwen, *op. cit.*

environment in this case. The vicious rivalry and conflict that can occur between agencies has been described by Miller in his "Interinstitutional Conflict as a Major Impediment to Delinquency Prevention," and there are echoes of his distressing analysis here.[8] Agencies everywhere seem to fear the loss of their autonomy and invasions of their domain. In a rare admission of problems on this score, the mayor of Collegetown noted that the community "must stop dividing itself." But the surprising thing is that the Youth Commission survived at all, threatening, as it did, the domain of other agencies. The formal powers of the second chairman, as a free agent without a local constituency, may have proved decisive here, though we are unable to document this point. Perhaps even more important was the fact that while most active members had constituencies they sought to serve, the organization itself, as an organization, had none beyond that of youth in general. Were it given a specific task in its charter, for example to study or promote racial integration, or recreational facilities, or health services, it would not have been as available for supporting ordinances, seminars, or protective services.[9]

But the significant generalization is related to the power that inheres in the very fact of an organization's existence. An organization can be a tool or weapon[10] to those outside of it as well as those who direct it. The uses to which some community organizations are put may be minor, as when they merely indicate "something is being done" about a problem even if they are expressly designed to do little beyond providing that indication. But a greater potential exists. A formal organization is visible and has an address to which communications can be sent; it has a legitimate, official area of relevant interest;[11] and it can speak with one voice, amplified by the size and prestige of its members and allies. It is equipped to be used for organized action even if its members wish to avoid action, as was the case with the Youth Commission. Reluctant as it may have been, the Commission had no choice but to exist for some time; and within a short time organizations turned to it as a source of support for their activities, exploiting the potential derived from its presence and broad purview, despite its self-imposed operative goals of merely existing and "listening."

8. Walter B. Miller, "Interinstitutional Conflict as a Major Impediment to Delinquency Prevention," *Human Organization,* 17 (1958), 20–23.
9. We are not inclined to attribute the survival of the Commission to crises such as the brawl or a growing awareness of real problems. Mounting concern is always present, particularly in retrospect. Every few years an opportunity such as the protective-service project presents itself, but unless it falls within the province of a group that already exists, the opportunity may not even be perceived by most observers.
10. This word is borrowed from Selznick who uses it in a much more dramatic sense in *The Organizational Weapon* (New York: McGraw-Hill, 1952). It has more general utility than has been recognized.
11. An organization powerful in its own right becomes, moreover, like the physician, a generalized wise man wielding influence over a variety of areas. See the example of the American Medical Association mentioned in the next paragraph.

All organizations can be used for purposes that go beyond their normal goals. In the process of meeting their goals and surviving, they generate power which can be put to uses that are independent of the achievement of normal goals. The potential power of a business firm is being utilized when it is a source of testimonials, sponsorship, or support for political, social, or economic activities that are unrelated to its basic task of providing goods or services. When the American Medical Association supports the farm organizations in their relentless war on daylight-saving time, or takes a stand on the treaty-making powers of the presidency, its power as a medical group is being used by other groups. When organized labor is drawn into a political camp, or liberal groups used by "front" organizations,[12] or when a PTA is used to spearhead political reform, or when an organization seeks to have its prestige claims validated by appropriate groups in an effort to control their dependency upon the environment,[13] existing tools are being activated and used by others.

Although such use of an organization often has no significant impact upon the organization, it can shape the organization and even constitute an unacknowledged or unwitting goal for the organization. Elsewhere, this has been labeled as a "derived goal"—derived from the normal activity of the organization and not essential to that activity.[14] Initially, the Youth Commission wished merely to exist and to provide a polite and sympathetic hearing to all agencies. But this was a weak and vulnerable mission in the face of demands from powerful groups, and the uses derived from its existence became the open and acknowledged goals of the Commission. This, at least, appears to be the significance of the newspaper report at the end of the third year. The organization was raising funds and hiring a staff, and thus would grow in the face of a presumably hostile environment, and it would pursue such services as overseeing the activities of other organizations and conducting and co-ordinating protective services. The width of its province—matters affecting youth—and the existence and legitimacy of its machinery for investigating, validating and organizing made it an available organizational weapon and transformed it.

Though its goals were changed by others, it need not be a captive of others. Presumably, among the possible options open to the once reluctant organization, after its third year of existence, is the one of

12. Philip Selznick, *The Organizational Weapon, op. cit.*
13. Charles Perrow, "Organizational Prestige, Some Functions and Dysfunctions," *American Journal of Sociology*, 66 (1961), 335–341.
14. Charles Perrow, "Organizational Goals," in David Sills (ed.), *International Encyclopedia of the Social Sciences* (rev. ed.; New York: Crowell-Collier, forthcoming). *Derived goals* are distinguished from *system goals*, which relate to system characteristics of the organization, such as its emphasis upon growth, stability, risk, etc., and from *product goals*, which relate to the type and characteristics of the goods or services produced, such as the emphasis upon quality, quantity, variety, etc. Derived goals may, in time, become system or product goals.

becoming a reasonably viable and powerful central agency in the community concerned with youth problems, free to utilize other agencies in the environment aggressively, even including the Probate Court.

----------------------- **13** -----------------------

ORGANIZATIONAL DEVELOPMENT

Peter M. Blau and W. Richard Scott

BUREAUCRATIZATION

Structural growth by its very nature involves increasing complexity. Boulding derives this conclusion from his "principle of nonproportional change": since the rates of growth of the various parts of an organization are not proportional, growth always entails internal adjustment and change.[1]   One of the most important changes that occurs as organizations become larger and more complex is the development of an administrative apparatus. Many observers have lamented the trend toward larger administrative overhead in organizations as indicative of overbureaucratization. Parkinson has satirized the presumably parasitic character of administrative personnel most wittily, suggesting that the less work there is in an organization, the greater are the increases in its administrative staff. He cites in support of his "law" the fact that while the number of officers and men in the Royal Navy decreased by 31 per cent between the years 1914 and 1928, the number of Admiralty officials increased by 78 per cent.[2] Haire also comments on "the remarkable resistance of the staff to negative growth," noting that in 19 cases of layoffs observed in four different firms only line workers were involved and that in a few instances new staff personnel was hired during the layoff period.[3] Powerful administrators undoubtedly can and often do protect their positions against being affected by reductions in staff. Parkinson's illustration, however, is quite misleading, since it unquestionably reflects in part technological advances in warfare and the changes that occur in a military service as it adjusts to peacetime—conscripts are discharged and regulars are gradu-

1. Kenneth E. Boulding, "Towards a General Theory of Growth," *Canadian Journal of Economics and Political Science,* 19 (1953), pp. 326–340.
2. C. Northcote Parkinson, *Parkinson's Law and Other Studies in Administration,* Boston: Houghton-Mifflin, 1957, pp. 7–8.
3. Mason Haire, "Biological Models and Empirical Histories of the Growth of Organizations," Mason Haire (ed.), *Modern Organization Theory,* New York: Wiley, 1959, pp. 292–293.

ally promoted, since it is important to maintain a core of staff officers for future emergencies.

It is widely assumed that large organizations tend to be over-bureaucratized, that is, that an increase in organizational size is accompanied by a disproportionate increase in administrative overhead; but the evidence does not support this assumption. To be sure, the average size of manufacturing firms has increased during the first half of this century, and so has the proportion of personnel devoted to administration rather than production.[4] These trends, which reflect basic changes in the organization of industrial concerns, may be responsible for the prevailing impression that size is associated with overbureaucratization. The growth of government services during the last few decades may also have contributed to this notion. Except for small firms, however, increases in size are not associated with increases in the proportion of administrative personnel. Only during an organization's early stages of growth does the proportion of administrative officials increase;[5] further growth is not accompanied by increases in administrative overhead. To cite specific cases, a study of 211 manufacturing firms in Ohio conducted by Baker and Davis found no relation between size of organization and proportion of administrative officials.[6] Melman's data on American manufacturing concerns even reveal an inverse relation between size and proportion of administrative personnel.[7] Data on German industries analyzed by Bendix also show an inverse relation between size and proportion of administrative staff; in 1933, for instance, the proportion of administrators was lower in firms employing more than 1,000 employees than in those employing between 51 and 200 workers.[8]

In industrial organizations, then, bureaucratization as indicated by proportion of administrative personnel is, contrary to prevailing impressions, not directly related to size, and may even be inversely related to it. Two studies of other types of organizations have also dealt with this problem. Terrien and Mills present the only systematic data confirming the popular conception: the size of school districts in California was directly related to the proportion of administrative personnel, although the relations observed were small.[9] Anderson and Warkov, on

4. Seymour Melman, "The Rise of Administrative Overhead in the Manufacturing Industries of the United States, 1899–1947," *Oxford Economic Papers*, 3 (1951), pp. 64–66, 89.
5. Haire, *op. cit.*, pp. 288–292, 305.
6. Alton W. Baker and Ralph C. Davis, *Ratios of Staff to Line Employees and Stages of Differentiation of Staff Functions,* Columbus: Bureau of Business Research. Ohio State University, 1954, pp. 14–15.
7. Melman, *op. cit.*, pp. 89–90.
8. Reinhard Bendix, *Work and Authority in Industry,* New York: Wiley, pp. 221–222. Bendix shows that the proportion of technicians does increase as a function of size of firm; but since administrative officers are the larger group, "the over-all tendency remains for bureaucratization to be highest in the smaller firms."
9. Frederic W. Terrien and Donald L. Mills, "The Effects of Changing Size upon the Internal Structure of Organizations," *American Sociological Review,* 20 (1955), pp. 11–13.

the other hand, examining 49 Veterans' Administration hospitals, found an inverse relation between the size of a hospital and the proportional size of its administrative staff.[10] Their analysis also suggests that complexity[11] as distinguished from size, although the two usually go together, is directly associated with the proportion of administrative personnel, and this distinction provides a possible reason for the discrepancy between the results of the school-district study and those of other research on this problem. Larger school districts were probably more complex than smaller ones—administering several schools in different locations rather than a single one—and this complexity, not size itself, may have been responsible for their larger administrative staffs. The conclusions that emerge from the research findings are that large organizations do not typically have disproportionately large administrative machineries; that, however, size tends to be directly related to complexity, and complexity to a large proportion of administrative personnel; and that the size of an organization, particularly if complexity is held constant, may actually be inversely related to the relative size of its administrative staff.

In mutual-benefit associations bureaucratization poses the special problem of oligarchy. The functions of this type of organization, where the members are expected to be the prime beneficiaries and to govern themselves, are placed in jeopardy by the development of a bureaucratic apparatus that centralizes power in the hands of administrative officials, as was shown in Michels' famous study of unions and social-democratic parties in Germany.[12] The egalitarian ideology and objectives of these organizations would lead one to expect them to be democratically governed by their membership. But the need for efficient administration to insure success in bargaining or in elections encourages the development of a bureaucratic machinery with effective control of the organization centralized in the leadership. Moreover, as the experience gained by the leaders makes them virtually indispensable for the successful implementation of organizational objectives, their dominant position is further strengthened. The examination of such consequences led Michels to propose his "iron law of oligarchy," according to which even initially egalitarian organizations invariably develop hierarchical structures in the interest of effective accomplishment of objectives. There can be little doubt that Michels directs attention to widely prevailing tendencies in mutual-benefit associations. The same developments that he describes have characterized the history of

10. Theodore R. Anderson and Seymour Warkov, "Organizational Size and Functional Complexity," *American Sociological Review*, 26 (1961), pp. 23–28.
11. Tuberculosis hospitals were considered noncomplex, whereas general hospitals, which serve other kinds of patients as well as tubercular ones, were considered complex. See *ibid.*, pp. 25–27.
12. Robert Michels, *Political Parties*, Eden Paul and Cedar Paul (trans.), Glencoe, Ill.: Free Press, 1949, (first published 1915).

many American unions. Contrary to his assumptions, however, these developments, though prevalent, are not inevitable, as the study of the International Typographical Union by Lipset and his colleagues demonstrates.[13] This union has successfully resisted domination by a self-perpetuating oligarchy, because it has maintained a two-party system which safeguards the democratic election of union leaders.

Bureaucratization entails the danger that the original objectives of the organization are lost sight of as the result of preoccupation with administrative problems. Thus, Michels observes that the radical programs of socialist unions and parties became increasingly modified and conservative once bureaucratic hierarchies had developed. For the leaders, interested in preserving and increasing the organization's strength, willingly abandoned radical objectives in favor of more moderate ones that did not threaten the organization's survival in a hostile society. Note the dilemma implied here: a party or a union must build a strong organization and assure its survival to achieve its objectives, yet preoccupation with such organizational problems leads to the surrender of these very objectives. Modifications of this kind in the organization and its program occur not only in mutual-benefit associations but also in other types of formal organizations.

Selznick's analysis of the process of cooptation illustrates how a different mechanism brought about similar changes in a government agency, namely the Tennessee Valley Authority.[14] The reform program of the TVA encountered strong opposition from powerful entrenched forces in the area, and the TVA's grass-roots policy required that it achieve success by coming to terms with these opposition forces rather than impose its will upon them by relying on the power of the federal government. As a means for adjusting to its hostile environment, the TVA coopted some representatives of the opposition into its management. However, since these new elements helped now to shape the policies of the organization in accordance with their own interests, the earlier objectives of the TVA were modified and transformed. For example, an initial policy of the TVA was to purchase large land strips around the reservoirs created by its dam-building operations in order to enable the public to benefit from the increased value of this land resulting from the expenditure of public funds. But the representatives of local agricultural interests who had been coopted into the policymaking bodies of the TVA succeeded in reversing this policy and adopting the procedure that only the minimum amount of land required for reservoirs and other facilities be acquired, thus enabling private investors to reap the benefits from the improved surrounding land.[15] Again,

13. Seymour M. Lipset *et al., Union Democracy,* Glencoe, Ill.: Free Press, 1956, pp. 201–269.
14. Philip Selznick, *TVA and the Grass Roots,* Berkeley: University of California Press, 1949.
15. *Ibid.,* pp. 196–204.

changes introduced to promote the adjustment of an organization to a hostile environment modified the organization's objectives.

The general principle illustrated by these changes is that in the course of adopting means to attain organizational goals the means may become ends-in-themselves that displace the original goals. In an innovating organization, whether political party, union, or government agency, this displacement tends to take the form, as we have just seen, of a retreat from the initial program to a more moderate and conservative program in the interest of maintaining the strength of the organization in an adverse environment. An example of this process in a voluntary association is furnished by Messinger, who describes how the fund-raising activities of the Townsend Organization were transformed from means into ends-in-themselves as new social conditions rendered its original objectives obsolete.[16] But in old and established bureaucracies the displacement of goals typically assumes a different form—the one to which Merton referred when he introduced the concept—namely, a rigid conformity with official procedures at the expense of the objectives they are designed to accomplish, which results from bureaucratic pressures and an overemphasis on discipline. In short, displacement of goals underlies the very tendencies associated with the stereotype "bureaucracy." In Merton's own words:

> Adherence to the rules, originally conceived as a means, becomes transformed into an end-in-itself; there occurs the familiar process of *displacement of goals* whereby "an instrumental value becomes a terminal value." Discipline, readily interpreted as conformance with regulations, whatever the situation, is seen not as a measure designed for specific purposes but becomes an immediate value in the life-organization of the bureaucrat. This emphasis, resulting from the displacement of the original goals, develops into rigidities and an inability to adjust readily.[17]

The very opposite processes, however, have also been observed in bureaucracies. For example, the orientations of officials in a government agency established to enforce New Deal legislation revealed a decade later not an inclination to retreat from the original reform program but a tendency to use it as a steppingstone for further reforms.[18] The earlier goals were not displaced by means that became ends-in-themselves but rather were succeeded by more advanced objectives. Officials advocated legislation that would make the agency responsible for administering more advanced reforms. While officials were in part guided by an idealistic attachment to furthering the pro-

16. Sheldon L. Messinger, "Organizational Transformation," *American Sociological Review,* 20 (1955), pp. 3–10.
17. Robert K. Merton, *Social Theory and Social Structure* (2d ed.), Glencoe, Ill.: Free Press, 1957. p. 199 (italics in original).
18. See Peter M. Blau, *The Dynamics of Bureaucracy,* Chicago: University of Chicago Press, 1955, pp. 193–200.

gram of the New Deal, their career interests provided additional strong incentives for their support of new programs. For once the original mission of getting the new laws generally accepted was accomplished, the task of continuing enforcement involved narrower and more routine responsibilities. These tasks were not as interesting as instituting new reforms and, furthermore, could be accomplished with a smaller staff. Indeed, reductions of staff had already taken place and more threatened to follow. New reform programs would create new challenges that would make the work more interesting and necessitate staff expansions that would avert the threat of layoff and improve the promotion chances of the present personnel. The economic as well as the psychological interests of these officials motivated them to advance new reform objectives.

This succession of goals, the opposite of the displacement of goals, has also been observed in labor unions. Hart's study of a local of the United Automobile Workers in Windsor shows that this union had expanded its activities far beyond the function of representing workers in relation to management by providing a variety of services to members, such as loans, counseling, consumer cooperatives, and health care.[19] This proliferation of goals apparently occurred when the accomplishment of the union's original objectives had become routine, because the industry was thoroughly organized and industry-wide collective bargaining was carried out by the international union. Local union leaders, consequently, had reason to fear that members might look upon them as dispensable, and this possibility threatened their position (just as the indispensability of union leaders strengthens their position, as Michels pointed out). To avert this threat and fortify their position, union leaders instituted various services to members that would make them and the local again important to the membership.[20] A final example of the succession of goals is furnished by a voluntary association. On the basis of his study of a large service organization staffed by volunteers—the National Foundation for Infantile Paralysis—Sills correctly predicted that this organization would turn to new programs with the accomplishment of its original objectives.[21] This prediction was based on the facts that the organization had received wide public acceptance, had successfully attained its initial objectives, and was governed by a corporate-type structure that had the capacity and interest to establish new policies as well as the power to implement them.

What conditions govern whether the displacement of goals or the

19. C. W. M. Hart, "Industrial Relations Research and Social Theory," *Canadian Journal of Economics and Political Science,* 15 (1949), pp. 53–73.
20. Lipset *et al. (op. cit.,* p. 407) have noted that an important latent consequence of the proliferation of activities in unions is to encourage more active participation by members.
21. David L. Sills, *The Volunteers,* Glencoe, Ill.: Free Press, 1957, pp. 253–268.

succession of goals is the prevailing trend in an organization? A crucial factor seems to be the organization's relation to its environment. As long as its very survival is threatened by a hostile environment, its officers will seek to strengthen the organization by building up its administrative machinery and searching for external sources of support. This process is often accompanied by a retreat from the original goal to more modest objectives, as exemplified by the history of the Tennessee Valley Authority and by the tendencies in socialist parties and unions in imperial Germany. But if the community permits an organization to succeed in achieving its initial objectives, the staff's interest in preserving the organization and expanding its jurisdiction will lead to the advocacy and adoption of more advanced goals, as illustrated by the federal agency, the Windsor local as well as other American unions, and the National Foundation. This explanation, however, does not account for the rigid conformity with procedures found in many old bureaucracies that are not at all threatened by the community. Perhaps the environment must supply stimulating challenges as well as support to organizations for flexibility and the succession of goals to develop, just as both these conditions seem to be needed for individual creativity.

Is it correct to speak of increased bureaucratization in those organizations where original goals are succeeded by more advanced ones? Yes, in the sense that the change involves increased scope and power for the bureaucracy; no, in the sense that it involves less preoccupation with administrative procedures as ends-in-themselves. The strain is toward innovation, not rigidity, and in this sense represents a debureaucratizing tendency. We turn now to a discussion of some other forms of debureaucratization.

DEBUREAUCRATIZATION

Less attention has been devoted to processes leading to reduced bureaucratization than to those leading to increased bureaucratization. A recent article by Katz and Eisenstadt analyzes some cases of debureaucratization reported in previous studies, most of which deal with tendencies to relax hierarchical authority.[22] It has been observed, for example, that army discipline, strict lines of authority, and social distance between officers and men were less pronounced in combat than in peacetime, particularly if the combat unit was isolated from other units. A study of an industrial concern found that miners were able successfully to resist attempts by management to increase bureaucratization while factory workers in the same company could not. Re-

22. Elihu Katz and S. N. Eisenstadt. "Some Sociological Observations on the Response of Israeli Organizations to New Immigrants," *Administrative Science Quarterly,* 5 (1960), pp. 113–133.

search also indicates that men on the night shift in industrial plants were less subject to hierarchical authority and discipline than men on the day shift. Katz and Eisenstadt suggest that the common elements in these situations are the presence of physical danger and the isolation of the unit from the larger organization. Both of these conditions make superiors in some respects dependent on their subordinates, and their dependence constrains them to refrain from using authoritarian or coercive measures in performing their duties and to rely, instead, on more personal, nonbureaucratic means of motivating cooperative effort. Katz and Eisenstadt infer from their secondary analysis that dependence of officials on their subordinates promotes debureaucratization, and that this principle applies to dependence on clients as well as on subordinates in an organization. They further extend this principle by following a lead of Parsons and including in the concept of dependence not only the fact that a client or subordinate has the power to influence the life-chances of an official but also the mere fact that the former is capable of disrupting the role performance of the latter.[23]

Data to illustrate this conclusion are gathered by Katz and Eisenstadt in their study of the contacts between immigrants and bureaucrats in Israel. Official-client relations depend on the abilities of both parties properly to perform their roles. Since immigrants who came to Israel from non-Western countries typically did not know what was expected of a bureaucratic client, their inability to act appropriately in this role disturbed the official-client relationship. For example, immigrants sometimes tried to bargain with the bus driver over the amount of the fare or to debate the route the bus was to travel. In such situations, an official was obliged to teach his clients how to play their role before he could properly perform his. Again, the public-health nurse had to teach her prospective clients which of their problems she could deal with and which ones were outside her sphere of competence. But the diffuse relations with clients that developed as officials assumed the role of teacher and counselor tended to impinge on their specific roles as representatives of a given bureaucracy. It led to debureaucratization and occasionally to entirely new role relationships independent of the initial bureaucratic ones. Some of the instructors sent by the government to immigrant villages, for instance, came to assume boundary roles mediating between the government and "their" village and, in the extreme case, turned into representatives of the immigrant group or even into leaders of movements furthering this group's interest.

The hypothesis that the dependence of officials on clients (or subor-

---

23. Parsons notes that although the parents have power over the life-chances of the child, they are also dependent on the child, because he or she is capable of disrupting the family system. See Talcott Parsons and Robert F. Bales, *Family Socialization and Interaction Process,* Glencoe, Ill.: Free Press, 1955, pp. 46–17, footnote 18.

dinates) lessens the degree of bureaucratization can be tested with data from County Agency previously presented in another connection. It will be recalled that in our comparison of the Public Assistance Division and the Child Welfare Division of County Agency it was noted that the clients of the latter were not only children but also foster parents, on whose cooperation operations in CWD were dependent, while there was much less dependence on the recipients of public assistance in PAD. The prediction is, therefore, that CWD should be less bureaucratized than PAD. The findings support this conclusion. Thus, caseloads were smaller in CWD, and there was more opportunity for casework in this division. Assignment of cases were less bureaucratic in CWD— not by geographic area, as in PAD, but by matching the severity of the problem with the experience of the worker. Since no case reassignments were necessary in CWD when the client changed residence, worker-client relations were more stable and workers were not considered to be interchangeable. Finally, the feelings of the client about the race of the worker were taken into account in CWD but not in PAD. (Note that lack of bureaucratization, even if in the interest of giving professional considerations wider scope, opens the door to racial discrimination.) These differences conform to the prediction. With only two cases, however, one cannot say with confidence whether these differences in bureaucratization actually were the result of the greater dependence of CWD on clients or were due to other conditions, such as the fact that CWD served children or that it had legal responsibility for their care.

Diamond presents an extreme case of debureaucratization in his discussion of an organization that became a society.[24] The Virginia Company was established in 1607 as a business concern to exploit the riches of a new continent and the labors of native peoples, Virginia, however, provided conditions different from those that had been faced by similar companies in India, Mexico, and Peru. Native labor refused to be mobilized, and mineral wealth was not to be found. Hence, it proved necessary to establish an agricultural community based on imported labor, and the company had to devote its efforts to recruiting the necessary voluntary labor from England. After these laborers had arrived, they were subjected to strict discipline enforced by a military regime and by religious sanctions. However, not enough men responded to the call, and the Company was forced to offer more and more concessions to serve as inducements for migrating. The terms under which the laborers could obtain land were eased, women were sent to Virginia to become the wives of the settlers, and martial law was

24. Sigmund Diamond, "From Organization to Society," *The American Journal of Sociology,* 63 (1958), pp. 457–475.

gradually limited as representatives of the settlers were given some voice in government. As a consequence of these changes settlers became involved in a complex network of statuses, many of them outside the organization of the Virginia Company.

> At one time in Virginia, the single relationship that existed between persons rested upon the positions they occupied in the Company's table of organization. As a result of the efforts made by the Company to get persons to accept that relationship, however, each person in Virginia had become the occupant of several statuses, for now there were rich and poor in Virginia, landowners and renters, masters and servants, old residents and newcomers, married and single, men and women; and the simultaneous possession of these statuses involved the holder in a network of relationships, some congruent and some incompatible, with his organizational relationship.[25]

Gradually, settlers felt that their statuses outside the Company were the more important, and they were no longer willing to accept organization position as the primary basis of legitimate authority. Thus, a society emerged where before there had been only a formal organization, a transformation that constitutes the polar case of debureaucratization.

25. *Ibid.*, p. 471.

14

DOMAIN CONSENSUS
A Key Variable in Interorganizational Analysis

Rita Braito, Steve Paulson, Gerald Klonglon*

The general purpose of this paper is to investigate the concept of domain consensus. The first objective will be to review the definition of domain consensus and the frameworks within which it has been discussed and to review the concepts which have been related to do-

*The work upon which this publication is based was performed persuant to Contract Number PH86-68-129 with the U.S. Public Health Service, Department of Health, Education and Welfare and was conducted by the Iowa Agricultural and Home Economics Experiment Station (Project 1703), Department of Sociology and Anthropology, Iowa State University of Science and Technology, Ames, Iowa.

The conclusions are those of the authors and should not be construed as representing the policy of any agency of the U.S. Government or of the Iowa Agricultural and Home Economics Experiment Station.

main consensus, i.e., variables which have been helpful in understanding and predicting domain consensus. The second objective will be to empirically investigate the relationships between domain consensus and selected variables which have been associated with the study of complex organizations in general and interorganizational relationships in particular. This will be done utilizing state level health related organizations which have national as well as intrastate components. The area of domain and domain consensus which will be investigated is in the participation and creation of an agency to deal with problems associated with smoking and health.

INTERORGANIZATIONAL ANALYSIS

During the decade of the sixties there has been an increasing interest in the behavior of organizations. The developing body of theoretical and empirical literature has not merely emphasized the structural bureaucratic perspective, as has traditionally been the case, but has focused upon the organization and its environment. Evan discussed the organization and organization set as analogous to role set.[1] The perspectives with which to view organizations *vis à vis* other organizations (as well as the environment in general) have proliferated since these early contributions.[2] It appears to us that any discussion of interorganizational analysis, either explicitly or implicitly, deals with the concepts of domain and domain consensus. We studied organizations as to their willingness to participate in the formation of an agency concerned with smoking and health (domain), and their endorsement as to whether other organizations should participate (domain consensus).

DOMAIN CONSENSUS AS BASIC TO AN EXCHANGE FRAMEWORK

Levine and White suggest organizations could be viewed within an exchange framework, in which organizational exchange is viewed as "any voluntary activity between organizations which has consequences, actual or anticipated for the realization of their respective goals or objectives and that exchange is contingent upon prior domain consensus."[3] Levine and White and Paul define domain of an organiza-

---

1. William M. Evan, "The Organization-Set: Toward a Theory of Interorganizational Relations," in James D. Thompson (ed.), *Approaches to Organizational Design*, Pittsburgh, Pennsylvania: University of Pittsburgh Press, 1966, pp. 173–191.

2. See for example: Shirley Terryberry, "The Evolution of Organizational Environments," *Administrative Quarterly*, 12, (1968), pp. 590–613; Charles Perrow, "A Framework for the Comparative Analysis of Organizations," *American Sociological Review*, 32, (1967), pp. 194–208; Ephraim Yuctman and Stanley E. Seashore, "A System Resource Approach to Organizational Effectiveness," *American Sociological Review*, 32, (1967), pp. 891–903; and James D. Thompson, *Organizations in Action*, New York: McGraw Hill, 1967.

3. Sol Levine and Paul E. White, "Exchange as a Conceptual Framework for the Study of Interorganizational Relationships," *Administrative Science Quarterly*, 4, (1961), pp. 588.

tion as "the specific goals it wishes to pursue and the functions it seeks to undertake in order to achieve these goals."[4]

Our indicator of domain is a statement of whether or not an organization should engage in the creation of an agency to deal with problems of smoking and health. We have also ascertained what activities the organization is currently engaging in relative to the smoking and health phenomena. In addition, we have determined what "contributions"— resources, people, etc., the organization is willing to allocate to such an agency if created. In this respect we have, at least as it relates to a particular program, operationalized the phenomenon which appears to have high face validity with the definition provided by Levine, White and Paul. Within the health field, Levine and White defined the domain as "diseases covered, population served, and services rendered."[5] Thompson suggests "with appropriate modifications in the specifics of the definition—for example, substituting "range of products" for "diseases covered"—the concept of domain appears useful for the analysis of all types of complex organizations."[6] However, as Thompson points out, domain establishment cannot be arbitrary.[7] It is dependent upon recognition by those who provide necessary support in the task environment. The organization in the process of establishing its domain must offer something desirable, thereby getting involved in the exchange process. Since organizations require inputs in order to survive, the concept of domain consensus not only influences the ability of an organization to establish itself, but also to maintain itself.

The question as to whether an organization requires domain consensus is contingent upon the purpose of an organization. A secret society, for example, requires only legitimation from its members. Therefore, we do not think domain consensus is essential for organizational establishment. To the degree that the organization is dependent upon designation of input related to its goals, it enters into the exchange process and domain consensus occurs. Seeking domain consensus may be pursued as along a continuum. The degree of domain consensus required would also be contingent upon dependency on the environment which is partly a reflection of the power of the organization itself as well as that of other organizations with which it "must interact."

Domain consensus between two agencies according to Levine, White, and Paul refers to the "degree to which they agree and accept each other's claims with regard to problem or diseases covered, services offered, and population served."[8] Thompson has defined domain con-

4. Sol Levine, Paul E. White and Benjamin D. Paul, "Community Interorganizational Problems in Providing Medical Care and Social Services," *American Journal of Public Health*, 53, (1963), pp. 1191.
5. Sol Levine and Paul E. White, *op. cit.*, p. 597.
6. James D. Thompson, *op. cit.*, p. 26.
7. *Ibid.*
8. Sol Levine, Paul E. White and Benjamin D. Paul, *op. cit.*, p. 1191.

sensus as a "set of expectations, both for members of an organization and for others with whom they interact, about what the organization will and will not do . . . it provides an image of the organization's role in a larger system, which in turn serves as a guide for the ordering of action in certain directions and not in others."[9] We operationalized domain consensus as an organization's statement as to whether or not a particular organization should be involved in an agency formed for reduction of the incidence of cigarette smoking. Our indicator represents one part of the concept as defined above. Thompson suggests that the establishment of a viable domain is a political problem.[10] As such, it can be seen that domain consensus may be both sought by an organization and granted by others. We have already commented on the fact that the seeking of it is on a continuum. The granting of it may also be conceived as on a continuum.

DOMAIN CONSENSUS WITHIN A DECISION MAKING FRAMEWORK

Warren suggests domain is a key variable in decision-making. He conceptualizes it as the "organization's locus in the interorganizational network," including access to necessary resources, and "right" to operate in a given geographical area.[11] He feels that his definition is broader than Thompson's definition as it includes the elements necessary for an organization to maintain itself in an environment. He relates, in propositional form, domains and organizational interaction with domain preservation and domain expansion. Viewed in this context, domain, by including "risk," appears to include both domain and domain consensus as used by Thompson. An organization may have a right and perhaps, if the organization is to survive, "need" to legitimate itself in the process of establishing a domain. As suggested earlier, the organization's actual legitimation is a function of other organizations. Warren, in his paper, is extending the definition of domain but appears to be leaving domain consensus, as defined by Thompson, unchanged.

DOMAIN AND DOMAIN CONSENSUS AS ASSOCIATED WITH STABILITY AND CHANGE IN AN ORGANIZATION

To the degree that domain and domain consensus are involved in exchange relationships between organizations and central to the decision-making framework, they are intimately associated with stability and change of an organization. (This is not to suggest that other factors internal and external to the organization do not influence the organization's stability and change, but rather, that domain and domain consen-

9. James D. Thompson, op. cit., p. 29.
10. Ibid., p. 36.
11. Roland L. Warren, "The Concerting of Decisions as a Variable in Organizational Interaction," Paper prepared for a Conference on Interorganizational Decision Making, Northwestern University, Evanston, Illinois, 1969.

sus are integrally associated with the phenomena.) Thompson and McEwen indicate that some processes by which changes occur are competition, bargaining, co-optation, and coalition.[12] The last three of these are co-operative strategies. Litwak and Hylton, to cite only one example, have taken competition as given in interorganizational analysis. They suggest both co-operation and conflict exist at any given point in time although they may have differential emphasis.[13] This suggests an interesting question, how are domain and domain consensus related to the form and process of interorganizational relationships? From this perspective, one might ask under what conditions would organizations cooperate? Co-operation implicitly suggests some agreement on an organization's domain and the phenomenon of domain consensus as it implies one or all of the following: (1) the sharing of domains, (2) the extension of domains, or (3) the control of domains.

Hollister utilizes data from police youth bureaus and juvenile court to suggest that organizations engage in exchange relationships (interorganizational relationships) because of similarity of functions and legal requirements.[14] In conditions of disagreement on domain consensus less information and fewer cases are exchanged. Hollister further suggests that three factors contribute to domain consensus: (1) ideological differences (disagreements about task performance), (2) low resources (affects resource allocation internal, and external), and (3) indeterminate technologies or "uncertainty in the cause and effect relationships."[15]

Indeterminate technology is a characteristic of the problem we have focused on: "the problem of smoking and health is not amenable to the facile solutions or ready made prescriptions . . . based on evidence it is safe to say that it is no easy matter to encourage large amounts of smokers to amend their health behavior."[16] It is probable that given such an area of ambiguity as indeterminate technology, and the ready availability of funds, organizations would be willing to share and extend their domains. Conversely, if a technology is such that a solution is apparent it is also likely that technology may be associated with a given organization, which if it could handle the problem itself, would not be willing to share its domain.

12. James D. Thompson and William J. McEwen, "Organizational Goals and Environment: Goal Setting as an Interaction Process," *American Sociological Review,* 23, (1958), pp. 23–31.
13. Eugene Litwak and Lydia F. Hylton, "Interorganizational Analysis: A Hypothesis on Coordinating Agencies," in Amitai Etzioni (ed.), *A Sociological Reader on Complex Organizations,* New York: Holt Rinehart and Winston, Inc., 1969, pp. 339–356.
14. David Hollister, "Interorganizational Conflict: The Case of Police Youth Bureaus and the Juvenile Court," A paper presented at the 65th Annual Meeting of the American Sociological Association, 1970.
15. James D. Thompson, *op. cit.,* p. 134.
16. Sol Levine, "Summary and Implications for Future Research," in Edgar F. Borgatta and Robert R. Evans (eds.), *Smoking, Health, and Behavior,* Chicago: Adeline Publishing Company, 1968, pp. 274–281.

In many areas such as health, pollution or crime, social problems in essence, it appears that domains could be claimed by multiple organizations—educational, health, economic, welfare, religious, and political. The greater the magnitude and scope of the problem the more resources needed in the solution. Associate all of these with an indeterminate technology and an arena of uncertainty exists within which all types of organizations may seek to establish domains.

STAKING AND MAINTAINING A CLAIM

An organization's history and its association with a particular problem should increase the possibility of the problem being in an organization's domain. We have obtained data as to the age of the organization as well as smoking and health activities currently engaged in. To the degree that an organization has been associated with the problem, the possibility increases that other organizations will legitimate its claim. On the other hand, simple association of an organization with a problem over time is not sufficient to maintain the domain consensus. The public, other organizations, etc., may become dissatisfied with the progress and technology of a particular organization, question its domain, and withdraw legitimation. For example, civic groups wanting more control over area schools have questioned the legitimation of teacher control as well as that of other functionaries.

Structural properties, internal to organizations, have been associated with their willingness to participate in interorganizational relationships through the establishment of joint programs. This involves the staking of new claims (domains) as well as the extension of claims (domains).

Some of the structural properties that have been identified with interorganizational relationships are complexity, innovativeness, active internal communication structures, and more decentralized decision-making structures.[17] A further hypothesis offered was that the "resources needed to support such innovations required interdependent relations with other organizations."[18] This need for resources has been posited by a number of authors as a basis for forming joint relationships associated with a sharing domain.[19] It appears that no direct assessment of this need has been made. Mott's study casts doubt on the need for resources through interorganizational cooperation as being the basic

---

17. Michael Aiken and Jerald Hage, "Organizational Interdependence and Intraorganizational Structure," *American Sociological Review,* 33, (1968), pp. 912–930.
18. *Ibid.,* p. 928.
19. Sol Levine and Paul E. White, *op. cit.;* Michael Aiken and Jerald Hage, *op. cit.;* Jerald Hage and Michael Aiken, "Program Change and Organizational Properties: A Comparative Analysis." *American Journal of Sociology,* 72, (1967), pp. 503–519; Roland L. Warren, "The Interorganizational Field as a Focus for Investigation," *Administrative Science Quarterly,* 12, (1967), pp. 396–419; Eugene Litwak and Lydia F. Hylton, *op. cit.;* and David C. Hollister, *op. cit.*

explanation for formation of councils, joint operations, or formation of new agencies.[20]

Mott identifies factors, internal and external to a council, which influence the co-operation of members of a council. The external factors are: (1) outside power groups—vested interest groups, the governor and (2) availability of federal funds. Factors internal to the organization are: (1) limited segments of the agencies total health responsibilities are involved (on the periphery of domain), and (2) special populations are involved which comprise the most difficult groups to help, and programs for them are less well developed in other areas, perhaps related to indeterminate technology. The reasons are that among the most difficult groups, agencies' responsibilities are less clear and programs for these difficult groups are less developed than in other areas. Another way of expressing this is that no consensus on domain as yet existed.

A constraint to the cooperation of organizations according to Hilleboe is: "an agency and his staff are unable to engage in cooperative endeavors with other organizations that threaten the agency's future and its capacity to meet the public needs to which its members and supporters are committed. Every public agency necessarily adopts a view of the public interest that reconciles its organizational needs with the needs of those it serves."[21] Friedman, Klein, and John also report that in general, public officials perceive their agencies as serving particular groups as opposed to the general public.[22] As it related to the staking and maintaining of a claim, it appears that there are both facilitative and constraining factors.

SUMMARY

Domain and domain consensus have been shown to be either implicit or explicit in various approaches to interorganizational analysis and appear useful in the understanding of processes associated with organizational stability and change. Variables internal and external to the organization which are facilitative and constraining as it relates to the establishment, extension and maintenance of a domain have been briefly referred to. An attempt has also been made to broaden the current perspective within which research related to interorganizational analysis could proceed. The general objective of this section has been a discussion of the concept of domain consensus. The objective of the second part of this article is an examination of the empirical relationship of domain consensus with other selected variables.

20. Basil J. F. Mott, *Anatomy of a Coordinating Council: Implications for Planning,* University of Pittsburg Press, 1968, p. 183.

21. Herman E. Hilleboe, "Preface," in Basil J. Mott (ed.), *Anatomy of a Coordinating Council,* University of Pittsburg Press, 1968, p. XXVII.

22. Robert S. Friedman, Bernard W. Klein, and John Romani, "Administrative Agencies and the Publics they Serve," *Public Administration Review,* 27, (1966), pp. 192–204.

SPECIFICATION OF THE RESEARCH PROBLEM

An assumption underlying the research to be presented was: An organization may be highly committed (self definition of domain) to the reduction of a specific problem, but unless they receive support from other organizations in their environment (domain consensus), they will have little success in working with other organizations in this problem area.[23]

Since the relationships to be discussed (in this article) have not been derived from a more general perspective, we have not explicitly stated them as hypotheses. Knowledge of the results, from the larger project, in which more levels of the organization as well as many other issues, theoretical and empirical, were present may have influenced our perception of what to expect. Because of the literature reviewed, and presented, we expect the following to be related to high domain consensus: (1) domain, (2) resource allocation, (3) activities, (4) resource level, and (5) age.

Since the problem is related to willingness to participate in a new program for smoking and health, three variables which are somewhat similar to those used by Aiken and Hage also seemed appropriate to explore within this context: (1) complexity, (2) formalization, and (3) occupational composition (broad composition).

Variables which are presented herein which have not been dealt with by others relate to the question, "Do organizations which endorse themselves endorse others more or less, and how is this related to domain consensus?" "Is willingness to participate in a program contingent upon organizational prerogatives and if so, what types?" The variables are: (1) endorsements given and (2) organizational prerogatives. Size as a variable is included because it has been shown to be related to organizational structure in a number of different studies.[24]

THE ORGANIZATIONAL SAMPLE AND DATA COLLECTION

The sample consists of 33 state level health organizations. The individual who occupied the highest administrative position in each organization was interviewed. Four types of organizations are included: (1) voluntary organizations which receive funds from private sources such as contributions and bequests (2) public organizations which receive funds from public tax revenue sources (3) professional organizations whose funds usually come in the form of dues from professionals

---

23. The particular research from which the data for this study were derived was concerned with the feasibility of coordination of health-related organizations to become active in reducing the incidence of cigarette smoking.

24. See for example: Richard Hall, J. E. Haas, and N. J. Johnson, "Organizational Size, Complexity, and Formalization," *American Sociological Review*, 32, (1967), pp. 903–911, and Michael Aiken and Jerald Hage, *op. cit.*

in specific fields and (4) interagency organizations which are funded by contributions from member organizations in the form of dues or assessments. This categorization is in terms of source of funds. The second general characteristic of the organizations selected is that they are federated. The chief characteristic of this type of organization is the existence of "parent bodies" and affiliation of local or state units within these. These types of organizations were chosen based on the assumption that for the concept of domain consensus, the organization's state level is the crucial level, for it is at this level that the major policy and program decisions are made. Furthermore, such a selection allows for an analysis across the nation of similar organizations. There are 9 voluntary, 7 public, 11 professional, and 6 interagency organizations represented in our sample.

MEASUREMENT OF THE CONCEPT OF DOMAIN CONSENSUS—DEPENDENT VARIABLE

The measure of domain consensus consists of one question as given here.

> If a new interorganizational program designed to reduce cigarette smoking was to be instigated in this state which organizations do you think *should* be involved in it?

The respondent was given a list of 33 organizations, which included his own, and asked to consider each of them in terms of the above question using the following responses: (1) definitely should not, (2) probably should not, (3) not sure, (4) probably should and (5) definitely should.

From these responses a domain consensus score was obtained by giving an organization one point every time it was indicated by other organizations as probably (4) or definitely should (5). Since each organization was evaluated by 32 administrators, the highest possible score (high domain consensus) was 32 and the lowest possible score was 0. The *actual* distribution of scores was 9 to 32 with a median of 27.

There are two considerations which should be noted in terms of this measure of domain consensus as it may *appear* to differ from theoretical implications discussed above.

(1) The concern is not with respect to an entire domain of an organization, rather it is related to a specific domain in a particular problem area, namely smoking and health.

(2) Consensus is not limited to general agreement on domain, but includes a *value orientation* in terms of positive consensus, where our "high" domain consensus is high agreement *and* high normative ranking of the organization re "should be" involved, and negative consensus where "low" domain is also high agreement but low normative ranking of the organization re "should be" involved.

Such an explication of this concept allows, we feel, a more realistic application of the findings for specific problem areas such as the health problem of cigarette smoking yet retains a necessary linkage to theory.

MEASUREMENT OF INDEPENDENT VARIABLES

In this section we will nominally and operationally define key independent variables of this research which will be examined to determine how they relate to the dependent variable of domain consensus. Note that the first two variables used the domain consensus question for their measurements.

(1) "Organizational domain" is defined as an organization's claim to a range of products, populations served and services rendered.[25] The measure consisted of the organization's response *about itself* to the question given above under domain consensus. The actual and possible range of responses are, thus a five point continuum of definitely should not (1) to definitely should (5).

(2) "Endorsements given" is defined as the extent to which an organization legitimates others as to others' involvement in a given problem area. This concept was measured by summing the number of other organizations endorsed by an organization (32 possible) in responding to the domain consensus question. By "endorsed" we mean the administrator responded that another organization "probably" or "definitely" should be involved. The possible range of this score, then, is 0 (no endorsements) to 32 (many endorsements), while the actual range was 4 to 32.

(3) "Resource allocation" is defined as the willingness to contribute various types of resources. The question and response framework used to measure this concept was as follows: "To what extent would you be willing to contribute each of the following resources to an interorganizational program in smoking and health: funds, administrator time, staff time, facilities, materials, endorsements." Responses: 5 = definitely would; 4 = probably would; 3 = not sure; 2 = probably would not; 1 = definitely would not. The resource allocation score was the average response given to all items resulting in a range of 1 – 5.

(4) "Organizational activities"—particular functions to which an organization allocates elements it controls. Eleven activities[26] were presented and the respondent was asked if his organization conducted such activities. The "activity score" is the sum, for each organization, of the number of activities involved in. The possible range is 0 to 11, while the actual range was 0 to 9.

(5) "Board composition" is defined as the occupational representation of board members of an organization. The measure of this concept

---

25. James D. Thompson, *op. cit.*, p. 26.
26. These are found in Table 2.

consisted of the total number of "health providers" (M.D.'s, nurses, etc.) on the board of directors. The actual range is 0 to 27.

(6) "Organizational prerogatives" are defined as preconditions for participation. In this study, participation was limited to smoking and health activities.[27] A summing score was arrived at by counting, for each organization, the number of these preconditions it felt was necessary for its involvement. The possible and actual range is 0 – 5.

(7) "Resource levels" refers to the quantity of inputs an organization owns at a given point and time. Only one resource, funds, was considered for this study and was measured by categories of amounts of annual expenditures. The categories were 0; $1 – 599; 600 – 4,999; 5,000 – 20,999; 21,000 – 99,999; 100,000 – 799,999; 800,000 and over. All categories were used.

(8) "Organization size" is defined as the total number of personnel involved in carrying out the organization's responsibilities. The actual number is used as a measure of this concept and ranged from 8 – 99.

(9) "Organization age" is defined as the number of years an organization has been in existence and was measured by recording the actual number of years, and ranges from 1 to 68.

(10) "Organizational complexity" is defined as " . . . the degree of internal segmentation—the number of separate parts of the organization as reflected by the division of labor, number of hierarchical levels and the spatial dispersion of the organization."[28] The measure of this concept consisted of recording, for each organization, the number of paid assistant *positions* in the organization. Such a measure, we feel, reflects the organizational horizontal division of labor. The actual range is from 0 to 20.

(11) "Organizational formalization" is defined by Aiken and Hage as " . . . degree of work standardization and derivation allowed from these standards."[29] The measure of organizational formalization consists of one question with a five point response category: How often do you (the organizational administrator) refer to written documents to carry out your duties (1 = never, 2 = seldom, 3 = occasionally, 4 = usually, 5 = always)? All categories are used.

FINDINGS

In this section we will discuss variable relationships among the data from two perspectives: (1) the inspection of correlation values and (2) selected descriptive cross-tabulations.

27. These are found in Table 3.
28. Richard Hall, J. E. Haas, and N. J. Johnson, *op. cit.,* p. 906.
29. Michael Aiken and Jerald Hage, *op. cit.,* p. 912.

CORRELATIONAL ANALYSIS

A matrix showing correlation values among the variables given above is found in Table 1. The 90% level of confidence was selected rather than the usual 95 or 99 because of the exploratory nature of the research; that is, at this point we would rather retain variables of marginal statistical significance until one can learn more about them.

At this level six of the eleven independent variables are significantly related to domain consensus. These include resource allocation, board composition, activities, domain, age, and formalization. Note that only the last two of these, age and formalization, were measured totally irrespective of the problem area of smoking and health. The other four are measured in terms of some dimension of an organization's involvement in the health problem area. This would suggest that high or low domain consensus is not necessarily a characteristic of particular organizational structures but is, primarily, a function of the organization's domain or claims to problem areas which it sets out for itself. This point becomes even more apparent upon inspection of the independent variables which are *not* related to domain consensus; complexity, size, resource levels, endorsements given, and prerogatives. That is, domain consensus is not related to general organizational characteristics or variables (endorsements and prerogatives) indicative of an organization's concern about other organization's activity in smoking and health. Domain consensus, then, as we have defined it, appears to be a function of an organization's domain rather than structural organizational characteristics. It is also important to note that the level of resources indicative of resources an organization has rather than need is not related. Based on the literature we had expected a relationship. It appears that concern with a problem (resource allocation) and activities engaged in (related to a particular problem) are the best predictors of domain consensus. Although the age of the organization is related, a better measure might be length of time an organization has been associated with a particular problem.

Domain is related to resource allocation and endorsements. This suggests that an organization which is involved with a given problem is also more apt to endorse others as "should" be involved. This suggests a willingness to share domain. This is not necessarily an indication that indeterminate technology is in any way, related to willingness to share a problem or nature of the problem or magnitude *per se*. It could be inferred that these variables contribute to willingness to share. Domain is also related to a third variable, activities, which some might argue is one measure of domain. It is interesting to note that, given this as an assumption, the magnitude of the relationship is not great.

Among the independent variables only eleven 2-variable relationships are found significant:

TABLE 1

Correlation Values for Relationships Among Organizational Variables

	Domain Consensus	Domain	Endorsements Given	Resource Allocation	Activities	Board Composition	Prerogatives	Resource Levels	Size	Age	Complexity	Formalization
Domain consensus	1.000	.375*	−.049	.571*	.533*	.359*	−.229	−.104	−.013	.308*	−.007	.331*
Domain		1.000	.310*	.523*	.351*	.179	.039	−.242	−.100	.129	−.223	.064
Endorsements given			1.000	.031	−.056	−.246	.051	−.308*	−.148	−.119	−.205	−.192
Resource allocation				1.000	.377*	.195	−.285	−.079	−.027	.159	.001	.200
Activities					1.000	.066	−.324*	−.102	−.147	.154	−.124	−.033
Board composition						1.000	.030	.006	.281	.116	.006	.225
Prerogatives							1.000	−.040	.034	−.145	−.153	.293
Resource levels								1.000	.637*	.170	.667*	.142
Size									1.000	.020	.528*	.308*
Age										1.000	−.077	.341*
Complexity											1.000	.000
Formalization												1.000

* = Significant at .900 level of confidence.

With 30 degrees of freedom: r of .296 significant at .900 level of confidence
r of .349 significant at .950 level of confidence
r of .448 significant at .990 level of confidence
r of .554 significant at .999 level of confidence

188

  (1)   Age and formalization
  (2)   Size and complexity
  (3)   Resource Level and complexity
  (4)   Resource level and size
  (5)   Formalization and size
  (6)   Activities and resource allocation
  (7)   Activities and prerogatives
  (8)   Activities and domain
  (9)   Endorsements given and domain
(10)   Resource allocation and domain
(11)   Resource level and endorsements given

     The reader will notice that the first five relationships are among general structural variables and the second five (6 through 10) are among problem (smoking and health) related variables. Only one significant relationship between structural variables and problem (smoking and health related) variables is found. This relationship is the last one listed above (11) and is negative where the others are positive; that is, the higher the resource level (expenditures) the less the willingness to extend endorsements to other organizations in the area of smoking and health. The negative relationship between resource level and endorsements given might reflect the desire, and perhaps ability, of the organization to control its domain. The fact that resource level is related to size would tend to support this interpretation.

     Notwithstanding the above exception, there is little relationship between organizational structural characteristics and the specific problem area. The general lack of relationship between the organizational characteristics and "problem" oriented variables support the contention that problem makes a difference as it relates to willingness to extend domains and innovativeness. Aiken and Hage have illustrated that particular organizational characteristics are related to a willingness to form and participate in new joint programs not necessarily related to a particular program.[30] Our findings suggest that the problematic nature of the joint program makes a difference.

CROSS-TABULATIONAL ANALYSIS

     The major concern of this section is to present and discuss the findings in terms of the multiple item measures of organizational activities and organizational prerogatives. For the correlational analysis given above, only summary scores for these concepts are used as described in the measurement section.

     Table 2 is a three-way cross-classification of: (1) specific activities, (2) the number of organizations (N = 33) responding "yes" or "no" to

30. *Ibid.*

Table 2

Number of Activities by Domain Consensus

| | Domain Consensus | | | |
| | Low | | High | |
Anti-Smoking Activities	No	Yes	No	Yes
Anti-smoking school programs	15	0	12	6
Promotion of TV and radio advertising advertisements	14	1	13	5
Sponsor smoking and health education for health professions	15	0	11	7
Sponsor smoking and health speakers	15	0	12	6
Sponsor smoking and health exhibits at public meetings	17	1	12	6
Provide information about nonsmoking substitutes for cigarettes	15	0	16	2
Provide individual counseling to problem smokers	15	0	16	2
Provide group withdrawal sessions	15	0	16	2
Conduct research to determine the effects of smoking	15	0	16	2
Conduct research to develop a less harmful cigarette	15	0	17	1
Apply pressure to change laws about smoking	15	0	13	5

the items and (3) "high" (above median) or "low" (below median) domain consensus score of the organization. Note that, generally, the activity of the organizations in smoking and health is very low (very few "yes" responses) but that those organizations with "high" domain consensus are slightly more likely to be active than those with "low" domain consensus.

Table 3 is also a three-way cross-classification consisting of: (1) specific prerogatives, (2) the number of organizations responding "yes" or "no" to the items and (3) "high" (above median) or "low" (below median) domain consensus score of the organization. In an overall sense there seems to be no clear trend of responses, rather the distinctions are by specific items. The distribution of item 3 suggests that knowledge of similarity of goal is important regardless of domain consensus level.

Table 3

Number of Organizational Prerogatives by Domain Consensus

| | Domain Consensus | | | |
| | Low | | High | |
Organizational Prerogatives	No	Yes	No	Yes
Assurance that your organization has clear administrative responsibility	14	1	13	5
Assurance that your organization has clear specific responsibility	7	8	6	12
Knowledge that the program goals are similar to those of your organization	5	10	3	15
Assurance that public recognition will be distributed among the organizations involved	1	14	12	6
Detailed knowledge of costs involved	11	4	6	12

Conversely the distribution of item 1 suggests that with regard to administrative responsibilities, organizations have very little concern with control regardless of domain consensus level. Two other distinctions are in terms of the last two items where: (1) public recognition is much more important among the organizations with low domain consensus than those with high domain consensus and (2) knowledge of costs appears to be more important for those with "high" domain consensus than those with "low" domain consensus.

CONCLUSION

This research was undertaken to learn something about the phenomena of domain and domain consensus. The literature review and our findings suggest an understanding of interorganizational relations is enhanced by consideration of these two variables. They account for over one-half of the statistically significant relationships in our correlation matrix. Domain consensus is more important than domain. The problem (smoking and health) rather than structural characteristics of organizations is more predictive of willingness to engage in co-operative interorganizational relations.

Organizations which have high domain consensus are those which are participating in activities related to smoking and health. The majority of organizations we studied do not participate in such activities which suggests activities are not as important as would be expected.

At a more general level organizational prerogatives as a precondition to exchange appears to be important. Our data limits us to smoking and health. The importance of similarity of goals as a condition of organizational exchange is required by twenty-five out of thirty-three organizations. Conversely, twenty-seven out of thirty-three organizations suggest that the assurance of clear administrative responsibility is not important. This latter variable then is not a precondition of or relevant to interorganizational exchange. The nature of the problem influenced the organizational prerogatives selected. For example, we did not include profit or assurance of success. This leaves us with questions: What are the basic preconditions to organizational exchange regardless of nature of problem or type of organizations?

Much of the past research in the area of interorganizational relations has been done in the (crime-health-welfare) problem arena. Our research has also been limited in this respect. Such research is usually concerned with areas defined as broad social problems and is associated with an indeterminate technology. There is a need to extend our research endeavors into areas in which technology is determinate, the scope is limited, and a variety of relationships, other than cooperative, are central to the investigation. Such research would allow for examination of interorganizational theory, irrespective of particular problem areas. This would allow for conclusions such as reached in this research to be further evaluated for their general applicability to the study of interorganizational relations.

CHAPTER FOUR

ORGANIZATIONAL CONTROL

Just as societies must maintain and regulate individual behavior, complex organizations must also employ control mechanisms. While socialization is important as a control device, the selections below tend to minimize this process. Rather, the focus of this book is directed toward structural controls. That is, organizational control is accomplished through various types of structured activities or relationships. The hierarchy of authority, specialization, and standardization of procedures are but a few of the structural elements which enhance organizational control.

Since complex organizations exist in a larger environment, they constantly encounter contingencies. Contingencies refer to the crises, emergencies, and disruptions which are endemic to all organizations. Some are internal, others external to the organization. Organizations must cope with these contingencies. Open systems-models of organization provide for the analyses of such contingencies.

Conflict, Scott maintains, is one type of contingency which is always present in organizations. This is generally institutionalized to insure organizational stability. This selection, from his larger study, examines four administrative alternatives: (1) authoritarian, (2) legalistic (internal), (3) legalistic (external), and (4) democratic. For each of these he discusses the objectives, judicial settlement standards, and sources of these standards. He concludes that formal appeal systems are often overlooked in favor of an informal system.

Control cannot be understood in its fullest sense without taking

193

into account the development through time and the impact of historical influences. Bordua and Reiss examine the police bureaucracy in terms of its historical development and change. They discuss some of the factors which tend to mitigate the personal charisma and influences of the police chief, such as the centralized communications system, due process of law, etc. The article examines selected ways in which bureaucratization of the police has served to commit police to the occupational organization, to an occupational community, and to norms of subordination and service.

Studies of organizational control have traditionally emphasized either structural considerations or supervisory patterns. The study by Rosengren attempts to relate these two variables by utilization of data obtained from eighty large governmental hospitals and fifty-two small private hospitals. The data lead Rosengren to conclude that maximum structural control tends to be associated with a limited employee control, whereas minimal structural control is related to more pervasive employee control. Rosengren discusses his findings using a Weberian model, and then he contrasts these with selected non-Weberian models.

The selection by Marcus and Marcus represents an attempt to combine findings from numerous studies, which were primarily conducted for other reasons, in order to examine organizational control. They utilize the tremendous depository of research at the Survey Research Center at the University of Michigan for secondary analysis. They conclude that the more *total control* within an organization (that is, the more the control is spread throughout the organization at various levels) the higher the morale, organizational effectiveness, and consensus regarding work. Where control tends to be maintained at the upper levels of the hierarchy, morale, organizational effectiveness, and work consensus tend to be lower. They found that dissatisfactions with organizational control tend to manifest themselves in higher turnover and absentee rates and in lower efficiency and production.

—————————————— **15** ——————————————

THE MANAGEMENT OF CONFLICT
Appeal Systems in Organizations

William G. Scott

CRY HARO

Adolf Berle in his book, *The 20th Century Capitalist Revolution,*[1] tells of the feudal practice allowing aggrieved people to approach the lord or king with the cry of "haro" which signified they were seeking redress of a wrong. These appeals were to the benevolence of the king's conscience because all other avenues for justice had been exhausted. Berle finds a similarity between appeals invoking the conscience of the king and appeals to the conscience of the corporation. But the problem, as he sees it, is that the rights and mechanisms necessary in calling upon the judicial conscience of the corporation are not well defined or firmly established. This does not mean that ways of resolving conflicts do not exist.

Conflicts of many descriptions, actual or potential, are present in organizations. Most of these conflicts are institutionalized to insure organizational stability. Regularized means are evolved to settle conflicts, or direct them into harmless channels, or to use them as constructive forces. Practically it makes little difference whether the means are formal or informal as long as conflicts are resolved before they erode the organization. Regularization does not imply administrative formalization. Evan has shown, for example, ". . . that a very high proportion of the respondents in the industrial laboratory—which does not have a formal appeal system—perceives a due process norm to be institutionalized and have internalized such a norm. This points to the functioning of an informal appeal system."[2]

Thus, in many organizations the cry of haro may be directed with ease and informality to key executives who act in the role of arbitrator in resolving conflicts among subordinates. But as the determinants of size and mobility are felt, informal conflict resolution is often paralleled by formalized procedures which serve similar ends. Formal systems of appeal may never fully supplant informal methods for settling complaints and ameliorating conflicts. However, the forces of bureaucrati-

1. A. A. Berle, Jr., *The 20th Century Capitalist Revolution* (New York: Harcourt, Brace and Company, 1954), chap. 3.
2. William M. Evan, "Due Process of Law in a Government and an Industrial Research Organization," *Proceedings of the Academy of Management,* 1965, p. 115.

zation which produce programs of procedural due process will cause administrators to reflect more carefully on their judicial function. This function has been subordinated in emphasis to the legislative (policy-making) and executive (action-evoking) in organizations, particularly business firms. The appeal systems which we have analyzed are formalized means through which the modern participant in a bureaucratic organization can "cry haro" if he feels his rights are jeopardized.

So just as the cry of haro, as an institutionalized system for the redress of grievances, was a restraint on the absolute power of the feudal ruler, so also are systems of appeal restraints on the power of administrators. However, it is indeed naive not to recognize that the amount of restraint depends entirely upon the judicial standards used by managers, where these standards come from, and the extent to which the executive and legislative functions of administration are separated from the judicial function.

While the process of bureaucratization may be the determinant of the formalization of appeal practices, it is *not* the determinant of the philosophy or spirit in which the system is administered. The goals of the system and the judicial standards which are used for appeal settlement may differ from organization to organization. The differences are attributable to the choices of the policy makers themselves. What these alternatives are is considered next.

THE JUDICIAL GOALS AND STANDARDS OF APPEAL SYSTEMS

Appeal systems are not inherently democratic or authoritarian. As products of an amoral *process*—formalization—they serve either philosophy, or some intermediate ones, equally well. The tone and spirit in which the system is administered depends on the philosophy of the executives in each organization. The philosophical alternatives upon which the administration of formal appeal systems can be based is shown in Figure 1.[3]

Before we take a closer look at each alternative, the reader is reminded that most appeal programs are anticipated to contribute to the effectiveness and efficiency goals which are essential in the cooperative system. This is true even though administrators may differ on appeal philosophy.

AUTHORITARIAN

While the major character of formal organizations is hierarchy, there are many, including those in high positions of authority, who feel that leadership must be benevolent. By formalizing the appeal process,

3. An approach suggested by Walter E. Oberer, "Union Democracy and the Rule of Law," *Democracy and Public Review* (New York: The fund for the Republic, 1960).

the authoritarian objective of benevolence is underscored. We might call it formalizing the access to the "conscience of the organization." Anyway, the right to formal redress is at least a modest restraint on arbitrary and unjust use of authority.

The authoritarian alternative would admit settlement of cases upon judicial standards which are derived internally from the organization's value system. That is, the "legitimate" criteria used in settling cases conform to organizational standards primarily, *although these criteria may not be uniformly applied from case to case by executives involved in the hearings.*

Administrative Alternatives	Objectives	Judicial Settlement Standards	Source of Standards
1. Authoritarian	1. Benevolence and control	1. *Ad hoc* standards of executives hearing cases, consistent with organization's value system	1. Internally derived from organization's value system
2. Legalistic (internal)	2. Uniform and impartial application of organization law	2. Organization policy rules, regulations, and precedents	2. Internally derived from organization's value system but unbiased application assured by outside participant in appeal system
3. Legalistic (external)	3. Dilution of authoritarianism by the regulation of policy legislation and execution	3. Organization values congruent with democratic public legal statutes and precedents	3. Internally derived but with an eye to correspondence with *external* values of a democratic society the enforcement of which in the organization is assured by an outside participant in the appeal system
4. Democratic	4. Equality of satisfactions a. Release from dependence b. Self-determination	4. Liberal, democratic humanitarianism within the framework of a system of organizational due process of law	4. Externally derived from the democratic organizational milieu. Will prevail as long as organizations retain hierarchical authoritarian bias

Figure 1. The Goals and Settlement Standards of Appeal Systems.

This situation must exist in many organizations with appeal programs. Settlement of complaints is based upon interpretations of employee "rights" which frequently either are not formally stated at all or are vaguely represented in handbooks and manuals. In any event, somewhere in the appeal network the "givers of rights" become also the "interpreters of the same rights." This arrangement prevents any serious objection from being raised against organizational values. At the same time, it gives managerial "judges" the chance to bend rules or modify precedents for the sake of benevolence in individual cases.

The authoritarian alternative has another aspect, besides benevolence, which cannot be ignored. Since the policies of an organization are executed by humans, the risk of mistakes, malpractice, injustice, and cheating is present in varying degrees. In view of this, appeal systems may also be correctly considered as control devices. This interpretation takes on added meaning when we reflect on the fact that the aggrieved party most often institutes his appeal action on technical, administrative, or personal grounds against an *agent* of the organization rather than the organization itself.

Control is certainly the point of several business policy statements I read which say that if a manager knows that his subordinates have a legitimate avenue of redress around him he will "watch his step." In other organizations, the control feature of appeal is strengthened by the institution of a control staff function like the military inspector general or the ecclesiastical visitor. It is not a coincidence that official documents in these organizations say that the soldier or the cleric has the *duty* to report administrative injustices or infractions. This statement of duty is calculated to reinforce organizational control through the appeal network.

LEGALISTIC (INTERNAL)

The philosophic foundation of the internal legalistic alternative is found neither in authoritarian benevolence nor in bureaucratic control. Instead this philosophy proposes the rule of law, not men, in organizations. Its goal is to insure that the law of the organization is kept through impartial hearings, objective interpretations, and equitable settlements of complaints. The aim of this philosophy is to insure administrative compliance with the policies which define the rights and govern the organization's affairs with its members.

The standards for judicial actions are derived internally from the organization's value system. In this respect, this alternative differs little from the authoritarian. *The distinction is that the internal legalistic approach seeks consistent and impartial application of organizational law to all organization members.*

The chief difficulty of this approach is implementation. In order for laws and policies to be administered impartially those who hear and decide appeal cases should not be members of the organizational hierarchy. This is probably too extreme to be realistic. So let us amend it and say that at least one decision stage, preferably the last in the appeal procedure, ought to be in the hands of responsible parties having no connection with the executive structure. They should have the power to interpret and enforce the laws and policies as these have evolved in the organization, and yet they must be detached from the hierarchy of the organization.

These provisions are necessary for the internal legalistic approach to work. First, there must be a statutory base provided by a constitution or some other kind of pact as the foundation for membership rights. In a business organization this could be as simple as a manual. Second, a file of decisions reached in all appeal cases at all steps in the procedure must be maintained as precedents for future cases. Neither of these requirements poses a problem. The third does. *It requires outside participation in conflict resolution.*

By opening the appeal procedure to an external uncommitted party in the settlement process, the crucial separation of judicial from other management activities occurs. This is an aspect of the legalistic approach which many policy makers would find hard to accept. Yet the separation of functions in the administration of an appeal network is essential if a modicum of organizational justice is sought. Just two business organizations were encountered in this study which employed this approach. The UAW's Public Review Board is a good example, structurally, of the alternative examined in this section.

LEGALISTIC (EXTERNAL)

This alternative differs in two ways from the internal legalistic.

1. It adopts standards of civil law as guides for those hearing organizational appeal cases. This is where the name external legalistic comes from.

2. It implies outside participation, or veto power, in legislative as well as judicial administrative activities.

The purpose of this alternative is to mold the settlements gained through the appeal procedure into conformance with the legal criteria of the democratic society at large. The dominance of internal authoritarianism is reduced by reference to external standards of legal custom and practice. Thus an appeal may be denied on the grounds of an organization's constitution or other rules of government. But if the section of the constitution or policies upon which the case is based is not consistent with analogous civil statute or precedent, then, under this approach, the rule itself might be invalidated and the appeal sustained.[4]

4. This is a difficult proposal so let us pose a hypothetical case. Suppose an employee objects to having his psyche probed by tests and analyses to determine his promotability within his corporation. Suppose further that his objection is grounded upon his opinion that this personnel policy and practice constitutes an invasion of his privacy. So he files an appeal, saying he should be promoted on, say, the basis of demonstrated competence in prior jobs, seniority, and the additional education he has undertaken to improve his functional expertness. *He feels that the organization invades his right to be let alone* if it goes beyond the objective concrete evidence of tenure and proficiency in establishing his promotability. Assuming the appeal goes the full route through the procedure, which it probably will, then

It is evident that the need for outside participation in the appeal process is as essential in this alternative as it is in the previous.

While this approach most certainly would dilute the authoritarianism of an organization's executive hierarchy, it would also reduce their sovereignty. If a policy is challenged in appeal and found inconsistent with or contrary to civil legal criteria, the law of organization could be overturned. It is doubtful that administrators would be willing to impose this degree of restraint upon their autonomy to legislate.

DEMOCRATIC

This alternative visualizes the objective of appeal as the enhancement of the individual's satisfactions as an organizational participant. Although this goal is implied in the other alternatives, the standards of democratic judgment are the most permissive of all because they propose to reduce individual dependence and extend the opportunity for self-determination.

The judicial criteria to accomplish this do not come entirely from formal organizational values or from public law. Instead the norms are found in the *spirit* of those who are liberal and humanitarian in outlook. Of these some would be selected to participate in the appeal activity, again as members unattached and uncommitted to the organization to which the system is appended.

The democratic alternative is difficult to conceptualize. Yet its aims are not much different from the more familiar methods recommended to humanize the organization. This alternative is consistent with, and might even be considered the *judicial* extension of, McGregor's Theory Y. This means that instead of a negative atmosphere surrounding the appeal activity in its authoritarian or legalistic forms, the democratic approach would promote a positive integration of organizational and individual goals.

It would do so by operating from a framework of behavioral assumptions which differ substantially from the traditional. The attitudes guiding appeal hearings and settlements would stem more from Theory Y behavioral criteria than from standards which are implicit in the authoritarian or legalistic notions of motivation.

The main point to be stressed in this section is when judicial criteria are internally derived and when there is no separation of the judicial

---

it is up to the outside party in the corporate appeal network to decide if there is any merit to the argument by reference to the external law of privacy.

The selection of this example is not an arbitrary choice since there is considerable literature building up on this issue of tests and privacy. However, to pursue it here would be an interesting but unnecessary digression. The reader might refer to an article in the *Wall Street Journal* of February 9, 1965, for a discussion of the subject. For a treatment of the legal status of the concept of privacy, see Morris L. Ernst and Alan U. Schwartz, *Privacy: The Right to be Let Alone* (New York: The Macmillan Company, 1962).

from the legislative and executive functions, it is hard to foresee that the standards of conflict management would more than mildly differ, if at all, from organizational values. This situation, represented by the authoritarian alternative, imposes the minimum restraint on the hierarchy. By the same token, it may also be the least efficient in Barnard's sense.

The degree of restraint on authority increases in the other alternatives, moving from the internal legalistic, through the external legalistic, and finally to the democratic. Presumably, too, the amount of dependence is reduced progressively in each of these alternatives while, simultaneously, the chances for individual self-determination increase.

Now although I carefully noted that these alternatives represent a spirit or philosophy of administration, there are procedural prerequisites which must exist to insure that the philosophy is more than talk. The minimum procedural requirement is separation of the functions which we have mentioned several times. Somewhere in the procedure, an outsider must exercise judicial authority or the appeal system comes to little more than a form of benevolence or paternalism.

It is safe to say, with the exceptions already described, that most of the organizations comprising the targets of this analysis have not gone beyond the second alternative, the internal legalistic, in the imposition of restraint on managerial authority through the appeal device. Even here, in business organizations, redress is generally not available to a disinterested outside third party. Instead, a representative of the personnel department is often used in this role. His job is to secure a tenuous compromise between the separation of legal power on the one hand with the maintenance of vested authority and secrecy about organizational affairs on the other. His success in this capacity, by securing a modicum of detachment from organizational values and demands, is a matter requiring research.

THE CHALLENGE TO FORMAL AUTHORITY

While formal organizations of every description in America are exerting a widening influence on the individual, the legitimacy of authority within these organizations is being questioned. It is not surprising though since part of our cultural heritage includes a suspicion of authority without counterbalancing regulation. This coupled with the desire to secure equal opportunity for self-development for all citizens would cause many to interpret bureaucratization as a threat to our democratic ideals. Thus the recommendations for authoritarian offsets multiply. So even though the process of formalization which accounts for appeal systems and the philosophies by which they may be administered are quite different matters, the melding of the two, process and philosophy, provides a vehicle for constraint upon internal organizational authority. As such these programs are in step with the modern mood of liberalism.

Administrators themselves have not ignored the potential effects this challenge of authority may have upon the organization. The broad acceptance of such administrative devices as participation, democratic leadership, sensitivity training, and so on is evidence that policy makers believe that the unmodified structure of formal authority creates dangerous inequalities in the distribution of satisfactions to people in the organization. Dangerous to the extent that if changes in the motivational climate are not introduced, the behavior of the organization as a cooperative system will be impaired.

An appeal system as part of the modified structure and motivational climate cannot, however, be a shallow substitute for self-determination. No one is fooled when it is. An appeal system based upon Machiavellian or paternalistic premises is usually avoided as a means for resolving conflicts. Instead conflicts are settled either informally or not at all.

The difficulty with many formal programs of redress is that their values and the values of the organization in which they function are not perceived by participants as different. This is why a grin is often provoked when a person is told he can go over his superior's head if he has a problem. He is telling you that he does not believe it will do him any good or that reprisals will not be visited upon him. In summary he does not see organizational justice implemented by the formal machinery of due process.

Our skeptical friend has not, in the language of the social psychologist, internalized the values of the formal appeal system. This reaction is caused in part by structural deficiencies, mainly the failure to separate the legal functions of the organization. But the problem is deeper because rejection of a formal system of appeal adds up to a vote of "no confidence" in the management's efforts to provide objective, accessible, and systematic grounds for adjudication of disputes.

I think cynicism characterizes the attitude of many people toward formalized appeal procedures or "open-door policies." To dispel this attitude fully a democratic approach to the administration of programs may be necessary. However, this is a little rich for contemporary executives. But the demands for more restraint on arbitrary authority and greater opportunities for personal development will not go unnoticed. They will become imperative as the character of the work force continues to change. The enlarging numbers of scientific, administrative, and technical personnel will reinforce the swelling desire for freedom and satisfaction within organizations.

The first step in this direction for most organizations probably is not the democratic one. More likely, it is some form of legalism. If the organization cannot be democratized, in the literal meaning of the word, it can at least be constitutionalized. I feel this is the direction in which not a few organizations are moving. And in this transition away from unfettered authoritarianism, procedural due process is essential for the settlement of disputes which arise "under the law."

----------------------------------- **16** -----------------------------------

COMMAND, CONTROL, AND CHARISMA
Reflections on Police Bureaucracy

David J. Bordua and Albert J. Reiss, Jr.

Bureaucratization can be regarded as an organizational technique whereby civic pressures are neutralized from the standpoint of the governing regime. In the development of the modern police, bureaucratization has been a major device to commit members to the occupational organization, to the occupational community, and to its norms of subordination and service to a degree where these commitments take precedence over extra-occupational ones to family and community.

The political neutrality and legal reliability of the police in modern societies are less a matter of the social sources of their recruitment than of the nature of internal organization, training, and control. While this, of course, is true for all government organizations under a civil service or tenure system, it is true for the police not primarily because they are civil servants in the restricted sense but because of their allegiance to an occupationally organized community that sets itself apart. The situation is particularly crucial for the police since they often are called upon to enforce laws that are unpopular with the public or for which they have no personal sympathy, while at the same time they are armed and organized. Perhaps this fundamental significance of police bureaucratization can be seen by the fact that given a well-organized, well-disciplined, and internally well-regulated police, civil authorities can count on the police if they are assured of the political loyalty or neutrality of the commander. Indeed, the modern police emerged under conditions whereby they were an organized source of stability between the elites and the masses, serving to draw hostility from the elites to themselves and thereby permitting more orderly relations among the elites and the masses.[1]

COMMAND SYSTEMS

To our knowledge, there is no detailed empirical description of command processes in a police department. It is necessary, therefore, to rely largely on published discourses that give information on the rhetoric of command and control and that are of variable and unknown validity as descriptions of behavior.[2]

Police literature emphasizes the quasimilitary nature of police-command relations, and casual observation in metropolitan police departments indicates that police officials are highly sensitive to "orders from above" and to probabilities of official disapproval of behavior. In principle and in rhetoric, a police organization is one characterized by strict subordination, by a rigid chain of command, by accountability of command, and more doubtfully, by a lack of formal provision for consultation between ranks.

Before accepting this description of its structure uncritically, it is necessary to say that such statements are meaningful only by comparison. We have relatively little data comparing the operating as opposed to the rhetorical nature of command in different types of organizations. In many ways, policing is a highly decentralized operation involving the deployment of large numbers of men alone or in small units where control by actual command, that is, by issuing orders, is difficult. This problem is generally recognized by top police administrators, leading to their stressing the importance of accountability of command to achieve control. O. W. Wilson puts it this way:

> Authority is delegated by some form of command; responsibility is effectively placed by some form of control. . . . The effective placing of responsibility or the act of holding accountable involves an evaluation of the manner in which the authority was exercised, hence the rule of control: *He who gives an order must ascertain that it has been properly executed.*
>
> It is relatively easy to delegate authority by giving a command, but to ascertain the manner in which the order was carried out so that the subordinate may be held responsible is often difficult.[3]

1. Alan Silver, "On the Demand for Order in Civil Society: A Review of Some Themes in the History of Urban Crime, Police and Riot in England" (to be published in David J. Bordua [ed.], *The Police* [New York: John Wiley & Sons, 1966]), p. 11.

2. See, for example, Bruce Smith, *Police Systems in the United States* (2d rev. ed.; New York: Harper & Brothers, 1960), esp. chaps. vii–ix.

3. O. W. Wilson, *Police Administration* (New York: McGraw-Hill Book Co., 1950), p. 59.

Other evidence from the police literature suggests that the description is overdrawn, that both internal and external transactions structure the effective range of command and control. Moreover, as J. Q. Wilson points out, it seems clear that the variations between "system-oriented" as opposed to "professionalized" departments includes fundamental differences in styles of control.[4]

Historical changes in the nature of police work and organization have increased the importance of more subtle and perhaps more important developments in methods of control. In the dialectic of dispersion versus centralization of command, every development in the technology for police control of the population is accompanied by changes in the capacity of the organization to control its members. Originally the bell, creaker, or rattle watches were limited in summoning help to the effective range of their "noise"; the addition of "calling the hours" served to monitor the behavior of the patrol (quite generally open to question).[5] Here we see evidence of a classic and continuing dilemma in organizations—that to control subordinates they must be required to make themselves visible. For the police, this means that when they become visible they likewise become more calculable to potential violators. Control of the dispersed police was really difficult before the call box that simultaneously enabled patrolmen to summon help and enabled commanders to issue calls and require periodic reporting.[6] The cruising car with two-way radio enabled still greater dispersion and flexibility in the allocation of patrols, while at the same time bringing the patrolman or team more nearly within the range of constant control. It is now a fundamental duty of the radio patrol officer to remain "in contact," that is, controllable.

More important, perhaps, is the fact that a centralized radio communication system, where telephoned complaints are received and commands given, makes it possible for top management to have independent knowledge of complaints and of who is assigned to them before either subordinate commanders or the patrol team does. A minimum of centralized control is available, then, not simply by the direct issuance of commands from superior to subordinate but by means of a paper-matching process whereby the complaint board's written record can be matched with the written record the patrolman is required to generate. This pattern of control by centralized communication and internal organizational audit is highly dependent upon the distribution

4. James Q. Wilson, "The Police and Their Problems: A Theory," in Carl J. Friedrich and Seymour E. Harris (eds.), *Public Policy, XII* (Cambridge, Mass.: Harvard University Press, 1963), pp. 189–216.
5. Selden D. Bacon, "The Early Development of American Municipal Police: A Study of the Evolution of Formal Controls in a Changing Society" (unpublished Ph.D. dissertation, Yale University, 1939).
6. The innovation of the police patrol and signal service in Chicago in 1880 brought forth considerable resistance and indignation from the police patrol precisely because it made possible closer supervision of the patrol (see John Joseph Flynn, *History of the Chicago Police: From the Settlement of the Community to the Present Time* [Chicago: Police Book Fund, 1887], chap. xx).

of telephones in the population. The citizen's telephone enables the police commander to enlist the complainant—on a routine basis—as part of the apparatus for control of the policeman. A citizen's opportunity to mobilize the police is intricately balanced with that of the commander.

Added to these matters of task organization, in large police departments, the chief's power to command and control is limited by a complex system of "due process" that protects subordinates. This, of course, is true of all civil service organizations. The strong interest in keeping the police "out of politics" coupled with the interest of the rank and file in job security, however creates a situation where, formally, the department head must contend with legally empowered authorities in the selection, promotion, and discharge of personnel. Even in matters of internal assignment and definition of task, decisions may impinge on the civil service classification system. Police employee organizations, likewise, are quite effective in seeing to it that the system of "due process" continues to protect them. The individual officer, furthermore, when accused of wrongdoing or a crime, demands all the legal safeguards he may deny to those whom he accuses of committing a crime.

Not all police operations are constituted in the fashion of this highly oversimplified picture of so-called routine patrol. Detectives, for example, are less subject to such control. But these considerations of due-process barriers to centralized command and historical changes in control procedures that rely less on actual command as a form of control are intended to raise questions about the sociological meaning of the stress generally placed on command and to lay the ground for a somewhat more systematic analysis of it.

FORMS OF LEGITIMATION

Thus far, "command" has been used in two senses. In one, "command" refers to a technique of control in organizations that consists of "giving commands." The directive communication between superior and subordinate may be called "a command," or, if more impersonally clothed, "an order." In another sense, however, "command" means neither a specific technique of control nor an instance of its use, but something more general—a principle that legitimates orders, instructions, or rules. Orders, then, are obeyed *because* they are "commanded."

Sociologists are familiar with discussions of this type ever since Weber.[7] In Weberian terms, the police department "as an order" is

---

7. Talcott Parsons (ed.), *Max Weber: The Theory of Social and Economic Organization* (New York: Oxford University Press, 1947), pp. 324 ff.

legitimated by the principle of command. Each form of legitimation, however, as Weber so clearly saw, has a correlative requirement of "attitude" on the part of those subject to its sway. In the case of "an order" legitimated by a rhetoric of command, the correlative expectation is "obedience"—again not as a situational expectation in the case of a given specific command but as a principle relating member to organization. To be "obedient" in this sense carries the same general sense of principle as in the "poverty, chastity, and obedience" of the monk's vow. In a system so legitimated, we can expect that commitment to obedience will be displayed as a sign of membership.

It is not surprising, then, that social scientists who are based in organizations where independence is legitimated, rehabilitation workers based in those where professional discretion and supportiveness are legitimated, and police who are based in organizations where obedience is legitimated so often fail to communicate with one another when they are engaged in exchanges of ideologies.

We may point out as well that in orders legitimated by command and exacting obedience, the classic status reward is "honor." The morale and public-relations problems of the American police can be more clearly understood as an attempt to substitute public prestige sought in an occupational performance market for the Weberian status regard sought and validated in the "honor market." The American police are denied both, for the public seems unwilling to accord the police status either in the European sense of status honor as representatives of the State or in the more typically American sense of prestige based on a claim to occupational competence.

Command as a basis for legitimacy can be located under any of the three basic types of legitimation discussed by Weber—the rational-legal, the traditional, and the charismatic. Inherently, however, command as a principle focuses on the commander, and the exact nature of the concrete "order" legitimated by the principle of command will depend on the role of the specific commander. Because of this commander focus, the command principle is likely to lead to a mystique of the personal commander and an organizational stress on legitimating specific orders or even general rules as emanating from him.

COMMAND AND TASK ORGANIZATION

To regard a metropolitan police system solely in terms of the classic features of the hierarchically oriented command bureaucracy would be mistaken, however. Although the more traditional police departments in American cities are organized on quasimilitary command principles, modernized ones display features of other control systems, particularly those of centralized and professional control structures.

The core of the modern metropolitan police system is the communications center, linking as it does by radio dispatch the telephoned demands of a dispersed population with a dispersed police in mobile units. The technology of the radio, the telephone, the recorder, and the computer permits a high degree of central control of operating units in the field. The more modern police departments, for example, have tape records of all citizen phone complaints, the response of dispatch to them, and the action of mobile units. This technology also makes possible reporting directly to a centralized records unit. Indeed, the more rationalized police-command systems make extensive use of the computer as a centralized intelligence system to which mobile units can make virtually direct inquiry, as a "decision-maker" about which units are to be dispersed for what service, and as a source of intelligence on the output of personnel and units in the department. Such a centralized and direct system of command and control makes it possible to bypass many positions in the hierarchical command structure, particularly those in the station command. More and more, those in the line of authority assume work supervision or informal adjudicatory rather than strictly command roles.

There undeniably is considerable variability among internal units of a police department in the degree to which they are centrally commanded such that routine patrol is more subject to central command than are tactical or investigation units. Yet, all in all, there is a growing tendency for all internal units to operate under programed operations of a central command rather than under local commanders. Orders not only originate with the central command but pass directly from it.

The centralization of command and control is one of the major ways that American police chiefs have for coping with the tendency toward corruption inherent in traditional hierarchically organized departments. Chiefs no longer need rely to the same extent upon the station commander to implement the goals of the department through the exercise of command. Indeed, a major way that corrupt departments are reformed these days is to reduce the command operations of local commanders, replacing them with centralized command and control. Yet it is precisely in those operations where corruption is most likely to occur, namely, the control of vice, that a centralized command is least effective. The main reason for this is that a centralized command lends itself best to a reactive strategy, whereas a professionalized or hierarchically organized command lends itself to a proactive strategy. Vice requires an essentially proactive strategy of policing in the modern metropolis, whereas the citizens' command for service demands an essentially reactive strategy and tactics.

A central command not only bypasses traditional hierarchical command relations but, like the hierarchical command, creates problems for the developing professionalized control in police systems. A professionalized model of control respects a more or less decentralized decision-making system where the central bureaucracy, at best, sets general policy and principles that guide the professional. Indeed, many police tasks and decisions would appear to lend themselves to a professional as well as technical role relationship with the client.

Yet, the institutionalized and legally defined role of the police formally denies professional discretion to them in decisions of prosecution and adjudication, granting them to professional lawyers. The "professionalizing" police, therefore, are formally left only with certain decisions regarding public order, safety, service, and arrest. These formal prohibitions coupled with the new technology and centralized command (developed under the banner of professionalization of the police) both serve to decrease rather than enhance discretionary decision-making by subordinates. Police organizations become "professionalized," not their members.

COMMAND AND OCCUPATIONAL CULTURE

The internal organizational life of American police departments displays features which distinguish the police from other organizations and which have important implications for the nature of organizational command. These features are the familial and/or ethnic inheritance of occupation, the almost exclusive practice of promotion from within, the large number of formal voluntary organizations that cut across organizational membership, and, finally, the existence of legal protections for tenure which inhere in civil service regulations.

Specific police jobs differ; yet it is quite important to recognize that, fundamentally, police status overrides these differentiations. Not only does the basic status override lateral differentiations, but it also tends to override differences in rank. Police occupational culture, unlike the situation in industry, unites rather than divides ranks.

This is perhaps the most fundamental significance of the practice of promoting from within. The fact that all police-command personnel came up through the ranks means not only that there is relatively little class distinction among police but that the sharp differences between managers and workers in industry is less apparent for the police.[8]

In addition to the vertical spread of police occupational culture due to promotion from within, local recruitment tends to entrench any specific department's version of the more general occupational culture.

8. The more professionalized a police department, however, the more it displays manager-worker differences common in industry. The police in the line symbolize this by referring to those on the staff as "empty holster———." The occupational culture holds, nevertheless, for police personnel in staff and line versus the non-sworn personnel, the latter commonly being referred to as "civilians."

This combination of occupational culture and organizational culture produces what J. Q. Wilson referred to as "system-oriented" departments.[9]

Interlinked with the features of local recruitment and internal promotion is the factor of familial and ethnic inheritance of the police occupation. Many occupations are strongly based in ethnicity, and many organizations have widespread kinship bonds; indeed, some companies advertise the fact. The consequences, however, are more exaggerated in the police, partly because police culture emphasizes distance between the occupation and the general community but, more importantly we suspect, because of the relative lack of vertical differentiation. Thus, police corruption can become spread up precisely because of this lack of differentiation.

Finally, the development of civil service can mean that a rather rigid formal, legal shell is erected around occupational and organizational cultures in a way that makes the exercise of command from the top even more difficult than it would otherwise be. The reform chief must choose his command from among those who began tenure under his predecessors. And except for retirement, "resignation," or formal dismissal proceedings, he is left with the cadre of the "old department."

It should be noted, however, that occupational and organizational cultures and the reinforcing solidarities provided by formal organizations like the Fraternal Order of Police and by the legal protections of civil service have another side. They make possible the existence of police systems which function at least moderately well over long periods in a society notoriously inhospitable to police; indeed, they are partially a defensive response to that inhospitability. While they may inhibit modernization and reform, they do insure that the job will get done somehow. More importantly, they provide the irreplaceable minimum structural conditions for at least the basic elements of status honor. They provide the essential precondition for a sense of honor— a relatively closed, secure community (not just organization) of functionaries who can elaborate and apply honor-conferring criteria.

These internal solidarities create special barriers to the effective exercise of command over and above the features of task organization previously discussed. They become particularly significant in attempts at modernization or reform. The police commander ignores this internal culture at his peril. It can confront him with an opposition united from top to bottom.

The modernizing chief is constrained, therefore, to make at least symbolic obeisance to police solidarity by demonstrating that he is a "cop's cop" as well as a devotee of systems analysis and psychological

9. James Q. Wilson, *op. cit.*

screening of applicants. One of the ways he does so is by emphasis in his dress and bearing—the policeman's chief social tool—the ability to command personal respect.[10] At least during a period of change, personal charisma and "presence" are of particular significance. He must also make his orders stick, of course.

The reform chief's charisma is of special significance because of the objective uncertainty of obedience but also because reform depends on the co-operation of a cadre of immediate subordinates whose careers may depend upon the chief's success. His certainty becomes their hope.

COMMAND AND CIVIL ACCOUNTABILITY

The structure of command is affected not only by elements of task organization and technology and by the features of occupational and organizational culture discussed above but also by the relationship between the chief and his civil superiors. In the case of the American municipality, police chiefs, at least traditionally, both at law and in practice, are politically accountable officials who ordinarily stand or fall with the fortunes of their civilian superiors (who are lodged in external systems). Given the often controversial nature of police work, and the often "irrational" and unpredictable nature of political fortunes in municipal government, the American police chief who is responsible to a politically elected official comes close to the position of a "patrimonial bureaucrat" in Weber's terms. His tenure as chief, though not necessarily his tenure in the department, depends on continuing acceptability to the elected official(s).

We have alluded to some of the dimensions along which police departments and their command processes seem to vary—using terms like "modernized," "rationalized," "reformed." It would be possible to indicate other dimensions which intersect these by referring to department age, growth rate, and other variables as well as environmental context variables such as variations in civic culture—comparing, for example, Los Angeles and San Francisco. It is not our intention, however, to attempt a systematic comparative scheme. In the case of the problem of civic accountability, however, it is possible to use some of the material presented thus far to begin development of such a scheme.

The relations of police commanders to civil superiors are actually more varied and complex than those depicted above. We shall discuss briefly only the two most important dimensions of variation: the security of tenure of the chief commander and the degree to which he is held strictly accountable by a mayor. Given strict accountability plus

10. The ability to command respect personally is more necessary in America than in Britain where police command more respect officially (see Michael Banton, *The Policeman in the Community* (New York: Basic Books, 1965).

insecurity of tenure, we can expect a kind of obsession with command and a seemingly "irrational" emphasis on the twinned symbols of the visibility of the commander and the obedience of the force. Some of the rhetoric of command in the police literature likely arises from an attempt to "protect" the chief by the compulsive effort to "overcontrol" subordinates, almost any of whom can get him fired. This amounts to saying that as civil superiors increase the formal accountability of the police chief *without changing* the tenure features of the role, the increasing bureaucratization of the American municipal police stressed by J. Q. Wilson leads to the development of an organization animated by a principle of the commanding person.[11] This "personalized subordination" to the "Hero Chief" can become an operating, if not a formal, principle of organization.[12]

Increased professionalization can be another accommodative strategy in such a situation, but this time aimed not at control of the force but at control of the mayor by changing the grounds of accountability. One of the first jobs of the "professionalizing" police chief often is to convince his civil superior that "you can't win 'em all" and that it is irrational and "unprofessional" to dismiss a police chief or commissioner because of failure to solve some particular crime. Perhaps, in the long run, it is hard to have a professionalized police without a professionalized mayor. Perhaps also, this would lead us to expect different kinds of command styles where a professional city manager intervenes between the chief and the mayor.

If the civil superior, for whatever reason, does not demand accountability from the chief, the quasi-formalized obsession with "command" as a principle of control may be replaced by a complex system of feudal loyalties. In this situation, ties of personal political fealty between chief and mayor—or between chief and the local "powers"—may become prominent and "keep your nose clean" the principle of subordination. When this trend goes beyond a certain point, the department is commonly described as politically corrupt. Finally, to the degree that the chief is secure in his tenure, we would expect the obsession with command and the emphasis on personalized subordination to decrease.

On the basis of this analysis of command and the position of the chief we may distinguish the four types of departments (Table 1).

We have consciously chosen words such as "feudality" with outrageously large quotas of surplus meaning since the concern here is to

11. James Q. Wilson, *op. cit.*
12. One study reports that, as compared with welfare workers and school teachers, policemen were more likely to personalize authority (Robert L. Peabody, "Perceptions of Organizational Authority: A Comparative Analysis," *Administrative Science Quarterly,* VI [March, 1962], 447–80; see also Elaine Cumming, Ian M. Cumming, and Laura Edell, "Policeman as Philosopher, Guide and Friend," *Social Problems,* XII [Winter, 1965], 276–97).

Table 1

Types of Police Departments

Relation to Mayor	Tenure of Chief	
	Secure	Insecure
Strictly account-able	Command bureaucracy	Personalized command bureaucracy
Feudal allegiance .	Command feudality	Personalized "political" feudality

direct attention to features of police organization that receive relatively little attention and to questions of fundamental differences in the consequences of organizational membership between police and other organizations.[13]

A word about two of these types seems in order. The command-feudality type seems a contradiction in terms (and indeed derives from the cross-classification itself). Some small municipal and sheriff's departments, where the tenure of the chief in the local "feudal political structure" is secure, may fall here. Because everyone is secure in a relatively non-bureaucratic system, the operating principle of subordination can be command. Such an arrangement possibly characterizes the exceptionally long-tenure chiefs discovered in Lunden's study in Iowa.[14]

The "personalized command bureaucracy" seems likely to occur where an insecure reform head is in office. To reform successfully he must bureaucratize and rationalize administrative operations. To do this against the inevitable internal resistance he must emphasize the principle of command. To make clear that status quo-oriented commanders have been superseded he must emphasize *his* command and his *capacity* to command. In *short,* he must exercise what Selznick defines as one of the crucial functions of leadership in administration. He must define the emerging character of the institution.[15]

CONCLUSION

We have discussed features of American police systems that may account for variations in and possible changes in command structures

13. This typology owes much to the analysis of labor unions in Harold L. Wilensky, *Intellectuals in Labor Unions* (Glencoe, Ill.: Free Press, 1956).
14. Walter A. Lunden, "The Mobility of Chiefs of Police," *Journal of Criminal Law, Criminology and Police Science,* XLIX (1958), 178–83.
15. Philip Selznick, *Leadership in Administration* (New York: Row, Peterson & Co., 1957).

and also features that account for both a rhetorical and behavioral emphasis not on one or the other formal command system but on something which seemingly appears as alien and contradictory—the personal charisma of the chief and the emphasis on personalized command as a symbolic, if not actual, principle of order.

Command, obedience, and honor ring strangely in analysis of organizational life in America except, perhaps, for the military. Yet it seems to us that meaningful analysis of the police must touch upon them as well as upon duty, courage, and restraint. The self-image of the police is different because of them. We have already alluded to the fact that the status reward for obedience is honor and that the maintenance of honor requires a status community—not simply a formal organization.[16]

The significance of honor is that it lies at the heart of the necessary police virtues—courage, devotion to duty, restraint, and honesty. In the absence of ritually symbolic auspices such as the European State or the English Crown, the personal charisma of chiefs is a necessary transitional step to an occupationally based community of honor. In the long run, such status honor, not only occupational prestige, is one fundamental answer to police corruption.[17] In the short run, it means that successful police commanders must attempt not to have the police reflect the society but transcend it.

16. Military honor is similarly communal and not just organizational (Morris Janowitz, *The Professional Soldier* [Glencoe, Ill.: Free Press, 1960], esp. chaps. iv and v).
17. M. McMullen, "A Theory of Corruption," *Sociological Review,* IX (1961), 181–201.

———————————————— **17** ————————————————

STRUCTURE, POLICY, AND STYLE
Strategies of Organizational Control

William R. Rosengren[1]

Studies of formal organizations turn more and more to the strategies of control that organizations use to make their employees or clients tractable to the organization. Investigations of control in formal organizations often focus upon two conceptually divergent though empiri-

1. This study was made possible through a Grant-in-Aid from the Institute for Health Sciences, and a Faculty Grant from Brown University. I am grateful to the 132 chiefs of service for completing a long questionnaire. Thanks are also due to Basil G. Zimmer Jr., who helped in the analysis of data, and to Charles Perrow for both devastating criticisms and helpful suggestions.

cally related issues. One deals with the kinds of internal structures that develop in organizations—the division of labor, task specialization, and systems of communication.[2] Included here are studies which view the structural properties of organizations as derived from the goals of the organization and the degree of autonomy it enjoys. A related approach takes account of size as a determinant of organizational structure.[3] Studies such as these are generally consistent with Weberian concepts, especially in their focus upon structural arrangements and how they are effected. The second issue is related to the strategies of administrative leadership and influence that control participants in desired ways— whether by loose or close supervision, by manipulation of rewards, by the degree of democratization of decision making, and so forth.[4] This aspect of organizational behavior has been investigated in case studies of single organizations undergoing change, reorganization, or other crisis situations.

Only recently, however, has the study of organizational control included both structural characteristics and supervisory styles. The contention here is that structural characteristics in organizations can themselves be regarded as mechanisms of control. Therefore, if participant control can be achieved either through structural characteristics or supervisory strategies, then it is of interest to find how these two means of control are related.

The distinction between supervisory or administrative strategies of control and organizational structure is noted in the difference between

2. See for example, S. N. Eisenstadt, Bureaucracy, Bureaucratization, and De-bureaucratization, *Administrative Science Quarterly,* 4 (1959), 302–320; A. Etzioni, "Organizational Control Structure," in J. March (ed.), *Handbook of Organizations* (Chicago: Rand-McNally, 1965); Sol Levine and P. E. White, Exchange as a Conceptual Framework for the Study of Interorganizational Relationships, *Administrative Science Quarterly,* 5 (March 1961), 583–601; Richard L. Simpson and H. W. Gulley, Goals, Environmental Pressures, and Organizational Characteristics, *American Sociological Review,* 27 (June 1962), 344–351; James D. Thompson and W. D. McEwen, Organizational Goals and Environment: Goal-Setting as an Interactional Process, *American Sociological Review,* 23 (February 1958), 23–31; T. Burns and G. Stalker, *The Management of Innovation* (London: Tavistock, 1961); Michael Crozier, *The Bureaucratic Phenomenon* (Chicago: University of Chicago, 1965); James Thompson (ed.), *Approaches to Organizational Design* (Pittsburgh: University of Pittsburgh, 1966); Stanley H. Udy Jr., Administrative Rationality, Social Setting, and Organizational Development, *American Journal of Sociology,* 68 (November 1962), 299–308.

3. Some studies conclude that bureaucratization increases with size; others find the reverse. Cf. Theodore R. Anderson and S. Warkov, Organizational Size and Functional Complexity: A Study of Administration in Hospitals, *American Sociological Review,* 26 (February 1961), 23–28; Theodore Caplow, Organizational Size, *Administrative Science Quarterly,* 1 (March 1957), 484–505; Frederick W. Terrien and D. L. Mills, The Effects of Changing Size upon the Internal Structure of Organizations, *American Sociological Review,* 20 (February 1955), 11–14; Oscar Grusky, Corporate Size, Bureaucratization, and Managerial Succession, *American Journal of Sociology,* 67 (November 1961), 261–269; Robert H. Guest, Managerial Succession in Complex Organizations, *American Journal of Sociology,* 68 (July 1962), 47–54; Louis Kriesberg, Careers, Organization Size, and Succession, *American Journal of Sociology,* 68 (November 1962), 355–359.

4. For example, Amitai Etzioni, *A Comparative Analysis of Complex Organizations* (New York: The Free Press, 1961); also "Organizational Control Structure," in J. March, *op. cit.;* Peter Blau, *The Dynamics of Bureaucracy* (Chicago: University of Chicago, 1955); Peter Blau and W. Richard Scott, *Formal Organizations* (San Francisco: Chandler, 1962); Richard McCleery, *Policy Change in Prison Management* (East Lansing: Michigan State University Governmental Research Bureau, 1957).

influence and authority. Authority is customarily regarded as legitimized power over others residing in organizational structure. Influence, conceived as nonlegitimized power, is more nearly what is meant by supervisory style, although the capacity to exercise influence over others can hardly be sharply distinguished from the prerogatives that attach to an office. Shils, for example, has argued that even in orderly bureaucracies, authority acquires a "charisma of status," which gives the office holder an increment of power beyond that which attaches to the position.[5] Thus, while structural arrangements may define the limits within which participants *must* act, the potential for supervisory influence allows discretion as to the boundaries within which incumbents *may* act.

This paper is concerned with the relationship between the structure of offices and supervisory styles as they relate to control of participants in organizations. More specifically, this study examines some relationships between size and sponsorship, specialization of tasks, operational policies, and supervisory control styles in 132 psychiatric hospitals.

ORGANIZATIONS STUDIED

A questionnaire was sent to the chiefs of psychiatric service in the 270 hospitals approved for psychiatric residency training in 1961 by the American Medical Association, with military hospitals excluded.[6] Responses were received from 152, or 56.3 percent, of these hospitals. Of this number, 12 were eliminated from the sample because they reported no in-patient psychiatric services and eight because they returned questionnaires with internal errors or inconsistencies. Of the total sent out, therefore, 48.8 percent were used.

Two indicators of the representativeness of the sample were used: the geographic location of the hospitals and the size of the in-patient populations. Location was determined on the basis of the nine standard

5. Edward Shils, Charisma, Order, and Status, *American Sociological Review,* 30 (April 1965), 199–213.
6. One of the problems connected with data from questionnaires is whether the respondents have taken seriously the task of completing such questionnaires. The indications used in this study were whether each respondent had reported the in-patient census in rounded-off figures, and whether he had gone beyond what was contained in the questions, and added further information. In the first instance, 33 questionnaires contained in-patient census figures which might be regarded as rounding or guessing about the in-patient census. Of these, however, 21 included other indications of respondent seriousness: erasures indicating correction or recalculations, explication of response, notations written on the questionnaire, or extensive comments and explanations written on the blank page which accompanied each questionnaire. Among the total 132 questionnaires, 83 percent contained such additions, explications, or corrections. In addition, 70 percent of the respondents wrote under separate cover commenting on the study and asking for publications and reports when available. In so far as such indicators are meaningful, most respondents appeared to complete the questionnaire thoughtfully and seriously. Also although findings are reported by a single respondent from each organization, the chief of services, though not a disinterested observer in his own institution, is a person in a position to know the kinds of information asked for.

census areas of the United States. The differences between the number sent and the number returned in eight areas ranged from 0.1 percent to 2.1 percent. The greatest difference (–5.0 percent) was found in the Middle Atlantic area. On the basis of returns, identified by postmark, this area appeared to be underrepresented largely because of fewer responses from the large metropolitan center in the area. For size the mean inpatient census among the 270 to which questionnaires were sent was 1,205; and the mean census among the 132 usable returns was 1,210. On the strength of these two factors, the hospitals on which this report is based might be regarded as representative of the sample.

CONCEPTS, INDICATORS, AND METHODS OF ANALYSIS

ORGANIZATIONAL SIZE AND AUTONOMY

Organizational size. The number of in-patients served was chosen as the criterion for size. In-patient populations ranged from 20 to 12, 000, with a break in the frequency distribution between 400 and about 1,000; 52 hospitals served patient populations under 400, and 80 served clienteles near 1,000 and above. On the basis of this distribution, a distinction between *small* and *large* hospitals is made in the discussion that follows.

Organizational autonomy. Differences in the relationship of the hospital to its external environment were indicated by type of sponsorship. Seven kinds of sponsorship were reported: state and municipal hospitals, private institutions operated on a proprietary basis, private hospitals functioning on a nonprofit basis, Veterans' Administration hospitals, hospitals under religious order or denominational control, and hospitals affiliated with a medical school. Because of the relatively small number of institutions in the municipal, private proprietary, and denominational categories (see Table 1), the analysis of data is based upon a comparison of *government* hospitals ($N = 87$) with *private* hospitals ($N = 45$).

The distinction between government and private hospitals is reinforced by the correlation with size; only seven of the government hospitals were small, and none of the private hospitals were large ($X^2 = 1050.037$). The correlation between size and sponsorship was so great that these two variables are here treated as one; references to "small" hospitals imply private sponsorship, and references to "large" hospitals imply government sponsorship. In examining relations between these variables and control mechanisms, tests of independence are based *strictly* on the small-large distinction.

Neither the distinction between government versus private sponsorship—nor its correlate of size—is fully adequate as a test of the degree of organizational autonomy. Organizational autonomy is better

Table 1

Organizational Size and Sponsorship

Sponsorship	Number of Patients*							
	20-200	201-500†	501-850	851-1150‡	1151-1500	1501-2500	2501 plus	N
Governmental								
Municipal/county	2	1	0	5	2	0	0	10
State	1	0	0	2	16	19	24	62
Veterans administration	2	1	0	1	8	3	0	15
Private								
Private proprietary	9	0	0	0	0	0	0	9
Private philanthropic	10	2	0	0	0	0	0	12
Religious-denominational	6	0	0	0	0	0	0	6
University/medical school	16	2	0	0	0	0	0	18

* 52 small hospitals (under 500); 80 large hospitals (over 850).
† The largest census in this category was 481.
‡ The smallest census in this category destinction was 918.

thought of as marking differences in the kinds of environmental pressures to which institutions in each category might be exposed. Government hospitals might be expected to have greater constraints imposed upon their structure of offices and communication patterns than private institutions. On the other hand, sponsors of private organizations might be expected to grant more autonomy in the structural arrangements for work, and exercise more control over operational policies in the organizations they support.[7]

INTERNAL STRUCTURES

Four aspects of internal structure were taken into account, all of which bear directly upon the issue of participant control.

Work assignments. The first relates to the work assignments. Each chief of service reported the work activities of employees in each occupational category. These included psychotherapy group therapy sessions, research, standardized patient assessment procedures, family counseling, administrative work, and others. In some hospitals, employees in each occupational category were held responsible for only a single task with different work assignments for each category of staff. In others, however, the work assignments within each occupational category were characterized by multiple and overlapping tasks that cut across occupational and professional lines. The mean number of work assignments was four. A distinction was therefore made between those

7. See Leonard Mayo, Relationships Between Public and Voluntary Health and Welfare Agencies, *American Journal of Public Health,* 49 (October 1959), 1307–1313.

organizations in which the mean number of assignments was four or more, and those in which it was three or less. The hospitals in which the work assignments were highly specific and which involved a minimum of overlap across occupational categories, that is, characterized by *specialized tasks* are here called *specialized systems.* Those characterized by a broad range of work assignments within occupational groups and therefore overlap across occupational categories, that is, *unspecialized tasks,* are called *unspecialized systems.*

Thus, in specialized systems occupational categories could be sharply distinguished on the basis of distinctive tasks in the organization, whereas in unspecialized systems, occupational title would be less of a distinguishing mark of work role. For example, in the unspecialized systems social workers and psychologists were as likely to provide individual psychotherapy as were psychiatrists; whereas in specialized systems psychotherapy was more often the exclusive task of psychiatrists.

Formal communication. The second aspect of structure involved the relative emphasis placed upon *formal* as opposed to *informal* communication. Formal communication included not only reliance upon information from regularly scheduled staff meetings, but also upon routinely prepared and regularly written reports, data from standardized testing procedures, and from existing records and documents. Informal communication included coffee-room discussions among staff, observation of patient and employee behavior, hastily written notes not intended as permanent hospital records, and other procedures unspecified as to procedure or content.

Communication across levels. The third structural feature was the range of occupational levels in the organization having direct communication with the chief of services. In some hospitals, the chief exchanged information principally with high-level professional personnel —psychiatrists, other physicians, psychologists, and social workers. In these organizations communications with line nurses, ward attendants, and other lower-level clinical personnel were routinely channelled through an employee at an intermediate staff level. This pattern of information flow is referred to as *lateral* communication. In other hospitals the chief exchanged information directly with lower-level staff members as well as with those of higher professional status. This suggests a less precise and less specified communication of information, with somewhat greater opportunity for contact and communication among all staff members than in lateral communication. This type of communication is called *institutional communication.*

Extent of communication. Finally, each respondent reported the kinds of information for which employees in each occupational category were held responsible. Such responsibilities included clinical infor-

mation about patients, information about behavior in the routines of
hospital life, about the family situation of patients, and about personnel
and administrative matters. The mean number of communication responsibilities in the 132 hospitals was four, with a range from one to
eight. Those hospitals with a score of four or more were said to have
diffuse communication systems; those with a score of three or less,
restricted communication systems. In a diffuse communication system
employees in each occupational category were responsible for a wide
range of information, much of it similar to that for which other employees were responsible. In such a system, ward attendants were as
likely to be knowledgeable about patient psychodynamics as psychiatrists. On the other hand, ward attendants working in restricted communication systems would be likely to be responsible only for
knowledge about patient behavior in hospital routines, while psychiatrists would be responsible only for psychodynamics.

In structural terms then, one implication of these distinctions is
that those organizations with specialized tasks, and lateral, formal, and
restricted communication have a greater potential for participant control than organizations with unspecialized tasks, and institutional, informal, and diffuse communication. In so far as these indicators may
suggest a distinction between bureaucratic and unbureaucratic organizations, they suggest that bureaucracies have a greater structural capacity for control than less bureaucratic institutions.

OPERATIONAL POLICIES

Patient care. Three indicators of operational policies were used.
The first was the emphasis on *Traditional treatment* as contrasted with
Innovative treatment of patients. Hospitals with traditional treatment
emphasized electric-shock, drug therapy, and arts and crafts—all of
which entail specific and routinized techniques. Those with more innovative treatment favored treatments such as group therapy, manipulation of peer relationships among the patients, and interpersonal
relations between staff and patients—treatments in which technique
and implementation are less specifically prescribed and routinized.

Patient subculture. A second indicator of operational policy was
the extent to which subcultural forms of patient conduct were judged
to be organizationally relevant. The forms of patient misconduct usually found in in-patient hospitals that were taken into account are listed
in Table 2. Each respondent indicated by "yes" or "no" whether each
form of patient behavior was regarded as sufficiently important to be
of interest and concern. Those institutions above the mean (3.5) were
said to have a *relevant patient subculture;* those below the mean were
said to have an *irrelevant patient subculture.*

Table 2

Questionnaire Items on Patient Subculture

Do you expect staff members in your hospital to be concerned about:
1. Leadership persistently exercised by a small group of patients?
2. Myths or stories which the patients tell about the hospital and the staff?
3. Special jargon or "catch" phrases among the patients?
4. Trading forbidden foods and other articles of value among the patients?
5. Periodic patient misconduct?
6. Ways of "hazing" new patients as they enter the hospital?
7. Ways of "getting around" rules and regulations?
8. Periodic fads and fashion in dress, recreation, and so forth among the patients?

Reaction to patient subculture. Lastly, regardless of the extent of the hospital's concern about patterned deviations among the patients, each respondent indicated how such forms of patient behavior were treated. The reactions of the hospitals are listed in Table 3. A distinction was made between reactions that involved the adjustment of the hospital system itself, allowing indigenous forms of patient conduct to persist (marked "*s*" in Table 3), as compared with the implementation of administrative tactics and policies to eliminate the behavior, or to dominate or control the patients (marked "*p*" in Table 3). Reactions allowing the patient subculture to persist, here called *permissive patient control,* led to methods such as the use of ward representatives, relaxation of hospital rules when they appeared to conflict with the patients' customary behavior, and ward meetings and discussions among the patients. Reactions leading to direct organizational intervention to control patients, here termed *suppressive patient control,* included suppressing patient misconduct through therapists or other personnel, filling loop-

Table 3

Questionnaire Items on Reactions to Patient Subculture

Which of the following methods are used in your hospital to deal with the kinds of patient behavior you indicated to be present in your institutions?
1. Use of patient ward representatives or patient government, (s).*
2. Handle through the use of therapists or other personnel on an individual basis, (p).†
3. Filling loopholes in administrative procedures, (p).
4. Adding more ward personnel when possible, (p).
5. Relaxing hospital rules where they appear to conflict with the patients' forms of conduct, (s).
6. Ward meetings and discussions among the patients, (s).
7. Making regulations effective, (p).

* s = allowing patient conduct to persist.
† p = controlling patient conduct.

holes in rules and procedures, adding more ward personnel to achieve greater supervision, and making regulations generally more effective.

SUPERVISORY STYLE

The supervisory style characterizing the exercise of discretionary power in these hospitals was indicated by (*1*) the extent of organizational control over employee conduct, and (*2*) the kinds of standards and criteria against which adequate work performance was judged.

Employee control. The first indicator was whether employees were subject to scrutiny and control in relation to the wide range of behaviors listed in Table 4.[8] Hospitals attempting to maintain control over only the few kinds of behaviors directly related to the work situation, that is, having *limited employee control* were interested in working hours, consumption of alcohol, and the cleanliness of employees' work places. Hospitals, attempting to control a broad scope of employee conduct, whether directly or indirectly related to the work situation, that is, having *pervasive employee control* exercised control in relation to the forms of address workers used in talking with one another, how much leisure time employees spent with superiors and subordinates, faithfulness of employees to their spouses, and in other ways.

Table 4

Questionnaire Items on Employee Control

Do you feel that your organization has a responsibility to take account of and supervise your employees with respect to the following kinds of behaviors?
1. Employees' working hours.
2. How much alcohol employees consume.
3. The kind of temperament employees exhibit on the job.
4. How much importance employees attach to getting along with other people.
5. How employees divide up their work day among their various duties.
6. The type of clothing employees wear at work.
7. The form of address employees use in talking with their colleagues.
8. How much leisure time employees spend with their subordinates.
9. The tidiness of employees' offices or work places.
10. How faithful an employee is to his wife.
11. How much leisure time employees spend with their superiors.
12. The amount of work employees take home with them.

Job criteria. The second indicator of supervisory style was related to the criteria the service chief used to evaluate employee performance. Criteria such as the ability to supervise subordinates and to execute directions efficiently, and the level of formal education are here

8. The items were drawn from: Edgar H. Schein and J. S. Ott, The Legitimacy of Organizational Influence, *American Journal of Sociology,* 67 (May 1962), 682–689.

called *categoric criteria*. Those which emphasized previous work history and experience, creativity and initiative, and ability to get along with people, are here called *interpersonal criteria*. Workers in limited-control institutions might be expected to know and to conform to the prevailing rules of relevance more than persons in pervasive-control organizations, in which the limits of conduct relevance would be less precise and circumscribed.

The analysis, then, is based upon (*1*) *organizational size and sponsorship*, comparing large governmental hospitals with small private ones; (*2*) *structural controls* including specialization of tasks and operational policies; and (*3*) *supervisory styles*, as shown by the scope of organizational control over employee conduct and the criteria by which employees were judged.

These dimensions of organization are considered in their bearing on the control of organizational members. Specifically, it is argued that hospitals with specialized tasks, formal, lateral, and restricted communication patterns, with traditional treatment, with irrelevant patient subculture and suppressive patient control patterns have great structural capacity for control. Finally, it is assumed that interpersonal criteria of work competence and pervasive employee control result in greater pressures toward employee control than categoric criteria and limited employee control.

The aim of the following analysis is to determine the relations between structural and supervising forms of control within the two size and sponsorship categories of organizations.

FINDINGS

To the extent that the dimensions of organizational structure and dynamics may be related to a bureaucratic conception of organizations, the following associations might be expected among these variables:

1. The *structural* characteristics most conducive to achieving participant control will occur more frequently in large government hospitals than in small private ones. Specifically, specialized tasks, and formal, lateral, and restricted communication will characterize large government hospitals.
2. The *operational* structures most conducive to maximizing participant control, i.e., traditional treatment, will vary independently of specialization of tasks and forms of communication systems.[9]
3. Hospitals with specialized tasks (and other structural characteristics

9. Studies about the relevance of bureaucracy to administration may have led to a neglect of its relevance for work functions. Weber has written, "The concept of administrative authority would include all the rules which govern the behaviour of the administrative staff, as well as that of the members vis-à-vis the corporate group." Cf. M. Weber, *Basic Concepts in Sociology* (London: Peter Owen, 1962), p. 113.

conducive to control) will exercise more pervasive employee control than organizations with structural dimensions less conducive to maximum control.

4. Hospitals with structural arrangements likely to maximize employee control will also attempt to maximize control over patients, i.e., will have relevant patient subcultures and suppressive patient control.

With expectations such as these guiding the analysis of data, the findings are reported as they bear upon them. Associations are tested by means of chi-square analysis.

SIZE AND SPONSORSHIP, AND STRUCTURAL CONTROLS

There were marked associations between size and diffuse-restricted communication ($X^2 = 62.490$), and between size and lateral-institutional communications ($X^2 = 56.000$). Restricted communication —limited and prescribed kinds of information for each level of employees—was the typical pattern in the large governmental hospitals. The reverse, diffuse communication, characterized small private hospitals.[10] Similarly organizational size and sponsorship was associated with lateral-institutional communication. Information appeared to pass to and from all occupational levels in the smaller institutions, whereas it was limited more strictly to rank equals in the larger hospitals ($X^2 = 61.684$). The close association between size and sponsorship precludes an explanation of this finding; however, these findings *are* in accord with the expectations about communication systems and specialization of tasks in large government organizations, which are derived from a classical conception of bureaucracy.[11]

Contrary to what might have been anticipated, however, specialized tasks were found no more frequently in the large hospitals than in the small ones, nor were unspecialized task assignments characteristic of the smaller hospitals. Therefore, although large size and government sponsorship appeared to result in structural control by restricted communication and the limitation of participants to lateral communication, they were not otherwise important determinants of structural control mechanisms.

TASK SPECIALIZATION AND COMMUNICATION SYSTEMS

Hospitals with specialized tasks were characterized by lateral communication, while those with unspecialized tasks more often had insti-

10. One factor which may account for this pattern was the difference in the physical settings between the large and small organizations. The small institutions tended to operate with all employees in a single building. Many of the larger hospitals, however, included several buildings, each with different activities, and in some instances, the hospital's work spaces were not even on the same grounds.
11. The coincidence of authority communication patterns is discussed by T. Hopkins, "Bureaucratic Authority: The Convergence of Weber and Barnard," in A. Etzioni (ed.), *Complex Organizations* (New York: Winston, 1961), pp. 82–98.

tutional communication ($x^2 = 7.526$). Furthermore, those with specialized tasks relied on formal means of communication, but those with unspecialized tasks used more informal methods of communication ($x^2 = 15.272$). There was no significant difference, however, between the specialized and unspecialized hospitals as to restricted-diffuse communication responsibilities ($x^2 = 1.550$).

The data indicated, therefore, that maximization of control through specialization of tasks tended to be associated with control through the systems of communication and information flow in these organizations. It should be emphasized, however, that the relations between task assignments and communication lines were more marked in the small private hospitals than in the large ones. The relevance of size as an intervening variable was observed throughout this study.

SPECIALIZATION OF TASKS AND OPERATIONAL POLICIES

The data on the specialization of tasks and operational policies are shown in Table 5. There was a consistent association between specialization of tasks and type of treatment; again, however, the association was more marked in the small hospitals than in the large hospitals. In both cases, however, hospitals with specialized tasks tended to favor traditional treatment, whereas those with unspecialized tasks emphasized innovative treatment. Therefore, maximization of structural control through specialization of tasks, especially in the small hospitals, was

Table 5

Task Specialization and Operational Policies
in Relation to Size*

Operational Policies	Specialized Hospitals†	Unspecialized Hospitals‡	x^2	p
Small hospitals (N = 52)				
Innovative treatment (N = 31)	25.8	74.2	24.122	.001
Traditional treatment (N = 27)	70.3	29.7	6.166	.05
Relevant patient subculture (N = 28)	39.2	60.8	5.181	.05
Suppressive patient control (N = 22)	81.8	18.2	11.988	.001
Large hospitals (N = 80)				
Innovative treatment (N = 41)	36.5	63.5	15.542	.001
Traditional treatment (N = 38)	65.7	34.3	2.033	——
Relevant patient subculture (N = 42)	50.0	50.0	2.115	——
Suppressive patient control (N = 45)	68.8	31.2	5.464	.05

*Data are shown in percentages, with the N for each indicator of operational policy used as the base. Only the top two cells of each four-fold contingency are reproduced in the table. Frequencies in the reciprocal lower two cells may be computed by subtracting from two N's under structure of offices.
† N = 28 for small hospitals; N = 46 for large hospitals.
‡ N = 24 for small hospitals; N = 34 for large hospitals.

associated with control of patients through the operational system of the hospitals. Perhaps the most striking difference is that hospitals with specialized tasks tended to maximize patient control; whereas hospitals with unspecialized tasks showed minimal recourse to organizational constraints designed to control and dominate patterned deviations, despite the high relevance of these deviations.

There was, therefore, a consistent association between the structure of offices, indicated here by specialization of tasks, and operational policies, these associations being somewhat more marked in the small private hospitals. In general, the structural mechanisms of control inherent in the specialization of tasks were consistent with those in the systems of communication. Lastly, both of these control-implementing structures were found in close association with operational policies that maximized structured control over patients.

SUPERVISORY STYLES, SPECIALIZATION OF TASKS, AND OPERATIONAL POLICIES

The association between the employee control and work criteria was sufficiently marked ($\chi^2 = 7.713$) to suggest that they related to similar ways of expressing supervisory influence. That is, if there was pervasive employee control, employees were also likely to be subject to interpersonal criteria of work competence. In view of this, data are reported only in terms of employee control, although similar patterns were found for standards of work competence. The findings are reported in Table 6.

There were marked differences in specialization of tasks, systems of communication, and operational policies—all significantly related to the prevailing style of supervisory control. Specifically, hospitals with pervasive employee control tended to have unspecialized tasks as well as institutional, informal, and diffuse communication. On the other hand, organizations with limited employee control tended to have more specialization of tasks as well as more restricted and formalized communication.

Those hospitals in which the style of supervision was characterized by limited employee control stressed traditional treatment, regarded indigenous patterns of patient subculture as irrelevant, and reacted to patterned deviations by suppressive patient control. On the other hand, hospitals with pervasive employee control had unspecialized tasks, valued innovative treatment, found the patient subculture highly relevant, although they reacted to this by permissive patient control.

The point to be emphasized here is that when employee control was patterned into structured specialization of tasks, procedures for

Table 6

Internal Structures and Operational Policies in Relation to Employee Control in Small and Large Hospitals.*

Structure and Operation	All Hospitals					Small Hospitals (N = 52)					Large Hospitals (N = 80)				
	Pervasive Control (N = 73)	Limited Control (N = 59)	χ^2	P	N	Pervasive Control (N = 32)	Limited Control (N = 20)	χ^2	P	N	Pervasive Control (N = 41)	Limited Control (N = 39)	χ^2	P	N
Internal structures															
Specialized tasks	32.4	67.6	35.536	.001	74	39.3	60.7	12.568	.001	28	28.3	71.7	23.001	.001	46
Restricted communication	47.3	52.7	4.331	.05	74	42.9	57.1	†	—	7	47.8	52.2	2.117	—	67
Lateral communication	50.8	49.2	.898	—	61	43.3	56.7	10.065	.01	30	58.1	41.9	.930	—	31
Formal communication	36.6	63.4	21.809	.001	71	30.4	69.6	12.055	.001	23	39.6	60.4	6.537	.01	48
Operational policies															
Innovative treatment	73.6	26.4	21.538	.001	72	71.0	29.0	7.130	.01	31	73.2	26.8	12.560	.001	41
Traditional treatment	35.4	64.6	7.556	.01	65	25.9	74.1	23.342	.001	27	42.1	57.9	3.904	.05	38
Relevant patient subculture	72.8	27.2	18.595	.001	70	78.6	21.4	11.038	.001	28	69.0	31.0	8.258	.01	42
Suppressive patient control	49.2	50.8	2.009	—	67	40.5	59.5	7.048	.01	22	48.9	51.1	.226	—	45

* Data are shown in percentages, with the N's for each indicator of structure and policy used as the base. Only the two top cells of each fourfold contingency are reproduced in the table. Frequencies in the reciprocal lower two cells may be computed by subtracting from the two N's listed under types of administrative style.

† Expected frequency in cell too small to compute χ^2.

work, and systems of communication, then supervisory control of employees was minimal. When the structural patterns for employee control were absent, supervisory strategies of control appeared to elicit pervasive and extended patterns of employee control. In short, employee control appeared to be patterned into specialization of tasks in specialized hospitals, but was imposed by processes of supervisory influence in hospitals not having structural characteristics making for employee control.

A related though somewhat different issue is the contrasting kinds of operational policies found in these two types of organizations. The hospitals with specialized tasks favored traditional treatment, which involves the intrusion of objects between patients and employees—drugs, machines, implements, and consensually validated theory systems. Under such circumstances, relationships between patients and employees are likely to be routinized—perhaps to the point of depersonalization. Employees in such organizations are required to invest less of their personal selves (though perhaps more of their professional selves), in the processes of work. Hence, organizations in which such treatment policies are found—quite apart from their specialization of tasks—are presented with only a narrow scope of employee conduct to be controlled. But the innovative treatment in hospitals with unspecialized tasks allows patients and employees to be in continuous contact and interaction without the intervention of either a studied and symbolic professional repertoire or an elaborate machine technology. Therefore, employees in unspecialized hospitals may have more of their personal selves in their work, and therefore to present organizational authorities with a greater variety of behaviors for supervisory control.[12]

Finally, although these associations were the general pattern, there remains the persisting issue of organizational size as an intervening variable, between structural and supervisory means of control.

SUPERVISORY CONTROLS AND ORGANIZATIONAL SIZE

The patterns just discussed were generally consistent in both large and small institutions, but there was sufficient variation related to size to justify reporting associations between style of employee supervision and structural characteristics separately in the large and small hospitals. These data are also shown in Table 6.

First, limited employee control was associated with specialized

12. Similar patterns were found with respect to types of work performance criteria. Hospitals in which categoric standards were used—educational level and ability to "take orders"—tended to be bureaucratically organized and to value therapies such as electric shock, and also exercised maximal control over clients. But hospitals which evaluated employee competence on the basis of interpersonal criteria tended to be less bureaucratic and to value less traditional forms of care, and also exercised less constraint over patients.

tasks and with suppressive patient control in both the large and small hospitals; pervasive employee control was the prevailing supervisory style in those institutions with unspecialized task assignments and permissive patient control. That is, pervasive employee control was associated with permissive patient control, and limited employee control with suppressive control of patients.

Aside from this, the principal difference between the large and small organizations was in operational policies. In *both* the large and small hospitals with pervasive employee control, innovative forms of treatment tended to be highly valued. However, while smaller hospitals with pervasive employee control devalued traditional treatment, the larger hospitals placed considerable emphasis on traditional treatment *as well* as upon more innovative treatment. Also, high relevance of the patient subculture was associated with pervasive employee control in both the large and small establishments, but permissive patient control was strongly related to pervasive employee control *only* in the small organizations.

The style of supervisory control was related to the specialization of tasks in both large and small hospitals, but was related to differences in operational policies somewhat more strongly only in the small hospitals. Thus, the control of clients appeared to be linked to the control of employees through operational policies in the small hospitals, but through specialization of tasks in the large organizations. That is, large hospitals relied operationally upon those forms of treatment which themselves function as control mechanisms over patient behavior. Therefore, although they may have incorporated innovative treatment into their operational policies, thus indicating a tendency away from suppressive patient control, they also retained those structural features (traditional treatment) which tended toward suppressive patient control.

The implication of this, therefore, is that in the small hospitals, the coincidence of unspecialized tasks and pervasive employee control was accompanied by a decrease in control over patients both in operational strategies and supervisory constraint. While there was a similar congruence between unspecialized tasks and pervasive employee control in the large hospitals, those operational structures conducive to the maintenance of suppressive patient control were retained.

SUMMARY AND DISCUSSION

This study was concerned with the relation of organizational size and sponsorship, organizational structures and operational policies and styles of administrative supervision. Both structural characteristics and styles of supervision have been regarded as mechanisms for maintaining participant control.

SUMMARY

The data indicated that restricted communication responsibilities characterized large governmental institutions. Because of the correlation between size and sponsorship it is possible only to speculate as to whether this characteristic is related to size or sponsorship. It could be argued that increased size places both ecological and internal limitations on the access employees have to information. It may also be contended that the extra-organizational responsibilities of government agencies leads to more restricted communication responsibilities than in private organizations.

In the associations between specialization of tasks and communications also, small hospitals with specialized tasks had formal and restricted communication, while those with unspecialized tasks had informal and diffuse communication. The patterns in the large hospitals were less clear. Furthermore, specialized hospitals implemented traditional kinds of treatment, whereas unspecialized hospitals emphasized innovative treatment. Here again the association was somewhat more marked in the smaller hospitals than in the large ones.

Size and sponsorship, however, are not as closely related to organizational structures and operational policies as styles of supervisory control. Hospitals with pervasive employee control tended to have unspecialized tasks and innovative treatment; those with limited employee control had specialized tasks and traditional treatment.

INTERPRETATION BASED ON WEBERIAN MODEL

The association between types of internal structures and the character of operational policies is of further interest when considered from the point of view of hospitals using treatment based upon a body of rational-technical knowledge, the implementation of which is likely in itself to result in client control. All formal organizations are to some extent faced with an imperfect body of knowledge and a clientele that is not entirely compliant. The absence of a body of reliable knowledge makes orderly specialization of tasks hard to devise; consequently, task assignments become unspecialized and employee control a structural problem. The lack of client control associated with this presents organizations with a further control problem. It would appear, then, that an understanding of the control of organizational employees can hardly be separated analytically from the control of clients.

In specialized hospitals, the control of employees appeared to be achieved by structural means, and the control of patients by treatment programs in which methods, tactics, and techniques were recurrent, reliable, and predictable. These organizations were also conducted as if indigenous forms of inmate behavior were not relevant except in so far as the hospital had devised specific structural means to control such patterned deviations. In short, the presence of a technology resting upon rational-technical knowledge seemed to lead to the control of both patients and staff through structural mechanisms with a minimum of reliance upon supervisory control strategies. In unspecialized hospitals, policies were based less upon predictable and recurrent knowledge and were therefore less likely to result in the structural mechanisms conducive to patient or employee control. This seemed to be correlated with a highly relevant patient subculture, and resulted in reacting to patient deviations in a less controlling and constraining way. An explanation of these attributes of the unspecialized organizations may be that a drift away from specialized to unspecialized organizations may be accompanied by the emergence of what might be called a humanitarian organizational ethic that rejects the use of force and coercion.

Therefore, while the specialized hospitals were mobilized structurally to maximize patient control, the scope of employee control was limited. In contrast, unspecialized hospitals had neither the structural nor the supervisory mechanisms to maintain control over patients, and employees were the principal targets for supervisory control. In Goffman's terms, the specialized hospitals were "total" for clients, but "minimal" for employees, whereas structurally unspecialized hospitals were "minimal" for patients, but "total" for employees.[13] The distinction emphasized here between structural and supervisory means of control implies alternate ways of achieving consistency in the ways in which participants engage in the tasks of organizations. If organizations conformed to an ideal construct of bureaucracy, it does not seem likely that the exercise of supervisory controls would be found empirically. In such a case, control of both client and staff would occur through self-control, effected by the rationality of knowledge and the consequent systematic specialization of tasks. But with partial client autonomy and an imperfect division of labor, means of control will be devised outside the organizational structure.

In this study, supervisory style appeared to function as the mechanism of control over the employees, while operational policies functioned as the mechanism of control over clients.[14] One implication of this is that the intrusion of styles of supervision into organizations and

13. E. Goffman, *Asylums* (New York: Doubleday-Anchor), 1961.
14. Differences in the control functions of structure, policy, and style, in organizations of different size raises the possibility that optimum size categories may be found within which control of employees *is* achieved within the division of labor itself. In such a case, one might expect that the use of control would not be necessary and that administrative styles would be mild and unobtrusive. It might further be expected that within such optimal size categories, the classic separation of policy from administration might indeed be found, since the operational aspects of the organization would not need to be mobilized to serve both goal achievement and system maintenance functions at the same time.

the adaptation of operational policies to control problems represent defective structural arrangements. This becomes an even more plausible explanation when these seeming incongruities are viewed from the perspective of a conceptually pure model of bureaucratic organization. A second implication relates to the emphasis upon pervasive employee control in the unspecialized organizations, and suppressive client control in the specialized ones. This apparent anomaly might reflect organizational priorities not revealed by the data presented. In both cases, however, such implications lead logically to the conclusion that these patterns deviate from what organizations *ought* to be—in both structural and supervisory ways—were it not for the fact that they fall short of what a bureaucratic model of organizations prescribes. There is a different point of view, however, which warrants consideration.[15]

Interpretation Based on Non-Weberian Models

In contrast to the previous position, it could be argued that the relationships between structural and supervisory control of clients and staff are not unexpected. Such an argument rests upon the assumption that organizations need not conform in all respects to a classical model of bureaucracy to be judged orderly and understandable. Such a position assumes that organizations may have different, although equally legitimate, conceptions of their work; and that they work upon materials, with chosen means, with differing degrees of tractability and uniformity. Given variations in these respects, it seems reasonable to expect that organizations will be confronted with different kinds of control problems and will deal with them in different ways.

Bennis contends that the traditional bureaucratic form seems peculiarly suited to organizations that deal not with persons in their more humanized capacities but rather with objects, or with persons seen as objects.[16] To this extent, the associations between unspecialized tasks, innovative treatment, and permissive patient control might be understandable—although the pattern of employee control remains unexplained. There is, in addition, a large body of literature dealing with the therapeutic milieu in hospitals, in which the goals of the organization seem to necessitate deviations from the traditional bureaucratic form.[17]

---

15. A further causal sequence suggested by an editorial reader is that administrators begin their work with a "technological theory," the implementation of which requires a particular style of administration. This then results in the emergence of the appropriate organizational structures through which the available technology can best be administered. Comparative and longitudinal studies of organizational growth would be one means of putting this to the test.

16. The importance of shifts in values in the structure and function of organizations is suggested in W. Bennis, Beyond Bureaucracy, *Trans-Action,* 2 (July/August 1965), 31–35.

17. See for example, Mark Lefton, S. Dinitz, and B. Pasamanick, Decision-Making in a Mental Hospital: Real, Perceived, and Ideal, *American Sociological Review,* 24 (1959), 822–829; Robert Rapoport, *et al., Community as Doctor* (London: Tavistock, 1960); W. Rosengren, Communication, Organization, and Conduct in the "Therapeutic Milieu," *Administrative Science Quarterly,* 9 (June 1964), 70–90; A. Stanton and M. Schwartz, *The Mental Hospital* (New York: Basic Books), 1954.

More recently, Perrow has taken the position that differences in organizational structure arise as a consequence of the organization's perception of the materials to be worked upon.[18] One aspect of this model consists of a continuum along which materials range from well-understood, uniform, and stable (the custodial institution), to not well-understood, nonuniform, and unstable (the elite psychiatric agency). The conception of organizations derived from such a model is that the institution dealing with unknown and unstable human materials will be characterized by high supervisory power, high interdependence of groups, high supervisory discretion, and flexible polycentralized authority. This cluster of characteristics—regarded as systematic and orderly from the perspective of Perrow's model—are not inconsistent with the characteristics of unspecialized hospitals found here. Conversely, the organization dealing with well-understood and stable materials is characterized by low supervisory power, low group interdependence, low-administrative discretion, and by formal-centralized authority, patterns consistent with the structural and supervisory controls found in the specialized hospitals.

Another pertinent conception of organizations is that outlined by Burns and Stalker.[19] They contrast the properties of "mechanical" and "organic" management systems. The mechanical system (similar to specialized here) appears particularly suited to the maintenance of organizational stability in the face of stable external conditions, accommodates programmed decision making, and allows the individual employee more freedom than does the organic. Furthermore, the administrator is less apprehensive and concerned about what others in the organization are doing, and employee loyalty is achieved through a "*presumed* [italics mine] community of interest with the rest of the working organization," whereas in the organic system it arises out of a "commitment to the concern's task."[20]

The Perrow and the Burns and Stalker models account for differences in the structural arrangements in organizations that may not be consistent with a classical Weberian conception of organizations. They differ, however, in that Perrow regards perceptions of the materials worked upon as determinants of structural arrangements, whereas Burns and Stalker regard the contingencies of "innovation" as the more important.

The structural properties, operational activities, and styles of supervisory controls examined in this paper can be regarded as deviations

18. Charles Perrow, "Hospitals: Technology, Structure, and Goals," in J. March (ed.), *op. cit.;* also "A Framework for the Comparative Analysis of Organizations," paper presented at the Annual Meetings of the American Sociological Association, Miami, 1966.

19. T. Burns and G. Stalker, *op. cit.*

20. *Ibid.,* pp. 121-122.

from an ideal type, and therefore incongruous and inconsistent. On the other hand, more recent models of organizations make it possible to understand deviations from a pure bureaucratic model.

The differential effect of size may be critical in choosing one explanation rather than the other. The increased use of organizations as units of analysis may provide the opportunity to document an explanation for at least two findings of this study which are of interest to students of formal organizations: (1) the inverse relation between the employee and client control, and (2) specification of the variant relationships between structural and supervisory controls.

18

CONTROL IN MODERN ORGANIZATIONS

Philip M. Marcus *and* **Dora Marcus**

Perhaps Cervantes' Don Quixote expresses a universal urge in his words, "I would have nobody to control me, I would be absolute." Never possible even in a feudal age, such aspirations today seem all the more unreal in the face of the pervasiveness of modern organizations. Yet control need not be exercised to bring misery to men, and recent research or organizational theory has examined the implications of control for the sometimes competing goals of individual adjustment and organizational performance.

In pre-World War II organization theory, efficiency was assumed to result from specialization of task and strict adherence to a hierarchic chain of command.[1] While much theoretical literature of this period contains broad and useful hypotheses on organization behavior, its propositions are often highly abstract and difficult to apply to specific organizational situations.[2] More recent investigations including those of the Organization Behavior Program at the Survey Research Center, have shown that greater initiative at lower levels, freer communication

This article and much of the current research cited within it was made possible by a grant from the Carnegie Corporation of New York to the Survey Research Center, Institute for Social Research, The University of Michigan. We are indebted to Robert S. Friedman, Glenn Jones, Stanley E. Seashore, and Arnold S. Tannenbaum of The University of Michigan for critically reading our earlier drafts.
1. A thorough critical evaluation of the early organization literature can be found in James G. March and Herbert A. Simon, *Organizations* (Wiley and Sons, 1958).
2. Examples of these abstract propositions are Robert Michel's "iron law of oligarchy" and Max Weber's "routinization of charisma."

between levels, and less specialization may simultaneously provide an organization with a tighter control structure and a more competent and satisfied staff.[3] The research program at The University of Michigan has focused on control because of its central importance in coordinating diverse specializations and integrating groups into functioning units. After examining some of the theoretical aspects of control, we will dwell on some representative findings concerning the control structures of various organizations.

SOME THEORETICAL ASPECTS OF CONTROL

Coordination in an organization is effected by the organization's control structure. What must be coordinated includes not only the various organizational units representing division of labor, or specialization, but also the diverse capabilities, temperaments, and attitudes of the people employed. Control may be defined as "that process in which a person (or group of persons or organization of persons) determines, i.e., intentionally affects, what another person, (or group, or organization) will do."[4] This definition is sufficiently inclusive to encompass unilateral control, whereby one person or group influences another, or bilateral control, whereby two parties mutually affect each other.

An attempt to clarify aspects of organizational control has been made by Arnold S. Tannenbaum and Robert L. Kahn in their development of the "control graph,"[5] (see Figure 1), which depicts two aspects of control operative within an organization. The horizontal axis represents hierarchical levels in an organization. The vertical axis represents the amount of control that each level exercises.[6]

Plotting control in this manner provides a picture of the *distribution,* as well as the *amount* of control at various levels. The distribution of control is the amount of control exercised by *each* level in the organization. The sum of levels of control at all hierarchical levels may be considered the *total amount of control* operative in an organization. The *total amount* of control exercised in an organization is a variable

---

3. Some of these more recent theorists would include Rensis Likert, Chris Argyris, Douglas McGregor and W. F. Whyte. Georges Friedmann, writing of the industrial situation in Europe, has come to very similar conclusions about the more traditional approaches to administration.

4. Arnold S. Tannenbaum, "Control in Organizations: Individual Adjustment and Organizational Performance," 2 *Administrative Science Quarterly* 236–257. (September 1962).

5. Arnold S. Tannenbaum and Robert L. Kahn, *Participation in Union Locals* (Row, Peterson, 1958).

6. The measure employed to derive these control curves is usually some variation of the following questionnaire item:

"In general, how much influence do you think the following groups or persons actually have in determining the policies and actions in (organization's name)?"

The question is asked for each group or level in the organization and the response categories range from "no influence" to "a very great deal of influence." "Total control" is usually derived by summing the amount exercised at all levels. The distribution of control is calculated by subtracting the control exercised by the upper echelons from that exercised by the lower.

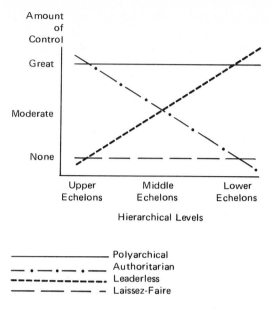

Figure 1. Control Curves for Four Different Types of Organizations.

frequently neglected in the literature. Control is most often viewed in terms of the position or person(s) exercising it.[7] Thus, there are analyses of "authoritarian" or "democratic" structures, or, in other words, analyses of the *distribution* of control. Such a conceptualization assumes that if control is redistributed and increased at the lower levels it is decreased at the top. But control removed from an upper level may result in a reduction of total control in the organization. For example, if executives, for some reason, issue fewer directives, it cannot be assumed that the discretion of lower echelons will necessarily be increased; it is more likely that fewer organizational demands will be met. Reducing the amount of total control beyond a certain level may endanger the coordination and effective functioning of an entire organization.

Different types of organizational control structure may be depicted on the control graph. An authoritarian organization would be represented by a negatively sloped line; a democratic or laissez-faire organi-

7. A few social scientists have begun to explore the possibility of social control as a non-fixed entity. It is quite explicit in Talcott Parsons, "On the Concept of Influence," 27 *Public Opinion Quarterly* 59–62 (Spring 1963). David Riesman implicitly makes a similar assumption in his analysis of the American power structure. David Riesman, "Who Has the Power?," in R. Bendix and S. M. Lipset (editors), *Class, Status and Power* (The Free Press, 1953), pp. 154–162. For a thorough discussion of control, see Rolf Dahrendorf, *Class and Class Conflict in Industrial Society* (Stanford University Press, 1959) pp. 157–240.

zation by a low flat line; and a polyarchical organization by a high flat line. Obviously, no organization would conform perfectly to any curve.

Although the *total amount* and the *distribution* of control are conceptually independent, subsequent research has not clearly indicated their empirical independence. In the Center study of the League of Women Voters,[8] the correlation between total amount of control and distribution of control was very small and statistically insignificant. David Bowers[9] also found a very low correlation between total control and distribution of control in his study of insurance agencies. On the other hand, a study of a large delivery company revealed a high and significant correlation between the two variables.[10]

In an analysis of membership participation in four labor unions it was reported that the membership as a whole exercised more influence than their presidents, i.e., the control curves tended to be positively sloped.[11] But when officers of the two most effective unions were compared with those of the other two, the membership reported that the more effective officers exercised more control. Members also reported that they exercised more control in the effective unions than in ineffective ones, thus affirming the assumption that effectiveness is related to the total amount of control exercised in an organization. Generally, all other organizations studied had negatively sloped control curves, i.e., officers were perceived as exercising more control than employees.

Self-ratings by the rank and file as to control they exercised showed variations among organizations.[12] On a five point scale of influence, for example, the lower skilled workers in a national delivery company felt they exerted the least control of the four hierarchical levels. League of Women Voters' members and insurance salesmen rated the amount of influence they exercised in their respective organizations about equally, and slightly above mid-points for the scale. Rank and file union members estimated their total influence to be very near the top of the scale.

In several studies respondents were asked to rate the amount of influence they *should have* (ideal control) in their organization as well as the amount of influence they did possess (actual control). The distributions of *ideal* and *actual* control responses for these studies have

8. Arnold S. Tannenbaum, "Control and Effectiveness in a Voluntary Organization," 68 *American Journal of Sociology* 33–46. (July 1961).
9. David G. Bowers, "Organizational Control in an Insurance Company," *Sociometry* 27, 2. (June 1964).
10. Clagett G. Smith and Ogus Ari, "Organization Control Structure and Member Consensus," 69 *American Journal of Sociology* 623–638. (May 1964).
11. Tannenbaum and Kahn, *op. cit.*
12. When making cross-organizational comparisons such as these self ratings, one of the limitations of the control graph should be kept in mind. The horizontal axis on the control graph representing the hierarchical levels varies for each graph since it depends upon the structure of each organization.

been plotted on control graphs and compared. A comparison of 32 stations in the delivery company showed negatively sloped curves for both actual and ideal control, i.e., workers felt they had and should have less control than their superiors. The workers' ideal curve also indicated they felt both they and their superiors should have more control.

In the League of Women Voters study, the ideal control curve was higher than the actual control curve; the actual and ideal slopes also differed in that members reported, on the one hand, that their officers had more control than the rank and file, and on the other hand, that members ought to have more control than either the president or the board. The amount of control the members thought the board should exercise was much greater than the amount they would grant the president, suggesting that League members see the role of president primarily as expediter, or representative to outside groups. In conclusion, it should be reported that most respondents of the organizations studied want more control, not only for themselves, but for others within the organization.

CONTROL AND INDIVIDUAL ADJUSTMENT

Distribution of control significantly affects individual behavior and adjustment to organizational life. Several studies made by the Center test the hypothesis that *morale* and *loyalty* to an organization and *participation* in it are high for those who desire to exercise control and are able to do so. Two experimental programs were set up in a clerical organization.[13] One was patterned after a *democratic model,* i.e., responsibility was increased and greater authority delegated to lower level personnel. At group meetings, decisions were made as to work distribution, length of recess, right to leave department during working hours, etc. The other experimental program was established along more *autocratic* lines, i.e., the clerks' routines were regulated more rigidly by "scientific management" principles, and decisions were made by upper level company officials. Results indicated that more clerks preferred the democratic model. However, there were persons in both programs who would have been more satisfied with the other type of control structure. What is needed is the integration of personality predispositions with the organizational pattern of control.

In the study of the League of Women Voters, loyalty to the League was measured by two questionnaire items concerning the degree of effort the respondent would make to prevent local leagues from failing from membership apathy or community opposition.[14] The amount of

13. Nancy C. Morse and Everett Reimer, "The Experimental Change of a Major Organizational Variable," 52 *The Journal of Abnormal and Social Psychology* 120–129. (January 1956).
14. Clagett G. Smith and Arnold S. Tannenbaum, "Organizational Control Structure: A Comparative Analysis," *Human Relations* 299–316. (in press, 1963).

influence and control exercised by League members was measured by a question concerning the influence exercised by members and officers. When the loyalty index was related to the control measure, it indicated that the more control League members exercised, the more loyalty they felt toward the organization.

Employees of 32 delivery stations were asked to rate the level of morale in their stations.[15] The mean of their responses regarding morale was computed for each station and was found to correlate with the measure of employee influence. Total control (i.e., the total amount of influence exerted within an organization) is also related to loyalty and morale. The delivery stations study showed that stations with more total control had higher employee morale. But this was also true for the four labor unions studied. No such relationship was found in the League study.

CONTROL AND ORGANIZATIONAL EFFECTIVENESS

Because goals vary from organization to organization and are often intangible, development of adequate measures of organizational effectiveness has been very difficult. Data on productivity, turnover, and absenteeism do not provide entirely satisfactory indices.[16] Measures of organizational effectiveness were related to measures of control in a number of studies. For example, in the study of the delivery stations, productivity records and ratings from questionnaire responses concerning the degree of intraorganizational strain and flexibility were used to determine effectiveness. Scores were assigned to each station. These scores correlated with scores on total control, but were found to be unrelated to the distribution of control.

In the study of the League of Women Voters, judges were asked to rate the individual leagues on a number of matters, e.g., success in fund-raising, quality of League publications, impact on the community, etc. Both total control and the distribution of control were found to be related to organizational effectiveness. The more influence exerted by lower levels of the League, the greater the effectiveness; the more reciprocal influence among all organizational levels, the greater the effectiveness.

In both studies, total control was related to organizational effectiveness; the distribution of control was found related to effectiveness only in the League study. This suggests that the total amount of control exercised in an organization is more crucial than the distribution of control.

15. Bernard Indik, Basil Georgopoulos, and Stanley E. Seashore, "Superior-Subordinate Relationships and Performance," 14 *Personnel Psychology* 357–374. (1951).
16. Basil Georgopoulos and Arnold S. Tannenbaum, "A Study of Organizational Effectiveness," 22 *American Sociological Review* 534–540. (1957).

The League however, must substitute psychological remunerations for the financial and status rewards offered to members of other organizations. The exercise of influence and control in League affairs is perhaps a major factor in maintaining the interest and activity of the membership and the effectiveness of the League as an organization.

Data from a nationwide survey of 30 automobile dealerships—highly competitive and reliant "individual enterprise" among their salesmen—suggest that the amount and distribution of control are more important in an organizational structure which emphasizes cooperation and coordination of its parts than in one which stresses competition and individual initiative.[17] Using sales records as a measure of effectiveness, it was discovered that there was no correlation with measure of total control or distribution of control.

Size may be another factor affecting the relationship between control and effectiveness. When the units of an organization are small and scattered, as are automobile dealerships, there is less likelihood of close personal ties. Group cohesiveness built upon these ties would not be enhanced, nor would norms governing production be sustained as motivating forces for the participants. Consequently, lower organizational effectiveness may result. In contrast, larger work units allow small subgroups to form among individuals with shared values and attitudes. Overlapping membership in small groups provides links with the larger organization and promotes greater member morale and loyalty, which, in turn, increases organizational effectiveness.[18]

CONTROL AND CONSENSUS

Consensus may be defined as uniformity in perceptions and attitudes.[19] Members of an organization may agree, for example, upon what jobs need to be done and the best ways of doing them. Such agreement among organizational participants produces judgments as to appropriate behavior and application of sanctions against those who do not conform. Consensus gives rise, then, to shared norms which govern the behavior and activities of members of an organization. Consensus should thus be positively related to organizational effectiveness.

A number of areas of consensus have been identified as relevant to

17. Martin Patchen, Stanley E. Seashore, and William Eckerman, "Some Dealership Characteristics Related to Change in New Car Sales Volume," Unpublished report (Institute for Social Research, 1961).

18. The relevance of work group size and its implications for social activity is explored in S. M. Lipset, M. A. Trow, and J. S. Coleman, *Union Democracy* (The Free Press, 1956), pp. 150–175. Stanley E. Seashore (*Group Cohesiveness in the Industrial Work Group,* Institute for Social Research, 1954), however, found a curvilinear relationship between size and group cohesiveness; small groups tended to have very low or very high cohesiveness scores. It is clear, then, that more research is needed to clarify this important point.

19. Clagett G. Smith and Ogus Ari, *op. cit.*

work groups, including work group standards, morale, adequacy of supervisory planning, general work group consensus, and amount of influence desire for various levels. In the stations of the delivery company, no significant correlations were found between *the distribution of control* and these variables. However, another variable, degree of trust and confidence in the supervisor, was significantly related. Even when the averages of these items were computed across hierarchical levels, they did not yield a relationship to the distribution of control. When the measures of consensus were correlated with *total amount of control* within each station, a different picture emerged. Four of these measures were found to be significantly related to total control: morale; trust and confidence in the supervisor; adequacy of supervisory planning; and general work group consensus. No relationship was found between work group standards or the influence desired for various levels and total control. When the amount of consensus *between* levels was analyzed, it was found that work group standards and morale were correlated with total control, while influence desired for various levels was not. Further, a general measure of consensus was found to relate to total control, but not to the distribution of control.

This indicates that total control, or the composite of mutual influence within a station, is related to the amount of consensus both between levels in the hierarchy and within the work group. Consensus, is necessary to the coordination and attainment of the goals of large scale organizations. Consensus makes possible a greater amount of decentralization of responsibility and delegation of tasks and, for this reason, is crucial to the effective operation of an organization.

Findings concerning control and consensus in the delivery company stations are consistent with those of the study of four labor unions. Twenty-four different items were used to measure union norms, including the willingness to do picket duty, the international's role, various passive and active sanctions, attitudes of member's friends, spouse, etc. In general, active members of the union showed a higher consensus on most of these norms than inactives. The four locals were ranked on their overall uniformity in nine content areas (representing a categorization of the 24 original items) and there was a very high correlation among the areas. Locals high in one area of uniformity tended to be high in others. A strong positive relationship was found when these measures were correlated with amount of total control in each local.

RESULTS FROM EXPERIMENTAL STUDIES

While some of the studies described yield findings of interest and potential value, it may be argued that the practical application of these findings is somewhat limited, that it would be an extremely difficult task to introduce new patterns of control into organizational settings. However, experimental studies are available which demonstrate that control variables and some of their correlates are capable of being implemented.

One such study conducted in a large white-collar organization has already been mentioned. In both the democratic and the autocratic experimental divisions, attempts to change the level of control and decision making, albeit in different directions, were successful. Along with the delegation of decision making, the amount of job involvement and company loyalty increased among members of the participative groups. The experimenters also reported that these employees continued to perform their jobs even in the absence of supervisors, and attitudes toward company management and high-producing workers became more favorable. The reverse was found among members of the hierarchically-controlled groups. These employees reported a decrease in job involvement, less loyalty to the company, and less feeling of job responsibility in the absence of their supervisors. Turnover also increased as did negative attitudes toward management and high-producers.

Yet productivity increased among both groups. In fact, the amount of increase was greater in the hierarchical groups than in the participative groups. While it is difficult to judge what the long run effects will be, it is suggested that effectiveness will decrease in the hierarchical groups because of the hostility and resentment developed toward high producers and management. ". . . [T]urnover and the adverse attitudes created by the hierarchically-controlled program tend typically to affect productivity adversely over a long period of time."[20]

Another experimental study cited earlier was conducted in a large manufacturing plant over a three-year period. Results of measures taken just prior to induced change indicated that all plant departments which had been selected to undergo no change, scored higher than the experimental departments on eleven independent variables. These variables involved various aspects of employee participation in decision making, peer interaction and influence, supportive behavior, and emphasis on the work group.[21] Measures taken at the end of the study revealed that all but one of the initial differences in variables reversed themselves. The experimental departments showed substantial improvement on ten of the variables,[22] while the others experienced negative change on seven variables.[23]

20. Rensis Likert, *New Patterns of Management* (McGraw-Hill, 1961), p. 68.
21. Of the eleven independent variables, only five differences between control and experimental departments were statistically significant. See Seashore and Bowers, *op. cit.,* Tables 3 and 4, pp. 73–74.
22. Of these ten independent variables, eight were found to be statistically significant.
23. Of these seven independent variables, four were found to be statistically significant.

An analysis of the dependent variables in this study revealed a more or less consistent pattern with that of the independent variables, i.e., generally favoring the experimental departments. An increase in measures of machine efficiency and employee satisfaction was found for the experimental groups, and a decrease in both variables was found for the control groups. While both the experimental and control departments increased in absentee rates, the increase was greater in the control groups.

CONCLUSION

The research described in these pages suggests that the concept of *total control* must be closely considered in a study of organizational behavior. Whether the criterion of a good organization is that of productivity or the intelligent utilization of human resources, the findings indicate that with greater *total control* there is a greater sharing in control at all levels, morale is higher, consensus regarding work is greater, and organizational effectiveness is facilitated.

It is virtually impossible for upper echelons to integrate and coordinate the lower levels in organizations characterized by increasing specialization, because persons in the upper echelons lack sufficient technical understanding. In fact, the subordinates who carry out the directives are often in a better position to make wise decisions.

In short, both organizational characteristics and humane considerations require that some control be delegated to the lower echelons. A greater amount of total control, whereby subordinates can actually influence their supervisors, will heighten, not lower, the organization's performance. However, when subordinates obtain a measure of expertise but are given no control, morale and willingness to contribute to the organization decrease. Dissatisfactions manifest themselves in high turnover and absentee rates, and in lower efficiency and production.

The comparisons made earlier between actual and ideal control curves showed that subordinates do not want more control and influence for themselves at the expense of higher levels in the organization. Rather, they desire more control for all levels over job activities, so that individuals know what is expected of them and what rewards or punishments they may receive. As society becomes increasingly dependent upon organization services, it needs also to become increasingly sensitive to the critical implications of control for individual adjustment and organizational performance.

CHAPTER FIVE

ORGANIZATIONAL AND
ENVIRONMENTAL INTERACTION

In the initial chapter of this book, several alternative theoretical approaches were presented. One of the criteria for selecting these particular approaches was that they focus on the organization as the unit of analysis. Organizations, as Parsons suggests, are parts of larger social systems, i.e., they exist within an environment which consists of physical elements, culture, other organizations, etc. An organization can only be partially understood unless it is considered within the context of its environment. Research demonstrates that there is reciprocal influence between the environment and the organization.

The selection by Lawrence and Lorsch examines the inter-relationship between the individual and the organization as well as the inter-relationship between the organization and the environment. As organizations get larger they tend to segment into departments. These departments, in turn, interact with the other parts of their environment. They find that the inter-relationship of the organization and the environment influences the goals, time orientation, interpersonal relations, and formality of structure. The types of environments affect the organization differentially just as the various types of organizations may be influenced differentially by the same environment.

Most organizational theorists in the past have treated goals as static. However, Thompson and McEwen conceptualize goals as recurring, dynamic problems which face the organization. Since the goals are dynamic, constant interaction between the organization and the environment is required. This article also hypothesizes that a power relation-

245

ship exists between the organization and the environment. At one extreme the organization clearly dominates the environmental relationships, whereas at the other extreme the organization is clearly dominated by the environment. In reality, most organizations fall somewhere between these extremes. Consequently, the organizations must adopt strategies for coming to terms with the environment.

Thompson and McEwen discuss two major forms or classes of strategy: competition and cooperation. They further subdivide cooperation into three subtypes: (a) bargaining, (b) cooptation, (c) coalition. Thompson and McEwen's strategy does not present competition and conflict as subtypes of cooperation, but they clearly may be so conceptualized. Just as bargaining requires rules, structure, normative behavior, etc., there are also these same kinds of elements involved with competition and conflict.

The article by Emery and Trist investigates organizational change as it especially relates to differences in the environment. The article introduces the concept "causal texture of the environment" which suggests that in order to understand exchange between the organization and the environment, it is first necessary to examine the interdependencies within the environment. They present four "ideal types" of environments which influence organizational adaptation: (1) placid, randomized environment, (2) placid, clustered environment, (3) disturbed-reactive environment, and (4) turbulent fields. The fourth type is of especial importance. It suggests that organizations increasingly encounter relevant uncertainty. Value consensus is of primary importance when the organization encounters high degrees of uncertainty, i.e., a turbulent field.

Rickson and Simpkins's original paper suggests that the cultural and structural properties of a society interact with the natural environment. They note that the very existence of complex organizations is dependent upon the physical and social environment. The article contends that water pollution and its control by industry must be examined within societal value systems. The authors strongly intimate that the values of the economic institution (profits) override the esthetic values within modern society—hence, pollution. Complex organizations must search for information to control pollution since they are among the most effective agents for change which deal with this problem. The organization is adaptive and therefore turns to the industrial scientists for information relevant to such change.

Some characteristics of organizations are more influential than others in affecting the successful relationship of the organization with its environment. Organizational prestige is one of these characteristics. Young and Larsen present empirical data from forty-three organizations in order to investigate selected correlates of organizational prestige. They find organizational prestige is related to such structural attributes as formal organization, program characteristics, internal and external contact, etc. Organizations high in prestige tend to also be high in complexity. They appear to function as channels of information in and out of the community to the greater society. The most important organizations also embody the value constellations of the community of which they are a part.

———————————————————— **19** ————————————————————

ORGANIZATION AND ENVIRONMENT
Managing Differentiation and Integration

Paul R. Lawrence and Jay W. Lorsch

THE ORGANIZATION AS A SYSTEM

At the most general level we find it useful to view an organization as an open system in which the behaviors of members are themselves interrelated. The behaviors of members of an organization are also interdependent with the formal organization, the tasks to be accomplished, the personalities of other individuals, and the unwritten rules about appropriate behavior for a member. Under this concept of system, the behavior of any one manager can be seen as determined not only by his own personality needs and motives, but also by the way his personality interacts with those of his colleagues. Further, this relationship among organization members is also influenced by the nature of the task being performed, by the formal relationships, rewards, and controls, and by the existing ideas within the organization about how a well-accepted member should behave. It is important to emphasize that all these determinants of behavior are themselves interrelated.

For example, a typical manufacturing executive behaves in a certain manner not only because of his own personality, but also because his job as a plant manager requires him to have contact with a certain group of subordinates and with a number of executives at his own level as well as with a particular superior. While the individual personalities of these other executives may influence his behavior, our man will probably also behave as he does because of some expectations he shares with all these other managers about how a plant manager in this company should behave. The behavior of this executive will also be influenced by the fact that there is an established control system that measures certain costs and certain quality characteristics. The exact nature of the control system may be closely related to the nature of the technology. In a job-order shop a plant manager might be concerned about somewhat different matters from those that would confront the manager of a chemical processing plant. Both the formal organization and the technology may also be related to the shared expectations of how managers should behave, and because of all these characteristics the organization may attract managers with certain personality needs.

This description of an organization as a system has, for illustration, focused on the influences affecting the behavior of a typical manager. Our interest, however, is in understanding the behavior of large numbers of managers in sizable organizations. This necessitates a central concern with two other important aspects of the functioning of systems. First, as systems become large, they differentiate into parts, and the functioning of these separate parts has to be integrated if the entire system is to be viable. As an analogy, the human body is differentiated into a number of vital organs, which are integrated through the nervous system and brain. Second, an important function of any system is adaptation to what goes on in the world outside. We, as human systems, are very much concerned about dealing with the people and things that make up our external environment.

DIFFERENTIATION AND INTEGRATION AND THE ORGANIZATION'S ENVIRONMENT

It is on the states of differentiation and integration in organizational systems that this study places major emphasis. As organizations deal with their external environments, they become segmented into units, each of which has as its major task the problem of dealing with a part of the conditions outside the firm. This is a result of the fact that any one group of managers has a limited span of surveillance. Each one has the capacity to deal with only a portion of the total environment. If we take as an example either a division of a large, diversified corporation or a medium-sized manufacturing firm, we readily observe sales, production, and design units, each of which is coping with a portion of the organization's external environment. The sales unit faces problems associated with the market, the customers, the competitors, and so on. The production unit deals with production equipment sources, raw materials sources, labor markets, and the like. Such external conditions as the state of scientific knowledge and opportunities for expanding knowledge and applying it are in the most general sense the purview of the design unit. These parts of the system also have to be linked together toward the accomplishment of the organization's overall purpose. This division of labor among departments and the need for unified effort lead to a state of differentiation and integration within any organization.

The concepts of differentiation and integration as applied to organizations are not novel. They have been discussed in one way or another by a number of organization theorists and researchers. The best way to understand the differences in our approach from those of the other writers on organizational topics is to point to the way these concepts have been used in the past. In so doing we acknowledge our intellectual debt to these earlier theorists, and also recognize that the limitations of their use of these concepts have become apparent only through increased knowledge about the functioning of organizations.

Early writers about organizations, who have been labeled the classicists, were concerned with differentiation and integration.[1] Fayol, Gulick, Mooney, and Urwick dealt with how best to divide the tasks of the organization and how to obtain integration within it. From our point of view, however, their major failing was that they did not recognize the systemic properties of organizations. As a consequence, they failed to see that the act of segmenting the organization into departments would influence the behavior of organizational members in several ways. The members of each unit would become specialists in dealing with their particular tasks. Both because of their prior education and experience and because of the nature of their task, they would develop specialized working styles and mental processes.[2] For example, research managers and their subordinates tend to develop a distinct pace of work and orientation to time and to technical achievement as they spend hours puzzling over ambiguous problems. Similar points could be made about the ways of thinking and behavior patterns of other functional groups, such as production and sales. By differentiation we mean these differences in attitude and behavior, not just the simple fact of segmentation and specialized knowledge.

The observation of these differences is, of course, not new. In the course of this study, however, we have gone beyond everyday observation to identify three specific dimensions of the differences in ways of thinking and working that develop among managers in these several

1. Henri Fayol, *Industrial and General Administration,* Part II, Chapter I, "General Principles of Organization"; Chapter II, "Elements of Administration" (Paris: Dunod, 1925).

Luther Gulick, "Notes on the Theory of Organizations," in *Papers on the Science of Administration,* Luther Gulick and Lyndall F. Urwick, eds. (New York: Institute of Public Administration, Columbia University, 1937).

Lyndall F. Urwick, "Organization as a Technical Problem," in *Papers,* op. cit.

James D. Mooney, "The Principles of Organization," in *Papers,* op. cit.

2. Research evidence of this can be found in James G. March and Herbert A. Simon, *Organizations* (New York: John Wiley & Sons, 1958).

functional units. First, we have investigated the differences among managers in different functional jobs *in their orientation toward particular goals.* To what extent are managers in sales units concerned with different objectives (*i.e.,* sales volume) from those of their counterparts in production (*i.e.,* low manufacturing costs)? Second, we have been interested in differences in the *time orientation* of managers in different parts of the organization. Might production executives not be more pressed by immediate problems than design engineers, who deal with longer-range questions? Third, we have been concerned with differences in the way managers in various functional departments typically deal with their colleagues, that is with their *interpersonal orientation.*[3] Are managers in one part of the organization more likely to be preoccupied with getting the job done when they deal with others, while those in another unit pay more attention to maintaining relationships with their peers? In selecting these three categories of orientations to examine, we are not suggesting that these are the only differences that might be found among managers in different parts of an organization, but only that they seemed to be three important dimensions which our own observations of managerial behavior and earlier behavioral science research have suggested might be important.

The early organization theorists also did not recognize that each of the functional units would develop different formal reporting relationships, different criteria for rewards, and different control procedures, depending on the task of each unit.[4] Thus, the production department might have many levels in the management hierarchy, rewards for performance in meeting cost and quality standards, and control systems that measure these criteria in detail. On the other hand, a research unit might have fewer supervisory levels for each supervisor, rewards for performance of a broad objective such as "contribution to knowledge," and a much less precise control system. The variation in the *formality of structure* is the fourth dimension of differentiation among functional units that we have attempted to investigate.

In summary, when we refer to differentiation among units, we will mean differences in goal orientation and in the formality of structure. While these four characteristics are not all-inclusive and homogeneous, they do provide us with shorthand measures of differentiation as we define it in this study—*the difference in cognitive and emotional orientation among managers in different functional departments.* When we describe pairs of units or organizations as having more or less differentiation, we will be referring to whether the managers in the various units

3. This difference was suggested by the work of Fiedler. For example, see Fred E. Fiedler, *Technical Report No. 10,* Group Effectiveness Research Laboratory, Department of Psychology, University of Illinois, May 1962.
4. R. H. Hall, "Intraorganizational Structure Variables," *Administrative Science Quarterly,* December 1962, pp. 295–308.

are quite different (more differentiation) in these four attributes or whether they are relatively similar (less differentiation).

As the early organization theorists did not recognize the consequences of the division of labor on the attitudes and behaviors of organization members, they failed to see that these different orientations and organizational practices would be crucially related to problems of achieving integration. Because the members of each department develop different interests and differing points of view, they often find it difficult to reach agreement on integrated programs of action.[5] A plant manager and a sales manager with different assigned responsibilities could quite naturally be expected to hold different views about the best price for a particular product. The plant manager might find a higher price, which would give him a wider latitude in production costs, desirable, while the sales manager might prefer a lower price, which would enable him to meet competition more effectively. This very elementary example of a built-in conflict of interests is compounded a hundred times over in a real organization, and the issues at stake are seldom so clear cut. It does, however, illustrate how we define integration—*the quality of the state of collaboration that exists among departments that are required to achieve unity of effort by the demands of the environment.* While we will be using the term "integration" primarily to refer to this state of interdepartmental relations, we will also, for convenience, use it to describe both the process by which this state is achieved and the organizational devices used to achieve it.

CONFLICT RESOLUTION TO ACHIEVE INTEGRATION

While the early theorists did not explicitly recognize the relationship between the states of differentiation and integration, they did emphasize the need for integration in the organization. Their view, however, was that integration is accomplished through an entirely rational and mechanical process. If the total task of the organization was divided up according to certain principles, the integration would be taken care of simply by issuing orders through the management hierarchy, "the chain of command."[6] Our view, on the other hand, is that integration is *not* achieved by such an automatic process. In fact, the different points of view held by various functional specialists are frequently going to lead to conflicts about what direction to take. To achieve effective integration these conflicts must be resolved. The man-

5. This point was first made by Muzafer Sherif in "Superordinate Goals in the Reduction of Intergroup Conflict," *American Journal of Sociology*, March, 1958, pp. 356–394, and *Intergroup Relations and Leadership*, Muzafer Sherif, ed. (New York: John Wiley & Sons, 1962); more recently in the context of industrial organizations by March and Simon, op. cit. It is put forth in an earlier report of part of this study by Jay W. Lorsch, *Product Innovation and Organization* (New York: The Macmillan Company, 1965).
6. Mooney, op. cit., and Urwick, op. cit. One exception was Gulick, op. cit.

agerial hierarchy provides one means through which this resolution can come about, but it is not the only means. In many organizations integrating committees and teams are established or individual integrators are designated to facilitate collaboration among functional departments at all management levels. Routine control and scheduling procedures also provide a means of achieving integration. Finally, much integrating activity is carried out by individual managers outside official channels.[7] In our investigation we have also attempted to learn what factors have created the need for these various integrating devices, and what factors may be related to their serving a useful function in resolving conflict and achieving integration under various external environmental conditions.

In learning what factors determine the effectiveness of these various integrative devices, we have focused on another shortcoming in the early organization theories. Because of their notion that the process of achieving integration is mechanical and entirely rational, the early writers ignored the feelings and emotions connected with the achievement of organizational collaboration. As a consequence, they did not concern themselves to any great extent with the interpersonal skills required to achieve integration.[8]

This issue of interpersonal skills and their relationship to organizational integration has been a central concern of many later theorists and researchers, particularly behavioral scientists. These students of human relations have pointed to a variety of conditions in interpersonal relationships that are necessary to attain effective collaboration.[9] One such condition is that the parties who are dealing with one another learn to be open and frank about their positions as they work together. This openness leads to a climate of trust among the parties, which results in more effective problem solving. Closely related to this is the idea that conflicts must be confronted and brought into the open, rather than suppressed through the power of one side or avoided by the tacit consent of all.

While we have attempted to build on these and related ideas, they do have two major limitations. First, these theorists and researchers have been so concerned with problems of achieving collaboration that many of them have overlooked the equally important need for differentiation within organizations.[10] As a consequence, they appear at times

---

7. These same points have been made by Joseph Literer in *The Analysis of Organizations* (New York: John Wiley & Sons, 1965).

8. One exception to this was Mary Parker Follett in *Dynamic Administration: The Collected Papers of Mary Parker Follett* (New York: Harper and Brothers, 1940).

9. A more comprehensive review of this literature and its sources is provided in Chapter VII of the book from which this selection was taken.

10. An important exception to this statement is A. K. Rice and his colleagues at Tavistock. For example, see A. K. Rice, *The Enterprise and Its Environment* (London: Tavistock Publications, 1963), pp. 186–198, March.

to view recurrent conflict and disagreement as an avoidable dissipation of human energy. It is our view, given the need for differentiated ways of working and points of view in various units of large organizations, that recurring conflict is inevitable. The important question which we have tried to answer is how the specifics of each conflict episode can be managed and resolved without expecting conflict to disappear. In other words, how can integration be facilitated without sacrificing the needed differentiation?

ENVIRONMENTAL AND TASK ATTRIBUTES

These are some of the essential ways in which our approach differs from the ideas of the classical theorists and from those of many of the human relations researchers. There is, however, one other difference —to us the most important of all. Until very recently, as we have suggested, organization researchers and theorists have tended to view the internal functioning of effective organizations as if there was one best way to organize. No attention was devoted to the problem in which we are interested—that different external conditions might require different organizational characteristics and behavior patterns within the effective organization.

Our conviction that this approach might be fruitful came from several sources. First, our observations in many organizations as we gathered case studies for teaching provided concrete examples of the fact that different types of organizations were effective under different conditions. A case study of a highly profitable fine-grade paper company revealed an organization with very little reliance on formal rules and procedures, and with only limited control at the top of the organization.[11] Many important decisions were reached at the lowest levels of management. On the other hand, a case study of a highly profitable meat packing firm uncovered a different type of organization.[12] Here we found highly detailed procedures, many levels in the hierarchy, and very strong and dominant control at the top. We were intrigued with the question of what differences in the production technologies and in the markets might be related to the different styles of these two highly effective organizations.

Our curiosity was further stimulated by the involvement of one of the authors in a recent research study of worker response to varying technologies.[13] Although this particular research was not designed to

11. "Marshall Company Case," in *Organizational Behavior and Administration,* Paul R. Lawrence and John A. Seiler, eds. (Homewood: Richard D. Irwin and the Dorsey Press, 1965).
12. "Pioneer Packing Company," Case No. 449 R, Copyright by the President and Fellows of Harvard College, 1964.
13. Arthur N. Turner and Paul R. Lawrence, *Industrial Jobs and the Worker* (Boston: Division of Research, Harvard Business School, 1965).

examine overall organizational patterns in relation to technological and market differences, as the data were gathered and the researchers were exposed to eleven different organizations in as many industries it became apparent that there were differences in organizational patterns among these firms. If there was one best way to structure and administer an organization, how could these companies, which by economic criteria were all reasonably effective, have such diverse organizational styles?

Two recent studies have more systematically addressed these questions and further stimulated our interest. Joan Woodward reported that successful organizations in different industries with different technologies are characterized by different organizational structures. For example, she found that the most successful firms in industries characterized by a unit or job-shop production technology had wider spans of supervisory control and fewer levels in the hierarchy than did successful firms in industries with continuous-process technology. A related finding was reported by Burns and Stalker in a study of firms in both a dynamic, changing industry and a more stable, established industry. Organizations in the stable industry tended to be what the authors called "mechanistic." There was more reliance on formal rules and procedures. Decisions were reached at higher levels of the organization. The spans of supervisory control were narrower. On the other hand, effective organizations in the more dynamic industry were typically more "organic." Spans of supervisory control were wider; less attention was paid to formal procedures; more decisions were reached at the middle levels of the organization, etc.

Both of these studies suggested that differing technical and economic conditions outside the firm necessitated different organizational patterns within it. More specifically these studies, particularly that of Burns and Stalker, suggested that the certainty of information or knowledge about events in the environment was one external dimension that impacted on the organizational variables in which we were interested. As we have already suggested, it might affect the organizational practices within departments, but it might also create different requirements for the way integration was achieved in the total organization. In more certain environments conflicts might be resolved and integration achieved at the upper levels through the management hierarchy. In less certain environments conflict resolution and the achievement of integration might have to take place at the lower levels of the hierarchy.

The questions raised by these two studies and our own observations of organizational situations can be summarized as follows:

1. How are the environmental demands facing various organizations

different, and how do environmental demands relate to the internal functioning of effective organizations?

2. Is it true that organizations in certain or stable environments make more exclusive use of the formal hierarchy to achieve integration, and, if so, why? Because less integration is required, or because in a certain environment these decisions can be made more effectively at higher organizational levels or by fewer people?

3. Is the same degree of differentiation in orientation and in departmental structure found in organizations in different industrial environments?

4. If greater differentiation among functional departments is required in different industries, does this influence the problems of integrating the organization's parts? Does it influence the organizational means of achieving integration?

As we considered these issues, we realized that many organizational theorists and researchers were asking the wrong question. There probably is no one best way to organize. If our observations were correct, better practicing managers, consciously or by natural selection, recognized this fact as they designed and administered organizations under different environmental conditions. If we could investigate and compare organizations in several different environments, we might provide a systematic understanding of what states of differentiation and integration are related to effective performance under different environmental conditions, and further, we might learn something about how these states are achieved.

20

ORGANIZATIONAL GOALS AND ENVIRONMENT
Goal Setting as an Interaction Process

James D. Thompson and William J. McEwen

In the analysis of complex organizations the definition of organizational goals is commonly utilized as a standard for appraising organizational performance. In many such analyses the goals of the organization are often viewed as a constant. Thus a wide variety of data, such as official documents, work activity records, organizational output, or statements by organizational spokesmen, may provide the basis for the definition of goals. Once this definition has been accomplished, interest in goals as a dynamic aspect of organizational activity frequently ends.

It is possible, however, to view the setting of goals (i.e., major organizational purposes) not as a static element but as a necessary and recurring problem facing any organization, whether it is governmental, military, business, educational, medical, religious, or other type.

This perspective appears appropriate in developing the two major lines of the present analysis. The first of these is to emphasize the interdependence of complex organizations within the larger society and the consequences this has for organizational goal-setting. The second is to emphasize the similarities of goal-setting *processes* in organizations with manifestly different goals. The present analysis is offered to supplement recent studies of organizational operations.[1]

It is postulated that goal-setting behavior is *purposive* but not necessarily *rational;* we assume that goals may be determined by accident, i.e., by blundering of members of the organization and, contrariwise, that the most calculated and careful determination of goals may be negated by developments outside the control of organization members. The goal-setting problem as discussed here is essentially determining a relationship of the organization to the larger society, which in turn becomes a question of what the society (or elements within it) wants done or can be persuaded to support.

GOALS AS DYNAMIC VARIABLES

Because the setting of goals is essentially a problem of defining desired relationships between an organization and its environment, change in either requires review and perhaps alteration of goals. Even where the most abstract statement of goals remains constant, application requires redefinition or interpretation as changes occur in the organization, the environment, or both.

The corporation, for example, faces changing markets and develops staff specialists with responsibility for continuous study and projection of market changes and product appeal. The governmental agency, its legislative mandate notwithstanding, has need to reformulate or reinterpret its goals as other agencies are created and dissolved, as the population changes, or as non-governmental organizations appear to do the same job or to compete. The school and the university may have unchanging abstract goals but the clientele, the needs of pupils or students, and the techniques of teaching change and bring with them

1. Among recent materials that treat organizational goal-setting are Kenneth E. Boulding, *The Organizational Revolution,* New York: Harper and Brothers, 1953; Robert A. Dahl and Charles E. Lindblom, *Politics, Economics, and Welfare,* New York: Harper and Brothers, 1953; and John K. Galbraith, *American Capitalism: The Concept of Countervailing Power,* Boston: Houghton Mifflin, 1952.

redefinition and reinterpretation of those objectives. The hospital has been faced with problems requiring an expansion of goals to include consideration of preventive medicine, public health practices, and the degree to which the hospital should extend its activities out into the community. The mental hospital and the prison are changing their objectives from primary emphasis on custody to a stress on therapy. Even the church alters its pragmatic objectives as changes in the society call for new forms of social ethics, and as government and organized philanthropy take over some of the activities formerly left to organized religion.[2]

Reappraisal of goals thus appears to be a recurrent problem for large organization, albeit a more constant problem in an unstable environment than in a stable one. Reappraisal of goals likewise appears to be more difficult as the "product" of the enterprise becomes less tangible and more difficult to measure objectively. The manufacturing firm has a relatively ready index of the acceptability of its product in sales figures; while poor sales may indicate inferior quality rather than public distaste for the commodity itself, sales totals frequently are supplemented by trade association statistics indicating the firm's "share of the market." Thus within a matter of weeks, a manufacturing firm may be able to reappraise its decision to enter the "widget" market and may therefore begin deciding how it can get out of that market with the least cost.

The governmental enterprise may have similar indicators of the acceptability of its goals if it is involved in producing an item such as electricity, but where its activity is oriented to a less tangible purpose such as maintaining favorable relations with foreign nations, the indices of effective operation are likely to be less precise and the vagaries more numerous. The degree to which a government satisfies its clientele may be reflected periodically in elections, but despite the claims of party officials, it seldom is clear just what the mandate of the people is with reference to any particular governmental enterprise. In addition, the public is not always steadfast in its mandate.

The university perhaps has even greater difficulties in evaluating its environmental situation through response to its output. Its range of "products" is enormous, extending from astronomers to zoologists. The test of a competent specialist is not always standardized and may be

2. For pertinent studies of various organizational types see Burton R. Clark, *Adult Education in Transition*, Berkeley and Los Angeles: University of California Press, 1956; Temple Burling, Edith M. Lentz, and Robert N. Wilson, *The Give and Take in Hospitals*, New York: G. P. Putnam's Sons, 1956, especially pp. 3–10; Lloyd E. Ohlin, *Sociology and the Field of Corrections*, New York: Russell Sage Foundation, 1956, pp. 13–18; Liston Pope, *Millhands and Preachers*, New Haven: Yale University Press, 1942; Charles Y. Glock and Benjamin B. Ringer, "Church Policy and the Attitudes of Ministers and Parishioners on Social Issues," *American Sociological Review*, 21 (April, 1956), pp. 148–156. For a similar analysis in the field of philanthropy, see J. R. Seeley, B. H. Junker, R. W. Jones, Jr., and others, *Community Chest: A Case Study in Philanthropy*, Toronto: University of Toronto Press, 1957, especially Chapters 2 and 5.

changing, and the university's success in turning out "educated" people is judged by many and often conflicting standards. The university's product is in process for four or more years and when it is placed on the "market" it can be only imperfectly judged. Vocational placement statistics may give some indication of the university's success in its objectives, but initial placement is no guarantee of performance at a later date. Furthermore, performance in an occupation is only one of several abilities that the university is supposed to produce in its students. Finally, any particular department of the university may find that its reputation lags far behind its performance. A "good" department may work for years before its reputation becomes "good" and a downhill department may coast for several years before the fact is realized by the professional world.

In sum, the goals of an organization, which determine the kinds of goods or services it produces and offers to the environment, often are subject to peculiar difficulties of reappraisal. Where the purpose calls for an easily identified, readily measured product, reappraisal and readjustment of goals may be accomplished rapidly. But as goals call for increasingly intangible, difficult-to-measure products, society finds it more difficult to determine and reflect its acceptability of that product, and the signals that indicate unacceptable goals are less effective and perhaps longer in coming.

ENVIRONMENTAL CONTROLS OVER GOALS

A continuing situation of necessary interaction between an organization and its environment introduces an element of environmental control into the organization. While the motives of personnel, including goal-setting officers, may be profits, prestige, votes, or the salvation of souls, their efforts must produce something useful or acceptable to at least a part of the organizational environment to win continued support.[3]

In the simpler society social control over productive activities may be exercised rather informally and directly through such means as gossip and ridicule. As a society becomes more complex and its productive activities more deliberately organized, social controls are increasingly exercised through such formal devices as contracts, legal codes, and governmental regulations. The stability of expectations provided by these devices is arrived at through interaction, and often through the exercise of power in interaction.

3. This statement would seem to exclude anti-social organizations, such as crime syndicates. A detailed analysis of such organizations would be useful for many purposes; meanwhile it would appear necessary for them to acquire a clientele, suppliers, and others, in spite of the fact that their methods at times may be somewhat unique.

It is possible to conceive of a continuum of organizational power in environmental relations, ranging from the organization that dominates its environmental relations to one completely dominated by its environment. Few organizations approach either extreme. Certain gigantic industrial enterprises, such as the *Zaibatsu* in Japan or the old Standard Oil Trust in America, have approached the dominance-over-environment position at one time, but this position eventually brought about "countervailing powers."[4] Perhaps the nearest approximation to the completely powerless organization is the commuter transit system, which may be unable to cover its costs but nevertheless is regarded as a necessary utility and cannot get permission to quit business. Most complex organizations, falling somewhere between the extremes of the power continuum, must adopt strategies for coming to terms with their environments. This is not to imply that such strategies are necessarily chosen by rational or deliberate processes. An organization can survive so long as it adjusts to its situation; whether the process of adjustment is awkward or nimble becomes important in determining the organization's degree of prosperity.

However arrived at, strategies for dealing with the organizational environment may be broadly classified as either *competitive* or *co-operative*. Both appear to be important in a complex society—of the "free enterprise" type or other.[5] Both provide a measure of environmental control over organizations by providing for "outsiders" to enter into or limit organizational decision process.

The decision process may be viewed as a series of activities, conscious or not, culminating in a choice among alternatives. For purposes of this paper we view the decision-making process as consisting of the following activities:

1. Recognizing an occasion for decision, i.e., a need or an opportunity.
2. Analysis of the existing situation.
3. Identification of alternative courses of action.
4. Assessment of the probable consequences of each alternative.
5. Choice from among alternatives.[6]

The following discussion suggests that the potential power of an

---

4. For the *Zaibatsu* case see Japan Council, *The Control of Industry in Japan,* Tokyo: Institute of Political and Economic Research, 1953; and Edwin O. Reischauer, *The United States and Japan,* Cambridge: Harvard University Press, 1954, pp. 87–97.
5. For evidence on Russia see David Granick, *Management of the Industrial Firm in the U.S.S.R.,* New York: Columbia University Press, 1954; and Joseph S. Berliner, "Informal Organization of the Soviet Firm," *Quarterly Journal of Economics,* 66 (August, 1952), pp. 353–365.
6. This particular breakdown is taken from Edward H. Litchfield, "Notes on a General Theory of Administration," *Administrative Science Quarterly,* 1 (June, 1956), pp. 3–29. We are also indebted to Robert Tannenbaum and Fred Massarik who, by breaking the decision-making process into three steps, show that subordinates can take part in the "manager's decision" even when the manager makes the final choice. See "Participation by Subordinates in the Managerial Decision-Making Process," *Canadian Journal of Economics and Political Science,* 16 (August, 1949), pp. 410–418.

outsider increases the earlier he enters into the decision process,[7] and that competition and three sub-types of co-operative strategy—*bargaining, co-optation,* and *coalition*—differ in this respect. It is therefore possible to order these forms of interaction in terms of the degree to which they provide for environmental control over organizational goal-setting decisions.

Competition. The term competition implies an element of rivalry. For present purposes competition refers to that form of rivalry between two or more organizations which is mediated by a third party. In the case of the manufacturing firm the third party may be the customer, the supplier, the potential or present member of the labor force, or others. In the case of the governmental bureau, the third party through whom competition takes place may be the legislative committee, the budget bureau, or the chief executive, as well as potential clientele and potential members of the bureau.

The complexity of competition in a heterogeneous society is much greater than customary usage (with economic overtones) often suggests. Society judges the enterprise not only by the finished product but also in terms of the desirability of applying resources to that purpose. Even the organization that enjoys a product monopoly must compete for society's support. From the society it must obtain resources—personnel, finances, and materials—as well as customers or clientele. In the business sphere of a "free enterprise" economy this competition for resources and customers usually takes place in the market, but in times of crisis the society may exercise more direct controls, such as rationing or the establishment of priorities during a war. The monopoly competes with enterprises having different purposes or goals but using similar raw materials; it competes with many other enterprises, for human skills and loyalties, and it competes with many other activities for support in the money markets.

The university, customarily a non-profit organization, competes as eagerly as any business firm, although perhaps more subtly.[8] Virtually every university seeks, if not more students, better-qualified students. Publicly supported universities compete at annual budget sessions with other governmental enterprises for shares in tax revenues. Endowed universities must compete for gifts and bequests, not only with other universities but also with museums, charities, zoos, and similar non-profit enterprises. The American university is only one of many organizations competing for foundation support, and it competes with other universities and with other types of organizations for faculty.

7. Robert K. Merton makes a similar point regarding the role of the intellectual in public bureaucracy. See his *Social Theory and Social Structure,* Glencoe: The Free Press, 1949, Chapter VI.
8. See Logan Wilson, *The Academic Man,* New York: Oxford University Press, 1942, especially Chapter IX. Also see Warren G. Bennis, "The Effect on Academic Goods of Their Market," *American Journal of Sociology,* 62 (July, 1956), pp. 28–33.

The public school system, perhaps one of our most pervasive forms of near-monopoly, not only competes with other governmental units for funds and with different types of organizations for teachers, but current programs espoused by professional educators often compete in a very real way with a public conception of the nature of education, e.g., as the three R's, devoid of "frills."

The hospital may compete with the mid-wife, the faith-healer, the "quack" and the patent-medicine manufacturer, as well as with neighboring hospitals, despite the fact that general hospitals do not "advertise" and are not usually recognized as competitive.

Competition is thus a complicated network of relationships. It includes scrambling for resources as well as for customers or clients, and in a complex society it includes rivalry for potential members and their loyalties. In each case a third party makes a choice among alternatives, two or more organizations attempt to influence that choice through some type of "appeal" or offering, and choice by the third party is a "vote" of support for one of the competing organizations and a denial of support to the others involved.

Competition, then, is one process whereby the organization's choice of goals is partially controlled by the environment. It tends to prevent unilateral or arbitrary choice of organizational goals, or to correct such a choice if one is made. Competition for society's support is an important means of eliminating not only inefficient organizations but also those that seek to provide goods or services the environment is not willing to accept.

Bargaining. The term bargaining, as used here, refers to the negotiation of an agreement for the exchange of goods or services between two or more organizations. Even where fairly stable and dependable expectations have been built up with important elements of the organizational environment—with suppliers, distributors, legislators, workers and so on—the organization cannot assume that these relationships will continue. Periodic review of these relationships must be accomplished, and an important means for this is bargaining, whereby each organization, through negotiation, arrives at a decision about future behavior satisfactory to the others involved.

The need for periodic adjustment of relationships is demonstrated most dramatically in collective bargaining between labor and industrial management, in which the bases for continued support by organization members are reviewed.[9] But bargaining occurs in other important, if less dramatic, areas of organizational endeavor. The business firm must bargain with its agents or distributors, and while this may appear at times to be one-sided and hence not much of a bargain, still even a

9. For an account of this on a daily basis see Melville Dalton, "Unofficial Union Management Relations," *American Sociological Review,* 15 (October, 1950), pp. 611–619.

long-standing agency agreement may be severed by competitive offers unless the agent's level of satisfaction is maintained through periodic review.[10] Where suppliers are required to install new equipment to handle the peculiar demands of an organization, bargaining between the two is not unusual.

The university likewise must bargain.[11] It may compete for free or unrestricted funds, but often it must compromise that ideal by bargaining away the name of a building or of a library collection, or by the conferring of an honorary degree. Graduate students and faculty members may be given financial or other concessions through bargaining, in order to prevent their loss to other institutions.

The governmental organization may also find bargaining expedient.[12] The police department, for example, may overlook certain violations of statutes in order to gain the support of minor violators who have channels of information not otherwise open to department members. Concessions to those who "turn state's evidence" are not unusual. Similarly a department of state may forego or postpone recognition of a foreign power in order to gain support for other aspects of its policy, and a governmental agency may relinquish certain activities in order to gain budget bureau approval of more important goals.

While bargaining may focus on resources rather than explicitly on goals, the fact remains that it is improbable that a goal can be effective unless it is at least partially implemented. To the extent that bargaining sets limits on the amount of resources available or the ways they may be employed, it effectively sets limits on choice of goals. Hence bargaining, like competition, results in environmental control over organizational goals and reduces the probability of arbitrary, unilateral goal-setting.

Unlike competition, however, bargaining involves direct interaction with other organizations in the environment, rather than with a third party. Bargaining appears, therefore, to invade the actual decision process. To the extent that the second party's support is necessary he is in a position to exercise a veto over final choice of alternative goals, and hence takes part in the decision.

Co-optation. Co-optation has been defined as the process of absorbing new elements into the leadership or policy-determining structure of an organization as a means of averting threats to its stability or existence.[13] Co-optation makes still further inroads on the process of

10. See Valentine F. Ridgway, "Administration of Manufacturer-Dealer Systems," *Administrative Science Quarterly,* 1 (March, 1957), pp. 464–483.
11. Wilson, *op. cit.,* Chapters VII and VIII.
12. For an interesting study of governmental bargaining see William J. Gore, "Administrative Decision-Making in Federal Field Offices," *Public Administration Review,* 16 (Autumn, 1956), pp. 281–291.
13. Philip Selznick, *TVA and the Grass Roots,* Berkeley and Los Angeles: University of California Press, 1949.

deciding goals; not only must the final choice be acceptable to the co-opted party or organization, but to the extent that co-optation is effective it places the representative of an "outsider" in a position to determine the occasion for a goal decision, to participate in analyzing the existing situation, to suggest alternatives, and to take part in the deliberation of consequences.

The term co-optation has only recently been given currency in this country, but the phenomenon it describes is neither new nor unimportant. The acceptance on a corporation's board of directors of representatives of banks or other financial institutions is a time-honored custom among firms that have large financial obligations or that may in the future want access to financial resources. The state university may find it expedient (if not mandatory) to place legislators on its board of trustees, and the endowed college may find that whereas the honorary degree brings forth a token gift, membership on the board may result in a more substantial bequest. The local medical society often plays a decisive role in hospital goal-setting, since the support of professional medical practitioners is urgently necessary for the hospital.

From the standpoint of society, however, co-optation is more than an expediency. By giving a potential supporter a position of power and often of responsibility in the organization, the organization gains his awareness and understanding of the problems it faces. A business advisory council may be an effective educational device for a government, and a White House conference on education may mobilize "grass roots" support in a thousand localities, both by focussing attention on the problem area and by giving key people a sense of participation in goal deliberation.

Moreover, by providing overlapping memberships, co-optation is an important social device for increasing the likelihood that organizations related to one another in complicated ways will in fact find compatible goals. By thus reducing the possibilities of antithetical actions by two or more organizations, co-optation aids in the integration of the heterogeneous parts of a complex society. By the same token, co-optation further limits the opportunity for one organization to choose its goals arbitrarily or unilaterally.

Coalition. As used here, the term coalition refers, to a combination of two or more organizations for a common purpose. Coalition appears to be the ultimate or extreme form of environmental conditioning of organizational goals.[14] A coalition may be unstable, but to the extent

14. Coalition may involve joint action toward only limited aspects of the goals of each member. It may involve the complete commitment of each member for a specific period of time or indefinitely. In either case the ultimate power to withdraw is retained by the members. We thus distinguish coalition from merger, in which two or more organizations are fused permanently. In merger one or all of the original parts may lose their identity. Goal-setting in such a situation, of course, is no longer subject to inter-organizational constraints.

that it is operative, two or more organizations act as one with respect to certain goals. Coalition is a means widely used when two or more enterprises wish to pursue a goal calling for more support, especially for more resources, than any one of them is able to marshall unaided. American business firms frequently resort to coalition for purposes of research or product promotion and for the construction of such gigantic facilities as dams or atomic reactors.[15]

Coalition is not uncommon among educational organizations. Universities have established joint operations in such areas as nuclear research, archaeological research, and even social science research. Many smaller colleges have banded together for fund-raising purposes. The consolidation of public school districts is another form of coalition (if not merger), and the fact that it does represent a sharing or "invasion" of goal-setting power is reflected in some of the bitter resistance to consolidation in tradition-oriented localities.

Coalition requires a commitment for joint decision of future activities and thus places limits on unilateral or arbitrary decisions. Furthermore, inability of an organization to find partners in a coalition venture automatically prevents pursuit of that objective, and is therefore also a form of social control. If the collective judgment is that a proposal is unworkable, a possible disaster may be escaped and unproductive allocation of resources avoided.

DEVELOPMENT OF ENVIRONMENTAL SUPPORT

Environmental control is not a one-way process limited to consequences for the organization of action in its environment. Those subject to control are also part of the larger society and hence are also agents of social control. The enterprise that competes is not only influenced in its goal-setting by what the competitor and the third party may do, but also exerts influence over both. Bargaining likewise is a form of mutual, two-way influence; co-optation affects the co-opted as well as the co-opting party; and coalition clearly sets limits on both parties.

Goals appear to grow out of interaction, both within the organization and between the organization and its environment. While every enterprise must find sufficient support for its goals, it may wield initiative in this. The difference between effective and ineffective organizations may well lie in the initiative exercised by those in the organization who are responsible for goal-setting.

The ability of an administrator to win support for an objective may be as vital as his ability to foresee the utility of a new idea. And his role as a "seller" of ideas may be as important to society as to his organization, for as society becomes increasingly specialized and heterogeneous,

15. See "The Joint Venture Is an Effective Approach to Major Engineering Projects," *New York Times,* July 14, 1957, Section 3, p. 1 F.

the importance of new objectives may be more readily seen by specialized segments than by the general society. It was not public clamor that
originated revisions in public school curricula and training methods; the
impetus came largely from professional specialists in or on the periphery of education.[16] The shift in focus from custody to therapy in mental
hospitals derives largely from the urgings of professionals, and the same
can be said of our prisons.[17] In both cases the public anger, aroused by
crusaders and muck-rakers, might have been soothed by more humane
methods of custody. Current attempts to revitalize the liberal arts curricula of our colleges, universities, and technical institutes have developed more in response to the activities of professional specialists than
from public urging.[18] Commercial aviation, likewise, was "sold" the
hard way, with support being based on subsidy for a considerable period
before the importance of such transportation was apparent to the larger
public.[19]

In each of these examples the goal-setters saw their ideas become
widely accepted only after strenuous efforts to win support through
education of important elements of the environment. Present currents
in some medical quarters to shift emphasis from treatment of the sick
to maintenance of health through preventive medicine and public
health programs likewise have to be "sold" to a society schooled in an
older concept.[20]

The activities involved in winning support for organizational goals
thus are not confined to communication within the organization, however important this is. The need to justify organization goals, to explain
the social functions of the organization, is seen daily in all types of
"public relations" activities, ranging from luncheon club speeches to
house organs. It is part of an educational requirement in a complicated
society where devious interdependence hides many of the functions of
organized, specialized activities.

GOAL-SETTING AND STRATEGY

We have suggested that it is improbable that an organization can
continue indefinitely if its goals are formulated arbitrarily, without cog-

16. See Robert S. and Helen Merrell Lynd, *Middletown in Transition,* New York: Harcourt Brace,
1937, Chapter VI.
17. Milton Greenblatt, Richard H. York, and Esther Lucille Brown, *From Custodial to Therapeutic
Patient Care in Mental Hospitals,* New York: Russell Sage Foundation, 1955, Chapter 1, and Ohlin,
loc. cit.
18. For one example, see the Report of the Harvard Committee, *General Education in a Free Society,*
Cambridge: Harvard University Press, 1945.
19. America's civil air transport industry began in 1926 and eight years later carried 500,000 passen-
gers. Yet it was testified in 1934 that half of the $120 million invested in airlines had been lost in spite
of subsidies. See Jerome C. Hunsaker, *Aeronautics at the Mid-Century,* New Haven: Yale University
Press, 1952, pp. 37–38. The case of Billy Mitchell was, of course, the landmark in the selling of military
aviation.
20. Ray E. Trussell, *Hunterdon Medical Center,* Cambridge: Harvard University Press (for the Commonwealth Fund), 1956, Chapter 3.

nizance of its relations to the environment. One of the requirements for survival appears to be ability to learn about the environment accurately enough and quickly enough to permit organizational adjustments in time to avoid extinction. In a more positive vein, it becomes important for an organization to judge the amount and sources of support that can be mobilized for a goal, and to arrive at a strategy for their mobilization.

Competition, bargaining, co-optation, and coalition constitute procedures for gaining support from the organizational environment; the selection of one or more of these is a strategic problem. It is here that the element of rationality appears to become exceedingly important, for in the order treated above, these relational processes represent increasingly "costly" methods of gaining support in terms of decision-making power. The organization that adopts a strategy of competition when co-optation is called for may lose all opportunity to realize its goals, or may finally turn to co-optation or coalition at a higher "cost" than would have been necessary originally. On the other hand, an organization may lose part of its integrity, and therefore some of its potentiality, if it unnecessarily shares power in exchange for support. Hence the establishment *in the appropriate form* of interaction with the many relevant parts of its environment can be a major organizational consideration in a complex society.

This means, in effect, that the organization must be able to estimate the position of other relevant organizations and their willingness to enter into or alter relationships. Often, too, these matters must be determined or estimated without revealing one's own weaknesses, or even one's ultimate strength. It is necessary or advantageous, in other words, to have the consent or acquiescence of the other party, if a new relationship is to be established or an existing relationship altered. For this purpose organizational administrators often engage in what might be termed a *sounding out process.*[21]

The sounding out process can be illustrated by the problem of the boss with amorous designs on his secretary in an organization that taboos such relations. He must find some means of determining her willingness to alter the relationship, but he must do so without risking rebuff, for a showdown might come at the cost of his dignity or his office reputation, at the cost of losing her secretarial services, or in the extreme case at the cost of losing his own position. The "sophisticated" procedure is to create an ambiguous situation in which the secretary is forced to respond in one of two ways: (1) to ignore or tactfully counter, thereby clearly channeling the relationship back into an already existing pattern, or (2) to respond in a similarly ambiguous vein (if not in a

21. This section on the sounding out process is a modified version of a paper by James D. Thompson, William J. McEwen, and Frederick L. Bates, "Sounding Out as a Relating Process," read at the annual meeting of the Eastern Sociological Society.

positive one) indicating a receptiveness to further advances. It is important in the sounding out process that the situation be ambiguous for two
reasons: (1) the secretary must not be able to "pin down" the boss with
evidence if she rejects the idea, and (2) the situation must be far enough
removed from normal to be noticeable to the secretary. The ambiguity
of sounding out has the further advantage to the participants that neither party alone is clearly responsible for initiating the change.

The situation described above illustrates a process that seems to
explain many organizational as well as personal inter-action situations.
In moving from one relationship to another between two or more
organizations it is often necessary to leave a well defined situation and
proceed through a period of deliberate ambiguity, to arrive at a new
clear-cut relationship. In interaction over goal-setting problems, sounding out sometimes is done through a form of double-talk, wherein the
parties refer to "hypothetical" enterprises and "hypothetical" situations, or in "diplomatic" language, which often serves the same purpose. In other cases, and perhaps more frequently, sounding out is done
through the good offices of a third party. This occurs, apparently, where
there has been no relationship in the past, or at the stage of negotiations
where the parties have indicated intentions but are not willing to state
their positions frankly. Here it becomes useful at times to find a discrete
go-between who can be trusted with full information and who will seek
an arrangement suitable to both parties.

CONCLUSION

In the complex modern society desired goals often require complex
organizations. At the same time the desirability of goals and the appropriate division of labor among large organizations is less self-evident
than in simpler, more homogeneous society. Purpose becomes a question to be decided rather than an obvious matter.

To the extent that behavior of organization members is oriented to
questions of goals or purposes, a science of organization must attempt
to understand and explain that behavior. We have suggested one classification scheme, based on decision-making, as potentially useful in
analyzing organizational-environmental interaction with respect to
goal-setting and we have attempted to illustrate some aspects of its
utility. It is hoped that the suggested scheme encompasses questions of
rationality or irrationality without presuming either.

Argument by example, however, is at best only a starting point for
scientific understanding and for the collection of evidence. Two factors
make organizational goal-setting in a complex society a "big" research
topic: the multiplicity of large organizations of diverse type and the
necessity of studying them in diachronic perspective. We hope that our

discussion will encourage critical thinking and the sharing of observations about the subject.

———————————————— 21 ————————————————

THE CAUSAL TEXTURE OF
ORGANIZATIONAL ENVIRONMENTS

F. E. Emery and E. L. Trist

IDENTIFICATION OF THE PROBLEM

A main problem in the study of organizational change is that the environmental contexts in which organizations exist are themselves changing, at an increasing rate, and towards increasing complexity. This point, in itself, scarcely needs labouring. Nevertheless, the characteristics of organizational environments demand consideration for their own sake, if there is to be an advancement of understanding in the behavioural sciences of a great deal that is taking place under the impact of technological change, especially at the present time. This paper[1] is offered as a brief attempt to open up some of the problems, and stems from a belief that progress will be quicker if a certain extension can be made to current thinking about systems.

In a general way it may be said that to think in terms of systems seems the most appropriate conceptual response so far available when the phenomena under study—at any level and in any domain—display the character of being organized, and when understanding the nature of the interdependencies constitutes the research task. In the behavioural sciences, the first steps in building a systems theory were taken in connection with the analysis of internal processes in organisms, or organizations, when the parts had to be related to the whole. Examples include the organismic biology of Jennings, Cannon, and Henderson; early Gestalt theory and its later derivatives such as balance theory; and the classical theories of social structure. Many of these problems could be represented in closed-system models. The next steps were taken when wholes had to be related to their environments. This led to open-system models.

A great deal of the thinking here has been influenced by cybernetics and information theory, though this has been used as much to extend

1. A paper read at the XVII International Congress of Psychology, Washington, D.C., U.S.A., 20–26 August 1963. A French translation appeared in *Sociologie du Travail*, 4/61.

the scope of closed-system as to improve the sophistication of open-system formulations. It was von Bertalanffy who, in terms of the general transport equation which he introduced, first fully disclosed the importance of openness or closedness to the environment as a means of distinguishing living organisms from inanimate objects.[2] In contradistinction to physical objects, any living entity survives by importing into itself certain types of material from its environment, transforming these in accordance with its own system characteristics, and exporting other types back into the environment. By this process the organism obtains the additional energy that renders it 'negentropic'; it becomes capable of attaining stability in a time-independent steady state—a necessary condition of adaptability to environmental variance.

Such steady states are very different affairs from the equilibrium states described in classical physics, which have far too often been taken as models for representing biological and social transactions. Equilibrium states follow the second law of thermodynamics, so that no work can be done when equilibrium is reached, whereas the openness to the environment of a steady state maintains the capacity of the organism for work, without which adaptability, and hence survival, would be impossible.

Many corollaries follow as regards the properties of open systems, such as equifinality, growth through internal elaboration, self-regulation, constancy of direction with change of position, etc.—and by no means all of these have yet been worked out. But though von Bertalanffy's formulation enables exchange processes between the organism, or organization, and elements in its environment to be dealt with in a new perspective, it does not deal at all with those processes in the environment itself which are among the determining conditions of the exchanges. To analyse these an additional concept is needed—*the causal texture of the environment*—if we may re-introduce, at a social level of analysis, a term suggested by Tolman and Brunswik[3] and drawn from S. C. Pepper.[4]

With this addition, we may now state the following general proposition: that a comprehensive understanding of organizational behaviour requires some knowledge of each member of the following set, where L indicates some potentially lawful connection, and the suffix 1 refers to the organization and the suffix 2 to the environment:

$$L_{11}, L_{12}$$
$$L_{21}, L_{22}$$

2. L. von Bertalanffy, "The Theory of Open Systems in Physics and Biology," *Science,* Vol. 3, 1950, pp. 23–29.
3. E. C. Tolman and E. Brunswik, "The Organism and the Causal Texture of the Environment," *Psychological Review,* Vol. 42, 1935, pp. 43–77.
4. S. C. Pepper, "The Conceptual Framework of Tolman's Purposive Behaviorism," *Psychological Review,* Vol. 41, 1934, pp. 108–133.

L_{11} here refers to processes within the organization—the area of internal interdependencies; L_{12} and L_{21} to exchanges between the organization and its environment—the area of transactional interdependencies, from either direction; and L_{22} to processes through which parts of the environment become related to each other—i.e. its causal texture—the area of interdependencies that belong within the environment itself.

In considering environmental interdependencies, the first point to which we wish to draw attention is that the laws connecting parts of the environment to each other are often incommensurate with those connecting parts of the organization to each other, or even with those which govern the exchanges. It is not possible, for example, always to reduce organization-environment relations to the form of 'being included in'; boundaries are also 'break' points. As Barker and Wright, following Lewin, have pointed out in their analysis of this problem as it affects psychological ecology, we may lawfully connect the actions of a javelin thrower in sighting and throwing his weapon; but we cannot describe in the same concepts the course of the javelin as this is affected by variables lawfully linked by meteorological and other systems.[5]

THE DEVELOPMENT OF ENVIRONMENTAL CONNECTEDNESS (CASE I)

A case history, taken from the industrial field, may serve to illustrate what is meant by the environment becoming organized at the social level. It will show how a greater degree of system-connectedness, of crucial relevance to the organization, may develop in the environment, which is yet not directly a function either of the organization's own characteristics or of its immediate relations. Both of these, of course, once again become crucial when the response of the organization to what has been happening is considered.

The company concerned was the foremost in its particular market in the food-canning industry in the U.K. and belonged to a large parent group. Its main product—a canned vegetable—had some 65 per cent of this market, a situation which had been relatively stable since before the war. Believing it would continue to hold this position, the company persuaded the group board to invest several million pounds sterling in erecting a new, automated factory, which, however, based its economies on an inbuilt rigidity—it was set up exclusively for the long runs expected from the traditional market.

The character of the environment, however, began to change while the factory was being built. A number of small canning firms appeared, not dealing with this product nor indeed with others in the

5. R. B. Barker and H. F. Wright, "Psychological Ecology and the Problem of Psychosocial Development," *Child Development,* Vol. 20, 1949, pp. 131–143.

company's range, but with imported fruits. These firms arose because the last of the post-war controls had been removed from steel strip and tin, and cheaper cans could now be obtained in any numbers—while at the same time a larger market was developing in imported fruits. This trade being seasonal, the firms were anxious to find a way of using their machinery and retaining their labour in winter. They became able to do so through a curious side-effect of the development of quick-frozen foods, when the company's staple was produced by others in this form. The quick-freezing process demanded great constancy at the growing end. It was not possible to control this beyond a certain point, so that quite large crops unsuitable for quick freezing but suitable for canning became available—originally from another country (the United States) where a large market for quick-frozen foods had been established. These surplus crops had been sold at a very low price for animal feed. They were now imported by the small canners—at a better but still comparatively low price, and additional cheap supplies soon began to be procurable from underdeveloped countries.

Before the introduction of the quick-freezing form, the company's own canned product—whose raw material had been specially grown at additional cost—had been the premier brand, superior to other varieties and charged at a higher price. But its position in the product spectrum now changed. With the increasing affluence of the society, more people were able to afford the quick-frozen form. Moreover, there was competition from a great many other vegetable products which could substitute for the staple, and people preferred this greater variety. The advantage of being the premier line among canned forms diminished, and demand increased both for the not-so-expensive varieties among them and for the quick-frozen forms. At the same time, major changes were taking place in retailing; supermarkets were developing, and more and more large grocery chains were coming into existence. These establishments wanted to sell certain types of goods under their own house names, and began to place bulk orders with the small canners for their own varieties of the company's staple that fell within this class. As the small canners provided an extremely cheap article (having no marketing expenses and a cheaper raw material), they could undercut the manufacturers' branded product, and within three years they captured over 50 per cent of the market. Previously, retailers' varieties had accounted for less than 1 per cent.

The new automatic factory could not be adapted to the new situation until alternative products with a big sales volume could be developed, and the scale of research and development, based on the type of market analysis required to identify these, was beyond the scope of the existing resources of the company either in people or in funds.

The changed texture of the environment was not recognized by an able but traditional management until it was too late. They failed entirely to appreciate that a number of outside events were becoming connected with each other in a way that was leading up to irreversible general change. Their first reaction was to make an herculean effort to defend the traditional product, then the board split on whether or not to make entry into the cheaper unbranded market in a supplier role. Group H.Q. now felt they had no option but to step in, and many upheavals and changes in management took place until a 'redefinition of mission' was agreed, and slowly and painfully the company re-emerged with a very much altered product mix and something of a new identity.

FOUR TYPES OF CAUSAL TEXTURE

It was this experience, and a number of others not dissimilar, by no means all of them industrial (and including studies of change problems in hospitals, in prisons, and in educational and political organizations), that gradually led us to feel a need for re-directing conceptual attention to the causal texture of the environment, considered as a quasi-independent domain. We have now isolated four 'ideal types' of causal texture, approximations to which may be thought of as existing simultaneously in the 'real world' of most organizations—though, of course, their weighting will vary enormously from case to case.

The first three of these types have already, and indeed repeatedly, been described—in a large variety of terms and with the emphasis on an equally bewildering variety of special aspects—in the literature of a number of disciplines, ranging from biology to economics and including military theory as well as psychology and sociology. The fourth type, however, is new, at least to us, and is the one that for some time we have been endeavouring to identify. About the first three, therefore, we can be brief, but the fourth is scarcely understandable without reference to them. Together, the four types may be said to form a series in which the degree of causal texturing is increased, in a new and significant way, as each step is taken. We leave as an open question the need for further steps.

STEP ONE

The simplest type of environmental texture is that in which goals and noxiants ('goods' and 'bads') are relatively unchanging in themselves and randomly distributed. This may be called the *placid, randomized environment.* It corresponds to Simon's idea of a surface over which an organism can locomote: most of this is bare, but at isolated, widely scattered points there are little heaps of food.[6] It also corre-

6. H. A. Simon, *Models of Man* (New York: Wiley, 1957), p. 137.

sponds to Ashby's limiting case of no connection between the environmental parts;[7] and to Schutzenberger's random field.[8] The economist's classical market also corresponds to this type.

A critical property of organizational response under random conditions has been stated by Schutzenberger: that there is no distinction between tactics and strategy, 'the optimal strategy is just the simple tactic of attempting to do one's best on a purely local basis.'[9] The best tactic, moreover, can be learnt only by trial and error and only for a particular class of local environmental variances.[10] While organizations under these conditions can exist adaptively as single and indeed quite small units, this becomes progressively more difficult under the other types.

Step Two

More complicated, but still a placid environment, is that which can be characterized in terms of clustering: goals and noxiants are not randomly distributed but hang together in certain ways. This may be called the *placid, clustered environment,* and is the case with which Tolman and Brunswik were concerned; it corresponds to Ashby's 'serial system' and to the economist's 'imperfect competition.' The clustering enables some parts to take on roles as signs of other parts or become means-objects with respect to approaching or avoiding. Survival, however, becomes precarious if an organization attempts to deal tactically with each environmental variance as it occurs.

The new feature of organizational response to this kind of environment is the emergence of strategy as distinct from tactics. Survival becomes critically linked with what an organization knows of its environment. To pursue a goal under its nose may lead it into parts of the field fraught with danger, while avoidance of an immediately difficult issue may lead it away from potentially rewarding areas. In the clustered environment the relevant objective is that of 'optimal location,' some positions being discernible as potentially richer than others.

To reach these requires concentration of resources, subordination to the main plan, and the development of a 'distinctive competence,' to use Selznick's[11] term, in reaching the strategic objective. Organizations under these conditions, therefore, tend to grow in size and also to become hierarchical, with a tendency towards centralized control and coordination.

7. W. Ross Ashby, *Design For a Brain* (London: Chapman and Hall, 1960), p. S15/4.
8. M. P. Schutzenberger, "A Tentative Classification of Goal-seeking Behaviors," *Journal of Mental Science,* Vol. 100, 1954, p. 100.
9. *Ibid.,* p. 101.
10. Ashby, p. 197.
11. P. Selznick, *Leadership in Administration* (Evanston: Row Peterson, 1957).

STEP THREE

The next level of causal texturing we have called the *disturbed-reactive environment.* It may be compared with Ashby's ultra-stable system or the economist's oligopolic market. It is a type 2 environment in which there is more than one organization of the same kind; indeed, the existence of a number of similar organizations now becomes the dominant characteristic of the environmental field. Each organization does not simply have to take account of the others when they meet at random, but has also to consider that what it knows can also be known by the others. The part of the environment to which it wishes to move itself in the long run is also the part to which the others seek to move. Knowing this, each will wish to improve its own chances by hindering the others, and each will know that the others must not only wish to do likewise, but also know that each knows this. The presence of similar others creates an imbrication, to use a term of Chein's,[12] of some of the causal strands in the environment.

If strategy is a matter of selecting the 'strategic objective'—where one wishes to be at a future time—and tactics a matter of selecting an immediate action from one's available repertoire, then there appears in type 3 environments to be an intermediate level of organizational response—that of the *operation*—to use the term adopted by German and Soviet military theorists, who formally distinguish tactics, operations, and stratgey. One has now not only to make sequential choices, but to choose actions that will draw off the other organizations. The new element is that of deciding which of someone else's possible tactics one wishes to take place, while ensuring that others of them do not. An operation consists of a campaign involving a planned series of tactical initiatives, calculated reactions by others, and counteractions. The flexibility required encourages a certain decentralization and also puts a premium on quality and speed of decision at various peripheral points.[13]

It now becomes necessary to define the organizational objective in terms not so much of location as of capacity or power to move more or less at will, i.e. to be able to make and meet competitive challenge. This gives particular relevance to strategies of absorption and parasitism. It can also give rise to situations in which stability can be obtained only by a certain coming-to-terms between competitors, whether enterprises, interest groups, or governments. One has to know when not to fight to the death.

STEP FOUR

Yet more complex are the environments we have called *turbulent*

12. I. Chein, "Personality and Typology," *Journal of Social Psychology,* Vol. 18, 1943, pp. 89–101.
13. Lord Heyworth, *The Organization of Unilever* (London: Unilever Limited, 1955).

fields. In these, dynamic processes, which create significant variances for the component organizations, arise from the field itself. Like type 3 and unlike the static types 1 and 2, they are dynamic. Unlike type 3, the dynamic properties arise not simply from the interaction of the component organizations, but also from the field itself. The 'ground' is in motion.

Three trends contribute to the emergence of these dynamic field forces:

1. The growth to meet type 3 conditions of organizations, and linked sets of organizations, so large that their actions are both persistent and strong enough to induce autochthonous processes in the environment. An analogous effect would be that of a company of soldiers marching in step over a bridge.
2. The deepening interdependence between the economic and the other facets of the society. This means that economic organizations are increasingly enmeshed in legislation and public regulation.
3. The increasing reliance on research and development to achieve the capacity to meet competitive challenge. This leads to a situation in which a change gradient is continuously present in the environmental field.

For organizations, these trends mean a gross increase in their area of *relevant uncertainty.* The consequences which flow from their actions lead off in ways that become increasingly unpredictable: they do not necessarily fall off with distance, but may at any point be amplified beyond all expectation; similarly, lines of action that are strongly pursued may find themselves attenuated by emergent field forces.

THE SALIENCE OF TYPE 4 CHARACTERISTICS (CASE II)

Some of these effects are apparent in what happened to the canning company of case I, whose situation represents a transition from an environment largely composed of type 2 and type 3 characteristics to one where those of type 4 began to gain in salience. The case now to be presented illustrates the combined operation of the three trends described above in an altogether larger environmental field involving a total industry and its relations with the wider society.

The organization concerned is the National Farmers Union of Great Britain to which more than 200,000 of the 250,000 farmers of England and Wales belong. The presenting problem brought to us for investigation was that of communications. Headquarters felt, and was deemed to be, out of touch with county branches, and these with local branches. The farmer had looked to the N.F.U. very largely to protect him against market fluctuations by negotiating a comprehensive deal with the government at annual reviews concerned with the level of price support. These reviews had enabled home agriculture to maintain a steady state during two decades when the threat, or existence, of war in relation to the type of military technology then in being had made it imperative to maintain a high level of homegrown food without increasing prices to the consumer. This policy, however, was becoming obsolete as the conditions of thermonuclear stalemate established themselves. A level of support could no longer be counted upon which would keep in existence small and inefficient farmers—often on marginal land and dependent on family labour—compared with efficient medium-size farms, to say nothing of large and highly mechanized undertakings.

Yet it was the former situation which had produced N.F.U. cohesion. As this situation receded, not only were farmers becoming exposed to more competition from each other, as well as from Commonwealth and European farmers, but the effects were being felt of very great changes which had been taking place on both the supply and marketing sides of the industry. On the supply side, a small number of giant firms now supplied almost all the requirements in fertilizer, machinery, seeds, veterinary products, etc. As efficient farming depended upon ever greater utilization of these resources, their controllers exerted correspondingly greater power over the farmers. Even more dramatic were the changes in the marketing of farm produce. Highly organized food processing and distributing industries had grown up dominated again by a few large firms, on contracts from which (fashioned to suit their rather than his interests) the farmer was becoming increasingly dependent. From both sides deep inroads were being made on his autonomy.

It became clear that the source of the felt difficulty about communications lay in radical environmental changes which were confronting the organization with problems it was ill-adapted to meet. Communications about these changes were being interpreted or acted upon as if they referred to the 'traditional' situation. Only through a parallel analysis of the environment and the N.F.U. was progress made towards developing understanding on the basis of which attempts to devise adaptive organizational policies and forms could be made. Not least among the problems was that of creating a bureaucratic elite that could cope with the highly technical long-range planning now required and yet remain loyal to the democratic values of the N.F.U. Equally difficult was that of developing mediating institutions—agencies that would effectively mediate the relations between agriculture and other economic sectors without triggering off massive competitive processes.

These environmental changes and the organizational crisis they induced were fully apparent two or three years before the question of

Britain's possible entry into the Common Market first appeared on the political agenda—which, of course, further complicated every issue.

A workable solution needed to preserve reasonable autonomy for the farmers as an occupational group, while meeting the interests of other sections of the community. Any such possibility depended on securing the consent of the large majority of farmers to placing under some degree of N.F.U. control matters that hitherto had remained within their own power of decision. These included what they produced, how and to what standard, and how most of it should be marketed. Such thoughts were anathema, for however dependent the farmer had grown on the N.F.U. he also remained intensely individualistic. He was being asked, he now felt, to redefine his identity, reverse his basic values, and refashion his organization—all at the same time. It is scarcely surprising that progress has been, and remains, both fitful and slow, and ridden with conflict.

VALUES AND RELEVANT UNCERTAINTY

What becomes precarious under type 4 conditions is how organizational stability can be achieved. In these environments individual organizations, however large cannot expect to adapt successfully simply through their own direct actions—as is evident in the case of the N.F.U. Nevertheless, there are some indications of a solution that may have the same general significance for these environments as have strategy and operations for types 2 and 3. This is the emergence of *values that have overriding significance for all members of the field.* Social values are here regarded as coping mechanisms that make it possible to deal with persisting areas of relevant uncertainty. Unable to trace out the consequences of their actions as these are amplified and resonated through their extended social fields, men in all societies have sought rules, sometimes categorical, such as the ten commandments, to provide them with a guide and ready calculus. Values are not strategies or tactics; as Lewin (1936) has pointed out, they have the conceptual character of 'power fields' and act as injunctions.

So far as effective values emerge, the character of richly joined, turbulent fields changes in a most striking fashion. The relevance of large classes of events no longer has to be sought in an intricate mesh of diverging causal strands, but is given directly in the ethical code. By this transformation a field is created which is no longer richly joined and turbulent but simplified and relatively static. Such a transformation will be regressive, or constructively adaptative, according to how far the emergent values adequately represent the new environmental requirements.

Ashby,[14] as a biologist, has stated his view, on the one hand, that examples of environments that are both large and richly connected are not common, for our terrestrial environment is widely characterized by being highly subdivided and, on the other, that, so far as they are encountered, they may well be beyond the limits of human adaptation, the brain being an ultra-stable system. By contrast the role here attributed to social values suggests that this sort of environment may in fact be not only one to which adaptation is possible, however difficult, but one that has been increasingly characteristic of the human condition since the beginning of settled communities. Also, let us not forget that values can be rational as well as irrational and that the rationality of their rationale is likely to become more powerful as the scientific ethos takes greater hold in a society.

MATRIX ORGANIZATION AND INSTITUTIONAL SUCCESS

Nevertheless, turbulent fields demand some overall form of organization that is essentially different from the hierarchically structured forms to which we are accustomed. Whereas type 3 environments require one or other form of accommodation between like, but competitive, organizations whose fates are to a degree negatively correlated, turbulent environments require some relationship between dissimilar organizations whose fates are, basically, positively correlated. This means relationships that will maximize cooperation and which recognize that no one organization can take over the role of 'the other' and become paramount. We are inclined to speak of this type of relationship as an *organizational matrix*. Such a matrix acts in the first place by delimiting on value criteria the character of what may be included in the field specified—and therefore who. This selectivity then enables some definable shape to be worked out without recourse to much in the way of formal hierarchy among members. Professional associations provide one model of which there had been long experience.

We do not suggest that in other fields than the professional the requisite sanctioning can be provided only by state-controlled bodies. Indeed, the reverse is far more likely. Nor do we suggest that organizational matrices will function so as to eliminate the need for other measures to achieve stability. As with values, matrix organizations, even if successful, will only help to transform turbulent environments into the kinds of environment we have discussed as 'clustered' and 'disturbed-reactive.' Though, with these transformations, an organization could hope to achieve a degree of stability through its strategies, operation, and tactics, the transformations would not provide environments identical with the originals. The strategic objective in the transformed cases could no longer be stated simply in terms of optimal location (as in type

14. Ashby, p. 205.

2) or capabilities (as in type 3). It must now rather be formulated in terms of *institutionalization.* According to Selznick (1957) organizations become institutions through the embodiment of organizational values which relate them to the wider society.[15] As Selznick has stated in his analysis of leadership in the modern American corporation, 'the default of leadership shows itself in an acute form when *organizational* achievement or survival is confounded with *institutional* success. . . . the executive becomes a statesman as he makes the transition from administrative management to institutional leadership.'[16]

The processes of strategic planning now also become modified. In so far as institutionalization becomes a prerequisite for stability, the determination of policy will necessitate not only a bias towards goals that are congruent with the organization's own character, but also a selection of goal-paths that offer maximum convergence as regards the interests of other parties. This became a central issue for the N.F.U. and is becoming one now for an organization such as the National Economic Development Council, which has the task of creating a matrix in which the British economy can function at something better than the stop-go level.

Such organizations arise from the need to meet problems emanating from type 4 environments. Unless this is recognized, they will only too easily be construed in type 3 terms, and attempts will be made to secure for them a degree of monolithic power that will be resisted overtly in democratic societies and covertly in others. In the one case they may be prevented from ever undertaking their missions; in the other one may wonder how long they can succeed in maintaining them.

An organizational matrix implies what McGregor has called Theory Y.[17] This in turn implies a new set of values. But values are psychosocial commodities that come into existence only rather slowly. Very little systematic work has yet been done on the establishment of new systems of values, or on the type of critera that might be adduced to allow their effectiveness to be empirically tested. A pioneer attempt is that of Churchman and Ackoff.[18] Likert[19] has suggested that, in the large corporation or government establishment, it may well take some ten to fifteen years before the new type of group values with which he is concerned could permeate the total organization. For a new set to

15. Since the present paper was presented, this line of thought has been further developed by Churchman and Emery (1964) in their discussion of the relation of the statistical aggregate of individuals to structured role sets:

Like other values, organizational values emerge to cope with relevant uncertainties and gain their authority from their reference to the requirements of larger systems within which people's interests are largely concordant.

16. Selznick, p. 154.

17. D. McGregor, *The Human Side of Enterprise* (New York, Toronto, London: McGraw Hill, 1960).

18. C. W. Churchman and R. L. Ackoff, *Methods of Inquiry* (St. Louis: Educational Publishers, 1950).

19. R. Likert, *New Patterns of Management* (New York, Toronto, London: McGraw Hill, 1961).

permeate a whole modern society the time required must be much longer—at least a generation, according to the common saying—and this, indeed, must be a minimum. One may ask if this is fast enough, given the rate at which type 4 environments are becoming salient. A compelling task for social scientists is to direct more research onto these problems.

SUMMARY

(a) A main problem in the study of organizational change is that the environmental contexts in which organizations exist are themselves changing—at an increasing rate, under the impact of technological change. This means that they demand consideration for their own sake. Towards this end a redefinition is offered, at a social level of analysis, of the causal texture of the environment, a concept introduced in 1935 by Tolman and Brunswik.

(b) This requires an extension of systems theory. The first steps in systems theory were taken in connection with the analysis of internal processes in organisms, or organizations, which involved relating parts to the whole. Most of these problems could be dealt with through closed-system models. The next steps were taken when wholes had to be related to their environments. This led to open-system models, such as that introduced by Bertalanffy, involving a general transport equation. Though this enables exchange processes between the organism, or organization, and elements in its environment to be dealt with, it does not deal with those processes in the environment itself which are the determining conditions of the exchanges. To analyse these an additional concept—the causal texture of the environment—is needed.

(c) The laws connecting parts of the environment to each other are often incommensurate with those connecting parts of the organization to each other, or even those which govern exchanges. Case history I illustrates this and shows the dangers and difficulties that arise when there is a rapid and gross increase in the area of relevant uncertainty, a characteristic feature of many contemporary environments.

(d) Organizational environments differ in their causal texture, both as regards degree of uncertainty and in many other important respects. A typology is suggested which identifies four 'ideal types,' approximations to which exist simultaneously in the 'real world' of most organizations, though the weighting varies enormously:

1. In the simplest type, goals and noxiants are relatively unchanging in themselves and randomly distributed. This may be called the placid, randomized environment. A critical property from the organization's viewpoint is that there is no difference between tactics

and strategy, and organizations can exist adaptively as single, and indeed quite small, units.

2. The next type is also static, but goals and noxiants are not randomly distributed; they hang together in certain ways. This may be called the placid, clustered environment. Now the need arises for strategy as distinct from tactics. Under these conditions organizations grow in size, becoming multiple and tending towards centralized control and coordination.

3. The third type is dynamic rather than static. We call it the disturbed-reactive environment. It consists of a clustered environment in which there is more than one system of the same kind, i.e. the objects of one organization are the same as, or relevant to, others like it. Such competitors seek to improve their own chances by hindering each other, each knowing the others are playing the same game. Between strategy and tactics there emerges an intermediate type of organizational response—what military theorists refer to as operations. Control becomes more decentralized to allow these to be conducted. On the other hand, stability may require a certain coming-to-terms between competitors.

4. The fourth type is dynamic in a second respect, the dynamic properties arising not simply from the interaction of identifiable component systems but from the field itself (the 'ground'). We call these environments turbulent fields. The turbulence results from the complexity and multiple character of the causal interconnections. Individual organizations, however large, cannot adapt successfully simply through their direct interactions. An examination is made of the enhanced importance of values, regarded as a basic response to persisting areas of relevant uncertainty, as providing a control mechanism, when commonly held by all members in a field. This raises the question of organizational forms based on the characteristics of a matrix.

(e) Case history II is presented to illustrate problems of the transition from type 3 to type 4. The perspective of the four environmental types is used to clarify the role of Theory X and Theory Y as representing a trend in value change. The establishment of a new set of values is a slow social process requiring something like a generation—unless new means can be developed.

———————————— **22** ————————————

INDUSTRIAL ORGANIZATIONS AND THE ECOLOGICAL PROCESS
The Case of Water Pollution

Roy E. Rickson and Charles E. Simpkins

Mastery over nature is one of the prerequisites of organized social life. In turn, the cultural and structural properties of a given society influence the relationship of society with the natural environment. The discovery of natural laws and the consequences of using such knowledge are sometimes contradictory. Thus, one result of advanced industrial production has been serious environmental pollution. In the following paper, we attempt to understand current problems of water pollution and control by analyzing the cultural priorities of modern industrial societies and the factors influencing the relationship of the industrial firm to the natural and social environment.

The rapid growth of our industrial technology and the emergence of heavily populated urban areas have placed serious strains on the quality of our natural resources. Water, for example, is a basic ingredient of industrial production, and when not a specific input the resource is often used for the elimination of waste.[1] At the very time the public needs an ever increasing supply of good quality water, it has experienced decline in both quantity and quality. Accordingly, water pollution has become socially unacceptable and its occurrence a focal issue in the relationship of public and private interests, industrial organizations, and their communities.[2] Industrial organizations are simultaneously faced with a deteriorating resource, water, upon which they are highly dependent and an increasingly hostile social environment in which powerful groups are attempting to regulate the industrial use of water and challenging, in many respects, the traditional decision-making autonomy of industry.

A fact of life for industrial organizations is that their autonomy and

1. Industry is the largest withdrawer of water in the United States and its total water withdrawals are expected to increase. Industry, in addition, is a major producer of liquid wastes. Given the normal functioning of the U.S. economy, both the absolute quantity of water used and the liquid wastes produced by industry will continue to increase as we experience economic growth. See Blair T. Bower, "The Economics of Industrial Water Utilization," in A. V. Kneese and S. C. Smith, *Water Research,* Baltimore: The Johns Hopkins University Press, 1965, pp. 143–73.

2. The quality of the natural environment has rapidly become a public issue. Four or five years ago, opinion pollsters heard almost no mention of it when they asked people about the major issues of the day. Today survey respondents frequently rank environmental pollution as the second or third most important issue. See Phillip J. Tichenor, *et. al.,* "Environment and Public Opinion in Minnesota," Mimeographed paper, Institute of Agriculture, Department of Sociology, University of Minnesota.

survival depends upon the nature of their relationship with the physical and social environment. An analysis of the role of industry in modern societies, therefore, requires that attention be given to the cultural assumptions of the societies in which they function, the social structure of industries, their technology, and power. Finally, a relationship that students of complex organizations have generally overlooked is the ultimate dependence of all human groups on the inanimate environment. The latter has increased importance given the existence of three contemporary conditions: (1) although the extent is not fully determined, serious damage has been done to the natural environment as the result of advanced industrial production; (2) to a considerable degree, the technology and the scientific knowledge needed by industries to reduce their pollution is available, and (3) the current debates over the definition of a quality environment and the general rules for the use of the physical environment directly involves industry and has far reaching consequences for the role of industrial production in contemporary society. The general question of interest to sociologists is "When do industries search for information to control pollution?" The question is more than one of public image for industries and is important for the development of organizational theory. Indeed, the future role of industrial organization is at stake. Their capacity to change the way in which they use natural resources is important to understanding the association, conflictual or cooperative, between industries and relevant social groups also dependent on the natural environment. The problem of water pollution and its control by industry can now be seen against a background of the values of the society in which they serve and their structural characteristics. The definition of water problems and solutions will eventually involve scientists whose role is encouraged and limited by the needs of the rational firm.

GENERAL FACTORS RELEVANT TO WATER POLLUTION CONTROL BY INDUSTRY

An inescapable business of all societies is the acquisition of energy for their sustenance and development. In industrial societies, this key function is performed primarily by giant, industrial organizations. Generally, modern industrial civilizations relate to the physical environment in terms of its utility for their institutional goals rather than for its intrinsic qualities.[3] Control over nature and the increasing capacity of societies to extract energy from nature have certainly been one of the foundations of modern development. Agricultural and industrial pro-

3. According to Hans Kelsen, *General Theory of Law and State,* New York: Russel and Russel, 1961, p. 47: the interpretation of nature had originally a social character. Primitive man considers nature to be an intrinsic part of his society. He interprets physical reality according to the same principles that determine his social relations. His social order for him is, at the same time, the order of nature. Just as men obey the norms of the social order, things obey the norms emanating from superhuman

duction as well as revolutions in health care have resulted from greater understanding of natural functions and more sophisticated technology that has both allowed and required the exploitation of natural energy. As more complex social structures have developed, the exploitation of natural resources and the ability to predict and control nature have become even more important. Indeed, the history of human societies can be interpreted in the framework of competition with nature in order to define "balance with nature" in terms of their own institutional problems. Balance with nature, after all, prevailed when men's lives were truly nasty, brutish, and short. Modern industrial technology is one source of social change that provides some solutions to problems of social and economic development, but which may also entail societal decline through widespread pollution. Consequently, the study of program changes in industrial organizations and the general direction of their interest is important to the study of the ecological process. A fundamental sociological problem is how existing cultural and structural patterns influence the way in which manufacturing firms respond to changing environmental conditions.

CULTURAL ASSUMPTIONS AND INDUSTRIAL USE OF NATURAL RESOURCES

The value patterns of American culture and similar western industrialized nations are generally compatible with the needs of an expanding industrial system and the goals of science. Mastery over the physical and social environment has been the consistent objective and recurring theme of the industrial and scientific communities. Extensive exploitation of natural energy and social order are basic requirements of industrial development. As a result, the political, educational, and economic institutions are intimately related.[4] The political institution insures order and support for long-term industrial investment and the educational institution is the primary source of scientific manpower and knowledge that contributes greatly to the sustenance and expansion of

personal beings. The fundamental social law is the norm according to which the good has to be rewarded, the evil punished. It is the principle of retribution which completely dominates primitive consciousness. The legal norm is the prototype of this principle. According to this principle of retribution, primitive man interprets nature. His interpretation has a normative-juristic character. It is in the norm of retribution that the law of causality originates and, in the way of a gradual change of meaning, develops.

Kelson goes on to argue that a utilitarian conception of the natural environment came from Greek philosophy of law and modern science. The separation of the law of the state and the law of nature created a basis for a utilitarian definition. The law of the state became dominant and the needs of the state became dominant. The condition of nature as a thing of intrinsic value was de-emphasized as a result. The rise of modern science and its notions of causality simply eliminated much of the explanation of physical phenomena that assumed inherent spirits in nature. Events could be explained by science and one need not fear retribution from physical things as they were inanimate and did not have motivation. See also Hans Kelsen, *Society and Nature: A Sociological Inquiry,* London: Kegan Paul, Trench, Trubner, 1946.
4. Robin Williams, *American Society,* New York: Alfred A. Knopf, 1970.

industrial technology. Consequently, the economic system of production and exchange functions in a fashion that is interdependent with other major social institutions and cultural value orientations. Finally, the behavior of the individual firm reflects the values and priorities of the economic institution. The resistance of industrial organizations to adoption of available pollution control technology can be explained as a product of the value hierarchy of an industrial economy, and a general value structure that is supportive of the industrial system.

As rational structures, industrial organizations relate to the physical environment as a means to an end—as inputs to production. A theoretical analysis of the values of the American industrial system by Galbraith proposes that the esthetic qualities of the society are not as important as is economic growth.[5] No other goal is as revered as is economic growth and its complement, full employment. Technological innovation is valued to the degree that it contributes to the economic growth or the stability of the industrial system, and therefore the mature corporation innovates in the direction that seemingly contributes to its growth and power while other concerns are given less importance.[6] With reference to water use, Bower contends that industries have given little consideration to: (1) the substitution possibilities among the components of industrial water utilization systems, (2) the relationship of water to other factor inputs to the production process, and (3) the impact of technological changes on industrial water utilization.[7]

If natural resources, e.g., water, are seen primarily as commodities,[8] the pollution problem has its roots partly in the contemporary organization of economic activities. Industries find that the price of everything they use—land, labor, material supplies, time—is increasingly dear. The power position of labor in industrial societies is, of course, related to industrial priorities. But clean water, though now deemed precious by some powerful groups, is still largely left out of the pricing system, and is still relatively free of charge.[9] The current pric-

5. John K. Galbraith, *The New Industrial State,* Boston: Houghton-Mifflin Company, 1967.
6. An example of this phenomena is recent evidence about the priorities of the United States Atomic Energy Commission reported in the *Wall Street Journal,* January 25, 1971, p. 1. According to the journal, a United States Senator has calculated that over the last 25 years, while the atomic agency spent billions of dollars to develop military and commercial applications of the atom, it spent only 50 million dollars on water disposal research. Today the nuclear power industry is growing rapidly. But, according to the report, one of the AEC's own advisory committees has characterized some of the agency's waste disposal practices as "expedients designed to make the best use of poor locations."
7. Blair T. Bower, *op. cit.*
8. William R. Burch, "Resources and Social Structure: Some Conditions of Stability and Change." *The Annals,* 386, (1970), pp. 27–35.
9. Industries that use water as an integral part of their production process, e.g., the brewing industry, do pay for water. The point that we wish to make is that in comparison to other costs, water as a direct input is very low. Furthermore, any discussion of industrial water use must consider the use of water, lakes, rivers, for taking industrial effluent. The widespread dumping of industrial effluent into bodies of water magnifies many times the overall importance of water to the industrial process. In general, industries in the past have not had to pay for water used by them for effluent purposes, except indirectly through paying taxes for municipal water plants and sewage disposal. See Blair T. Bower, *op. cit.*

ing system, a cultural fact,[10] works against the conservation of natural resources. Logically, a manufacturer attempts to offset rising labor costs by developing new techniques for the conservation of labor. Firms also adopt new techniques for purposes of social control. The predictability of events internal to the organization is sometimes enhanced when procedures can be standardized through machine technology. The extent to which automated techniques replace bureaucratic rules has clear implications for standardization and internal control. Large labor unions representing the firm's work force also comprise a solution to the problems of organizational uncertainty. Firms are considerably more secure in dealing with a work force represented by a few powerful unions than they would be if power among workers were more dispersed and "wildcat" strikes were common. There has been no comparable pressure until very recently in the use of natural resources such as water. Not surprisingly, techniques for the conservation of this resource and the adoption of available technology have developed very slowly. The effect of omitting nominally free resources from the pricing system has made the economy as a whole pay a considerable subsidy to those activities that put a great deal of pressure on resources. In short, contemporary economic organization reflecting the cultural values of the industrial system as a whole provides a huge, unintentional market incentive to pollution.[11]

Although some dominant cultural values of the American industrial society promote pollution of water resources, other dominant values conflict with such a trend. The humanitarian mores and the value on individualism and freedom in American culture provide bases for change in the way natural resources are used.[12] The values of the industrial system and the latter are in conflict when large groups in the society begin suffering from visible and extensive pollution. Water pollution in particular can be something that inhibits individual freedom to use waterways for leisure time and recreational purposes. Pollution, unlike racism, affects almost everyone in large urban areas. The middle classes generally suffer the same effects as lower class members. If we remember the most successful social movements in American society have had a middle class through the formation of voluntary organiza-

10. Robin Williams, *op. cit.*

11. It should be added that we are speaking of industrial systems and not capitalist as opposed to socialist systems of production. Although the dynamics of the pricing system differs among the two, the goals of their industrial systems and the organization of their respective economies become strikingly similar. See Joseph Alois Schumpeter, *Capitalism, Socialism, and Democracy,* New York and London: Harper and Row, 1942, and John K. Galbraith, *op. cit.* Industrial pollution, particularly water pollution, is a problem in the Soviet Union for substantially the same reasons as in the United States.

12. Robin Williams, *op. cit.*

tions,[13] the modern conservationist movement is a potentially powerful source of change. It is not by accident that public support for the conservationist movement, formerly an upper-middle class past-time, has increased.

The concept of equilibrium as defined by human ecologists also suggests a basis for change and, perhaps, conflict. Societies are open systems engaged in transactions with the physical and social milieu. When there are drastic changes in the physical environment some change in the internal structure of the social organization will result. According to Hawley:

> A system founded on nonreplaceable resources is faced with "imminent change"; sooner or later it will either pass into decline or shift perforce to a different resource base. Such, for instance has been the experience of innumerable mining communities; in a similar manner agricultural communities often alter the soil composition of their lands by the uses they practice, with the ultimate result that the lands will no longer support the systems as they are constituted.[14]

The continued flow of materials, energy, and information into a system allows some adaptation; and to the extent that the adaptation is effective, system integration is partially assured. The response to the natural environment is, therefore, tempered by the kind of information that organizations seek, how information enters the structure, and what information is seen as relevant to its functioning. As formal or rational organizations are one of the most basic action units in modern society, the process whereby organizations gather, process, interpret, and communicate information about the consequences of their technology for environmental pollution is a starting point for sociological analysis. Inevitably, industrial organizations must respond to drastic changes in the quality of the physical environment when those changes threaten to disturb their production process. They must also react to the demands of powerful conservationist groups and government agencies. It may be argued that the disparity of power between groups promoting conservationist values rather than "business" interests is decreasing as public support for their activities grows. Issues fundamental to the role of industry in a modern capitalist state are directly involved, e.g., the right of industries to be relatively autonomous in decisions about their standards of production. Industry, as a dominant institution in American society can be expected to resist movements that threaten its traditional autonomy and power. The response of individual firms to such

13. Alexis de Tocqueville, *Democracy in America,* Vol. I. Vintage Books, 1954. Max Weber, *From Max Weber: Essays in Sociology,* Hans Gerth and C. Wright Mills, (eds.), New York: Oxford University Press, 1946, pp. 159–262.

14. Amos H. Hawley, "Human Ecology," *International Encyclopedia of the Social Sciences,* 1969.

pressure, we propose, is associated with the nature of their technology, their social structure, and power.

INDUSTRIAL CAPACITY FOR CHANGE AND THE USE OF WATER RESOURCES TECHNOLOGY

Organizations of any type do not readily change their structures or their technologies. The change requires considerable reorientation and cost. The rational behavior of industry is, therefore, directed to develop the type of relationship with the environment that will not require frequent and extensive change. Thompson proposes that industrial organizations attempt to control their environment so that a compatible relationship between input activities, output activities, and technological activities will prevail.[15] The importance of a compatible balance of these factors is seen to be the following:

> To the extent that environmental fluctuations are unanticipated, they interfere with the orderly operation of the core technology and thereby reduce its performance. When such influences are anticipated and considered for a particular period of time, the technical core can operate as if it enjoyed a closed system.[16]

Rational organizations, therefore, seek to buffer environmental influences from the core technology. Technology is of two types: (1) the tools, machines, instruments involved in the production process and (2) the body of ideas and knowledge which express the goals of the work.[17] As long as the organization is not dependent upon an immediately diminishing resource, e.g., the fishing industry, the influence of the physical environment can be relatively ignored. If the production process is relatively routine, then procedures can be standardized so that the core technology can operate as if it were a closed system. In such an instance, innovativeness is not critical to the operation of the core technology and a norm for innovativeness or the search for new techniques is not likely to appear.

Innovativeness should be most characteristic of organizations where the work process requires continual attention to exceptional events or cases[18] and where there are few or no programmed solutions to the exceptional cases. A critical problem for organizations frequently faced with exceptional or relatively uncontrollable events (nuclear power plants, hospitals) is to search for ways to standardize operative procedures. One answer to this problem is the creation of innovation

15. James D. Thompson, *Organizations in Action,* New York: The McGraw-Hill Book Company, 1967.
16. *Ibid.,* p. 22.
17. Robert Dubin, "Working Union-Management Relations," *The Sociology of Industrial Relations,* Englewood Cliffs, New Jersey: Prentice Hall, 1967.
18. Charles Perrow, "A Framework for the Comparative Analysis of Organizations," *American Sociological Review,* 32, (1967), pp. 194–209.

sub-systems for research and development. The protection of the core technology is, therefore, based on the development of new technology or ideas about the principle input leading eventually to standardization. The functioning of the core technology and its revisions to meet changing conditions make the organization highly dependent on scientific knowledge. For example, there is a great deal of uncertainty as to the impact of nuclear power production on the physical environment. In order for industries to apply nuclear energy to their production process, considerable research is required to predict the multiple consequences of utilizing nuclear energy.[19]

We have already established that water is a principal input to industrial production. Industrial organizations do have water quality standards for the operation of their production process, and they sponsor and conduct research themselves to further understand the relationship between water type and their product. Process and production engineers, with the advice of production personnel, are the arbiters of water quality in each industrial plant. There are several different minimum qualities for various processes including: product mix, heat exchange, barometric condensing, fire protection, dilution, sanitation, boiler makeup, material transport. According to a publication of the National Association of Manufacturers:

> Deciding what kind of treatment to give which portions of water intake is an engineering and economic decision. By far the most common problems are turbidity and hardness, and both are amenable to relatively inexpensive treatment by conventional methods.[20]

Industries, therefore, engage in the filtration of water, softening, demineralization, settling and sedimentation, chlorination, distillation, etc. The internal logic of the core technology will not be interrupted when there is knowledge about the water condition that is most appropriate to the functioning of the technology. When the production process is complex, i.e., a large range of products with many different types of processing units, then the search process could be expected to include the research expertise of scientists and engineers.[21] Other things being equal, we would expect that organizations that are highly dependent on scientific knowledge for their functioning will be more innovative or have the capacity to be more innovative in their use of water than organizations without such a knowledge base. Thompson and

19. Frank Barnaby, "Is Nuclear Power Worth the Risk?" *Science Journal,* 6, (1970), p. 3–26.
20. National Association of Manufacturers, "Water in Industry: A Survey of Water Use in Industry," by the National Association of Manufacturers and the Chamber of Commerce of the United States in cooperation with the National Technical Task Committee on Industrial Wastes, New York.
21. This proposition is somewhat supported by data showing that such industries as food and kindred products, paper and allied products, chemicals and allied products, petroleum refining and extraction, primary metals, rubber products, are more involved with basic and applied research than such industries as machinery production, electrical equipment, and motor vehicles. *National Science Foundation Reviews of Data on Science Resources,* No. 7, January, 1966.

Bates define the adaptability or "innovative capacity" of a technology as "the extent to which the appropriate mechanics, knowledge, skills, and raw materials can be used for other products."[22] The capacity of an organization to adapt to a deteriorating water supply should also be related to its knowledge base.

Generally, quality requirements of the production process direct industrial innovations. Scientific research when it concerns water, has traditionally emphasized the relationship of water quality to production requirements rather than the water polluting consequences of production. Extensive quality control over industrial effluents could disrupt seriously the core technology. For example, one of the means of reducing the polluting effects of production is to modify the production process itself by speeding up chemical reactions, manipulating chemical composition, or giving up certain lines of production. When the production technology is relatively standardized as the result of considerable research and investment, there will be resistance to change for the sake of purifying wastes, an interest that was not present in the early stages of standardizing procedures. The point is that the effluent process cannot be separated from the functioning of the core technology, if we are to effectively study the use of water pollution control technology by industry. Although innovative structures have a knowledge base that allows them to make a sophisticated search for ideas and alternatives to reduce their pollution, it is also the case that the requirements of the core technology are powerful internal stimuli that influence the industrial search for information and the research of industrial scientists and engineers.

SOCIAL STRUCTURE

Information or cybernetic theory classifies formal organizations as learning or innovative structures. That is, as bodies capable of gathering information about their environment, storing the information, recalling past experience, and applying it to present circumstances.[23] Organizations are adaptable to change, according to this perspective, when their structures are organized so that feedback from the environment readily enters the organization's structure and influences decision-making. Burns and Stalker found, in a survey of British electronic firms, that in the adaptive firms there was a social structure that readily reacted to market fluctuations.[24] Technological or market information flowed from the research and development departments directly to those parts

22. James D. Thompson and F. L. Bates, "Technology, Organization, and Administration," *Administrative Science Quarterly,* 2, (1957), pp. 323–343.
23. M. L. Cadwallader, "The Analysis of Change in Complex Social Organizations," in W. L. Buckley (ed.), *Modern Systems Theory for the Behavioral Scientists,* Chicago: Aldine Publishing Company, 1968, pp. 437–441.
24. T. Burns, and G. M. Stalker, *The Management of Innovation,* London: Tavistock, 1961.

of the production department where the information was needed to re-program the routine operations. Other students of organization substantiate the conclusions by Burns and Stalker with their findings that the rate of program change is greatest in organizations high in complexity, low in centralization and formalization.[25] In different studies, Price and Blau found that the use of new knowledge was most likely in organizations where the responsibilities of scientists and administrative decision makers were highly integrated.[26]

The core technologies of organizations rest on closed systems of logic.[27] The norm of rationality that is present in formal organizations serves to provide inputs and outputs to the production process so that some of the conditions of a closed system will prevail. That is, so the production process can operate without major disturbance. Although the needs of the core technology relate to the social structure of the organization, they are not wholly determinate of organizational structure.[28] Such needs do comprise a powerful internal stimulus for action, however, and when the core technology is not very adaptable to changes in the way it uses water, then resistance to innovations in water use are anticipated.

Another independent variable that relates to the ability of organizations to innovate is their internal organization of knowledge. We might suggest that the roles performed by industrial scientists vary according to their autonomy or their desire to introduce new knowledge into the ongoing system. It may also be argued that the research activities of industrial scientists is associated with the needs of the core technology. However, it is also expected the social structures where scientists have power have the capacity to be more innovative because of the norm for research as a means to solve the problems of product or market uncertainty. When organizations lack such a norm or have the type of structure that inhibits the administrative involvement of scientists, then the norm of rationality will limit the degree to which the organization will respond to changes in water quality.

Industrial organizations as rational systems will, therefore, attempt to influence the definition of water quality and compete and cooperate with other public and private groups so that the logic of their production process will suffer only minimal change and that the social environ-

25. P. R. Lawrence and J. W. Lorsch, *Organizations and Environment,* Boston: Division of Research, Graduate School of Business Administration, Harvard University, 1967. J. Hage and M. Aiken, *Social Change in Complex Organizations,* New York: Random House, Inc., 1970.
26. James Price, "Use of New Knowledge in Organizations," *Human Organization,* 23, (1964), pp. 224–234. Peter M. Blau, "The Hierarchy of Authority in Organizations," *American Journal of Sociology,* 73, (1968), pp. 453–467.
27. James D. Thompson, *op. cit.,* p. 23.
28. D. J. Hickson, D. S. Pugh, and D. C. Pheysey, "Operations Technology and Organization Structure," *Administrative Science Quarterly,* 14, (1969), pp. 378–398.

ment will remain predictable. We propose that the vigourousness by which they exercise their power to influence water legislation and resist innovation is related to their innovative capacity. The less adaptable or innovative they are, the more apt are industrial organizations to use their power to define water quality and affect the general rules for water use. Consequently, a reasonable study of the emerging definitions of water quality, requires a sociological analysis of the power relationship among public and private social units mutually dependent on water but with different interests.

Organizational rationality necessarily refers to more than just technological rationality since the technological activities and the social structure of organizations is ultimately dependent on resources from the social environment as well as the physical milieu. The activities of the organization including the way it uses resources must be legitimated by other social groups and the general society. The result is that rationality requires negotiation with the social environment so that the critical inputs, materials, supplies, knowledge, water, can be maintained. The contribution of structural analysis in sociology has been to give us a model whereby the definition of problems and the enactment of solutions can be associated with the distribution of power and influence within a social system. A study of the power relationships among organizations attempting to define water quality is suggested as important for further analysis.[29]

29. A general study of the power relationships between public interests and industrial organizations is now under way at the University of Minnesota, Department of Sociology. The study, Social and Economic Aspects of Industrial Use of Water Pollution Control Technology, is funded by the United States Department of the Interior and the Agricultural Experiment Station, University of Minnesota, St. Paul, Minnesota.

---------------------------- **23** ----------------------------

THE CONTRIBUTION OF VOLUNTARY ORGANIZATIONS TO COMMUNITY STRUCTURE

Ruth C. Young and Olaf F. Larson

When voluntary organizations are considered as units contributing to the total structure of communities, a whole series of questions follows. Is there a prestige hierarchy among organizations, and is it independent of the prestige of the individuals who are members? What is the relationship, if any, of such secondary organizations to primary social relations? What is their role with respect to external community relations, to internal stability, and to change? While the context in which these questions are examined is admittedly a single, small New York community they are nonetheless of such a general nature that findings attest to the value of studying groups as such rather than the conventional method of making inferences about groups largely from the characteristics of the membership.

METHOD

The principal source of data was a series of structured interviews[1] conducted with at least one major officer of each of forty-three formal organizations in a New York community of about 2,300 persons. An organization was defined as a named group which had a meeting place in the community and at least fifteen members.[2] The initial discussion about size and prestige includes some thirty more organizations which did not meet the two defining criteria. The organizations studied included churches; school-centered adult groups; out-of-school organizations for youth; agricultural and business organizations; fraternal, athletic, and other social groups; women's clubs; and homemaking groups.

The schedule asked the informant to report on the organization as a whole. Most of the questions were factual, but others involved judgments. In particular, each officer was asked to name and rank the five most important organizations in the community. Each choice was assigned a weight of from one (for the lowest ranking organization) to five, and the total score was computed. When the informants gave generic categories like "church" or "school," the scores for particular churches were all combined with the score for "church." This procedure may have inflated the standing of some particular churches, but, in general, it reflected more accurately the actual categories of thought used by the informants.

The resulting prestige rank of organizations is the criterion variable against which the many other organizational characteristics are compared. The prestige variable derived from the pooled estimates of all officers lays claim to representing the social reality of the community

1. These interviews were collected by Harold R. Capener, who originally used them in another study. See his "A Study of Organizational Processes in an Experimental Community Approach to Extension Program Planning" (unpublished Ph.D. thesis, Cornell University, 1951).
2. Based upon male heads and homemakers, included in a complete enumeration of the community, who reported membership. At least fifteen members were required by the larger structural analysis of which this study was a part. See Ruth C. Young, "Community Structure and Individual Integration: A Test of the Group Effect Hypothesis in Neighborhoods and Formal Organizations" (unpublished Ph.D. thesis, Cornell University, 1958). This thesis was based on data collected in several New York State communities in a study directed by Olaf F. Larson. See his "Research for Experimental Community Projects in New York," *Rural Sociology*, XV (1950), 67–69.

reflected in statements by articulate representatives of the organizations.

THE "J" CURVE OF ORGANIZATIONAL PRESTIGE

Figure 1 shows the curve derived from plotting the prestige scores by the number of organizations with given scores. (This figure is based on more than seventy organizations, those that do not as well as those that do meet the criteria.) The result is a *J* curve of organizational prestige quite similar to the curves based on sociometric choices. The top organizations with scores from 120 to 58 were: church, village business club, farm and home extension organizations, school and related organizations, a particular youth organization, and the farm fraternal clubs. Falling in a second category scoring from 57 to 16 were the patriotic and service organizations and all but one of the youth organizations. The low prestige group scoring 15 or less contained fraternal groups and local women's clubs. Organizations with a zero score were excluded from the remainder of the analysis. In this respect the analysis was biased against the hypotheses of the study as detailed below.

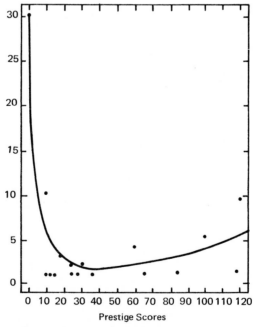

Figure 1. Number of organizations or organizational types.

The significant difference between the high-prestige organizations and the rest is that they represent what most persons think of as the main institutions of the community: religious; economic, both commercial and agricultural; family, and youth training and education.

The distribution of organizations by size of membership formed a similar J curve.[3] The membership data were independently derived from the answers to a schedule administered to male heads of households and homemakers at the same time as the organization study and are therefore independent of the estimates of prestige.

The two variables are related: 50 per cent of the high-prestige organizations had fifty or more members, as compared with 36 per cent of the medium and 18 per cent of the low prestige. It is to be noted, however, that while low-prestige organizations tend to be small, not all high-prestige organizations are large. This suggests that certain organizations accrue large memberships because they are important to the community, rather than the reverse.

Another correlate of prestige is the age of the organization. Among high-prestige organizations, 60 per cent are twenty-five or more years old, in contrast to 55 per cent for the middle category and 34 per cent for the low-prestige organizations. These relations of prestige to age and size may be regarded as something of a validity check on the criterion variable in that they also reflect organizational importance.[4]

STRUCTURAL CORRELATES OF ORGANIZATIONAL PRESTIGE

Formal structure and programs.—In general, high-prestige organizations show greater formality and elaboration of structure than middle- or low-prestige groups, but at the same time they are more specialized in their program. For instance, the high-prestige organizations have an average of 11.3 officers, while the medium prestige average 8.1 and the low prestige 5.1. The findings with respect to number of committees are roughly similar: high-prestige organizations average 3.5 committees, medium prestige 3.6 committees, and low 0.9. Moreover, as Table 1 shows, the organizations differ with respect to the

3. The J curve of organizational size was previously noticed and discussed by F. Stuart Chapin in his "The Optimum Size of Institutions: A Theory of the Large Group," *American Journal of Sociology,* LXII (March, 1957), 449–60.
4. Mhyra S. Minnis has reported a prestige ranking of women's organizations in some ways comparable to this one. She used four types of data in arriving at her over-all judgment of five degrees of organizational prestige. The data types were: residential area; occupation of husband or, if single, of women members; education; and the social prestige or reputation of the organization. The last was based on the reports of officers in the organizations including items on type of organization, date of founding, how membership is secured, frequency of newspaper publicity, etc. Although her analysis is mainly concerned with the characteristics of the members in the five prestige levels and although she does not separate prestige from the characteristics of the organizations, her results are generally congruent with those of this study. See her "Cleavage in Women's Organizations: A Reflection of the Social Structure of a City," *American Sociological Review,* XVIII (1953), 47–53.

Table 1

Committees Classified by Prestige of Organizations
and by Duties of Committees

Prestige of Organizations	No. of Committees	Percentage of Committees by Main Duties			
		Administrative	Service	Entertainment	Total
High	70	50	23	27	100
Medium	40	25	50	25	100
Low	11	18	27	55	100

functions performed by the committees. The predominant functions
are administrative for the high-prestige groups, service for the medium
prestige, and entertainment for the low prestige.

The informants also gave their judgments of the main purposes of
their organization, taken as a whole. The first-named main functions are
tabulated in Table 2 according to the main common-sense categories
that emerged from the responses.

Table 2

Organizations Classified by Prestige and by
First-Named Chief Function Performed

Chief Function	Prestige of Organizations (%)		
	High (N = 20)	Medium (N = 11)	Low (N = 12)
Agricultural	20		33
Religious, moral	40	27	42
Homemaking	30		
Youth education	5		
Economic	5		
Social		73	25
Total	100	100	100

The greatest proportion of high-prestige organizations have a religious function, followed by homemaking and agricultural functions;
among the middle-prestige organizations and the greatest proportion
have a social function; the low-prestige groups are spread over agricultural, religious, and social functions. In addition to what may be considered a contrasting value emphasis in the three categories, the degree
of concentration of their emphasis differs with prestige. Among the
high-prestige organizations 65 per cent report only one important function, while 18 per cent of the middle and 30 per cent of the low-prestige

organizations have only one. Much of the evidence, however, shows that high-prestige organizations may in fact perform multiple functions but have developed a more general way of characterizing the main purpose of the organization (i.e., "religious") so that the many special functions are subsumed. For example, churches do support programs for youth, charity, community development, etc.

Relations with other organizations and the community.—Leaders of organizations were asked to describe the relations of their organization with others in the community. Their replies were classified with respect to whether the organization originated action for other groups, received directions, or had no relation. The distribution is shown in Table 3. The high-prestige organizations are the originators of interorganizational activity. The low-prestige organizations have no relation or tend to receive stimulation, while the middle-prestige organizations tend to stand apart from other organizations or to originate activity. Only one organization co-operated with any other. A similar pattern is indicated by the classification of organizations with respect to the direction of their efforts. Some 50 per cent of the high-prestige organizations are outer-directed toward non-members, in contrast to 0 and 8 per cent, respectively, for the middle- and low-prestige categories. The latter direct most of their efforts inward toward their own members. Other indications of efforts and ability to influence the community are reflected in the presence of a membership committee (50, 27, and 0 per cent for the three categories) and the presence of a program for teaching the young (50, 18, and 17 per cent for the three categories).

Table 3

Organizations Classified by Prestige and by Type of
Relation with Other Community Organizations

Prestige	N	Type of Relations with Other Organizations			
		Originates (%)	Receives or Co-operates (%)	No Relation (%)	Total (%)
High	20	50	10	40	100
Medium	11	27	9	64	100
Low	12	8	42	50	100

The high-prestige organizations hold more ritual programs that are open to the public, as one might expect from the fact that churches account for about half of the high-prestige organizations, but they do not maintain their position with respect to social programs open to the community at large. When it comes to dances, bingo, plays, fairs, and the like, the medium-level organizations (which include the fraternal groups) are busier than the others. Thirty per cent of the high-prestige organizations hold some such open social function at least occasionally, while 63 per cent of the medium-prestige and 58 per cent of the low-prestige groups do so.

The same variant pattern is apparent when the organizations in the several prestige levels are classified according to whether they at least occasionally perform charitable services for the community. The medium-prestige organizations are somewhat more likely to perform community services, such as raising money for the fire department, and are quite a bit more likely to be concerned with the welfare of individuals.

It appears, then, that the middle-prestige organizations are not simply paler editions of the high-prestige organizations but are concerned with different functions—social, charity, and fraternal. In addition, they have the greatest number of age-sex requirements for membership, a characteristic that goes hand in hand with activities that require homogeneous groups for their success.

Relations outside the community.—Outside affiliations imply a flow of communications from a state or national office, and perhaps once a year the local groups provide feedback by sending delegates to a convention or "workshop." In contrast, the purely local groups are not attentive to, controlled by, or stimulated by an outside body or staff of specialists, nor are they directly connected to the national society in other ways. High-, medium-, and low-prestige organizations differ in respect to outside affiliation; the proportions with affiliation are 100, 82, and 33 per cent, respectively, for the three categories.

Stability-change functions.—The responses concerning activities and programs were classified according to four types of changes introduced by organizations: general changes introduced into the community as a whole, such as a new swimming pool; new practices introduced to individuals or families; establishment of new units of existing organizations, such as a new scout troop where one already exists; and finally, improvement of the organization's own physical plant. The distribution of these introduced changes by prestige is given in Table 4.

The high-prestige organizations lead the others in the proportion introducing some type of innovation and with respect to general community innovations, new practices, and new units. They are almost matched by medium-prestige organizations in the introduction of community-wide innovations. One may question the quality or beneficial effect of the changes, but it is the high-prestige organizations, representing the main institutions, that most often engage in innovative activity in the community setting.

Table 4

Organizations Classified by Prestige and by Type of
Changes Introduced into the Community

Type of Changes Introduced	Prestige of Organizations (%)		
	High (N = 20)	Medium (N = 11)	Low (N = 12)
General for community as whole*	25	18	
Individual practices*	35		8
New units of existing organizations*	50	27	25
Improvement of own property*	5	9	8
Sponsors no change of any kind	5	54	58

*An organization can introduce more than one type of innovation. These categories are not mutually exclusive, and columns do not add up to 100 per cent. Each is a proportion of the total number of organizations which are high, medium, or low prestige introducing a given type of change.

If new people bring new ideas, the high-prestige groups should have more ideas available. While 70 per cent of the leaders of high-prestige organizations stated that they had officers who had moved into the community in the last five years, only 27 per cent of the medium- and 17 per cent of the low-prestige groups had newcomers as officers.

It does not follow that the low-prestige groups are therefore more stable. The findings that the high-prestige groups are older and have more ritual activities have already been reported. The question, "Does this organization tend to place the same people in the same jobs repeatedly?" obviously does not put an organization in a favorable light. Yet the high-prestige organizations acknowledge this type of stability more frequently than the other two categories (75 per cent as compared to 45 and 42 per cent). The high-prestige groups have both more change and more continuity in their leadership.

PRIMARY RELATIONS IN SECONDARY ORGANIZATIONS

The organizational attributes discussed so far are ordinarily considered "secondary" because that term is used to refer to the formal, impersonal relations of groups to their members and implies organizational formality, impersonality, and complexity. But in this modern rural community the formal organizations *contain* primary relationships as well. It is not simply a matter of primary and secondary relations existing side by side in separate structures; the finding of this study is that primary relationships are most likely to occur among people who participate in the high-prestige organizations.

Such a conclusion is suggested initially by the data on opportunities for family participation. The high-prestige organizations are much more likely to offer opportunities for family participation (60 per cent), while only 18 per cent of the medium-prestige and none of the low-prestige groups make such provisions. The medium- and low-prestige groups provide a pattern of individual rather than family participation.

Table 5

Organizations Classified by Prestige and by
Visiting Choices Among Members

Prestige	N	Percentage of Most Visited Choices Among Members			
		Under 30	30-49	50 and Over	Total
High	20	10	52	38	100
Medium	11	18	82	0	100
Low	12	83	17	0	100

More direct evidence of the presence of primary relationships operating in the context of secondary groups is presented in Table 5. By using the independently collected survey data, which included information on family visiting choices, it was possible to compute the proportion of people named by the members of a given organization as "most visited" who were also members of that organization. The proportions naming fellow members are divided into three categories as shown. Then the proportion of organizations in each prestige group that fell into each of these three categories was calculated. The result is clear: The high-prestige organizations have a good proportion with a membership-visiting overlap of 50 per cent or over, a category in which the medium- and low-prestige organizations are not even represented. The medium-prestige organizations show up strongly in the middle category. The low-prestige organizations are composed of members who tend not to visit each other very often. Admittedly, the larger size of the high-prestige organizations increases the chances that personal friends will be found within the boundaries, but the other prestige categories have compensating advantages, such as the social emphasis of the medium and the possibilities for greater interaction in the small or low-prestige groups. If any variable should be considered explanatory, it is prestige and its correlates.

SUMMARY AND DISCUSSION

Taking all these findings together, what general picture of voluntary organizations do they suggest? First and foremost, there is evidence that those in the best position to know—the officers of the organizations—discriminate among organizations with respect to their "importance." It turns out that the most important organizations are those that embody the main institutional or value constellations of the community. They particularly fit Chapin's definition of nucleated institutions,[5] but because of their more general significance and wider connections outside the community they also embody most of the meaning usually ascribed to institutions in the more diffuse sense. Thus, when the officers report on these organizations, they are reporting, to a large degree, on the structure of social meanings that are maintained and upheld by the community as a whole.

The high-prestige organizations, which are central to this structure of meaning, are the largest and oldest and appear to serve as links between the community and the wider society. By their affiliation with state and national centers, and through them with other communities, they receive a stream of ideas, information, and innovations and perhaps help to integrate one community with another. Thus, the information stored in many other communities and organizations is potentially available, and what is actually received is passed on to the rest of the community by way of the large memberships of high-prestige groups, their more active public influence, and through ties to other organizations within the local community. These high-prestige organizations are specialized in the sense that the work of their relatively elaborate and carefully administered structure converges on a delimited sphere of activity, but the greater number of subgroups they contain or foster, and their encouragement of family participation, indicate that the overall goal may be attained by a variety of avenues. The high-prestige groups not only appear to introduce change but also, through continuity of leadership, ritual performances, and general institutional "weight," as indexed by their persistence as organizations, exercise a stabilizing function in the community. They are, then, the gatekeepers of change. They are also characterized by close ties of friendship among their members.

A middle-prestige group appears to differ in type and function. These are the specialized age-sex clubs with a strong program emphasis on socializing and entertainment and with another emphasis, possibly by way of integrating themselves into the community, on charitable services. These groups do not represent major institutional areas, they have selective memberships, and their relations with other groups in or

---

5. Chapin defines nucleated institutions in terms of four criteria: common reciprocating attitudes of individuals and their conventionalized behavior patterns; cultural objects of symbolic value; cultural objects possessing utilitarian value; a code of oral or written symbols preserving the institution's specifications. Nucleated institutions are attached to a restricted locus by means of property ownership. See F. Stuart Chapin, *Contemporary American Institutions* (New York: Harper & Bros., 1935), pp. 13–23.

out of the community are restricted. They make few efforts to influence anyone, and their expressed and apparent program is entertainment. What is of considerable theoretical interest in these groups is that, *in toto,* their characteristics nullify the interpretation of the prestige hierarchy as a simple dimension in all respects. They are generally "medium" in their organization, as compared with the high and low groups, but they are variant in accentuating another dimension: a combination of fraternalism, ritual (but different from that of the churches), activity orientation (as in athletics or other high interaction types of entertainment), and a delimitation of organizational interest to the group itself. It may be that they have sacrificed organizational flexibility and adaptation to group integration and enhancement of membership prestige.

The low-prestige organizations are marginal in most respects and have little in common except their lack of recognition. This lack of position in the prestige structure is accounted for in two ways. Some of the groups are fraternal groups or church auxiliaries which are dying out. Others are ephemeral clusters which are just getting started but probably will not go very far beyond thinking up a name for themselves. Some of these groups may be innovative, despite the findings of this study, but in general they represent tiny and transient subcultures.

Taken as a whole, this structure of voluntary organizations and its associated web of social meanings is quite a different way of viewing the community from that to which years of household surveys have accustomed us. This approach emphasizes the group as a unit of analysis rather than the individual and considers the consequences of thinking about communities as an organized structure of social meanings and relationships rather than as a collection of individuals who possess social characteristics.[6]

When the focus is on the community structure as such, it becomes easier to deal with communities defined other than by the territory they occupy. One can imagine finding communities within larger cities by an analysis of the institutional structure derived from reports of the officers of organizations. Even spatially separate organizations may be considered a part of the "community" if they are included in a particular prestige hierarchy. Moreover, in those communities where territory is coterminous with interaction patterns, that fact should show up in the organizational analysis.

Studying a community through its institutional organization permits the analysis of dimensions not available through a study focused on individuals. Such dimensions include the total pattern adjustment of

6. Another paper will deal with the relations between voluntary organizations and social class.

organization, hierarchies, organizational complexity, growth, stability, innovation, ritual, and relations to the state and nation. Still another implication of this institutional approach bears on the possibility of generalizing about communities. When the data consist of family reports, it is difficult to say anything general about communities. In contrast, this analysis suggests at least one generalization that may hold for all communities. It is that they all have a prestige-complexity hierarchy of organizations in which high-prestige groups embody community institutions, while the medium-prestige groups elaborate integrative activities. Obviously, the present data do not test this generalization, but a general knowledge of American communities supports the proposition as an encapsulation of a widespread pattern.

Ultimately, this analysis assumes that communities are collection and processing structures for information obtained from a much larger information pool to which they also feed back information.[7] But the formal organization located in a community is not simply a link in a wider network. In a more abstract sense, taken as a structure of social meaning, it serves as a frame of reference with which the members of organizations and their families can make sense out of their own activity and the environment. By providing sets of cognitive categories, vocabularies of motives, and stereotyped judgments, it organizes individual activity in relation to other efforts that may be occurring far away and completely unknown to the people of a particular community. In an era of vast urban interpenetration of communities—a process that operates concretely through networks of formal organizations—an approach to community structure that stresses these ought to advance our understanding.

---

7. Two authors have recently discussed this "information" conception of community. See Morris Freilich, "Toward an Operational Definition of Community," *Rural Sociology,* XXVIII (1963), 117–27, and Charles L. Cleland, "Characteristics of Social Systems within Which Selected Types of Information Are Transmitted," *Rural Sociology,* XXV (1960), 212–18.

CHAPTER SIX

INTERORGANIZATIONAL ANALYSIS

While there is an extensive literature on *intra*organizational relationships, work on *inter*organizational relations has been, and still is, largely underdeveloped. As sociologists have recognized the paucity of work in this area, they have called for more theory and research. Currently, it appears that there is a trend towards *inter*organizational analysis.

Warren's article specifies interorganizational analysis as a field of investigation. By the use of empirical data from community decision organizations, he develops a typology of contexts for inclusive decision making. The typology, which is based on the ways organizational units interact in the decision making process, includes four types: unitary, federative, coalitional, and social choice. Warren further suggests that the interorganizational field (interaction among community organizations) may be useful for optimization of a mix of community values and goals.

"Organization-set" is a useful concept for interorganizational analysis. It is an extension of Merton's important article on role-set. Organization-set treats the organization as the unit of analysis and traces its interactions within the network of organizations in its environment. That organization, which is the major point of reference, is termed the "focal" organization. Evan's article explores both the conceptual and methodological problems of interorganizational analysis much as Gross, Mason, and McEachern have done for role analysis.

Evan presents seven dimensions of organizational sets and then

305

suggests several hypotheses relative to organizational analysis. He discusses some of the methodological problems in organizational analysis and advocates the use of two kinds of tools: graph theory and input-output analysis.

The selection by Levine and White treats organizational exchange as voluntary activity between two organizations which has consequences for their respective goals and objectives. Levine and White stress resources as a crucial linkage between organizations. Resource scarcity in one organization makes interorganizational exchange essential. Organizational interdependence is contingent upon three major factors: (1) accessibility of resources, (2) organizational objective and functions, and (3) the degree of domain consensus. They examine selected dimensions of exchange including the direction of exchange.

Organizational boundaries have long been a point of consideration not very well handled by theorists who have emphasized goals of the organization. Levine and White's discussion of organizational domain deals with this boundary problem which we refer to in the theory section and in selected articles throughout the book.

Clark's examination of the educational institution utilizes a case study of the Physical Science Study Committee to emphasize the necessity of federation among small agencies or organizations. Federation is a mechanism to gain power for the "struggle" with other organizations. It provides competitive advantage. The tendency toward federation indicates that the agency may fear loss of autonomy or diminution of its power. While Clark concerns himself primarily with the educational institution, he also explores problems which are significant to many other types of organizations.

The article by Clark explores organizational means which may be employed by any organization in order to stabilize or enhance its position in society. This selection also suggests rather uniquely the possibility of one organization lending its power to another.

Aiken and Hage present an empirical examination of organizational interdependence. It utilizes as an indicator of interdependence the number of joint programs. They examine the relationship between interdependence and internal organizational behavior in a study of sixteen social welfare and health organizations. An increase in interdependence results in increases in complexity, innovativeness, the activity of internal communications channels, and a somewhat greater increase in the decentralization of decision-making. They hypothesize that with an increase in the division of labor, organizations will become more complex and more innovative. Furthermore, Aiken and Hage present data which indicate that scarcity of resources, which results from increased innovativeness, tends to promote greater cooperation and, as a consequence, greater interdependencies among organizations.

Kunz employs the concept "sponsorship" as a special case of interorganizational relations in which the sponsored organization utilizes other organizations to implement its own program. Sponsorship implies the following two conditions: (1) the *beneficiary* organization must have sufficiently distinct boundaries from the *sponsoring* organization, and (2) The beneficiary organization legitimately makes use of the organizational facilities of the sponsor to achieve its ends. He empirically investigates selected implications of this concept with data from Boy Scout Troops. He concludes that the effects upon the beneficiary organization vary according to the nature of the sponsoring organization. For example, Scout troops which are sponsored by large, bureaucratic organizations have increased probability of persistence as compared with troops sponsored by small, *ad hoc* neighborhood committees.

24

THE INTERORGANIZATIONAL FIELD
AS A FOCUS FOR INVESTIGATION

Roland L. Warren

There is a growing literature of research and conceptualization on the relation of organizational behavior to various aspects of the environment and, more specifically, on the interaction of specific organizations, especially on exchanges that occur between them.[1] This paper attempts to indicate the need for research focusing deliberately on the "field" within which organizations interact.[2] It depicts the American

1. Richard L. Simpson and William H. Gulley, Goals, Environmental Pressures, and Organizational Characteristics, *American Sociological Review*, 27 (June 1962); James D. Thompson and William J. McEwen, Organizational Goals and Environment: Goal-Setting as an Interaction Process, *American Sociological Review*, 23 (February 1958); William R. Dill, "The Impact of Environment on Organizational Development," in Sydney Mailick and E. H. Van Ness (eds.), *Concepts and Issues in Administrative Behavior* (Englewood Cliffs, N.J.: Prentice-Hall, 1962); Eugene Litwak and Lydia F. Hylton, Interorganizational Analysis: A Hypothesis on Coordinating Agencies, *Administrative Science Quarterly*, 6 (March 1962); James D. Thompson, Organizations and Output Transactions, *American Journal of Sociology*, 68 (November 1962); Sol Levine and Paul E. White, Exchange as a Conceptual Framework for the Study of Interorganizational Relationships, *Administrative Science Quarterly*, 5 (March 1961); Sol Levine, Paul E. White, and Benjamin D. Paul, Community Interorganizational Problems in Providing Medical Care and Social Services, *American Journal of Public Health*, 53 (August 1963); William M. Evan, "The Organization-Set: Toward a Theory of Interorganizational Relations," in James D. Thompson (ed.), *Approaches to Organizational Design* (Pittsburgh: University of Pittsburgh, 1966); Bernard Olshansky, *Planned Change in Interorganizational Relationships* (Doctoral dissertation, Florence Heller Graduate School for Advanced Studies in Social Welfare, Brandeis University, June 1961). Other recent publications in this field are cited in the course of this paper.
2. The term "field" is used here essentially in Lewin's sense: "a totality of coexisting facts which are conceived of as mutually interdependent." Cf. Kurt Lewin, *Field Theory in Social Science: Selected Theoretical Papers* (New York: Harper, 1951), p. 240 and *passim*.

metropolitan community as a special instance for interorganizational field analysis and presents a simplified conceptual model for the analysis of this field. It then raises some questions about further research to determine specific modes of organizational interaction in the community field, and also, about possible changes that might increase the overall usefulness of interorganizational decision making.[3]

CONCEPT OF INTERORGANIZATIONAL FIELD

The concept of interorganizational field is based on the observation that the interaction between two organizations is affected, in part at least, by the nature of the organizational pattern or network within which they find themselves. For example, the interaction between two department stores of a given size will be somewhat different if they are the only two department stores in a medium-sized city from what it would be if they constituted two out of twenty different department stores of approximately the same size in a metropolis.

Mannheim has taken, as a central condition in his consideration of social planning, the concept of "density of events." Using the example of the traffic light, which becomes necessary only after the density of traffic reaches a certain point, he says: "This simple illustration enables us to see precisely how the increasing *density of events (Dichtigkeit des Geschehens)* makes the possibility of a natural balance through competition or through mutual adaptation more and more hopeless."[4]

The density of events, even among the same type of actors, increasingly focuses attention on the structure of their interaction, but it may, in addition, relate different types of actors in new modes of interaction. Thus, a local department store and a local bank, which formerly interacted in terms of exchanges involving loans and repayments, or deposits and withdrawals, now may find themselves interacting with other units in a larger group setting up an industrial development corporation or attempting to influence the course of urban renewal in the downtown area.

Elsewhere, Mannheim uses the concept of "field structure" for a situation in which various parties interact in such a way that their mutual influence tends to exceed the borders of structured institutional and organizational channels. He adds: "Whenever society instead of expanding in concentric circles, develops new spheres of action which traverse the boundaries of the concrete groups, we speak of a field structure.[5] One need not reify this field structure into an entity inde-

3. The research on which this paper is based was supported by a Public Health Service research career program award No. K3-MH-21-869 and supplementary grant No. MH-11085-02.
4. Karl Mannheim, *Man and Society in an Age of Reconstruction: Studies in Modern Social Structure* (New York: Harcourt, Brace, 1951) p. 157.
5. *Ibid.,* p. 297.

pendent of the behavior of its constituent parts in order to concede the importance of studying it as a more inclusive level than that of the exchange behavior of an individual organization with other actors in its environment.

Emery and Trist made the point that "the environmental contexts in which organizations exist are themselves changing, at an increasing rate, and towards increasing complexity."[6] With such change, the environmental contexts themselves become an important subject for analysis. "In a general way it may be said that to think in terms of systems seems the most appropriate conceptual response so far available when the phenomena under study—at any level and in any domain—display the character of being organized, and when understanding the nature of the interdependencies constitutes the research task."[7] But can the environmental field in which organizations interact be considered to be organized, and if so, what can be said about such environmental organization systematically?

Emery and Trist answered the first question affirmatively and developed a typology of four different environmental "textures," extending from the placid, randomized environment to the turbulent field environment. They analyzed these in terms of strategy, tactics, and operations; the complexity of actors in the field and their similarity or dissimilarity; and the types of behavior necessary for organizational survival in each case. The turbulent field had, in addition to the increased complexity of interorganizational relationships characteristic of the third stage, a new emergent in that "the dynamic properties arise not simply from the interaction of the component organizations, but also from the field itself. The 'ground' is in motion."[8] In these circumstances, "individual organizations, however large, cannot expect to adapt successfully simply through their own direct actions."[9]

COMMUNITY DECISION ORGANIZATIONS

An exploratory project on the interrelationship of community-level[10] planning organizations in three cities—Philadelphia, Detroit,

6. S. E. Emery and E. L. Trist, The Causal Texture of Organizational Environments, *Human Relations,* 18 (February 1965), 21.
7. *Ibid.*
8. *Ibid.,* 26.
9. *Ibid.,* 28.
10. The term "community level" is used here loosely to denote both the city itself and the metropolitan area. Community decision organizations included in the present analysis may have either of these domain boundaries. The distinction between the two, though extremely important in many contexts, is not important in the present one. Furthermore, although the present analysis confines itself to interaction among organizations at this community level, the vertical relations to organizational systems outside of the community, as, for example, the federal government, should not be overlooked. The term "community level" does not imply a discretely identifiable level, except for purposes of analysis. One of the aspects of the turbulence within which community decision organizations interact is the fluid admixture of organizations from all levels, both more inclusive than the community, such as state and federal, and less inclusive than the community, such as neighborhood organizations.

and Boston, considered organizations such as community welfare councils, urban renewal authorities, antipoverty organizations, housing authorities, chambers of commerce, federations of churches, municipal health and welfare departments, boards of education, and so on. It became apparent that the term "planning," in addition to its ambiguity and current semantic explosiveness, did not accurately distinguish these organizations from others. But all the organizations mentioned purported to—and in varying degrees were legitimated to—represent the interests of the community in some segment of broad community concern; therefore the term community decision organizations (CDO's) was adopted.[11]

Such organizations constitute the means through which the community attempts to concert certain decisions and activities. Presumably a higher aggregate utility is attainable through joint decision making and action within the respective CDO's than if decisions within each field of concern were left to what Banfield calls "social choice."[12] Most cities today have many and varied CDO's. Many of them receive strong financial support and program stimulus from the federal government or other extra-community sources, and their spheres of activity, although differentially defined, overlap in various relationships.[13]

It has often been observed that communities do not have a single organizational structure, but rather are constituted of many formal structures (including that of the municipal government) as well as interaction patterns through which locality-relevant decisions are made. The process through which this occurs is bewilderingly complex. Norton Long has sought to capture it as an ecology of games "in the local territorial system [which] accomplishes unplanned but largely functional results,"[14] and Banfield has treated the process in terms of an elaborate analysis of "political influence."[15] Greer sums it up as follows:

> The over-all polity is, however, a sum of efforts ranging from those of neighborhood improvement associations to the negotiations between

11. Field work in Philadelphia and Detroit was extremely limited, being confined to a limited number of interviews with leaders of such community decision organizations, principally for the purpose of qualitative comparison with the more intensive exploratory field work conducted in Boston. The term "community decision organization" was suggested by James J. Callahan, a doctoral candidate at Brandeis University.
12. Banfield has developed the concept of social choice, as opposed to central decision. "*A social choice* ... is the accidental by-product of the actions of two or more actors—'interested parties,' they will be called—who have no common intention and who make their selections competitively or without regard to each other. In a social choice process, each actor seeks to attain his own ends; the aggregate of all actions—the situation produced by all actions together—constitutes an outcome for the group, but it is an outcome which no one has planned as a 'solution' to a 'problem.' It is a 'resultant' rather than a 'solution.'" Cf. Edward C. Banfield, *Political Influence* (New York: The Free Press of Glencoe, 1961), pp. 326–327.
13. Roland L. Warren, The Impact of New Designs of Community Organization, *Child Welfare*, 44 (November 1965).
14. Norton E. Long, The Local Community as an Ecology of Games, *American Journal of Sociology*, 64 (November 1958), 254.
15. *Ibid.*

central city mayor and the plenipotentiaries of powerful organizations. In the absence of a central arena and polity, the public decisions are made in response to the politically potent demands of a fragmented electorate and the professional concerns of the political managerial elite. They suffice to accomplish a minimal ordering.[16]

But the perennial question is whether that "minimal ordering" is an optimal ordering, and if not, how an optimal ordering may be achieved. The time when the community welfare council could aspire to be *the* instrument of the community for social planning has long since passed, as the texture of the organizational environment has become complicated by the multiplicity of organizations exercising a planning function in this field. A recent trend toward closer collaboration between physical planners and social planners in the urban field is apparent in the professional literature and behavior of each. Earlier attempts, such as the Syracuse and Onondaga County Post-War Planning Council, to bring the existing CDO's into one organization for centralized decision making have largely been abandoned. A newer trend is the function of mayors—and their development coordinators —as a locus not only for some integrated centralized decision making, but also as a decision-making resource when the conflict of CDO interests threatens an impasse.

CHARACTERISTICS OF INTERORGANIZATIONAL FIELD

It is of little interest to investigate the interorganizational field in which the activities of one CDO—say the health department—can be carried on with little relation to those of another, such as the chamber of commerce or the metropolitan transit authority. Altshuler has concluded:

The most distinguishing feature of the bureaucratization of society in recent generations has perhaps been the extent to which planning at the level of governments and large private organizations has gradually become more and more systematized. The proliferation of specialized research and planning staffs in large bureaucracies of all kinds is symptomatic of this trend. Planning becomes "political" only when the efforts of some men and organizations to plan come into conflict with those of others.[17]

Litwak and Hylton distinguish interorganizational analysis from intraorganizational analysis by "(*1*) the operation of social behavior under conditions of partial conflict and (*2*) the stress on factors which

16. Scott Greer, *The Emerging City: Myth and Reality* (New York: The Free Press of Glencoe, 1962), p. 200.
17. Alan Altshuler, *The City Planning Process: A Political Analysis* (Ithaca, N.Y.: Cornell University, 1965), p. 409.

derive equally from all units of interaction rather than being differentially weighted by authority structure."[18]

In getting at some of the other distinguishing characteristics of interorganizational interaction, Burton R. Clark considers three patterns of concerting influence. The first is the organizational, or bureaucratic pattern. At the other extreme is that "found in political arenas characterized by a formal decentralization of authority, and therefore to be understood by a theory of political influence," such as Banfield's.[19] Between the two are patterns of confederative organization or organizational alliance which "converge with and become somewhat a part of political influence, in that they are the result of efforts to co-ordinate autonomous agencies, to unite effort *without* the authority of formal hierarchy and employee status. They are somewhat different in that they develop away from formal political arenas and often escape the constraints of political accountability."[20] He contrasts such interorganizational patterns with bureaucratic (intraorganizational) ones, as indicated in Table 1.[21]

Table 1

Bureaucratic and Interorganizational Patterns As
Depicted by Clark

	Bureaucratic Patterns	Interorganizational Patterns
Authority and supervision	Inherent in the office	Less through formal structure and more shared by specific agreement
Accountability	Accountability up the line, supervision down the line	Looser accountability and supervision; provided by general agreement, limited in scope and in time
Standards of work	Explication, formalization, universal application	Less formal, more indirect; often through manipulating resources and incentives in a large market or economy of organizations
Personnel assignment	Periodic review of performance, replacement or reassignment where appropriate	Other methods of strengthening weak sectors, including supplying resources
Research and development	Usually provided for in organizational chart	Subsidizing private innovative groups by major agencies, facilitating dissemination of innovations to the field

18. Litwak and Hylton, *op. cit.*, 398.
19. Burton R. Clark, Interorganizational Patterns in Education, *Administrative Science Quarterly*, 10 (September 1965), 233.
20. *Ibid.*
21. Adapted by the writer from Clark, *op. cit.*, 234–236.

INCLUSIVE CONTEXTS FOR DECISION MAKING

A preliminary study in Boston analyzing the highly complex context in which community decision organizations operate indicated that decisions were being made in the most varied organizational contexts, and that the difference in contexts seemed to be related to the behavior of the CDO's in the interaction process. Four such contexts were discernible and may be of general applicability in examining organizational and interorganizational behavior.

The context typology distinguishes between the ways in which organizational units interact in the decision-making process as these are influenced by their relationships to an inclusive decision-making structure. The four types of context are: (*1*) unitary, (*2*) federative, (*3*) coalitional, and (*4*) social choice.

These are distinguished from each other on the basis of a number of dimensions: (*1*) relation of units to an inclusive goal, (*2*) locus of inclusive decision making, (*3*) locus of authority, (*4*) structural provision for division of labor, (*5*) commitment to a leadership subsystem, and (*6*) prescribed collectivity orientation of units. These dimensions all vary in ordinal fashion, in the same direction from one extreme—the unitary context, to the other—the social-choice context.

The *unitary context* is exemplified by a city health department or transportation authority. The units (divisions, bureaus, and so on) are deliberately organized for the achievement of inclusive goals. Decision making, as to policy and program, takes place at the top of the structure and final authority over the units rests there. The units are structured in a division of labor for the achievement of the inclusive goals. Norms call for a high commitment to following the orders of a leadership subsystem.[22] The units are expected to orient their behavior toward the well-being of the inclusive organization, rather than toward their own respective subgoals.[23]

The *federative context* for inclusive decision making is exemplified by a council of social agencies (to a lesser extent by the newer type community welfare council), or by a council of churches. The units (member organizations, rather than integral departments) have their individual goals, but there is some formal organization for the accomplishment of inclusive goals, and there is formal staff structure for this purpose. Decision making is focused in a specific part of the inclusive

---

22. Ramsöy has made an extensive analysis in largely Parsonian terms of the relation of units that can be considered as subsystems of a more inclusive system. In it, he specifically analyzes the development of a leadership subsystem within the inclusive system which contains the units. Cf. Odd Ramsöy, *Social Groups as System and Subsystem* (New York: The Free Press of Glencoe, 1963).

23. Organizational literature is replete with exceptions to this statement; that is, examples of departments or other units within organizations which develop and pursue their own goals even when these are at variance with the goals of the inclusive organization. Nevertheless, the unitary organization is specifically designed to avoid this, regardless of the extent to which it may fail.

structure, but it is in effect subject to ratification by the units. Authority remains at the unit (member) level, with the exception of some administrative prerogatives which are delegated by the units to a formal staff. The units are structured autonomously, but they may agree to a division of labor that may affect their structure although not making them "departments" of an inclusive organization, as in the unitary context. The norms are for moderate commitment of the (member) units to the inclusive leadership subsystem, but considerable unit autonomy is tolerated and expected. A moderate degree of collectivity orientation— consideration of the well-being of the inclusive organization—is expected.

The *coalitional context* for inclusive decision making is exemplified by a group of organizations cooperating more or less closely to attain some desired objective, such as persuading a new industry to locate in the community or developing a federally sponsored project. Each organization has its own set of goals, but collaborates informally and on an *ad hoc* basis where some of its goals are similar to those of other organizations in the group. There is no formal organization or staff for inclusive decision making. Rather, decision making takes place at the level of the units themselves, as they interact with each other. Also, the coalition itself has no authority, the authority for its behavior resting with the units. The units are autonomously structured to pursue their own various purposes, but they may agree to *ad hoc* division of labor in order to accomplish their inclusive goal. Such division of labor ordinarily involves a minimum of restructuring of the cooperating units. There are no norms of commitment to an inclusive leadership, but there are general norms that govern the interaction of the unit leaders involved. There is only a minimal prescription of collectivity-orientation by the units, it being understood that the units are concerned primarily with their own goals, and only secondarily with the loose interactional structure in which they happen to be collaborating.

The *social-choice context* for inclusive decision making is exemplified by the autonomous behavior of a number of organizations and individuals in the community as they relate themselves and their behavior to any particular issue which concerns more than one of them —as, for example, the issue of Medicare or of housing desegregation, or highway location.[24] They do not necessarily share any inclusive goals, and indeed, their goals with respect to the issue may be discordant. There is no formal inclusive structure within which the units make their decisions; rather, decisions are made at the level of the units themselves, many of which may be inclusive organizations of a unitary, federative, or coalitional type. Likewise, authority rests at the unit

24. *Op. cit.;* see note 12.

level. There is no formally structured provision for division of labor within an inclusive context, each unit pursuing its own goals and organizing itself for that purpose as it deems appropriate. There is no expected commitment to a leadership system other than that of the individual units.[25] Finally, there is little or no prescribed collectivity-orientation of units, the units being highly self-oriented as they pursue their goals, and there being no structure to whose well-being such collectivity-orientation would be addressed.[26]

As indicated, there is a progression in these four types of context from that in which various units are integrally organized for division of labor and centralized decision making to that in which there is no identifiable central decision-making body, and the units are related to each other only within a general interactional field, without provision for centralized decision making or centralized authority. Table 2 illustrates the relationships. The four contexts should be understood as points along the various dimensions, rather than as discrete states.

The typology is useful in categorizing CDO's. Poverty agencies, community planning councils, city planning commissions, urban renewal authorities, city health departments, and similar organizations are either unitary or federative. Presumably, the variation in the dimensions analyzed accounts for some of the differences in the behavior of CDO's toward each other. The federation, depending ultimately on the continued assent of its autonomous constituent organizations, is under great constraint to operate on a consensus basis. Since innovations and major system changes are likely to threaten this consensus, they are under constraint to avoid them. On the other hand, coalitions, because their existence is based solely upon a convergence of interests around some particular issue, may engage freely in controversy, but have little persistence beyond the immediate issue. By contrast, unitary organizations show much greater stability and persistence, even in conflict situations.

RELATIONS AMONG CDO'S

What of the relation of CDO's to each other? Almost by definition, the context in which two or more CDO's interact cannot take the form

25. In a sense, the power structure may be considered as a leadership subsystem within the community where the social choice is being made. To the extent that a power structure actually centralizes decision making among the CDO's of a community, it would represent evidence contrary to the statement. But one should not overlook the plurality of power structures found in many large cities. Even in cities with monolithic power structures, these would seem to serve primarily a diffuse function of general policy constraints with an actual centralization of decision making only occasionally, where the social choice process has resulted in an impasse or an undesirable outcome.

26. Although there is no formal inclusive structure, it can still be said that the community is a meaningful focus for collectivity-orientation among CDO's. In addition, CDO's often make explicit claim to be representing "community welfare" or the "public interest" in pursuing their own goals. The final section of this article discusses the interrelation of CDO goals from the standpoint of a more inclusive "community" interest.

Table 2

Types of Inclusive Context

Dimension	Type of Context			
	Unitary	Federative	Coalitional	Social Choice
Relation of units to an inclusive goal	Units organized for achievement of inclusive goals	Units with disparate goals, but some formal organization for inclusive goals	Units with disparate goals, but informal collaboration for inclusive goals	No inclusive goals
Locus of inclusive decision making	At top of inclusive structure	At top of inclusive structure, subject to unit ratification	In interaction of units without a formal inclusive structure	Within units
Locus of authority	At top of hierarchy of inclusive structure	Primarily at unit level	Exclusively at unit level	Exclusively at unit level
Structural provision for division of labor	Units structured for division of labor within inclusive organization	Units structured autonomously, may agree to a division of labor, which may affect their structure	Units structured autonomously, may agree to *ad hoc* division of labor, without restructuring	No formally structured division of labor within an inclusive context
Commitment to a leadership subsystem	Norms of high commitment	Norms of moderate commitment	Commitment only to unit leaders	Commitment only to unit leaders
Prescribed collectivity-orientation of units	High	Moderate	Minimal	Little or none

of a unitary organization, but frequently takes the form of a federation —as in the case of the various social agencies that unite in a council of social agencies or a federation of municipalities which performs certain minimal functions in a metropolitan area. It may also take the form of a coalition, as in the case of the collaborative efforts of three or four specific organizations to establish some new service or secure passage of a new piece of legislation. Or it may take the form of a social-choice context, with various parties seeking to advance their own goals with whatever outcome the total combination of actions may produce.

The four-fold typology lends itself readily to the wheels-within-wheels phenomenon; for a unitary organization may be a member of a federation which, in turn, may be a member of a coalition which is acting to some extent in concert in a larger social-choice decision. Other combinations also occur. At whatever level the analysis is being made, however, the dynamics of the structure of the field are pertinent in attempting to assess the interaction processes taking place.

The first two contexts, especially, are of great potential usefulness in studying the behavior of CDO's toward each other. Although a rigorous systematic study has not been made, a cursory examination of the Detroit and Philadelphia settings and a more extensive examination of the Boston setting indicate that the behavior of CDO's is directly related to their position with respect to some of the six inclusive context dimensions just considered. Research is needed to indicate the extent to which various kinds of unitary organizations behave in similar ways under similar conditions in community decisions and to contrast this behavior with that of federations and coalitions. Research is also needed on the characteristic structure of a specific type of CDO, e.g., an urban renewal authority, to determine whether the organization in the various cities approaches the unitary or the federative type of structure, and the accompanying differences, if any, in its interorganizational behavior.

The CDO's that are the subject of this paper are typically unitary or federative organizations. Each has its own legitimate segment of interest and operations which sometimes overlaps that of other CDO's. Occasionally, short-term issues bring the most diverse kinds of CDO's together in their interest in the same issue. But on any particular issue, whether short-term or long-term, an interested CDO might be able to classify all other CDO's into one of the following categories: (1) not involved in the issue, (2) involved in the issue in a manner that supports the first CDO in its pursuit of its goals, and (3) involved in the issue in a manner that hampers the first CDO in its pursuit of its goals.

Many of the CDO's have specific financial and bureaucratic support through a federal grant-in-aid agency, as well as an accompanying set of federal constraints. Each CDO has a local input constituency, consisting of those parties to which it acknowledges a responsibility in determining its policy and program; and an output constituency consisting of those parties which are acknowledged by the organization as being the appropriate targets of the organization's activity.

MAXIMIZING VALUES IN THE INTERORGANIZATIONAL FIELD

Let us consider the seminal point about "partial conflict" characterizing the interorganizational field. Litwak and Hylton write that:

> Values may be theoretically consistent, but limited resources force individuals to choose between them without completely rejecting either choice. (This is one of the classic problems of economics.) Or it may be that a given task requires several specialties, i.e., a division of labor, and limited resources at times of crisis force a choice between them, although all are desirable (for example, the conflicts between the various military services). In such cases organizational independence might be given to the specialties to preserve their essential core despite competition.[27]

They then point out that all societies must have a situation of partial conflict, "because of limited resources for maximizing all values simultaneously."[28]

This important point can be helpful in conceptualizing the nature of the interorganizational field of CDO's. But first, a modification of this statement suggests itself. It may well be, especially in particular situations, that regardless of resources, certain value combinations are compatible only within limits, beyond which one tends to interfere with the other. Leys, for example, has listed six moral standards: happiness, lawfulness, harmony or consistency, survival, integrity, and loyalty, "any one of which may be in conflict with any other." Each has served as the keystone of a complete ethical system of occidental philosophy, and although he does not himself choose a *summum bonum* among these values, he states: "But I do propose a rather loose-jointed system, in the sense that sound decision-making will involve successive reviews of the decision from the standpoint of each of these six standards."[29]

Such value conflicts characterize not only the interorganizational field, but also the intraorganizational field. In each case they pose the problem of "optimal mix," the determination of the best combination of investment in various values. In the intraorganizational context, this is determined largely by centralized decision making. In the interor-

27. Litwak and Hylton, *op. cit.,* 397.
28. *Ibid.,* 399.
29. Wayne A. R. Leys, "The Value Framework of Decision-Making," in Mailick and Van Ness (eds.), *op. cit.,* p. 87.

ganizational context, decision making is allowed to form out of the interaction of various organizations. These organizations make various investments in one value or another, from differing pools of resources.

In national planning, Fisher indicates some considerations in program budgeting:

> Major allocative decisions involve such questions as, Should more resources be employed in national security in the future, or in national health programs, or in preservation and development of natural resources, etc. Ideally, the decision makers would like to plan to allocate resources in the future so that for a given budget, for example, the estimated marginal return (or utility) in each major area of application would be equal. But this is more easily said than done; and at the current state of analytical art, no one really knows with any precision how the "grand optimum" might be obtained.[30]

Yet despite this uncertainty, allocations are made annually, rather routinely, through the budgetary process which no one claims is optimal, but which serves as partly an organizational and partly a social-choice means of making the theoretically impossible decisions.[31]

Within the profit-making organization, the simplest model for the allocation process is that which considers only one value—the maximization of profits, so that the problem of weighting conflicting values does not arise. Values that limit profit maximization are considered as constraints, rather than as competitive values, although other values, such as firm prestige or individual career considerations do, of course, affect the allocative process.

The nonprofit organization (whether governmental or non-governmental) does not have, even theoretically, this simple criterion for allocational decisions. It is somewhat freer in the sense of not having to show a profit, but like the profit organizations, it makes decisions which, even though essentially based on intuition and subjective value assumptions, are nevertheless centralized.

By contrast, the social-choice context puts such allocative decisions into a competitive arena. Here, social processes are equated with a presumably "rational" dialectic, and that which emerges in the free interplay of parties, and values, and resources is the agreed-upon solution. Where the solution is not acceptable to significant parties, there are such recourses as trying to get the City Council to pass a law, or getting the mayor to serve as mediator, or setting up an *ad hoc* mech-

30. Gene H. Fisher, "The Role of Cost-Utility Analysis in Program Budgeting," in David Novick (ed.), *Program Budgeting* (Rand Corporation; Washington, D.C.: U.S. Government Printing Office, 1964–1965), p. 35.
31. Aaron Wildavsky, *The Politics of the Budgetary Process* (Boston and Toronto: Little, Brown, 1964). The present analysis applies specifically to organizational behavior that is oriented toward the attainment of explicit goals. It allows for the widely acknowledged fact that organizational behavior is frequently oriented toward system maintenance as well as toward goals other than the explicit organizational ones. Cf. Amitai Etzioni, Two Approaches to Organizational Analysis: A Critique and a Suggestion, *Administrative Science Quarterly,* 5 (September 1960).

anism for meliorating the unacceptable solution, or, in the last analysis, a public struggle.

Thus, the community interorganizational field shares with the intraorganizational context the inability to calculate rationally the optimum mix from a field of competing values, but differs from it in not having a structure for centralizing decision making and implementing strategy. While this lack of centralization is bemoaned in some community social and physical planning quarters, it is not universally deplored. Banfield, for example, concluded that in the major issues that he studied in Chicago, this process led to decisions which he himself would have favored, even though these decisions were made for what he considered the "wrong" reasons. [32]

HEURISTIC MODEL OF THE INTERORGANIZATIONAL FIELD OF CDO'S

It may help to summarize by presenting a brief "model" of interorganizational decision making in the community arena. Let us conceptualize the situation on an "as if" basis.[33] It is "as if" the people of the community, concerned with a number of different kinds of "values"[34] —such as adequate housing, a viable economic base, the rejuvenation of the city's core, adequate transit, an appropriate array of social services, good schools, and so on—had parcelled these values out among a number of CDO's, giving to each the responsibility for maximizing its particular value—not absolutely, but in interaction with other CDO's. The CDO's have different, partially overlapping value configurations, with different types and amounts of resources at their disposal. Not all the values can be maximized simultaneously, either because of inadequate resources or because some—like adequate low-cost housing, may conflict with others—like eliminating segregation, when they are pressed beyond certain limits. Furthermore, the people of the community have acknowledged the right of these CDO's to speak for the community in their respective fields (i.e., given them legitimation) and have allocated to them money, personnel, and other resources with which to do it.

Although the joint decision usually satisfies no one completely, it produces a resolution well within the bounds of acceptability for most important parties to the community dialogue. Such changes as are

32. *Op. cit.*, p. 238.
33. Obviously, it is not being asserted here that deliberate community decisions are made in a unitary context. Quite the contrary. Most of the decisions involved here are made in a social-choice context. Nevertheless the "as if" approach would seem to have heuristic advantages. Cf. Hans Vaihinger, *The Philosophy of "As If,"* translated by C. K. Ogden (London: K. Paul, Trench, Trubner & Co., Ltd. New York: Harcourt Brace & Co., Inc., 1924).
34. The term "value" is used here not in the normative sense but rather in the sense of an object having the capacity to satisfy a desire.

needed occur incrementally through the waxing and waning of the various CDO's (resource reallocation) and through changes in legitimation (shifting domain). Where the attempts of the CDO's to press incompatible values result in a crisis, the mayor or some other "deus ex machina" is called in to resolve the immediate dispute and perhaps to reallocate resources.

In the long run, if the people of the community do not like the mix they are getting in their current investment of resources and legitimation, they can simply change the mix, through budget reallocation, through the legal setting up or dissolution of a CDO, through shifts in voluntary donation patterns, through new legislation, and so on. Such shifts may be fairly easy or extremely difficult to bring about. They do not determine the specific decisions that will eventually be made in the interaction of CDO's, but they may influence them. What such shifts do is to change the situation within which the decisions arise. They provide a way for the people of the community to intervene in the interorganizational field, but then to withdraw as it were and monitor the continuing struggle for value ascendancy among the various CDO's.

Deliberate changes in this field of CDO interaction are likewise influenced by the various possibilities of resource input from outside the community, principally from various federal agencies. The availability of such federal financial support, distributed unevenly among the values represented by the various CDO's, constitutes an important component of the decisional field. Thus, the availability of 50 percent or 80 percent reimbursement for an expanded program of a particular CDO may be important in influencing the local decision as to how local resources are to be allocated.

To summarize briefly, the people of a metropolitan community are not organized for making centralized rational choices among values which cannot be maximized simultaneously. Various values are allocated to specific CDO's for maximization. These CDO's, in turn, are the protagonists in a sort of sociodrama in which the "mix" gets worked out in some relation to respective resources and skill in their use, and within the framework of the range of acceptability of the composite decision to the large and important sectors of the community.

SATISFICING VERSUS MAXIMIZING

In this process, the excessive pressing of a particular value by any one of the CDO's is made virtually impossible by the conflicting claims of the other CDO's. This can be related to Aristotle's principle of the golden mean, adduced from his observation of the deterioration of a value when pushed in either direction beyond a certain threshold.[35] If

35. Aristotle, *Ethics.*

our current analysis is valid, there may be a definite relationship between this type of rationalistic approach in ethics and the "satisficing"
behavior described by Simon, which he exemplifies in terms of "share
of market," "adequate profit," and "fair price."[36] Banfield has observed
that organizations satisfice instead of maximizing, not because they
"lack the wits to maximize," as Simon has suggested, but because they
"lack the will."[37] In the present context, they lack the will to maximize
any particular value and therefore satisfice, because they are constrained by the fact that maximization of one of their values would
jeopardize an acceptable degree of achievement of another value. They
thus satisfice in order to keep goal achievement in their value cluster
within an acceptable set of limits.

Within the intraorganizational context, this process of satisficing
occurs as a centralized decision-making process. In the interorganizational field of CDO's, it occurs through the competition of various
CDO's to advance their particular values. Their respective satisficing
thus makes possible a composite result, which is usually acceptable,
though never maximal, and perhaps seldom optimal for the community.

Leys presented an analysis which helps further to explain this
satisficing process among a number of competing values sought by
competing CDO's in the community. On any particular issue, he says,
there will be both partisans and bystanders. Some of the partisans want
to press a particular value to a point where it jeopardizes the values of
other partisans. The bystanders are not specifically concerned with the
issue in dispute, but are concerned that the issue does not result in
damaging side-effects. Because of the wider variety of values that the
bystanders represent, they will commonly enforce a resolution of the
immediate controversy, usually to the complete satisfaction of none of
the partisans.[38] In this way, the dynamic interaction of CDO's constitutes a series of satisficing resolutions in which values are mixed more
or less in keeping with community preferences, as indicated operationally by resource allocations. The outcome is not calculable, given the
resource allocations, but it is obviously manipulable through such resource allocations. Mannheim writes:

> If one wishes to interfere in these fields (where conflict and competi-
> tion are the usual forms of adjustment) without doing violence to the
> spontaneity of events, a specific kind of regulation is necessary. Regula-

---

36. Herbert A. Simon, *Administrative Behavior: A Study of Decision-Making Process in Administrative Organization* (New York: The Free Press, 1965), p. xxv.
37. Edward C. Banfield, "Ends and Means in Planning," in Mailick and Van Ness (eds.), *op. cit.,*
p. 78.
38. Wayne A. R. Leys; *Ethics and Social Policy* (New York: Prentice-Hall, 1941), chs. 12–14. Coleman
treats this phenomenon in somewhat different terms; cf. James S. Coleman, *Community Conflict*
(Glencoe, Ill.: The Free Press, 1957).

tions which are adapted to the nature of the field structure intervene only at certain points in the course of events. They do not determine the line of action in advance as in custom or administration.[39]

The same can be said of resource allocation.

OPTIMIZING THE "MIX"

Since the outcome of the interaction of CDO's is not predetermined, but emerges in a social-interaction process within the interorganizational field, the question arises as to whether different structuring of this interactional field might produce a more desirable mix.

What would a more desirable mix mean? It would mean, presumably, that satisficing levels on each value would be higher. Presumably, this could occur in one of two ways: either through a more efficient use of resources, where lack of resources had figured largely in the lower satisficing levels; or in finding ways in which higher satisficing levels on particular values could be found that did not jeopardize satisficing levels on other values. Thus, an improvement of the mix would simply mean an advance in the direction of maximization of some values without jeopardizing other values. Our question then becomes whether aggregate value can be increased through manipulating the interorganizational field.

In his analysis of anomie, Durkheim offers a clue to this problem in referring to the interrelation of roles in a division of labor, the resultant of which is facilitated by a body of clearly understood rules governing the interaction. He states:

> But, on the contrary, if some opaque environment is interposed, then only stimuli of a certain intensity can be communicated from one organ to another. Relations, being rare, are not repeated enough to be determined; each time there ensues new groping. The lines of passage taken by the streams of movement cannot deepen because the streams themselves are too intermittent. If some rules do come to constitute them, they are, however, general and vague, for under these conditions it is only the most general contours of phenomena that can be fixed. The case will be the same if the contiguity, though sufficient, is too recent or has not endured long enough.[40]

The interorganizational field of CDO's would seem to approximate this condition. In many large cities today, large CDO's are all seeking, within a unitary or federative context, to rationalize some aspects of decision making in their respective legitimated spheres, but interacting in loose coalitional or social-choice contexts in ways which often affect one another adversely or favorably, but with little or no concert, and

39. Karl Mannheim, *op. cit.,* p. 297.
40. Emile Durkheim, *The Division of Labor in Society,* transl. by George Simpson (New York: The Free Press of Glencoe, 1964), pp. 368–369.

with few clearly defined norms governing the interaction. The interorganizational environment is crowded and turbulent in the sense of Emery and Trist, but at the same time it is opaque in the sense of the Durkheim statement just quoted.

It is precisely this condition which leads many urban experts to advocate more centralized planning—in this instance, a more inclusive centralization of the already centralized planning of the respective CDO's. Aside from the feasibility or desirability of such centralization, are there changes in the CDO interorganizational field which might improve joint decision making? From the foregoing analysis, one way that suggests itself would be to make the interactional field less opaque, so that the respective CDO's would be better able to adapt their behavior to each other in a more deliberate way. They could retain their present relative autonomy, but through more comprehensive knowledge of each other's policies, plans, and programs, could better influence decisions where their respective values reinforced each other, and perhaps even reduce some of the value conflicts.

A number of such changes in the interorganizational field of CDO's could be made:

1. The organization of common data banks and systems for retrieval and analysis, so that disparities are not needlessly caused by the use of different sets of figures and projections as a basis for planning, and so as to facilitate the examination of the reciprocal side effects of plans of the CDO's.
2. Prompt communication of proposed policy or program changes, so as to facilitate anticipatory adjustment in the behavior of other CDO's.[41]
3. Specific procedures among CDO's for feedback and incremental reformulation of proposed changes in their respective policies or programs.
4. Specific procedures for feedback or feed-in from output constituencies, so that respective fields of activity can be focused together as they are checked against responses from various significant groups in the community.
5. Procedures to improve the process of resource reallocation among CDO's where the "mix" is perceived as less than optimal.
6. Procedures for overlapping board and committee members, thus providing important bridging roles for people who are competently familiar with two or more CDO's.
7. Deliberate broadening of the scope of interaction among CDO's to include personnel at different hierarchical levels, where more or

41. This is unrealistic to expect in zero-sum situations, but probably only a minority of inter-CDO situations are zero-sum.

less inclusive policy or implementing decisions are made, including the lending of staff members to other CDO's for specific *ad hoc* collaborative ventures.

8. Deliberate establishment of procedures for joint participation in planning among CDO's in major developments that involve the interests of more than one CDO.

9. Specific provision of methods for central decision making to break impasses or resolve conflicts among CDO's.

An examination of these suggestions may lead to the premature conclusion that they should be accepted as dicta. Perhaps they should, but this cannot be concluded from the present analysis. The suggestions listed could improve the mix through a more efficient use of resources, or by discovering ways in which higher satisficing levels on particular values could be found without jeopardizing other values. But there is no assurance that gains from increased coordination among CDO's through these suggestions might not be offset by losses in innovativeness, intensity, or quality of individual CDO programs. There is some indication that excellence in a city's urban renewal program, or public school system, or transit system is often brought about largely through the passionate commitment of relatively single-minded individuals and /or organizations. Implementation of the suggestions above, while bringing about an improvement in the two ways indicated, might conceivably lose more through the "smoothing out" of peaks of excellence along with the obvious nadirs of ineptness. In other words, it is a question for empirical determination, rather than for logical analysis, to discover whether the gains in raised satisficing levels on the various values involved could actually take place without losses on others.

It is believed that most, if not all, of the suggestions can be made operational for research purposes and that a means for controlling many of the other pertinent variables is available. It is hoped that certain aspects of this question will therefore lend themselves to empirical investigation in the near future.

25

THE ORGANIZATION–SET
Toward a Theory of Interorganizational Relations

William M. Evan

Social science research on organizations has been concerned principally with *intraorganizational* phenomena. Psychologists have studied the individual in an organization; social psychologists, the relations among the members of a group in an organization and the impact of a group on the attitudes and behavior of group members; and sociologists, informal groups, formal subunits, and structural attributes of an organization.[1] With relatively few exceptions, social scientists engaged in organizational research have not taken the organization in its environment as a unit of observation and analysis. Selznick's[2] work on the TVA is a notable exception, as are Ridgeway's[3] study of the manufacturer-dealer relationships, Dill's[4] comparative study of two Norwegian firms, Levine and White's[5] research on health and welfare agencies, Elling and Halebsky's[6] study of hospitals, and Litwak and Hylton's[7] study of community chests and social service exchanges.

The relative neglect of *interorganizational* relations is all the more surprising in view of the fact that all formal organizations are embedded in an environment of other organizations as well as in a complex of norms, values, and collectivities of the society at large. Inherent in the relationship between any formal organization and its environment is the fact that it is to some degree dependent upon its environment;

1. C. Argyris, *Integrating the Individual and the Organization,* New York: Wiley, 1964. M. Haire, *Psychology in Management,* 2nd ed., New York: McGraw-Hill, 1964. W. G. Bennis, E. H. Schein, D. E. Berlew, and F. I. Steele, *Interpersonal Dynamics: Essays and Readings on Human Interaction,* Homewood, Ill.: Dorsey, 1964. P. M. Blau, *The Dynamics of Bureaucracy,* Chicago: University of Chicago Press, 1955. W. M. Evan, "Indices of the Hierarchical Structure of Industrial Organizations," *Management Science,* 1963, 9, pp. 468–477. T. W. Costello and S. S. Zalkind, *Psychology in Administration: A Research Orientation,* Englewood Cliffs: Prentice-Hall, 1963.
2. P. Selznick, *TVA and the Grass Roots: A Study in the Sociology of Formal Organization,* Berkeley and Los Angeles: University of California Press, 1949.
3. V. F. Ridgeway, "Administration of Manufacturer-Dealer Systems," *Administrative Science Quarterly,* 2, 1957, pp. 464–483.
4. W. R. Dill, "Environment as an Influence on Managerial Autonomy," *Administrative Science Quarterly,* 2, 1958, pp. 409–443.
5. S. Levine and P. E. White, "Exchange as a Conceptual Framework for the Study of Interorganizational Relationships," *Administrative Science Quarterly,* 5, 1961, pp. 583–601.
6. R. H. Elling and S. Halebsky, "Organizational Differentiation and Support: A Conceptual Framework," *Administrative Science Quarterly,* 6, 1961, pp. 185–209.
7. E. Litwak and L. F. Hylton, "Inter-organizational Analysis: A Hypothesis on Coordinating Agencies," *Administrative Science Quarterly,* 6, 1962, pp. 395–426.

in other words, it is a subsystem of the more inclusive social system of society. As distinct from a society, which in some respects is relatively self-sufficient in that it runs the gamut of all human institutions, a formal organization is a partial social system inasmuch as it defines only a specific set of goals and statuses as relevant to its functioning.

The phenomena and problems of interorganizational relations are part of the general class of boundary-relations problems confronting all types of social systems, including formal organizations. All such boundary relations tend to be enormously complex. Apart from sheer complexity, problems of interorganizational relations have been neglected by organizational analysts in part because of the concepts and propositions of various theories of organization. For example, the Weberian theory of bureaucracy is concerned largely with internal structural attributes and processes such as specialization of functions, allocation of authority, and formalization of rules. Taylorism and other kindred theories are all oriented toward internal relations among personnel. And the inducement-contribution theory of Barnard[8] and Simon[9] also has an intraorganizational focus.[10] A notable exception to the intraorganizational focus is the theoretical work of Parsons[11] on formal organizations. As a social system theorist, Parsons is concerned with how organizations differing in their primacy of functions solve four system problems: adaptation, goal attainment, pattern maintenance, and integration. Any attempt to investigate how a particular organization solves these problems immediately involves considerations of interorganizational relations.

Notwithstanding the general neglect of interorganizational phenomena by organization theorists, managers are greatly preoccupied with interorganizational relations. Some well-known examples of interorganizational practices are allocation of resources to public relations, cooptation of personnel of environing organizations into leadership positions in order to reduce the threat they might otherwise pose, acquisition of and merging with competitors, use of espionage against competitors, and recourse to litigation, arbitration, and mediation to resolve interorganizational disputes. These and many other interorganizational phenomena and processes await systematic inquiry by organization theorists. Millett's[12] general observation about organization theory is particularly relevant to this problem area: ". . . our practice has far outrun our theory. . . . The art of organization has much more to its credit . . . than has the science of organization." Impeding

8. C. I. Barnard, *The Functions of the Executive,* Cambridge: Harvard University Press, 1938.
9. H. A. Simon, *Administrative Behavior,* New York: Macmillan, 1945.
10. J. March and H. A. Simon, *Organizations,* New York: Wiley, 1958, p. 83.
11. T. Parsons, "General Theory in Sociology," in R. K. Merton, Leonard Broom, and Leonard S. Cottrell, Jr., (eds.), *Sociology Today,* New York: Basic Books, 1959, pp. 60–65.
12. J. D. Millett, *An Essay on Organization: The Academic Community,* New York: McGraw-Hill, 1962.

progress are problems of conceptualizing and measuring interactions among organizations. Prevailing organizational concepts and theories concerned with intraorganizational phenomena are probably not adequate for a study of interorganizational phenomena.

The purpose of this paper is to explore in a preliminary manner some conceptual and methodological problems of interorganizational relations. In the process we hope to extend the scope of organization theory and to draw attention to the potentialities of comparative research on interorganizational relations.

THE ROLE-SET

One point of departure in the study of interorganizational relations is to examine the utility of the concept of the "role-set," developed by Merton,[13] for analyzing role relationships.[14] A role-set consists of the complex of roles and role relationships that the occupant of a given status has by virtue of occupying that status. A professor, for example, interacts not only with students but also with other professors, with the head of his department, with the dean of his school, and occasionally with the president or with the members of the board of trustees.

In all organizations the occupants of some statuses perform a liaison function with other organizations. Top executives in industrial organizations frequently confer with government officials, with executives of other firms within and without the industry, with members of trade associations, with officials in the local community. As guardians of the "public image" of the organization,[15] they are probably wary of delegating to subordinates contacts with representatives of other organizations that might have critical significance for the welfare of their own organizations.

The difference in orientation and behavior between liaison and non-liaison personnel is clearly brought out in a study by Macaulay.[16] In a study of the use of contract law among business firms, Macaulay found a high incidence of noncontractual relations. Among his other findings was a difference in orientation among the various departments in business firms toward the use of contracts, with the sales department being more negatively disposed to contracts and the comptroller departments being more positively disposed. When interdepartmental

13. R. K. Merton, *Social Theory and Social Structure,* rev. ed., Glencoe, Ill.: Free Press, 1957.
14. N. Gross, W. S. Mason, and A. W. McEachern, *Explorations in Role Analysis: Studies of the School Superintendency Role,* New York: Wiley, 1958.
15. J. W. Riley, Jr., and M. F. Levy, (eds.), *The Corporation and Its Publics: Essays on the Corporate Image,* New York: Wiley, 1963.
16. S. Macaulay, "Non-Contractual Relations in Business: A Preliminary Study," *American Sociological Review,* 29, 1963, pp. 55–67.

conflicts arise about the use of contracts, the house counsel, Macaulay observes, occasionally performs the function of an arbitrator.

A role-set analysis of the sales personnel as compared with the personnel of the comptroller departments suggests a possible explanation for the observed difference in attitudes toward the use of contracts.[17] As the "foreign affairs" personnel of an organization, sales department employees come into recurrent contact with their "role partners" in other organizations, i.e., purchasing agents, with the result that nonorganizational norms develop, making for less recourse to contracts. In contrast, the role-sets of comptroller personnel involve a higher degree of interaction with others within the organization, thus reinforcing organizational norms—including the use of contracts. We may infer from Macaulay's study that systematic inquiry into the role-sets of boundary personnel will shed light on interorganizational relations as it bears on organizational decisions, whether pertaining to the use of contracts or other matters.

THE ORGANIZATION-SET

Analogous to the role-set concept is what I propose to call the "organization-set." Instead of taking a particular status as the unit of analysis, as Merton does in his role-set analysis, I shall take as the unit of analysis an organization, or a class of organizations, and trace its interactions with the network of organizations in its environment, i.e., with elements of its organization-set. In analyzing a particular organization-set I shall refer to the organization that is the point of reference as the "focal organization."[18] In order to avoid the danger of reifying interorganizational relations, the relations between the focal organization and its organization-set are conceived as mediated by (a) the role-sets of its boundary personnel, (b) the flow of information, (c) the flow of products or services, and (d) the flow of personnel. As in the case of the role-set, conflicting demands by members of the organization-set may be handled by the focal organization with the help of mechanisms analogous to those described by Merton,[19] e.g., by preventing observation of behavior and by concerted action to counter the demands of other organizations.

An analysis of the organization-set of a focal organization (or of a class of focal organizations), could help explain: (a) the internal structure of the focal organization; (b) its degree of autonomy in decision-making; (c) its degree of effectiveness or "goal attainment"; (d) its identity, i.e.,

17. W. M. Evan, "Comment on Stewart Macaulay's 'Non-Contractual Relations in Business: A Preliminary Study,'" *American Sociological Review*, 28, 1963, pp. 67–69.
18. *Op. Cit.*, N. Gross, W. S. Mason, and A. W. McEachern.
19. *Op. Cit.*, Robert K. Merton.

its public image and self-image; (e) the flow of information from the focal organization to the elements of its organization-set and vice versa; (f) the flow of personnel from the focal organization to the elements of its organization-set and vice versa; and (g) the forces impelling the focal organization to cooperate or compete with elements of its organization-set, to coordinate its activities, to merge with other organizations, or to dissolve. As an example of the possible explanatory utility of the organization-set concept we shall presently consider the effects of structural variations in the organization-set on the decision-making autonomy of the focal organization.

SOME DIMENSIONS OF ORGANIZATION-SETS

If we are to make any progress in analyzing interorganizational relations, we shall have to identify strategic attributes or dimensions of organization-sets. With the aid of such attributes we can formulate empirically testable propositions about interactions among organizations.

A provisional listing of dimensions of organization-sets follows; its principal value may lie in illustrating a possibly useful direction of conceptual analysis. Whether these dimensions are more heuristic than others that might be abstracted can be determined only by means of empirical research.

1. *Input vs. output organization-sets.* The focal organization's environment consists of an input and an output organization-set. As a partial social system, a focal organization depends on input organizations for various types of resources: personnel, matériel, capital, legality, and legitimacy.[20] The focal organization in turn produces a product or a service for a market, an audience, a client system, etc. For example, a private hospital may have in its input organization-set the community chest from which it obtains financial support, an association of hospitals from which it receives accreditation, and the department of public health of the local or state government from which it receives one or more licenses granting it the right to function. Its output organization-set may include other hospitals with which it cooperates or competes, medical research organizations, government agencies to which it sends data, etc.

2. *Comparative vs. normative reference organizations.* As in the case of an individual, the focal organization may evaluate its performance by using one or more organizations in its set—input or output, more likely the latter—as a standard for comparison, i.e., as a "comparative reference organization." On the other hand, if a focal organization

20. W. M. Evan, and M. A. Schwartz, "Law and the Emergence of Formal Organizations," *Sociology and Social Research,* 48 (1964): 276–279.

incorporates the values and goals of one or more of the elements of its organization-sets, we would refer to it as a "normative reference organization."[21] For example, a firm manufacturing a particular kind of bomber might compare the quality of its product with other firms manufacturing bombers. Such outside firms would then be deemed "comparative reference organizations." Suppose, however, the Department of Defense indicates that the rapid production of a newly developed unmanned decoy bomber is urgently required by the United States. If the firm decided to convert its current bomber production into the production of an unmanned decoy bomber, it will have in effect incorporated as its goal the goal of the government and would be using a representative of the government, the Department of Defense, as a "normative reference organization."

3. *Size of the organization-set.* A focal organization may have a relatively large or a relatively small number of elements in its set. Whether it interacts with few or with many organizations presumably has significant consequences for its internal structure and decision-making. The size of the organization-set is to be distinguished, of course, from the size of the focal organization, although the two are presumably correlated.

4. *Concentration of input organizational resources.* The focal organization may depend on few or many elements in its input organization-set for its resources. Whether the concentration of input organizational resources is high or low would probably affect the structure and functioning of the focal organization.

5. *Overlap in membership.* Not infrequently there is an overlap in membership of the focal organization with one of the organizations in its set. This is manifestly the case with (a) employees of an industrial organization who belong to a trade union with which the focal organization has a collective bargaining agreement, (b) scientists or engineers who are affiliated with a professional society from or through which an employing organization recruits its employees, and (c) members of the board of directors of the focal organization who are also directors of organizations in its set.

6. *Overlap in goals and values.* The goals and values of the focal organization may overlap with those of the elements in its set. To the extent that this occurs it probably affects the nature of the interorganizational relations that develop. For example, hostility might be engendered between an American military base overseas and a political party in the country in which the base was situated if the party did not share the assessment that the base was performing a "protective and deterrent" function rather than an "offensive and provocative" function.

21. *Op. Cit.,* R. K. Merton.

7. *Boundary personnel.* Classifying the personnel of an organization into those concerned principally with domestic matters and those preoccupied with "foreign affairs" is difficult, though not impossible.[22] In a study of four manufacturing organizations, Haire[23] analyzes the growth of external personnel in relation to internal personnel. Parsons[24] distinguishes among three levels of personnel and functions in a formal organization: institutional, managerial, and technical. The first and third category probably involve a higher proportion of boundary personnel than the second category. In other words, top executives and some staff specialists such as sales, public relations, and house counsel are more likely to be engaged in boundary-maintenance functions than are junior and middle executives.

SOME HYPOTHESES ABOUT ORGANIZATION-SETS

Whether or not our preliminary consideration of some conceptual problems of interorganizational relations will prove useful only empirical research can establish. In the interest of stimulating inquiry in this relatively neglected area, several hypotheses on organization-sets, each assuming a *ceteris paribus* condition, will be formulated with the aid of the attributes enumerated in the foregoing section.

1. *The higher the concentration of input organizational resources, the lower the degree of autonomy in decision making of the focal organization.* A case in point is the difference in degree of independence between a public and private university. A public university probably has fewer sources of revenue than a private university, and one member in its organization-set, the state legislature, probably accounts for the greatest part of its revenue. Consequently, public universities with a high concentration of input organizational resources probably exercise a lower degree of decision-making autonomy than private universities with a low concentration of input organizational resources.

2. *The greater the size of the organization-set, the lower the decision-making autonomy of the focal organization, provided that some elements in the set form an uncooperative coalition that controls resources essential to the functioning of the focal organization, or provided that an uncooperative single member of the set controls such resources.* Where there is a high degree of conflict among the elements of the organization-set, such conflict may tend to cancel out their effect

22. J. D. Thompson and W. J. McEwen, "Organizational Goals and Environment: Goal-setting as an Interaction Process," *American Sociological Review,* 23, 1958, pp. 23–31.
23. M. Haire, "Biological Models and Empirical Histories of the Growth of Organizations," in M. Haire, (ed.), *Modern Organization Theory,* New York: Wiley, 1959.
24. *Op. Cit.,* T. Parsons. T. Parsons, *Structure and Process in Modern Societies,* Glencoe, Ill.: Free Press, 1960.

on the focal organization, thus affording it more autonomy than would otherwise be the case. On the other hand, to the extent that there are coalition formations and to the extent that these coalition formations provide essential resources for or services to the focal organization, this does impose significant constraints on the degree of independence of the focal organization.

A striking example of a coalition formation against a focal organization is the boycott by druggists—organized by their trade association—of the Pepsodent Company when the latter withdrew its California fair-trade contracts.[25] Also impressive is the action of the National Automobile Dealers Association, in the courts and in legislatures, to curb the power of the three large automobile manufacturers to dictate the terms of contracts and to cancel contracts.[26] By means of concerted action this trade association has become a countervailing power in the automobile industry. But size of organization-set, through an alternative sequence of variations, may produce an increase in the decision-making autonomy of the focal organization as well as the decrease hypothesized above. Quite likely there is a positive association between size of the organization-set and size of the focal organization. The larger the organization, the greater the specialization in liaison functions, the greater the number of boundary personnel, and so the greater the decision-making autonomy of the focal organization. However, some qualifications are necessary. To the extent that the proportion of boundary personnel is indicative of the *actual* rather than the *attempted* impact on the elements of its set, the greater the proportion of such personnel in the focal organization—relative to the proportion of such personnel in the set—the greater is its decision-making autonomy. Thus it may be seen that different mediators of the effects of size of organization-set yield opposite consequences for decision-making autonomy of the focal organization.

3. *The greater the degree of similarity of goals and functions between the organization-set and the focal organization, the greater the amount of competition between them, and hence the lower the degree of decision-making autonomy of the focal organization.* In their study of health and welfare agencies, Levine and White observe that:

> . . . intense competition may occur occasionally between two agencies offering the same services, especially when other agencies have no specific criteria for referring patients to one rather than the other. If both services are operating near capacity, competition between the two tends to be less keen, the choice being governed by the availability of service. If the services are being operated at less than capacity, competition and conflict often occur. Personnel of referring agencies

25. J. C. Palamountain, Jr., *The Politics of Distribution*, Cambridge: Harvard University Press, 1955.
26. *Ibid.*

in this case frequently deplore the "duplication of services" in the community.[27]

Another illustration of this hypothesis is the enactment of a law by Congress in 1959 requiring legislative authorization of major weapons programs of the armed forces. The enactment, Section 412 of the Military Construction Authorization Act of Fiscal 1960, substantially affects the process of policy-making in military affairs. Previously, major weapons procurement was authorized on a continual basis. Section 412, however, required that procurement of aircraft, missiles, and ships by all the services would require renewed authorization on an annual basis. Section 412 was authorized by the Senate Armed Services Committee, which was seeking to expand Congress' participation in defense policy-making. Here it may be seen that the common goal of the Defense Department and of the Armed Services Committee was the adequate defense of the nation, and that efforts to achieve that goal brought them into conflict, lowering the decision-making autonomy of the Department of Defense.[28]

4. *The greater the overlap in membership between the focal organization and the elements of its set, the lower its degree of decision-making autonomy.* A case in point is the overlapping membership of industrial organizations and trade unions. Overlapping membership, if accompanied by overlapping goals and values, may engender a conflict of loyalties that in turn probably diminishes the autonomy of the focal organization.

In Africa trade unions have become closely associated with nationalist parties, which have almost invariably provided governments of newly independent states with important personnel. Overlapping membership then occurs between a ministry of the central government and a trade union. These union leaders then face a dilemma in the concurrent needs to meet their members' demands for higher living standards and to cooperate with the government in promoting economic expansion. Their decision-making autonomy is thus reduced relative to the autonomy present when they were only union officials.

5. *Normative reference organizations have a greater constraining effect on the decisions of the focal organization than do comparative reference organizations.* The relations between trade unions of federal civil servants and the government illustrates this hypothesis. In the American public service it has been traditional not to strike; instead public servants have been satisfied to have working conditions determined by legislation or unilateral administrative action. This is probably due in large measure to the fact that the government department for

27. *Op. Cit.,* S. Levine and P. E. White.
28. R. H. Dawson, "Congressional Innovation and Intervention in Defense Policy: Legislative Authorization of Weapons Systems," *American Political Science Review,* 56, 1962, pp. 42–57.

which the civil servant works constitutes a very strong normative reference organization. Civil servants have apparently incorporated the goals of government, one of which is to maintain the continuity of the government in all circumstances. A trade union of office workers outside the government that threatens to strike will be seen only as a comparative reference organization whose members perform parallel duties with government workers. In the case of the civil servant, a normative reference organization clearly determines behavior to a greater extent than a comparative reference organization.[29]

The foregoing hypotheses are but illustrations of the kinds of hypotheses that might be formulated with the help of the properties of organization-sets. These hypotheses revolve around the dependent variable of autonomy in decision making of the focal organization. Clearly, similar hypotheses are needed for various interorganizational processes, e.g., coordination, cooperation, competition, conflict, innovation, amalgamation.[30] Several examples of such hypotheses will be briefly considered:

1. *The greater the size of the organization-set, the greater the degree of centralization of authority in order to prevent the "displacement of goals"[31] generated by subunit loyalties and actions. In turn, an increase in centralization of authority results in an increase in the formalization of rules within the focal organization as a means of guarding against the displacement of goals.*

2. *The greater the similarity of functions between the focal organization and the members of its set, the greater the likelihood that it will compete with them. Overlapping membership, however, probably tends to mitigate competition. If overlapping membership is combined with overlapping goals and values, cooperative action that could lead to amalgamation might ensue.*

3. *The greater the complementarity of functions between the focal organization and the members of its set, the greater the likelihood of cooperative action.*

4. *The greater the capacity of the focal organization to invoke sanctions against the members of its set, the greater the likelihood of coordination and cooperation, provided that members of the set do not succeed in uniting in opposition to the focal organization.*

5. *The greater the shortage of input resources on the part of the focal*

29. S. D. Spero, "Collective Bargaining in Public Employment: Form and Scope," *Public Administration Review,* 22, 1962, pp. 1–4.
30. J. D. Thompson, and W. J. McEwen, "Organizational Goals and Environment: Goal-setting as an Interaction Process," *American Sociological Review,* 23, 1958, pp. 23–31.
31. *Op. Cit.,* R. K. Merton. D. Cartwright, "The Potential Contribution of Graph Theory to Organization Theory," in M. Haire, (ed.), *Modern Organizational Theory,* New York: Wiley, 1959. F. Harary and R. Z. Norman, *Graph Theory as a Mathematical Model in Social Science,* Ann Arbor: University of Michigan Institute for Social Research, 1953. C. Flament, *Application of Graph Theory to Group Structure,* Englewood Cliffs: Prentice Hall, 1963.

organization, the greater the likelihood that it will cooperate with the input organizations in its set and the more favorable its disposition toward amalgamation with one or more of them. The academic "common market" being formed among midwest universities to pool their resources in graduate education is a case in point.

6. *The greater the competition between the focal organization and the members of the output organizations in its set, the more favorable is its disposition toward amalgamation, provided that the goals and values of the respective organizations are compatible.*

7. *If the members of the organization-set exhibit a high rate of technological change, the focal organization, in order to remain competitive, will be highly receptive to innovations.*

SOME METHODOLOGICAL PROBLEMS

Apart from the conceptual problems awaiting analysis in this area of research, there are measurement problems of considerable difficulty. Describing and measuring networks of interorganizational relations presents a substantial methodological challenge. Some gross behavioral indicators of interorganizational relations are number of contracts, number of clients or customers, volume of sales or services, volume of telephone calls made and received, volume of mail sent and received. Mapping interactions of organizations would require special attention to boundary personnel, as noted above, and to the patterns of interaction of organizational decision-makers. Such mapping operations of the behavior of boundary personnel and decision-makers could also yield sociometric data on which of the elements in an organization-set are perceived by different categories of members of the focal organization as "comparative reference organizations" or as "normative reference organizations." Two closely related methodological tools that may prove useful in the mapping of interorganizational relations are graph theory and input-output analysis.

GRAPH THEORY

One possible use of graph theory[32] is in the construction of an index measuring the amount of decision-making autonomy of a focal organization or of any of the elements in its set. Let us consider three highly simplified organization-set configurations approximating a "wheel," a "chain," and an "all-channel network."[33] In the three diagrams shown in Figure 1, each point represents an organization, each

---

32. *Ibid.,* D. Cartwright. *Ibid.,* F. Harary and R. Z. Norman. *Ibid.,* C. Flament.

33. A. Bavalas, "Communication Patterns in Task-Oriented Groups." In H. Lasswell and D. Lerner, (eds.), *The Policy Sciences,* Stanford, California: Stanford University Press, 1951. H. J. Leavitt, *Managerial Psychology,* rev. ed., Chicago: University of Chicago Press, 1964.

I. Wheel

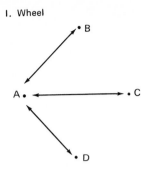

II. All-Channel Network

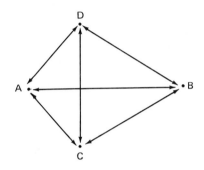

III. Chain

Figure 1. Three Organization-Set Configurations.

line a type of interaction (a flow of information, of goods, of influence, or of personnel), and an arrow the direction of interaction.

If we take A as the focal organization in the three configurations, how do they differ in their degree of decision-making autonomy? Intuitively, we would expect that I_A ranks first in autonomy, II_A ranks second, and III_A ranks third. In the automobile industry the supplier-manufacturer-dealer sequence of organizational relationships would suggest that the supplier is in a position comparable to III_A and that the manufacturers are in a position comparable to I_A.[34] Can we

34. V. F. Ridgeway, "Administration of Manufacturer-Dealer Systems," *Administrative Science Quarterly*, 2, 1957, pp. 464–483.

construct an index that would yield a "coefficient of interconnected-ness" of elements in an organization-set—and hence decision-making autonomy—that would discriminate not only among the three sim-plified organization-sets shown in Figure 1 but also among other possi-ble configurations?

INPUT-OUTPUT ANALYSIS

One input-output model that may prove useful in the study of interorganizational relations is that developed by Leontief.[35] In the study of the structure of the American economy, Leontief and his as-sociates have, of course, concerned themselves with economic parame-ters such as prices, investments, and incomes. Is this mode of analysis applicable to noneconomic parameters of interorganizational relation-ships with which sociologists, social psychologists, and political scientists are concerned? Are the obstacles to an input-output analysis of interor-ganizational relations insuperable because the data most social scien-tists work with do not take the form of ratio scales, as is true of the data of economists? In most cases the data used by social scientists studying organizations—other than economists—frequently take the form of nominal or ordinal scales and, occasionally, interval scales, e.g., flows of information, flows of personnel, or flows of influence. Apart from the level of measurement, do noneconomic data permit the construction of "technical coefficients" of inputs to the outputs of the focal organiza-tions?

One way of raising the question of the applicability of input-output analysis is to consider a highly simplified relationship between the members of an oligopolistic industry, such as automobile manufactur-ing. In Figure 2 we present a hypothetical input-output matrix consist-ing of the flow of influence on management decisions regarding the styling of new automobiles. It would appear from the hypothetical data in Figure 2 that G.M. is the "style leader." It receives the largest num-ber of praiseworthy "mentions" in the minutes of management meet-ings of its competitors, and it in turn makes the fewest praiseworthy mentions in its meetings of its competitors' styles. Would an input-output analysis of matrices of the type shown in Figure 2—possibly in conjunction with additional data, e.g., share of the market—suggest any further operations for analyzing the data or yield any additional insights into the decision-making process concerning automobile styles?

An analogous matrix that might lend itself to an input-output analy-sis is shown in Figure 3. Once again it is clear from the hypothetical data that G. M. enjoys a commanding position: it has the smallest outflux of engineering personnel and the largest influx from the other automobile

35. Wassily W. Leontief, et al., *Studies in the Structure of the American Economy,* New York: Oxford University Press, 1953.

Number of Praiseworthy Mentions Received by

Number of Praiseworthy Mentions Made by	A.M.	Ford	Chrysler	G.M.	Total
A.M.		10	5	15	30
Ford	2		5	15	22
Chrysler	3	8		13	24
G.M.	0	4	6		10
Total	5	22	16	43	

Figure 2. Hypothetical Matrix of Flow of Influence on Styling Decisions in the Automobile Industry (as Indexed by Frequency of Praiseworthy Mentions in the Minutes of Management Meetings).

Flow of Engineering Personnel to

Flow of Engineering Personnel from	A.M.	Ford	Chrysler	G.M.	Total
A.M.		15	5	40	60
Ford	5		5	25	35
Chrysler	7	8		35	50
G.M.	2	12	6		20
Total	14	35	16	100	

Figure 3. Hypothetical Flow of Engineering Personnel, 1955-1960.

companies. Would an input-output analysis of this matrix, supplemented by data on other characteristics of the organizations, contribute to our understanding of the data?

The matrices shown in Figures 2 and 3 involve one point in time. Assuming that data are available for two or more time periods, can we apply a Markov chain model to analyze the processes of change in interorganizational relations?

CONCLUSION

The foregoing methodological discussion together with the theoretical analysis may provide guidelines for new research on interorganizational relations. Of particular promise is comparative research on the organization-sets of different classes of organizations. How different are the organization-sets of economic, political, religious, educational, and cultural organizations? And what are the consequences of variations in organization-sets for the internal structure and for the decision-making process of different types of organizations? Do "coercive" organizations have a network of interactions with other organizations different from "utilitarian" and "normative" organizations?[36] How different are the organization-sets of habit, problem solving, indoctrination, and service types of organizations?[37]

Within the confines of any one class of organizations, how different are the organization-sets of, say, industrial organizations classified by industry? Similarly, what structural variations in organization-sets are observable among therapeutic versus custodial prisons[38] or among hospitals differing in the importance they attach to the goals of treatment, teaching, and research?

Another possible use of organization-set analysis is in the study of intraorganizational dynamics. If each of the major functional areas in a business organization—production, sales, engineering, personnel, etc. —is taken as a unit of inquiry, an organization-set analysis would be applicable in studying interdepartmental relations. Such an approach would probably be especially useful in investigating the problem of innovation in industrial organizations.[39]

As is generally recognized, a formal organization is a particular type of social system. The study of interorganizational relations hence involves an analysis of intersocial system relations. Systematic inquiry into the interactions among various types of organizations may not only unearth new intraorganizational phenomena and processes, but may also provide the wherewithal for bridging the gap between the microscopic *organizational* and the macroscopic *institutional* levels of analysis. The solution of intersystem problems of the most aggregate level, viz., interrelations among societies, presupposes a knowledge of the nature of interorganizational interactions within and between the several institutions of a society.

36. A. Etzioni, *A Comparative Analysis of Complex Organizations*, New York: Free Press, 1961.
37. W. G. Bennis, "Leadership Theory and Administrative Behavior: The Problem of Authority," *Administrative Science Quarterly*, 4, 1959, pp. 259–301.
38. R. A. Cloward, D. R. Cressey, G. N. Grosser, R. McCleery, L. E. Ohlin, G. Sykes, and S. L. Messinger, *Theoretical Studies in Social Organization of the Prison*, New York: Social Science Research Council, 1960; S. Wheeler, "Role Conflict in Correctional Communities," In D. Cressey, (ed.,), *The Prison: Studies in Institutional Organization and Change*, New York: Holt, Rinehart & Winston, 1961.
39. W. M. Evan, "Organizational Lag," *Human Organization* (in press).

---------------------- **26** ----------------------

EXCHANGE AS A CONCEPTUAL FRAMEWORK FOR THE STUDY OF INTERORGANIZATIONAL RELATIONSHIPS

Sol Levine and Paul E. White

Sociologists have devoted considerable attention to the study of formal organizations, particularly in industry, government, and the trade union field. Their chief focus, however, has been on patterns within rather than between organizations. Studies of interrelationships have largely been confined to units within the same organizational structure or between a pair of complementary organizations such as management and labor. Dimock's study of jurisdictional conflict between two federal agencies is a notable exception.[1] Another is a study of a community reaction to disaster by Form and Nosow in which the authors produce revealing data on the interaction pattern of local health organizations. The authors observe that "organizational cooperation was facilitated among organizations with similar internal structures."[2] March and Simon suggest that interorganizational conflict is very similar to intergroup conflict within organizations but present no supporting data.[3] Blau has commented on the general problems involved in studying multiple organizations.[4] In pointing up the need to study the organization in relation to its environment, Etzioni specifies the area of interorganizational relationships as one of the three meriting further intensive empirical study.[5]

Health and social welfare agencies within a given community offer an excellent opportunity for exploring patterns of relationship among organizations. There are an appreciable number of such organizations in any fairly large urban American community. Most of them are small so that relatively few individuals have to be interviewed to obtain information on their interaction. Within any community setting, vary-

1. Marshall E. Dimock, "Expanding Jurisdictions: A Case Study in Bureaucratic Conflict," in Robert K. Merton, Ailsa P. Gray, Barbara Hockey, Hanan C. Selvin, eds. *Reader in Bureaucracy* (Glencoe, 1952).
2. William H. Form and Sigmund Nosow, *Community in Disaster* (New York, 1958), p. 236.
3. James G. March and H. A. Simon, *Organizations* (New York, 1958).
4. Peter M. Blau, Formal Organization: Dimensions of Analysis, *American Journal of Sociology,* 63 (1957), 58.
5. Amitai Etzioni, New Directions in the Study of Organizations and Society, *Social Research,* 27 (1960), 223–228.

ing kinds of relations exist between official and voluntary organizations concerned with health and welfare. Thus welfare agencies may use public health nursing services, or information on the status of families may be shared by such voluntary organizations as the Red Cross and the Tuberculosis and Health Association.

Facilitating communication between local organizations has been a major objective of public health administrators and community organizers. Their writings contain many assertions about the desirability of improving relationships in order to reduce gaps and overlaps of medical services to the citizens, but as yet little effort has been made to appraise objectively the interrelationships that actually exist within the community.

In the following pages we should like to present our theoretical interpretation of interorganizational relationships together with a discussion of our research approach and a few preliminary findings, pointing up some of the substantive areas in organizational sociology for which our study has relevance. Our present thinking is largely based on the results of an exploratory study of twenty-two health organizations in a New England community with a population of 200,000 and initial impressions of data on a more intensive study, as yet unanalyzed, of some fifty-five health organizations in another New England community of comparable size.[6]

The site of our initial investigation was selected because we found it fairly accessible for study and relatively independent of a large metropolis; moreover, it contained a range of organizations which were of interest—a full-time health department, a welfare department, autonomous local agencies, local chapters or affiliates of major voluntary health and social welfare organizations, and major community hospitals. Of the twenty-two health organizations or agencies studied, fourteen were voluntary agencies, five were hospitals (three with out-patient clinics and two without) and three other were official agencies—health, welfare, and school. Intensive semistructured interviews were conducted with executive directors and supervisory personnel of each organization, and information was obtained from members of the boards through brief semistructured questionnaires. In addition, we used an adaptation of an instrument developed by Irwin T. Sanders to locate the most influential leaders in the community for the purpose of determining their distribution on agency boards.[7] The prestige ratings that the

6. The project is sponsored by the Social Science Program at the Harvard School of Public Health and supported by Grant 8676-2 from the National Institutes of Health. Professor Sol Levine is the principal investigator of the project snd Benjamin D. Paul, the director of the Social Science Program, is coinvestigator. We are grateful for the criticisms and suggestions given by Professors Paul, S. M. Miller, Irwin T. Sanders, and Howard E. Freeman.
7. Irwin T. Sanders, The Community Social Profile, *American Sociological Review,* 25 (1960), 75–77.

influential leaders assigned to the organizations constituted one of the independent variables of our study.

EXCHANGE AS A CONCEPTUAL FRAMEWORK

The complex of community health organizations may be seen as a system with individual organizations or system parts varying in the kinds and frequency of their relationships with one another. This system is enmeshed in ever larger systems—the community, the state, and so on.

Prevention and cure of disease constitute the ideal orientation of the health agency system, and individual agencies derive their respective goals or objectives from this larger orientation. In order to achieve its specific objectives, however, an agency must possess or control certain elements. It must have clients to serve; it must have resources in the form of equipment, specialized knowledge, or the funds with which to procure them; and it must have the services of people who can direct these resources to the clients. Few, if any, organizations have enough access to all these elements to enable them to attain their objectives fully. Under realistic conditions of element scarcity, organizations must select, on the basis of expediency or efficiency, particular functions that permit them to achieve their ends as fully as possible. By function is meant a set of interrelated services or activities that are instrumental, or believed to be instrumental, for the realization of an organization's objectives.

Although, because of scarcity, an organization limits itself to particular functions, it can seldom carry them out without establishing relationships with other organizations of the health system. The reasons for this are clear. To fulfill its functions without relating to other parts of the health system, an organization must be able to procure the necessary elements—cases, labor services, and other resources—directly from the community or outside it. Certain classes of hospitals treating a specific disease and serving an area larger than the local community probably most nearly approximate this condition. But even in this case other organizations within the system usually control some elements that are necessary or, at least, helpful to the carrying out of its functions. These may be money, equipment, or special personnel, which are conditionally lent or given. Usually agencies are unable to obtain all the elements they need from the community or through their individual efforts and, accordingly, have to turn to other agencies to obtain additional elements. The need for a sufficient number of clients, for example, is often more efficiently met through exchanges with other organizations than through independent case-finding procedures.

Theoretically, then, were all the essential elements in infinite supply there would be little need for organizational interaction and for subscription to co-operation as an ideal. Under actual conditions of scarcity, however, interorganizational exchanges are essential to goal attainment. In sum, organizational goals or objectives are derived from general health values. These goals or objectives may be viewed as defining the organization's ideal need for elements—consumers, labor services, and other resources. The scarcity of elements, however, impels the organization to restrict its activity to limited specific functions. The fulfillment of these limited functions, in turn, requires access to certain kinds of elements, which an organization seeks to obtain by entering into exchanges with other organizations.

Interaction among organizations can be viewed within the framework of an exchange model like that suggested by Homans.[8] However, the few available definitions of exchange are somewhat limited for our purposes because they tend to be bound by economics and because their referents are mainly individual or psychological phenomena and are not intended to encompass interaction between organizational entities or larger systems.[9]

We suggest the following definition of organizational exchange: *Organizational exchange is any voluntary activity between two organizations which has consequences, actual or anticipated, for the realization of their respective goals or objectives.* This definition has several advantages. First, it refers to activity in general and not exclusively to reciprocal activity. The action may be unidirectional and yet involve exchange. If an organization refers a patient to another organization which then treats him, an exchange has taken place if the respective objectives of the two organizations are furthered by the action. Pivoting the definition on goals or objectives provides for an obvious but crucial component of what constitutes an organization. The co-ordination of activities of a number of individuals toward some objective or goal has been designated as a distinguishing feature of organizations by students

8. George C. Homans, Social Behavior as Exchange, *American Journal of Sociology,* 63 (1958), 597–606.

9. Weber states that "by 'exchange' in the broadest sense will be meant every case of a formally voluntary agreement involving the offer of any sort of present, continuing, or future utility in exchange for utilities of any sort offered in return." Weber employs the term "utility" in the economic sense. It is the "utility" of the "object of exchange" to the parties concerned that produces exchange. See Max Weber, *The Theory of Social and Economic Organization* (New York, 1947) p. 170. Homans, on the other hand, in characterizing interaction between persons as an exchange of goods, material and nonmaterial, sees the impulse to "exchange" in the psychological make-up of the parties to the exchange. He states, "the paradigm of elementary social behavior, and the problem of the elementary sociologist is to state propositions relating the variations in the values and costs of each man to his frequency distribution of behavior among alternatives, where the values (in the mathematical sense) taken by these variables for one man determine in part their values for the other." See Homans, *op cit.,* p. 598.

in the field.[10] Parsons, for example, has defined an organization as a "special type of social system organized about the primacy of interest in the attainment of a particular type of system goal."[11] That its goals or objectives may be transformed by a variety of factors and that, under some circumstances, mere survival may become primary does not deny that goals or objectives are universal characteristics of organizations.

Second, the definition widens the concept of exchange beyond the transfer of material goods and beyond gratifications in the immediate present. This broad definition of exchange permits us to consider a number of dimensions of organizational interaction that would otherwise be overlooked.

Finally, while the organizations may not be bargaining or interacting on equal terms and may even employ sanctions or pressures (by granting or withholding these elements), it is important to exclude from our definition, relationships involving physical coercion or domination; hence emphasis is on the word "voluntary" in our definition.

The elements that are exchanged by health organizations fall into three main categories: (1) referrals of cases, clients, or patients; (2) the giving or receiving of labor services, including the services of volunteer, clerical, and professional personnel, and (3) the sending or receiving of resources other than labor services, including funds, equipment, and information on cases and technical matters. Organizations have varying needs of these elements depending on their particular functions. Referrals, for example, may be seen as the delivery of the consumers of services to organizations, labor services as the human means by which the resources of the organization are made available to the consumers, and resources other than labor services as the necessary capital goods.

THE DETERMINANTS OF EXCHANGE

The interdependence of the parts of the exchange system is contingent upon three related factors: (1) the accessibility of each organization to necessary elements from sources outside the health system, (2) the objectives of the organization and particular functions to which it allocates the elements it controls, and (3) the degree to which domain consensus exists among the various organizations. An ideal theory of organizational exchange would describe the interrelationship and relative contribution of each of these factors. For the present, however, we will draw on some of our preliminary findings to suggest possible relationships among these factors and to indicate that each plays a part in affecting the exchange of elements among organizations.

10. Talcott Parsons, Suggestions for a Sociological Approach to the Theory of Organizations—I, *Administrative Science Quarterly*, 1 (1956), 63–85.
11. *Ibid.*, p. 64.

Gouldner has emphasized the need to differentiate the various parts of a system in terms of their relative dependence upon other parts of the system.[12] In our terms, certain system parts are relatively dependent, not having access to elements outside the system, whereas others, which have access to such elements, possess a high degree of independence or functional autonomy. The voluntary organizations of our study (excluding hospitals) can be classified into what Sills calls either corporate or federated organizations.[13] Corporate organizations are those which delegate authority downward from the national or state level to the local level. They contrast with organizations of the federated type which delegate authority upwards—from the local to the state or national level.

It appears that local member units of corporate organizations, because they are less dependent on the local health system and can obtain the necessary elements from the community or their parent organizations, interact less with other local agencies than federated organizations. This is supported by preliminary data presented in Table 1. It is also suggested that by carrying out their activities without entering actively into exchange relationships with other organizations, corporate organizations apparently are able to maintain their essential structure and avoid consequences resulting in the displacement of state or national goals. It may be that corporate organizations deliberately choose functions that require minimal involvement with other organizations. An examination of the four corporate organizations in our preliminary study reveals that three of them give resources to other agencies to carry out their activities, and the fourth conducts broad educational programs. Such functions are less likely to involve relationships with other organizations than the more direct service organizations, those that render services to individual recipients.

An organization's relative independence from the rest of the local health agency system and greater dependence upon a system outside the community may, at times, produce specific types of disagreements with the other agencies within the local system. This is dramatically demonstrated in the criticisms expressed toward a local community branch of an official state rehabilitation organization. The state organization, to justify its existence, has to present a successful experience to the legislators—that a minimum number of persons have been successfully rehabilitated. This means that by virtue of the services the organization has offered, a certain percentage of its debilitated clients are

12. Alvin W. Gouldner, Reciprocity and Autonomy in Functional Theory, in Llewellyn Gross, ed., *Symposium on Sociological Theory,* (Evanston, Ill., 1959); also The Norm of Reciprocity: A Preliminary Statement, *American Sociological Review,* 25 (1960), 161–178.
13. David L. Sills, *The Volunteers: Means and Ends in a National Organization,* (Glencoe, 1957).

Table 1

Weighted Rankings of Organizations Classified by Organizational Form on Four Interaction Indices*

Interaction Index	Sent by	N	Sent to					
			Voluntary		Hospitals		Official	Total Interaction Sent
			Corporate	Federated	Without Clinics	With Clinics		
Referrals	Vol. corporate	4	4.5	5	3.7	4.5	5	5
	Vol. federated	10	3	4	3.7	3	4	3
	Hosps. w/o clinics	2	4.5	3	3.7	4.5	3	4
	Hosps. w. clinics	3	1	1	1.5	2	1	1
	Official	3	2	2	1.5	1	2	2
Resources	Vol. corporate	4	5	2	1	4	5	3.5
	Vol. federated	10	4	3	3	4	4	3.5
	Hosps. w/o clinics	2	2	4.5	4.5	5	3	5
	Hosps. w. clinics	3	1	1	2	1	2	1
	Official	3	3	4.5	4.5	2	1	2
Written and verbal communication	Vol. corporate	4	5	3	2	4	5	4
	Vol. federated	10	3	1	3	3	3	2.5
	Hosps. w/o clinics	2	2	5	4.5	5	4	5
	Hosps. w. clinics	3	4	4	4.5	1	1.5	2.5
	Official	3	1	2	1	2	1.5	1
Joint activities	Vol. corporate	4	4.5	4	3	5	3.5	5
	Vol. federated	10	3	3	5	3	1	3
	Hosps. w/o clinics	2	2	5	1	2	3.5	4
	Hosps. w. clinics	3	4.5	2	2	1	5	1.5
	Official	3	1	1	4	4	2	1.5

*Note: 1 indicates highest interaction; 5 indicates lowest interaction.

347

again returned to self-supporting roles. The rehabilitative goal of the organization cannot be fulfilled unless it is selective in the persons it accepts as clients. Other community agencies dealing with seriously debilitated clients are unable to get the state to accept their clients for rehabilitation. In the eyes of these frustrated agencies the state organization is remiss in fulfilling its public goal. The state agency, on the other hand, cannot commit its limited personnel and resources to the time-consuming task of trying to rehabilitate what seem to be very poor risks. The state agency wants to be accepted and approved by the local community and its health agencies, but the state legislature and the governor, being the primary source of the agency's resources, constitute its significant reference group. Hence, given the existing definition of organizational goals and the state agency's relative independence of the local health system, its interaction with other community agencies is relatively low.

The marked difference in the interaction rank position of hospitals with out-patient clinics and those without suggests other differences between the two classes of hospitals. It may be that the two types of hospitals have different goals and that hospitals with clinics have a greater "community" orientation and are more committed to the concept of "comprehensive" care than are hospitals without clinics. However, whether or not the goals of the two types of hospitals do indeed differ, those with out-patient departments deal with population groups similar to those serviced by other agencies of the health system, that is, patients who are largely ambulatory and indigent; thus they serve patients whom other organizations may also be seeking to serve. Moreover, hospitals with out-patient clinics have greater control over their clinic patients than over those in-patients who are the charges of private physicians, and are thereby freer to refer patients to other agencies.

The functions of an organization not only represent the means by which it allocates its elements but, in accordance with our exchange formulation, also determine the degree of dependence on other organizations for specific kinds of elements, as well as its capacity to make certain kinds of elements available to other organizations. The exchange model leads us to explain the flow of elements between organizations largely in terms of the respective functions performed by the participating agencies. Indeed, it is doubtful whether any analysis of exchange of elements among organizations which ignores differences in organizational needs would have much theoretical or practical value.

In analyzing the data from our pilot community we classified agencies on the basis of their primary health functions: resource, education, prevention, treatment, or rehabilitation. Resource organizations attempt to achieve their objectives by providing other agencies with the means to carry out their functions. The four other agency types may be conceived as representing respective steps in the control of disease. We have suggested that the primary function determines an organization's need for exchange elements. Our preliminary data reveal, as expected, that treatment organizations rate highest on number of referrals and amount of resources received and that educational organizations, whose efforts are directed toward the general public, rate low on the number of referrals (see Table 2). This finding holds even when the larger organizations—official agencies and hospitals—are excluded and the analysis is based on the remaining voluntary agencies of our sample. As a case in point, let us consider a health organization whose function is to educate the public about a specific disease but which renders no direct service to individual clients. If it carries on an active educational program, it is possible that some people may come to it directly to obtain information and, mistakenly, in the hope of receiving treatment. If this occurs, the organization will temporarily be in possession of potential clients whom it may route or refer to other more appropriate agencies. That such referrals will be frequent is unlikely however. It is even less likely that the organization will receive many referrals from other organizations. If an organization renders a direct service to a client, however, such as giving X-ray examinations, or polio immunizations, there is greater likelihood that it will send or receive referrals.

An organization is less limited in its function in such interagency activities as discussing general community health problems, attending agency council meetings or co-operating on some aspect of fund raising. Also, with sufficient initiative even a small educational agency can maintain communication with a large treatment organization (for example, a general hospital) through exchanges of periodic reports and telephone calls to obtain various types of information. But precisely because it is an educational agency offering services to the general public and not to individuals, it will be limited in its capacity to maintain other kinds of interaction with the treatment organization. It probably will not be able to lend or give space or equipment, and it is even doubtful that it can offer the kind of instruction that the treatment organization would seek for its staff. That the organization's function establishes the range of possibilities for exchange and that other variables exert influence within the framework established by function is suggested by some other early findings presented in Table 3. Organizations were classified as direct or indirect on the basis of whether or not they provided a direct service to the public. They were also classified according to their relative prestige as rated by influential leaders in the community. Organizations high in prestige lead in the number of joint

Table 2

Weighted Rankings* of Organizations, Classified by Function on Four Interaction Indices

Interaction Index	Received by	N	Received from					Total Interaction Received
			Education	Resource	Prevention	Treatment	Rehabilitation	
Referrals	Education	3	4.5	5	5	5	5	5
	Resource	5	3	4	2	4	1	3
	Prevention	5	2	1	3	2	2.5	2
	Treatment	7	1	2	1	1	2.5	1
	Rehabilitation	2	4.5	3	4	3	4	4
Resources	Education	3	4.5	5	4	5	4.5	5
	Resource	5	1.5	3	3	4	3	3.5
	Prevention	5	1.5	4	2	3	4.5	3.5
	Treatment	7	3	2	1	2	2	1
	Rehabilitation	2	4.5	1	5	1	1	2
Written and verbal communication	Education	3	4	5	4.5	5	5	5
	Resource	5	3	2	2	3	2	2.5
	Prevention	5	2	4	3	4	4	3
	Treatment	7	1	1	1	2	3	1
	Rehabilitation	2	5	3	4.5	1	1	2.5
Joint activities	Education	3	4	4	1	3	4.5	4
	Resource	5	2	1	3	4	1	3
	Prevention	5	1	2	2	2	3	1
	Treatment	7	3	3	4	1	2	2
	Rehabilitation	2	5	5	5	5	4.5	5

*Note: 1 indicates highest interaction; 5 indicates lowest interaction.

350

Table 3

Weighted Rankings* of Organizations Classified by Prestige of Organization and by General Type of Service Offered on Four Interaction Indices

Interaction Index	Received by	N	Received from				Total Interaction Received
			High Prestige		Low Prestige		
			Direct Service	Indirect Service	Direct Service	Indirect Service	
Referrals	High direct	9	1	1	1	1	1
	High indirect	3	3	3.5	3	3.5	3
	Low direct	6	2	2	2	2	2
	Low indirect	4	4	3.5	4	3.5	4
Resources	High direct	9	2	2	2	2	2
	High indirect	3	3	3	3	3.5	3
	Low direct	6	1	1	1	1	1
	Low indirect	4	4	4	4	3.5	4
Written and verbal communication	High direct	9	2	2	3	1	2
	High indirect	3	3	3	1	3	3
	Low direct	6	1	1	2	2	1
	Low indirect	4	4	4	4	4	4
Joint activities	High direct	9	1	1.5	2	2	2
	High indirect	3	2	1.5	1	1	1
	Low direct	6	4	3	3	4	3
	Low indirect	4	3	4	4	3	4

*Note: 1 indicates highest interaction; 5 indicates lowest interaction.

activities, and prestige seems to exert some influence on the amount of verbal and written communication. Yet it is agencies offering direct services—regardless of prestige—which lead in the number of referrals and resources received. In other words, prestige, leadership, and other organizational variables seem to affect interaction patterns within limits established by the function variable.

An obvious question is whether organizations with shared or common boards interact more with one another than do agencies with separate boards. Our preliminary data show that the interaction rate is not affected by shared board membership. We have not been able to ascertain if there is any variation in organizational interaction when the shared board positions are occupied by persons with high status or influence. In our pilot community, there was only one instance in which two organizations had the same top community leaders as board members. If boards play an active role in the activities of health organizations, they serve more to link the organization to the community and the elements it possesses than to link the organization to other health and welfare agencies. The board probably also exerts influence on internal organizational operations and on establishing or approving the primary objective of the organization. Once the objective and the implementing functions are established, these functions tend to exert their influence autonomously on organizational interaction.

ORGANIZATIONAL DOMAIN

As we have seen, the elements exchanged are cases, labor services, and other resources. All organizational relationships directly or indirectly involve the flow and control of these elements. Within the local health agency system, the flow of elements is not centrally co-ordinated, but rests upon voluntary agreements or understanding. Obviously, there will be no exchange of elements between two organizations that do not know of each other's existence or that are completely unaware of each other's functions. Even more, there can be no exchange of elements without some agreement or understanding, however implicit. These exchange agreements are contingent upon the organization's domain. The domain of an organization consists of the specific goals it wishes to pursue and the functions it undertakes in order to implement its goals. In operational terms, organizational domain in the health field refers to the claims that an organization stakes out for itself in terms of (1) disease covered, (2) population served, and (3) services rendered. The goals of the organization constitute in effect the organization's claim to future functions and to the elements requisite to these functions, whereas the present or actual functions carried out by the organization constitute *de facto* claims to these elements. Exchange agreements rest upon prior consensus regarding domain. Within the health agency system, consensus regarding an organization's domain must exist to the extent that parts of the system will provide each agency with the elements necessary to attain its ends.

Once an organization's goals are accepted, domain consensus continues as long as the organization fulfills the functions adjudged appropriate to its goals and adheres to certain standards of quality. Our data show that organizations find it more difficult to legitimate themselves before other organizations in the health system than before such outside systems as the community or state. An organization can sometimes obtain sufficient elements from outside the local health system, usually in the form of funds, to continue in operation long after other organizations within the system have challenged its domain. Conversely, if the goals of a specific organization are accepted within the local agency system, other organizations of the system may encourage it to expand its functions and to realize its goals more fully by offering it elements to implement them. Should an organization not respond to this encouragement, it may be forced to forfeit its claim to the unrealized aspect of its domain.

Within the system, delineation of organizational domains is highly desired.[14] For example, intense competition may occur occasionally between two agencies offering the same services, especially when other agencies have no specific criteria for referring patients to one rather than the other. If both services are operating near capacity, competition between the two tends to be less keen, the choice being governed by the availability of service. If the services are being operated at less than capacity, competition and conflict often occur. Personnel of referring agencies in this case frequently deplore the "duplication of services" in the community. In most cases the conflict situation is eventually resolved by agreement on the part of the competing agencies to specify the criteria for referring patients to them. The agreement may take the form of consecutive handling of the same patients. For example, age may be employed as a criterion. In one case three agencies were involved in giving rehabilitation services: one took preschool children, another school children, and the third adults. In another case, where preventive services were offered, one agency took preschool children and the other took children of school age. The relative accessibility of the agencies to the respective age groups was a partial basis for these divisions. Another criterion—disease stage—also permits consecutive treatment of patients. One agency provided physical therapy to bedridden patients; another handled them when they became ambulatory.

14. In our research a large percentage of our respondents spontaneously referred to the undesirability of overlapping or duplicated services.

Several other considerations, such as priorities in allocation of elements, may impel an organization to delimit its functions even when no duplication of services exists. The phenomenon of delimiting one's role and consequently of restricting one's domain is well known. It can be seen, for instance, in the resistance of certain universities of high prestige to offer "practical" or vocational courses, or courses to meet the needs of any but high-status professionals, even to the extent of foregoing readily accessible federal grants. It is evidenced in the insistence of certain psychiatric clinics on handling only cases suitable for psychoanalytic treatment, of certain business organizations on selling only to wholesalers, of some retail stores on handling only expensive merchandise.

The flow of elements in the health system is contingent upon solving the problem of "who gets what for what purpose." The clarification of organizational domains and the development of greater domain consensus contributes to the solution of this problem. In short, domain consensus is a prerequisite to exchange. Achieving domain consensus may involve negotiation, orientation, or legitimation. When the functions of the interacting organizations are diffuse, achieving domain consensus becomes a matter of constant readjustment and compromise, a process which may be called negotiation or bargaining. The more specific the functions, however, the more domain consensus is attained merely by orientation (for example, an agency may call an X-ray unit to inquire about the specific procedures for implementing services). A third, less frequent but more formalized, means of attaining domain consensus is the empowering, licensing or "legitimating" of an organization to operate within the community by some other organization. Negotiation, as a means of attaining domain consensus seems to be related to diffuseness of function, whereas orientation, at the opposite extreme, relates to specificity of function.

These processes of achieving domain consensus constitute much of the interaction between organizations. While they may not involve the immediate flow of elements, they are often necessary preconditions for the exchange of elements, because without at least minimal domain consensus there can be no exchange among organizations. Moreover, to the extent that these processes involve proferring information about the availability of elements as well as about rights and obligations regarding the elements, they constitute a form of interorganizational exchange.

DIMENSIONS OF EXCHANGE

We have stated that all relationships among local health agencies may be conceptualized as involving exchange. There are four main dimensions to the actual exchange situation. They are:

1. *The parties to the exchange.* The characteristics we have thus far employed in classifying organizations or the parties to the exchange are: organizational form or affiliation, function, prestige, size, personnel characteristics, and numbers and types of clients served.

2. *The kinds and quantities exchanged.* These involve two main classes: the actual elements exchanged (consumers, labor services, and resources other than labor services), and information on the availability of these organizational elements and on rights and obligations regarding them.

3. *The agreement underlying the exchange.* Every exchange is contingent upon a prior agreement, which may be implicit and informal or fairly explicit and highly formalized. For example, a person may be informally routed or referred to another agency with the implicit awareness or expectation that the other organization will handle the case. On the other hand, the two agencies may enter into arrangements that stipulate the exact conditions and procedures by which patients are referred from one to another. Furthermore, both parties may be actively involved in arriving at the terms of the agreement, or these terms may be explicitly defined by one for all who may wish to conform to them. An example of the latter case is the decision of a single organization to establish a policy of a standard fee for service.

4. *The direction of the exchange.* This refers to the direction of the flow of organizational elements. We have differentiated three types:

    (a) *Unilateral:* where elements flow from one organization to another and no elements are given in return.

    (b) *Reciprocal:* where elements flow from one organization to another in return for other elements.

    (c) *Joint:* where elements flow from two organizations acting in unison toward a third party. This type, although representing a high order of agreement and co-ordination of policy among agencies, does not involve the actual transfer of elements.

As we proceed with our study of relationships among health agencies, we will undoubtedly modify and expand our theoretical model. For example, we will attempt to describe how the larger systems are intertwined with the health agency system. Also, we will give more attention to the effect of interagency competition and conflict regarding the flow of elements among organizations. In this respect we will analyze differences among organizations with respect not only to domain but to fundamental goals as well. As part of this analysis we will examine the orientations of different categories of professionals (for example, nurses and social workers) as well as groups with varying experiences and training within categories of professionals (as nurses with or without graduate education).

In the meantime, we find the exchange framework useful in ordering our data, locating new areas for investigation, and developing designs for studying interorganizational relationships. We feel that the conceptual framework and findings of our study will be helpful in understanding not only health agency interaction but also relationships within other specific systems (such as military, industrial, governmental, educational, and other systems). As in our study of health agencies, organizations within any system may confidently be expected to have need for clients, labor, and other resources. We would also expect that the interaction pattern among organizations within each system will also be affected by (1) organizational function, (2) access to the necessary elements from outside the system, and (3) the degree of domain consensus existing among the organizations of the system. It appears that the framework also shows promise in explaining interaction among organizations belonging to different systems (for example, educational and business systems, educational and governmental, military and industrial, and so forth). Finally, we believe our framework has obvious value in explaining interaction among units or departments within a single large-scale organization.

27

INTERORGANIZATIONAL PATTERNS IN EDUCATION

Burton R. Clark

Among the many social trends that swirl around the school and college, three broad sets of forces stand out: the first is economic, the second demographic, and the third political. These forces create problems to which educational authorities must respond, and, in responding, initiate effects that reverberate through the system and alter its structure. The direction and style of this change is only partly predicted by the traditional theory of bureaucracy and associated conceptions of administrative behavior. This paper[1] explores some of the changes taking place that, if followed, lead to a research perspective at a tangent from the study of bureaucracy.

---

1. Paper presented at Fifty-ninth Annual Meeting, American Sociological Association, Montreal, September, 1964.

First the primary trends and outside forces that confront education are reviewed, then the way these external social changes affect the school and college. Next a relatively new pattern of influences on educational decision making and practice in the United States is specified in detail as illustration of the adaptation of organizations to social trends. Finally a research perspective is presented that will help in understanding education in the modern world and at the same time contribute to theories of influence and organization. Both interorganizational analysis[2] and intraorganizational analysis are needed to comprehend the concert of action in American education. In any attempt to compare centralized and decentralized systems of action, it is necessary to understand the similarities and differences between influence within a bureaucracy and influence among bureaucracies, communication within the organization and communication between organizations, initiative and innovation within an organization and parallel effort in a loosely joined federation or alliance or *ad hoc* confluence of interests.

SOCIAL TRENDS

The primary force of the economy on education lies in the increasing need for educational preparation and repreparation for work.[3] One qualifies for work through education, and the threshold of qualification constantly rises as the bottom of the occupational structure shrinks (decrease in unskilled jobs), the middle is upgraded in skills, and the top (professional and technical) expands rapidly. The organizations for formal instruction are charged with qualifying people for work and allocating them to an ever wider spectrum of job specialties. They thus come under heavy pressure to be continually oriented to the provision of expert labor. This pressure, already greatly expanded since 1945, is intensified by the emerging task of keeping men qualified to work through repreparation, as a rapidly changing technology makes obsolescent old skills and jobs and new demands on competence. With this, education becomes more a part of the economic order than ever before. Seen as investment in human resources,[4] education is thereby increasingly viewed as part of both the local economy and the state economy, but particularly the national economy.

2. On interorganizational analysis, see Sol Levine and Paul E. White, "Exchange and Interorganizational Relationships," *Administrative Science Quarterly*, 5 (1961), 583–601; Eugene Litwak and Lydia F. Hylton, "Interorganizational Analysis," *Administrative Science Quarterly*, 6 (1962), 395–420; James D. Thompson and William J. McEwen, "Organizational Goals and Environment," *American Sociological Review*, 23 (1958), 23–31.
3. A. H. Halsey, Jean Floud, and C. Arnold Anderson (eds.), *Education, Economy, and Society* (New York: Free Press, 1961, Pts. I and II); Burton R. Clark, *Educating the Expert Society* (San Francisco: Chandler, 1962), ch. ii.
4. See special issue on "Investment in Human Beings," *Journal of Political Economy*, 70 (October, 1962).

The pressures generated on education by the growing economic utility of the years spent in formal instruction are intensified by the growth in the general population and by the growing participation in education. A much enlarged school population results from a combination of high birth rate, which widens the population base, and high aspiration and high enrollment rate, which results in the school population more fully representing the base. Mass education is extending farther up the ladder of the school grades.[5]

The growing economic and demographic relevance of education contributes to a third major trend: the growth of political concern with education. If education is investment rather than consumption, if it is a major form of economic capital, then it must become a concern of those responsible for public policy. If there is growing involvement of the population in the schooling process, then, especially in democratic societies, education becomes a political issue on which parties and candidates can appeal to the electorate. The educational system is now probably the most important single issue in community government in the United States, and its importance as an issue in state government is growing rapidly. Most important, education has emerged as a national concern in the last fifteen years. Spokesmen for the national interest have come forth from many quarters. These include nationally visible individuals (e.g., James T. Conant, Admiral Rickover), major private foundations (Carnegie, Ford), established national associations (National Education Association, American Council on Education), and newly formed groups (Physical Science Study Committee, Council for Basic Education).

The national concern has its most potent form in the interest of the Federal government in the outputs of education. The Federal interest is, of course, actually an array of interests.[6] They have to do with manpower and unemployment, leadership and creativity, and urban and rural renewal, thus involving the Office of Education which has a general mandate to serve education, the Department of Labor, and even the Bureau of the Budget. The critical interest is in the role of education in training men for work, with a particular focus on scientists and engineers for research and development. Here the National Science Foundation has a general mandate to strengthen science. The interest in scientists and engineers is sharply defined by diplomatic posture, military strength, and the missions, maintenance needs and organizational character of the Department of Defense, together with

---

5. Martin Trow, "The Democratization of Higher Education in the United States," *European Journal of Sociology*, 3 (1962), 231–262.

6. Homer D. Babbidge, Jr., and Robert M. Rozenzweig, *The Federal Interest in Higher Education* (New York: McGraw-Hill, 1962); Charles V. Kidd, *American Universities and Federal Research* (Cambridge: Harvard University Press, 1959).

the Atomic Energy Commission and the National Aeronautics and Space Agency. These interests that have emerged at the national level in the last twenty years are strong, central, permanent, and genuine. They are compelling enough to call forth attempts at national programs. Such programs must either be effected through the existing educational structure, by changing that structure, or bypassing it.

Economic, demographic, and political trends of the last two decades have, therefore, eliminated the economic and political irrelevance of education. No longer is education seen to have only long-run, indirect, and undifferentiated consequences, the effects subsumed under the global terms of cultural transmission and socialization of the young. Education is implicated in the training of experts for the labor force of a few years hence and is involved in present innovation efforts in research and development. It is a large and rapidly growing public expenditure in which the needs of allocation, co-ordination, and responsibility demand the attention of politicians and planners. It thereby becomes part of a larger order, that of political economy.

THE ORGANIZATIONAL RESPONSE

As modern social forces recast education as part of the economic and political institutions of society, numerous adjustments and adaptations are bound to occur within the single school system, in major segments of the educational system, and in the educational system as a whole. Examples of adjustments within the single educational organization are the adaptation of new technologies and the elaboration and professionalization of public relations, fund raising, and other boundary roles and activities. An adjustment among different units is the alliance of private colleges (Great Lakes Association, Associated Colleges of the Midwest, College Center of the Finger Lakes). The impulse here comes from the search for competitive advantage, particularly the need of small colleges to share expensive facilities and faculties and engage in joint fund raising as they compete with the large university, as well as with others of their size. This tendency to band together has in a few years proceeded sufficiently far that officials involved refer to it self-consciously as a movement.[7] The colleges that move toward confederation are attempting to solve organizational problems: how to grow and yet remain small; how to co-ordinate across a larger pool of activity while protecting unit autonomy.

No attempt is made here to catalog the many adjustments. Instead, one major line of adjustment in the over-all educational system is considered: the structure of influence and control. This has implications for

7. John J. Wittich (ed.), *College and University Interinstitutional Co-operation* (Corning, N. Y.: College Center of the Finger Lakes, 1962).

educational administration and for research on organizations. The decentralized educational control in the United States has, through a long history, become tuned to the concerns of the individual school or college, the local community, and the separate state. What major changes can we discern in this decentralized control as it comes under increasingly heavy pressure to accommodate to modern social forces, particularly to the concerns that are national in scope and are defined by federal agencies and private national bodies?

There is some shift upward in the formal locus of educational decision making, from the local to state level in public education, and from local and state to the national level in such programs as the National Defense Education Act of 1958. But much of the change taking place is in arrangements that lie in part outside the hierarchy of public offices. Indirect and subtle means of influence are being developed by many groups. The emerging patterns depend on voluntary relations among public agencies and private groups. In some degree, these arrangements serve as substitutes for or as alternatives to formal internal administration, that is, to the national-state-local line of ministerial authority found in many countries. The patterns represent ways of influencing the grass-roots level of operation in a field where no formal authority can impose co-operation.

One pattern is that of the private committee serving as connector between public authorities, notably between federal agencies and local authorities, as in the curriculum reform movement. The prototype was the work of the Physical Science Study Committee, the group of professors and secondary school science teachers under Professor Zacharias of MIT, who worked on changes in the instruction of high school physics.[8] The Committee was financed by a Federal agency, the National Science Foundation, and committees of the agency reviewed its work. The purpose of the Committee was to improve the teaching of physical sciences in the secondary schools of the nation which was considered inadequate at the time and was viewed as a national weakness.[9] The granting of funds for this purpose was well within the broad missions of the National Science Foundation, established by Congress in 1950, to strengthen basic research and education in the sciences. The first major component in the pattern of influence, then, was an agency in the executive branch of the Federal government, whose breadth of

8. Paul E. Marsh and Ross A. Gortner, *Federal Aid to Science Education: Two Programs* (Syracuse: Syracuse University Press, 1962); Roald F. Campbell and Robert A. Bunnell (eds.), *Nationalizing Influence on Secondary Education* (Chicago, Ill.: Midwest Administration Center, The University of Chicago, 1963); *Innovation and Experiment in Education* (Washington, D.C.: U.S. Government Printing Office, 1964); John I. Goodlad, *School Curriculum Reform in the United States* (New York: Fund for the Advancement of Education, 1964); Matthew B. Miles (ed.), *Innovation in Education* (New York: Teachers College, Columbia University, 1964), especially ch. x, Paul E. Marsh, "Wellsprings of Strategy: Considerations Affecting Innovations by the PSSC."
9. Marsh and Gortner, *op. cit.,* ch. x.

mandate allowed initiation of influence without seeking legislative approval of specific formal programs. Private foundations also soon entered into the financial support of the curriculum reform group.

The Committee to which the problem was delegated and the funds allotted was private and voluntary, having some of the attributes of an independent and impartial group of civic leaders. The Committee set out to write a course for national school use, something that no federal agency could do directly because of probable Congressional and popular opposition. Working at MIT away from the political arena, the Committee in two years' time (1956–1958), provided a "complex of schoolbooks, homework assignments, laboratory guides, films, teacher's guides, laboratory apparatus, and classroom and college-entrance tests."[10]

The Committee then saw to it that these materials would be actively promoted and made widely available throughout the nation by putting them into normal commercial channels. During the winter of 1959–1960, the Committee gave its printed materials to a schoolbook publisher, its new scientific equipment to a manufacturer of scientific apparatus, and its films to an educational film distributor.[11] By these simple moves, the Committee became an important mechanism of national influence. It had, in effect, made itself a research and innovation arm of the textbook industry—more broadly, the course-materials industry—doing the research and development that the industry itself was not doing. No publisher has four and a half million dollars of venture capital (the cost of the physical science program) to develop the instructional materials for a course. The course-materials industry had been relatively passive, gearing innovation largely to market research and very little to research and development.[12] Thus the commercial market itself provided little money and little impulse for improving courses. In the absence of national standards, where there are no nationwide governmental prescriptions about instructional materials, it is the national market for course materials that determines the quality of these materials.[13] The Committee affected American education by changing what was available on the market, and, more important in the long run, by changing the passive relation of the course-materials industry to the market. The Committee, incorporated as Educational Services, Inc. and broadened to include other disciplines in the sciences and social sciences (an important organizational phenomenon in itself) promises to revise its materials periodically and thus to remain an active, innovative arm of the industry. It is a national center of textbook revision.

10. *Ibid.*, p. 30.
11. *Ibid.*, p. 63.
12. *Ibid.*, pp. 9–14.
13. *Ibid.*, p. 14.

Teachers had to be taught how to use the new materials. The National Science Foundation initiated and supported a program of summer institutes that were voluntary throughout—for the colleges that offered them, the professors who directed and staffed them, and the teachers who came as students. The curriculum and the students of the institutes were made the responsibility of the individual colleges. The Committee had to convince the directors of these institutes to use its materials. The directors were looking for the latest and best materials; they adopted the new materials and the institutes became part of the implementation of the new physics course. Finally, local educational authorities entered the pattern. They retained the formal choice as to whether to adopt the new materials, and their decision to enter was voluntary.

In summary, this pattern of influence was set in motion from the top, by a Federal agency and a national private committee. The object was to affect general educational practice, which was seen as a national weakness. The flow of influence was downward, through a chain of independent groups and organizations who found it to their interest to enter the alliance or compact. A Federal agency provided the funds; a private nonprofit group received the money and developed a new course; commercial organizations made the new materials available to all units of the decentralized educational system; dispersed universities and colleges used the new materials to train teachers in all regions of the country; existing local authorities adopted the materials and allowed their teachers to reshape the local courses. In this pattern, decision making was strongly influenced by the prestige of expertise. The National Science Foundation was expert and prestigeful; so also were the Committee, the Institutes, the teachers trained in the new materials. The very materials themselves traveled under the same aura.

Considering the voluntary character of the participation of each party, especially that of adoption by the local school district, the outcome of this pattern of influence is impressive. The new materials did not become available until after 1958; yet 40 to 50 percent of the students taking high school physics in 1963–1964 and 1964–1965 were studying with the new materials.[14] Given the educational backwardness of some of the states, some of the rural areas, and some of the slums, it is doubtful if a national ministry with full authority over a national curriculum could have changed the study of physics more in the same period. The voluntaristic pattern has a major dysfunction in its present form, however, in that it undoubtedly increases the inequalities of education between the rich and the poor, and the progressive and the backward school districts. The forward-looking districts will seek to

14. Goodlad, *op. cit.,* p. 24; *Educational Services Incorporated: A Review of Current Programs, 1965* (Watertown, Mass.: 1965), p. 5.

adopt improved curricula, the backward will be less interested. The weakness suggests the remedy, a compensatory distribution of incentives to encourage and help the backward districts to catch up.

INTERORGANIZATIONAL PATTERNS

This pattern of influence, in which private groups serve as connectors between large public organizations and levels of government, is one that, with minor variations, is now widespread in the curriculum reform movement that is rapidly altering educational practice in the United States. (The secretariats of national academic organizations, such as the American Association for the Advancement of Science, are increasingly important agents in these relations.) The pattern is a way of concerting action without bureaucracy. It is one of a class of patterns whose growing importance points up the fact that unitary bureaucratic structure is just one way of consciously concerting action to achieve a goal.[15] These patterns, interorganizational in character, lie somewhat between the ways of concerting action that are commonly found within organizations, hence to be understood by a theory of formal organization; and the ways of concerting action that are commonly found in political arenas characterized by a formal decentralization of authority, and therefore to be understood by a theory of political influence, such as that which Edward Banfield has so brilliantly attempted to construct.[16] We need a theory of confederative organization or organizational alliance. Generalizations developed toward such a theory would reveal many points of contact and overlap in ideas about influence derived from the study of politics as well as from the study of internal administration. These interorganizational patterns converge with and become somewhat a part of political influence, in that they are the result of efforts to co-ordinate autonomous agencies, to unite effort *without* the authority of formal hierarchy and employee status. They are somewhat different in that they develop away from formal political arenas and often escape the constraints of political accountability. They move public policy away from the overt politician; in return, of course, some of their own members become covert public politicians.

One way to approach these new patterns is to think of them as in lieu of bureaucracy. This is a useful approach for comparative analysis of educational influence, since in some countries the study of influence in education must begin with the fact that there is a national organization of education with important elements of hierarchical and formal control from national ministries to the region, the community, and the individual school or college. In such countries, educational organization

---

15. Edward C. Banfield, *Political Influence* (New York: Free Press, 1961), *passim.*, particularly ch. xi.
16. *Ibid.*

or educational administration or educational policy is related to this
formal national system. This relationship is lacking in the United States,
but an attempt is now being made to exert influence from the national
center, and much of this influence flows outside bureaucratic channels.[17] It is fruitful to compare the patterns of influence among agencies
with well-known features of bureaucratic organization, in each case
suggesting the kind of relation between organizations in alliance that
approximates the internal device.

Authority and Supervision

In a bureaucracy, authority and responsibility are delegated internally from position to position, office to office, to handle problems effectively. In interorganizational patterns, where leverage of position is
reduced, the handling of problems is less through formal structure, and
more shared by specific agreement or are presented by those who have
responsibilities and problems but no rights of command to those who
possess competence and such means of accomplishment as access to a
necessary population. The shared or farmed-out responsibilities and
problems are received by co-operating organizations which discover
advantage in the relationship. Delegation is largely lateral rather than
vertical and voluntary rather than mandatory. It is heavily adaptive to
the technical authority of experts, even more than the new forms of
lateral co-ordination developing within modern organizations to accommodate professionalism.

A corollary of the internal delegation of authority in a bureaucracy
is accountability up the line and supervision by those who occupy positions higher up the line. In the patterns that function in lieu of bureaucracy, a looser accountability and supervision is provided by a general
agreement. Two or more independent organizations bind themselves
together for a limited time and limited activities, often by the terms of
a contract.[18] Then, in lieu of a superior official who commands and
reviews, there are the legally enforceable stipulations of the contract.

In short, the sharing of problems, and hence of domains of work,
under limited agreement is a counterpart to authority. It is an organizational invention, or rather an interorganizational invention, of no slight
consequence for webs of organizations where authority is very decentralized.

Standards of Work

In a bureaucracy, there is explication, formalization, and universal
application of standards of work, from the administrators' code to the

17. It has been argued that the United States already has a national educational system because of
the extensive linkage provided by "ancillary structures." See Sloan R. Wayland, "Structural Features
of American Education as Basic Factors in Innovation," in Miles, *op. cit.*, ch. xxiii.
18. On "federalism by contract," see Don K. Price, *Government and Science* (New York: Oxford
University Press, 1962); ch. iii.

standards of the inspectors at the end of the production line. In interorganizational patterns, the setting of standards is less formal and more indirect. Standards setting often takes the form of manipulating resources and incentives in a large market or economy of organizations. One device is to improve the quality of materials available on the market, through subsidized innovation, and then accord prestige for the use of the improved materials. Where the source of prestige behind the improved materials is very strong, as from leading scientists, foundations, or public officials, the prestige may be semicommanding. A second device is to construct models of performance and encourage imitation, with prestige again a significant element of leverage.

PERSONNEL ASSIGNMENT

Within a bureaucratic organization, administrative performance is periodically reviewed and officials are replaced and reassigned to correct weaknesses in the organization. In interorganizational patterns, weak sectors are strengthened in other ways. The authority to reshuffle and replace men directly is lacking, but certain units of the alliance support weak sectors with resources they do possess—money and prestige. When officials in federal or private agencies thought they saw a national weakness in the curriculum of the secondary school, they were in no position to make changes in state and local personnel. They *were* in a position to use the leverage of money as well as the prestige of science to influence local authorities toward certain kinds of teachers and certain kinds of teaching materials.

RESEARCH AND DEVELOPMENT

In the modern organization, a research and development wing is often created to guarantee a flow of new ideas and innovations. In the patterns that are in lieu of bureaucracy, major agencies subsidize private innovative groups, contract for innovation, and then facilitate dissemination of the innovations to the field. Since this combination of subsidized research and dissemination of results is characteristic of many private foundations, this can be called "the foundation mechanism."

DECISION MAKING

In a bureaucracy, solutions to problems take the form of deliberate decision. The organization assembles the elements of the problem, weighs the alternatives, and makes a purposeful or deliberate decision. In the patterns of influence that connect autonomous organizations, on the other hand, solutions to problems are less formally and consciously determined. The solutions approach those found in decentralized political systems, where the solution is a social choice; that is, a resultant of the interaction of interested, autonomous organizations.[19] Influence exerted in a web of autonomous organizations often involves a decision that occurs in increments over time. In the pattern of curriculum reform, all the interested parties did not come together at one time. Their self-interest was not relevant at every stage. Different organizations were involved in the stages of creating new materials, retraining teachers, and adopting the new physics curriculum in the local school district. There was a rolling federation or alliance; the proposal for action was never a unified proposal but one composed of increments determined at different times; the decision resulted from the interaction of different parties at different stages.

These few sketchy parallels between bureaucratic and interorganizational patterns are sufficient to suggest one way of exploring the extensive area of social action, which lies outside of the formal organization and formal political arenas, but in which human effort is organized in quasi-formal or quasi-conscious ways by organizational agents. At least in education, social forces are greatly increasing the importance of this area that is not bounded by the kind of structures that have usually been designated as organizations. Leadership is moving into the interagency compact, the limited alliance, the consortium, the grants committee, the federation. Those who believe that the study of organizations is a valuable part of social inquiry need to extend their research perspectives so as to understand influence in interorganizational activity and comprehend the determinants of policy and practice among loosely joined organizations. To comprehend the shift to interorganizational administration and leadership would be to understand better the changing nature of administration inside the giant organization where large size and deepening expertise have fragmented command. Since many complex single organizations resemble the more structured interorganizations, there is no sharp line between the conceptions appropriate to such formal organizations and those necessary to the interorganizational scene.

19. Banfield, op. cit., pp. 326–327.

━━━━━━━━━━━━━━━━━━━━━━ **28** ━━━━━━━━━━━━━━━━━━━━━━

ORGANIZATIONAL INTERDEPENDENCE AND INTRAORGANIZATIONAL STRUCTURE

Michael Aiken and Jerald Hage

The major purpose of this paper is to explore some of the causes and consequences of organizational interpendence among health and welfare organizations. The aspect of organizational interpendence that is examined here is the joint cooperative program with other organizations. In particular, we are interested in relating this aspect of the organization's relationships with its environment to internal organizational behavior.

Thus this paper explores one aspect of the general field of interorganizational analysis. The effect of the environment on organizational behavior as well as the nature of the interorganizational relationships in an organization's environment are topics that have received increasing attention from scholars in recent years. Among studies in the latter category, there are those that have attempted to describe the nature of organizational environments in terms of the degree of turbulence.[1] and in terms of organizational sets.[2] Others have emphasized transactional interpendencies among organizations.[3] Still others have empha-

This is a revised version of a paper read at the annual meetings of the American Sociological Association, San Francisco, California, August 30, 1967. This investigation was supported in part by a research grant from the Vocational Rehabilitation Administration, Department of Health, Education, and Welfare, Washington D.C. We are grateful to Charles Perrow for helpful comments on an earlier version of this paper. In addition, we would like to acknowledge the cooperation and support of Harry Sharp and the Wisconsin Survey Laboratory during the interviewing phase of this project.
1. F. E. Emery and E. L. Trist, "The Causal Texture of Organizational Environment," *Human Relations*, 18, 1965, pp. 21–31.
2. William M. Evan, "The Organization-Set: Toward a Theory of Interorganizational Relations," pp. 173–191 in James D. Thompson (ed.), *Approaches to Organizational Design*, Pittsburgh, Pa.: University of Pittsburgh Press, 1966.
3. Phillip Selznick, *TVA and the Grass Roots*, Berkeley, Cal.: University of California Press, 1949. V. F. Ridgeway, "Administration of manufacturer-dealer systems," *Administrative Science Quarterly*, 1, 1957, pp. 273–295. William R. Dill, "The Impact of Environment on Organizational Development," in Sidney Mailick and Edward H. Van Ness (eds.), *Concepts and Issues in Administrative Behavior*, Englewood Cliffs, N.J.: Prentice-Hall, Inc., pp. 94–109, 1962. Sol Levine and Paul E. White, "Exchange as a Conceptual Framework for the Study of Interorganizational Relationships," *Administrative Science Quarterly*, 5, 1961, pp. 583–601. Sol Levine and Paul E. White and Benjamin D. Paul, "Community Interorganizational Problems in Providing Medical Care and Social Services," *American Journal of Public Health*, 53, 1963, pp. 1183–1195. Harold Guetzkow, "Interagency Committee Usage," *Public Administration Review*, 10, 1950, pp. 190–196. Eugene Litwak, "Models of Bureaucracy which Permit Conflict," *American Journal of Sociology*, 67, 1961, pp. 177–184. James D. Thompson, "Organizations and Output Transactions," *American Journal of Sociology*, 68, 1962, pp. 309–324.

sized the importance of an understanding of interorganizational relationships for such problem areas as education,[4] medical care,[5] rehabilitation and mental health,[6] delinquency prevention and control,[7] services for the elderly,[8] community action,[9] and community response to disasters.[10]

Few studies, however, have examined the impact of the environment on internal organizational processes. One such study by Thompson and McEwen[11] showed how the organizational environment can affect goal-setting in organizations, while a study by Dill[12] examined how environmental pressures affect the degree of managerial autonomy. Simpson and Gulley[13] found that voluntary organizations with diffuse pressures from the environment were more likely to have decentralized structures, high internal communications, and high membership involvement, while those having more restricted pressures from the environment had the opposite characteristics. Terreberry[14] has hypothesized that organizational change is largely induced by forces in the environment, and Yuchtman and Seashore[15] have defined organizational effectiveness in terms of the organization's success in obtaining resources from the environment. Recently, James D. Thompson[16] and Lawrence and Lorsch[17] have suggested some ways in which elements in the environment can affect organizational behavior. There are also other studies which argue that another aspect of the environment—variations in cultural values and norms—may also affect the

R. H. Elling and S. Halbsky, "Organizational Differentiation and Support: A Conceptual Framework," *Administrative Science Quarterly,* 6, 1961, pp. 185–209. William Reid, "Interagency Coordination in Delinquency Prevention and Control," *American Sociological Review,* 32, 1967, pp. 418–428.

4. Burton R. Clark, "Interorganizational Patterns in Education," *Administrative Science Quarterly,* 10, 1965, pp. 224–237.

5. Sol Levine and Paul E. White, "The Community of Health Organizations," in Howard E. Freeman, S. E. Levine, and Lee G. Reeder (eds.), *Handbook of Medical Sociology,* Englewood Cliffs, New Jersey: Prentice-Hall, 1963, pp. 321–347.

6. Bertram J. Black and Harold M. Kase, "Inter-agency Cooperation in Rehabilitation and Mental Health," *Social Service Review,* 37, 1963, pp. 26–32.

7. Walter B. Miller, "Inter-institutional Conflict as a Major Impediment to Delinquency Prevention," *Human Organization,* 17, 1958, pp. 20–23. *Op. Cit.,* William Reid.

8. Robert Morris and Ollie A. Randall, "Planning and Organization of Community Services for the Elderly," *Social Work,* 10, 1965, pp. 96–102.

9. Roland L. Warren, "The Interorganizational Field as a Focus for Investigation," *Administrative Science Quarterly,* 12, 1967, pp. 396–419.

10. William H. Form and Sigmund Nosow, *Community in Disaster,* New York: Harper and Row, 1958.

11. James D. Thompson and William J. McEwen, "Organizational Goals and Environment Goal-Setting as an Interaction Process," *American Sociological Review,* 23, 1958, pp. 23–31.

12. William R. Dill, "Environment as an Influence on Managerial Autonomy," *Administrative Science Quarterly,* 2, 1958, pp. 409–443.

13. Richard L. Simpson, and William H. Gulley, "Goals, Environmental Pressures, and Organizational Characteristics," *American Sociological Review,* 27, 1962, pp. 344–351.

14. Shirley Terreberry, "The Evolution of Organizational Environments," *Administrative Science Quarterly,* 12, 1968, pp. 590–613.

15. Ephraim Yuchtman and Stanley E. Seashore, "A System Resource Approach to Organizational Effectiveness," *American Sociological Review,* 32, 1967, pp. 891–903.

16. James D. Thompson, *Organizations in Action,* New York: McGraw-Hill, 1967.

17. Paul R. Lawrence and Jay W. Lorsch, *Organization and Environment,* Boston: Graduate School of Business Administration, Harvard University, 1967.

internal structure of organizations.[18] Each of these studies, then, suggests ways in which the organization's environment affects the internal nature of the organization. The purpose of this study is to show how one aspect of the organization's relationship with its environment, i.e., the interdependence that arises through joint cooperative programs with other organizations, is related to several intra-organizational characteristics. We shall do this by describing a theoretical framework about organizational interdependence and then by examining some results from an empirical study of organizational interdependence.

A second objective in calling attention to this relatively neglected area of organizational analysis is to suggest that the processes of both conflict and cooperation can be incorporated into the same model of organizational interdependence. The concept of interdependence helps us to focus on the problem of interorganizational exchanges. At the same time, the exchange of resources, another aspect of the relationships between organizations, is likely to involve an element of conflict. While Simmel has made the dialectic of cooperation and conflict a truism, as yet there has been little work that explains interorganizational cooperation and conflict. Caplow[19] has suggested a model of conflict involving the variables of subjugation, insulation, violence, and attrition, but this model focuses neither on the particular internal conditions that give rise to interorganizational relationships nor on the consequences of them for organizational structure. These are key intellectual problems in attempting to understand exchanges among organizations.

The models of pluralistic societies described by Tocqueville[20] and more recently by Kornhauser[21] underscore the importance of autonomous and competing organizations for viable democratic processes. Such theoretical models assume that the processes of conflict as well as cooperation inhere in social reality. Recent American social theory has been criticized for its excessive emphasis on a static view of social processes and for failing to include conflict in its conceptual models.[22] The study of interorganizational relationships appears to be one area which can appropriately incorporate the processes of both conflict and cooperation. Therefore the concept of organizational interdependence becomes a critical analytical tool for understanding this process.

18. Stephen A. Richardson, "Organizational Contrasts on British and American Ships," *Administrative Science Quarterly,* 1, 1959, pp. 189–207. Frederick H. Harbison, E. Kochling, F. H. Cassel and H. C. Ruebman, "Steel Management on Two Continents," *Management Science,* 2, 1955, pp. 31–39. Michel Crozier, *The Bureaucratic Phenomenon,* Chicago: The University of Chicago Press, 1964.
19. Theodore Caplow, *Principles of Organization,* New York: Harcourt, Brace & World, Inc., 1964.
20. Alexis de Tocqueville, *Democracy in America,* New York: Alfred A. Knopf, Inc., 1945.
21. William Kornhauser, *The Politics of Mass Society,* Glencoe, Ill.: The Free Press of Glencoe, 1959.
22. Ralf Dahrendorf, "Out of Utopia: Toward a Reorientation of Sociological Analysis," *American Journal of Sociology,* 64, 1958. Lewis Coser, *The Functions of Social Conflict,* Glencoe, Ill.: The Free Press of Glencoe, 1956. Dennis Wrong, "The Oversocialized Conception of Man in Modern Society," *American Sociological Review,* 26, 1961, pp. 183–193.

Most studies of organizational interdependence essentially conceive of the organization as an entity that needs inputs and provides outputs, linking together a number of organizations via the mechanisms of exchanges or transactions.[23] Some types of organizational exchanges involve the sharing of clients, funds, and staff in order to perform activities for some common objective.[24] The measure of the degree of organizational interdependence used here is the *number of joint programs* that a focal organization has with other organizations. The greater the number of joint programs, the more organizational decision-making is constrained through obligations, commitments, or contracts with other organizations, and the greater the degree of organizational interdependence.[25]   This type of interdependence among health and welfare organizations has variously been called "functional co-operation" by Black and Kase[26] and "program co-ordination" by Reid,[27] and is considered a more binding form of interdependence   and   therefore   a   more   interesting   example   of interorganizational cooperation. This does not suggest that the cooperation that is involved in joint programs is easily achieved. On the contrary,   there   are   a   number   of   barriers   to   establishing   such interdependencies among organizations,[28] and the probability of conflict is quite high, as Miller[29] and Barth[30] point out.

The reader may wonder why the concept of the joint program is apparently such an important kind of interorganizational relationship. The answer is that, unlike exchanges of clients or funds (which may only imply the *purchase* of services) or other types of organizational cooperation, a joint program is often a relatively enduring relationship, thus indicating a high degree of organizational interdependence.

The *joint program* needs to be carefully distinguished from the *joint organization*. The latter refers to the situation in which two or more organizations create a separate organization for some common purpose. For example, the Community Chest has been created by health and welfare organizations for fund-raising purposes. Similarly, Harrison[31] has noted that the Baptist Convention was created by the

---

23. *Op. Cit.,* V. F. Ridgeway. *Op. Cit.,* R. H. Elling and S. Halbsky. *Op. Cit.,* Sol Levine and Paul E. White, 1961. *Op. Cit.,* William R. Dill, 1962. *Op. Cit.,* James D. Thompson, 1962.
24. *Op. Cit.,* Sol Levine, Paul E. White and Benjamin D. Paul.
25. Harold Guetzkow, "Relations among Organizations," in Raymond V. Bowers (ed.), *Studies on Behavior in Organizations,* Athens, Ga.: University of Georgia Press, 1966, pp. 13–44.
26. *Op. Cit.,* Bertram J. Black and Harold M. Kase.
27. *Op. Cit.,* William Reid.
28. Ray E. Johns and David F. de Marche, *Community Organization and Agency Responsibility,* New York: Association Press, 1951.
29. *Op. Cit.,* Walter B. Miller.
30. Ernest A. T. Barth, "The Causes and Consequences of Inter-Agency Conflict," *Sociological Inquiry,* 33, 1963, pp. 51–57.
31. Paul M. Harrison, *Authority and Power in the Free Church Tradition,* Princeton, N.J.: Princeton University Press, 1959.

separate Baptist churches for more effective fund raising. Guetzkow[32] has described interagency committees among federal agencies, representing a special case of the joint organization. Business firms have created joint organizations in order to provide service functions. These are clearly different from the joint program because these joint organizations have separate corporate identities and often their own staff, budget, and objectives.

Some examples of joint programs in organizations other than those in the health and welfare field are the student exchange programs in the Big Ten. Harvard, Columbia, Yale, and Cornell Universities are developing a common computerized medical library. Indeed, it is interesting to note how many universities use joint programs of one kind or another. We do not believe that this is an accident; rather, it flows from the characteristics of these organizations. In our study, which includes rehabilitation centers, we have observed the attempt by one organization to develop a number of joint programs for the mentally retarded. These efforts are being financed by the Department of Health, Education, and Welfare, and evidently reflect a govermental concern for creating more cooperative relationships among organizations. Even in the business world, where the pursuit of profit would seem to make the joint program an impossibility, there are examples of this phenomenon. Recently, Ford and Mobil Oil started a joint research project designed to develop a superior gasoline. This pattern is developing even across national boundaries in both the business and nonbusiness sectors.

It is this apparently increasing frequency of joint programs that makes this form of interdependence not only empirically relevant, but theoretically strategic. In so far as we can determine, organizational interdependence is increasingly more common,[33] but the question of why remains to be answered.

THEORETICAL FRAMEWORK

The basic assumptions that are made about organizational behavior and the hypotheses of this study are shown in Figure 1. These assumptions provide the argument, or model, to use Willer's[34] term, for the hypotheses to be tested below.

The first three assumptions deal with the basic problem of why organizations, at least health and welfare organizations, become involved in interdependent relationships with other units. The type of interdependency with which we are concerned here is the establish-

32. *Op. Cit.,* Harold Guetzkow.
33. *Op. Cit.,* Shirley Terreberry.
34. Willer, *Scientific Sociology: Theory and Method,* Englewood Cliffs, New Jersey: Prentice-Hall, 1967.

Assumptions:

   I. Internal organizational diversity stimulates organizational innovation.
  II. Organizational innovation increases the need for resources.
 III. As the need for resources intensifies, organizations are more likely to develop greater interdependencies with other organizations, joint programs, in order to gain resources.
 IV. Organizations attempt to maximize gains and minimize losses in attempting to obtain resources.
  V. Heightened interdependence increases problems of internal control and coordination.
 VI. Heightened interdependence increases the internal diversity of the organization.

Hypotheses:

  1. A high degree of complexity varies directly with a high number of joint programs.
  2. A high degree of program innovation varies directly with a number of joint programs.
  3. A high rate of internal communication varies directly with a high number of joint programs.
  4. A high degree of centralization varies inversely with a high number of joint programs.
  5. A high degree of formalization varies inversely with a high number of joint programs.

Figure 1. Assumptions and Hypotheses about Organizational Interdependence.

ment of joint, cooperative activities with other organizations. If we accept Gouldner's[35] premise that there is a strain toward organizations maximizing their autonomy, then the establishment of an interdependency with another organization would seem to be an undesirable course of action. It is the view here that organizations are "pushed" into such interdependencies because of their need for resources—not only money, but also resources such as specialized skills, access to particular kinds of markets, and the like.

One source of the need for additional resources results from a heightened rate of innovation, which in turn is a function of internal organizational diversity. In several ways internal diversity creates a strain towards innovation and change. The conflict between different occupations and interest groups, or even different theoretical, philosophical, or other perspectives, results in new ways of looking at organizational problems. The likely result of this is a high rate of both proposals for program innovations as well as successful implementation of them.[36] But organizational diversity also implies a greater knowledge and awareness of the nature of and changes in the organizational environment, particularly when organizational diversity implies not only a spectrum of occupational roles in the organization, but also involvement in professional societies in the environment by the incumbents of those occupational roles, itself a type of organizational interdependency. Together the internal conflicts and awareness of the nature

35. Alvin Gouldner, "Reciprocity and Autonomy in Functional Theory," in Llewellyn Gross (ed.), *Symposium on Sociological Theory,* New York: Harper and Row, 1959, pp. 241–270.
36. Jerald Hage and Michael Aiken, "Program Change and Organizational Properties: A Comparative Analysis," *American Journal of Sociology,* 72, 1967, pp. 503–519.

of the organization's environment create strains towards organizational change.

But innovation has its price. There is a need for more resources to pay the costs of implementing such innovations—not only money, but staff, space, and time. The greater the magnitude of the change or the number of changes within some specified period of time, the greater the amounts of resource that will be needed and the less likely that the normal sources will be sufficient. Some have called organizations that successfully accomplish this task effective ones.[37] Thus, the leaders of innovating organizations must search for other possibilities, and the creation of a joint, cooperative project with another organization becomes one solution to this problem.

This mechanism for gaining resources, i.e., the establishment of a joint program, is best viewed as a type of organizational exchange. The leaders sacrifice a small amount of autonomy for gains in staff, funds, etc. While there are strong organizational imperatives against such exchanges, since they inevitably involve some loss of autonomy, as well as necessitate greater internal coordination, the increased intensification of needs for greater resources makes such an alternative increasingly attractive. Still another factor involved here is that some objectives can only be achieved through cooperation in some joint program. The goal may be so complicated or the distribution of risk so great that organizations are impelled to enter into some type of joint venture. Of course the creation of interdependencies with other organizations also has its costs. The organization must utilize some of its own resources in order to perform whatever coordination is necessary. Hence an organization with no surplus resources available could hardly afford a joint program. Thus there must be some slack in the resource base in the organization before any innovation or cooperative venture is likely.

This is not to argue for the perfect rationality of organizational leaders. Some decisions about change or the choice of a cooperative activity may be quite irrational, and perhaps non-logical.[38] Indeed much of our argument about the conditions that lead to organizational innovation, i.e., conflict among different occupations, interest groups, or perspectives, is that this is hardly the most rational way to bring about change. Perhaps it is best to view the process as a series of circumstances that propel such events.

While we feel that this line of reasoning is a valid explanation of why organizations enter into interdependent relationships with other organizations via such mechanisms as the joint program, alternative

---

37. *Op. Cit.*, Ephraim Yuchtman and Stanley E. Seashore.
38. Harold L. Wilensky, *Organizational Intelligence.* New York: Basic Books, Inc. 1967.

explanations have been offered and must be considered. Lefton and Rosengren[39] have suggested that the lateral and longitudinal dimensions of organizational commitment to clients are factors, at least in health and welfare organizations. These are probably not the primary factors in other types of organizations, such as economic ones. However, our concern has been to attempt to find the most general argument possible to explain organizational interdependence. At the same time we have left unanswered the question of why organizations become diverse in the first place, and their framework may provide one possible answer. Reid[40] has indicated that complementary resources are also an important factor in understanding organizational interdependence. Without necessarily agreeing or disagreeing with these points of view, we do believe that the first three assumptions in Figure 1 represent *one* causal chain showing why organizations become involved in more enduring interorganizational relationships.

The next theoretical problem is what kind of organization is likely to be chosen as a partner in an interdependent relationship. Here we assume that organizations attempt to maximize their gains and minimize their losses. This is our fourth premise. That is, they want to lose as little power and autonomy as possible in their exchange for other resources. This suggests that they are most likely to choose organizations with complementary resources, as Reid[41] has suggested, or partners with different goals, as Guetzkow[42] has indicated. This reduces some of the problem of decreased autonomy, because the probability of conflict is reduced and cooperation facilitated in such symbiotic arrangements.[43] This assumption also implies that other kinds of strategies might be used by the leaders of the organization once they have chosen the joint program as a mechanism of obtaining resources. Perhaps it is best to develop interdependent relationships with a number of organizations in order to obtain a given set of resources, thus reducing the degree of dependence on a given source. Again, we do not want to argue that organizational leaders will always choose the rational or logical alternative, but rather that they will simply *attempt* to minimize losses and maximize gains. Under circumstances of imperfect knowledge, some decisions will undoubtedly be irrational.

Our last theoretical problem is consideration of the consequences for the organization of establishing interdependent relationships as a means of gaining additional resources. Such joint activities will necessitate a set of arrangements between the participating organizations to

39. Mark Lefton and William Rosengren, "Organizations and Clients: Lateral and Longitudinal Dimensions," *American Sociological Review*, 31, 1966, pp. 802–810.
40. *Op. Cit.*, William Reid.
41. *Ibid.*
42. *Op. Cit.*, Harold Guetzkow.
43. Amos H. Hawley, *Human Ecology*, New York: The Ronald Press, 1951.

carry out the program. This will mean commitments to the other organization, resulting in constraints on some aspect of organizational behavior. This in turn will mean an increase in problems of internal coordination, our fifth assumption. It is often difficult to work with outsiders, i.e., the partner in a joint activity. In this circumstance a number of mutual adaptations in a number of different areas will become necessary. One solution to this problem is the creation of extensive communication channels, such as a broad committee structure which meets frequently.

But perhaps a more interesting consequence of the joint program is that it can in turn contribute to organizational diversity. There is not only the likelihood of the addition of new staff from other organizations, but, more importantly, the creation of new communication links with other units in the organization's environment. New windows will have been opened into the organization, infusing new ideas and feeding the diversity of the organization, which means that the cycle of change, with all of its consequences, is likely to be regenerated.

In this way a never-ending cycle of diversity—innovation—need for resources—establishment of joint programs—is created. What may start as an interim solution to a problem can become a long-term organizational commitment which has a profound impact on the organization. In the long run, there is the tendency for units in an organizational set to become netted together in a web of interdependencies.[44]

With these six assumptions, a large number of testable hypotheses can be deduced. Indeed this is one of the advantages of a general theoretical framework. Not only does it provide the rationale for the hypotheses being tested, but it can suggest additional ideas for future research. Since we are mainly concerned with the factors associated with high interdependency, and more particularly the number of joint programs, all of the hypotheses in Figure 1 are stated in terms of this variable.

Organizational diversity implies many different kinds of variables. We have examined three separate indicators of it: diversity in the number of occupations or the degree of complexity; diversity in the number of power groups or the degree of centralization; and diversity in the actual work experience or the degree of formalization. If assumptions I–III are correct, then the stimulation of change, and more particularly innovation brought about by each of these kinds of diversity, should be associated with a large number of programs. But this is not the only way in which these variables can be related; and that observation only emphasizes how the internal structure of the organization affects the extent of the enduring relationships with other organizations. The

44. *Op. Cit.*, Shirley Terreberry.

problems of internal coordination and the increased diversity, assumptions V and VI, are also related. Both mechanisms of coordination—communication and programming— are undoubtedly tried, but communication is probably preferred. This increases the advantages of diversity and also helps to bring about greater decentralization and less formalization. Similarly, the greater awareness of the environment, via the infusion of staff from other organizations, feeds this cycle of cause and effect relationships. Therefore, we have hypothesized that the number of joint programs varies directly with the degree of complexity (Hypothesis 1) and inversely with the degree of centralization and formalization (hypotheses 4 and 5).

Since our arguments also involve statements about the stimulation of innovation, which in turn heightens the need for resources, it is clear that we would expect the degree of innovation to co-vary with the number of joint programs. This is hypothesis 2 of Figure 1. While program change is only one kind of organizational innovation, it is probably the most important, at least from the standpoint of generating needs for additional resources, and thus it goes to the heart of the argument presented in Figure 1. Program innovation in turn has consequences for the degree of centralization and formalization in the organization, but here we are mainly concerned about the relationship between the rate of organization innovation as reflected in new programs and the number of joint programs, and not about these other mediating influences.

The degree of attempted internal coordination is measured by only one variable, namely the rate of communication, but again we feel that this is an important indication of this idea. Given the desire to minimize the loss of autonomy (assumption IV), organizational members must be particularly circumspect when dealing with staff and other kinds of resources from their organizational partners. This largely reduces the options about programming and encourages the elite to emphasize communication rates. Probably special "boundary spanning" roles[45] are created; these men negotiate the transactions with other organizations and in turn keep their organizational members informed. The problems of interpenetration by other organizational members will keep the communication channels open and filled with messages as internal adjustments are made. Thus this is the rationale for the third hypothesis.

STUDY DESIGN AND METHODOLOGY

The data upon which this study is based were gathered in sixteen social welfare and health organizations located in a large midwestern

45. *Op. Cit.,* James D. Thompson, 1962.

metropolis in 1967. The study is a replication of an earlier study conducted in 1964. Ten organizations were private; six were either public or branches of public agencies. These organizations were all the larger welfare organizations that provide rehabilitation, psychiatric services, and services for the mentally retarded, as defined by the directory of the Community Chest. The organizations vary in size from twenty-four to several hundred. Interviews were conducted with 520 staff members of these sixteen organizations. Respondents within each organization were selected by the following criteria: (a) all executive directors and department heads; (b) in departments of less than ten members, one-half of the staff was selected randomly; (c) in departments of more than ten members, one-third of the staff was selected randomly. Non-supervisory administrative and maintenance personnel were not interviewed.

Aggregation of Data. This sampling procedure divides the organization into levels and departments. Job occupants in the upper levels were selected because they are most likely to be key decision-makers and to determine organizational policy, whereas job occupants on the lower levels were selected randomly. The different ratios within departments ensured that smaller departments were adequately represented. Professionals, such as psychiatrists, social workers and rehabilitation counselors, are included because they are intimately involved in the achievement of organizational goals and are likely to have organizational power. Non-professionals, such as attendants, janitors, and secretaries are excluded because they are less directly involved in the achievement of organizational objectives and have little or no power. The number of interviews varied from eleven in the smallest organization to sixty-two in one of the larger organizations.

It should be stressed that in this study the units of analysis are *organizations,* not individuals in the organizations. Information obtained from respondents was pooled to reflect properties of the sixteen organizations, and these properties were then related to one another. Aggregating individual data in this way presents methodological problems for which there are yet no satisfactory solutions. For example, if all respondents are equally weighted, undue weight is given to respondents lower in the hierarchy. Yet those higher in the chain of command, not the lower-status staff members, are the ones most likely to make the decisions which give an agency an ethos.[46]

We attempted to compensate for this by computing an organizational score from the means of social position within the agency. A social position is defined by the level or stratum in the organization and the

---

46. For a discussion of some of the basic differences between individual and collective properties, see Lazarsfeld and Menzel (1960) and Coleman (1964).

department or type of professional activity. For example, if an agency's professional staff consists of psychiatrists and social workers, each divided into two hierarchical levels, the agency has four social positions: supervisory psychiatrists, psychiatrists, supervisory social workers, and social workers. A mean was then computed for each social position in the agency. The organizational score for a given variable was determined by computing the average of all social position means in the agency.[47]

The procedure for computing organizational scores parallels the method utilized in selecting respondents. It attempts to represent organizational life more accurately by not giving disproportionate weight to those social positions that have little power and that are little involved in the achievement of organizational goals.

Computation of means for each social position has the advantage of avoiding the potential problem created by the use of different sampling ratios. In effect, responses are standardized by organizational location—level and department—and then combined into an organizational score. Computation of means of social position also has a major theoretical advantage in that it focuses on the sociological perspective of organizational reality.

We make no assumption that the distribution of power, regulations, or rewards is random within any particular social position. Instead, each respondent is treated as if he provides a true estimate of the score for a given social position. There is likely to be some distortion due to personality differences or events unique in the history of the organization, but the computation of means for each social position hopefully eliminates or at least reduces the variation due to such factors. By obtaining measures from all levels and all departments, the total structure is portrayed and reflected in the organizational score.

The Measurement of Organizational Interdependence. The degree of organizational interdependence is measured by the number of joint programs with other organizations. There are several possible

---

47. One advantage of this procedure is that it allows for the cancellation of individual errors made by the job occupants of a particular position. It also allows for the elimination of certain idiosyncratic elements that result from the special privileges a particular occupant might have received as a consequence. An alternative procedure for computing organizational means is to weight all respondents equally. These two procedures yield strikingly similar results for the variables reported in this paper. The product-moment correlation coefficients between the scores based on these two computational procedures were as follows for the variables indicated:

Hierarchy of authority 0.93
Participation in decision making 0.85
Job codification 0.89
Rule observation 0.89
Index of specificity of jobs 0.93
Index of routinization of technology 0.94
Professional training 0.90
Professional activity 0.93

measures of the nature and degree of organizational interdependence among social welfare and health organizations. Among these are:

1. The number of cases, clients or patients referred or exchanged.
2. The number of personnel lent, borrowed, or exchanged.
3. The number, sources, and amounts of financial support.
4. The number of joint programs.

The first two of these were used in an earlier study of interorganizational relationships.[48] In our research we found that organizations such as rehabilitation workshops and family agencies simply did not keep records of the number of walk-ins or calls referred by other organizations. Similar problems were encountered with exchanges of personnel. Thus, we found great difficulty in using these measures of interdependence. While the nature and amounts of financial support are interesting and important aspects of interorganizational analysis, they are not included in this study.

We asked the head of each organization to list every joint program in which his organization had been involved in the past ten years, whether terminated or not. A profile of each program was obtained, including the name of participating organizations, goals of the program, number and type of clients or patients involved, and source of financial and other resources for the program. Only existing programs and those involving the commitment of resources by all participating organizations—such as personnel, finances, space—were included in our analysis.

Since a number of our sixteen organizations had participated in joint programs with each other, it was possible to check the reliability of their responses. We did not find any difficulties of recall for this period of time. In part this is probably because most of the joint programs, once started, tended to continue over time. Some organizations had maintained their organizational relationships for as many as twenty years. Then too, the fact that the joint program is not a minor incident in the life of an organization also facilitates recall. We did discover that organizational leaders tended to think of the purchase of services as a joint program. To solve this problem we included in our interview schedule a series of follow-up questions about the amount of staff shared and the amount of funds contributed by each organization involved in the joint program.

Another problem of measurement centered on the difficulty of defining separate joint programs. For example, there was a tendency for an organization with a history of successful relationships (those that endured for more than two years) to develop a number of joint pro-

48. *Op. Cit.,* Sol Levine and Paul E. White, 1961.

grams with the same organization. The relationships would grow in scope and depth in much the way that one would predict from Homans[49] hypotheses about the interaction between people. This raised the problem of whether joint programs with the same organization should be counted as separate programs. Our solution was to count the program separately if it involved different activities. Thus a research program and an education program with the same organization, two common kinds of programs, would be counted as separate joint programs. The key in making this decision was the idea of separate activities. In fact, programs were usually developed at different dates, suggesting again that our solution was a correct one. At the same time, if an organization developed the same joint program with three organizations, this was counted only once. From a practical standpoint these attempts at refinement were not so important because it is clear that the differences in number of joint programs among the sixteen organizations in our study are so great that similar ranking would occur regardless of how one counted the programs.

The number of existing joint programs among these sixteen organizations ranged from none to 33. Rehabilitation centers had the highest average number of joint programs, although the range was quite extensive among some other kinds of organizations in our study (Table 1). The special education department and the hospitals had an intermediate range of programs. Social casework agencies and homes for the emotionally disturbed had the least number of joint programs. In every case,

Table 1

Average Number of Joint Programs
by Type of Organization

Type of Organizations	Number of Organizations	Average Number of Joint Programs	Range
Rehabilitation centers	3	20.7	8-33
Special education department—public schools	1	15.0	15
Hospitals	3	8.3	6-12
Homes for emotionally disturbed	3	2.3	1-3
Social casework agencies	6	1.2	0-4
All organizations	16	7.3	0-33

49. George Homans, *The Human Group,* New York: Harcourt, Brace and World, Inc., 1950.

however, there was some variation within each organizational category.

FINDINGS

A strict interpretation of data would allow us to discuss only the consequences of interorganizational relationships on the internal structure and performance of an organization. This is true because the period of time during which measurement of the number of joint programs, our measure of organizational interdependence, was made occured prior to most of our measures of structure and performance. Yet the reasoning in our theoretical framework suggests that these variables are both causes and effects in an on-going process. Strictly speaking, our data reflect the consequences of increased joint programs, but we shall still make some inferences about their causes.

1. *Organizations with many joint programs are more complex organizations, that is, they are more highly professionalized and have more diversified occupational structures.* By complexity we do not mean the same thing as Rushing's[50] division of labor, a measure of the distribution of people among different occupations, but rather the diversity of activities. There are essentially two aspects of complexity as we have defined it: the degree to which there is a high number of different types of occupational activities in the organization; and the degree to which these diverse occupations are anchored in professional societies.[51] One of the most startling findings in our study is the extremely high correlation between the number of different types of occupations in an organization and the number of joint programs ($r=0.87$).

The relationship between the occupational diversity of the organization and the number of joint programs in 1967 is very high, whether we use the number of occupations in 1959 ($r=0.79$), the number of occupations in 1964 ($r=0.83$), or the number of occupations in 1967 ($r=0.87$). While time sequence is not the same as causation, this does suggest that occupational diversity is not solely a function of new programs. Rather it suggests that organizations that have a high number of joint programs are organizations that have been occupationally diverse for a number of years.

The addition of joint programs evidently makes an organization

50. William A. Rushing, "The Effects of Industry Size and Division of Labor on Administration," *Administrative Science Quarterly*, 12, 1967, pp. 273–295.
51. It should be noted that our count of occupational specialties is not based on the number of specific job titles. Instead, each respondent was asked what he did and then this was coded according to the kind of professional activity and whether it was a specialty. This procedure was used for two reasons. First, it allows for comparability across organizations. Second, it avoids the problem of task specialization where one activity might be divided into many specific and separate tasks.

aware of the need for still more specialties. One rehabilitation center used social workers in a joint program involving the mentally retarded with several other agencies. It then decided to add social workers to a number of its other programs. The addition of new specialties may also be necessary in order to help solve some of the problems of coordination created by the joint programs.

The dependent variable, number of joint programs, is quite dispersed with a range from 0 to 33 and a mean of 7.3. It is entirely possible that the unusually high correlations for some variables in Table 2 are

Table 2

Relationships Between the Number of Joint
Programs and Organizational Characteristics

Organizational Characteristic	Pearsonian Product-Moment Correlation Coefficients between Each Organizational Characteristic and the Number of Joint Programs
1. Degree of Complexity	
Index of professional training	.15
Index of professional activity	.60**
Number of occupations: 1967	.87****
2. Degree of Organizational Innovation: 1959-1966	
Number of new programs (including new programs that are joint programs)	.71***
Number of new programs (excluding new programs that are joint programs)	.74****
3. Internal Communication	
Number of committees	.47*
Number of committee meetings per month	.83****
4. Degree of Centralization	
Index of participation in decision-making	.30
Index of hierarchy of authority	.33
5. Degree of Formation	
Index of job codification	.13
Index of rule observation	−.06
Index of specificity of job	−.06

* $P < .10$.
** $P < .05$.
*** $P < .01$.
**** $P < .001$.

simply a function of a highly skewed distribution on this variable. Therefore, we computed two non-parametric measures of correlation, Spearman's rank order correlation coefficient (rho) and Kendall's rank correlation coefficient (tau) for the relationship between number of occupations in 1967 and the number of joint programs as shown in Table 3. The relationship between these two variables remains strong even when using the non-parametric statistics.

Table 3

Comparison of Pearsonian Correlation Coefficient (R),
Spearman's Rank Order Correlation Coefficient (RHO),
and Kendall's Rank Correlation Coefficient (TAU) for
the Four Largest Correlations Shown in Table 2

Organizational Characteristics	Correlation Coefficient between Number of Joint Programs and Organizational Characteristics		
	r	rho	tau
Number of Occupations: 1967	.87	.81	.74
Number of New Programs: 1959-1966 (including new programs that are joint programs)	.71	.84	.75
Number of New Programs: 1959-1966 (excluding new programs that are joint programs)	.74	.80	.70
Number of Committee meetings per month	.83	.61	.54

The objection could be raised that the very strong relationship between number of occupational specialties and the number of joint programs may also be a function of the type of organization. In Table 1, it was shown that rehabilitation centers had the most joint programs, followed by the special education department, hospitals, homes for the emotionally disturbed, and finally social casework agencies. The observation that there is a positive relationship between these two variables is valid within three of the four categories of organizations shown in Table 4. That is, within the categories of rehabilitation centers, mental hospitals, and homes for the emotionally disturbed the organizations having the highest number of occupations have the most joint programs while those having the fewest occupational specialties have the smallest number of joint programs. Only among social casework agencies does the relationship not hold. It might be noted that only one social casework organization had more than one interorganizational tie.

384

INTERORGANIZATIONAL ANALYSIS

Table 4

Number of Occupations In 1967 and Number of
Joint Programs by Type of Organization

	Number of Occupations 1967	Number of Joint Programs
Rehabilitation Centers		
Rehabilitation Center A	27	33
Rehabilitation Center B	24	21
Rehabilitation Center C	13	8
Department of Special Education		
Educational Organization D	19	15
Mental Hospitals		
Mental Hospital E	18	12
Mental Hospital F	18	7
Mental Hospital G	11	6
Homes for Emotionally Disturbed		
Home H	11	3
Home I	10	3
Home J	7	1
Social Casework Agencies		
Casework Agency K	7	1
Casework Agency L	6	0
Casework Agency M	5	1
Casework Agency N	5	1
Casework Agency O	4	4
Casework Agency P	1	0

The degree to which an organization is professionalized is also strongly related to the number of joint programs. We measured the degree of professionalism in organizations in two ways: first, the degree to which the organizational members received professional training; and second, the degree to which organizational members are currently active in professional activities, i.e., attending meetings giving papers, or holding offices. The measure of current professional activity was also quite highly related to our measure of the number of joint programs $(r=0.60)$.[52] The degree of professional training had little relationship with the number of joint programs $(r=0.15)$.[53]

52. The index of professional activity, which ranged from 0 to 3 points, was computed as follows: (a) 1 point for belonging to a professional organization; (b) 1 point for attending at least two-thirds of the previous six meetings of any professional organization; (c) 1 point for the presentation of a paper or holding an office in any professional organization.
53. The index was scored as follows: (a) high school graduates or less education, with no professional training, received a score of 0; (b) high school graduates or less education, with some professional training, received a score of 1; (c) Staff members with a college degree or some college, but an absence of other professional training, received a score of 2; (d) staff members with a college degree or some college, and the presence of some other professional training, received a score of 3; (e) the presence

Table 5

Partial Correlation Coefficients between Number of
Joint Programs and Organizational Innovation,
Controlling for Indicators of Complexity

Control Variables	Partial Correlation between Number of Joint Programs and Number of New Programs 1959-1966 (Excluding New Programs that Are Joint Programs), Controlling for the Variable Indicated
Indicators of Complexity	
Index of professional training	.77
Index of professional activity	.55
Number of occupations: 1967	.46

2. *Organizations with many joint programs are more innovative organizations.* The degree of organizational innovation is measured by the number of new programs that were successfully implemented in the organization during the eight-year period from 1959 to 1966. The correlation coeffieient between joint programs and new programs is 0.71, as shown in Table 2. Of course, there is an element of spuriousness in this relationship, since some of the new programs are joint programs. If the correlation coefficient is recomputed, eliminating all new programs that are also joint programs, we find the same result (r=0.74).

As in the case of number of occupational specialties in the organization, the finding based on non-parametric measures of association between each of these two measures of organizational innovation and the number of new programs is little different from the results based on the parametric statistical measure (See Table 3).

It could be that the above relationships between degree of organizational innovation and number of joint programs may simply be a function of complexity. We have argued that the degree of complexity gives rise not only to joint programs, but also to new programs. While there is no relationship between professional training and the number of new programs (r=−0.18), there are relatively strong relationships between this variable and professional activity (r=0.74) as well as occupational diversity (r=0.67). When the relationships between the number of joint programs and the number of new programs (excluding new programs that are joint programs) is controlled for each of these three indicators separately, the relationship between these two variables remains relatively strong (see Table 5). This illustrates that the number

of training beyond a college degree, and the absence of other professional training, received a score of 4; (f) the presence of training beyond a college degree, and the presence of other professional training, received a score of 5.

of new programs is related to the number of joint programs independently of these various indicators of complexity.

The key idea in our interpretation is that it is the rate of organizational innovation that intensifies the need for new resources. The higher this rate, the more likely organizations are to use the joint program as a mechanism for cost reduction in such activities. The fact that some new programs are joint programs only strengthens our argument that the joint program is a useful solution for the organization seeking to develop new programs.

This interplay between new programs and joint programs can be made clear with several examples from our study. One rehabilitation center with a high rate of new programs developed joint programs with several organizations that were primarily fund-raising organizations, as a solution for funding its growth. But in turn these organizations recognized new needs and asked the organization to develop still more new programs in areas for their clients. This particular agency is presently exploring the possibility of developing special toys for the mentally retarded because one of its joint programs is with an organization concerned with this type of client.

We may also re-examine the relationships between indicators of complexity and the number of joint programs. As shown in Table 6, only the relationship between the number of occupations and the number of joint programs remains strong when the number of new programs (excluding new programs that are joint programs) is controlled (partial $r=0.75$).

3. *Organizations with many joint programs have more active internal communication channels.* We measured the degree of internal communication in two ways. First, the number of committees in the organization and, second, the number of committee meetings per month. An active committee structure in an organization provides the potential for viable communication links in an organization. As shown in Table 2, there was a moderately strong relationship between the number of organizational committees and joint programs ($r=0.47$) and a very strong relationship between the number of committee meetings per month and the number of joint programs ($r=0.83$).

The relationship between the number of joint programs and the number of committee meetings per month remains moderately strong when the two non-parametric measures of association are computed. (See Table 3.)

Actually the system of communication for joint programs is even more complex than this. For example, one rehabilitation agency with the largest number of joint programs had a special board with the university with which it had many joint programs and was in the process of establishing another joint board with a second university. An-

Table 6

Partial Correlation Coefficients between Number of
Joint Programs and Indicators of Complexity, Con-
trolling for Number of New Programs (Excluding
New Programs that Are Joint Programs)

Indicators of Complexity	Partial Correlation between Number of Joint Programs and Indicators of Complexity, Controlling for Number of New Programs (Excluding New Programs that Are Joint Programs)
Index of professional training	.32
Index of professional activity	.11
Number of occupations: 1967	.75

Table 7

Partial Correlation Coefficients between Number of Joint
Programs and Indicators of Internal Communication,
Controlling for Indicators of Complexity and Innovation

Control Variables	Partial Correlation between Number of Joint Programs and Number of Committees, Controlling for the Variable Indicated	Partial Correlation between Number of Joint Programs and Frequency of Committee Meetings, Controlling for the Variable Indicated
Indicators of Complexity		
Index of professional training	.45	.83
Index of professional activity	.13	.76
Number of occupations: 1967	.11	.57
Indicator of Organizational Innovation		
Number of new programs: 1959-1966 (excluding new programs that are joint programs)	.08	.64

other rehabilitation agency created a special steering committee to suggest and supervise joint programs: the members of this committee were representatives from other organizations.

Controlling for the indicators of complexity and program change reduces the relationship between the number of committees and number of joint programs almost to zero in every case except that of professional training. Thus, the number of committees is evidently a function of these factors. On the other hand, the very strong relationship between the number of joint programs and the frequency of committee meetings is only moderately reduced when these controls are applied as shown in Table 7. This shows that the frequency of committee meetings is not simply a function of the complexity of the organization or the degree of organizational innovation, but has an independent relationship with the number of joint programs.

4. *Organizations with many joint programs have slightly more decentralized decision-making structures.* In our study, staff members were asked how often they participated in organizational decisions about the hiring of personnel, the promotion of personnel, the adoption of new organizational policies, and the adoption of new programs or services. The organizational score was based on the degree of participation in these four areas of decision-making.[54] As shown in Table 2, there is a weak, positive relationship between the degree of participation in agency-wide decisions and the number of joint programs ($r=0.30$). This appears to be measuring the way resources are controlled. A second kind of decision-making concerns the control of work. We measure the degree of decision-making about work with a scale called the "hierarchy of authority."[55] This scale had a relationship with the number of joint programs in the opposite direction to our expectation ($r=0.33$). While highly interdependent organizations have slightly more decentralization of decisions about organizational resources, there is slightly less control over work in such organizations. It is difficult to account for this other than that the organizations with a high degree of program change during the period 1964–1966 had less control over work decisions in 1967 than in 1964. This suggests that the rate of change was so high in such organizations during this period that some more rigid mechanisms of social control were adopted in these organizations. Since the highly innovative organizations were also those with more joint programs, this helps to explain the reversal.

Partial correlations between the number of joint programs and the degree of participation in decision-making, controlling for each of the

54. The index of actual participation in decision making was based on the following four questions: (1) How frequently do you usually participate in the decision to hire new staff? (2) How frequently do you usually participate in the decisions on the promotion of any of the professional staff? (3) How frequently do you participate in decisions on the adoption of new policies? (4) How frequently do you participate in the decisions on the adoption of new programs? Respondents were assigned numerical scores from 1 (low participation) to 5 (high participation), depending on whether they answered "never," "sometimes," "often," or "always," respectively, to these questions. An average score on these questions was computed for each respondent, and then the data were aggregated into organizational scores as described above.

55. The empirical indicators of these concepts were derived from two scales developed by Richard Hall (1963), namely, hierarchy of authority and rules. The index of hierarchy of authority was computed by first averaging the replies of individual respondents to each of the following five statements: (1) There can be little action taken here until a supervisor approves a decision. (2) A person who wants to make his own decisions would be quickly discouraged here. (3) Even small matters have to be referred to someone higher up for a final answer. (4) I have to ask my boss before I do almost anything. (5) Any decision I make has to have my boss's approval. Responses could vary from 1 (definitely false) to 4 (definitely true). The individual scores were then combined into an organizational score as described above.

indicators of complexity, innovation, and internal communication, are shown in Table 8.

The relatively low relationship between these two variables is reduced, and in one case reversed, when these other factors are controlled by using partial correlations. Only in the case of frequency of committee meetings is the relationship strengthened. What this means is that the degree of particpation in decision-making is largely a function of some of the previously discussed variables—professional activity, number of occupations, and number of committees. Thus, it has little independent relationship with the number of joint programs.

The relationship between hierarchy of authority and the number of joint programs is little affected by indicators of complexity, but somewhat more by the indicators of internal communication. (See Table 8.) On the other hand, the relationship between these two variables is reversed when the number of new programs is controlled, and the relationship is now in the expected direction, i.e., members of organizations with many joint programs having more control over individual work tasks. This finding buttresses our earlier interpretation that it was the dramatic increase of new programs that brought about less control

Table 8

Partial Correlation Coefficients between Number of Joint Programs and Indicators of Centralization of Decision-Making, Controlling for Indicators of Complexity, Innovation, and Internal Communication

Control Variables	Partial Correlations between Number of Joint Programs and Participation in Decision-Making, Controlling for the Variable Indicated	Partial Correlations between Number of Joint Programs and Hierarchy of Authority, Controlling for the Variable Indicated
Indicators of Complexity		
Index of professional training	.27	.33
Index of professional activity	.01	.21
Number of occupations: 1967	−.10	.31
Indicator of Organizational Innovation		
Number of new programs: 1959-1966 (excluding new programs that are joint programs)	.20	−.28
Indicators of Internal Communication		
Number of committees	.16	.17
Number of committee meetings per month	.43	.22

over individual work decisions in organizations with many joint programs.

5. *There is no relationship between formalization and the number of joint programs.* Rules and regulations are important organizational mechanisms that are often used to insure the predictability of performance. There are several important aspects of rules as mechanisms of social control. One is the number of regulations specifying who is to do what, when, where, and why; this we call job codification.[56] A second is the diligency with which such rules are enforced; this we call rule observation.[57] A third is the degree to which the procedures defining a job are spelled out; this we call the index of specificity of jobs.[58]

Two of these three indicators of formalization, the degree of rule observation and the degree of specificity of jobs, had very small inverse relationships with the number of joint programs (r=–0.06 in each case), but each of these is hardly different from zero. The index of job codification was directly related to the number of joint programs (r=0.13), but it too is little different from zero, although it is in the opposite direction to our expectation.

We conclude from these findings that formalization is unrelated to the degree of organizational interdependence, suggesting that either this kind of internal diversity is not very important or that we do not have valid measures of this phenomenon. However, there is some problem of interpretation because there was also some movement of the highly innovative organizations toward greater formalization. For example, there is a negative partial correlation between the number of joint programs and each of the indicators of formalization, i.e., job codification (partial r=–0.11), rule observation (partial r=–0.37), and degree of specificity of jobs (partial r=–0.29), when the number of new programs during the period 1959–1966 is partialled out.

56. The index of job codification was based on responses to the following five statements: (1) A person can make his own decisions without checking with anybody else. (2) How things are done here is left up to the person doing the work. (3) People here are allowed to do almost as they please. (4) Most people here make their own rules on the job. Replies to these questions were scored from 1 (definitely true) to 4 (definitely false), and then each of the respondent's answers was averaged. Thus, a high score on this index means high job codification.
57. The index of rule observation was computed by averaging the responses to each of the following two statements: (1) The employees are constantly being checked on for rule violations. (2) People here feel as though they are constantly being watched, to see that they obey all the rules. Respondents' answers were coded from 1 (definitely false) to 4 (definitely true), and then the average score of each respondent on these items was computed. Organizational scores were computed as previously described. On this index, a high score means a high degree of rule observation.
58. The index of specificity of job was based on responses to the following six statements: (1) Whatever situation arises, we have procedures to follow in dealing with it. (2) Everyone has a specific job to do. (3) Going through the proper channels is constantly stressed. (4) The organization keeps a written record of everyone's job performance. (5) We are to follow strict operating procedures at all times. (6) Whenever we have a problem, we are supposed to go to the same person for an answer. Replies to these questions were scored from 1 (definitely false) to 4 (definitely true), and then the average score of each respondent on these items was computed as the other measures. A high score means a high degree of specificity of the job.

Controls for Size, Auspices, Age, and Technology. The sixteen organizations included in this study are, from one point of view, relatively homogeneous. All of them provide either psychiatric, social, or rehabilitation services of one kind or another. In comparison to economic organizations, they are indeed homogeneous. In addition, they are all located in a single metropolitan area. The reader might wonder, therefore, how far we can generalize from our study to other kinds of organizations or to organizations in other communities.

There are several ways in which some estimate of the generality can be made. One approach would be to divide the organizations into different categories, as was done in Tables 1 and 4. Here we emphasized the differences among a set of organizations that, considering the range of all organizations, are relatively homogeneous. The difficulty with this approach is that we are making comparisons among so few cases in each category.

An alternative approach is to look at some general variables that describe the conditions of all organizations. The size of the organization is one such variable. Similarly the auspices of the organization, i.e., whether private or public, is another. And the age of the organization may also be an important factor here. Perrow[59] has recently suggested another variable, the degree of routinization of technology. Undoubtedly there are others, but these represent some of the variables that one is likely to encounter in the literature and, therefore, are a good starting place for controls.

Since there were such great differences in the size of organizations in the study, a rank ordering of size is used. The correlation coefficient between size and the number of joint programs is positive and moderate ($r=0.34$), which means that larger organizations have slightly more joint programs.

The auspices of the organization is measured by a dummy variable of private (1) versus public (0). The correlation coefficient between auspices and number of joint programs is 0.20, meaning that private organizations have slightly more joint programs.

The age of the organization was measured by constructing a trichotomous variable: (0), the organization was started in the post-Depression years (1938 to present); (1), the organization was started in the years following World War I (1918–1923); and (2), the organization was started prior to 1900. The correlation coefficient between age of the organization and the number of joint programs is -0.15, indicating that the younger organizations have slightly more joint programs.

Finally we looked at the type of technology, measured by the

59. Charles Perrow, "A Framework for the Comparative Analysis of Organizations," *American Sociological Review*, 32, 1967, pp. 194–208.

degree of routineness of work activities. By routineness of work we mean the degree to which organizational members have non-uniform work activities.[60] The correlation coefficient between routineness of work and the number of joint programs is –0.24, meaning the organizations with many joint programs have less routine technologies.

None of these four variables has strong relationships with the number of joint programs. When each of the relationships between the number of joint programs and the indicators of complexity, organizational innovation, internal communication, centralization, and formalization are controlled by each of these four variables separately, the relationships shown in Table 2 are little affected. (See Table 9.) This means that the factors of organizational size, auspices, age, and technology (as we have measured them) have little or no effect on the findings of this study.

DISCUSSIONS AND CONCLUSIONS

We now return to the issues raised at the outset of this paper. How are organizational structure and interdependence related? How can the study of an organization and its environment be combined? What kinds of organizations are more cooperative and integrated with other organizations?

We noted that there is a greater degree of complexity, i.e., more occupational diversity and greater professionalism of staff, in those organizations with the most joint programs. The participation in joint programs is evidently one mechanism for adding new occupational specialties to the organization at a reduced cost. By combining the resources of the focal organization with one or more others, there is the possibility of adding new occupational specializations to the organizational roster. This is especially true because joint programs are likely to be of a highly specialized nature, providing services and activities that the focal organization cannot support alone.

The involvement of staff in interorganizational relationships introduces them to new ideas, new perspectives, and new techniques for solving organizational problems. The establishment of collegial relationships with comparable staff members of other organizations provides them with a comparative framework for understanding their own organizations. This is likely to affect their professional activities—atten-

60. *Ibid.* Joan Woodward, *Industrial Organization,* London: Oxford University Press, 1965. The index of routinization of technology was based on responses to the following five statements: (1) People here do the same job in the same way every day (reversed). (2) One thing people like around here is the variety of work. (3) Most jobs have something new happening every day. (4) There is something different to do every day. (5) Would you describe your job as being highly routine, somewhat routine, somewhat non-routine, or highly non-routine? The first four items were scored from 1 (definitely true) to 4 (definitely false). On the fifth item scores ranged from 1 (highly non-routine) to 4 (highly routine).

Table 9

Partial Correlations between the Number of Joint Programs and
Indicators of Complexity, Innovation, Internal Communication,
Centralization, and Formalization, Controlling Separately for
Organization Size, Auspices, Age, and Technology

	Partial Correlation Coefficient between Number of Joint Programs and the Organization Characteristic Indicated, Controlling for			
	Size	Auspices	Age	Technology
Complexity				
Index of professional training	.35	.14	.16	.02
Index of professional activity	.56	.61	.64	.60
Number of occupations: 1967	.88	.86	.89	.86
Innovation				
Number of new programs: 1959-1966 (excluding new programs that are joint programs)	.73	.76	.74	.75
Internal Communication				
Number of committees	.41	.45	.48	.48
Number of committee meetings per month	.81	.82	.82	.83
Centralization				
Index of participation in decision-making	.25	.27	.40	.18
Index of hierarchy of authority	.38	.35	.29	.33
Formalization				
Index of job codification	.18	.12	.07	.19
Index of rule observation	−.27	.00	−.10	−.02
Index of specificity of job	−.19	.03	−.16	.12

dance at meetings of professional societies—as well as reinforce professional standards of excellence. In these ways the involvement of organizations in joint programs has the effect of increasing the complexity of these social and health welfare organizations.

The heightened interdependence has other important implications for the internal structure of organizations. The partial or total commitment of organizational resources to other organizations is likely to affect various departments and the business office as well as the central programs of such an organization. Problems of coordination are likely to become particularly acute under such circumstances. The organization is forced to overcome these problems by heightening the frequency of internal communication. A more diverse committee structure and more committee meetings are mechanisms for handling such problems.

We would have expected that the heightened rates of communication would have resulted in more decentralization than appears to be the case. It is entirely possible that the problems of internal coordination may be reflected in some attempts to tighten the power structure, thus leading to less movement towards decentralization than we had expected. Also, the problems of internal coordination may be reflected in greater programming of the organization, or at least attempts in that direction, and this may be the reason why there is a small relationship between heightened interdependency, as we have measured it, and the degree of centralization.

Diversity in occupations (the degree of complexity) and power groups (the degree of decentralization) are related to the number of joint programs, but diversity in work, as reflected in the absence of rules, is not related to this measure of interdependence. In part this may be a consequence of the sudden increase in the rate of program innovation. But it may also be that the degree of formalization is not a good measure of diversity. It is the diversity of occupations, including their perspectives and self-interests, along with the representation of these points of view in a decentralized structure, that allows for diversity with the most critical consequences.

Our assumptions help to explain the steadily increasing frequency of organizational interdependency, especially that involving joint programs. As education levels increase, the division of labor proceeds (stimulated by research and technology), and organizations become more complex. As they do, they also become more innovative. The search for resources needed to support such innovations requires interdependent relations with other organizations. At first, these interdependencies may be established with organizations with different goals and in areas that are more tangential to the organization. Over time, however, it may be that cooperation among organizations will multiply, involving interdependencies in more critical areas, and involve organizations having more similar goals. It is scarcity of resources that forces organizations to enter into more cooperative activities with other organizations, thus creating greater integration of the organizations in a community structure. The long range consequence of this process will probably be a gradually heightened coordination in communities.

———————————————— **29** ————————————————

SPONSORSHIP AND ORGANIZATIONAL STABILITY
Boy Scout Troops

Phillip R. Kunz

One device for implementing a large-scale organization is the utilization of a pre-existing organizational structure as a "sponsor." The chief problem of this paper[1] is to analyze the relationship of the sponsored or "beneficiary" organization and the sponsoring organization through a study of the Boy Scouts and their sponsors.

Sponsorship as it is understood here includes two defining elements: (1) the beneficiary organization retains its distinct boundaries from the sponsoring organization, and (2) the beneficiary organization legitimately makes use of the sponsoring organization's facilities.[2]

Much of what is called sponsorship in everyday parlance will not be included in this definition. For example, United Fund would *not* be a sponsor of all the recipients of its financial aid. It would be more correctly seen as a sponsored or beneficiary organization encompassed by an organizational context. The various organizations used to raise money for United Fund would be its sponsors. While this definition of sponsorship may depart somewhat from common usage, it will be serviceable for the purposes of this paper.

THE BOY SCOUTS OF AMERICA

The Boy Scouts of America, under the auspices of a federal charter granted by Congress, has had phenomenal success in the extension of its program to eligible boys throughout America. This growth in scouting, especially in the middle class, has taken place without the national organization having had to build a vast organizational structure of its own. The national scouting organization has rather utilized the device of sponsorship to extend its program to the approximately two million boys currently enrolled.

The Boy Scouts of America provides its "character building and

1. Adapted from Phillip Ray Kunz, "Sponsorship as an Organizational Device: The Case of the Boy Scouts of America" (unpublished Ph.D. dissertation, University of Michigan, 1967). I am indebted to Leon H. Mayhew and Gerald Suttles for reading the manuscript, suggesting ideas which improved the paper, and encouraging publication.
2. While both organizations "benefit" from the relationship in some sense, the organization being sponsored is designated as the beneficiary organization here, since we are looking at the organization specifically.

citizenship training program" to various local organizations which are chartered annually by the Boy Scouts to use the program. This is much the same as a company which offers a franchise to someone to sell its nationally advertised product. The local organizations are expected to provide and maintain the leadership and meeting place for the troop. How well the troop functions depends to a great extent on this sponsor, which essentially "owns" the troop. In this way, the Boy Scouts of America utilizes an already existing organizational structure to obtain membership, leadership, and access in general to what is necessary for its continuous existence as an organization.

DATA

Data for this study were based on information obtained from a national probability sample of scout troops collected by the Survey Research Center of the University of Michigan.[3] In addition, I obtained information in 1966 relative to the same troops sampled by the Survey Research Center in 1959. This additional information provided for analysis of the troops over a seven-year period. Other information was obtained from the annual reports of the Boy Scouts of America to Congress.

The sponsoring organizations were differentiated in three ways: (1) goal alignment with the Boy Scouts, (2) inclusion of troop members within the sponsoring organization, and (3) organizational resources of the sponsors. If the major purpose of the organization was directed toward youth, for example, a school, it was listed as "youth oriented." Those organizations which had some subunit directed toward youth were listed as "partially youth oriented," like the Rotary Club, which has a committee organized to deal specifically with youth. Those organizations with goals other than youth oriented, like a fire department, were designated as "non-youth oriented." The sponsoring organizations were divided into these three divisions after examining their organization and purpose as given in *The Encyclopedia of Associations.*[4] Inclusion refers to a person being a member of both the sponsoring *and* the beneficiary organizations, for example, a student of the sponsoring school who is also a troop member.

Organizational resources refer not only to financial resources but more especially to the organizational structure which can be used to implement the activity and make the changes that are from time to time necessary in the sponsorship relation. An *ad hoc* committee of

3. Survey Research Center, *A Study of Boy Scouts and their Scoutmasters* (Ann Arbor, Mich.: Institute for Social Research, 1960).
4. *The Encyclopedia of Associations,* ed. Frederick Ruffner *et al.* (4th ed.; Detroit: Gale Research, 1964), Vol. I.

parents would not have organizational resources because they would not have the facilities to replace themselves. Contrast this with the Mormon ward, where with some type of divine authority the bishop "calls" a new scoutmaster to "serve."

Each of these variables was employed to ascertain the effect of sponsorship upon stability of the scout troop. Stability was operationalized as (1) whether a troop was still organized after eight years, and (2) whether the troop had changed its sponsor during the same period of time.

HYPOTHESES AND FINDINGS

Where the sponsoring organization and the beneficiary organization have the same general goals, they have a common interest in maintaining the relation. It can be expected, then, that changes in sponsorship will vary negatively with the goal alignment of the beneficiary and sponsoring organizations.

The hypothesis was tested by analysis of the relationship between change in sponsorship and youth orientation. These data are presented in Table 1. The percentage of troops with a change is negatively related to youth orientation as the hypothesis predicts. The χ^2 is 13.62, with two degrees of freedom, which is significant at the .01 level. Looking at the extremes, it may be noted that 69 per cent of the troops sponsored by youth-oriented organizations had not changed sponsor, whereas only 36 per cent of the troops with non-youth-oriented sponsors had retained the same sponsor.

Where the sponsoring organization has organizational resources, it will be able to call upon these resources in maintaining the beneficiary organization. The assumption was made that those organizations with

Table 1

Change in Sponsor by Youth Orientation
(Percentage Distribution)

Youth Orientation	Change in Sponsor		Total (%)	Total N
	No Change (%)	Change (%)		
Youth oriented	69	31	100	226
Partially youth oriented	62	38	100	81
Non-youth oriented	36	64	100	33
Total N	218	122		340

$$\chi^2 = 13.62; \; 2 \; \text{d.f.}; \; p < .01$$

a national affiliation, and especially those with hierarchical superordinants, have more organizational resources.

Table 2 represents the findings of this relationship. The X^2 in this case is 30.39 (4 d.f.), which achieves the .001 level of significance. As can be observed from Table 2, 79 per cent of the national denominations (religious organizations with a national affiliation) retained sponsorship of their troops. But schools and PTA's were found to be higher in retaining their troops than national civic and service organizations, with 66 and 62 per cent, respectively. This finding indicates that the sponsors with greater organizational resources will reduce the problem of sponsor turnover for the sponsored organization. The value of this type of sponsor for a national organization such as the Boy Scouts is especially evident.

Table 2

Change in Sponsor by Type of Sponsor
(Percentage Distribution)

Type Sponsor	Change in Sponsor		Total (%)	Total N
	Same Sponsor (%)	New Sponsor (%)		
National denomination	79	21	100	126
National civic and service	62	38	100	82
School and PTA	66	34	100	38
Local denomination[a]	50	50	100	60
Local civic and parents	35	65	100	34
Total N	218	122		340

$$\chi^2 = 30.39;\ 4\ \text{d.f};\ p < .001$$

[a] Local denomination refers to religious organizations that are autonomous and without national affiliation.

The argument can be made that once organizations with high organizational resources were sponsoring scout troops, they would be better able and more willing to continue sponsorship. National organizations with many local units acting as sponsors would tend to implement such sponsorship as a policy. Thus, it could be expected that change in sponsorship will vary positively with the proportion of an organization's locals which act as sponsors. To test this hypothesis, an Index of Sponsorship for denominational-type sponsors was constructed by considering the total number of local church units in the denomination (within the United States) and the total number of troops sponsored by the denomination in 1965. The Index of Sponsorship was computed by first dividing each denomination's local church units by all local church units. This percentage was then divided into the percentage of all troops sponsored by that denomination. Thus, the Church of Christ has 6.2 per cent of all the local church units in the United States; however, it sponsors only 0.5 per cent of all the troops sponsored by religious denominations. Dividing 0.5 by 6.2 yields its index score of 0.08, which indicates that this denomination does not sponsor as many troops as it should, based on the number of local church units it has. Table 3 presents this Index of Sponsorship.

This index was dichotomized into High and Low, with High referring to 1.00 or above, that is, for a denomination which has sponsorship

Table 3

Selected Denominations by Percentage of Total Local Church Units in the United States, Percentage of Scout Troops Sponsors in 1965, and Index of Sponsorship[a]

Denomination	Total Church Units (%)	All Religion-Sponsored Troops (%)	Index of Sponsorship
African Methodist Episcopal	1.8	0.9	0.50
African Methodist Episcopal Zion	1.3	0.4	0.31
Assemblies of God	0.3	0.2	0.67
Baptist	25.9	12.3	0.48
Christian Church (Disciples of Christ) Congregational	2.5	3.4	1.36
Christian Methodist Episcopal	0.8	0.2	0.25
Church of Christ	6.2	0.5	0.08
Church of God	3.0	0.7	0.23
Church of the Brethren	0.4	0.3	0.75
Church of the Nazarene	1.4	0.3	0.21
Eastern Orthodox	0.6	0.2	0.33
Evangelical United Brethren	1.3	1.5	1.15
Friends	0.3	0.1	0.33
Jewish	1.4	1.3	0.93
Latter-Day Saints	1.3	8.7	6.69
Lutheran	5.7	9.2	1.61
Methodist	9.9	20.6	2.08
Moravian	0.1	0.1	1.00
Presbyterian	4.5	10.3	2.29
Protestant Episcopal	2.3	4.1	1.78
Reformed	0.5	0.6	1.20
Roman Catholic	7.3	16.4	2.25
Salvation Army	0.4	0.8	2.00
Unitarian Universalist	0.3	0.1	0.33
United Church of Christ	2.2	4.2	1.91
Other Churches	18.3	2.6	0.14
Total %	100.0	100.0	

[a]The Index of Sponsorship was computed by dividing each denomination's percentage of all local units by the percentage of all troops sponsored by a religious denomination in 1965.

of troops proportional to its number of local units, and Low referring to those with fewer troops than would be expected on the basis of their number.

This dichotomized Index of Sponsorship was then compared with the outcome of the troop. As Table 4 indicates, the X^2 is 4.41 (1 d.f.), which is large enough to be significant at the .05 level. This indicates that those denominational type sponsors with a proportionally high number of troops have fewer discontinued troops.

Table 4

Index of Sponsorship for Denominational Type Sponsors
by Outcome of Troop (Percentage Distribution)

Index of Sponsorship	Outcome of Troop		Total (%)	Total N
	Organized (%)	Discontinued (%)		
High	85	15	100	101
Low	73	27	100	84
Total N	147	38		185

$$\chi^2 = 4.41; \text{1 d.f}; p < .05$$

This same influence, then, can be expected to prevent sponsors from discontinuing the relation. It follows that discontinuation of sponsorship will vary positively with the proportion of an organization's locals which act as sponsors.

The Index of Sponsorship is also highly related to change of sponsor, as Table 5 indicates. In this case, 81 per cent of the denominational sponsors within the High Index category retained sponsorship of their troops, whereas only 57 per cent of those within the Low category retained sponsorship. The X^2 was 12.69 (1 d.f.) and attained the .001 level of significance.

Where a change of sponsorship occurs, the beneficiary organization incurs a certain cost in that resources must be utilized to obtain a new sponsor. Those responsible for paying this cost would tend to obtain a new sponsor with greater probability of being stable in the relation. It is expected that when change of sponsorship occurs, it will tend to be in the direction of increased stability.

This hypothesis was tested by comparing the type of sponsor for the 340 troops from the national probability sample at two points in time: 1958 and 1966. As was indicated above, 122 of the troops still intact in 1966 had changed sponsor during that period of time. Table 6, which

Table 5

Change of Sponsor by Index of Sponsorship
(Percentage Distribution)

Index of Sponsorship	Change of Sponsors		Total (%)	Total N
	No (%)	Yes (%)		
High	81	19	100	101
Low	57	43	100	84
Total N	130	55		185
	χ^2 = 12.69; 1 d.f; $p < .001$			

presents this data, is divided into three parts. The first presents a frequency distribution; the second presents a percentage distribution, by row; and the third gives the ratios of the observed to the expected frequencies. The expected frequencies were computed by the row and column marginal totals. A ratio of 2.7, for example, indicates that the observed frequency for that cell is 2.7 times the expected frequency for that cell. A ratio less than 1.0 means that the observed frequency was less than the expected frequency for that cell.

One should note the strong tendency for the sponsor in Time 2 to be within the same type of organization as it was at Time 1, as the diagonal cell from the top left to the bottom right in each part of the table indicates. In order to understand this tendency better, a diagonalization ratio[5] was computed. Laumann gives the following formula:

$$\text{Ratio}_d = \frac{(X_o - X_e) \cdot}{X_o}$$

Laumann explains: "Where X_o is the observed frequency in diagonal cell O, and X_e is the expected frequency for that cell. This ratio might be interpreted as the proportion of the observed frequency falling in the diagonal cells that exceeds (or is less than) the frequency to be expected by chance to fall in the diagonal cells."[6]

The diagonalization ratio for Table 6 equals 0.652. Thus, when troop sponsors do change, there is a strong tendency to obtain a new sponsor of the same type. One possibility which may obtain is that

5. I am especially indebted to Edward Laumann for the method of analysis in this section. All of the techniques used here are explained in more detail in Edward O. Laumann, *Prestige and Association in an Urban Community: An Analysis of an Urban Stratification System* (Indianapolis: Bobbs-Merrill Co., 1966), chap. v.
6. *Ibid.*, pp. 81–82.

organizations within each category are linked by some ties which would give the old sponsor or the Boy Scout Council access to the same type of organization as a new sponsor. Note especially the ratios of observed to expected frequencies in the diagonal cells for types (3), (4), and (5) in Table 6. These three types of organizations are much more likely to retain sponsorship within their own category. Because of the small sample size one should not place too much confidence in details, but the over-all structure is important.

The frequencies on the diagonal represent sponsors with *no* change in stability. Our current interest lies especially with the direction of change for those cases off the diagonal. The cases in the upper right-hand side of the matrix represent sponsors with less stability, while those in the lower lefthand side represent sponsors with increased stability at Time 2. A symmetry ratio was computed by dividing the sum of the frequencies on the left of the diagonal by the sum of the frequencies on the right. A symmetrical table would yield a ratio of 1.00. The symmetry ratio for Table 6 is 1.98, which means that the left side has 1.98 times the frequency of the right side. This is the direction of movement predicted by the hypothesis.[7]

While the frequency in most of the cells is small, by inspecting the individual cells on the left-hand side and comparing them with their counterparts on the right-hand side, one can more fully understand the data. For example, the frequency distribution shows that five troops sponsored by local civic or parents groups in Time 1 changed to national denominations in Time 2. On the other hand, no troops initially sponsored by national denominations changed to local civic or parents groups. Five troops sponsored by local civic or parents groups in Time 1 changed to national civic and service organizations, while only one case is shown for the opposite type of move.

Another way of observing this trend is to note that the marginal totals in the frequency table for (1), (2), and (3) *increased* from Time 1 to Time 2, while (4) and (5) *decreased,* again indicating a shift toward more stable sponsors.

7. One should use caution with this finding, however, for another test of asymmetry of the matrix fails to achieve significance. This test is described by Laumann as follows: "The asymmetry test is based on the Chi-square distribution. The Chi-square is calculated according to the following formula:

$$ \chi^2 = \sum \frac{(X_1 - Y_1)^2}{(X_1 + Y_1)} $$

where X_1 is the frequency in a cell on the right-hand side of the diagonal cells and Y_1 is the frequency in the comparable or counterpart cells on the left-hand side of the diagonal cells. With a five-by-five matrix, there are ten such pairs of cells; and, consequently, there are 10 degrees of freedom. When such a Chi-square achieves an acceptable level of significance, it indicates that the probability of observing such an imbalance between the right-hand and left-hand cell due to chance alone is quite small" (*ibid.,* pp. 82–83). In this case, the χ^2 was 12.79, with ten degrees of freedom, which yields a $p < .30$.

Table 6

Type of Troop Sponsor in 1966 by Type of Sponsor in 1958
for Those Troops Which Had Changed Sponsor

Frequency Distribution

1958 Sponsor (Time 1)	Type	1966 Sponsor (Time 2)					Total
		(1)	(2)	(3)	(4)	(5)	
National denomination	(1)	20	3	2	1	0	26
National civic and service	(2)	5	20	2	3	1	31
School and PTA	(3)	1	1	9	1	1	13
Local denomination	(4)	4	6	1	17	2	30
Local civic and parents	(5)	5	5	2	1	9	22
Total		35	35	16	23	13	122

Percentage Distribution

	Type	(1)	(2)	(3)	(4)	(5)	Total
National denomination	(1)	76.9	11.6	7.7	3.8	0.0	100.0
National civic and service	(2)	16.2	64.5	6.4	9.7	3.2	100.0
School and PTA	(3)	7.7	7.7	69.2	7.7	7.7	100.0
Local denomination	(4)	13.3	20.0	3.3	56.7	6.7	100.0
Local civic and parents	(5)	22.7	22.7	9.1	4.6	40.9	100.0

Ratio of Observed to Expected Frequencies

	Type	(1)	(2)	(3)	(4)	(5)
National denomination	(1)	2.7	0.4	0.6	0.2	0.0
National civic and service	(2)	0.6	2.2	0.5	0.5	0.3
School and PTA	(3)	0.3	0.3	5.3	0.4	0.7
Local denomination	(4)	0.1	0.7	0.3	3.0	0.6
Local civic and parents	(5)	0.8	0.8	0.7	0.2	3.9

The argument was made above that sponsors with high organizational resources would be more likely to retain this relationship over a period of time. In addition, it was argued that the beneficiary organization would attempt to obtain more stable sponsors when changes in sponsorship did occur. It is expected, then, that historically the Boy Scouts of America will have shifted from sponsors with fewer organizational resources to sponsors with more of such resources.

This hypothesis was examined by plotting the total number of troops (less a few troops classified as miscellaneous each year) sponsored by the five different types of sponsors for a period of fifty-one years. These data were obtained from the Boy Scouts' annual reports to congress for

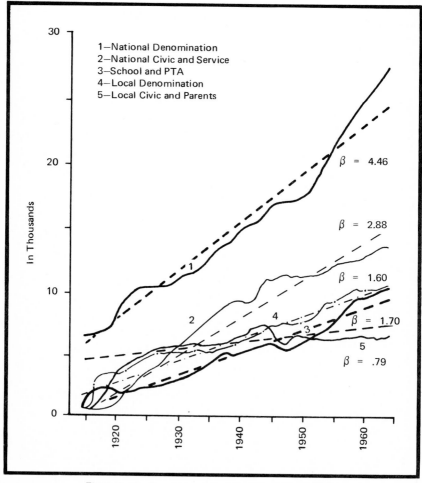

Figure 1. Boy Scout troops by type of sponsor 1915-65.

those years in which they were published and from the private reports for the years prior to that. Data was not available for three years: 1919, 1924, and 1928. In these three instances the figures for the preceding and following years were used to interpolate the data for the missing years. A regression slope was then computed for each type of sponsor. The beta coefficients are reported in each case in Figure 1. As can be observed there, the slope of the line for national denominational type sponsors ($\beta = 4.46$) is greater than for the others: $\beta = 2.88$ for national civic and service organizations, 1.60 for social denominations, 1.70 for schools and PTA, and, finally, 0.79 for local civic and parents groups. As Figure 1 indicates, the local civic and parent group type sponsors are most marked in decrease, and the national denominational types have increased the most.

Other hypotheses relative to these variables, for which the data were in the predicted direction, but *not significantly* so, were the following:

Discontinuation of the beneficiary organization will vary negatively with the degree of inclusion of the beneficiary's members in the sponsoring organization.

Turnover in sponsorship will vary negatively with the degree of inclusion of the beneficiary's members in the sponsoring organization.

Discontinuation of the beneficiary organization will vary negatively with the goal alignment of the sponsoring and beneficiary organizations.

Discontinuation of the beneficiary organization will vary negatively with the organizational resources of the sponsoring organization.

None of the hypotheses relative to these variables discloses data in a direction other than that which was predicted.

DISCUSSION

As a society, we are increasingly involved in large-scale organizations. Many commentators on modern social life have observed widespread organizational involvement as a basic and pervasive characteristic of our current society. Modern man is man in organizations.

Because of this, large-scale programs can be carried out for our mutual benefit. Furthermore, complex organizations, as social realities, often relate to other organizations and utilize them to attain some purpose or goal. In this age of large-scale organization, the application of sponsorship, as a means of introducing some stability and support to local small-scale activity, is an important device.

A large organization can limit its own need to build up a vast organizational structure by utilizing other organizations with already existent structures. More important, however, the large organization can gain access via sponsorship to members and other resources which might not otherwise be available.

This device permits the extension of an organization to the grassroots level without extensive bureaucratic organization of the beneficiary. Sponsorship provides facilities such as membership, training, and monitoring of small-scale activity by an existing organizational system, thus relieving the beneficiary organization of these various functions.

Thus, United Fund with only a very skeletal organization can mobilize once every year with its various community-based sponsors to fund its many recipients. In this case, United Fund is able to maintain itself without maintaining extensive personnel and, in addition, can swell its coffers with whatever pressuring tactics its sponsors can employ upon their own members.

Or, one may examine the National Institute of Mental Health (NIMH) in a like manner. The NIMH provides, among other things, training stipends for students in various universities. The university, as the keeper of the money and the trainer of the student, is in this sense a sponsor of NIMH.

It is easy to see the implication for the possible future extension of this type of organization on the national level. Thus, health programs which are basically the responsibility of the federal government can be carried out by the local existing organizations. Federal projects to inoculate against a disease can utilize local medical associations and carry out the program. The federal government could utilize local police systems to train a force for riot control.

Apparently one could utilize such an organizational device to bring any large-scale program to the local level. The case of the Boy Scouts of America also indicates the possibility of using such a device without hampering a program with similar values and goals as those held by the sponsors. The stability of the local sponsor apparently is of importance for a continuing organization and influences the success of the program. Thus, we conclude that large-scale organizations could avoid many organizational costs by using the device of sponsorship. This device seems to have much potential for future understanding and development of interorganizational relationships.

It should be pointed out, however, that sponsorship appears to have some inherent weaknesses. That is, this type of organizational device implies restrictions on target populations. In the case of the Boy Scouts of America it is apparent that certain types of boys will not be reached.

Thus, lower-class boys are not equally represented with middle-class boys in the scouting organization. For a number of reasons the Boy

Scouts of America has been a middle-class organization, and lower-class boys are more prone to join boys' clubs. In addition, the organization is not keeping up with the increasing numbers of boys of scout age.[8] Perhaps boys living in a more affluent society have other avenues to the same type of activity which the scout organization formerly provided. Also, the increased homogeneity of the sponsors may limit access to memberships. Other reasons undoubtedly exist.

Another of the weaknesses of sponsorship seems to be its inability to accommodate a beneficiary organization to a very pluralistic society. Despite the great potential in sponsoring organizations in the United States, only a limited number can be used by the scouts for their own organizational goals. Partly this is because of the scouts' demand that only organizations with similarities to the scouts be used as sponsors. In addition, there is self-selection by certain types of organizations which want to use the scout program and are therefore more likely to become sponsors; and, finally, certain types of organizations are more likely to survive as sponsors. All of these factors tend to maintain the homogeneity of the sponsors as a whole in the scout organization. In spite of these weaknesses, however, the Boy Scouts of America has utilized the device of sponsorship to its advantage.

8. Kunz, *op. cit.*, pp. 98–100.

Bibliography

The rather extensive bibliography which follows will assist in further study of the topics presented in this book. It should be recognized that this is not a definitive presentation of the work done in the study of organization. It includes many of the earlier works which are considered important and also contains a somewhat more inclusive list of the recent works. The selections which have been included in the bibliography are those which stress the topics covered in the sections of this book. In addition, however, important works with which every student of complex organization should be familiar are also included.

No attempt has been made to order these entries into a systematic presentation other than to alphabetize them by author. The overriding consideration which directs this alphabetic presentation is that almost every selection included can be placed in multiple listings, dependent upon the aspect of the selection to which one wants to pay attention.

Bibliography

ABEGGLEN, JAMES C. *The Japanese Factory*. New York: The Free Press of Glencoe, 1958.

AIKEN, MICHAEL, and HAGE, JERALD. "The Organic Organization and Innovation." *Sociology*, Vol. 5, No. 1 (January 1971):63–82.

ALDRICH, HOWARD E. "Sociable Organization: A Case Study of Mensa and Some Propositions." *Sociology and Social Research*, Vol. 55, No. 4, (July 1971): 429–441.

ALGER, CHADWICK F. "Research on Research: A Decade of Quantitative and Field Research on International Organizations." *International Organization*, Vol. XXIV, No. 3 (Summer 1970):414–450.

ANDERSON, THEODORE R., and WARKOV, SEYMOUR. "Organizational Size and Functional Complexity: A Study of Administration in Hospitals." *American Sociological Review*, Vol. 26 (February 1961):23–28.

ANDRESKI, STANISLAV. *Military Organization and Society*. London: Routledge and Kegan Paul, 1968.

ARGYRIS, CHRIS. *Executive Leadership*. New York: Harper & Row, Publishers Inc., 1953.

———. *Organization and Innovation*. Homewood, Ill.: Richard D. Irwin, Inc., and the Dorsey Press, 1965.

———. *Organization of a Bank*. New Haven, Conn.: Labor and Management Center, Yale University, 1954.

Arneson, B. A. *The Democratic Monarchies of Scandinavia*. New York: Van Nostrand, 1939.

ATKINSON, JOHN W. "Motivational Determinants of Risk-Taking Behavior." *Psychological Review*, Vol. 64 (November 1957):359–372.

BALDRIDGE, J. VICTOR. *Power and Conflict in the University*. New York: John Wiley, 1971.

BALES, R. F. *Interaction Process Analysis: A Method for the Study of Small Groups*. Cambridge, Massachusetts: Addison-Wesley, 1950.

BANFIELD, E. *The Moral Basis of a Backward Society*. Glencoe, Ill.: Free Press, 1958.

BARNARD, CHESTER I. *Functions of the Executive*. Cambridge: Harvard University Press, 1938.

———. *Organization and Management*. Cambridge: Harvard University Press, 1948.

BARTON, ALLEN H. *Organizational Measurement and Its Bearing on the Study of College Environments*. New York: College Entrance Examination Board, 1961.

411

BARTH, ERNEST A. T. "The Causes and Consequences of Interagency Conflict."
    Social Service Review 37 (1963):51–57.
BAUER, O. *Die Nationalitätenfrage und die Sozialdemokratie.* Vienna: Verlag
    der Wiener Volksbuchhandlung, 1924.
BAUM, B. H. *Decentralization of Authority in a Bureaucracy.* Englewood Cliffs:
    Prentice-Hall, 1961.
BAUM, BERNARD H.; SORENSEN, JR., PETER F.; and PLACE, WILLIAM S. "Patterns
    of Consensus in the Perception of Organizational Control." *Sociological
    Quarterly* 10 (1969):335–340.
BEAL, GEORGE, and KLINGLAN, GERMOLD E. et al. *System Linkages Among
    Women's Organizations.* Ames: Dept. of Soc. & Anthro. Iowa State Univer-
    sity, 1967.
BECKER, SELWYN W., and BALOFF, N. "Organization Structure and Complex
    Problem Solving." *Administrative Science Quarterly* 14 (1969):260–271.
BECKER, SELWYN W., and GORDON, GERALD. "An Entrepreneurial Theory of
    Formal Organizations Part I: Patterns of Formal Organizations." *Adminis-
    trative Science Quarterly* 11 (1966):315–345.
BELL, GERALD D. ed. *Organizations and Human Behavior: A Book of Read-
    ings.* Englewood Cliffs, New Jersey: Prentice-Hall, Inc., 1967.
BENDIX, R. *Max Weber: An Intellectual Portrait.* Garden City, N.Y.: Doubleday,
    1960.
BENDIX, REINHARD, and LIPSET, S. M. *Class, Status and Power: Social Stratifica-
    tion in Comparative Perspective,* 2nd ed. New York: The Free Press, 1966.
BELL, WENDELL, and FORCE, MARYANNE T. "Social Structure and Participation
    in Different Types of Formal Associations." *Social Forces* 34 (1956):345–
    350.
BENNIS, WARREN G. ed. *American Bureaucracy. Trans-Action Book No. 14.*
    Chicago: Aldine Publishing Co., 1970.
————. *Changing Organizations: Essays on the Development and Evolution of
    Human Organization.* New York: McGraw Hill, 1966.
————; SCHEIN, EDGAR H.; STEELE, FRED I.; and BERLEW, DAVID E. eds. *Inter-
    personal Dynamics: Essays and Readings on Human Interaction.* Home-
    wood, Illinois: The Dorsey Press, 1968.
————, and SHEPARD, H. A. "A Theory of Group Development." *Human Rela-
    tions* 9 (1956):415–437.
BERELSON, BERNARD, and STEINER, GARY A. *Human Behavior: An Inventory of
    Scientific Findings.* New York: Harcourt, Brace and World, Inc., 1964.
BERG, CURT. "Case Studies in Organizational Research and Education." *Acta
    Sociologica* 11 (1968):1–11.
BERGER, MORROE. "Bureaucracy East and West." *Administrative Science Quar-
    terly* 1 (1957):518–529.
BERGER, MORROE. *Bureaucracy and Society in Modern Egypt: A Study of the
    Higher Civil Service.* Princeton, New Jersey: Princeton University Press,
    1957.
BERKOWITZ, NORMAN H., and BENNIS, WARREN G. "Interaction Patterns in For-
    mal Service Oriented Organizations." *Administrative Science Quarterly* 6
    (1961):25–50.
BERRIEN, F. KENNETH. *General and Social Systems.* New Brunswick, New Jer-
    sey: Rutgers University Press, 1968.
BIDWELL, CHARLES E. "The School as a Formal Organization," James G. March
    (ed.), *Handbook of Organizations.* Chicago: Rand McNally & Company,
    1965.

BIDWELL, CHARLES E. "Values, Norms and the Integration of Complex Social Systems." *Sociological Quarterly* 7 (1966):119–136.

BLACK, BERTRAM J., and KASE, HAROLD M. "Interagency Cooperation in Rehabilitation and Mental Health." *Social Service Review* 37 (1963):26–32.

BLAKE, JOSEPH A. "The Organization as Instrument of Violence: The Military Case." *Sociological Quarterly* 11 (1970):331–350.

BLAKE, ROBERT R., and MOUTON, JANE S. *The Managerial Grid.* Houston: Gulf Publishing Company, 1964.

BLAU, PETER M. *The Dynamics of Bureaucracy.* Chicago: University of Chicago Press, 1955.

BLAU, PETER M. "The Comparative Study of Organizations." *Industrial and Labor Relations Review* 18 (1965):323–338.

BLAU, PETER M. *Exchange and Power in Social Life.* New York: John Wiley & Sons, 1964.

BLAU, PETER M. "A Formal Theory of Differentiation in Organizations." *American Sociological Review* 35 (1970):201–218.

BLAU, PETER M. *Bureaucracy in Modern Society.* New York: Random House, 1956.

BLAU, PETER M., and SCOTT, W. RICHARD. *Formal Organizations.* San Francisco: Chandler Publishing Co., 1962.

BLAU, PETER, and DUNCAN, OTIS DUDLEY. *The American Occupational Structure.* New York: John Wiley & Sons, 1967.

BLAU, PETER M., and SCHOEN, HERR. *The Structure of Organizations.* New York: Basic Books, 1971.

BLAU, PETER M. "A Theory of Social Integration." *American Journal of Sociology* 65 (1960):545–556.

BLAUNER, ROBERT. *Alienation and Freedom.* Chicago: University of Chicago Press, 1964.

BLAUNER, ROBERT. "Work Satisfaction and Industrial Trends." *Labor and Trade Unionism: An Interdisciplinary Reader.* New York: John Wiley & Sons, 1960, pp. 339–360.

BLEGEN, HANS MARIUS. "The Systems Approach to the Study of Organizations." *Acta Sociologica* 11 (1968):12–30.

BLUMER, HERBERT. "Industrialization and the Traditional Order." *Sociology and Social Research* 48 (1963):129–138.

BOGUSLAW, ROBERT. *The New Utopians: A Study of System Design and Social Change.* Englewood Cliffs, New Jersey: Prentice-Hall, 1965.

BORDUA, DAVID J., and REISS, ALBERT J. "Command, Control and Charisma: Reflections of Police Bureaucracy." *American Journal of Sociology* 72 (1966):68–76.

BORHEK, J. T. "Role-orientations and Organizational Stability." *Human Organization,* Vol. 24, No. 4 (Winter, 1965):332–38.

BOULDING, KENNETH E. *The Organizational Revolution.* New York: Harper & Row, 1953.

BOULDING, KENNETH E. "A Pure Theory of Conflict Applied to Organizations," George Fisk (ed.), *The Frontiers of Management Psychology.* New York: Harper & Row, Publishers, Inc., 1964.

BOWERS, RAYMOND V. *Studies on Behavior in Organizations: A Research Symposium.* Athens: University of Georgia Press, 1966.

BRACHER, K. D. *Die Auflösung der Weimarer Republik.* Stuttgart und Düsseldorf: Ring-Verlag, 1957.

BRAGER, GEORGE. "Commitment and Conflict in a Normative Organization." *American Sociological Review* 34 (1969):482–491.

BRAGER, GEORGE. "Organizing the Unaffiliated in a Low-Income Area." *Social Work* 8 (1963):34–40.

BRETON, R. "Ethnic Communities and the Personal Relations of Immigrants." Unpublished doctoral dissertation, Johns Hopkins University, 1961.

BRIDGES, EDWIN; DOYLE, WAYNE; and MOHAN, DAVID. "Effects of Hierarchical Differentiation on Group Productivity, Efficiency and Risk Taking." *Administrative Science Quarterly,* Vol. 13 (1968):305–319.

BROUILLETTE, JOHN R., and QUARANTELLI, E. L. "Types of Patterned Variation in Bureaucratic Adaptations to Organizational Stress." *Sociological Inquiry* 41 (1971):39–46.

BROWN, J. S. "Union Size as a Function of Intra-union Conflict." *Human Relations* 9 (1956):75–89.

BROWN, W. *Exploration in Management.* London: Heinemann Educational Books, 1960, and Harmondsworth: Penquin Books, 1965.

BROX, OTTAR. "Recruitment and Organizational Stability in Industrially Underdeveloped Areas." *Acta Sociologica* 12 (1969):20–28.

BRUCE, GRADY D.; BONJEAN, CHARLES M.; and WILLIAMS, JR., J. ALLEN. "Job Satisfaction Among Independent Businessmen: A Correlative Study." *Sociology and Social Research* 52 (1966):195–204.

BUCKLEY, WALTER. *Modern Systems Research for the Behavioral Scientists.* Chicago: Aldine Publishing Co., 1968.

BUCKLEY, WALTER. *Sociology and Modern Systems Theory.* Englewood Cliffs, New Jersey: Prentice-Hall, 1967.

BURGESS, E. W., and LOCKE, H. J. *The Family: From Institution to Companionship.* New York: American Book, 1945.

BURNS, TOM. *Industrial Man: Selected Readings.* Baltimore, Maryland: Penquin Books, 1969.

BURNS, T., and STALKER, G. M. *The Management of Innovation.* London: Tavistock Pubs., 1961.

CADWALLADER, MERVYN L. "The Cybernetic Analysis of Change in Complex Social Organizations." *American Journal of Sociology* 65 (1959):154–157.

CAMPBELL, FREDERICK L., and AKERS, RONALD L. "Organizational Size, Complexity, and the Administrative Component in Occupational Associations." *Sociological Quarterly* 11 (1970):435–451.

CAPLOW, THEODORE. "Organizational Size." *Administrative Science Quarterly* 1 (1957):484–505.

CAPLOW, THEODORE. *Principles of Organization.* New York: Harcourt, Brace & World, 1964.

CAPLOW, T. *The Sociology of Work.* Minneapolis: University of Minnesota Press, 1954.

CARLSON, RICHARD O. "Environmental Constraints and Organizational Consequences: The Public School and its Clients," *Behavioral Science and Educational Administration.* Chicago: National Society for the Study of Education, 1964.

CARLSON, RICHARD O. *Executive Succession and Organizational Change.* Chicago: Mid-West Administration Center, University of Chicago, 1962.

CARLSON, RICHARD O. "Succession and Performance Among School Superintendents." *Administrative Science Quarterly* 6 (1961):210–227.

CARTWRIGHT, DORWIN ed. *Studies in Social Power.* Ann Arbor: Institute for Social Research, University of Michigan, 1959.

CARTWRIGHT, DORWIN, and ZANDER, A. *Group Dynamics: Research and Theory.* Evanston, Illinois: Row, Peterson, 1953.

CARZO, ROCCO, JR., and YANOUZAS, JOHN N. *Formal Organization: A Systems Approach.* Homewood, Illinois: Richard D. Irwin, and Dorsey Press, 1967.

CHANDLER, ALFRED D., JR. *Strategy and Structure.* Cambridge, Mass.: The M.I.T. Press, 1962.

CHAPIN, F. STEWART, and TSOUDEROS, JOHN E. "Formalization Observed in Ten Voluntary Associations: Concepts, Morphology, Process." *Social Forces* 33 (1955):306–309.

CHAPIN, F. STEWART, and TSOUDEROS, JOHN E. "The Formalization Process in Voluntary Organizations." *Social Forces* 34 (1956):342–344.

CHILDERS, GRANT W.; MAYHEW, JR., BRUCE H.; and GRAY, LOUIS N. "System Size and Structural Differentiation in Military Organizations: Testing a Baseline Model of the Division of Labor." *American Sociological Review* 76 (1971): 813–830.

CHINOY, ELY. *Automobile Workers and the American Dream.* Garden City, New York: Doubleday & Company, 1955.

CICOUREL, AARON V. *The Social Organization of Juvenile Justice.* New York: John Wiley and Sons, 1968.

CLARK, BURTON R. "Interorganizational Patterns in Education." *Administrative Science Quarterly* 10 (1965):224–237.

CLARK, BURTON R. "Organizational Adaptation and Precarious Values: A Case Study." *American Sociological Review* 21 (1956):327–336.

CLARK, PETER A., and FORD, JANET R. "Methodological and Theoretical Problems in the Investigation of Planned Organizational Change." *Sociological Review* 18 (1970):29–52.

CLARK, TERRY N. *Community Structures and Decision-Making: A Comparative Analysis.* San Francisco: Chandler Publishing Company, 1968.

CLARK, TERRY N. "Institutionalization of Innovations in Higher Education: Four Models." *Administrative Science Quarterly* 13 (1968):1–25.

CLARK, TERRY N. "Power and Community Structure: Who Governs, Where and When." *Sociological Quarterly* 8 (1967):291–316.

CLOWARD, RICHARD A. et al. *Theoretical Studies in Social Organization of the Prison.* New York: Social Science Research Council, 1960.

COE, RODNEY M. ed. *Planned Change in the Hospital: Case Studies of Organizational Innovation.* New York: Praeger Publishers, 1970.

COHEN, HARRY. "Bureaucratic Flexibility: Some Comments on Robert Merton's 'Bureaucratic Structure and Personality'." *The British Journal of Sociology* 21 (1970):390–399.

COHEN, HARRY. *The Demonics of Bureaucracy: Problems of Change in a Government Agencies.* Ames, Iowa: Iowa State University Press, 1965.

COLEMAN, J. S. "Community Disorganization." R. K. Merton & R. A. Nisbet eds. *Contemporary Social Problems.* New York: Harcourt, Brace, 1961, pp. 553–604.

COLEMAN, JAMES S.; KATZ, E.; and MENZEL, H. "Diffusion of an Innovation Among Physicians." *Sociometry* 20 (1957):253–270.

COLEMAN, JAMES S. "Relational Analysis: The Study of Social Structure with Survey Methods." *Human Organization* 17 (1958–59):28–36.

COMMONS, J. R. *Legal Foundations of Capitalism.* New York: Macmillan, 1924.

CONRAD, A. H. "Income Growth and Structural Change." S. E. Harris (ed.), *American Economic History.* New York: McGraw-Hill, pp. 26–64, 1961.

COOLEY, C. H. *Social Organization.* New York: Scribners, 1909.

COOPER, WILLIAM W.; LEAVITT, HAROLD J.; and SHELLY II, MAYNARD W. eds. *New Perspectives in Organization Research*. New York: John Wiley & Sons, Inc., 1964.

CORWIN, RONALD G. "Patterns of Organizational Conflict." *Administrative Science Quarterly* 14 (1969):507–521.

COSTELLO, TIMOTHY W.; KUBIS, JOSEPH F.; and SHAFFER, CHARLES L. "An Analysis of Attitudes toward a Planned Merger." *Administrative Science Quarterly*, Vol. 8 (September, 1963):235–250.

COTTRELL, LEONARD S. "Death by Dieselization: A Case Study in the Reaction to Technological Change." *American Sociological Review* 15 (1951):358–365.

COX, R. W. "Towards a General Theory of International Organization." *Industrial and Labor Relations Review* 19 (1965):99–106.

CRAYPO, CHARLES "The National Union Convention as an Internal Appeal Tribunal." *Industrial and Labor Relations Review* 22 (1969):487–511.

CRESSEY, DONALD R. ed. *The Prison: Studies in Institutional Organization and Change*. New York: Holt, Rinehart & Winston, 1961.

CROZIER, MICHEL. *The Bureaucratic Phenomenon*. Chicago: University of Chicago Press, 1964.

CUMMINGS, LARRY L., and SCOTT, WILLIAM E. *Readings in Organizational Behavior and Human Performance*. Homewood, Illinois: Dorsey Press, 1969.

CYERT, R. M., and MARCH, J. G. *Behavioral Theory of the Firm*. Englewood Cliffs: Prentice-Hall, 1963.

DAHL, R. A. "The Concept of Power." *Behavioral Science* 2 (1957):201–215.

DAHL, R. A., and LINDBLOM, C. E. *Politics, Economics and Welfare*. New York: Harper, 1953.

DAHRENDORF, R. *Class and Class Conflict in Industrial Society*. Stanford, Calif.: Stanford University Press, 1959.

DALTON, GENE W.; BARNES, LOUIS B.; and ZALEZNIK, ABRAHAM. *The Distribution of Authority in Formal Organizations*. Boston: Harvard University, 1968.

DALTON, MELVILLE. *Men Who Manage*. New York: John Wiley & Sons, 1959.

DAVIS, JAMES A.; SPAETH, JOE L.; and HUSON, CAROLYN. "A Technique for Analyzing the Effects of Group Composition." *American Sociological Review* 26 (1961):215–225.

DAVIS, K., and BLOMSTROM, ROBERT L. *Business and Its Environment*. New York: McGraw-Hill, 1966.

DAVIS, STANLEY N. "Managements' Effects on Worker Organizations in a Developing Country." *Human Organization*, Vol. 27, No. 1 (Spring, 1968):21–29.

DE JOUVENEL, B. *Power*. London: Batchworth, 1952.

DELANY, WILLIAM. "Some Field Notes on the Problem of Access in Organizational Research." *Administrative Science Quarterly* 5 (1960):448–457.

DENHARDT, ROBERT B. "Bureaucratic Socialization and Organizational Accommodation." *Administrative Science Quarterly* 13 (1968):441–450.

DENHARDT, ROBERT B. "Leadership Style, Worker Involvement, and Deference to Authority." *Sociology and Social Research* 54 (1969):172–180.

DEUTSCH, K. *Nationalism and Social Communication*. New York: Wiley, 1953.

DILL, WILLIAM R. "Desegregation or Integration? Comments about Contemporary Research on Organizations," W. W. Cooper, Harold J. Leavitt, and Maynard W. Shelly II eds. *New Perspectives in Organization Research*. New York: John Wiley & Sons, Inc., 1964.

DILL, WILLIAM R. "Environment as an Influence on Managerial Autonomy." *Administrative Science Quarterly* 2 (1958):409–443.

DILL, WILLIAM R.; HILTON, THOMAS L.; and REITMAN, WALTER R. *The New Managers.* Englewood Cliffs, N.J.: Prentice-Hall, Inc., 1962.

DILLMAN, DONALD ANDREW. "Analysis of Interorganizational Relations." James D. Thompson ed. *Approaches to Organizational Design.* Pittsburgh, Pennsylvania: University of Pittsburgh Press, 1969, pp. 173–191.

DICKSON, DONALD T. "Bureaucracy and Morality: An Organizational Perspective on a Moral Crusade." *Social Problems* 16 (1968):143–156.

DORE, R. P. "Agricultural Improvement in Japan: 1870–1900." *Econ. Developm. Cult. Change* 4 (1960) (1, part 2):69–91.

DOWNS, ANTHONY. *Inside Bureaucracy.* Boston: Little, Brown and Company, 1967.

DRABEK, THOMAS E. *Laboratory Simulation of Police Communications under Stress.* Columbus, Ohio: Ohio State University College of Administration, 1969.

DRABEK, THOMAS E., and HASS, J. EUGENE. "Laboratory Simulation of Organizational Stress." *American Sociological Review* 34 (1969):222–236.

———. "Realism in Laboratory Simulation: Myth or Method?" *Social Forces* 45 (1967):337–346.

DUBIN, ROBERT. "Industrial Conflict: The Power of Prediction." *Industrial and Labor Relations Review* 18 (1965):352–363.

DUBIN, ROBERT. "Power and Union-Management Relations." *Administrative Science Quarterly* 2 (1957):60–81.

DUBIN, ROBERT. "Stability of Human Organizations," Mason Haire ed. *Modern Organization Theory.* New York: John Wiley & Sons, Inc., 1959.

DUFF, RAYMOND S., and HOLLINGSHEAD, AUGUST B. *Sickness and Society.* New York: Harper & Row, Publishers, 1968.

DURKHEIM, EMILE. *The Division of Labor in Society.* New York: Free Press of Glencoe, 1964.

DUTTON, JOHN M., and WALTON, RICHARD E. "Interdepartmental Conflict and Cooperation: Two Contrasting Studies." *Human Organization* 25 (1966): 207–220.

DUVERGER, M. *Political Parties.* New York: Wiley, 1954.

DYNES, RUSSELL R. "The Relation of Community Characteristics to Religious Organization and Behavior." Marvin B. Sussman ed. *Community Structure and Analysis.* New York: Crowell, 1959, pp. 253–268.

EASTON, DAVID. *A Framework for Political Analysis.* Englewood Cliffs, New Jersey: Prentice-Hall, 1965.

EINSTADTER, WERNER J. "The Social Organization of Armed Robbery." *Social Problems,* Vol. 17, No. 1 (Summer, 1969):64–83.

EISENSTADT, S. N. *The Absorption of Immigrants.* Glencoe, Illinois: Free Press, 1955.

———. "Bureaucracy, Bureaucratization, and Debureaucratization." *Administrative Science Quarterly* 4 (1959):302–320.

———. "Some Reflections of the Variability of Development and Organizational Structures." *Administrative Science Quarterly* 13 (1968):491–497.

EISENSTADT, S. N. et al. *Social Factors which Promote or Impede Changes in Agricultural Organization and Production.* Final report submitted to the United States Department of Agriculture. Jerusalem, Israel: Department of Sociology, Hebrew University.

ELKINS, S. *Slavery.* Chicago: University of Chicago Press, 1959.

ELLING, RAY H., and HALEBSKY, SANDOR. "Organizational Differentiation and Support: A Conceptual Framework." *Administrative Science Quarterly*, Vol. 6, (September, 1961):185–209.

EMERY, F. E., and TRIST, E. L. "The Causal Texture of Organizational Environments." *Human Relations* 18 (1965):21–31.

ENGEL, GLORIA. "Professional Autonomy and Bureaucratic Organization." *Administrative Science Quarterly*, Vol. 15, No. 1 (March, 1970):12–21.

ETZIONI, AMITAI. *A Comparative Analysis of Complex Organizations.* New York: The Free Press of Glencoe, 1961.

―――. *Modern Organizations.* Englewood Cliffs, New Jersey: Prentice-Hall, 1964.

ETZIONI, AMITAI. ed. *Readings on Modern Organizations.* Englewood Cliffs, New Jersey: Prentice-Hall, 1969.

―――. *The Semi-Professions and Their Organization.* New York: The Free Press, 1969.

EVAN, WILLIAM M. "Organizational Lag." *Human Organization,* Vol. 25, No. 1, (Spring, 1966):51–53.

―――. "The Organization-Set: Toward a Theory of Interorganizational Relations." James D. Thompson ed. *Approaches to Organizational Design.* Pittsburgh: University of Pittsburgh Press, 1967, pp. 173-191.

EVAN, WILLIAM M., and SCHWARTZ, MILDRED A. "Law and the Emergence of Formal Organization." *Sociology and Social Research* 48 (1964):270–280.

FALLERS, LLOYD A. "Bureaucracy in a Particularistic Setting." *Bantu Bureaucracy, A Century of Political Evolution Among the Basoga of Uganda.* Chicago: University of Chicago Press, 1965, pp. 238–247.

FAUNCE, WILLIAM A., and FORM, WILLIAM H. *Comparative Perspectives on Industrial Society.* Boston: Little, Brown and Company, 1969.

FLANDERS, A. *Industrial Relations, What is Wrong with the System?* London: Faber & Faber, 1965.

FOX, DOUGLAS M. "The Identification of Community Leaders by the Reputational and Decisional Methods." *Sociology and Social Research* 54 (1969): 94–102.

FREEMAN, L. C.; FARARO, T. J.; BLOOMBERG, W.; and SUNSHINE, M. H. *Metropolitan Decision-making.* Syracuse, N.Y.: Syracuse University Press, 1962.

FRIEDMAN, ROBERT S.; KLEIN, BERNARD W.; and ROMANI, JOHN. "Administrative Agencies and the Publics They Serve." *Public Administration Review* 27 (1966):192–204.

GAMSON, ZELDA F. "Organizational Responses to Members." *Sociological Quarterly* 9 (1968):139–149.

GEERTZ, C. *The Religion of Java.* Glencoe, Illinois: Free Press, 1960.

GEORGOPOULOS, BASIL S., and TANNENBAUM, ARNOLD S. "A Study of Organizational Effectiveness." *American Sociological Review* 22 (1957):534–540.

GERSON, WALTER M. "The College Sorority as a Social System." *Sociology and Social Research* 53 (1969):385–394.

GERTH, H. H., and MILLS, C. WRIGHT. eds. *From Max Weber: Essays in Sociology.* New York: Oxford University Press, 1958.

GINZBERG, E., and REILLEY, E. W. *Effecting Change in Large Organizations.* New York: Columbia University Press, 1957.

GLASER, BARNEY. ed. *Organizational Careers: A Sourcebook for Theory.* Aldine Publishing Co., 1968.

GLASER, BARNEY. *Organizational Scientists: Their Professional Careers.* New York: Bobbs-Merrill, 1964.

GLASER, WILLIAM A. *Social Settings and Medical Organization.* New York: Atherton Press, 1970.

GLASER, WILLIAM A., and SILLS, DAVID L. eds. *The Government of Associations.* Totowa, New Jersey: Bedminister Press, 1966.

GLASS, DAVID C. ed. *Environmental Influences.* New York: Rockefeller University Press, 1968.

GOFFMAN, ERVING. "The Characteristics of Total Institutions." *Symposium on Preventive and Social Psychiatry* (Walter Reed Institute of Research). Washington, D.C.: U.S. Government Printing Office, 1957, pp. 43–84.

GOLDNER, FRED H. "Demotion in Industrial Management." *American Sociological Review,* Vol. 30 (October, 1965):714–724.

GOLDNER, FRED H. "Organizations and Their Environment: Roles at Their Boundary." Unpublished paper read at the meetings of the American Sociological Association, New York, 1960.

GOLEMBRIEWSKI, ROBERT T. *Organizing Men and Power: Patterns of Behavior and Line-Staff Models.* Chicago: Rand McNally, 1967.

GOLEMBIEWSKI, ROBERT T., and CARRIGAN, STOKES B. "The Persistence of Laboratory-Induced Changes in Organization Styles." *Administrative Science Quarterly* 15 (1970):330–340.

GOLEMBIEWSKI, ROBERT T., and CARRIGAN, STOKES B. "Planned Change in Organization Style Based on the Laboratory Approach." *Administrative Science Quarterly,* Vol. 15, No. 1, (March, 1970):79–93.

GOODE, W. J. "Illegitimacy, Anomie, and Cultural Penetration." *American Sociological Review* 26 (1961):910–925.

GOODMAN, PAUL S. "The Natural Controlled Experiment in Organizational Research." *Human Organization,* Vol. 29, No. 3 (Fall, 1970):197–203.

GORDON, R. A. "The Executive and the Owner Entrepreneur." R. K. Merton et al (eds.), *Reader in Bureaucracy.* Glencoe, Illinois: Free Press, 1952, pp. 158–164.

GORE, WILLIAM J. *Administrative Decision-making.* New York: John Wiley & Sons, 1964.

GOULD, NATHAN, and MELBIN, MURRAY. "Formal Structure and Rational Organization Theory." *Human Organization,* Vol. 23, No. 4 (Winter, 1964):305–311.

GOULDNER, ALVIN W. "Metaphysical Pathos and the Theory of Bureaucracy." *American Political Science Review* 49 (1955):496–507.

————. "Organizational Analysis." Robert K. Merton et al eds. *Sociology Today.* New York: Basic Books, 1959, pp. 400–428.

————. *Patterns of Industrial Bureaucracy.* Glencoe, Illinois: The Free Press, 1954.

GRANICK, D. *Management of the Industrial Firm in the U.S.S.R.* New York: Columbia University Press, 1959.

GRANICK, DAVID. *The Red Executive: A Study of the Organizational Man in Russian Industry.* Garden City, New York: Doubleday, 1960.

GREENBERG, MARTIN H. *Bureaucracy and Development: A Mexican Case Study.* Lexington, Mass.: Heath Lexington Books, 1970.

GREGG, ROBERT W. ed. *International Organization in the Western Hemisphere.* Syracuse, New York: Syracuse University Press, 1968.

GREINER, LARRY E. "Antecedents of Planned Organizational Change." *The Journal of Applied Behavioral Science* 3 (1967):61–85.

GRODZINS, M. *The Loyal and the Disloyal.* Chicago: University of Chicago Press, 1956.

GROSS, BERTRAM. *Organizations and Their Managing.* New York: The Free Press, 1968.

GROSS, EDWARD. "The Definition of Organizational Goals." *British Journal of Sociology* XX (1969):277–294.

———. *Industry and Social Life.* Dubuque, Iowa: Wm. C. Brown Company, Publishers, 1965.

———. "Some Functional Consequences of Primary Controls in Formal Work Organizations." *American Sociological Review* 18 (1959):368–373.

———. "Universities as Organizations: A Research Approach." *American Sociological Review* 33 (1968):518–544.

GROSS, EDWARD, and GRAMBSCH, PAUL V. *University Goals and Academic Power.* Washington, D.C.: American Council on Education, 1968.

GRUSKY, OSCAR. "Managerial Succession and Organizational Effectiveness." *The American Journal of Sociology* 69 (1963):21–30.

GRUSKY, OSCAR. "Role Conflict in Organization: A Study of Prison Camp Officials." *Administrative Science Quarterly* 3 (1959):452–472.

GRUSKY, OSCAR, and MILLER, GEORGE A. *The Sociology of Organizations: Basic Studies.* New York: The Free Press, 1970.

GUEST, ROBERT H. *Organizational Change.* Homewood, Illinois: Dorsey Press, 1962.

GUETZKOW, H., and DILL, W. R. "Factors in the Organizational Development of Task-Oriented Groups." *Sociometry* 20 (1957):175–204.

GUETZKOW, H., and SIMON, H. A. *Simulation in Social Science.* Englewood Cliffs, New Jersey: Prentice-Hall, 1962.

GULICK, LUTHER, and URWICK, L. eds. *Papers on the Science of Administration.* New York: Institute of Public Administration, 1937.

GUSFIELD, JOSEPH R. "Social Structure and Moral Reform: A Study of the Women's Christian Temperance Union." *American Journal of Sociology* 61 (1955):221–232.

HAAS, ERNST. *Beyond the Nation-State: Functionalism and International Organization.* Stanford, Calif.: Stanford University Press, 1964.

HAAS, EUGENE; HALL, RICHARD H.; and JOHNSON, NORMAN J. "The Size of the Supportive Component in Organizations: A Multi-Organizational Analysis." *Social Forces* 42 (1963):9–17.

HAGBURG, EUGENE C. "Correlates of Organizational Participation: An Examination of Factors Affecting Union Membership Activity." *Pacific Sociological Review,* Vol. 9, No. 1 (Spring, 1966):15–21.

HAGE, JERALD, and AIKEN, MICHAEL. *Social Change in Complex Organizations.* New York: Random House, 1970.

———. "Routine Technology, Social Structure, and Organizational Goals." *Administrative Science Quarterly* 14 (1969):366–377.

———. "Program Change and Organizational Properties: A Comparative Analysis." *American Journal of Sociology* 72 (1967):503–519.

HAGE, JERALD. "Axiomatic Theory of Organizations." *Administrative Science Quarterly,* Vol. 10 (1963):289–320.

HAIRE, M. (ed.) *Modern Organization Theory.* New York: Wiley, 1959.

HAIRE, M. "Size, Shape, and Function in Industrial Organizations." *Human Organization* 14 (1955):17–22.

HALL, RICHARD H. "Bureaucracy and Small Organizations." *Sociology and Social Research* 48 (1963):38–46.

———. "Professionalization and Bureaucratization." *American Sociological Review* 33 (1968):92–104.

HALL, RICHARD H.; JOHNSON, NORMAN J.; and HAAS, EUGENE J. "Organizational Size, Complexity, and Formalization." *American Sociological Review* 32 (1967):903–912.

HARVEY, EDWARD. "Technology and the Structure of Organization." *American Sociological Review* 33 (1968):247–258.

HAVENS, A. EUGENE, and POTTER, HARRY R. "Organizational and Societal Variables in Conflict Resolution: An International Comparison." *Human Organization,* Vol. 26, No. 3 (Fall, 1967):126–131.

HAWLEY, AMOS H.; BOLAND, WALTER; and BOLAND, MARGARET. "Population Size and Administration in Institutions of Higher Education." *American Sociological Review,* Vol. 30 (April, 1965):252–255.

HEGLAND, TORE JACOB, and NYLEHN, BÖRRE. "Adjustment of Work Organizations to Critical Environmental Factors." *Acta Sociologica* 11 (1968):31–54.

HERZBERG, FREDERICK. "The New Industrial Psychology." *Industrial and Labor Relations Review* 18 (1965):364–376.

HICKSON, D. J. "A Convergence in Organization Theory." *Administrative Science Quarterly* 11 (1966):224–237.

HICKSON, DAVID J., and PUGH, D. S. "Operations Technology and Organization Structure: An Empirical Reappraisal." *Administrative Science Quarterly,* Vol. 14, No. 3 (September, 1969):378–396.

HILL, WALTER A., and EGAN, DOUGLAS M. eds. *Readings in Organizational Theory: A Behavioral Approach.* Boston, Mass.: Allyn and Bacon, 1967.

HILLERY, GEORGE A., JR. *Communal Organizations: A Study of Local Societies.* Chicago: University of Chicago Press, 1968.

HILLS, R. JEAN. *Toward a Science of Organization.* Eugene, Oregon: University of Oregon Center for the Advanced Study of Educational Administration, 1968.

HININGS, C. R., and LEE, GLORIA L. "Dimensions of Organization Structure and Their Context: A Replication." *Sociology,* Vol. 5, No. 1 (January, 1971): 83–93.

HOBSBAWM, E. J. *Primitive Rebels.* Manchester, Eng.: Manchester University Press, 1959.

HOFFMANN, STANLEY. "International Organization and the International System." *International Organization,* Vol. XXIV, No. 3 (Summer, 1970):389–413.

HOLDAWAY, EDWARD A., and BLOWERS, THOMAS A. "Administrative Ratios and Organization Size: A Longitudinal Examination." *American Sociological Review* 36 (1971):278–286.

HOLFORD, SIR W. *The Built Environment* (Tavistock Pamphlet No. 2). London: Tavistock Publications, 1965.

HOLLISTER, C. DAVID. "Interorganizational Conflict: The Case of Police Youth Bureaus and the Juvenile Court." A paper presented at the 65th Annual Meeting of the American Sociological Association, 1970.

HOMANS, GEORGE C. *The Human Group.* London: Routledge & Kegan Paul, 1957.

———. "Social Behavior as Exchange." *American Journal of Sociology* 63 (1958):597–606.

———. *Social Behavior: Its Elementary Forms.* New York: Harcourt, Brace, and World, 1961.

HOSELITZ, B. F. "Some Problems in the Quantitative Study of Industrialization." *Econ. Devlopm. Cult. Change* 9 (1961):537–546.

HOWTON, WILLIAM F. *Functionaries.* 2nd ed. Chicago: Quadrangle Books, 1971.

HUMBLE, J. W. *Improving Management Performance.* London: B.I.M., 1965.

HUSKANEN, ILHKA. *Theoretical Approaches and Scientific Strategies in Administrative and Organizational Research: A Methodological Study.* Helsinki: Commentutiones Humanarum Litterarum, Societas Scientiarum Finnica, Vol. 39, No. 2, 1967.

HUTCHINSON, E. P. *Immigrants and Their Children.* New York: Wiley, 1956.

INGHAM, GEOFFREY K. *Size of Industrial Organization and Worker Behaviour.* Cambridge: Cambridge University Press, 1970.

INKSON, J. H. I.; PUGH, D. S.; and HICKSON, D. J. "Organization Context and Structure: An Abbreviated Replication." *Administrative Science Quarterly* 15 (1970):318–329.

JACOBY, E. H. *Agrarian Unrest in Southeast Asia.* New York: Columbia University Press, 1949.

JANOWITZ, MORRIS. "Changing Patterns of Organizational Authority: The Military Establishment." *Administrative Science Quarterly,* Vol. 3 (March, 1959):473–493.

———. Review of Samuel Huntington, "Changing Patterns of Military Politics." *American Journal of Sociology* 68 (1962):377–380.

———. "Social Stratification and Mobility in West Germany." *American Journal of Sociology* 64 (1958):6–24.

———. *Sociology and the Military Establishment.* New York: Russell Sage Foundation, 1959.

JÁSZI, O. *The Dissolution of the Hapsburg Monarchy.* Chicago, University of Chicago Press, 1929.

JAQUES, ELLIOT. *The Changing Culture of a Factory.* New York: The Dryden Press, 1952.

JONES, GARTH. *Planned Organizational Change: A Study in Change Dynamics.* London: Routledge and Kegan Paul, 1969.

JOHNS, ROY. *Confronting Organizational Change.* New York: New York Association Press, 1963.

JULIAN, JOSEPH. "Some Determinants of Dissensus on Role Prescriptions within and between Four Organizational Positions." *Sociological Quarterly* 10 (1969):177–189.

JURIS, HERVEY A., and HUTCHISON, KAY B. "The Legal Status of Municipal Police Employee Organizations." *Industrial and Labor Relations Review* 23 (1970):352–366.

KAHN, R. L. *Conflict and Ambiguity: Studies in Organizational Roles and Personal Stress.* New York: Wiley, 1964.

KAHN, R. L.; WOLFE, D. M.; QUINN, R. P.; SNOEK, J. D. (in collaboration with Rosenthal, R. A.) *Organizational Stress.* New York: Wiley, 1964.

KANTER, ROSABETH MOSS. "Commitment and Social Organization: A Study of Commitment Mechanisms in Utopian Communities." *American Sociological Review* 33 (1968):499–518.

KAPLAN, URTON H. "Notes on a Non-Weberian Model of Bureaucracy: The Lease of Development Bureaucracy." *Administrative Science Quarterly,* Vol. 13 (1968):471–483.

KATZ, D., and KAHN, R. L. *The Social Psychology of Organizations.* New York: John Wiley & Sons, 1966.

KATZ, ELIHU; BLAU, P. M.; BROWN, M. L.; and STRODTBECK, F. L. "Leadership Stability and Social Change: An Experiment with Small Groups." *Sociometry* 20 (1957):36–50.

KATZ, FRED E. "Do Administrative Officials Believe in Bureaucracy? A Pilot Study." *Sociological Inquiry,* Vol. 37, No. 2 (Spring, 1967):205–209.

KATZ, FRED E. *Autonomy and Organization: The Limits of Social Control.* New York: Random House, 1968.

KAUFMANN, CARL B. *Man Incorporate: The Individual and His Work in an Organized Society.* Toronto: Doubleday, 1967.

KAUFMAN, HERBERT, and SERDMAN, DAVID. "The Morphology of Organizations." *Administrative Science Quarterly,* Vol. 15, No. 4 (December, 1970):439–451.

KELLY, JOE. *Organizational Behaviour.* Homewood, Illinois: Dorsey Press, 1969.

KEPHART, WILLIAM M. "Experimental Family Organization: An Historico-Cultural Report on the Oneida Community." *Journal of Marriage and Family Living* 25 (1963):261–271.

KERR, CLARK. *Labor and Management in Industrial Society.* New York: Doubleday (Anchor Books), 1964.

KERR, CLARK; DUNLOP, J. T.; and HARBISON, F. H. *Industrialism and Industrial Man.* London: Heinemann Educational Books, 1962.

KEY, V. O., JR. *Politics, Parties and Pressure Groups* (3rd ed.). New York: Crowell, 1952.

KLATSKY, S. R. "Organizational Inequality: The Case of the Public Employment Agencies." *American Journal of Sociology* 76 (1970):474–491.

———. "Relationship of Organizational Size to Complexity and Coordination." *Administrative Science Quarterly,* Vol. 15, No. 4 (December, 1970):428–438.

KOLARZ, W. *Myths and Realities in Eastern Europe.* London: Drummond, 1946.

KOONTZ, HAROLD, and O'DONNELL, CYRIL. *Principle of Management: An Analysis of Managerial Functions.* New York: McGraw-Hill, 1968.

KRAMER, RALPH M., and SPECHT, HARRY. *Readings in Community Organization Practice.* Englewood Cliffs, New Jersey: Prentice-Hall, 1969.

KRAUSE, ELLIOTT A. "Functions of a Bureaucratic Ideology: 'Citizen Participation'." *Social Problems* 16 (1968):129–142.

KROHN, ROGER. "Conflict and Function: Some Basic Issues in Bureaucratic Theory." *The British Journal of Sociology* 22 (1971):115–132.

KRUPP, SHERMAN. *Pattern in Organization Analysis: A Critical Examination.* New York: Holt, Rinehart & Winston, 1961.

KUETHE, JAMES L., and LEVENSON, BERNARD. "Conceptions of Organizational Worth." *American Journal of Sociology* 70 (1964):342–348.

KUHN, ALFRED. *The Study of Society: A Unified Approach.* Homewood, Illinois: Richard D. Irwin, and Dorsey Press, 1963.

KUNKEL, J. H. "Economic Autonomy and Social Change in Mexican Villages." *Econ. Developm. Cult. Change* 10 (1961):51–63.

KUNZ, PHILLIP R. "The Relation of Sponsorship and Activity." Unpublished paper read at the American Sociological Association Annual Meeting, 1969.

———. *Sponsorships as an Organizational Device: The Case of the Boy Scouts of America.* Ann Arbor, Michigan: University Microfilms, 1967.

———. "Sponsorship and Organizational Stability: Boy Scout Troops." *American Journal of Sociology* 74 (1969):666–675.

———., and BRINKERHOFF, MERLIN B. "Growth in Religious Organizations: A Comparative Study." *Social Science,* Vol. 45, No. 4 (Oct., 1970):215–221.

LAMMERS, CORNELIS J. "Strikes and Mutinies: A Comparative Study of Organizational Conflicts between Rulers and Ruled." *Administrative Science Quarterly* 14 (1969):558–572.

LANDSBERGER, HENRY A. *Comparative Perspectives on Formal Organizations.* Boston: Little, Brown and Company, 1970.

LANE, MICHAEL. *Introduction to Structuralism.* New York: Basic Books, 1970.

LAWRENCE, PAUL R., and LORSCH, JAY W. "Differentiation and Integration in Complex Organizations." *Administrative Science Quarterly* 12 (1967):1–47.

LAWRENCE, PAUL R., and LORSCH, JAY W. *Organization and Environment: Managing Differentiation and Integration.* Boston: Division of Research, Graduate School of Business Administration, Harvard University, 1967.

LAWRENCE, PAUL R., and SEILER, JOHN A. *Organizational Behavior and Administration: Cases, Concepts, and Research Findings* rev. ed. Homewood, Illinois: Richard D. Irwin and Dorsey Press, 1965.

LAWRENCE, PAUL R. *The Changing of Organizational Behavior Patterns: A Case Study of Decentralization.* Boston: Graduate School of Business Administration, Harvard University Press, 1958.

LEARNED, EDMUND P., and SPROAT, AUDREY T. *Organizational Theory and Policy.* Homewood, Illinois: Richard D. Irwin, 1966.

LEAVITT, H. J. ed. *The Social Science of Organizations.* Englewood Cliffs: Prentice-Hall, 1963.

LEFTON, MARK, and ROSENGREN, WILLIAM. "Organizations and Clients: Lateral and Longitudinal Dimensions." *American Sociological Review* 31 (1966): 802–810.

LEHMAN, EDWARD W. "Opportunity, Mobility and Satisfaction within an Industrial Organization." *Social Forces* 46 (1968):492–501.

LENSKI, G. *The Religious Factor.* Garden City, N.Y.: Doubleday, 1961.

LERNER, D. *The Passing of Traditional Society.* Glencoe, Illinois: Free Press, 1958.

LEVINE, SOL.; WHITE, PAUL E.; and PAUL, BENJAMIN D. "Community Interorganizational Problems in Providing Medical Care and Social Services." *American Journal of Public Health* 53 (1963):1183–1195.

LEVINE, SOL., and WHITE, PAUL E. "The Community of Health Organizations." *Handbook of Medical Sociology* ed. Howard E. Freeman, S. E. Levine, and Leo G. Reeder. Englewood Cliffs, New Jersey: Prentice-Hall, 1963, pp. 321–347.

――――. "Exchange as a Conceptual Framework for the Study of Interorganizational Relationships." *Administrative Science Quarterly* 5 (1961):583–601.

LEVENSON, HARRY. "Reciprocation: The Relationship between Man and Organization." *Administrative Science Quarterly,* Vol. 9 (1964–65):370–390.

LEVY, PHILIP, and PUGH, DEREK. "Scaling and Multivariate Analyses in the Study of Organizational Variables." *Sociology,* Vol. 3, No. 2 (May, 1969):193–213.

LIEBERSON, STANLEY. "An Empirical Study of Military-Industrial Linkages." *American Journal of Sociology* 76 (1971):562–584.

LIEBOW, ELLIOT. *Tally's Corner: A Study of Streetcorner Men.* Boston: Little, Brown & Company, 1967.

LIKERT, RENSIS. *New Patterns of Management.* New York: McGraw-Hill, 1961.

LIKERT, RENSIS, and KATZ, D. "Supervisory Practices and Organizational Structures as They Affect Employee Productivity and Morale." *American Management Association, Personnel Series* No. 120, 1948.

LINTER, J. "The Financing of Corporations." E. S. Mason ed. *The Corporation in Moderate Society.* Cambridge, Mass.: Harvard University Press, 1959.

LIPSET, S. M. *Political Man.* Garden City, N.Y.: Doubleday, 1960.

LIPSET, S. M., and BENDIX, R. *Social Mobility in Industrial Society.* Berkeley: University of California Press, 1959.

LIPSET, S. M.; TROW, M.; and COLEMAN, J. S. *Union Democracy.* Glencoe, Illinois: Free Press, 1956.

LITTERER, JOSEPH A. *Organizations: Structure and Behavior.* New York: John Wiley & Sons, 1963.

LITWAK, EUGENE. "Models of Bureaucracy that Permit Conflict." *American Journal of Sociology* 67 (1961):177–184.

LITWAK, EUGENE, and HYLTON, LYDIA R. "Interorganizational Analysis: A Hypothesis on Co-ordinating Agencies." *Administrative Science Quarterly* 6 (1962):395–415.

LITWAK, EUGENE, and MEYER, HENRY J. "A Balance Theory of Coordination Between Bureaucratic Organizations and Community Primary Groups." *Administrative Science Quarterly* 11 (1966):33–58.

LITWIN, GEORGE H., and STRINGER, ROBERT A. *Motivation and Organizational Climate.* Division of Research, Graduate School of Business Administration, Harvard University, 1968.

LOCKWOOD, D. *The Blackcoated Worker.* London: Allen & Unwin, 1958.

LORSCH, JAY W., and LAWRENCE, PAUL R. "Organizing for Product Innovation." *Harvard Business Review* 43 (1965):109–122.

———. *Studies in Organizational Design.* Homewood, Illinois: Dorsey Press, 1970.

LOVE, LESTER B. *Technological Change: Its Conception and Measurement.* Englewood Cliffs, New Jersey: Prentice-Hall, 1966.

LYDEN, FREMONT J.; SHIPMAN, GEORGE A.; and KROLL, MORTON. eds. *Policies, Decisions, and Organization.* New York: Appleton-Century-Crofts, 1969.

LYNTON, ROLF D. "Linking an Innovative Subsystem into the System." *Administrative Science Quarterly,* Vol. 14, No. 3 (Sept., 1969):398–414.

MACGUIRE, JILLIAN M. "The Function of the 'Set' in Hospital Controlled Schemes of Nurse Training." *The British Journal of Sociology* 19 (1968): 271–283.

MACKENZIE, W. J. M. "Technology and Organization." *Politics and Social Science.* London: Penquin Books Ltd. (1967):262–267.

McCLEERY, R. N. *Policy Change in Prison Management.* East Lansing: Government Research Bureau, Michigan State University, 1957.

McEWEN, WILLIAM J. "Position Conflict and Professional Orientation in a Research Organization." *Administrative Science Quarterly* 1 (1956):208–224.

MAIOLO, JOHN R. "Organization for Social Action: Some Consequences of Competition for Control." *Sociological Quarterly* 11 (1970):463–473.

MALE, D. J. *Russian Peasant Organization Before Collectivism.* New York: Cambridge University Press, 1971.

MANIHA, JOHN, and PERROW, CHARLES. "The Reluctant Organization and the Aggressive Environment." *Administrative Science Quarterly* 10 (1965): 238–257.

MARCH, JAMES G. ed. *Handbook of Organizations.* Chicago: Rand McNally, 1965.

MARCH, JAMES G., and SIMON, HERBERT A. *Organizations.* New York: John Wiley and Sons, 1958.

MARCUS, PHILIP M., and MARCUS, DORA. "Control in Modern Organizations." *Public Administration Review* 25 (1965):121–127.

MARCUS, PHILIP. "Expressive and Instrumental Groups: Toward a Theory of Group Structure." *American Journal of Sociology* 66 (1960):54–59.

MAREK, JULIUS. "Technological Development, Organization and Interpersonal Relations." *Acta Sociologica*, Vol. 10 (1967):224–257.

MARTINDALE, DON. *Institutions, Organizations, and Mass Society.* Boston: Houghton Mifflin Company, 1966.

MARWELL, GERALD, and HAGE, JERALD. "The Organization of Role-Relationships: A Systematic Description." *American Sociological Review* 35 (1970): 884–900.

MATHIESEN, THOMAS. *Across the Boundaries of Organizations: An Exploratory Study of Communication Patterns in Two Penal Institutions.* Berkeley, California: The Glendessary Press, 1971.

MAYER, K., and GOLDSTEIN, S. *The First Two Years: Problems of Small Firm Growth and Survival.* Small Business Research Series, No. 2, Washington, D.C.: U.S. Govt. Printing Office, 1961.

MAYHEW, LEON H. *Law and Equal Opportunity: A Study of the Massachusetts Commission Against Discrimination.* Cambridge, Mass.: Harvard University Press, 1968.

MAYHEW, LEON H., and REISS, ALBERT J. "The Social Organization of Legal Contracts." *American Sociological Review* 34 (1969):309–318.

MELIO, NANCY. "Health Care Organizations and Innovation." *Journal of Health and Social Behavior,* Vol. 12, No. 2 (June, 1971):163–173.

MERTON, ROBERT K. "Bureaucratic Structure and Personality." *Social Forces* 18 (1940):560–568.

———. "The Role Set: Problems in Sociological Theory." *British Journal of Sociology* 8 (1957):106–120.

———. *Social Theory and Social Structure.* New York: The Free Press, 1968.

MERTON, ROBERT K.; READER, GEORGE C.; and KENDALL, PATRICIA L. eds. *The Student Physician: Introductory Studies in the Sociology of Medical Education.* Cambridge, Mass.: Harvard University Press, 1957.

MESSINGER, SHELDON L. "Organizational Transformation: A Case Study of a Declining Social Movement." *American Sociological Review,* Vol. 20 (Feb., 1955):3–10.

MEYER, JOHN W. "Collective Disturbances and Staff Organizations on Psychiatric Wards: A Formalization." *Sociometry,* Vol. 31 (1968):180–199.

MEYER, MARSHALL W. "Automation and Bureaucratic Structure." *American Journal of Sociology* 74 (1968):256–264.

———. "Two Authority Structures of Bureaucratic Organization." *Administrative Science Quarterly,* Vol. 13 (1968):211–228.

MILLER, DELBERT C. *International Community Power Structures: Comparative Studies of Four World Cities.* Bloomington, Indiana: Indiana University Press, 1970.

MILLER, DELBERT C., and FROM, WILLIAM C. *Industrial Sociology: The Sociology of Work Organizations* 2nd ed. New York: Harper & Row, 1964.

MILLER, E. J., and RICE, A. K. *Systems of Organization: The Control of Task and Sentient Boundaries.* New York: Tavistock Publications, 1967.

MOORE, WILBERT E. "On the Nature of Industrial Bureaucracy." *Industrial Relations and the Social Order.* New York: Macmillan, 1950.

MORSE, N. C., and REIMER, E. "Experimental Change of a Major Organizational Variable." *Journal of Abnormal and Social Psychology* 52 (1955):120–129.

MOTT, PAUL E. *The Organization of Society.* Englewood Cliffs, New Jersey: Prentice-Hall, 1965.

MOUZELIS, NICOS P. *Organization and Bureaucracy: An Analysis of Modern Theories.* Chicago: Aldine Publishing Company, 1967.

MULDER, NAUK; RITSEMA VAN ECK, JAN R.; and DE JONG, RENDEL D. "An Organization in Crisis and Non-Crisis Situations." *Human Relations,* Vol. 24, No. 1 (Feb., 1971):19–41.

MULFORD, CHARLES L. "Consideration of the Instrumental and Expressive Roles of Community Influentials and Formal Organizations." *Sociology and Social Research* 51 (1967):141–147.

MUSGRAVE, P. W. *The School as an Organization.* London: Macmillan, 1968.

MYERS, CHARLES A. ed. *The Impact of Computers on Management.* Cambridge, Mass.: M.I.T. Press, 1968.

O'CONNELL, JEREMIAH. *Managing Organizational Innovation.* Illinois: Irwin-Dorsey Press, 1968.

O'DONOVAN, THOMAS R., and DEEGAN, ARTHUR X. "A Comparative Study of the Orientations of a Selected Group of Church Executives." *Sociology and Social Research* 48 (1964):330–339.

OLSEN, MARVIN E. ed. *Power in Societies.* New York: The Macmillan Company, 1970.

OLSEN, MARVIN E. *The Process of Social Organization.* New York: Holt, Rinehart, Winston, 1968.

PALISI, BARTOLOMEO. "Some Suggestions about the Transitory-Permanence Dimensions of Organizations." *British Journal of Sociology* 21 (1970):200–206.

PALOLA, ERNEST G. "Organizational Types and Role Strains: An Experimental Study of Complex Organizations." *Sociology and Social Research* 51 (1967):171–184.

PARKINSON, C. NORTHCOTE. *Parkinson's Law and Other Studies in Administration.* Boston: Houghton Mifflin Company, 1957.

PARSONS, TALCOTT. *Politics and Social Structure.* New York: Free Press, 1969.

————. *The Social System.* Glencoe, Illinois: Free Press, 1951.

————. *Structure and Process in Modern Societies.* Glencoe, Illinois: Free Press, 1960.

————. *The Structure of Social Action.* New York: Free Press, 1967.

————. "Suggestions for a Sociological Approach to Theory of Organizations." *Administrative Science Quarterly* 1 (1956):63–85, 225–239.

PARSONS, TALCOTT; BALES, ROBERT F.; and SHILS, EDWARD. *Working Paper in the Theory of Action.* New York: Free Press, 1966.

PARSONS, TALCOTT, and SMELSER, N. *Economy and Society.* New York: Free Press, 1957.

PATTEN, THOMAS H. JR. "Organizational Processes and the Development of Managers: Some Hypotheses." *Human Organization,* Vol. 26, No. 4 (Winter, 1967):242–255.

PELZ, D. C. "Some Social Factors Related to Performance in a Research Organization." *Administrative Science Quarterly* 1 (1956):310–325.

PENALOSA, FERNANDO. "Ecological Organization of the Transitional City: Some Mexican Evidence." *Social Forces* 46 (1967):221–229.

PENROSE, EDITH TILTON. *The Theory of the Growth of the Firm.* New York: John Wiley & Sons, 1959.

PERROW, CHARLES. "A Framework for the Comparative Analysis of Organizations." *American Sociological Review* 32 (1967):194–208.

————. "Hospitals: Technology, Structure, and Goals." In James G. March (ed.), *Handbook of Organizations.* Chicago: Rand McNally, 1965.

————. *Organizational Analysis: A Sociological View.* Belmont, Calif.: Wadsworth Publishing Company, 1970.

————. "Organizational Prestige: Some Functions and Dysfunctions." *American Journal of Sociology* 66 (1961):335–341.

PERRUCCI, ROBERT, and RICHARD A. MANNWEILER. "Organization Size, Complexity, and Administrative Succession in Higher Education." *Sociological Quarterly* 9 (Summer, 1968):343–355.

PIRENNE, H. "Stages in the Social History of Capitalism." R. Bendix and S. M. Lipset eds. *Class, Status, and Power.* Glencoe, Ill.: Free Press, 1953, pp. 501–517.

PONDY, LOUIS R. "Organizational Conflict: Concepts and Models." *Administrative Science Quarterly* 12 (1967):296–320.

————. "Varieties of Organizational Conflict." *Administrative Science Quarterly* 14 (1969):499–506.

PRESTHUS, ROBERT. "Authority in Organizations." *Public Administration Review* 20 (1960):86–91.

————. *The Organizational Society.* New York: Alfred A. Knopf, Inc. and Random House, 1962.

PRICE, JAMES L. "Design of Proof in Organizational Research." *Administrative Science Quarterly* 13 (1968):121–134.

————. *Organizational Effectiveness: An Inventory of Propositions.* Homewood, Illinois: Richard D. Irwin, 1968.

PUGH, D. S.; HICKSON, D. J.; HINNINGS, C. R.; and TURNER, C. "The Context of Organizational Structures." *Administrative Science Quarterly* 14 (1969): 91–114.

————. "Dimensions of Organizational Structure." *Administrative Science Quarterly* 13 (1968):65–105.

RANDELL, SEPPO. "On some Social Influences of the Military Organization." *Acta Sociologica,* Vol. 10 (1967):274–298.

REID, WILLIAM. "Interagency Coordination in Delinquency Prevention and Control." *Social Service Review* 38 (1964):418–428.

REISS, ALBERT J., JR. *Schools in a Changing Society.* New York: The Free Press of Glencoe, 1965.

RHENMAN, ERIC. "Organizational Goals." *Acta Sociologica,* Vol. 10 (1967):275–87.

RICE, A. K. *The Enterprise and Its Environment.* London: Tavistock Publications, 1963.

————. *The Modern University: A Model Organization.* London: Tavistock Publications, 1970.

RICHARDSON, STEPHEN A. "Organizational Contrasts on British and American Ships." *Administrative Science Quarterly,* Vol. 1 (Sept., 1956):189–207.

RIGGS, Fred W. *Administration in Developing Countries.* Boston: Houghton Mifflin Company, 1964.

RITZER, GEORGE, and HARRISON M. TRICE. *An Occupation in Conflict.* Ithaca: New York State School of Industrial and Labor Relations, Cornell University, 1969.

RIZZO, JOHN R.; HOUSE, ROBERT J.; and LIRTZMAN, SIDNEY I. "Role Conflict and Ambiguity in Complex Organizations." *Administrative Science Quarterly* 15 (1970):150–163.

ROBERTSON, LEON S., and ROGERS, JAMES C. "Distributive Justice and Informal Organization in a Freight Warehouse Work Crew." *Human Organization* 25 (1966):221–224.

ROETHLISBERGER, F. J. *Man in Organization*. Cambridge, Mass.: Harvard University Press, 1968.

ROETHLISBERGER, F. J., and DICKSON, W. J. *Management and the Worker*. Cambridge, Mass.: Harvard University Press, 1939.

ROGERS, E. M. *Diffusion of Innovations*. New York: Free Press of Glencoe, 1962.

ROKEACH, MILTON. *Beliefs, Attitudes, and Values: A Theory of Organization and Change*. San Francisco: Jossey-Bass Inc., 1968.

ROSE, JERRY D. "The Attribution of Responsibility for Organizational Failure." *Sociology and Social Research* 53 (1969):323–332.

ROSEN, R. A. HUDSON. "Foreman Role Conflict: An Expression of Contradictions in Organizational Goals." *Industrial and Labor Relations Review* 23 (1970):541–552.

ROSENBLOOM, RICHARD S., and WOLEK, FRANCIS W. *Technology and Information Transfer: A Survey of Practice in Industrial Organizations*. Boston, Mass.: Harvard University Press, 1970.

ROSENGREN, WILLIAM R. "Communication, Organization and Conduct in the 'Therapeutic Milieu'." *Administrative Science Quarterly*, Vol. 9 (June, 1964):70–90.

ROSENGREN, WILLIAM R. "The Rhetoric of Value Transfer in Organizations." *Sociological Inquiry* 41 (1971):47–56.

ROSENGREN, WILLIAM R., and LEFTON, MARK. eds. *Organizations and Clients: Essays in the Sociology of Service*. Columbus, Ohio: Charles E. Merrill Publishing Company, 1970.

ROSENGREN, WILLIAM R., and LEFTON, MARK. "Structure, Policy and Style: Strategies of Organization Control." *Administrative Science Quarterly* 12 (1967):140–164.

ROSNER, MARTIN M. "Economic Determinants of Organizational Innovation." *Administrative Science Quarterly* 12 (1968):614–625.

ROSOVSKY, H., and OHKAWA, K. "The Indigenous Components in the Modern Japanese Economy." *Econ. Developm. Cult. Change* 9 (1961):476–497.

ROTHMAN, ROBERT A., and PERRUCCI, ROBERT. "Organizational Careers and Professional Expertise." *Administrative Science Quarterly*, Vol. 15, No. 3 (Sept., 1970):282–293.

ROYAL INSTITUTE OF INTERNATIONAL AFFAIRS. *Nationalism*. London: Oxford University Press, 1939.

RUBENSTEIN, ALBERTA H., and HABERSTROH, CHADWICK J. *Some Theories of Organization*. Homewood, Ill.: Dorsey Press, 1966.

RUITENBEEK, HENRICK M. ed. *The Dilemma of Organizational Society*. New York: E. P. Dutton, 1963.

RUSHING, WILLIAM A. "Organizational Size and Administration: The Problems of Causal Homogeneity and a Heterogeneous Category." *Pacific Sociological Review*, Vol. 9, No. 2 (Fall, 1966):100–108.

SADLER, P. F., and BARRY, B. A. *Organizational Development*. London: Longman Group, 1970.

SAMUEL, YITZHAK, and MANNHEIM, BILHA F. "A Multidimensional Approach Toward a Typology of Bureaucracy." *Administrative Science Quarterly* 15 (1970):216–229.

SAWTHROP, LOUIS. *Bureaucratic Behavior in the Executive Branch: An Analysis of Organizational Change*. New York: Free Press, 1969.

SAYLES, LEONARD R. *Managerial Behavior: Administration in Complex Organizations*. New York: McGraw-Hill, 1964.

SCHON, DONALD A. *Technology and Change*. New York: Delacorte Press, 1967.

SCHULMAN, JAY. *Remaking an Organization: Innovation in a Specialized Psychiatric Hospital.* Albany, New York: State University of New York Press, 1969.

SCHUMPETER, J. A. *Business Cycles.* New York: McGraw-Hill, 1939.

SCHUMPETER, J. A. *Imperialism and Social Classes.* New York: Kelley, 1951.

SCHUMPETER, J. A. *Theory of Economic Development.* Cambridge, Mass.: Harvard University Press, 1934.

SCOTT, JOSEPH W., and EL-ASSAL, MOHAMED. "Multiversity, University Size, University Quality and Student Protest." *American Sociological Review* 34 (1969):702–722.

SCOTT, WILLIAM A. *Values and Organizations: A Study of Fraternities and Sororities.* Chicago: Rand McNally & Company, 1965.

SCOTT, WILLIAM G. *The Management of Conflict.* Homewood, Illinois: Richard D. Irwin, Inc., and Dorsey Press, 1965.

———. *Organization Concepts and Analyses.* Belmont, Calif.: Dickinson, 1969.

———. *Organization Theory: A Behavioral Analysis for Management.* Homewood, Ill.: Richard D. Irwin, Inc., 1967.

SCOTT, W. RICHARD. "Field Methods in the Study of Organizations." James G. March (ed.), *Handbook of Organizations.* Chicago, Ill.: Rand McNally & Company, 1965, pp. 272–282.

———. "Field Work in a Formal Organization." *Human Organization* 22 (1963):162–168.

SEILER, JOHN A. *Systems Analysis in Organizational Behavior.* Homewood, Ill.: Dorsey Press, 1967.

SELZNICK, PHILIP. "Foundations of the Theory of Organization." *American Sociological Review* 13 (1948):25–35.

———. *Leadership in Administration.* New York: Row, Peterson & Company, 1957.

———. *The Organizational Weapon.* New York: McGraw-Hill, 1952.

———. *TVA and the Grass Roots: A Study in the Sociology of Formal Organization.* New York: Harper & Row, 1966.

SHILS, E., and JANOWITZ, M. "Cohesion and Disintegration in the Wehrmacht in World War II." *Public Opinion Quarterly* 12 (1948):280–315.

SHIRER, W. L. *The Rise and Fall of the Third Reich.* New York: Simon & Schuster, 1960.

SHULL, FREMONT A., JR.; DELBECQ, ANDRÉ; and CUMMINGS, L. L. *Organizational Decision Making.* New York: McGraw-Hill, 1970.

SIEGFRIED, A. *Tableau Politique de la France de l'ouest sous la Troisième République.* Paris: Colin, 1913.

SILLS, DAVID L. *The Volunteers.* Glencoe, Illinois: Free Press, 1957.

SILVERMAN, DAVID. *The Theory of Organizations.* New York: Basic Books, 1971.

SIMON, HERBERT A. *Administrative Behavior: A Study of Decision-making Processes in Administration Organization,* 2nd ed. New York: The Free Press of Glencoe, 1965.

———. "A Behavioral Model of Rational Choice." *Quarterly Journal of Economics* 69 (1955):99–118.

———. *The New Science of Management Decision.* New York: Harper, 1960.

———. "On the Concept of Organizational Goal." *Administrative Science Quarterly* 9 (1964):1–22.

SIMPSON, RICHARD L., and SIMPSON, IDA HARPER. *Social Organization and Behavior.* New York: John Wiley & Sons, 1964.

SJOBERG, GIDEON; BRYMER, RICHARD A.; and BUFORD, FARRIS. "Bureaucracy and the Lower Class." *Sociology and Social Research* 50 (1966):325-337.

SLESINGER, JONATHAN A., and HARBURG, ERNEST. "Organizational Change and Executive Behavior." *Human Organization* Vol. 27, No. 2 (Summer, 1968): 95-109.

SMELSER, N. *Theory of Collective Behavior.* New York: Free Press, 1963.

SMIGEL, ERWIN O. "The Impact of Recruitment on the Organization of the Large Law Firm." *American Sociological Review* 25 (1960):56-66.

SMITH, CLAGETT G. "A Comparative Analysis of Some Conditions and Consequences of Intra-organizational Conflict." *Administrative Science Quarterly* Vol. 10 (1965):504-529.

SMITH, DAVID HORTON. "The Importance of Formal Voluntary Organizations for Society." *Sociology and Social Research* 50 (1966):483-495.

SMITH, MICHAEL A. "Process Technology and Powerlessness." *British Journal of Sociology* 19 (1968):76-88.

SOFER, C. *The Organization from Within.* Chicago: Quadrangle Books, 1963.

SPEIER, H. "Eighteenth Century Militarism." *Social Order and the Risks of War.* New York: G. W. Stewart, 1952.

SPENCER, MARTIN A. "Weber on Legitimate Norms and Authority." *The British Journal of Sociology* 21 (1970):123-134.

SPIRO, MELFORD E. *Kibbutz: Venture in Utopia.* Cambridge, Mass.: Harvard University Press, 1956.

SPRADLEY, JAMES P. *You Owe Yourself a Drunk: An Ethnography of an Urban Nomad.* Boston: Little, Brown and Company, 1970.

SPREITZER, ELMER A. "Organizational Goals and Patterns of Informal Organization." *Journal of Health and Social Behavior,* Vol. 12, No. 1 (March, 1971): 73-80.

STARBUCK, WILLIAM H. "Organizational Growth and Development," James G. March (ed.), *Handbook of Organizations.* Chicago: Rand McNally, 1965.

STEPHAN, G. EDWARD. "Variation in County Size: A Theory of Segmental Growth." *American Sociological Review* 36 (1971):451-461.

STINCHCOMBE, ARTHUR L. "Agricultural Enterprise and Rural Class Relations." *American Journal of Sociology* 67 (1961):165-176.

———. "Bureaucratic and Craft Administration of Production: A Comparative Study." *Administrative Science Quarterly* 4 (1959):168-187.

———. "Social Structure and Organizations." James G. March (ed.), *Handbook of Organizations.* Chicago: Rand McNally, 1965, pp. 142-193.

———. "The Sociology of Organization and the Theory of the Firm." *Pacific Sociological Review* 3 (1960):75-82.

STINCHCOMBE, ARTHUR L.; MCDILL, MARY SEXTON; and WALKER, DOLLIE R. "Demography of Organizations." *American Journal of Sociology* 74 (1968):221-229.

STODDARD, ELLWYN R. "Some Latent Consequences of Bureaucratic Efficiency in Disaster Relief." *Human Organization* 28 (1969):177-189.

STOUFFER, SAMUEL A., et al. *The American Soldier.* Princeton, N.J.: Princeton University Press, 2 vols. 1949.

STYMNE, BENGT. "Interdepartmental Communication and Intraorganizational Strain." *Acta Sociologica* 11 (1968):82-100.

TANNENBAUM, A. S. "The Concept of Organizational Control." *Journal of Social Issues* 12 (1956):50-60.

———. *Control in Organizations.* New York: McGraw-Hill, 1968.

————. "Control Structure and Union Functions." *American Journal of Sociology* 61 (1956):536–545.

TANNENBAUM, A. S., and KAHN, R. L. "Organizational Control Structure: A General Descriptive Technique as Applied to Four Local Unions." *Human Relations* 10 (1957):127–140.

TAUB, RICHARD P. *Bureaucrats Under Stress.* Berkeley and Los Angeles: University of California Press, 1969.

TAUSKY, CURT. *Work Organizations: Major Theoretical Perspective.* Itasca, Ill.: F. E. Peacock, 1970.

TAYLOR, JAMES C. "Some Effects of Technology in Organizational Change." *Human Relations,* Vol. 24, No. 2 (April, 1971):105–123.

TAYLOR, FREDERICK W. *Scientific Management.* New York: Harper & Brothers, 1947.

TERREBERRY, SHIRLEY. "The Evolution of Organizational Environments." *Administrative Science Quarterly* 12 (1968):590–613.

THOMPSON, JAMES D. *Approaches to Organizational Design.* Pittsburgh: University of Pittsburgh Press, 1966.

————. "Organizations and Output Transactions." *American Journal of Sociology* 68 (1962):309–324.

————. *Organizations in Action.* New York: McGraw-Hill, 1967.

THOMPSON, JAMES D., and BATES, FREDERICK L. "Technology, Organization, and Administration." *Administrative Science Quarterly,* Vol. 2 (December, 1957):325–342.

THOMPSON, JAMES D., and McEWEN, W. J. "Organizational Goals and Environment: Goal-Setting as an Interaction Process." *American Sociological Review* 23 (1958):23–31.

THOMPSON, VICTOR A. *Bureaucracy and Innovation.* Alabama: University of Alabama Press, 1969.

————. *Modern Organization.* New York: Alfred A. Knopf, 1961.

THORNTON, RUSSELL. "Organizational Involvement and Commitment to Organization and Profession." *Administrative Science Quarterly,* Vol. 15, No. 4 (Dec., 1970):417–425.

THRUPP, S. *The Merchant Class of Medieval London, 1300–1500.* Chicago: University of Chicago Press, 1948.

TRICE, HARRISON M.; BELASCO, JAMES; and ALUTTO, JOSEPH A. "The Role of Ceremonials in Organizational Behavior." *Industrial and Labor Relations Review* 23 (1969):40–51.

TRIST, ERIC L., et al. *Organizational Choice.* London: Tavistock Institute of Human Relations, 1963.

TROTSKY, L. *History of the Russian Revolution.* Ann Arbor: University of Michigan, 1957.

TROTSKY, L. *Their Morals and Ours.* New York: Pioneer, 1942.

TSE, N. Q. "Industrialization and Social Adjustment in Hong Kong." *Sociology and Social Research* 52 (1966):237–251.

TULLOCK, GORDON. *The Politics of Bureaucracy.* Washington, D.C.: Public Affairs Press, 1965.

TURK, HERMAN. "The Interorganizational Networks in Urban Society: Initial Perspectives and Comparative Research." *American Sociological Review* 35 (1970):1–19.

UDY, STANLEY H., JR. "Administrative Rationality, Social Setting, and Organizational Development." *The American Journal of Sociology* 68 (1962):299–308.

————. " 'Bureaucracy' and 'Rationality' in Weber's Theory." *American Sociological Review* 24 (1959):791–795.

————. *Organization of Work.* New Haven, Conn.: Human Relations Area File Press, 1959.

————. "Technical and Institutional Factors in Production Organization." *American Journal of Sociology* 67 (1961):247–260.

ULLMAN, LEONARD P. *Institution and Outcome: A Comparative Study of Psychiatric Hospitals.* Oxford: Permagon Press, 1967.

U.S. BUREAU OF THE CENSUS. *Population Census 1950, Vol. 2, Part 1.* Washington, D.C.: U.S. Government Printing Office, 1952.

VAN DEN BERGHE, PIERRE L. *South Africa: A Study in Conflict.* Middletown, Conn.: Wesleyan University Press, 1965.

VAN DE VALL, MARK. *Labor Organizations: A Macro- and Micro- Sociological Analysis on a Comparative Basis.* New York: Cambridge University Press, 1970.

VON BERTALANFFY, LUDWIG. *General Systems Theory: Foundations, Development, Applications.* New York: George Graziller, 1968.

VROOM, VICTOR H. "The Effects of Attitudes on Perception of Organizational Goals." *Human Relations* 13 (1960):229–240.

————. *Methods of Organizational Research.* Pittsburgh: University of Pittsburgh Press, 1967.

WADE, L. R. "Professionals in Organizations: A Neoteric Model." *Human Organization,* Vol. 26, Nos. 1/2 (Spring/Summer, 1967):40–46.

WAGER, L. WESLEY. "The Expansion of Organizational Authority and Conditions Affecting its Denial." *Sociometry,* Vol. 34, No. 1 (March, 1971):91–113.

————. "Leadership Style, Hierarchical Influence and Supervisory Role Obligations." *Administrative Science Quarterly,* Vol. 9 (1965):391–420.

WAGER, L. WESLEY, and PALOLA, ERNEST G. "The Miniature Replica Model and Its Use in Laboratory Experiments of Complex Organizations." *Social Forces* 42 (1964):418–428.

WALKER, CHARLES R.; GUEST, ROBERT H.; and TURNER, ARTHUR N. *The Foreman on the Assembly Line.* Cambridge: Harvard University Press, 1956.

WALKER, CHARLES R. *Toward the Automatic Factory.* New Haven: Yale University Press, 1957.

WALLACE, MICHAEL D., and SINGER, J. DAVID. "Intergovernmental Organization in the Global System, 1815–1964: A Quantitative Description. *International Organization,* Vol. XXIV, No. 2 (Spring, 1970):239–287.

WALTON, RICHARD E., and DUTTON, JOHN N. "The Management of Interdepartmental Conflict: A Model and Review." *Administrative Science Quarterly* 14 (1969):73–90.

WARD, DAVID A., and KASSEBAUM, GENE G. *Women's Prison: Sex and Social Structure.* Chicago: Aldine, 1965.

WARD, J. T. *The Factory System.* New York: Barnes and Noble, 1970.

WARNER, W. KEITH, and HAVENS, A. EUGENE. "Goal Displacement and the Intangibility of Organizational Goals." *Administrative Science Quarterly* 12 (1968):539–555.

————. "The Interorganizational Field as a Focus for Investigation." *Administrative Science Quarterly* 12 (1967):396–419.

WARNER, MALCOLM. "Organizational Context and Control of Policy in the Television Newsroom." *British Journal of Sociology* 22 (1971):283–294.

WARNER, W. LLOYD; UNWALLA, DARAB B.; and TRIMM, JOHN H. eds. *The Emergent American Society: Large-scale Organizations.* New Haven, Conn.: Yale University Press, 1967.

WARREN, DONALD I. "The Effects of Power Bases and Peer Groups on Conformity in Formal Organizations." *Administrative Science Quarterly* 14 (1969):544–557.

———. "Power, Visibility, and Conformity in Formal Organizations." *American Sociological Review* 33 (1968):951–970.

WARRINER, CHARLES K. "The Problem of Organizational Purpose." *Sociological Quarterly* 6 (1965):139–146.

WEBER, M. *The City.* Glencoe, Ill.: Free Press, 1958.

———. *General Economic History.* New York: Greenberg, 1927.

———. *Gesammelte Aufsätze zur Sozialund Wirtschaftsgeschichte.* Tübingen: Mohr, 1924.

———. "Gutachten des Herrn Professor Max Weber." *Verhandlungen des deutschen Juristentages* 24 (1897):15–32.

———. *The Protestant Ethic and the Spirit of Capitalism.* New York: Scribner, 1930.

———. *The Theory of Social and Economic Organization.* Glencoe, Ill.: Free Press, 1947.

WEILAND, GEORGE F. "The Determinants of Clarity in Organization Goals." *Human Relations,* Vol. 22, No. 2 (April, 1969):161–172.

WEISS, ROBERT S. *Processes of Organization.* Ann Arbor: Institute for Social Research, University of Michigan Press, 1956.

———. "A Structure-Function Approach to Organization." *Journal of Social Issues* 12 (1956):61–67.

WEISSENBERG, PETER. *Introduction to Organizational Behavior.* Scranton, Penn.: The International Textbook Company, 1971.

WESTBY, DAVID L. "A Typology of Authority in Complex Organizations." *Social Forces* 44 (1966):484–492.

WHISLER, THOMAS L. *Information Technology and Organization Change.* Belmont, Calif.: Wadsworth Publishing Company, 1970.

WHISLER, THOMAS L. "Measuring Centralization of Control in Business Organizations." W. W. Cooper et al eds. *New Perspectives in Organization Research.* New York: John Wiley & Sons, 1964.

WHITE, HARRISON. *Chains of Opportunity: System Models of Mobility in Organizations.* Cambridge, Mass.: Harvard University Press, 1970.

WHYTE, WILLIAM FOOTE. "A Field in Search of a Focus." *Industrial and Labor Relations Review* 18 (1965):305–322.

———. *Human Relations in the Restaurant Industry.* New York: McGraw-Hill, 1948.

———. *Men at Work.* Homewood, Ill.: Richard D. Irwin, and Dorsey Press, 1961.

———. "Models for Building and Changing Organizations." *Human Organization,* Vol. 26, No. 1/2 (Spring/Summer, 1967):22–31.

WHYTE, WILLIAM FOOTE, et al. *Money and Motivation.* New York: Harper, 1955.

WHYTE, WILLIAM H., JR. *The Organization Man.* New York: Simon and Schuster, 1956.

WILENSKY, HAROLD L. *Intellectuals in Labor Unions.* Glencoe, Ill.: Free Press, 1956.

———. *Organizational Intelligence.* New York: Basic Books, 1967.

WILSON, JAMES Q. "Innovation in Organization: Notes Toward a Theory." James D. Thompson ed. *Approaches to Organizational Design.* Pittsburgh, Pa.: The University of Pittsburgh Press, 1966.

WITTES, SIMON. *People and Power: A Study of Crisis in Secondary Schools.* Ann Arbor, Mich.: University of Michigan Institute for Social Research, 1970.

WOLCOTT, HARRY F. "An Ethnographic Approach to the Study of School Administrators." *Human Organization* 29 (1970):115–122.

WOLIN, SHELDON S. "A Critique of Organizational Theories." *Politics and Vision: Continuity and Innovation in Western Political Thought.* Boston: Little Brown, 1960.

WOODWARD, J. *Industrial Organization: Theory and Practice.* London: Oxford University Press, 1965.

WOODWARD, JOAN. *Management and Technology.* London: Her Majesty's Printing Office, 1958.

WOOTON, GRAHAM. *Workers, Unions and the States.* New York: Schocken Books, 1967.

WUNDERLICH, F. *Farm Labor in Germany.* Princeton: Princeton University Press, 1961.

YANORIZAS, JOHN V. "A Study of Work Organization and Supervisory Behavior." *Human Organization,* Vol. 23, No. 3 (Fall, 1964):245–253.

YETLEY, MERVIN J.; MULFORD, CHARLES L.; and BEAL, GEORGE M. "Voluntary Associations and Social Change: A Suggested Analytical Framework." Paper read at Rural Sociological Society Meetings, Washington, D.C., 1970.

YOUNG, F., and YOUNG, R. "Social Integration and Change in Twenty-four Mexican Villages." *Econ. Developm. Cult. Change.* 8 (1960):366–377.

YOUNG, RUTH C., and LARSON, OLAF F. "The Contribution of Voluntary Organizations to Community Structure." *American Journal of Sociology* 71 (1965):178–186.

YUCHTMAN, EPHRAIM, and SEASHORE, STANLEY E. "A System Resource Approach to Organizational Effectiveness." *American Sociological Review* 32 (1967): 891–903.

ZALD, MAYER N. "The Power and Functions of Boards of Directors: A Theoretical Synthesis." *American Journal of Sociology* 75 (1969):97–111.

———. *Power in Organizations.* Nashville, Tenn.: Vanderbilt University Press, 1970.

———. "Who Shall Rule? A Political Analysis of Succession in a Large Welfare Organization." *Pacific Sociological Review,* Vol. 8, No. 1 (Spring, 1965): 52–60.

ZALD, MAYER N., and ASH, ROBERTA. "Social Movement Organizations: Growth, Decay, and Change." *Social Forces* 44 (1966):327–341.

ZALD, MAYER N., and DENTON, PATRICIA. "From Evangelism to General Service: The Transformation of the YMCA." *Administrative Science Quarterly,* Vol. 8, (Sept., 1963):214–234.

ZWERMAN, WILLIAM L. *New Perspectives in Organizational Theory: An Empirical Reconsideration of the Classical and Marxian Analyses.* Minneapolis: Greenwood Publishing Corporation, 1970.